D0881192

Implementing Public Policy

Implementing Public Policy

Ruth Levitt

CROOM HELM LONDON

© 1980 Ruth Levitt
Croom Helm Ltd, 2-10 St John's Road, London SW11

British Library Cataloguing in Publication Data

Levitt, Ruth, *b. 1950*
    Implementing public policy
    1. Environmental policy – Great Britain
    2. Great Britain – Politics and government –
    1964-
    I. Title
    628.5   HC260.E5

ISBN 0-7099-0068-6

Printed and bound in Great Britain by
Redwood Burn Limited
Trowbridge & Esher

CONTENTS

To **PR**

PREFACE

The review of a recently published book stated that: 'Social scientists should address themselves directly to questions of social importance instead of, as so often happens, to the writings of other social scientists' (*Economist*, 8 December 1979). This book tries to take such advice seriously and concentrate on the particular subject of implementing public policies. However it would be unwise and wrong to ignore the important and growing body of academic literature in this area, and readers will find plenty of references in the text to other studies. The approach throughout has been to express ideas and observations clearly and concisely, without assuming an advanced level of technical knowledge. There has been a conscious attempt to describe more fully any aspects of the policies or processes in question which may not be widely known or readily appreciated from another single source.

It is customary for academic studies of policy analysis to be written for an academic market, leaving more popular expositions to the magazines and papers read by those with day-to-day involvement in the specific policy area. This book tries to bridge the gap in so far as it has been written to be immediately accessible to practitioners and academics alike. In the attempt, a number of compromises have had to be made. From the strictly 'academic' point of view, the book could be said to discuss the relevant literature insufficiently in places and to refer too narrowly to other studies. From the strictly 'practical' viewpoint, it could be said that the book is too long and offers insufficient evidence from detailed research in the field. I hope nevertheless that readers will put to one side these reservations and assess the book for what *it is* rather than what it is not. And it is: an attempt to generalise about the nature and process of public policy implementation through an investigation of aspects of pollution policy.

The temptation to make judgements about the effectiveness or success of policies has largely been resisted, as has the possibility of interpreting motives and behaviour attributable to individuals and organisations whenever it might have been done. The idea has rather been to observe, clarify and draw attention to relevant detail; to set the ideas and evidence in context and to make the most of propositions and linkages that may shed more light on what is happening both at the immediate and symbolic levels.

Preface

I am most grateful to the many people who have given me information and advice so generously. A number provided personal interviews and access to private material. I have also used published documents and sources very widely. The research has been supported by a grant from the Social Science Research Council (grant no. RB 7/12/14). The completed text has been seen by many specialists, and I have taken note of their comments as far as possible. Because some of these individuals asked not to be identified I have not named anyone here. My debt to them is great, and any errors of fact, interpretation and omission that remain are entirely my responsibility. Nevertheless I hope that these do not get in the way of readers' enjoyment of what follows.

Ruth Levitt

Part One

THE IMPLEMENTATION PROBLEM

1 ANALYSING PUBLIC POLICIES

The subject of this book is public policy. By that is meant the scope of activity associated with government and its agents. Public policies occur in connection with government's responsibilities in a democratic society such that the members of a society (individuals and groups) explicitly delegate certain powers and duties to government institutions and expect to be affected by some of the outcomes of government action. Other actions are performed by government on the implicit assumption that they are legitimate and appropriate, in the interests of that society. These arrangements are, however, dynamic, and at any moment government agents may be both initiating action and responding to moves made by certain members of society.[1]

Public policies occur within the 'public sector' but are not synonymous with what that term covers. Usually, the public sector includes organisations and individuals whose actions are supported and controlled by government's money and/or resources. It also includes voluntary and non-profit-making enterprises of certain kinds. The private sector, by way of contrast, includes firms, companies and other organisations formed independently of government, and usually these function and are controlled by different rules from those for public sector bodies. Public policies can be directed at either or both of these sectors. But it is worth noting that not all public sector bodies are necessarily involved in public policies directly, and most private sector bodies are only indirectly concerned with public policies. However, these generalisations are difficult to sustain since the definitions of sectors are themselves vague. It is more useful to identify the key features of government action.

As commonly used, the term 'government' includes the activities of central government (the institutions of Parliament, politicians and civil servants), local government (elected members and officials), and other central and local agencies (e.g. health authorities, water authorities, commissions, corporations and other specially appointed bodies). All these agencies derive the legitimacy for their existence and actions from the laws and democratic principles prevailing in society. The distinction between agencies of government and other kinds of organisation also tends to be blurred by the existence of bodies or offices which are intermediate in their independence—the so-called 'quangos'.[2]

Public policies—the intentions and actions of government—range widely over many fields of endeavour, and may affect many members of society. It is said that the scope of public policy is enlarging rapidly as governments seek to or are persuaded to become further involved in aspects of society's affairs. As a result the physical presence of government is said to be more apparent — increasing numbers of people work for government agencies, and have their lives and work affected by the actions of these agencies. In 1970 the UK government itself observed that:

> ... government has been attempting to do too much. This has placed an excessive burden on industry, and on the people of the country as a whole, and has also overloaded the government machine itself. Public administration and management in central government has stood up to these strains, but the weakness has shown itself in the apparatus of policy formulation and in the quality of many government decisions over the last 25 years.[3]

With this growth in the domain of public policy has come uncertainty about the benefits that are produced and the trends being encouraged. Not only governments themselves but other organisations within society have increasingly been questioning the value of conducting social and economic affairs in this style. Alternatives after all do exist, theoretically. The scope of public policy could be radically curtailed such that much less control over the rights and powers of groups within society was permitted to be exercised legitimately by government. Equally, government could extend its scope of influence yet more widely such that far more power was permitted to be expressed through public policies.

Either way, it is widely held now that the value and effectiveness of public policies should be more thoroughly assessed, with a view to identifying successes and failures, areas meriting more or less attention, and setting out priorities for future concern. Self explains:

> Plainly, the number of public measures to be implemented has vastly grown, and the problems of implementation and enforcement (especially the latter) have increased because of shortage of resources, pressures for measures which are intrinsically hard to prosecute successfully, and probably reduced popular willingness to comply with administrative edicts. However, administrators are also strongly exhorted to achieve positive and prompt results. Hence tension between the demands for more participation and more rational

decision-making, on the one hand, and greater effectiveness on the other. The pressures pull strongly in opposite ways.[4]

In this context the analysis of public policies by practitioners and theoreticians has become increasingly popular, and attempts are being made to improve the accuracy and vigour of such policy studies. The main benefits of this work on public policies should fall into two categories. First, the cost of pursuing ineffective policies may become unacceptable to societies and their governments. As economic conditions place increasingly formidable constraints on the consequences of government action, it seems less and less likely that public policies will be tolerated unless their costs can be adequately accounted for. Second, the structural and organisational relationships within society already depend significantly on the constraints reflected in and acknowledged by public policies. If public policies in the future are to provide an acceptable minimum (or maximum) of influence on these relationships—and hence on the perceived stability of society—they are going to have to be capable of expression in these terms.[5] Policy analysis will, if it can contribute to these practical components of the policy system, provide some of the support now needed to enable the system to operate legitimately and acceptably.

Within that framework, this book looks at public policy in terms of implementation. Much has and will be written, attempting to pin down exactly what policy implementation is, how and whether it differs from formulation or action, and when and where it occurs. Gunn, for example, has compiled a checklist of questions which, from the position of establishing a model of perfect administration, aims to identify the preconditions of achieving completely effective implementation of public policies. In doing this he acknowledges the approach described by Hood. Many American studies have traced specific policies and programmes, and notable examples include those by Pressman and Wildavsky and Bardach. The literature on implementation studies has been usefully reviewed elsewhere.[6] The study of implementation can readily proceed by adopting two courses. It can focus on evidence arising in particular areas of public policy (e.g. health, housing, defence, education, pollution), highlighting different characteristics of the areas and explaining their position and function in the policy process. But it can also look at particular aspects of implementation itself (e.g. the influence of interorganisational relationships, discretion, enforcement) and thereby explain their relevance to the overall process.

So this study sets out evidence from one major area of public policy –

pollution control and protection of the environment – and also investigates aspects of implementation. The methodology is set out in Chapter 2, and more about the perspective adopted in the study is said there. Chapters 11 and 12 draw together the evidence presented and try to maximise the value of combining these routes to the study of implementation. It remains in this chapter to identify activity and investigation relevant to policy analysis generally.

The study of policy by theoreticians is not new, it having most frequently occurred in academic research departments within the disciplines of political science, economics and sociology and more extensively in the United States than Europe. However, in the last 25 years, academic interest has escalated if indicators such as new journals, symposia and postgraduate degree and research openings are anything to go by. Excellent critical reviews of the academic literature have been published recently by Jenkins[7] and Dunsire[8] which helpfully draw attention to the approaches and insights prevailing within the academic community.

It is apparent that several questions are relevant to this work. For example, can 'implementation' be separated from 'policy-making' or from 'impact'? Also, can discrete policies be identified? What is the relevance of the hierarchical relationships between organisations involved in implementation? What is the distinction between the 'output' and the 'impact' of policy? Various theoretical frameworks have been constructed and applied to these questions with a view to clarifying the nature of the policy process and the significance of implementation in it.

Within the practical sphere, monitoring and evaluation studies have been less broadly pursued but this may be because efforts have been concentrated in a smaller number of areas. As far as central government in the UK is concerned, economic aspects of policies have probably been subjected to the most internal scrutiny and evaluation. For example, the PESC (Public Expenditure Survey Committee) forward planning system for allocating resources to government departments, the pro-gramme budgets developed within some departments, and the Treasury's involvement in much policy-making show some facets of government's attempts to learn from experience and plan the future use of resources accordingly.[9] From the parliamentary perspective, the Select Committees generally and the Public Accounts and Expenditure Committees par-ticularly have provided politicians (and the general public) in the past with some means of judging the efficacy of policies. (Now with the re-arrangement of Select Committees to shadow departments more closely it remains unclear what the outcome of the committees' deliberations will provide.)[10]

It could be said that the ballot box represents one vehicle for the electorate to demonstrate its view of public policies relating to both central and local government. But interpretations of voting behaviour are notoriously unreliable so this claim needs to be made with care.[11] What is less contentious is that elections give most members of the public who choose whether and how to vote the chance of making a gesture of power, in relation to the policy system. That is to say, the accountability that elected politicians (MPs and councillors) are supposed to be subject to is only generally put to the test at election time. Most electors' knowledge of the candidate's past performance (if any) is so lacking in detail that it is difficult to see how the act of voting represents anything more than the symbolic exercise of power. Election manifestos are short and selective, designed to persuade and please, and often deal rather more with the future in general than the past in detail. So all but the most conscientious electors have too little information to go on to assess the candidate's role in public policies.[12] But general elections are sometimes called when a government wishes to establish or improve its mandate for certain policies, and in this setting the vote is explicitly cast in support of or opposition to those policies, even though the constituency and candidate details prevail. Only at referenda are voters spared the local dimension, although party lines would still be expressed. At any rate, voting on the scale of local or national elections or referenda can only provide at best a blunt instrument for the evaluation of policies or policy intentions.

In quite a different way, the practical consequences and outcomes of public policies can be subject to searching and authoritative analysis by the news media, and thus made evident to the widest audience. Exposés of scandals and shortcomings are not rare, and they can cause considerable embarrassment to the responsible parties. This ability to declare evidence and to 'point the finger' or act as society's watchdog over the actions of powerful bodies is held to be the most treasured value of a free press in a democratic society.[13] There are some legal constraints on the exercise of this freedom, and these continue to be a matter of contention. Nevertheless the role of the press in drawing attention to policy problems is undoubtedly crucial, even though it is not fully developed and used by those groups concerned with public policy that could usefully enlist its support.

Other ways of assessing policy implementation exist in the practical sphere (even though this may not be the original reason why they were established). In particular the consultations systems within organisations between employers/managers and their staff can serve this purpose.

Although terms and conditions of work are likely to be the most immediate subject of concern to individuals, a definite trend towards greater discussion of the objectives and performance of the organisation is evident. In the private sector, firms are beginning to share more management information with workers and to invite participation in decision-making. In the public sector too, although perhaps less widely, opportunities are being developed to involve employees more in these wider policy issues. But in so far as public policies involve large bureaucratic organisations with marked hierarchical structures, the likelihood of this being a prominent vehicle for policy analysis seems low.[14]

Instead, trade unions and professional associations can act as a mouthpiece for groups of workers identified by skill or type of work, and comment more generally on events in the policy system. Indeed most large bodies of this kind see it as part of their duty not only to protect the position of individual members, but also to claim on behalf of the collectivity of their members the right to express judgements, hopes and expectations of public policies for all to hear, but directed particularly to government agencies.[15]

Yet another method in the practical (as opposed to academic or theoretical) sphere involves special commissions or committees of enquiry. This device is commonly used in the public sector by government and government bodies to put policies or problems under a spotlight with a view to suggesting future action as a result. Through these means the experience of skilled and expert individuals can be put to work, and where the issues may be contentious, a balance or representation acceptable to the interested parties can be achieved. Because individual members may be specially authoritative or respected, these bodies can have strong influence on policies. However, the device can be used less creditably by government to sidestep a difficult issue or defuse opposition.[16]

The above list, although far from being comprehensive, gives an indication of the potential for policy assessment existing within the practical sphere where the policies are relevant. Much of this potential is ignored or misused, and as a result the forcefulness of evaluation is low. This is experienced for example as the same mistakes being made again or familiar problems continuing to reappear; difficulties that could be analysed and overcome tend to be perceived as 'inevitable' and the complexity of the policy system is given as the reasons why inertia or disagreement cannot be overcome. The expectations that people and their organisations have of what is possible (in policy terms) is a vital and overlooked feature of policy implementation.

In characterising policy-making as a rational and sequential system in which inputs are converted into outputs that have an impact, this important quality is overlooked. Discussions of the rational model demonstrate that this approach in itself is not without disagreements. A spectrum from the 'objective rationality' of Simon to the 'successive limited comparisons' model of Lindblom can be identified, and contrasted with Dror's 'normative-optimum' model and Lundqvist's discussion of 'steering'.[17] Some academic writers (not notably in the United States) have recognised this difficulty and called for a much less rigid model of policy-making and thereby drawn attention again to the implementation dimension. This is one example:

> ... policy making may be seen as an inescapably *political* activity into which the perception and interests of individual actors enter at all stages. In this case implementation becomes a problematic activity rather than something that can be taken for granted as in the rational process model; policy is seen as a bargained outcome, the environment as conflictual and the process itself is characterised by diversity and constraint.[18]

Writing of policy-making in local government, Vickers amplified another aspect:

> Policy is not made in a vacuum. It is made in a situation structured not only by facts, but also by norms and values ... Policy making, in other words, is not like playing chess—though some good minds insist that it is. For in playing chess both the nature of success and the rules of the game are defined and are not alterable by the players, whilst in managing human affairs at any level from the personal to the planetary, the nature of success and the rules of the game are what have to be achieved.[19]

It is worth emphasising here that this study is not concerned to explain success or failure in the sense implied by a rigidly rational model of the policy system. In the conventional 'top-down' view, it is assumed that policy is made in one place (the top or centre) and implemented lower down (at the bottom or periphery). From there it is claimed that policies have been implemented successfully if the centre's intentions are faithfully reflected in actions at the periphery; failure is constituted by distortion of these intentions or lack of action. Although this is something of a caricature it still exists as a perspective informing much policy analysis. Yet success and failure so perceived are unhelpful concepts for policy analysis if they do not do justice to the complexity of objectives and achievements in the policy system. It is features such as the centre/ periphery relationship, the characteristics of implementing agencies, the social, behavioural, political and economic environment and the dynamics of the process, that hold most promise in explaining what happens when implementation goes wrong or policies falter, and that may be attended to in order to put matters right.

Notes

1. Rose puts it this way: 'In contacts between pressure groups and government, influence moves in two directions. Governments seek to influence pressure groups, just as the latter press claims on the former. An exchange of influence occurs because each has things that the other wants, and each can offer things that the other needs.' R. Rose, *Politics in England Today* (Faber, London, 1974), p. 261.

2. These organisations, which are neither completely private nor completely public, are examined in detail in D.C. Hague, W.J.M. Mackenzie and A. Barker, *Public Policy and Private Interests* (Macmillan, London, 1975). The authors argue that quangos 'sprang from the need for piecemeal adjustment to radical change in politics, economics, society and culture . . . The pressing need was to solve new problems by new expedients and the establishment of quasi-non-governmental organisations was a result' (p. 13).

3. *The Reorganisation of Central Government*, Cmnd. 4506 (London, HMSO, October 1970), para. 2.

4. P. Self, *Administrative Theories and Politics* (Allen & Unwin, London, 1972), p. 278.

5. Rose, *Politics in England Today*, p. 328, draws attention to this in discussing the power of central government relative to the institutions of society. He quotes, for example, the case of the steel industry which was nationalised, denationalised and renationalised in the space of 15 years. Bodies such as the National Economic Development Council have been used from time to time to try to clarify the connections between public policies and key groups (unions, business and financial interests, government, consumers), through such devices as the sector working parties and the industrial strategy.

6. *Central Local Relationships: a Panel Report to the Research Initiatives Board* (SSRC, London, 1979), Appendix to the Report contains a representative selection of the literature, including references for Gunn, Hood, Pressman and Wildavsky and Bardach.

7. W.I. Jenkins, *Policy Analysis: a Political and Organisational Perspective* (Martin Robertson, London, 1978).

8. A. Dunsire, *The Execution Process* (Martin Robertson, Oxford, 1978): Vol. I: *Implementation in a Bureaucracy*; Vol. II: *Control in a Bureaucracy*.

9. The new Conservative Government elected in 1970 proposed to improve the efficiency of government by encouraging a more systematic approach to the formulation of central policies and by enhancing the effectiveness of strategic planning. Its ideas were set out in the White Paper Cmnd. 4506, *Reorganisation of Central Government*. For a further discussion see G. Gustafsson and J.J. Richardson, 'Concepts of Rationality and the Policy Process', *European Journal of Political Research*, vol. 7 (1979), pp. 415-36.

10. The reforms were set out in *First Report from the Select Committee on Procedure*, 1977-78 HC588 vol. I, and the new select committees started work in December 1979.

11. Rose discusses this in *Politics in England Today*, pp. 178-85.
12. See E. Lakeman, *How Democracies Vote*, 4th edn (Faber, London, 1974). She observes that our electoral system 'cannot be relied upon, either to give a Parliament reflecting all the main trends of opinion, or to place in power a government backed by the majority of the electorate, or even by the largest single body of voters', p. 57.
13. See J. Whale, *The Politics of the Media* (Fontana/Collins, Glasgow, 1977), pp. 114-17.
14. The Bullock Committee looked at some aspects of this. See Department of Trade, *Report of the Committee on Industrial Democracy*, Cmnd. 6706 (HMSO, London, January 1977). Further examples are discussed by David Watkins in *Industrial Common Ownership*, Fabian Tract 455 (Fabian Society, London, 1978).
15. '. . . the trade union movement is regularly consulted by the Government on a wide range of public issues, whilst its published statements and private representations profoundly affect public opinion and official and business policy'. Manpower and Employment in Britain, *Trade Unions*, COI Reference Pamphlet 128 (HMSO, London, 1975), p. 1.
16. These aspects are examined in R.A. Chapman (ed.), *The Role of Commissions in Policy-making* (Allen & Unwin, London, 1973), pp. 176-80 and 184-7.
17. Gustafsson and Richardson, 'Concepts of Rationality and the Policy Process'. Schon discusses the application of the rational model to the USA and analyses its limitations: D. Schon, *Beyond the Stable State* (Temple Smith, London, 1971), pp. 144-79.
18. I. Gordon, J. Lewis and K. Young, 'Perspectives on Policy Analysis', *Public Administration Bulletin*, vol. 25 (December 1977), p. 29.
19. G. Vickers, 'Policy Making in Local Government', *Local Government Studies* (February 1974), pp. 8-9.

2 ANALYSING POLLUTION POLICY

> The most formidable barrier to controlling pollution is
> probably not technology, population or public attitudes, but
> the politics of power.[1]

This observation, made by expert American environmental economists,
gives expression to the theme of this chapter. The following pages will
set out why pollution control policy is relevant to the study of
implementation and will explain the methodology employed in examining the evidence.

First then, it is necessary to demonstrate the connection between
effective pollution control policies and 'the politics of power'. Another
observation by American experts asserted

> Environmental policy research has tended to overlook the complex and
> deceptive dynamics of implementation, focussing instead on the pol-
> itics of securing legislative enactment and on the expected impacts of
> legislative programmes which it is simply assumed will function as
> planned. [We believe] that legislative goals and program impacts are
> fundamentally altered by the course which implementation takes.[2]

Here they reiterate the views of Vickers and others quoted at the end
of Chapter 1[3] about the inappropriateness of a rigid rational model of
policy-making, and illustrate the point by quoting their experience of
the environmental policy field. In fact the American academic literature
on policy studies and implementation commonly uses examples from
the pollution control field. In the UK there is growing interest now, and
a number of studies have explored the area.[4]

In choosing pollution control as the field of policy for this study,
two assumptions have been made. First, that pollution control policies
in the UK can be taken as useful examples of public policy, and secondly
that observations about pollution control policies will hold true to a
very great extent for policies of other fields, within the public sphere.
In other words, in the pages that follow, it is going to be considered quite
acceptable to suggest insights for public policy implementation generally
even though detailed study of pollution control policy is the basis of
the evidence for these insights. The idea that public policies are each
unique, special, dissimilar will not find support here.[5] Of course some of

the detailed scientific or technical or even administrative features of pollution control policies are absolutely special to the field. But the fundamental themes and principles, the pattern of observations and the evidence of explanatory factors will all be found to extend quite readily to other areas of public policy. Chapters 8, 11 and 12 will demonstrate this by drawing examples extensively from the study.

The first assumption – that pollution control policies are reasonable examples of public policies – needs further support here. It will be seen from the definitions advanced in Chapter 1 that pollution control policies have the general characteristics of public policies: they fall easily within the scope of action associated with government and its agents. Indeed the UK has a reputation in Europe and elsewhere for being the earliest into the field. This was largely as a result of the sudden and cumulative deterioration in environmental quality brought about by rapid and unregulated industrial development, beginning in the eighteenth century. As measured by legislation, there were formidable policy developments during the nineteenth century, particularly to control air and water pollution, and these have been continuously modified and added to in this century; land protection and noise have also become issues for policy.

Another way of placing pollution policies in the wider context of public policies is to identify their type or nature. A number of typologies and classifications exist; for example Lowi has described three groups: distributive, redistributive and regulative.[6] Much pollution control policy concerns regulation and control and thus its particular implementation problems may be useful in understanding and analysing other types of regulatory policies.

Pollution control policies now range very widely and include air, fresh and seawater, noise, waste management on land, radioactivity, pesticides and the general protection of amenity in the environment. Europe and the United States have on the whole caught up with the UK in formulating policies for these problems and have in some instances taken the lead. Pollution policies, although they are identifiable in this way, do overlap and interact with other areas of policy. Land-use planning and public/environmental health are the most closely associated. Gustafsson and Richardson have argued that policy-making is carried out by independent 'communities' within relatively autonomous policy sectors (e.g. one each for transport, health, employment and environment policy). The 'communities' contain four categories of participants: citizens, politicians, clients and civil servants. They point out that problems arise when the policies of different sectors conflict, and these sorts of co-ordination difficulties may be exported by central government to policy communities at the regional and local levels.[7]

But in so far as pollution is produced by human domestic and industrial activity it is these aspects that become involved in pollution control, and subject to the overlapping of policies. Taking manufacturing industry as just one example, the activities of this sector are heavily influenced by several public policy areas—economic, employment, industrial development, trade and pollution control, to name the obvious ones—and each can modify and enhance or interfere with the implementation of the other. These policies form one part of the context in which individual firms operate as private organisations. Other aspects include competition (at home and overseas), finance and investment, technical developments, industrial relations and corporate strategy. These present additional forces acting on and within the firm, and shaping its role in the policy system.[8]

So to separate out areas of public policy, although it is commonly done and certainly aids analysis, in fact distorts the true picture. Public policies are more accurately perceived as overlapping and interlocking influences that interact with each other as well as with other forces. The compartmentalisation of policies and the description of boundaries between them is often more imagined than real, although it can be convenient for descriptive reasons. Hence pollution policy will be discussed here as if it were a discrete entity, just as it is by those concerned with it. But the underlying reservation about this is that it oversimplifies reality and ignores the blurred edges between areas of public policy. However it emphasises the validity of the study's second assumption — that investigating pollution control policies will assist our understanding of public policies generally.

Pollution has of course long been recognised as a problem for society, but the appropriate style and level of governmental action (and therefore of public policies) continues to be problematic. Looking at comparable countries, their chosen approaches vary considerably, and there is no evident blueprint, since achievements of policy are similarly varied, and causal factors are complicated to identify. However comparative studies have tried to clarify the position, and in this the Organisation for Economic Co-operation and Development (OECD) has produced a number of excellent examples.[9]

It is also important to consider why pollution issues arrive 'on the agenda' of government, given the fact that they may have existed and been recognised as hazards or nuisances for some time. Solesbury has described an issue as a 'situation which by common consent is bad and could be better' and responses as 'what the government decides and is urged to do'.[10] Then he identifies various types of responses such as a more vigorous approach to the execution of established policy, or an incremental extension of existing powers, or an explicit revision of policy or a complete legislative recasting of the powers, institutions and finances which underpin policy. He observes that the desirability of one or other kind of response may well be an important consideration in the recognition of new issues.

But he concludes 'the more important question is not how ideas and issues originate but what gives them force . . . Issues only begin to become powerful once institutions within the political system become associated with them.'[11] Issues must therefore command attention, claim legitimacy and invoke action – 'One does not follow automatically from the other.'[12]

These remarks give some clue to the complexity surrounding the choice of action, and are particularly interesting since the author, Solesbury, is a senior civil servant in central government. Another observer, a journalist, commented more starkly on this question (in connection with the consequences for pollution control policies of the change of government in 1970); he wrote: '[The Conservatives] are the party of less government and a clean environment demands more government – constant official vigilance over industry and local government.'[13] A third perspective is offered by another journalist writing recently about the Control of Pollution Act: he maintained that the Act had prompted a shift from the question 'how unpolluted do we want to be?' through 'how polluted can we afford to be?' to 'how unpolluted should we realistically be?'[14]

These writers illustrate the shifting base of policy and action in this field. The implication is that the context of policy at particular moments in time will give important information about the possibilities for implementation. Certainly in the case of pollution this is a relevant factor (as will be demonstrated) since the staggered progress of legislative implementation, accompanied by phased introduction of policies over many years is a prominent feature. On this the OECD has said: 'the timing of the implementation of such programmes is important because in several cases traditional problems of adjustment may occur which could be considerably minimised by an adequate length of the adjustment period.'[15]

In selecting pollution control then, the field still needs to be narrowed down a little more to make investigation manageable. The historical context has been mentioned, and the extent of governmental action has been referred to. The need to control pollution is not now being ignored by any developed country although the subject is complex because:

1. the environmental consequences of certain activities or processes may not be known until damage has already been done;
2. the cost of controls may be unacceptably high; and
3. the benefits of control policies may not be fully realised because of difficulties in securing satisfactory implementation.[16]

Furthermore, there are supranational consequences arising not only from pollution itself but also as a result of the steps taken to control it.[17]

So in order to conduct a useful study of public policy implementation drawing on evidence from the pollution control field, the following objectives have been set:

1. the study should describe the origins, scope and objectives of key aspects of pollution control policies in the UK;
2. it should identify the extent of adoption of those policies; and
3. analyse significant features of their implementation;
4. the study should thereby offer a framework for analysing the implementation of public policies, generally; and
5. draw attention to the principal steps that may be taken to improve policy analysis and implementation.

To that end, the study will examine pollution control policies using the Control of Pollution Act 1974 as a focus. This recent piece of legislation offers a particularly fruitful basis for the study because it not only consolidates many of the much older policies but provides a variety of new powers for dealing with current and anticipated problems, thus embodying much of the breadth and variation of policy in this field. It is also a very practical focus for the study of implementation because it is being introduced in stages, and not all of its provisions are operational yet; also its introduction highlights clearly some of the principal components of implementation—interorganisational relationships, standards, rules, enforcement, discretion and so on.

Chapter 3 is devoted to an exposition of the Control of Pollution Act 1974, and deals more fully with its origins, how it came to be formulated, what the policies relating to it concern and who is affected by them, and what the policies are designed to achieve. It is followed by four case studies looking closely at key aspects of each of the four substantive areas covered by the Act: waste management on land, water, noise and air. The remaining chapters draw on this case material to discuss the implementation problems and offer some explanations to account for the evidence.

So, unlike a number of other policy studies which have examined causes of 'failure', where things went wrong or were subverted, this present study has chosen to use material which is much harder to label success or failure. In many ways (which will be discussed) the Control of Pollution Act and the policies that relate immediately to it are very difficult to judge—partly because they are very recent, partly because they have not produced much observable action, partly because the focus of initiative is not clear, partly because the objectives can be expressed in several different ways, and so on. Intentionally, therefore, the study will not produce any simple conclusions that silence all uncertainty. What it should do though is emphasise the conditions of reality in which policies occur—where success and failure are not self-evident, and where intentions and objectives change and influence each other, often producing unanticipated results. The concluding chapters will try to analyse these conditions so that common patterns, systems or interrelationships can be identified.

Notes

1. A. Freeman, R.H. Haveman and A.V. Kneese, *The Economics of Environmental Policy* (Wiley, New York, 1973), p. 170.
2. F.R. Anderson, A.V. Kneese, P.D. Reed, R.B. Stevenson and S. Taylor, *Environmental Improvement through Economic Incentives* (Johns Hopkins University Press for Resources for the Future, Baltimore, 1977), p. viii.
3. See Chapter 1, p. 19
4. See for example: R. Gregory, *The Price of Amenity* (Macmillan, London, 1971); N. Gunningham, *Pollution, Social Interest and the Law* (Martin Robertson, London, 1974); R. Parker, 'The Struggle for Clean Air', in *Change, Choice and Conflict in Social Policy*, ed. P. Hall, H. Land, R. Parker, A. Webb (Heinemann, London, 1975); *Pollution and Environment*, Open University, Decision Making in Britain Block V D203 (The Open University Press, Milton Keynes, 1977); R. Kimber and J.J. Richardson, *Campaigning for the Environment* (Routledge and Kegan Paul, London, 1974).
5. According to Gregory, for example: 'There is no point in pretending that cases concerned with amenity problems and the use of land tell us much about traditional aspects of public administration' (*The Price of Amenity*, p. xv). But in a critical review of Gregory's case studies Webb observes 'The way forward for the case-study is in adopting two related strategies. The first is the production of "sets" of cases centring on a particular field of study. The second is the comparative approach.' A. Webb in *Policy and Politics*, vol. 1, no. 1 (September 1972), pp. 65-8.
6. Jenkins discusses this usefully (*Policy Analysis*, Ch. 3).
7. See Gustafsson and Richardson, 'Concepts of Rationality and the Policy Process'. The pollution-planning relation is discussed by the Royal Commission on

Environmental Pollution in Ch. XI of its *Fifth Report: Air Pollution Control: an Integrated Approach*, Cmnd. 6371 (HMSO, London, 1976). The pollution-environmental health relation is discussed in Unit 2 of the Open University's second level technology course: 'Environmental Control and Public Health PT 272', *Environmental Health* (The Open University Press, Milton Keynes, 1977).

8. 'Most managers in industry, commerce and finance must be acutely aware that they face a new political environment, which is bringing new pressures on to them, as well as the new possibilities made available to them by the development of the technology of management'. Hague, Mackenzie and Barker, *Public Policy and Private Interests*, p. 22.

9. Some of these are: *Economic Implications of Pollution Control* (1974); *Pollution Charges: an Assessment* (1976); *Review of Agricultural Policies in OECD Member Countries* (1977); *Energy Production and the Environment* (1977); *Objectives, Concepts and Strategies for the Management of Radioactive Waste* (1977); *Long-range Transport of Air Pollutants* (1977); *Employment and Environment* (1978); *Reducing Noise in OECD Countries* (1978); *The State of the Environment in OECD Member Countries* (1979). For further discussion of 'styles' in pollution policy-making, see J.J. Richardson, 'Agency Behaviour: the Case of Pollution Control in Sweden', *Public Administration*, vol. 57 (Winter 1979), pp. 471-82.

10. W. Solesbury, 'The Environmental Agenda', *Public Administration*, no. 54 (Winter 1976), p. 381. See also: A. Downs, 'Up and Down with Ecology – the "issue attention cycle"', *Public Interest*, vol. 28 (1972), pp. 38-50.

11. Solesbury, 'The Environmental Agenda', pp. 382-3.

12. Ibid., p. 384, and compare with Downs, 'Up and Down with Ecology'.

13. J. Whale, 'Whitehall Diary', *Your Environment* (Spring 1980), pp. 34-6.

14. D. White, 'How Polluted are We – and How Polluted do we Want to Be?', *New Society* (11 January 1979), p. 66.

15. OECD, *Economic Implications of Pollution Control* (OECD, Paris, 1974), p. 9.

16. For example, (a) the widespread use of DDT as a pesticide, resulting in new strains of insects evolving resistant to its effects, as well as sublethal concentrations in living matter causing ecological disturbance; (b) abolishing lead in petrol would require redesign of motor engines, so policy is rather to reduce the concentration of lead in existing fuels; (c) the litter acts have not produced adequate controls. See also A. Downs, 'Up and Down with Ecology'.

17. For example the 'tall chimneys' policy in the UK for dispersing sulphur dioxide from industrial emissions is said to cause 'acid rain' to fall in Scandinavia, because of airborne transport of the pollutants. The use of the Rhine as a disposal site for industrial processes in Germany results in water of very low pollution-absorbing quality being available in Holland.

3 CREATING POLLUTION POLICY: THE CONTROL OF POLLUTION ACT 1974

The specific and the broader contexts of the Control of Pollution Act can be identified fairly readily, and they give some idea of the environment in which this piece of legislation took its place. In general terms, concern with the threat from industrialised society to health and natural resources grew noticeably during the 1960s, in the UK as well as in Europe, the United States and other 'advanced' societies. The subject was raised with increasing frequency by those in authority so that the media were encouraged to handle it seriously. Scares and the gloomy predictions about the destruction of the environment were not then generally believed; nevertheless they could not always be dismissed by sceptics as the ravings of cranks. As the 1970s approached, protection of the environment came to be aired more and more in such 'opinion-forming' settings as the Reith Lectures, Penguin specials, articles in newspapers and journals,[1] and particularly the report prepared for the Club of Rome called *The Limits to Growth*.[2] Internationally, the United Nations decided to hold a 'Conference on the Human Environment' in Stockholm in June 1972, so member-states set to work to prepare briefings for their delegations a couple of years in advance.[3]

In the UK, two important official actions indicated the arrival of environmental protection as a legitimate issue for government's attention. The first was a White Paper presented to Parliament in May 1970 by the (Labour) Secretaries of State for local government and regional planning, Scotland and Wales, called *The Protection of the Environment – the Fight against Pollution*.[4] This dealt with the major categories of pollution (air, noise, land, fresh water, sea and beaches, and radioactivity), representing a 'progress report and discussion of government intentions, aimed at stimulating public debate'.

In June of 1970 a general election removed the Labour Government and replaced it with a Conservative one, which did not delay in acting in this sphere by announcing, in October, the creation of the new Department of the Environment, under a Secretary of State, out of the former Ministries of Housing and Local Government, Public Building and Works and Transport. Its functions were to include 'the preservation of amenity, the protection of the coast and countryside and the control of air, water and noise pollution'.[5]

However there was a lull until 1972 when the government was forced
to respond to pressures on it concerning the dumping of toxic waste (this
is discussed fully in Chapter 4, and see also Chapter 9, note 28). It had
been alerted to the problem as a result of expert committees' evidence of
difficulties and clear evidence from the Royal Commission on Environmental Pollution. But these were insufficient to speed up the policy-
making system. Only after a vigorous campaign initiated by amenity
groups and taken up by the media was the government embarrassed into
responding. It announced through its junior Environment Minister,
Eldon Griffiths MP, that additional statutory powers, 'perhaps interim
ones', might be required pending the introduction of a comprehensive
anti-pollution Bill.[6] The government's Protection of the Environment
Bill was then mentioned in the Queen's Speech at the start of the
1973-4 parliamentary session.[7] It was first introduced, interestingly, in
the House of Lords. Most Bills start their life in the House of Commons,
but there are two main reasons why this pattern is sometimes changed.
First, the timetable for dealing with business becomes overloaded if every
piece of legislation has to start in the Commons, then go to the Lords
and come back to the Commons again. It leaves the Lords with little of
substance to do at the start of the session, and puts pressure on them
and the Commons to rush through outstanding business at the end of the
session. By starting a Bill in the Lords the workload can be shared more
evenly, and the progress of each House can be scheduled more smoothly.
Secondly though, the House of Lords contains a number of people who
have accumulated considerable expertise, knowledge and authority in
certain fields during the course of their working lives, which can usefully
be brought to bear on the specialist issues arising in parliamentary
business. This is not so often the case in the Commons, so where a
matter has considerable technical content, it can be worthwhile to
clarify the major problems early on with the help of appropriate expertise in the Lords.

Both these reasons fitted the circumstances in which the Protection
of the Environment Bill appeared. The government had ambitious
legislative plans for the 1973-4 session, the Bill undoubtedly dealt with
technical matters where specialist knowledge could be helpful, and the
House of Lords did then contain a number of individuals with knowledge
and interest in environmental problems, while the House of Commons
seemed relatively less well endowed.

Lord Windlesham[8] introduced the Protection of the Environment
Bill in the House of Lords on 14 November 1973 and it received its first
reading. This was followed on 27 November 1973 by the second reading

debate after which the Bill was committed to a Committee of the whole House. It was subsequently debated in Committee on eight occasions between 13 December 1973 and 4 February 1974, when its Committee Stage was completed.[9] However the rest of the usual sequence was interrupted in February 1974 by the sudden general election which forced all unfinished parliamentary business at that point to be abandoned and replaced the Conservative Government with a new Labour one. But the delay was not long, because the Queen's Speech on 12 March 1974 introducing the new parliamentary session promised further 'work for the protection and improvement of the environment'.[10]

This was followed by the introduction of a new measure: the Control of Pollution Bill. Again, it started in the House of Lords, this time introduced by Lord Shepherd,[11] and obviously built on the foundations laid in the previous session. The first reading was given on 30 April 1974 and the second reading debate took place on 7 May when the Bill was committed to a Committee of the whole House. Two periods of Committee debate were needed this time, on 14 and 16 May followed by the report in the House on 21 May and the third reading of the Bill.[12]

The House of Commons first became involved with the Control of Pollution Bill on 17 June 1974 when they gave it a second reading debate and committed it to a Standing Committee. The report stage and third reading was reached a month later, on 19 July 1974, and returned to the House of Lords where Commons amendments were considered on 25 July. The Bill was then agreed and received Royal Assent on 31 July 1974.[13] Because of the strike at Her Majesty's Stationery Office, some of the *Hansard* reports and the Act itself were not immediately available.[14]

Some interesting comments on implementation of policy were made during the parliamentary debates. Going back to November 1973, Lord Windlesham described the Protection of the Environment Bill in these terms: 'Each part of the Bill rests on foundations laid by a wide range of committees, studies and working parties.'[15] Part I dealt with waste on land, and introduced the new system of waste disposal based on much existing law as well as redefining activities within local authorities. Part II covered water pollution, and strengthened and extended water authorities' powers. Part III dealt with noise by trying out some experimental proposals to help contain this form of pollution. Part IV introduced relatively minor additions concerning pollution of the atmosphere. The penalties for offences committed under the new arrangements would be 'fairly standard in form' although increased severity of punishments was included.[16]

In the second reading debate, Lady White[17] for the Opposition

pointed out a number of the Bill's deficiencies including the omission of
any 'general declaration of a general duty to avoid pollution or to take
this into account in decisions reached by public bodies',[18] thus
acknowledging the interrelatedness of different spheres of policy and
its consequences for implementation. She also pointed out the absence
of measures to clarify the responsibility for wider aspects of environmental protection – such as the Environmental Protection Agency is
meant to do in the United States – suggesting that a body concerned with
surveillance and enforcement may be necessary in addition to legislation,
if implementation is to be ensured.[19]

Lord Henley[20] expressed concern about implementation too as he
said he was worried that inactivity would result where the measures were
difficult or expensive to operate. Lord Ashby,[21] however, was more
satisfied. In his maiden speech he said 'the abatement of pollution in this
country has been, with a number of reservations, a success story. But
very serious gaps and flaws have been left and this Bill goes a long way to
repairing these, e.g. derisory penalties, control of estuaries and tidal
waters and toxic waste dumping'.[22] Each of these three items is dealt
with in later chapters.

Other comments of relevance to later chapters were also made by
Lord Beeching,[23] then Chairman of Redland Ltd, parent company of
Redland Purle Ltd, which features in the case study on toxic waste. He
spoke in detail about Part I of the Bill, raising several practical issues
and relating the different views of what is possible to the outcome of
implementation. For example he criticised the Bill for not being explicit
enough: 'the waste disposal authorities who have to implement the
provisions of the Bill by regulatory and direct discharge of responsibility
within their own areas may not have the same understanding and viewpoint as those who drafted the legislation'.[24]

Viscount Amory[25] dealt with the timetable for introducing the
provisions of the Bill. He advised that since the costs would be falling on
local authorities (which he thought had been underestimated in the
financial memorandum) 'because of public pressure to implement
provisions plus central government pressure not to escalate expenditure,
I hope the government will be realistic when they come to fix the dates
for the implementation for these new costs'.[26]

Lady Young,[27] replying for the government defended a number of
criticisms point by point and she also observed that two themes had
been apparent in the debate: the need for information, and publicity.
When the Bill began its Committee Stage there were 91 government
amendments tabled, although few arose from the second reading debate –

they came mostly from advice to the DoE received during the continuing consultations it was having with other interested parties (such as the local authority associations, CBI and professional bodies). Many opposition amendments were proposed, Lady White and Lord Garnsworthy[28] doing most of the work in committee. Some of them were dropped after the government's undertaking to meet them in the report stage. Others were debated and won or lost on a vote.

When the Bill fell on dissolution of Parliament, it had been substantially amended in matters of detail, although no major provisions were added or removed. Its successor, the Control of Pollution Bill, had the same structure — Parts I to IV — and the same aims, as Lord Shepherd had described them: 'it is not a revolutionary Bill. It takes its place in the long and respectable history of public health legislation which has been developing since the 19th century to deal with these problems . . . in the main it represents a development of existing legislation in the waste disposal, water pollution, noise and air pollution fields'.[29] Lord Shepherd referred to a memorandum which described the actual changes between the Protection of the Environment and Control of Pollution Bills.[30] It showed where the earlier work done in the Lords had been accommodated, and where some new measures had been added by the new government.

The second reading debate met with support from the opposition, although Lord Zuckerman[31] and Lord Ashby expressed reservations about some details. They raised these later in the Committee Stage (14 and 16 May 1974) when the Bill was worked through clause by clause.[32] When the third reading was given, the government discussed the financial and economic aspects of the Bill. There would be direct effects on public expenditure because of the need that water and local authorities would have to employ more specialist staff (e.g. chemists, planners, hydro-geologists, etc.) and because of the need to improve the waste collection service, totalling £8 million to £9 million per annum. But because of the government's wish to contain growth of public expenditure, it was decided that the implementation of the Bill should not take place until after April 1975. In the intervening months the government would 'consult with local authorities and water authorities about how best limited resources can be used to carry out the new functions'.[33]

It was also recognised that consumers, industry and agriculture might also have to bear extra costs at a difficult time, but 'this must be done even if it is gradually and step by step'.[34] So an important feature of the implementation of the legislation was determined at this stage, without apparent opposition in Parliament — namely that the policy covering public expenditure was a greater priority than the policy dealing with pollution control, and that the rate of progress would be determined by central government, with little provision for exercise of local discretion.[35] Not that a date for implementation was *not* fixed – 'the government intend to delay the implementation until after 1 April 1975' – only the earliest possible date was identified, not the latest.

In the House of Commons second reading debate, Margaret Thatcher MP[36] stated: 'I cannot think of any Bill which I have seen introduced in the House which has been preceded by more investigation, research, discussion and consultation than this bill . . . there is a great gap between legislation and its enforcement on the one hand, and legislation and the habits of people on the other. There is only a limited amount that we in Parliament can do to improve the environment.'[37] Nevertheless the Commons did make a number of minor amendments and additions to the Bill before returning it to the Lords, all of which were agreed to.

The Control of Pollution Act 1974 has 109 sections and is divided into 6 parts with 4 schedules. Its provisions can be summarised as follows:

Part I Waste on Land

Section 1	Waste disposal arrangements
Section 2	Waste disposal plans
Sections 3-11	Licensing of disposal of controlled waste
Sections 12-17	Collection and disposal of controlled waste
Sections 18-19	Waste other than controlled waste
Sections 20-21	Reclamation, etc. of waste
Sections 22-24	Street cleaning and litter
Sections 25-30	Supplemental

Part II Pollution of Water

Sections 31-33	Control of entry of polluting matter and effluents into the water
Sections 34-40	Consents for discharges
Sections 41-42	Ancillary provisions relating to control of discharges
Sections 43-45	Control of discharges of trade effluent into public sewers
Sections 46-54	Miscellaneous
Sections 55-56	Supplemental

Part III Noise

Section 57	Periodical inspections by local authorities
Sections 58-59	Summary proceedings to deal with noise

Sections 60-61   Construction sites
Section 62   Noise in streets
Sections 63-67   Noise abatement zones
Section 68   Noise from plant or machinery
Sections 69-74   Supplemental

Part IV Pollution of the Atmosphere

Sections 75-78   Prevention of atmospheric pollution
Sections 79-83   Information about atmospheric pollution
Section 84   Interpretation

Part V Supplementary Provisions

Sections 85-88   Legal proceedings
Sections 89-90   Financial provisions
Sections 91-98   Miscellaneous

Part VI Miscellaneous and General

Sections 99-103   Miscellaneous
Sections 104-109 General

Schedules

1. Noise abatement zones
2. Alterations of penalties
3. Minor and consequential amendments of enactments
4. Repeals

Since the government wished to delay implementation as had been described, the Act is written in such a way that its provisions lie dormant until they are activated by Commencement Orders. These are a form of statutory instrument made by Parliament which bring specified sections of the Act into force on a given date. In addition some sections then also need to be amplified by regulations before they can be implemented. The timetable for introducing the Act's provisions is shown in Figures 3.1-3.3.

In the Department of the Environment's words 'there has been gradual implementation of parts of the Control of Pollution Act 1974 due to the uncertain economic climate. Provisions of the Act which introduce only discretionary powers or which do not involve significant public expenditure were implemented and came into force on 1 January 1976 in England and Wales.'[38] There is some confusion here over interpreting the meanings of the terms 'implemented' and 'came into force'. Those

Figure 3.1: Control of Pollution Act – Commencement Orders

No.	Ref.	Made	Commencement	Sections England/Wales	Scotland
1	1974 No 2039	5.12.74	12 Dec 1974	43, 44, 95, 104, 105, 107, 108(1), 109	104, 105, 109
2	1974 No 2169	20.12.74	1 Jan 1975	108(1-2)	–
3	1975 No 21	21.2.75	3 Mar 1975	–	108(2)
4	1975 No 2118	10.12.75	1 Jan 1976	12(5-7), 17, 19, 20, 21, 25, 26, 27 (1a, 2), 28, 29, 30, 49, 50, 56, 57-87, 89-94, 96-103, Sch I, II	12(5), 25, 29-30, 75-77, 99-103, 106, Sch II
5	1976 No 731	12.5.76	14 Jun 1976	3-11, 16, 18(1-2), 22, 23, 88	–
6	1976 No 956	10.6.76	20 Jul 1976	108(2, 11)	–
7	1976 No 1080	7.7.76	18 Jul 1976	–	17, 27(1a, 2), 57(a), 58-9, 62, 68, 69, 70, 71(1, 3), 72, 73, 74, 76, 84, 87, 89-94, 96, 98, 108(11)
8	1977 No 336	1.3.77	1 Apr 1977	12(5), 14(9-11), 108(2) Inner London only	–
9	1977 No 476	11.3.77	1 Apr 1977	24(4), 108(2)	24(4)
10	1977 No 1587	21.9.77	1 Jan 1978	–	3-11, 16, 17(3a), 18(1-2), 20, 88
11	1977 No 2164	20.12.77	1 Jul 1978	2	–
12	1978 No 816	31.5.78	1 Sep 1978	–	2
13	1978 No 954	4.7.78	1 Aug 1978	13(3, 5-8)	–

Figure 3.2: Control of Pollution Act – Regulations

Year	No.	Title	Commencement	CPA Section
1974	none			
1975	2115	Code of Practice for Construction Sites	1 Jan 1976	60
	2116	Control of Noise (Appeals) Regs.	1 Jan 1976	58, 60-1, 64-7
1976	37	Control of Noise (Measurement & Registers) Regs.	13 Feb 1977	64
	732	Control of Pollution (Licensing of Waste Disposal) Regs.	14 Jun 1976	3, 5, 6, 10, 11, 30
	957	Control of Pollution Act 1974 (Appointed Day) Order	19 Jul 1976	44(5)
	958	Control of Pollution (Discharges into Sewers) Regs.	20 Jul 1976	43-4
	1866	Motor Fuel (Lead content of petrol) Regs.	30 Nov 1976	73
	1988	Oil Fuel (Sulphur content of gas oil) Regs.	29 Dec 1976	76
	1989	Motor Fuel (Gas content of gas oil) Regs.	29 Dec 1976	75, 104(1)
1977	17	Control of Atmospheric Pollution (Appeals) Regs.	7 Feb 1977	80
	18	Control of Atmospheric Pollution (Exempted Premises) Regs.	7 Feb 1977	80
	19	Control of Atmospheric Pollution (Research and Publicity) Regs.	7 Feb 1977	80
	1185	Control of Pollution (Licensing of Waste Disposal)(Amendment) Regs.	16 Aug 1977	Amends 1976/732
1978	none			
1979	1	Motor Fuel (Lead content of petrol)(Amendment) Regs.	1 Feb 1979	Amends 1977/1866

Figure 3.3: Timetable for Introducing Each Section of the CPA

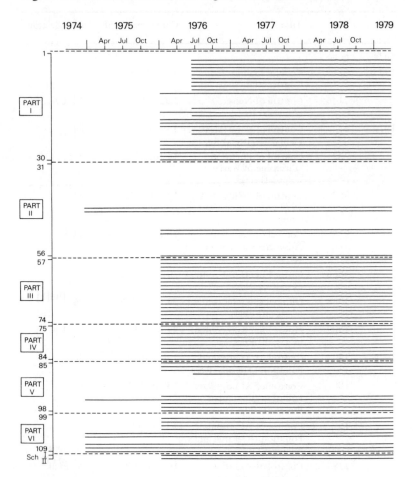

sections requiring regulations *as well as* Commencement Orders for full operational use by whatever bodies are involved are described in this way by the DoE, even if the regulations had not yet been made. The DoE does acknowledge this by saying that, for example, 'most of [Part IV of] the Act will not be fully effective until regulations are made later . . .'.[39] So the terms 'implementation' and 'come into force' should not be taken necessarily to mean that the sections of legislation in question are 'fully effective'. The gradation of statutory and operational status this imparts because of styles of legislative and administrative action is not unique to pollution control policy (the Medicines Act 1968, for example, is very similar). But it is a relatively recent phenomenon being used very dramatically in the case of the Control of Pollution Act, which creates a number of consequences for the policies and for the agencies and individuals involved in the implementation.

It has already been noted that the role of central government in bringing forward legislation to control pollution was not simply that of a single authority determined to lay down hard and fast rules for the implementation of its wishes. Not only is the Control of Pollution Act informed by the reports of several expert committees, evidence of research and expressions of public opinion in the tradition stretching back over a hundred years,[40] but the timing and mode of its transition from Act to fully effective policy are designed to allow variations and amendment arising from consultation and negotiation as the interested parties work on the policy. The interested parties vary, depending on the particular sections in question, and their perceptions of the meaning and purpose of the legislation will colour how they are affected by it and how they may try to interpret or modify it.

There is an added dimension here, in the sense that three important contextual features have shaped perceptions held by those in the pollution control policy system quite measurably, even though these factors are not directly or principally concerned with pollution control. One is the UK's recent (1973) membership of the European Community.[41] Secondly, the reorganisation of local government in the same year as the passing of the Act, and the reorganisation of the water authorities one year earlier.[42] And third, the period of stringency in public expenditure, provoked from about 1972 by the UK's poor economic performance and the world economic recession. These features will be returned to again during the discussion of the case studies.

Whatever the context of the Control of Pollution Act, though, it directly affects a number of parties in different ways. Part I, dealing with the disposal of waste on land, gives the county councils of England and

Wales several specific jobs to do in connection with the disposal of waste
from domestic, commercial and industrial sources, including hazardous
and toxic wastes. They have to survey the arisings (i.e. the wastes
originating) as well as the disposal facilities in their areas and operate a
licensing system for the use of disposal facilities. In Scotland and Wales
these duties rest with the district councils as well, as do responsibilities
for the collection of waste, street cleaning and litter abatement, which
the English district councils manage. Part II, concerning water pollution
control, gives the ten regional water authorities the responsibility of
protecting most inland waters including streams and underground sources,
as well as tidal coastal waters, from pollution. They have to operate a
consent system for regulating permitted discharges to be made into controlled waters, and the sewage effluents which they themselves create
from treatment works are not exempt from regulation.

Part III covers noise control and as well as reiterating the district
council's general public health duties to control nuisances it provided
them with specific powers to control noise from construction sites,
plant and machinery; and to deal with the problem of neighbourhood
noise through the creation of noise abatement zones. District councils
are also involved in Part IV of the Act which deals with atmospheric
pollution since they are given new powers to investigate industrial
emissions and publish their findings. The Secretary of State can regulate
pollution from fuel oils by making statutory orders to restrict the level
of sulphur, lead and other chemicals in them. Part V gives the Secretary
of State powers to hold a local public enquiry on any matter under the
Act that in his opinion warrants it, and he is also responsible for considering appeals against decisions to impose controls made under Parts I to IV
by the statutory authority. He may direct authorities who have failed to
perform their proper function to carry out certain duties or he may
transfer specific functions to himself. He also has the general power to
restrict the import and use of any substance that may be 'injurious'. The
government's White Paper, *Central Government Controls over Local
Authorities* (Cmnd. 7634, London, HMSO, September 1979), identified
a number of powers under the Control of Pollution Act 1974 which it
proposed to repeal. The case studies identify the relevant ones.

Apart from these statutory authorities identified in the Act, and their
official representative bodies—the Association of County Councils, the
Association of Metropolitan Authorities, the Association of District
Councils and the National Water Council—other parties are also directly
affected. Under Part I all waste producers and waste disposal contractors
are subject to the site licensing provisions. All manufacturing industry

produces waste continually and either has to treat and dispose of it on its own premises or hire a contractor to provide this service. Under the Act, very detailed rules about the methods of treatment, transport, site management and protection of amenity are laid down, and firms in breach of these are liable to prosecution. Industrial wastes that are discharged into water are also controlled by the Act so that firms using rivers and seas for disposal are prohibited from permitting anything other than the discharge specified in the consent from the water authority to enter the water. They may be prosecuted if their effluents breach the consent conditions. Industry also produces noise and gases or other types of air pollution and these are controlled in certain circumstances by the Act. So private industry of all types – manufacturing and service – is affected by the Act and obliged to comply with a number of controls imposed by the statutory authorities. For this reason the Confederation of British Industry has taken a strong interest in environmental legislation generally and the Control of Pollution Act in particular. One of its central committees is concerned with this, and there is a section of technical experts at the London headquarters to brief CBI spokesmen and to negotiate directly with government about the evolution and implementation of pollution control policies. The CBI's regional organisation also has specialist committees to deal with environmental matters and to negotiate with the regional and local authorities.

Individual industries also take pollution legislation seriously and many of them have specialist staff or advice to assist them in keeping track of developments and making representations where necessary. The Chemical Industries Association is particularly skilled at this, and other examples are the Road Haulage Association and the National Association of Waste Disposal Contractors. They lobby MPs and civil servants, brief their membership, produce bulletins and news-sheets, hold conferences and do whatever else they feel is necessary to protect their interests.

In contrast to this sophisticated level of organisation, the general public has a lot less to show, although its interests are very substantially influenced by the Control of Pollution Act. In each of the main parts of the Act the public is given new rights to obtain and act on information about controls. The details of waste disposal site licences and plans, of consents for discharges into water, of noise levels from premises and plant and of emissions into the air are all becoming available to the public to see. The obligation to maintain registers and publish data is newly imposed on the statutory authorities by the Act, and in effect it gives members of the public a chance to find out more about the uses to which the environment is being put, as well as the opportunity to draw deficiencies to the attention of the authorities and, in some cases, to institute prosecutions against firms, individuals or the authorities themselves.

Yet the pattern of public involvement in pollution control is very patchy. Elected representatives in Parliament and local authorities specialising in this aspect of policy are not generally a very conspicuous force, except sporadically where there may be scandals or incidents of particular significance. The appointed representatives on water authorities and advisory bodies have also not tended to be significantly active. One exception is the Royal Commission on Environmental Pollution which has consistently proposed measures to protect and enhance the rights of the general public.[43] The other medium through which public opinion is expressed is via voluntary or pressure groups, and here there is evidence of activity. Several groups have national as well as local organisations: this applies to Friends of the Earth, the Conservation Society and the Civic Trust, for example. But most public activity centres on immediate local issues such as a public enquiry about particular plans to develop facilities or after things have gone wrong. This is not to say public involvement is insignificant, but that it is a great deal less streamlined or continuous than that from private industry. In fact it tends to be erratic; yet it needs to be harnessed to particular subjects at particular times to be most effective – and this is not generally the style of voluntary bodies.

Newspapers, television and radio also obviously play an important part in pollution control and the increased availability of information under the Control of Pollution Act could help these organisations to pursue their investigations and report on their findings. And as with many subjects it is the sensational and dramatic aspects that most often appeal to newspaper editors and programme producers. In their preoccupation with circulation and audience figures, they tend to present the issues in an oversimplified way that does not reflect the complexity of the problems that form the basis of the need for effective policy. So the comprehensive coverage of pollution control issues that the media could provide is not really evident.

Other interested parties, although at some distance removed from those so far described, can be grouped into two categories. There are the international government and policy organisations, and the domestic, scientific or professional organisations. In the first group the most prominent bodies are the European Economic Community (EEC) and the Organisation for Economic Co-operation and Development (OECD), followed by the United Nations Environment Programme (UNEP) and the World Health Organisation (WHO).

The EEC has, since 1973, been committed to environmental action programmes which are designed through national and community action to protect the environment from abuse and conserve natural resources.[44] The influence of this on UK policies is investigated in the case on water set out in Chapter 5. OECD advises its member countries on a wide range of policy and since 1970[45] has had an environment directorate comparing and evaluating different approaches to pollution control. OECD publishes surveys, assessments and advice which are generally regarded as authoritative, and which inform the decision-making in member countries. In addition, 1970 was declared 'Conservation Year' by the Council of Europe, and this was the first demonstrable international step to put environmental questions into the limelight.

Following the United Nations Conference in 1972 the UNEP was established to report periodically on progress, and this has taken the form of several publications. WHO has a general responsibility to advise on public health protection and has set standards for a number of pollutants that countries use in fixing their own controls.[46]

The second group covers scientific, technical and professional organisations, and although they are not directly governed by the Control of Pollution Act they have an interest or involvement in the interpretation and application of certain of its provisions. This is referred to in detail in each of the case studies. Scientific bodies such as the Hazardous Materials Advisory Service provided by the Atomic Energy Research Establishment of the UK Atomic Energy Authority at Harwell, or the Water Research Centre at Stevenage offer advice to the authorities about the management of substances or pollutants, and this is used to set standards and monitor the effectiveness of controls. *Ad hoc* committees may also be set up by the government and by industry to advise on a particular problem, e.g. those concerned with disposal or transport of certain hazardous materials and chemicals or with the control of certain gas or dust emissions. Professional bodies exist for all the technical staff involved in pollution control. These include the Institute of Solid Waste Management, the Institute of Water Pollution Control, the Environmental Health Officers Association and the Institute of Public Health Engineers. They may be consulted and may make representations on all sorts of detail contained in the Act or in advice from the authorities about the operational policies that flow from it.

Those then are the significant bodies directly and indirectly affected by or interested in the Act. Others certainly exist, but are probably not widely significant, and the case studies identify some of these. Chapter

8 also returns to the interorganisational relationships and charts some of the influences these may have on implementation.

Notes

1. According to one observer, 'The press, the Royal Commission on Environmental Pollution, and weekly and monthly magazines such as *New Scientist*, the *Ecologist* and *Social Audit* had all helped to expose the dangers inherent in the shielding of pollution control administration from the critical eye of the public.' F. Sandbach, 'Has this Act any Teeth?', *Ecologist* (March 1977), p. 62. See also R. Carson, *Silent Spring* (Hamish Hamilton, London, 1963); F.F. Darling, *Wilderness and Plenty*, Reith Lectures 1969 (OUP, Oxford, 1970); B. Commoner, *The Closing Circle* (Cape, London, 1972); J. Bugler, *Polluting Britain* (Penguin, Harmondsworth, 1972); The Ecologist, *Blueprint for Survival* (Penguin, Harmondsworth, 1972); J. Bray, *The Politics of the Environment* (Fabian Society, London, 1972).

2. D.H. Meadows, *et al.*, *The Limits to Growth: a Report for the Club of Rome's Project on the Predicament of Mankind* (Earth Island Books, London, 1972).

3. United Nations Conference of the Human Environment, Stockholm, 1972. *The Human Environment: the British View* consists of five basic papers and four working party reports, published by HMSO, 1972:

1. The UK experience in dealing with oil pollution of the sea
2. Development, aid and the environment
3. International surveillance and monitoring of the environment
4. Marine pollution
5. International standards for pollution control.

Working party reports:

1. On the control of pollution: *Nuisance or nemesis*
2. On the management of natural resources: *Sinews for survival*
3. On the human habitat: *How do you want to live?*
4. On the role of voluntary movements and youth in the environment: *Fifty million volunteers.*

4. *The Protection of the Environment – the Fight against Pollution.* Presented to Parliament by the Secretary of State for Local Government and Regional Planning, the Secretary of State for Scotland and the Secretary of State for Wales. Cmnd. 4373 (HMSO, London, May 1970).

5. *The Reorganisation of Central Government.* Presented to Parliament by the Prime Minister and Minister for the Civil Service. Cmnd. 4506 (HMSO, London, October 1970).

6. *Hansard* 27 January 1972, House of Commons col. 1747-50, quoted by R. Kimber, J.J. Richardson and S.K. Brookes, in the Deposit of Poisonous Wastes Act 1972; a case of government by reaction. *Public Law*, Autumn 1974, p. 208. See also: Department of the Environment Press notice 1041, 26 September 1973.

7. House of Lords, vol. 346 col. 4, 30 October 1973.

8. Lord Windlesham, b. 1932, Member Westminster City Council (Cons) 1958-62. Minister of State, Home Office 1970-2. Minister of State, Northern Ireland 1972-3. Lord Privy Seal, Leader of House of Lords, 1973-4.

9. House of Lords, 13 December, vol. 347, cols. 1303-52, 15 January 1974, vol. 348, cols. 875-946, 17 January, cols. 1081-169, 22 January, cols. 1286-301, 1318-73, 1395-431, 24 January, cols. 1584-5, 1592-700, 28 January, vol. 349,

cols. 115-60, 29 January, cols. 185-257, 265-361, 4 February, cols. 564-91, 595-700.

10. House of Lords, 12 March 1974, vol. 350, col. 10.

11. Lord Shepherd, b. 1918. Chief Whip 1964-7. Minister of State, Foreign and Commonwealth Office Office 1967-70. Leader of the House of Lords 1970-4. Lord Privy Seal and Leader 1974-6.

12. Committee Stage: House of Lords, 14 May 1974, vol. 351, cols. 869-82, 890-992; 16 May, cols. 1161-231, 1325-6. Report and third reading: 21 May, cols. 1343-98, 1398-406.

13. House of Commons: 17 June 1974, vol. 875, cols. 94-167. 19 July 1974, vol. 877, cols. 906-1000. House of Lords: 25 July 1974, vol. 353, cols. 1866-86, 31 July 1974, col. 2366.

14. The Act was eventually published on 24 October 1974.

15. House of Lords, 27 November 1973, vol. 347, col. 13.

16. Ibid., col. 19.

17. Lady White (life peer 1970), b. 1909. Labour MP for East Flint 1950-70. Parliamentary Secretary Colonial Office 1964-6, Minister of State for Foreign Affairs 1966-7, Minister of State, Welsh Office 1967-70. Chairman, Advisory Committee on Oil Pollution at Sea 1973-7. Member, Royal Commission on Environmental Pollution 1974- . Member, British Waterways Board 1974-

18. House of Lords, 27 November 1973, vol. 347, col. 21.

19. This is discussed further in Chapter 11, pp. 196-7.

20. Lord Henley, b. 1914. Chairman of the Council for the Protection of Rural England 1972-

21. Lord Ashby (Sir Eric Ashby, created life peer 1973), b. 1904. Master of Clare College 1959-75. Chairman Royal Commission on Environmental Pollution 1970-3. Member and Chairman of numerous advisory committees concerned with scientific research, university education, etc. Chairman, Working Party on Pollution Control for UN conference on the Environment, Stockholm 1972.

22. House of Lords, 27 November 1973, vol. 347, col. 35.

23. Lord Beeching (life peer 1965), b. 1913. Joined ICI 1948, Deputy Chairman 1966-8. Chairman British Railways Board 1963-5. Chairman, Redland Limited 1970-7.

24. House of Lords, 27 November 1973, vol. 347, col. 59.

25. Viscount Amory (Derick Heathcoat Amory created Viscount 1960), b. 1899. Conservative MP Tiverton 1945-60. Several ministerial positions before Chancellor of the Exchequer 1959-60. President, County Councils Association 1961-74.

26. House of Lords, 27 November 1973, vol. 347, col. 65.

27. Lady Young (life peer 1971), b. 1926. Government Whip 1972-3. Parliamentary Under Secretary of State, DoE 1973-4. Councillor and Alderman, Oxford City Council.

28. Lord Garnsworthy, 1907-74. Created life peer 1967.

29. House of Lords, 7 May 1974, vol. 351, col. 373.

30. The memorandum, in the House of Lords library, itemised changes in each part of the new Bill. House of Lords, 7 May 1974, vol. 351, col. 374.

31. Lord Zuckerman (Sir Solly Zuckerman, life peer 1971), b. 1904. Chief Scientific Adviser to Secretary of State for Defence 1960-6, to HM Government 1964-71. Chairman Central Advisory Committee for Science and Technology, 1965-70. Member Royal Commission on Environmental Pollution 1970-4.

32. See note 12.

33. House of Lords, 21 May 1974, vol. 351, col. 1394.

34. Ibid.

35. See Chapter 11, p. 187; also A. Downs, 'Up and Down with Ecology'.

36. Rt. Hon. Margaret Thatcher, b. 1925, Conservative MP Finchley (Barnet)

1959. Joint Parliamentary Secretary, Minister of Pensions and National Insurance 1970-4. Secretary of State for Education and Science 1970-4. Leader of Opposition 1975-9. Prime Minister 1979- .

37. House of Commons, 17 June 1974, vol. 875, col. 106.

38. Department of the Environment, *Pollution Control in Britain: How it Works*, Pollution Paper no. 9, 2nd edn (HMSO, London, 1978), Annex B, para. 1, p. 94.

39. Ibid., para. 7.

40. The main ones are included in the bibliography to Pollution Paper no. 9, pp. 98-107.

41. The United Kingdom formally became a member of the European Economic Community, Euratom and the European Coal and Steel Community on 1 January 1973 as a result of signing the Treaty of Accession on 22 January 1972. The European Communities Act received Royal Assent on 17 October 1972. UK membership was confirmed in the UK by a referendum on 5 June 1975.

42. The Water Act 1973 c. 37 and the Local Government Act 1972 c. 70 gave legislative authority to these reorganisations. For fuller discussion of the former see: The Open University, 'Environmental Control and Public Health PT 272 Unit 8', *Administrative Control* (The Open University Press, Milton Keynes, 1978) and Ch. 5. For the latter see: *Local Government* (Community Service Volunteers School and Community Kits, London, 1978).

43. The standing Royal Commission was established in 1970 to advise on matters, both national and international, concerning the pollution of the environment; on the adequacy of research in this field; and the future possibilities of danger to the environment. It has to date published seven reports, dealing with such matters as air pollution, pesticides, nuclear power, estuaries and coastal waters, toxic waste and staffing questions. See the reports themselves for further details: Royal Commission on Environmental Pollution. *First Report*, Cmnd. 4585 (HMSO, London, 1971); *Second Report: Three Issues in Industrial Pollution*, Cmnd. 4894 (HMSO, London, 1972); *Third Report: Pollution in Some British Estuaries and Coastal Waters*, Cmnd. 5054 (HMSO, London, 1972); *Fourth Report: Pollution Control: Progress and Problems*, Cmnd. 5780 (HMSO, London, 1974); *Fifth Report: Air Pollution Control: an Integrated Approach*, Cmnd. 6371 (HMSO, London, 1976); *Sixth Report: Nuclear Power and the Environment*, Cmnd. 6618 (HMSO, London, 1976); *Seventh Report: Agriculture and Pollution*, Cmnd. 7644 (HMSO, London, 1979).

44. The intention to establish the community's first environment programme was announced at the Paris summit meeting in October 1972, which was agreed at a Council of Ministers meeting in July 1973. The text is published in the *Official Journal of the European Communities*, vol. 16, no. C112 (20 December 1973). This was followed by the second action programme which was adopted in May 1977. The text is published in vol. 20, no. C139 of 13 June 1977.

45. The Organisation for Economic Co-operation and Development was set up under a convention signed in Paris on 14 December 1960. The members are Australia, Austria, Belgium, Canada, Denmark, Finland, France, Federal Republic of Germany, Greece, Iceland, Ireland, Japan, Luxembourg, The Netherlands, New Zealand, Norway, Portugal, Spain, Sweden, Switzerland, Turkey, the United Kingdom and the United States of America. Its environment directorate was set up in 1970.

46. The World Health Organisation was established on 7 April 1948. Through its advisory services it helps member governments to strengthen environmental health (among other things). It also undertakes epidemiological surveillance, medical research and scientific publications.

Part Two

INVESTIGATING POLLUTION POLICY

4 TOXIC WASTE DISPOSAL

Defining Terms

It is no longer sufficiently precise to use the term 'toxic' when referring to dangerous waste. Several other terms are now in current usage and permit more careful definition, although there is still a lot of variation.

Figure 4.1: Categories of Waste

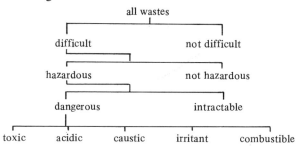

Figure 4.1 sets out the usual categories. Wastes are mostly, in volume terms, straightforward to dispose of. The rest can present problems because they are *hazardous* (i.e. present some sort of threat or risk) or simply because they are troublesome to get rid of (perhaps because of size or quantity). There are two broad kinds of hazardous waste, that which is *dangerous* because it will harm living things or natural resources, and that which is *intractable* because it is hard to reduce, neutralise or eliminate. Dangerous wastes are *toxic* if they will harm human, animal or plant life. They may also or alternatively be *acidic, caustic, combustible* or *irritant*, thus posing serious problems for safe handling or disposal. There may well be some overlap between these groups and categories, even though distinctions are clearly possible. It is important to stress that wastes may be unsightly, intrusive and unwelcome even if they are not particularly difficult or dangerous to dispose of. The problems of definition are further complicated by the fact that wastes may arise as *solids, liquids* or *sludges* — each requiring different methods of transport, handling and disposal. Within the *dangerous* category the actual components causing the risk may be present in *complex mixtures*, and depending on their properties they may pose a threat only in high or low *concentrations* or at certain *temperatures* or when *mixed* with other

substances. So the more precise definitions of toxicity are a technical matter of some complexity which nevertheless have to be used and appreciated by people involved in waste management even though they may possess varying amounts of technical knowledge.

The Deposit of Poisonous Wastes Act 1972 introduced a control procedure for waste disposal, but exempted from it any waste which did not contain 'any hazardous quantity or hazardous concentration of any poisonous, noxious or polluting substance'.[1] From the discussion above it can be seen that a number of questions are begged by this exemption since current knowledge does not always permit substances to be identified or categorised with sufficient confidence in those terms. Nevertheless a broadly acceptable classification system was drawn up and has been modified, so that all wastes can be grouped according to the activity that produces them (e.g. household, industrial, building) and also according to their chemical composition.

Waste Classification[2]

1. Household and commercial waste (including street sweepings, litter, market waste and gulley contents, but not local authority construction wastes, or waste falling into classifications 8/10/11 or 12 below).
2. Medical, surgical and veterinary waste.
3. Industrial waste.
4. Mine and quarry waste.
5. Radioactive waste.
6. Farm waste (including wastes from livestock markets).
7. Waste from construction and demolition.
8. Sewage sludge (including screenings), and cesspool and pail closet contents.
9. Old cars, vehicles and trailers.
10. Pulverised household and commercial waste.
11. Screenings from household and commercial waste.
12. Ash from incineration.

Classification of Difficult Wastes[3]

(a) Inorganic acids.
(b) Organic acids and related compounds.
(c) Alkalis.
(d) Toxic metal compounds.
(e) Non-toxic metal compounds.
(f) Metals (elemental).

(g) Metal oxides.
(h) Inorganic compounds.
(j) Other inorganic materials.
(k) Organic compounds.
(l) Polymeric materials and precursors.
(m) Fuel oil, oils and greases.
(n) Fine chemicals and biocides.
(p) Miscellaneous chemical waste.
(q) Filter materials, treatment sludge and contaminated rubbish.
(r) Interceptor wastes, tars, paints, dyes and pigments.
(s) Miscellaneous wastes.
(t) Animal and food wastes.

In order to describe toxic wastes more clearly though, work is currently underway to identify for a list of certain substances more precisely what concentrations, etc., are to be defined as toxic.[4]

The Control of Pollution Act 1974 does not use the term 'toxic', but categorises controlled waste (i.e. waste within the scope of the Act) into: 'household', 'commercial', 'industrial' and 'special'.[5] Special wastes are covered by Section 17 which requires certain additional controls to be introduced for 'certain dangerous or intractable waste'. So it is within this that 'toxic' wastes are most likely to fall.

Waste Management

Organised and controlled disposal of waste is a recent development which has been made necessary because of three factors:

1. The increasing volumes of waste being produced by domestic life and commercial and industrial activity.
2. Increasing knowledge about the harm to life, natural resources and environments caused by inappropriate disposal methods.
3. Increasing concern to protect the environment from abuse.

There are several ways in which wastes can be disposed of acceptably, depending on their properties, the nature of the disposal site, and the cost of disposal. Table 4.1 shows the volume of waste arising annually.

These are very considerable amounts and they are all increasing. The commonest method of disposal is controlled tipping on landfill sites, and it is the cheapest. More waste is disposed of in this way than in any other.

Table 4.1: Volume of Waste, England 1976

	Million tonnes	%
household & commercial	18	4
general industrial	45	10
power station	12	3
building	3	1
mining	60	14
quarrying	50	11
farming	250	57
	438	100

Source: *Digest of Environmental Pollution Statistics*, no. 1 and Open University Course. PT272 Environmental Control and Public Health, Unit 9.

To reduce its volume before tipping it is sometimes treated by compaction, shredding or baling. Some wastes have to be treated to reduce their danger before tipping, by incineration, chemical treatment or drying for example. Incineration is an alternative form of disposal, although the residual ash has to be dealt with. Other wastes are dumped at sea in bulk or in drums, are treated before being disposed of in fresh water through the sewage system, or are dumped on land in drums. Policies to develop recycling and reclamation from waste have been debated, and there are certain moves to use suitable wastes as a source of fuel for heating.[6]

Looking specifically at waste disposal on land, there are two clearly defined sectors in the business. The public sector consists of the county councils in England (and the Greater London Council) and the district councils in Wales and Scotland. (In England the district councils are only responsible for waste collection.) Part I of the Control of Pollution Act 1974 gives them powers and duties to control the disposal of all wastes to land arising or arriving in their areas. The private sector consists of waste producers who treat and dispose of material arising from their own processes, and private contractors who offer transportation, treatment and disposal services on a commercial basis to other producers. In addition, waste from mines, quarries, farms and radioactive waste has to be disposed of, much of it on land, but this is governed by other legislation and so will not be discussed further here.

The public authorities handle most of the domestic and commercial waste, leaving private contractors to deal with industrial arisings (Figure 4.2).

Figure 4.2: Waste Disposal on Land, Public and Private Sector (England, 1976)

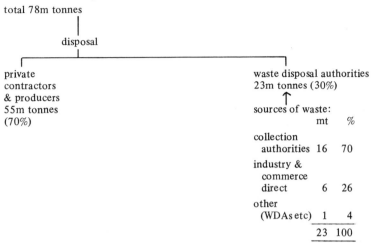

total 78m tonnes

disposal

private
contractors
& producers
55m tonnes
(70%)

waste disposal authorities
23m tonnes (30%)

sources of waste:

	mt	%
collection authorities	16	70
industry & commerce direct	6	26
other (WDAs etc)	1	4
	23	100

Source: *Digest of Environmental Pollution Statistics*, no. 1 and Open University Course PT272, Unit 9, and Waste Management Paper, no. 1.

Their control powers in Part I have been mentioned in Chapter 3, and to summarise they are required to license landfill sites and treatment plants in their areas that meet certain operating conditions and are run satisfactorily, so that it is an offence to deposit or treat waste anywhere other than at a licensed site. The authorities also have to survey arisings and disposal facilities and produce a plan. They will eventually be required to ensure that adequate arrangements exist in their areas, whether made by themselves or by others, to dispose of all categories of waste covered by the Act.[7]

This administrative control system is an innovation which developed from the recommendations of two important committees set up in the 1960s. The Working Group on the Disposal of Solid Toxic Waste[8] and the Working Group on Refuse Disposal[9] identified a number of major failings:

(a)   the lack of any machinery or responsibility for strategic planning of waste disposal over wide areas;

(b)   the poor siting and offensive operation of certain waste disposal facilities so as to damage amenity;

(c)   the danger of pollution, for example of water supplies, by
       abandoned wastes, especially toxic industrial wastes;
(d)   the failure to take full advantage of the best modern technology,
       of opportunities for integration of waste disposal facilities and
       of possibilities for recycling materials and reclaiming land;
(e)   the need for more research.

The two reports concluded that the necessary improvement to waste
disposal required greater public control exercised by local authorities,
and that this could integrate waste disposal well with land-use planning
and other environmental requirements. The 1972 Local Government
Act reallocated certain duties between district and county councils so
that waste collection and development control currently rests with the
districts in England and Wales (and London boroughs) while waste
disposal and strategic planning is a county (and Great London Council)
responsibility. In Scotland collection and disposal functions are handled
by the districts while planning is also split between regional and district
councils.

Advantages and disadvantages arising from these administrative changes
have been identified or claimed in relation to waste disposal. The main
advantage is that counties, as the disposal authorities, can plan and
control disposal over a more practical (i.e. larger) area. The main disadvantage is that the districts' exercise of planning powers can conflict
with the intentions of the counties in relation to developing disposal
facilities. This will be discussed further in the case material, as it is an
essential point of difficulty.

In order to assist local authorities to fulfil their responsibilities under
Part I of the Control of Pollution Act, the DoE issues circulars and
letters in the usual way, but it has also introduced a series of pamphlets
called Waste Management Papers.[10] The early ones dealt with aspects
of the administrative task that have been mentioned, viz.:

1.   Reclamation, treatment and disposal of wastes—an evaluation on
      available options.
2.   Waste disposal surveys.
3.   Guidelines for the preparation of a waste disposal plan.
4.   The licensing of waste disposal sites.
5.   The relationship between waste disposal authorities and private
      industry.

Others deal with the technical problems of handling specific wastes, e.g.

7.   Mineral oil wastes.
13.   Tarry and distillation wastes and other chemical based residues.

To produce detailed implementation guidelines such as this the DoE sets up a number of working groups and teams, several with outside advice, which complement the work of its technical and administrative staff within the waste division. Where it is appropriate to do so, advice is issued jointly with the Welsh and Scottish Offices. The Waste Management Advisory Council was established in 1974, chaired by ministers from the Departments of the Environment and Industry. It has mainly concentrated on the possibility of reducing waste and increasing reclamation and recycling to date.[11]

In addition to central and local government bodies, a number of other significant groups have an interest in waste disposal. The Institute of Solid Waste Management is the professional body for waste collection and disposal staff, and its membership is drawn mainly from local authorities. Its annual conferences have over the years provided useful evidence of views held in and between public and private sectors. The National Association of Waste Disposal Contractors is a trade association to which many private contractors belong. It acts as a spokesman for the private sector, particularly to central government, and attempts to improve standards within the industry. Its role will be discussed more fully later in the case material, because it holds an important role. It has formed local links with the Road Haulage Association in order jointly to improve public-private sector relations.

Amenity groups have a record of activity in the waste disposal area, too, although much of it is very localised, to do with individual developments or problems that might affect small groups of residents. National activity has tended to be, appropriately, concerned with more general issues. For example Friends of the Earth is very active on questions of reclamation and recycling.[12] The Civic Amenities Act 1967 was enacted largely as the result of the Civic Trust's efforts to improve facilities for dumping awkward household wastes. The Keep Britain Tidy Group is another well-established organisation and will have special responsibilities in relation to litter plans under Section 24 of the Control of Pollution Act.[13] The Conservation Society's role in connection with cyanide dumping is discussed later on.

This then is a summary of the operational and administrative arrangements for waste disposal on land, which sets the scene for an examination of the case study material on hazardous wastes. Despite the apparent developments of the last five to ten years, waste disposal is still a new field for public and private sector endeavour on any planned or rational basis. Many of the people currently involved can remember the comparatively disorganised and *laissez-faire* way in which disposal used to be conducted. The business still suffers from an 'inferiority complex' because it is a dirty and dangerous activity that most people prefer not to know much about. On the public side, investment has been low and little thought was given prior to the Control of Pollution Act to strategic planning for the provision of facilities. On the private side, financial rewards have been substantial for those firms able to develop their capital (sites, plant and transport fleets) and many more large firms are now developing waste disposal subsidiaries. There has been antipathy between the sectors born largely out of ignorance and suspicion, and although the Control of Pollution Act requires their collaboration to make waste management a sound and secure activity, a lot of attitudes still need to change. This point is at the heart of the case study material and is taken further later on.

Toxic Waste Disposal

Before 1972 when the Deposit of Poisonous Waste Act was passed there was no legislation covering industrial waste disposal. Eight years earlier a Technical Committee on the Disposal of Solid Toxic Wastes (the Key Committee) had been set up to investigate problems that were coming to light.[14] Some of these problems are described in the report, such as a case of dumping of fluoracetamide and the death of farm animals after drinking water that had become contaminated by dumped toxic substances. Several incidents of fly tipping drums of cyanide and other wastes, their contents sometimes unidentified, had been reported in the press, and cases of illegal tipping of toxic wastes in municipal refuse tips were also noted. The press helped to increase public awareness and concern about these incidents, and by the time the Key Committee reported in 1970 the issue was firmly on the agenda of public opinion.[15] Concern about all aspects of environmental protection was also at its peak at that time, so this assisted the pressure on the government to stop illegal disposal of toxic wastes.

The Royal Commission on Environmental Pollution, which had been established in that year, singled out toxic waste for particular mention in its first report. It urged the government to act on the recommendations of the Key Committee — to introduce controls without delay.[16] The Key Committee explained some of the problems it had uncovered in its long investigation. These included the technical difficulties of defining toxic waste, and the particular properties of solid, semi-solid and liquid wastes; the natural barriers to pollution of underground water sources were described, and the committee explored good methods of disposal practice that would protect surface and underground waters. It concluded that the system then existing offered too many opportunities to those who were concerned merely to get rid of waste rather than to dispose of it safely. It suggested public disposal authorities should be established to ensure proper methods of operating toxic waste tips.

The Royal Commission in its second report again urged the government (which had not yet taken any action in response) to act without delay.[17] It claimed the Key Committee had understated the problem and the need for urgency. The government appeared to want to introduce comprehensive proposals to co-ordinate the disposal of all waste on land more gradually, to take effect when the new authorities created by the imminent reorganisation of local government had been established, probably by 1974.[18] The Royal Commission nevertheless urged introduction of an interim measure, but it took further incidents of illegal tipping to force the government to act. In December 1971 the Warwickshire branch of the Conservation Society received information from a tanker driver working for one of the biggest firms of waste disposal contractors, concerning occasions when the driver had been required to engage in illegal tipping. The driver sought their support because he and his fellow employees were unhappy about perpetuating such dangerous practices. The Conservation Society made the facts known to the Secretary of State for the Environment, MPs and the press, and national radio and television took the story up in a major way in January 1972. The Secretary of State expressed concern but did not promise early action. In a debate that month in the House of Commons the minister gave assurances that the problems were under control by his department. However more and more cases were by now coming to light, not just in the West Midlands, and were being quite actively pursued by the media. The final straw was the discovery in February 1972 of 36 drums of cyanide dumped illegally in a brickyard at Nuneaton and of further drums at Coventry. The minister did then undertake to introduce measures 'at the earliest possible opportunity'.[19]

The Deposit of Poisonous Waste Bill was introduced in the House of Commons on 3 March 1972, and received Royal Assent on 30 March 1972, thus being one of the fastest handled pieces of legislation in Parliament.[20]

The Deposit of Poisonous Waste Act made it an offence to dispose of noxious or polluting waste in any place where it might cause an environmental hazard. The Act also introduced a notification system for every movement of a load of poisonous waste as follows:[21]

The notices have to be served by the waste producer at least three days in advance and have to specify the source and destination of the waste, its nature and chemical composition, the quantity and description of containers and the name of the person undertaking the removal. All loads except those exempted in a schedule to the regulations[22] have to follow the notification procedure, and the local and water authorities in the area where the waste for disposal is lying and in the area where it is to be deposited have to be informed. The same authorities have to be informed within three days by the tip operator that the specified waste has been deposited. A 'season ticket' procedure exists for regular disposal of similar consignments so that paper work may be reduced for genuinely consistent loads of notifiable wastes.[23]

Local authorities were made responsible for enforcement and have to keep records of all deposits in their areas. The notification system is a negative one in that it controls all substances except those exempted in the schedule. There is no positive identification of poisonous or dangerous substances. The schedule exempts innocuous domestic and commercial waste and then lists activities (e.g. highway construction, brewing) and items (e.g. plastics, coal, soaps) from which waste is also exempted from notification.[24] This has put a considerable burden on the local authorities to enforce the controls in a 'grey' area of knowledge. In many cases it may be uncertain whether or not a particular consignment poses a potential risk and the technical expertise available may be inadequate for the authorities to exercise confident judgements.

The Deposit of Poisonous Waste Act has remained in force since 1972 and will continue until regulations made under Section 17 of the Control of Pollution Act supersede it. The Secretary of State is given a duty under Section 17 to make provision by regulations for disposal of more difficult or toxic wastes in addition to the controls introduced by the site licensing system. The DoE is currently preparing draft regulations, having consulted with the relevant interests, with a view to issuing regulations in 1980.[25] The intention is to set up a revised notification procedure for consignments of any waste positively identified in the regulations. The aim will be to ensure that each consignment of 'special' waste can be tracked from its point of production to point of disposal; and that consignments of special waste are destined for appropriately licensed sites. An outline of the new arrangements was prepared as early as 1973 when the DoE issued a consultative document on the provisions of the forthcoming legislation on waste disposal.[26] These provisions will take into account the obligations created under the terms of an EEC directive.[27] The directive applies to waste containing or contaminated by 26 named substances and requires anyone handling the waste to maintain a record of this; the waste must be accompanied by a consignment note when it is moved; sites receiving these wastes must keep records. Competent authorities must be established to control the disposal of these substances, although member-states have discretion in prescribing the form, quantities and concentrations which would bring wastes within the directive's scope. The DoE proposes that consignment notes are 'receipted' by each party handling the 'special' waste and copies are sent to the appropriate waste disposal authorities. Each party will also be required to maintain a register showing details of each transaction.[28]

However, the final form of the consignment note system set out in the regulations made under Section 17 cannot be predicted because a number of modifications may be agreed in the course of consultations. The discussions are inevitably controversial because several conflicting interests are having to negotiate compromises to arrive at an agreed system. The consignment note procedure will not, however, create additional administrative work because it is officially expected to apply to fewer consignments than are caught by the blanket provisions of the 1972 Act. These and other facets will be discussed further in the case material. The point of note here is that when regulations under Section 17 of the Control of Pollution Act come into force and the Deposit of Poisonous Waste Act 1972 is repealed, the ideal administrative and legislative framework for hazardous waste disposal will probably be some way from being achieved. Not only technical knowledge about the behaviour of toxic substances will advance, but the working methods of the public authorities and private firms and their interrelationships will change as they gain experience.[29] The 1972 Act was introduced in unusually hurried circumstances but that cannot be said of Section 17 of the Control of Pollution Act. One question for later chapters to address is whether this difference in timescale offers particular insights about the implementation of resulting policies. In this chapter the description of toxic waste management now continues with an analysis of the private waste disposal industry before the problems uncovered in the case material are set out.

According to the National Association of Waste Disposal Contractors it is impossible to say how many firms are operating in the business, nor what percentage of them belong to the Association. NAWDC's 1979 Trade Directory lists 91 full members (waste disposal contractors and landfill site operators); 36 associate members (equipment manufacturers, research, experimental and advisory bodies); and 15 affiliate members (waste producers).[30] The full members clearly vary in the scale of their operations in terms of their numbers of employees, sites and what capital they employ and turnover they achieve. The waste disposal business is said to be like the construction industry where a small minority of the firms account for most of the employees and activity.[31] Waste disposal is a much younger industry though and still in a state of flux, with frequent mergers and acquisitions, and several new firms entering for the first time. The Director of NAWDC has said that waste disposal is 'a Steptoe activity moving up market'. It is according to him becoming more sophisticated, yet it still has to lose the 'rag and bone man' image.[32] Looking back to the early days of waste disposal around the 1930s one man recalled:

> although today we use the term 'waste disposal industry', it seems but a short time ago that waste disposal was but a fragmentary activity and an occupation which often attracted the less acceptable fringe of society. For those people who were connected with that occupation and who can recall the circumstances which existed in the early days, it is still a near miracle that today waste disposal is a recognised, well established, respectable and, in many cases, highly sophisticated industry in its own right . . . the ethics and indeed the rules which govern what could be tipped and where, were as minimal as the general efficiency. In far too many cases it was proved that where there was muck there was money, especially when that muck required shifting . . . today it seems inconceivable that at one time local authority vehicles shared tipping sites with those who could pay the tipping fee, and that local domestic rubbish often floated in waste oil, spent acid, latex and similar industrial liquids—in fact there was a vague optimism that one would 'soak up the other'.[33]

The industry developed through firms offering tanker services to industry, such as cesspool emptying and solvent removal. Very few treatment plants or landfill sites were run by the private sector. Loads were usually dumped within factory grounds or in a nearby quarry. The contractors depended on local authorities for alternative tipping sites, and the local authorities could accept or refuse loads without obligation. Very often they refused to have anything to do with industrial waste. The beginnings of organisation in the industry were partly stimulated by the licensing powers of local traffic authorities. A transport operator used to have to apply for a licence for his vehicles: if another established operator in the area felt the granting of the licence would harm his business he could lodge an objection and explain his case in court.[34] Some operators thought it would be better to settle the arguments in private through regular meetings between firms. This then developed in quarterly meetings where the negotiations were settled – sometimes quite vigorously: 'they joined in combat over some issues – usually concerning the A4 which each seemed to recognise as borderline to his operating area while at the same time managing to cross it if the job was lucrative enough'.[35]

But other matters of common concern were also raised at the meetings including relations with the public authorities, and technical developments in disposal services. Competition between operators handling wet and dry wastes was quite acute, rivalry between firms thereby preventing a united voice from emerging. The initiative was then taken by Tony Morgan of Purle Brothers Ltd in 1968, when he persuaded others that it was desirable to join him in setting up a trade association to represent their collective interests. The Road Haulage Association had previously had a waste disposal functional group within its structure but apart from that, the new National Association of Waste Disposal Contractors gave the industry a public identity for the first time, and only as recently as twelve years ago.[36]

A condition of NAWDC membership is the undertaking to abide by a code of practice which sets out the minimum acceptable standards of operation for collection, transporting and disposal of waste to be observed.[37] NAWDC also provides information and training facilities and operates a network of regional committees in conjunction with the Road Haulage Association. It is consulted by the DoE and other government departments on matters of national policy to do with waste disposal. It has an office in London with three staff and publishes a bimonthly newsletter called *NAWDC News.*

Standards of practice are improving now. The level of public concern in the 1970s, the Deposit of Poisonous Waste Act, and now the site licensing system of the Control of Pollution Act are expected to make it harder for unscrupulous operators to continue in the business. NAWDC admits there will always be some 'cowboys' who are prepared to take the risks of disposing of waste carelessly or illegally. It seems agreed amongst most firms involved in hazardous waste disposal (only a proportion of NAWDC members, since some handle straightforward wastes only) that a degree of legal control exercised by the government and public authorities is desirable. Not so easily agreed is how extensive these controls should be, how much discretion local waste disposal authorities should have in interpreting and fulfilling their responsibilities, and what degree of influence on the system should be permitted for public opinion. One pessimistic observer wrote recently: 'God forbid that we should get into a situation where pollution control is left to the discretion of industry. We've tried that system before and the nation still has the scars to prove it.'[38]

Until recently the very cautious attitude adopted by local authorities in accepting industrial toxic waste on their landfill tips was partly defended on the grounds that the amount of damage done to underground water sources was uncertain. But in 1973 the DoE initiated a large-scale research programme into this problem, and its final report was published in 1978.[39] It concludes that 'an ultra cautious approach is not justified, although some substances are not suitable for landfill and each case has to be treated on its merits'.[40] The report emphasises the natural processes that can dilute and thereby reduce the toxicity of hazardous substances between their deposit on a landfill tip and leakage down through ground layers to underground waters, provided the capacity of the natural systems is respected.

Three types of landfill site have been identified: those that contain the waste and leachates (i.e. water percolating through the tip containing substances dissolved from the waste); those that allow slow leachate movement away, and those allowing rapid migration of leachates. The sites suitable for toxic waste also depend on the form in which the waste is deposited – dry solid, sludge or liquid. To evaluate the potential of a site, thorough surveys of the rock and water systems have to be made, often with a bore hole drilling programme. This takes time and money and needs the skills of competent scientists. Provided a particular site appears suitable for toxic wastes, the contractor requires planning permission from the district council followed by a site licence from the county council before the site can be brought into operation. Providing adequate preliminary geological and hydrogeological studies are undertaken therefore, the report says there seems no reason why the major role that landfill plays should not continue. The DoE has recommended these findings to local authorities and water authorities since they do provide reassuring evidence.[41]

Another publication through which the DoE has encouraged local authorities to adopt a more positive approach to co-operation with private industry is Waste Management Paper no. 5[42] on the relations between them. This suggests a number of specific areas for collaboration and in relation to toxic waste mentions the difficulty of finding suitable sites and the need to look outside the local authority's area if this occurs. Sharing of landfill sites and treatment facilities is another possibility. For example a number of local authorities have incinerators which are operated at less than full capacity if only their local domestic and commercial waste is put into it. Running costs are high so it would be sensible to make the facility available (for a charge) to private contractors, particularly if they have toxic waste, unsuitable for landfill, which could be disposed of in that way. The DoE goes as far as to say that 'the provisions of the Control of Pollution Act depend on collaboration',[43] thereby making clear its view that it is local authorities who ought to take the initiative. But generalising about the unwillingness of local authorities to help private contractors obscures the fact that a number of them have had much more enlightened policies for many years, and did not require exhortations from the DoE or anyone else to develop collaboration further. Two of the authorities deserving special mention in this context are West Midlands and Essex County Councils. For many years the only two sites in England acknowledged to be suitable for large and continuing deposits of toxic waste have been Pitsea, near Basildon in Essex, operated by Land Reclamation Ltd, and Walsall Wood near Walsall in the West Midlands operated by Effluent Disposal Ltd. In each case the operating companies are subsidiaries of much larger companies— Redland Purle Ltd owned by Redland Ltd, and Leigh Interests Ltd, respectively. Redland had had an interest for many years in waste disposal, particularly since 1972 when it acquired Purle Brothers Holdings Ltd, which was mentioned in connection with the establishment of the National Association of Waste Disposal Contractors. Leigh Interests is, like Redland, a large diversified company, specialising in supplying the construction industry with products and services. With so few such sites toxic wastes from all over the country have been transported to them for disposal. Pitsea takes 40,000 tonnes of solid and 35 million gallons of liquid hazardous waste per annum, with 366,000 tonnes of barged in domestic refuse for the basis of the site.[44]

Case Study: The Private Sector's Problems

Since most toxic waste is produced and disposed of by private firms, the case study focuses on their perspective in examining the problems that arise. It consists of evidence from and about private firms' experience of toxic waste disposal, in the context of the earlier descriptive material. From the waste producers' point of view, the three most significant problems are:

(a)   legislative controls;
(b)   rising costs of disposal;
(c)   uncertainty about landfill sites.

From the disposal contractors' point of view the most significant problems are:

(a)   shortage of geologically suitable sites;
(b)   planning permission difficulties;
(c)   restricted use of sites.

These will be discussed in turn.

Legislative Controls

In the space of just a few years a network of responsibility has been created which now attempts to control the actions of hazardous waste producers in the interests of public and environmental protection. The notification system of the Deposit of Poisonous Waste Act, the site licensing and proposed consignment note system of the Control of Pollution Act require waste producers to plan and record their disposal arrangements in considerable detail. They are no longer free to pay anyone who will take a load of waste off their premises, without accepting responsibility for the consequences. They are now obliged to identify the contents of loads as specifically as possible and to ensure that conditions for handling them safely are made known. Those producers who treat their own waste may also be required to obtain licences for their plant from the waste disposal authority. The Health and Safety at Work Act 1974 also imposed responsibilities on the producers (as it does on others) to ensure employees' safety is adequately protected. In these and other ways recent legislation is having a considerable impact on waste producers.

Producers have to be sure they are (a) aware of their responsibilities and (b) capable of fulfilling them adequately. All sorts of information systems and technical advice are available to the firm that is properly organised in this respect (e.g. the Chemical Industries Association's *Environment Newsletter*,[45] services offered by NAWDC to its affiliate members,[46] the advice service run by the AERE at Harwell[47]). The major producers—chemical manufacturers and firms making iron and steel products, for example—will not have undue difficulty, although Mr Singleton of CIBA-Geigy maintained that even with their own pollution control departments larger industries could find the process of discovering their duties a daunting one.[48] But smaller firms, with less experience and staff, may find the new responsibilities even more onerous. For all firms however the legislation orders their priorities for them in a particular way that may or may not be welcome. According to a CBI spokesman, for example, 'the Deposit of Poisonous Waste Act did the country a disservice by drying up facilities which had been available. Industry is glad to see the back of it.'[49] As a contrast, though, Redland Ltd said in its 1972 Annual Report, 'this welcome legislation [the Deposit of Poisonous Waste Act] followed a long period of lobbying by responsible elements in the industry for higher standards to be set for safe disposal. However the rapidity of its introduction made producers of waste uncertain of their position under the new rules . . .'[50]

Many producers for example welcomed the Deposit of Poisonous Waste Act because they agreed that more information about hazardous wastes should be provided to the public authorities. But they also resent the administrative time that has to be spent on complying with the notification procedure. Responsible though these firms feel themselves to be (in the sense that they desire and support environmental protection policies), they are not always content with the detailed obligations that they are thereby expected to observe.

In the case of the consignment note system to be introduced under Section 17 of the Control of Pollution Act, for example, the Confederation of British Industry has been arguing vigorously with the DoE not to introduce a system based on notification because it feels that if the site licensing system is made to work properly there should be no need for such additional control. It maintains that any paper work system of notification can be abused, particularly since it is impossible to police every consignment of hazardous waste; yet the administrative load is heavy. It says that the responsible attitude of its members coupled with an effective site licensing system and co-operative relations between the public and private sectors will be the best insurance for reliable hazardous waste disposal.[51]

In addition to these criticisms of legislative controls, it has also been pointed out that in spite of consultation documents, guidelines and codes of practice, Part I of the Act can be interpreted in different ways. One waste disposal authority may adopt an entirely different attitude on a particular section to another, and the company may have to deal with more than one authority because it has several factories in different counties.[52]

Disposal Costs

The UK adheres to the 'polluter pays' principle as established by international agreement. This holds that the person or organisation creating
the pollution should be financially responsible for controlling it.[53] For
all waste producers the consequence of this is that disposal costs represent
a net charge on revenue. This can be passed on proportionately to
customers as increased prices, but with the risk that it reduces the
competitiveness of the product in question. For net costs that the
producer incurs at the margin the burden can seem considerable. Capital
costs of treatment plant for producers treating their own waste can also
be heavy (but for the chemical industry at least, much of the capital
expenditure was made in the 1960s). Accordingly the view of one CBI
spokesman was reported to be that 'the cheapest methods consistent
with safety should be used to get rid of poisonous wastes, but industry
should neither have to chafe under the bridle of those whose job it is to
err on the side of safety nor have to pay for work which would make
calculating the risks easier'.[54]

Accurate figures for industry's spending on hazardous waste disposal
are hard to obtain, but it is certain that costs have been rising in money
terms. One firm quotes a 2.6-fold rise between 1971 and 1972 and a
5.5-fold rise between 1971 and 1978.[55] It is thought transport costs
may have increased more rapidly than other elements because of the
closure of several sites caused by the more stringent legislation. One firm
quotes this experience: 'it is common throughout the country for hazardous wastes to be transported further and further to their final resting
place. With rising transport costs and stricter standards imposed on
landfill operations, expenditure on waste disposal is now a major item
in many industries.'[56] Table 4.2 shows the relative cost of different
disposal methods, and from this it can be worked out as a rough estimate
that 5 million tonnes of hazardous waste disposed of each year
produces a total cost in the region of £50 million which is less than one
quarter per cent of manufacturing industry's annual turnover.

Landfill Sites

Manufacturing industry needs long-term certainty that there will be
adequate facilities for the disposal of its wastes. There is always going to
be difficulty as far as hazardous wastes are concerned, since the unwanted
environmental consequences of disposal are still being discovered. Although
incineration and other treatments are available at a price, and even if
opportunities for recycling and reclamation increase, controlled landfill

Table 4.2: Hazardous Waste Disposal/Treatment Costs (1978)

Treatment/disposal	Cost/tonne (or per drum)
Near sea dumping of acids in bulk	£5-10
Land dumping of compacted hydroxides	£3-6
Neutralisation of acids and land dumping of the compacted solids	£20-40
Cracking of emulsions, dumping of compacted solids	
Encapsulation of toxic metal sludges and dumping of the solid polymer:	
solid catalysts	£10
50% toxic metal pastes	£100
Incineration of mixed foul solvents	£35-50
Incineration of highly chlorinated organics (depending on state and degree of chlorination)	£75-200
Deep sea disposal of cyanide residues	£75-100
Oxidation of cyanides, compaction of solids and land dumping of residues	£200-250
Bulk liquid incineration costs:	
capable of burning unsupported	£10-30
aqueous requiring support fuel	£30-40
requiring incineration with gas scrubbing	£40-120
Encapsulation of 40-gallon (180-litre) drums and sea dumping	£50-70 per drum
Drummed liquid wastes:	
5-gallon (23-litre) drums	£1 minimum per drum
45-gallon (207-litre) drums	£10-80 per drum

Source: Open University Course PT272, Unit 9.

is going to remain the commonest disposal method for a long time. This makes it imperative from the producer's point of view that there are sufficient landfill sites available. At the moment there are only about a dozen major ones (i.e. those accepting over 400 tonnes of toxic wastes per week) and these do not have unlimited capacities. Much therefore depends on collaboration between waste disposal authorities, planning authorities and disposal contractors to work out a sensible strategy for coping with the problem and this is discussed further below. It is of some comfort to waste producers that when Section 1 of the Control of Pollution Act comes into force, waste disposal authorities will have statutory responsibility to ensure that there are adequate arrangements, whether made by themselves or others, to dispose of all controlled waste in their areas.[57] But they are concerned that the different interpretations different authorities may make of this responsibility will perpetuate some of the uncertainties. They feel local authorities are still ill informed of industry's problems and rigidly assume that industry should be self-sufficient in waste management. The Sumner Report echoes this: 'the Association of Metropolitan Councils told us that industry could best look after its own waste disposal and local authorities should not be responsible for it'.[58] If this approach prevails there is little optimism that mutually acceptable solutions can be generated. Producers admit they could sometimes do more to modify the processes that produce difficult wastes. This is theoretically the best prevention of pollution. But research and development costs for this can be heavy, and carry high risk, so few producers are keen to invest substantially in this way. Smaller producers will in any case be unable to do a great deal of in-house waste treatment or process modification if they have limited capital, space and expertise, and will therefore be particularly concerned about finding economic disposal facilities elsewhere.

Geologically Suitable Sites

Apart from Pitsea, Walsall Wood and a site in Scotland there are only a few other landfill sites currently accepting significant quantities of toxic wastes. It is difficult to know the impact of the claimed shortage of geologically suitable sites. The County Project Officer of Essex County Council maintained that Pitsea was not a freak. Plenty more sites existed in other parts of the country and should be used, he said, to relieve the burden on Essex.[59] Other evidence suggests that toxic wastes are still being deposited on sites that are not suited to them.[60] Whatever the situation, private contractors are in no doubt that to do their business satisfactorily, further safe sites are needed, and they are concerned that too few of them are becoming available. The former marketing director of Redland Purle Ltd, Dr David Davies, has for some years tried to promote the idea of regional hazardous waste management as a solution to the problem. He argues that the availability of suitable sites, the generation of sufficient quantities to make them viable and the need to run the sites under close and skilful supervision argues for areas larger than counties to take this on and plan an appropriate strategy.[61]

Planning Permission

The traditionally cautious attitude of local planning authorities in allowing contractors to operate landfill sites and treatment plants in their areas has been a problem for a long time. It has not been helped by the bad reputation the business is acknowledged to have earned for itself. Planning committees are much more careful now in permitting more of their areas to be given over to landfill sites or treatment plants. Even in areas containing well-established and well-managed sites, contractors cannot be sure of obtaining new permissions as a matter of course. As one industrialist puts it:

> the two tier planning structure between district and county councils certainly does not help the development of waste disposal facilities. A private operator applying for planning permission for a landfill site may be refused by the district council while the county council . . . may support the application. The result means that the number of new schemes becoming available is very small and may be achieved only after years of persistence.[62]

An example of this occurred when Redland Purle Ltd applied to East Cambridgeshire District Council for planning permission to use its own brick clay pits outside Burwell for tipping non-hazardous wastes. Its proposals were backed by Cambridge County Council (the waste disposal authority) but the district council refused permission. The Burwell villagers had been vigorously opposing Redland Purle's application because they feared they might be getting another Pitsea on their doorstep.[63]

In cases such as these, the contractors suspect the councillors on planning committees in their concern to retain electoral support are unduly swayed by the emotive fears and rumours that local people may express. They also suspect many planning authorities have insufficient knowledge or expertise on hand to understand what the environmental impact of a proposed site would really be. A circular issued by the DoE to the planning authorities in 1972 could not have expressed contractors' views better for them:

> the Secretaries of State urge local planning authorities to take into account the overall need for such facilities and the general environmental benefits likely to accrue from the achievement of a reduction in the quantity and toxicity of waste. This is of particular importance when considering commercial proposals intended to cater for the needs of industries both inside and outside the area of the local planning authority concerned.[64]

Waste Management Paper no. 5 published four years later reiterated the advice:

> It must also be recognised however that firms do often run into difficulties when trying to obtain planning consent for disposal sites and there exists and will continue to exist, a competitive element between the [public and private] sectors. Neither of these factors is conducive to the development of a spirit of cooperation and the tensions they create will have to be overcome.[65]

Restricted Use of Sites

This problem relates to the use of existing treatment and disposal sites for hazardous wastes, where the sites may be operated either by the local disposal authority or a private contractor. Here again the contractors feel that the planning authorities have been overcautious in their response to applications for changes or extensions in the use of sites. The Standing Conference on London and South East Regional Planning reported that 'the use of quite safe sites has often been restricted, or even prevented altogether, by planning authorities who did not possess sufficient technical expertise properly to judge the risks involved in disposing of hazardous wastes, and who have therefore tended to "err on the safe side"'.[66]

In Redland Purle's own experience of operating the site at Pitsea there have been a series of arguments with Basildon District Council. According to a press report: 'it is no secret that Basildon DC wants to stop the deposit of hazardous liquids and sludges at Pitsea. And on its own behalf, and also responding to pressure from the local residents' association, are using every legal device available to achieve that end.'[67] One recent cause of disagreement between the district council and Redland Purle Ltd concerned the access road to the site. There were about 200 vehicle movements a day and the council considered the risk to residents unacceptable. So when the lease on the road expired, Redland's application for a new lease was turned down. A series of appeals were made against the decision, and after protracted argument the company was given permission to build its own road. The dispute took almost three years and was accompanied by 'public demonstration, bitterness and recrimination, largely brought about through fear and mis-information'.[68] Commenting on these sorts of difficulties in 1975 the chairman of Redland Ltd said: 'waste disposal does involve serious environmental considerations and socially acceptable national plans tend to produce local problems which are all too apparent, for the sake of widespread benefits which are often invisible'.[69]

Leigh Interests' Walsall Wood site has also been the cause of dispute between the company and the planning authorities. In 1976 the site, which is a disused mine, was closed when a shaft became blocked. The operating company, Effluent Disposal Ltd, applied to Walsall District Council for planning permission to use another nearby shaft for depositing liquid toxic waste instead. The response was not favourable because at an earlier planning enquiry concerning Walsall Wood the company was found to have flouted some of the consent conditions under which it was meant to operate. This relatively minor issue left a persisting and deep suspicion of the company even though the planning enquiry recommended mainly in its favour. It was simultaneously having trouble with both the planning and waste disposal authorities about its continuing and extended use of another nearby facility – Mitco site – for pre-treatment of industrial waste. Permission was eventually granted, although several conditions were imposed on the consent.[70] A statement that gives an idea of the flavour of the dispute was made by Leigh Interests on the planning enquiry inspector's report: 'the report is a significant document in the modern waste disposal industry's struggle to obtain consents for facilities in the teeth of opposition from local residents and environmentalists'.[71] Without a great deal more information it is difficult to identify who is responsible for things going wrong in such cases. But clearly the operators can have a busy time in court and at enquiries trying to establish agreement for them to conduct their business in the way they want.

Local authorities have also been accused of unnecessarily restricting the use of their own sites and treatment plants. Dr Feates, formerly of the AERE Hazardous Waste Service, said:

I do not think anyone would dispute the fact that at the present time there is an acute shortage of adequate disposal facilities for potentially hazardous material. Local authorities have some of the most sophisticated chemical treatment plants in the country at their disposal of sewage works and also in incinerators; they also control a wide range of tips on land of all kinds of geological structure. They must consider very seriously the extent to which these could be used in the short or long term to alleviate the problems faced by industry.[72]

Analysis

The above description of waste producers' and disposers' problems can
be illuminated by looking at the issues from a contrasted standpoint. The
descriptions, after all, do not contain a fully argued case; they simply set
out the preoccupations of the people most actively involved. There are
three dimensions to consider: scientific and technical features of the
management processes in waste disposal; the reputation or image that
the different parties hold of each other; and the appropriate roles various
parties might play.

On the first point, the scientific and technical issues will continue to
be the subject of continuing research and investigation, but financial
incentives are a significant determinant of progress. At the moment and
certainly in the medium term it is agreed that landfill will remain the
prime disposal method for hazardous waste in the UK, mainly because
it is the cheapest and easiest method, but also because it seems to be
fairly safe if properly managed. Research on other methods will continue, waste-producing processes will be modified, and some toxic wastes
may thus be reduced. But these are all unlikely to have a large impact on
the scale of the disposal problem. The difficulties with landfill will arise
therefore if good standards of practice are not introduced and maintained.

Secondly, the stereotyped images that the parties—industry, local
authorities, central government and local amenity groups—hold of each
other influence to a considerable degree the potential for progress in
eliminating difficulties. These have already been referred to: industry seen
as an irresponsible sector motivated by profit and careless about environmental damage; local authorities as blinkered, overcautious amateurs
dabbling ineffectually and interfering with progress; central government
as slow, indecisive and introducing excessively bureaucratic and inappropriate controls; and amenity groups as hysterical Luddites ready
to block any progress.

These are obviously highly selective caricatures and each group could
offer a defence of its real stance—industry's defence has already been
described. They see themselves doing a difficult job responsibly—economic
benefits accrue to society as a whole from this. In the face of technical
and financial problems and lack of co-operation from others, they are
doing reasonably well. The few 'lapses' that do occur are now very rare,
and not more than any other sector suffers. Local government's defence
is that local government reorganisation and a lot of new legislation and
responsibilities to shoulder in the context of severe financial difficulties
are bound to diminish their rate of progess. It is still justified to be

cautious about industry's advances because recent history illustrates the damage that can be done. For example in 1977 South Yorkshire County Council succeeded in persuading the DoE to contribute £650,000 towards the cost of land reclamation at Myletts Tip at Silverwood quarry near Rotherham. The site had been used by private tippers illicitly to dump acid, tars and other toxic wastes. Known locally as the 'bubbling cauldron', it was fenced off by South Yorkshire County Council after dangerous fumes began to be given off and several children and a dog had been burned. The county's difficulty was that the site had had a succession of owners over the past 20 years and it was impossible to find anyone on whom to pin responsibility.[73] Central government agrees that it is cautious but thinks this is appropriate for 'pioneering legislation such as the Deposit of Poisonous Waste Act and Section 17 of the Control of Pollution Act'.[74] It tries to introduce workable policies yet does not interfere in local implementation as this is beyond its responsibilities. Local amenity groups defend their approach by pointing to the disruption and nuisance some people have to suffer because no one has succeeded in preventing irresponsible developments.

So to contrast these with the private sector perspective, there seems to be an important issue recurring – the suspicion that whatever the private sector says and does to improve the acceptability of its practice, just one 'lapse' will harm its chances of relying on co-operation. Even in the case of a firm as large and as experienced as Redland Purle this is true. At the Pitsea enquiry recently, outside experts commended the firm for its good standards of practice. Yet only a few years earlier at the same site a tanker driver had died when he was overcome by fumes he had unknowingly created by mixing loads of incompatible toxic wastes. At their Metallic Tileries tip in Staffordshire, Redland Purle caused the Lyme Brook to be polluted some years ago, before local government reorganisation, by leakage from the tip where the top of the clay bowl fell away after it had been filled to capacity.[75] Leigh Interests was fined for a number of offences under the Deposit of Poisonous Waste Act in its operations at Walsall through the operating company Effluent Disposal Ltd.[76]

These incidents are probably rare in the context of the total amount of toxic waste handled effectively and safely every day, although it still seems quite possible to dump toxic wastes readily. The chances of getting caught and the vigilance of local authorities may be lower than is officially acknowledged. However, incidents that do come to light are very worrying to local authorities and communities and show to anyone reading newspaper accounts of them how imperfect the control systems are. It is agreed by the 'responsible' disposal contractors that a few 'cow-boys' do still exist and make a living from dangerous and illegal practices, although this distinction may sometimes become blurred. Even if it is beyond the power of legislation or the industry itself to eliminate the few cowboys, it seems important that the respectable firms will not allow themselves to 'lapse'. Since incidents such as the ones just quoted do appear to be avoidable it is not surprising that local people should remain suspicious of the firms' claims to be responsible. On the other side, though, some of the obstacles from local authorities encountered by private firms do seem unnecessary, and this has long been recognised by central and local government as a whole. For example in Circular 39/76 DoE urges waste disposal and water authorities to

> bear in mind, firstly the possibility that over restrictive attitudes may result in fly tipping by unscrupulous operators and this in turn may lead to the serious pollution problems site licensing seeks to avoid, and second-ly that unnecessary increases in the cost of waste disposal, which could be substantial, could in certain circumstances limit the money available for other environmental measures.[77]

The DoE expects that planning responsibilities will in time become located with the counties and thus relieve many of the difficulties encountered in England.[78] Also the Control of Pollution Act is acknowledged to be a force for good in the sense that it brings the private and public sectors into closer contact with each other and this in itself is the basis on which it is to be hoped that co-operation will be fostered.

One area where a problem may yet arise has to do with local authorities' charging policies. Although districts and counties generally collect and dispose of only tiny amounts of hazardous waste at the moment, the foregoing discussion has indicated that they may take on a bigger share. They are required to charge producers and contractors for this service, so that the service will be self-financing and not a charge on public money (through the rates). Waste Management Paper no. 5 spells this out quite clearly by stating that local authorities should ensure their disposal charges are realistic in fairness both to those operating in the private sector and to their own ratepayers.[79] But already some disposal firms are worried that this charging structure is not being adhered to and local authorities are not setting truly cost-reflective rates, thus under-cutting the private sector scale of charges which cannot be subsidised in a similar way. Evidence is not widely available to illustrate this problem although several firms say it goes on.[80] If it is substantiated then local authorities guilty of this are not complying with the guidance commended to them by the DoE. If the contractors are mistaken or are exaggerating the real scale of the problem then it seems their lack of trust of the local authorities is still strong. From an outside viewpoint it would appear unlikely that local authorities would want to compete with private contractors on any significant scale as far as hazardous waste disposal is concerned. They are not meant to make any profit from handling industrial waste, and this activity should not interfere in any way with their principal responsibility to collect and dispose of household and commercial waste.

The third analytic factor is the 'appropriate' role for each of the interested parties concerned with toxic waste disposal. From the evidence it emerged that a number of opportunities for reducing the private sector's difficulties were not being used to the full. The position of the National Association of Waste Disposal Contractors (NAWDC) is one example of this. Although its code of practice (which members undertake to observe) is a responsible and comprehensive one, 'lapses' from it are not severely punished, if the Association even gets to know of infringements. Scope for an internal NAWDC enquiry exists, but no effective deterrent sanctions are imposed on the guilty firm. This gives the impression that the industry is unable or unwilling to regulate itself, and by deduction therefore outside powers (public authorities, licences and regulations) are necessary. In addition the Association is unable to say how many private firms there are in the business or what proportion of them it represents. This may genuinely be difficult to ascertain but without some reasonable evidence of its position as a representative body NAWDC cannot necessarily expect to appear very convincing as a forceful spokesman – the fact that it is consulted by central government does not detract from this point. It has been shown that a major problem facing the industry is to convince local authorities and local communities that it is conscientious. This requires individual firms, large and small, to behave well since the best public relations the industry can enjoy will be a function (it has been suggested) of the number of 'lapses' that occur.[81] If the National Association of Waste Disposal Contractors can become a more powerful factor within the industry and back its claims for the industry with solid and convincing evidence, much suspicion will be defused.

Another area where NAWDC could perhaps do more relates to the effectiveness with which the smaller waste producers and disposers fulfil their statutory responsibility. There is evidence that many firms were ignorant of their obligations under the Deposit of Poisonous Waste

Act 1972 long after it was enforced. To quote one waste producer: 'there are still without doubt many industrial concerns who are unaware of existing and impending legislation and the only significant impact that waste disposal has made on them has been the rapidly increasing costs'.[82] Equally there have been many firms quite unaware of the site licensing provisions of the Control of Pollution Act. Keith Brackley, the Deputy Waste Disposal Officer of South Yorkshire County Council said, after his department had held a seminar to inform local contractors and private tip operators of the implications of these provisions:

> nearly all sectors of the private waste disposal industry in Yorkshire were blissfully unaware of the implications of both the Control of Pollution and the Health and Safety at Work Act. I am sure that when site licensing begins to bite the number of tips in the county will be reduced by more than half. We [the Waste Disposal Authority] were able to reduce the number of our tip sites from more than 50 to 16 and I suspect the private sector might have to do the same.[83]

NAWDC does sponsor a series of training courses for junior and middle managers, but there is clearly more widespread need for training: new legislative developments (e.g. Section 17 regulations when they are introduced, and future EEC legislation) are bound to emphasise this.

Another body which could perhaps play an enhanced part in improving public-private sector relations is the Institute of Solid Waste Management. This body is still dominated by local authorities staff (it was founded in 1898 and until recently used to be called the Institute of Public Cleansing) although more people from private firms are taking an interest in it now. But it still has a rather introspective and old fashioned image like many other professional associations and does not appear to take much interest in creating a more dynamic impression or improving the public's understanding of the difficulties its members face. As one ISWM member sadly explained, 'the parochial attitude previously held by many waste managers merely reflects on the one hand the meagre financial allocation made for local authority waste disposal, and on the other the "head in the sand" approach by some waste producers who wanted the waste taken away at the cheapest possible price with no thought to possible environmental dangers . . .'[84]

Lastly the role that public opinion plays in the private sector's problems should be recognised. Unless people live near to treatment plants or landfill sites or by the access roads to them the problems of hazardous waste disposal are unlikely to make much impact on them in the ordinary

way. Quite understandably there is a low level of public interest. But if
anything goes wrong—tanker accident, illegal tipping, water polluted by
leakages for example—then there is quite likely to be considerable local
response. Several types of serious damage done by toxic substances in
recent years have also made a strong impression: according to a senior
member of the Health and Safety Executive these include cases of bladder
cancer in the rubber and cable industries (1965); body absorption of
lead at Avonmouth and the Isle of Dogs (1972); angiosarcoma (cancer)
in plastics manufacture (1974); asbestos related diseases in Hebden
Bridge employees (1975); the release of TCDD at Seveso (1976).[85] The
general press reports very little about waste disposal unless accidents
occur. Then it often goes in for the splash headlines treatment and this
applies to television too. However the technical press does cover day-to-
day affairs more consistently as well as providing more background
information and informed comment when things do go wrong. The
most comprehensive journal in this context is *Municipal Engineering*—
a well-established fortnightly publication covering the technical side of
local government affairs.[86] Its Deputy Editor Rudy Singh has been
writing about waste management for many years and has earned a good
reputation for his comments. He has his own strong views and is not
afraid to criticise some of the people involved from either side but he
nevertheless succeeds in covering the subject fairly thoroughly and has
done a lot to inform readers of the issues. *Surveyor*[87] is a competitor
of *Municipal Engineering*, aiming at much the same local authority
readership (members and staff) and it too has good informative articles
on waste management, but rather less frequently nor with the same degree
of authority that *Municipal Engineering* manages. The Institute of Solid
Waste Management produces a monthly magazine *Solid Waste*[88] which
consists mainly of articles and papers written by local authority and
other operational staff on technical and practical questions of waste
management. It also reprints discussions of papers from its annual conferences which provide an interesting barometer of opinions. However
the journal is not so widely read by other people so it is mainly an
internal point of reference for local authority technical staff. Other
technical papers in related fields—environmental health, water-cycle
management, local planning—occasionally have pieces on hazardous
waste questions too.

From this it can be seen that there is little from the media helping
the public to develop a well-informed view of waste management. The
job has been taken up instead by certain amenity groups, but with a
built-in bias to their particular concerns, naturally. Friends of the Earth

for example are active in the recycling and reclamation field. The Conservation Society's role in the Deposit of Poisonous Waste Act 1972 has already been described. There are numerous residents' groups in towns and villages where treatment and disposal sites exist or are planned, who take a very lively part in the debate, campaigning vigorously against developments they oppose.[89] Generally public knowledge is very restricted, so there is more scope for public knowledge to improve planning authorities' grasp of the different issues and to reduce some of the unfounded fears that industry feels exist. Whether this is a job for industry, local authorities or the media is not exactly clear – but unless it is done, significant areas of support for industry will not be exploited.

Notes

1. Deposit of Poisonous Waste Act, Schedule Regulation 3.
2. Department of the Environment. *Waste Disposal Survey*, Waste Management Paper no. 2 (HMSO, London, 1976).
3. Department of the Environment Circular 55/76. Control of Pollution Act 1974, Part I (Waste on Land) *Disposal Licences.* Annex B. London, May 1976.
4. The Department of the Environment and Commission of the European Economic Communities are engaged in this; similar work is in hand in the United States, under the auspices of the Environmental Protection Agency.
5. Control of Pollution Act 1974, s30(1), 30(3) and 17(1).
6. See for example Department of the Environment, *War on Waste. Policy for Reclamation*, Cmnd. 5727 (HMSO, London, 1974); Report of the Institute of Municipal Engineers on wastes recycling in *Municipal Engineering* (7 November 1978), pp. 156-9; and Friends of the Earth, *Waste – Problem or Resource?* (FoE, London, December 1977); and B. Gulley 'Waste Treatment Systems – Options for the 1980s', *Municipal Engineering* (14 August 1979), pp. 602-4.
7. This power, contained in Section 1 of the Act, will not be invoked for the time being as the government announced indefinite postponement of its implementation on 17 September 1979.
8. Department of the Environment, *Refuse Disposal*, Report of the Working Party on Refuse Disposal (Chairman J. Sumner) (HMSO, London, 1971). The Working Party was appointed in 1967 to 'consider the various methods available for the disposal of refuse and to ascertain how satisfactorily they are being operated; to evaluate these methods with particular regard to the increasing quantities and changing character of refuse; and to consider what advice should be given to local authorities and others concerned on the choice of methods best suited to local conditions on the practical aspects of waste disposal generally'.
9. Ministry of Housing and Local Government and Scottish Development Department, *Report of the Technical Committee on the Disposal of Solid Toxic Wastes* (Chairman Dr A. Key) (HMSO, London, 1970). The Technical Committee was appointed in 1964 to 'consider present methods of disposal of solid and semi-solid toxic wastes from the chemical and allied industries, to examine suggestions for improvement and to advise what, if any, changes are desirable in current practice in the facilities available for disposal and in the control arrangements in order to ensure that such wastes are disposed of safely and without risk of polluting water supplies and rivers'.
10. Complete list in: Department of the Environment, *Pollution Control in Great Britain: How it Works*, Pollution Paper no. 9, 2nd edn (HMSO, London,

1978), para. 189.

11. Its terms of reference are: 'To keep under review the development of waste management policies in the United Kingdom having regard to the need to secure the best use of resources, and the safe and efficient disposal of wastes; to give particular attention to ways of reclaiming materials from waste, recycling materials from waste, recycling techniques, the interrelationship of waste utilisation and waste disposal, and the reduction or transformation of waste arising; to consider the technical, economic, administrative and legal problems involved; to consider the programme of research and development; and to make recommendations.' Its published reports include a study of waste paper collection by local authorities (1976) and an economic case study of waste oil. In a government announcement in September 1979, the Council's future existence was identified for review, as part of the pruning of 'quangos'.

12. For example, its publications include: *The Paper Chains* (FoE, London, 1977); *Ecological Paper Buying* (FoE, London, 1978); *Material Gains*, 2nd edn (FoE, London, 1979).

13. Under Section 24 local authorities will have a statutory obligation to set out in a published statement the steps intended to be taken within their areas for the abatement of litter. The Keep Britain Tidy Group will extend the information, advice and assistance it already provides to local authorities, to assist in this. The implementation of Section 24 was postponed, in a government announcement made in September 1979. The group is not a typical amenity body since its membership consists of companies and trade associations, national, professional and voluntary bodies and central and local government interests.

14. See note 9.

15. See the accounts in R. Kimber, J.J. Richardson and S.K. Brookes, 'The Deposit of Poisonous Waste Act 1972: a Case of Government by Reaction?', *Public Law* (Autumn 1974), pp. 198-219; and The Open University, 'Environmental Control and Public Health PT272 Unit 10', *Hazardous Wastes* (The Open University Press, Milton Keynes, 1978), pp. 14-58 and 140-4. Kimber *et al.* observed: 'The public awareness generated by the media transformed what had previously been a rather unexciting administrative matter into a sensitive political issue' (p. 204).

16. Royal Commission on Environmental Pollution, *First Report*, Cmnd. 4585 (HMSO, London, 1971), para. 72(1).

17. Royal Commission on Environmental Pollution, *Second Report: Three Issues in Industrial Pollution*, Cmnd. 4894 (HMSO, London, 1972), para. 31(2).

18. The government's reply was set out in a pamphlet in the Pollution Paper series: Department of the Environment, Central Unit on Environmental Pollution, *Controlling Pollution: a Review of Government Action Related to Recommendations by the Royal Commission on Environmental Pollution*, Pollution Paper no. 4 (HMSO, London, 1975).

19. As quoted in *The Times*, 25 February 1972.

20. See Kimber, Richardson and Brookes, *Deposit of Poisonous Waste Act*; Open University, *Hazardous Wastes* for further details of these events.

21. Although the Act received Royal Assent at the end of March, it was July before regulations exempting certain categories of waste had been made, and August before the notification system had been introduced. See Statutory Instrument 1972 No. 1016, *Deposit of Poisonous Waste Act (Commencement) Order* (6 July 1972) and Statutory Instrument 1972 No. 1017, *Deposit of Poisonous Waste Act 1972 (Notification of Removal of Deposits) Regulations* (1972).

22. See Schedule to Section 1 1972, No. 1017.

23. See Department of the Environment, *Deposit of Poisonous Waste Act 1972*, Circular 70/72.

24. Section 1 1972, No. 1017.

25. This timetable was accurate at the time of writing.

26. Department of the Environment, Welsh Office, Scottish Office, *Waste*

Disposal: Proposals for a New Framework (DoE, London, January 1973). Part V on pages 36-41 covers 'special controls for toxic or dangerous substances'.

27. The EEC Council of Ministers agreed a Directive on Toxic and Dangerous Waste on 12 December 1977, published in the Official Journal OJ No. L84 of 31 March 1978.

28. See Department of the Environment, Circular 29/78, *The Control of Pollution Act 1974. Part I – Waste on Land* (5 April 1978), particularly paras. 12-15.

29. Indeed, some observers already feel that the site licensing provisions of the Control of Pollution Act may have a greater impact on the safe disposal of toxic waste than the 1972 Act and the Section 17 regulations that succeed it.

30. National Association of Waste Disposal Contractors, *Trade Directory 1979* (NAWDC, London, revised April 1979).

31. W. Stapleton, Director of NAWDC in personal interview with author.

32. In the October 1979 issue of NAWDC, publication of the Association's first brochure was announced in these terms: 'For too long . . . we have stared at horrific historical slides of tinker-operated tips as evidence of the private sector's contribution to the waste industry. Now we have assembled pictorial proof positive of advances made in the private sector of waste management for all to see.' *NAWDC News* (October 1979), p. 3.

33. H. Mould, 'And in the Beginning . . .', *NAWDC News* (October 1978), p. 20.

34. Ibid., p. 20.

35. Ibid., p. 21.

36. NAWDC was established in 1968. The Royal Commission on Environmental Pollution had recommended that the government should stimulate and encourage a strong national association. (*Solid Wastes Management* (July 1974), p. 384).

37. National Association of Waste Disposal Contractors, *Code of Practice* (NAWDC, London, revised May 1978).

38. B. Randall, 'Randall Writes', *Municipal Engineering* (5 June 1979), p. 447.

39. Department of the Environment, *Final Report of the Co-operative Programme of Research on the Behaviour of Hazardous Wastes in Landfill Sites* (HMSO, London, 1978).

40. Quoted in Department of the Environment, Circular 29/78, *The Control of Pollution Act 1974. Part I – Waste on Land* (DoE, London, 5 April 1978), para. 3.

41. Ibid.

42. Department of the Environment, Waste Management Paper no. 5. *The Relationship between Waste Disposal Authorities and Private Industry* (HMSO, London, 1976).

43. Department of the Environment, Circular 3/76, *Waste Management Papers* (DoE, London, 26 March 1976), para. 10.

44. *Municipal Engineering* (5 June 1979), p. 396.

45. Chemical Industries Association Limited, *Environment Newsletter* (CIA, London, occasional).

46. See p. 61.

47. The DoE sponsors an Industrial Waste Information Bureau (at the Hazardous Materials Service run by the Atomic Energy Research Establishment at Harwell) which has been working since 1976. It issues regular bulletins to subscribers (local authorities, industry, contractors) and also offers emergency and consultancy services. Further details in *NAWDC News* (December 1979), pp. 12-14.

48. K.G. Singleton, *The Waste Producer's Viewpoint on Hazardous Substances in Treatment and Disposal of Hazardous Wastes*, Conference Transcript (Oyez International Business Communications Ltd, London, 1978), p. 45.

49. H.C. Butcher, at the Institute of Water Pollution Control Conference on Disposal of Municipal and Industrial Sludges and Solid Toxic Wastes, quoted in *Municipal Engineering* (7 December 1973), p. 2703.

50. Redland Ltd, *Report 1972*, p. 12.
51. According to Roy Martindale, Senior Technical Adviser, Confederation of British Industry, in personal communication with author.
52. Singleton, *The Waste Producer's Viewpoint*, p. 45.
53. This was agreed by OECD member countries in 1972. It implies that public money should not be given to polluters to assist directly with their pollution control costs. See OECD, *The State of the Environment in Member Countries* (OECD, Paris, 1979), p. 128 and pp. 133-8.
54. Account of H.C. Butcher's remarks in *Municipal Engineering* (7 December 1975), p. 2703.
55. Singleton, *The Waste Producer's Viewpoint*, p. 47.
56. Ibid.
57. But see note 7.
58. Department of the Environment, *Refuse Disposal: Report of the Working Party on Refuse Disposal* (HMSO, London, 1971), para. 574.
59. Quoted from Annual Report of Essex County Council's Project Officer, Bryan Beckett, in *Municipal Engineering* (30 October 1975), p. 1885.
60. See for example the Low Moor Farm case, *Municipal Engineering* (30 January 1979), p. 46.
61. D.R. Davies, *National Facilities for Waste Disposal and Disposal of Hazardous Wastes*, Conference Transcript (Oyez International Business Communications Ltd, London, 1978), pp. 128-9.
62. Singleton, *The Waste Producer's Viewpoint*, p. 46.
63. *Municipal Engineering* (26 July 1976), p. 1028.
64. Department of the Environment, Circular 70/72, *Deposit of Poisonous Waste Act* (July 1972), para. 29.
65. Ibid., para. 1.1.
66. Standing Conference on London and South East Regional Planning, *Waste Disposal in South East England*, Report SC909 (London, May 1978), para. 7-19.
67. Pitsea faces serious threats of closure. *Municipal Engineering* (19 December 1978), pp. 885-6.
68. *Municipal Engineering* (5 June 1979), p. 399.
69. Redland Ltd, *Annual Report 1975*, p. 9.
70. *Surveyor* (4 January 1979), p. 2.
71. 'Two-year Fight for Right to Continue Use of Walsall Wood Mines', *NAWDC News* (April 1979), p. 11.
72. F.S. Feates, *Disposal of Difficult Materials*, Paper presented to Institute of Public Cleansing symposium on The Collection and Disposal of Hazardous Wastes, Manchester (12 January 1973), p. 16.
73. *Municipal Engineering* (5 July 1977), p. 756 and (2 August 1977), p. 89.
74. Michael Ross, Administrative Trainee, Wastes Division DoE in personal interview with the author.
75. Quoted by Glyn Perry, Chairman, South-West and South Wales Group, ISWM, personal interview with author.
76. *Municipal Engineering* (14 January 1977), p. 45.
77. Department of the Environment, Circular 39/76, *The Balancing of Interests between Water Protection and Waste Disposal* (13 April 1976), para. 9.
78. According to Anthony Fagin, Wastes Division, DoE, in a personal interview with the author, in May 1979. In November 1979 the DoE Working Group on Land Wastes received a note from its Secretariat indicating that development control over waste disposal would indeed become a county matter, this being achieved by means of a statutory instrument under the provisions of subparagraph 32(f) of Schedule 16 to the Local Government Act 1972.
79. Waste Management Paper no. 5, paras 7.1-7.3.
80. Quoted by W. Stapleton, Director of NAWDC, in personal interview with author.
81. Thus according to Rudy Singh, 'The private sector of the waste management industry is fighting a dignified battle for survival in the face of a plethora of

recent legislation which, at worst, promises to sink it without trace, or, at best, to ensure survival only of the fittest'. *Municipal Engineering* (23 July 1976), p. 1136.

82. Singleton, *The Waste Producer's Viewpoint*, p. 44.

83. *Municipal Engineering* (2 April 1976), p. 505.

84. H.G. Shallcross, *The Relationship between the Public and Private Sectors of Solid Wastes Management in the Light of New Legislation*, Paper presented to Institute of Solid Wastes Management Conference (1975), p. 2.

85. Audrey Pittom, *The Control of Toxic Hazards: the way ahead. Chemistry and Industry* (4 February 1978), pp. 77-80.

86. *Municipal Engineering*, published by Municipal Journals Ltd.

87. *Surveyor*, published by IPC Business Press Ltd.

88. *Solid Wastes*, published by the Institute of Solid Wastes Management, 26 Portland Place, London W1N 4PE. Monthly journal of the Institute.

89. Nigel Haigh, formerly of the Civic Trust, commented in a personal interview with the author, that there could be more co-ordinated action by voluntary groups at county level. The strength of the amenity movement is its local attachment but this blinds it to wider considerations. The Civic Trust holds an annual meeting for amenity society federations and in 1978 this included a session on waste management. One such federation – the Berkshire Environmental Forum – held its own one-day seminar in September 1979 on this subject, entitled 'Our throwaway society'. Haigh commented that this was a welcome if rare example of voluntary group initiative at the appropriate level for having an impact on waste management questions.

5 THE BATHING WATER DIRECTIVE

Water Pollution Control

The Control of Pollution Act introduced a few new provisions for water pollution control; but most of Part II extends and improves the very extensive arrangements already established by legislation enacted during the previous 100 years. There have been two important trends in this legislation – one has been to integrate administrative responsibility for each part of the water cycle: previously water conservation and distribution, sewerage, sewage disposal and pollution control were managed by quite independent organisations. Now the Regional Water Authorities control all these functions within their areas. Secondly the trend away from local towards central determination of policy for water-cycle management (including pollution control) has been emphasised. The National Water Council is charged with the development of this policy, in consultation with other interested parties.[1]

The Public Health Act 1875 for the first time made local authorities responsible for the provision of an adequate public water supply and collection and disposal of sewage. In the next year the Rivers (Pollution Prevention) Act prohibited dumping of domestic, industrial and mining wastes and the disposal of sewage in rivers. Local authorities were not uniformly effective in implementing these changes and the 1936 Public Health Act reiterated that they should do this. Then in 1945 the Water Act made the Ministry of Health responsible for evolving and directing a national policy – although it did not provide an administrative framework for management of other uses of water apart from public supply.

In 1948, 32 River Boards were set up to manage land drainage, fisheries and to monitor effluents, but no longer following local authority boundaries and for the first time acknowledging the natural ones. The Board acquired pollution control duties from local authorities by virtue of the Rivers (Prevention of Pollution) Act 1951 and these were extended to cover estuaries and coastal waters from 1960 by the Clean Rivers (Estuaries and Tidal Waters) Act. Further strength was given to the Boards by the 1961 Rivers (Prevention of Pollution) Act because it enabled them to revise and review the consent standards allowed for discharge of effluents and brought under control pre-1951 discharges to inland waters. Administrative reorganisation was produced by the Water Resources Act 1963 which redrew the boundaries to create 27 new River

Authorities (plus the Thames and Lee Conservancies) and extended the Minister of Housing and Local Government's power to include a national water supply policy, implemented through a Water Resources Board and the River Authorities. Ten years later another complete reorganisation was created by the Water Act 1973. This replaced the River Boards by nine Regional Authorities in England and a new Welsh National Water Development Authority. The new water authorities have since then managed conservation, water supply, sewerage and sewage treatment, river pollution, fisheries, land drainage and water recreation, and thus took on functions that had previously been exercised by about 1,600 separate bodies in England and Wales (1,400 local authorities, 29 river authorities and 200 water undertakings).

Most local authorities design, construct and maintain sewers on the water authority's behalf, and in about 25 per cent of the country statutory water companies may still supply water as agents of the water authority.[2] The regional water authorities have to be financially self-supporting and charge those for whom they provide services. Central government (through the Department of the Environment) sets a limit for their capital borrowing, and takes advice from the National Water Council on national water policy issues. Part II of the Control of Pollution Act 1974 covers water, and its provisions have been outlined in Chapter 3. In summary, it brings under control all inland and coastal waters, and ensures that discharges of trade or sewage effluents into them are approved by the water authority through a system of consents. Consent conditions have to be set for the water authority's own sewage effluents too, and approved by the Secretary of State. Records of all applications and consents have to be kept by the water authority in registers which the public may consult. Only agricultural discharges that may be polluting are exempt from this control provided they arise from 'good agricultural practice'.[3]

The Secretaries of State for Scotland and Wales are responsible for water policy similarly (the Control of Pollution Act applies to Scotland although most of the previously mentioned Acts covered England and Wales only, separate provision being made for Scotland). However, the Minister of Agriculture, Fisheries and Food deals with policy matters relating to land drainage and fisheries and 'good agricultural practice'.

The major provisions of Part II have not yet been brought into force because of the 1974-9 government's decision to delay implementation of those sections of the Act that would involve significant public expenditure.[4] Part II is expected to cause water authorities substantial capital spending, and private industry is likely to be similarly affected. Water authorities will be obliged to increase their charges as a result and in the already severe economic circumstances the government wanted to delay this event. Before the 1979 general election DoE ministers had announced the intention of setting Part II in motion by the end of 1979,[5] and since the change of government there have not been any further public announcements.[6] In parallel the water authorities have been making preparations to revise the consent conditions they set so as to meet short- and long-term quality objections for each river, major stream and canal in their region.[7]

These three factors, the setting of river quality objectives, revision of consent conditions and control powers under Part II of the Act together represent a major effort to improve the condition of natural water resources and to plan the use and treatment of water on a more rational basis. Public water supply is currently about 300 litres per day per head of population. Water for all uses (domestic, industrial, agricultural) is derived from three sources in roughly equal proportions.

Figure 5.1: Water Sources

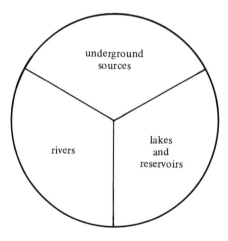

The volume of water being used is rising at 2 to 3 per cent each year, due to modernisation of kitchens and bathrooms, greater use of washing and dish-washing machines, and the expansion of industry. Of industrial users, power stations use twice as much as all others together (although mostly for cooling rather than consumption). Public sewers remove 95 per cent of domestic waste water and 80 per cent of the population is served by water authorities' treatment works. Not all waste water is treated—the need depends on where sewage effluents are being discharged. The natural capacity of the sea and tidal waters to dilute and disperse polluting matter can be exploited so that little or no treatment is required. Inland rivers, on the other hand, particularly those receiving high volumes of effluents if they serve large industrial towns, will require much more purifying of effluents if their quality is to be protected from deterioration. Three grades of sewage treatment are identified:[8]

Preliminary	screening, separation of grit and storm water
Primary	settling out suspended solids
Secondary	biological treatment by percolating through filters or aeration.

The 4,400 sewage treatment works of significant size in England and Wales remove 93 per cent of the polluting load for inland discharge of sewage effluent and 51 per cent of the polluting load for tidal discharge. Thirty million tonnes of sludge is produced annually from primary treatment, equivalent to about one million tonnes dry weight which is disposed of (as a thick scum or partially dried) in the following ways:

50%	spread on farmland
30%	dumped on landfill sites
20%	dumped at sea
<1%	incinerated

A system of assessing water pollution has been developed and used in national surveys of rivers[9] — there are four classes:

Class I	unpolluted: suitable for human consumption
Class II	of doubtful quality: suitable for fisheries
Class III	of poor quality
Class IV	grossly polluted

In 1975 77.6 per cent of non-tidal river mileage was of Class I standard, and 92.7 per cent was of Class I and Class II standard. The aim of pollution control is not necessarily to eliminate all rivers in Classes III and IV. This would be very costly (requiring much more expensive pre-treatment of effluents) and unnecessary for stretches of water not being used for public supply or fisheries. Some industrial users for example can accept polluted water without any disadvantage — e.g. power stations which require water for cooling. The aim of setting river quality objectives is therefore to match the conditions of the water to the functions it has to perform. This permits more selective programmes of improvement to be introduced.

For all water authorities their priority is to ensure sufficient quantity of wholesome water for human consumption in their regions. Those regions more dependent on rivers than other sources for their supply and disposal will have the heavier burden as far as this is concerned. Authorities with a sea coast and plentiful underground supplies may need less improvement to effluent standards. But throughout England and Wales there are sewage treatment works of insufficient capacity, many of them having to process far greater volumes than they were originally designed for. This is where the capital programme is more curtailed: even though the UK enjoys better conditions of supply and waste water disposal than many other countries, much of the stock of treatment works as well as sewerage (the pipes conducting sewage away) is elderly and in need of urgent replacement.

Another capital spending problem water authorities face is connected with continuity of supply. Although annual rainfall exceeds the annual volume needed for abstraction a lot of water is lost through evaporation and run-off into the sea. Often those areas with greatest demand enjoy lower rates of rainfall. In addition natural variations in rainfall (which have been extreme in recent years) put pressure on limited reserves at certain times of the year; water authorities therefore also need water resource development schemes to improve their resource management programmes.

Finally in this section it should be emphasised that water pollution control is done in order to prevent gross nuisance (e.g. smell), to protect the use of watercourses for fishing and their amenity value. The public health aspect of water supply is dealt with by chlorination and other treatment of abstracted water. If rivers only had to be protected where abstractions for public supply are made, most discharges to rivers could be allowed to go untreated since only a minority of rivers in this country are used for public water supply. It is the other uses that require pollution control effort.

EEC Pollution Legislation

The European Economic Community has agreed two 'Environmental Action Programmes' which are shaping the pollution legislation it is producing. The first programme was agreed on 22 November 1973 and ran until 1977. The second programme has a five-year span (1977-81).[10]

The first action programme involved:

1. Action to reduce and prevent pollution and nuisances;
2. Action to improve the environment and the quality of life;
3. Community action or, where applicable, common action by the member-states in international organisations dealing with the environment.

The second programme provided for these measures to be continued and adds a fourth category:

4. Non-damaging use and rational management of space, the environment and natural resources.

In the EEC's own words, 'it will not bring a "great leap forward" in the environment field but perhaps just as important it should lay the firm foundations of a Community Environment Policy capable of steering the Community to a growth model based more firmly on considerations of quality than of quantity'.[11]

The justification for the action programmes comes from a concern to modify the effects of Article 2 of the Treaty of Rome establishing the Communities in 1957 which stated that one task of the EEC was to 'promote throughout the Community the harmonious development of economic activities and a continuous and balanced expansion . . .' By 1972 it was clear that the indiscriminate pursuit of growth this suggested was likely to reduce the earth's natural finite resources unfairly and un-acceptably, thus making it impossible for the Community to achieve its essential objective under the Treaty of Rome: the constant improvement of living and working conditions. The EEC summit conference in Paris in October 1972 therefore agreed that Article 2 concerning growth 'could not henceforth be conceived of without an effective campaign to combat pollution and nuisances or an improvement in the quality of life and the protection of the environment'.[12]

The method by which the EEC goes about pursuing the action programme is for the staff of the Commission to produce proposals for implementation to the Council of Ministers. Proposals can be in the form of draft regulations, directives and decisions. *Regulations* are binding throughout the Community and directly applicable to all member-states. *Directives*, once adopted by the Council, are binding on member-states as regards the results to be achieved although they leave the method and means of implementation to the discretion of the national authority.

Decisions are usually concerned with specific problems and do not necessarily affect more than one member-state. The Council can also make resolutions and *recommendations* for member-states to consider. Under the first action programme (1973-6) the Council adopted the proposals shown in Table 5.1.[13]

Table 5.1: Proposals Adopted by the EEC Council of Ministers, 1973-6

	Waste	Water	Noise	Air	Chemicals in the environment	Research & information	Other	TOTAL
Regulations	–	–	–	–	–	–	–	–
Directives	3	3	–	2	12	–	1	20
Decisions	1	4	–	–	–	4	1	10
Resolutions	–	–	–	–	1	–	3	4
Recommendations	–	–	–	–	–	–	2	2
Other	–	1	–	–	2	–	1	5
TOTAL	4	8	–	2	15	4	8	41

Of particular relevance to the case study material which follows is the process through which a directive must go before it becomes adopted and may then be implemented. The sequence may vary a little, but in general the Commission works out and publishes a draft directive which is put before the Council. The Council consists of the minister from each member state within whose area of responsibility the subject of the proposal falls, e.g. the finance minister, minister of agriculture, environment minister. Before the Council discusses the proposal in detail it will ask the European Parliament and the European Economic and Social Committee for their opinions about it. The European Parliament will argue about the proposal, possibly on the basis of recommendations that one or more of its sub-committees have been asked to make. Its opinion is conveyed to the Council in writing together with the Economic and Social Committee's views. Simultaneously there are extensive negotiations to amend the draft in such a way that it will most likely be acceptable to the Council of Ministers. The negotiations may be lengthy and difficult, particularly since the aim is to achieve unanimity. One of the Council's working groups takes this on and, with assistance from Commission officials and the Council and national officials who constitute the working group, it discusses each part of the draft in fullest detail. The Council Secretariat prepares a report of the deliberations and any remaining differences of opinion are put to the Committee of Permanent Representatives (Coreper). Finally it is for the Council of Ministers themselves to achieve any necessary compromises to permit the proposal to be adopted. The text of the directive is then published in the Official Journal of the European Communities[14] and each member-state is notified by the President of the Council.

The Presidency of the Council rotates between members every six months, and whichever state holds the presidency at a particular time provides the Chairman of the Council of Ministers meetings as well as those of the Council's working groups and Coreper.[15] There is thus national as well as political scope to influence the agenda, priorities and timetable of work on draft proposals. Once a directive has been adopted and notified, it is for member-states to bring into force any legal provisions that may be necessary to implement it, usually within a time limit set by the directive. Some directives also build in a requirement for reporting back to the Council on progress, and may set long-term target dates for the achievement of particular objectives.

It is important for the UK government to follow each stage of this process carefully, both so that ministers and officials may make effective contributions where they have the opportunity, and also so that other relevant interests may be informed and consulted sufficiently before proposals become binding. Both the Houses of Parliament have established Select Committees to screen all Commission proposals for legislation and other documents and to draw their members' attention to any matters that need discussion and examination. The House of Commons Select Committee on European Legislation, etc. and the House of Lords Select Committee on the European Communities do this work through a system of frequent meetings of their full and sub-committees. At present these are as follows:[16]

House of Lords Select Committee on the European Communities
Sub-Committees   a: finance, economics, regional policy
                 b: trade and treaties
                 c: health, employment, education, social affairs
                 d: agriculture, consumer affairs
                 e: law
                 f: energy, transport, research, environment
House of Commons Select Committee on European Legislation, etc.
Sub-Committees
                 Sifting
                 I
                 II

Figure 5.2: How the EEC Works

Source: *Observer*, 18 November 1979.

The procedure is for the government to produce explanatory memoranda as quickly as possible after a proposal is published by the Commission in the Official Journal. These are sifted in batches every fortnight by the Chairman of the Lords Select Committee and the sifting Sub-Committee of the Commons Select Committee and provisionally allocated to one of the following categories:[17]

(a)   Proposals not requiring special attention
(b)   Proposals remitted to sub-committees for information or further consideration
(c)   Proposals having been remitted to sub-committees which are not to be reported to the House
(d)   Proposals having been remitted to sub-committees which are to be reported to the House for information
(e)   Proposals having been remitted to sub-committees which are to be reported to the House for debate.

The sub-committees then consider the proposals, calling for information from departments where necessary, and sometimes taking oral evidence. They report back to the full Select Committee which in turn reports to the full House. The House of Lords system has the additional advantage of being able to call for advisory briefs prepared by a small full-time staff seconded from the Civil Service.[18] To avoid unnecessary duplication of work the Lords and Commons Select Committees may confer with each other, share evidence and reports and deliberate together. This joint working follows recommendations of the Foster and Maybray King Committees, and is without precedent.[19] From special reports on their method of work that the Select Committees have produced for their respective Houses (as opposed to regular reports on European Community proposals) it is possible to see how this system is developing. At first (i.e. in 1973-4 at the start of UK membership of the Community) there were tremendous backlogs of proposals waiting to be considered. These were gradually eliminated so that by 1976 the Commons Committee could be sure of considering proposals within three weeks of the explanatory memorandum being made available. The Committees were able to pay more attention then to the effectiveness of their work and in 1977 the Lords Committee identified two problems: (1) the lack of public information about progress within the EEC institutions on proposals which had been subject to report and debate by Parliament; and (2) post-legislative scrutiny. The Commons Committee identified two others: (3) getting the government to allow time for debate on important

proposals speedily enough to permit ministers and officials to take the
views expressed into account in the course of their negotiations within
the Council; and (4) relations with the UK delegation to the European
Parliament. Debate of these special reports has taken place in the respective Houses and ministers have been able to give assurances or take note
of these points.[20]

As the consequences of membership of the Community for UK
policy and legislation becomes more fully appreciated, the scrutiny
procedure and the work of ministers and officials both at home and
within the Community's institutions is becoming more routine.[21] Until
now there has been a discernible note of uncertainty and even resentment
that has not helped the various interests to feel at ease with the opportunities
and responsibilities resulting from membership. In the specific context of
the environmental action programmes there has been strong evidence of
this kind of ambivalence. The first programme was prepared before UK
membership became effective, but its provisions and those of the second
programme have been willingly endorsed by the UK. But on matters of
detail there has often been acrimonious argument, with the UK earning
for itself the reputation of being difficult and unco-operative. The case
study looks in detail at the events surrounding one particular piece of
legislation—the Bathing Water Directive. Before describing these findings
it will be helpful to set out the wider context in which the UK has
dealt with the EEC environmental proposals.

At the heart of pollution control policies in the UK are two long-
established and widely-accepted principles: first, that more economical
and effective control can be achieved through the setting of environmental
quality objectives than through rigid fixing of universal emission standards;
and secondly, that the 'best practical means' would be sufficient basis on
which to achieve the control standards that are set.[22] These principles
contrast with approaches adopted elsewhere in Europe and on other
continents. Fixed emission standards are much more popular, and the
'best practical means' defence is not always allowed for offenders who
fail to keep within set controls. This is how Michel Carpentier, Director
of the Environment and Consumer Protection Service of the Commission
described the difference:

> we certainly recognise the long experience of Britain in environmental
> matters . . . at the previous meetings of the EEC Environment Council
> . . . the other nations have properly paid homage to Britain's long
> experience in this area. But . . . incredible as it may seem the rest of
> the Community do not necessarily agree on the absolute paramountcy

of axioms which are close to the heart of British experts and officials. For example the 'continentals' tend to believe more in standards defined on the basis of *best technical means* and applied through mandatory instruments. They mistrust systems based on goodwill and voluntary compliance, especially where toxic and dangerous substances are involved. They have serious doubts about the absorptive capacity of the environment and, this being so, do not believe that this is a 'resource' which can justifiably be 'exploited' in accordance with classic economic theory. They also tend to believe that where the scientific and medical evidence is inconclusive, we should err on the side of caution.[23]

The disagreement may have been misleadingly exaggerated. The essence of the British approach is to tackle each pollution problem case by case but with a consistent general approach. This means that introducing quality objectives necessarily implies control by emission standards. But the standards will be tailored to achieve the quality objectives set for the environment (river, lake) in the light of particular circumstances (e.g. tidal or static) and the uses made of the medium (e.g. water for human consumption, industrial use, etc.).

So emission standards do play a vital part in the controls—for each effluent discharged into waters controlled now by the Rivers (Prevention of Pollution) Acts and in the future by the Control of Pollution Act, for example, the consent conditions specify this standard in terms of content, volume, temperature and acidity and so on. But the standards for similar effluents will vary according to the circumstances and functions of the receiving waters. There are other kinds of standards though: 'we apply a complete range of control mechanisms from absolute bans, through statutory standards, negotiated agreements and voluntary schemes, to guidelines and recommendations, choosing carefully the instrument most appropriate to the need'.[24]

The differences are matters of nuance and interpretation rather than fundamental and irreconcilable positions, although in practice problems have been encountered within the Community's legislative processes because of the overriding need to aim for unanimity for the proposals of the kind being discussed. According to the environmental action programmes, pollution control will be exercised first by way of agreed environmental quality objectives for the receiving environment and on human health criteria. Then arising from these and from economic and social conditions, uniform emission standards will be imposed 'as a preferred method of control'.[25] This shows the compromise in the framework—it allows deviation from uniform emission standards, although not as a matter of course. Further aspects of this will be brought out through an examination of the case material, where further dimensions to do with the relative costs of introducing monitoring standards, as well as the different environmental circumstances in different member states will be brought out.

The Bathing Water Directive

The case study chosen here to provide material for an examination of the influence on UK water pollution control of EEC legislation is the Bathing Water Directive. Its passage through the Commission, Parliament and Council of the Community are described, as is the UK Parliament's scrutiny and subsequent implementation of its provisions.

The problem that the directive addresses is the quality of sea and fresh water for bathing. It is a long-established practice to dispose of sewage directly into the sea, often without pre-treatment. The resulting pollution is said to be a risk to health and a reduction of amenity. However these are controversial points and of different salience in different parts of the Community. Nevertheless the directive seeks to introduce bold measures to reduce this pollution. In the Commission's words, 'given existing levels of pollution around the coast of Europe the undertaking by member states to obtain the quality objectives ... within ten years is an impressive one: substantial investment in purifying and diffusers will be necessary.'[26]

The directive began as a draft prepared by the Commission under the terms of first environmental action programme. It was published in the Official Journal in March 1975[27] and the President of the Council wrote to the European Parliament asking for its opinion. The President of the Parliament referred the draft initially to the Committee on Public Health and the Environment. Members considered it at meetings on 21 March and 21 April 1975 and adopted a motion for a resolution embodying their opinions.[28] This was transmitted to the full Parliament which debated it on 13 May 1975. The Committee's resolution was accompanied by an explanatory statement which said:

... this Directive is of particular importance since polluted bathing water can cause dangerous forms of infectious diseases. This is confirmed by the large number of beaches which are closed to bathing every year because they exceed the permissible limit. As regards the technical and bacteriological analysis in the Directive the parameters would seem satisfactory, even if we cannot give a definite judgement at this point.[29]

The debate in Parliament on the resolution consisted entirely of consideration of amendments proposed by the UK delegates. The resolution forwarded by the Committee on Public Health and the Environment consisted of the following points:

(a)   Regret no provision to cover swimming pools.
(b)   Proposed bathing should be formally prohibited in waters found to exceed the stipulated parameters.
(c)   Provisions should be extended by Community measures to improve bathing water quality, and possibly to provide Community funds for the purchase by local Communities of diffusers and purifiers for sewage effluents.
(d)   Approve proposal in principal.
(e)   Suggest that (because of the connection between tourism and sea water pollution) the Community should align itself with International Organisations in order to secure the wider introduction of protective measures laid down in the proposal.

In the debate Sir Derek Walker-Smith[30] opened by drawing attention to the practical and logistical difficulties involved in implementing the directive as then drafted. These points were defended by Scarascia Mugnozza[31] (for the Commission). Lord Bethell[32] then spoke to his tabled amendments which dealt with the method of identifying designated beaches. He explained how different the systems of permitting and prohibiting bathing were in North and South Europe and claimed that unless the draft was modified, implementation would be very difficult in the UK as well as Ireland, Denmark and Germany.

Commissioner Mugnozza replied that the Commission was opposed to this amendment since the directive permitted application to take account of specific national situations. Walker-Smith objected that a directive would nevertheless be binding as to the whole of its substance and that national discretion only related to the form in which it was implemented. He thought a legal opinion was needed. Mugnozza replied that nothing had prevented the Parliament asking its Legal Affairs Committee for an opinion – this was a matter of internal procedure. Peter Kirk[33] then proposed the matter should be referred to the Legal Affairs Committee. Monsieur Giraud[34] (on behalf of the Socialist Group) criticised this tactic. The proposal was then put to the vote and lost, as was Lord Bethell's amendment. James Spicer[35] then proposed an amendment which would recommend bathing was discouraged rather than banned in waters with a higher level of pollution than stipulated in the draft directive, because he felt a ban could not be enforced. He said:

about four years ago a national newspaper undertook a survey of 12 major resorts in the UK — graded them filthy, more filthy and even more filthy. The direct result of that campaign was that it was taken to heart because it hit the pockets of those whose livelihood depended on the attraction of tourists to seaside resorts during the summer months. Action was taken and certainly in many parts of the country it was very effective.

However, there was no other contribution, it being announced that the Commission opposed the amendment. It was put to the vote and defeated, and the whole resolution was adopted.

The remaining steps to convert the draft directive into a piece of legislation adopted by the Council of Environment Ministers therefore were those taken within the Council's working group on the environment and the Coreper. Simultaneously with this sequence the UK scrutiny was taking place. In fact as soon as the draft directive was published in March 1975 the DoE prepared an explanatory memorandum and the Select Committees began their work on the drafts. The House of Commons Select Committee required further information, and this is recorded in its report of 29 April 1975.[36] On 1 July the Committee took oral evidence from the Minister, Dennis Howell MP,[37] two DoE officials and a medical officer from the DHSS. They covered issues raised by the draft as it then was, relating to the problems of implementation in the UK. Mr Howell said:

we contemplate no circumstances under which we shall prohibit bathing . . . in this country . . . the EEC is proposing to create absolute standards which is not exactly the way in which we have operated our environmental legislation and our projects in this country . . . nevertheless although we have a lot of reservations about the way they are proceeding with the timescale on the whole we are in general support of the direction in which they are moving . . . We would therefore resist any attempts to try to create priorities which are very desirable in themselves but to which we could not give as much weight as the cleaning up of drinking water.[38]

In response to a question about creating a league table of beaches Howell replied 'the truth of the matter is that until the Control of Pollution Act becomes operative and regional water authorities get operative we really do not know the extent of the problem in this country'.[39] Another question asked whether the UK would have to comply with the criteria laid down by the directive, and Howell said we would if the directive was accepted as drafted. In negotiations, however, UK representatives would press for better definition of bathing waters and for the right to be in control of the national pro- grammes. A member (Julius Silverman MP)[40] then said, 'does that mean, Minister, you would make those reservations before you gave your vote . . . in Council?' Howell replied: 'it means that . . . I shall instruct our representatives to pursue that policy within the EEC. One must wait and see of course what comes out of those discussions, and if at the end of the day all else fails we have the power of veto . . . we think it ought to be reasonable to reach agreement.'[41]

As a result of this session, the Select Committee said in their report published on 8 July:

> the committee have considered the instrument and seek further information. They understand so far as sea water is concerned the maintenance of adequate public health standards would not present any particular difficulties in the UK. They note there might be difficulties in maintaining the higher amenity standards envisaged in the Directive as drafted. The Committee therefore proposes to defer their decision until further information is available on the progress of the instrument, particularly the extent to which the instrument in its final form places obligations on central and local government in the UK.[42]

About two weeks before the Commons Committee had taken oral evidence the Lords Select Committee Sub-Committee F had listened to three officials (two of whom were also at the Commons Committee's session).[43] They asked about the problems from the DoE's point of view. These were described as (1) how bathing water should be defined by the authorities; (2) interpreting the term 'bathing season'; (3) meeting the bacteriological limits—a rough estimate of £100m of capital expend- iture would be required to improve the sewage treatment and outfalls to beaches to this degree; (4) the health risk was thought to be slight 'unless contamination is of such a level that it would be aesthetically almost impossible to swim there'; (5) the measurement standards and methods proposed would have to be defined more clearly by a technical committee; (6) timetable for implementation:

> Where the guidelines turn into imperative standards which one must achieve at a particular time everywhere, the divergence with a general approach becomes most acute. We put forward the view that one wants to know why an eight year programme is considered sensible across the whole community – it may be appropriate in some areas where there may be an identifiable health risk in bathing and where one would very much like, as a British tourist, to see beaches improved.[44]

The Select Committee published a report on 29 July giving its view on the draft directive:

> the UK is committed to a policy of general improvement of water quality, an intention supported by the recent reorganisation of water authorities and by legislation including the Control of Pollution Act 1974 . . . But restrictions appropriate to the organised beaches of Southern Europe and the Mediterranean coastline and other semi enclosed and almost tideless seas may be quite inapplicable to the tidal regime around our coast. Furthermore, uniform or universal emission or quality standards for air or water play no part in our pragmatic administration.[45]

In particular the Select Committee drew three points to the Lords' attention: inappropriate stringent conditions; an ill-worded draft; and the possibility that bathing might be prohibited. The House of Lords debated this report in October but before that on 16 September the House of Commons Select Committee was able to comment further, in its report on its deliberations. It said: 'the committee have now received further information on the progress of the instrument and understand that changes are likely to be made that will meet some of the points of difficulty that were raised'. They referred to the definition of bathing water which would now be in terms of 'significant numbers of bathers', and to the removal of any suggestion of prohibiting bathing in waters where there was a risk to health. On the question of complying with the directive's standards within eight years they said it was not yet clear whether this would be amended. But they concluded: 'in the Committee's opinion the instrument raised questions of political importance but there is no recommendation for further consideration by the House'.[46] So that is where the House of Commons involvement ended.

On 13 October 1975 the House of Lords held a debate 'to take note' of its Select Committee's Report. This covered a number of, by now, familiar issues: the applicability of the definitions to UK beaches, the question over health risk, the method of setting standards, etc.[47] Replying for the government, Lady Birk said[48]

> whatever criticisms we may have of the draft, we entirely support the proposal to define quality criteria for sea or fresh water bathing and to improve waters in which people bathe until satisfactory standards are met. This is not because there is any significant health risk in sea bathing in British waters—... nevertheless water off some of our beaches, even if not dangerously polluted can be extremely offensive ... Even so we do not want standards which are too rigid. As I think has been pointed out, we do not all start from the same point.[49]

She dealt with all the points raised and referred to the latest revision of the draft which was reassuring on most of the problems. She concluded 'the time limit of eight years is the remaining major problem to be solved—what we want is a power for member states to make an exception from the normal eight year timetable in areas where improvements do not necessarily have a high priority, and it is on this point we shall be arguing our case very strongly with the EEC'.[50]

At its meeting on 16 October 1975 the Council of Environment Ministers approved the final revision of the text of the Bathing Water Directive and formally adopted it at their meeting on 8 December 1975. It was notified to member states on that date which is thus the reference point for all time deadlines set in the directive.

In summary the directive contains the following points:

Article 1   The Directive concerns the quality of bathing water (which is water where bathing is 'explicitly authorised' or 'traditionally practised by a large number of bathers'); therapeutic and swimming pools are excluded.

Article 2   The Annex to the Directive indicates the physical, chemical and microbiological parameters.

Article 3   Values shall be set for the parameters in the bathing areas and may not be less stringent than the mandatory (I) values listed in the Annex. Guideline (G) values may be used.

Article 4   These values shall be observed within ten years of notification for existing bathing waters. (I) values must apply instantly for new areas. The ten-year time limit may be extended on certain conditions and the Commission must be informed of this not later than six years after notification (i.e. December 1981).

Article 5   Conformity will have been achieved if 95% of samples correspond to the (I) values or 90% or 80%, depending on the parameter (details in the Annex).

Article 6   Specifies the sampling method, and the Annex lays down minimum frequencies for sampling and a reference method of analysis or inspection.

Article 7   Implementation may not lead to the deterioration of current water quality. More stringent values than those laid down by the Directive may be fixed by member states.

Article 8   Exemptions from the requirements of the Directive for certain parameters may be waived because of exceptional weather or geographic conditions and generally where natural enrichment of the water occurs. The Commission will be notified of all waivers.

Article 9   Adaptations to the (G) and (I) values may be made in the light of technical progress.

Articles 10-11   A Committee on Adaptations to Technical Progress may be set up; its method of proceeding is described.

Article 12   Laws, regulations and administrative provisions relating to this Directive must be made by member states within two years of notification (i.e. December 1977).

Article 13   Four years after notification (i.e. December 1979) and regularly thereafter member states must submit comprehensive reports on bathing water.

In order to assist the water authorities in implementing the directive, the DoE circulated a note in March 1977. This stated that no new legislation would be required although at that time there was 'doubt how far water authorities will have the statutory means to implement the Directive in respect of coastal waters until Part II of the Control of Pollution Act 1974 is implemented'. In particular, the pollution control functions of water authorities do not yet include coastal waters. Also until the consent system applies to all coastal waters, achievement of the required water quality could not be guaranteed. So the DoE concluded that although full implementation of the directive would have to await the bringing into force of the 1974 Act, 'it will be necessary for the UK to show in the meantime that all possible steps are being taken to meet our obligations'.[51]

The note describes the parameters and the Annex as 'in many cases more stringent than required to protect public health, or not related to that purpose'. Apart from the water authorities, district councils will be concerned with the implementation of the directive, 'both through their public health responsibilities and, particularly in the case of maritime resorts, through their general concern for the amenities of the area'. So there should be joint consultations in order to identify bathing waters and the bathing season, and to set values for the parameters. The note discusses sampling and monitoring arrangements and suggests that water authorities should include details of bathing water in the registers they will be maintaining under Section 41 of the Control of Pollution Act, which will be available for the public to consult.

The cost of implementing the directive is said in the note to be 'potentially significant' both from the required monitoring programme and from any need to improve existing discharges or impose limitations on new ones. 'In view of the large proportion of sewage effluents in discharges to coastal waters, most of the latter would fall on the water authorities' the note says. Although waivers may be made under Article 4, 'to take advantage of this could have an adverse effect on tourism'.

Further guidelines from the DoE[52] asked the water authorities: (a) to gather data which would help decisions on which waters should be designated bathing waters; (b) to sample and analyse water from these areas; and (c) by the end of 1978 to designate bathing waters. It was suggested that bathers should be counted on a number of occasions under favourable conditions and all beaches with over 1,000 bathers per kilometre would definitely be designated while those with 500 to 1,000 bathers per kilometre could be designated following negotiations between the water authorities and district councils. All designations would be confirmed by the DoE by the end of 1978.

In Wessex Water Authority for example, the members discussed this in some detail and agreed that £5,000 should be voted for spending on aerial photographic surveys of five potential 'Euro-beaches' during July and August 1978, and that sampling of these waters should go ahead. It was also emphasised by the authority that 'improvement of sewage discharge to coastal waters is considered a desirable long-term goal, but first priority must be given to public health needs and the provision of services to new housing and industry. For these reasons this directive is bound to be implemented selectively . . .'[53] Much the same was probably being said in the other authorities, but in June 1978 further local activity was postponed because the Secretary of State for the Environment, Peter Shore MP,[54] instructed the matter to be called in for his personal decision. Subsequently a letter from the DoE to the water authorities said that designation of 'Euro-beaches' should be agreed locally between water authorities and district councils, and that the department would only become involved if agreement could not be reached. The water authorities rejected this since they felt it would put them in a difficult position with the district councils. They asked the DoE to give them guidelines according to its interpretation of the directive. After the general election, ministers at the DoE decided to go ahead with implementation of the directive as quickly as possible. The department's final advice was issued on 9 July 1979.[55] Water authorities and local authorities conducted a joint identification exercise over the summer, and by December the list of identified beaches had been established, subject to formal confirmation in one or two cases.[56] The list of bathing waters and the technical data relating to them was sent to the EEC Commission on 18 December 1979. A DoE minister also listed the bathing waters in answer to a Parliamentary Question on 14 December 1979.[57]

Analysis

This section works through a number of points raised by the case material on bathing water quality and discusses them in the context of the background information covered earlier in the chapter. The points relate to both practical and organisational considerations:

1. evidence of health risk;
2. interpretation of the directive;
3. role of the Community in relation to national policies;
4. contribution of UK representatives;
5. ordering of priorities;
6. effect on the Control of Pollution Act;
7. enhanced role for DoE.

Evidence of Health Risk

Although the Bathing Water Directive has been promoted partly as a public health measure, there is in the UK considerable doubt about the risk to health of bathing in sewage-polluted sea water. According to a Medical Research Council report published 21 years ago in 1959, there was no significant health risk to bathers unless the water was heavily fouled, and no valid evidence to the contrary has been produced since then.[58] This does not lead all British experts to dismiss the idea though. For example Mr Guiver of Southern Water Authority said in 1978 that he had qualms about denying to the public that there were any health risks from high bacteriological counts, although he accepted the lack of conclusive evidence.[59] Some evidence of a link between high bacteriological counts in bathing water and the incidence of gastro-intestinal disorders has recently been published following detailed studies in America.[60] However the prevailing view is that British beaches are not on the whole dangerously contaminated and therefore compliance with the bacteriological counts specified in the directive will not constitute a move to improve public health conditions. But there is no shortage of evidence that some British beaches could be brought up to higher amenity standard: Mr Hammerton, Director of the Clyde River Purification Board, for example, said that the Medical Research Council's report had set the clock back by making it more difficult for authorities such as his own to press for the cleaning up of beaches which were seriously polluted by any standards. They were not seeking it on health grounds but purely on environmental pollution grounds. His authority had found 'little scientific rationale behind the figures chosen, [in the directive] but nevertheless the mandatory coliform [i.e. bacteriological] standards are a very good compromise', and less stringent than values they were setting for themselves in order to achieve the desired environmental improvement.[61] Other experts agree that the standards set by the directive can be achieved, not by treating sewage more thoroughly before it is discharged into the sea, but by improving the design and location of submerged outfalls.

'The sea provides cost free and efficient sewage purification, and so long as this does not conflict with amenity or public health it seems sensible to take advantage of the fact'—this was the advice published in 1975 by the DoE from the Coastal Pollution Research Committee.[62] Translated into practical terms by Mr Ridley of Northumbrian Water Authority: 'the sea is bactericidal to an extent unattainable in sewage works without chemical treatment though a full treatment plant of normal design cannot purify the effluent to the EEC required pathogen free standards. A suitably designed sea outfall, preferably with fine prescreening, is the only reasonable solution.'[63] The experts also agree that setting bacteriological values for sea water is a reasonable method of improving amenity standards. The Select Committees understandably found this a difficult point to grasp at first hearing. For example Mr Percival MP[64] put it to Mr Howell (at the oral session on 1 July 1975 of the Commons Committee) 'whether the Directive is acceptable or not may depend to a large extent on whether the standards laid down in the Directive are limited to danger to health or whether they are wider and include amenity standards – could the Minister give us any indication of what the standards are likely to be in the final Directive?' Mr Howell replied: 'I am told they are amenity standards and this is one of the areas in which we shall be entering into discussion.'[65] However once the directive had been adopted, the European Commission reported that 'there was a growing body of opinion in the member states that the quality of bathing water should satisfy other criteria besides those of public health such as amenity, aesthetic attractiveness and the improvement of the quality of the environment in general. No provisions of the same scope and degree of technicality already existed in the national legislation.'[66]

The conclusion from this seems to be that the directive is acceptable as an amenity-improving instrument, and irrelevant as a public health measure. However, the next sub-section should throw more light on this because it introduces another dimension – the different physical conditions in the UK, Western Denmark, Holland, Belgium, Northern and Western France and Ireland, compared with the rest of Europe.

Interpretation of the Directive

Putting to one side the public health versus amenity argument, the directive also poses two further categories of problem. One relates to its relevance to the physical conditions that characterise British beaches; the other relates to the practical methods of sampling and analysing bathing water to monitor its conformity with the values specified in the directive.

One obvious difference, on the first count, is the features of the Atlantic Ocean and North Sea compared with the Mediterranean Sea and continental European inland lakes. In the expert committee's view, 'particularly favourable hydrographic conditions occur in most areas around the UK; current velocities in coastal waters are significantly greater than in many other countries . . . but in higher water temperatures than around the UK and in areas where the rate of dispersion is less higher standards should be required'.[67] When sewage is discharged into sea or other waters it is first diluted by the water then moved in the water mass by any tides or currents, and further dispersed by eddies. Some bacteria will die because of the action of strong sunshine and some will remain alive in the water that reaches the shore. So depending on these factors – tide, wind, sunshine – a lot of differences in bathing water quality will be explained.

In addition the popularity of bathing varies greatly – few British beaches are thought to qualify for designation under the directive solely on the criterion of having over 1,000 bathers per kilometre at the height of the season. Most 'popular' British beaches have much lower counts. On the Mediterranean coast however, and on the Italian Adriatic beaches, numbers are much higher. It could be argued then that the need to protect these hotter, more static bathing waters where greater numbers of people bathe is much more pressing than the need to tackle the problem in the UK. This is a view commonly held in the UK, but there is nevertheless an underlying worry about the consequences for tourism.

The DoE note of 1977 referred to this – the advantages of seeking exemption from the directive's conditions could be outweighed by the damage to tourism if beaches were not designated.[68] Others have spelt this out a little more:

> coastal resorts can be divided into four categories: those which are or are not designated, and those which do or do not comply with the Directive. A resort which is designated and does comply is likely to highlight this information in its brochure for attracting visitors; whereas if the quality does not meet with the requirements of the Directive, adverse publicity may well affect the tourist industry until remedial action has been taken. A resort which is not designated but where the quality is known or believed to conform with the Directive, may well press to be designated, since non-designation would seem to imply that the resort is not one of the country's major bathing areas. If it remains undesignated, there may still be a desire to publicise the acceptability of the waters. The remaining category – undesignated bathing waters which do not comply – cause for little comment, since the local authority will not wish to advertise the non-compliance except for the purpose of ensuring improvements are made.[69]

The key to this is that expenditure on outfalls in order to make improvements will be the responsibility of the water authorities. They are worried about being urged by many local authorities simultaneously (and perhaps publicly) to incur this expenditure and hence they were most unwilling to 'let the DoE off the hook' in the matter of designating beaches. As one water authority official put it, 'any resort with pretensions will want to be a Euro-beach'.[70]

The second issue of interpretation relates to the rules and methods laid down in the directive for testing samples of water. The problem is the combination of fine detail with considerable vagueness. For example on the one hand, values are expressed very precisely: e.g. the (I) value for faecal coliforms is 2,000 per 100 ml. But on the other hand, no one method of culturing the bacteria is described. The experts say that the methods of sampling and testing have a gross influence on the results obtained: 'all the time during those years of investigation at Stevenage [the Water Research Centre's laboratory] we were bewildered by the fact that coliform counts were so variable and hardly reproducable'.[71] '. . . by the judicious choice of sampling time and place, method of transport to the laboratory and analytic technique, doubtful beaches could appear to comply with the mandatory limits'.[72] Lord Ashby expressed his criticism more forthrightly: 'this is no trivial technical matter but a matter of high principle which affects our relationship with the community. Some pressure should be brought to bear on the people in Brussels who draft these Directives which are incomplete, ambiguous, not to say half baked.'[73] Yet Lord Ashby was, as first Chairman of the Royal Commission on Environmental Pollution, a formidable champion of the cause to control and reduce pollution.[74] In relation to the directive's coliform values he maintained they could not possibly serve as an index of sewage pollution and that they were 'positively misleading because they would give people an absolutely spurious impression of scientific accuracy'. He concluded: 'I agree with the Medical Research Council that the realistic test of whether a beach is good enough to bathe in is that it looks clean and does not smell.'[75] It does not appear that a solution to this difficulty is immediately available. The DoE indicated it would be issuing guidelines to the water authorities on these technical aspects of implementation,[76] so workable interpretations may evolve. The directive itself contains in Article 9 the provision to amend parameters, possibly on the advice of its Committee on Adaptation to Technical Progress. At the time of writing it appeared unlikely that this committee would be set up.[77] So the gloomy conclusion of the Water Research Centre, which is probably shared by many, is: 'the EEC Directive poses problems of interpretation and implementation, the methodology of enumerating coliform bacteria is in a state of confusion, and methods of predicting bacteriological counts on bathing beaches leave much to be desired'.[78]

Role of the Community in Relation to National Policies

Given the rather persuasive criticisms of the directive so far described (confusion about health and amenity objectives, obstacles to interpretation and implementation), it is important to know why the directive did become adopted and has stimulated action in the UK. One theory that emerges from the case material is that there are other, 'political' motives at work particularly in relation to the Commission's influence. A hint of this was apparent in evidence given by one official to the House of Lords Select Committee.

Mr McQuillan, a Principal at the DoE, in reply to a question raising the possibility that the directive might be unnecessary, said:

> Our attitude is that this is a sensible and useful endeavour to draw up quality objectives for different types of water according to use. It fits in fairly well with our general approach to matters of pollution control. If you say at what level ought these to be enforced, should they be drawn up at Community level as measures which must be met without any great flexibility at national level, they certainly agree this is a question which is debatable. The answer that the Commission would give at any rate, and certainly some member states would give, is that if we want environmental improvement it is not always entirely effective to leave entire discretion on these matters with each individual member state, because history, they would say, shows it does not always achieve anything. So there is a school of thought in the community which wants to have directives of this kind which are basically aimed not at protecting the bather.[79]

Another DoE official, D.C. Renshaw, writing of his experience in dealing with the Community over the Bathing Water Directive has said,

> the fact that it is fundamentally a political process is sometimes forgotten; when people say, as they occasionally do, that the Council in agreeing a directive seems to have ignored or played down the agreed advice of experts, they perhaps need to remember that Ministers in Council may be under pressure to reach agreement at any price that is remotely reasonable to pay, even if the result is less than ideal from the technical or expert viewpoint.[80]

Renshaw explained how political considerations often play a large part in the selection of business, the sources of advice chosen, the timetable of negotiations and the level at which decisions are taken:

even matters which may seem to the ordinary observer to require a dispassionate technical solution (such as the limit value to be fixed for a particular parameter defining water quality) are not exempted from this process. Often a Minister must decide not whether something is technically right or ideal but whether he and the interests he represents in his country can live with something less than ideal for the sake of agreement.[81]

This suggests that national interests cannot be guaranteed protection in the Community's negotiating processes even when there are ministers and officials there to look after them. Further comment on the role of UK representatives follows, but a point to note here is that the consequences for national policies of even a relatively minor issue such as the quality of bathing water can be significant. The time, money and energy that is diverted to dealing with the directive before, during and after it has been adopted represents a substantial cost. The influence of the Community is strong in this respect and not, from the evidence of the case material, necessarily unwelcome.

Contribution of UK Representatives

The Bathing Water Directive's history has shown the considerable range of people who have become involved from the UK—government department officials and ministers, experts from various agencies, the UK diplomats of Coreper and the UK delegates to (now popularly elected members of) the European Parliament. But in some quarters it was felt they did not do as much as was necessary to ensure the directive was well designed: 'it is unfortunate that the final stages of its drafting proceeded too fast for the representatives of the UK (then a new member state) to be able to effect many substantial changes'.[82] Others however have pointed out the advantages of making a strong contribution earlier in the process. According to D.C. Renshaw, 'as a relative newcomer to the EEC the UK has only recently begun to learn the significance of this stage [before the draft directive is agreed by the Commission] and how to play a full part in it, but the UK voices are now increasingly being heard'.[83]

Parliament's Select Committees added to this view in their special report. They suggested that there were two stages where national governments could try to influence the Council of Ministers:

1. after an instrument had been transmitted by the Commission to the Council and was published; and

2. when an instrument was known to be ready for final consideration and adoption by the Council.

The Committees thought their most effective input could be made at the first stage, so that the Houses could be informed early on if there were issues for debate. The Committees could take a second look at the instrument later on in cases where there had been substantial amendment during the passage through Council. But to achieve this the government would have to be more helpful in providing supplementary explanatory memoranda, and allowing time for debate in Parliament promptly if the Committees recommended this.[84]

The UK delegates to the European Parliament also have a particular slot in the timetable where they can make their views known. In the Bathing Water Directive's case they certainly did this, but not particularly persuasively. One problem may have been the difficulty of building up a good case and knowing how best to make it in the light of the Commission's strength. There is seen to be a division of labour here, with the delegates at the European Parliament trying to influence the Commission while the national Parliaments and scrutiny committees should influence the Council of Ministers through their national Parliaments. Somewhere in between the two are the government officials, experts and Coreper representatives who work away from public view throughout the legislative process. These distinctions are important and need to be recognised by representatives in order to make an appropriate contribution.

Clearly in the bathing water example the changes made to the directive during 1975 turned it from something which the UK was very critical of into an instrument which is, although far from perfect, regarded as an acceptable base for implementation. The concessions on definitions of bathing areas and seasons, exemptions for certain beaches, and scope to change technical elements are important achievements of negotiation. It is difficult to know who was responsible for this, but from the description it was not until after the European Parliament's debate that these modifications began to be made – i.e. within the Council's working group negotiations. Furthermore, it is difficult to be sure what effect the scrutiny committees and the House of Lords debate might have had. At the Council meeting in November 1975 the text was agreed so that quite little may have been achieved. But whether further modifications were made before the December Council of Ministers meeting is also not clear. In the circumstances it is possible to ask what price the UK has paid or would pay for this measure of influence in the process. If, as seems probable, the Council of Ministers' decisions do constitute essentially political compromises, what has the UK gained or lost from agreeing to the directive? Without making a value judgement it is possible to point out consequences for UK legislation and policy implementation which would not otherwise have existed – this is discussed next.

Ordering of Priorities

The most obvious effect of the Bathing Water Directive's adoption, with its associated timetable for implementation, has been the preparatory work undertaken by the DoE and water authorities. The DoE's note of 1977 and subsequent guidance, water authorities' discussions with district councils, monitoring programmes and bathing number surveys are all attributable to the directive. Indeed, as soon as there was talk in 1974, of a directive on bathing water being made, water authorities in some places started their own quality monitoring programmes in the most popular beaches.[85]

It has already been said that the capital expenditure consequences of the directive are likely to be heavy for water authorities. Many British bathing waters do not meet the directive's bacteriological criteria. To do so would usually require building new submerged pipelines to carry sewage effluents out to sea and improving existing diffusers. The estimated cost of a new outfall is in the region of eight million pounds and while water authorities' borrowing limits are constrained this may not be the way they want to spend their money.[86]

Amenity and recreation are important to the water authorities, but not more important in general than improving the supply of water for industrial and domestic uses. Yet it seems that they will be obliged to attend to bathing water unless exemptions from the directive's timetable are sought. From the case material this seems to be welcomed by some and resented by others. The National Water Council's position is that 'the least satisfactory EEC directive on water quality to emerge up to now [1978] is that on the quality of water for bathing. It is not well judged scientifically and may well be costly to administer; it could also lead to a distortion of investment in environmental improvement.'[87] Thus it appears that in at least some places unless compliance with the directive is deferred, bathing water quality will have been made a higher priority than it otherwise would be.

Effect on the Control of Pollution Act

There are two further consequences worth mentioning because of their specific effect on the Control of Pollution Act. The first relates to Section 41 which obliges water authorities to keep registers of consents, applications and the results of analysis of samples which the public may consult. The DoE note of 1977 suggested that water authorities would want to widen this interpretation to include information about the application of the directive to bathing waters, since 'it would be in keeping with the spirit of the Act'. And water authorities seem to have accepted the logic of this.

However in discussing Section 41 in other contexts, the water authorities have sometimes been less than enthusiastic about the obligations under which it puts them. They fear the information in the registers may be used in a troublesome way by overzealous environmentalists, and may force them into defensive positions over the discharges for which they themselves are responsible.[88] It would of course be in the interests of those district councils who control bathing resorts and who seek their designation as 'Euro-beaches' to draw attention to the information on the registers. This could be used powerfully to embarrass an unwilling water authority into action. Thus an added dimension has been attached to Section 41 as a result of the Bathing Water Directive.

The second matter concerns water authorities' jurisdiction over tidal water, as a result of Part II of the Act. Until the outstanding (and major) sections of Part II of the Control of Pollution Act are brought into force, water authorities cannot exercise general pollution control duties over tidal and coastal waters, since the relevant legislation (Rivers (Prevention of Pollution) Acts 1951 and 1961 and Clean Rivers (Estuaries and Tidal) Act 1960) does not give them adequate powers.

The terms of the directive require member states to have made the necessary legislative and administrative arrangements to implement the provisions by December 1979. The DoE note of 1977 said that no *new* legislation would be required in this context although until Part II was fully operational, there would be a problem. In 1978 the minister responsible (Mr Howell) announced that the outstanding sections of Part II would be brought into force by 1979. As this coincides neatly with the directive's deadline it seems reasonable to think the directive influenced the minister's announcement. It is therefore a matter of speculation whether any other factor, apart from the Bathing Water Directive, would have had this effect.

Enhanced Role for DoE

One final effect of the Bathing Water Directive to be covered in this chapter concerns the DoE's role. It has been shown earlier that the regional reorganisation of the water industry in 1973 was intended to integrate the control of water-cycle functions over large naturally defined areas, while giving the Secretary of State for the Environment responsibility for overall national policy. However, the tendency with negotiations on Community proposals, as with their application inside the UK, is to give the DoE a more prominent involvement in the detail of local affairs.

The steps being taken to achieve designation of 'Euro-beaches' illustrate this, but paradoxically since water authorities did not wish to have as much discretion as the Secretary of State appeared to want them to have. Conversely, the opportunities available to the DoE to influence Community proposals so that UK interests are protected do not seem to have been used sufficiently, over the matter of bacteriological standards. The National Water Council sits between the water authorities and the DoE in these matters, and indicated in its evidence to the House of Commons Select Committee on nationalised industries what it was proposing to do to influence European proposals through direct contact with Commission officials, and through Eureau – the organisation of water industries in Europe.[89] The point is that although the DoE does consult the National Water Council and others about European water proposals, the political pressures acting on the minister (and his own attitude towards UK involvement with the European Community) can have an influence on implementation that the water authorities may resent. Yet because, in constitutional terms, the DoE ministers and officials must be agents for the Community, the effect of Community legislation can be felt in unpredictable and sometimes unwelcome ways. This is certainly the case with the Bathing Water Directive where the stop-go activity in the UK since 1977 has been attributed particularly to the lack of enthusiasm the Secretary of State at the time (Peter Shore) had for European matters.

Notes

1. For a fuller description see: Department of the Environment, *Pollution Control in Great Britain: How it Works*, Pollution Paper no. 9, 2nd edn (HMSO, London, 1978), para. 87.

2. For example, the Bristol Waterworks Company supplies water on behalf of the Wessex Water Authority, and bills customers directly.

3. Pollution Paper no. 9, para. 84.

4. See Chapter 3, p. 33.

5. These important implementation decisions are discussed further in Chapters 11 and 12. The timetable was announced by the Minister on 13 April 1978. See DoE Press Notice no. 199, *Water Pollution Controls Extended*.

6. In September 1979 D.C. Renshaw, Assistant Secretary DoE responsible for

implementation of the water provisions of the Control of Pollution Act, was quoted as saying that the timetable was currently being considered by ministers, particularly in the light of resource implications. It must be obvious, he said, that the timetable announced previously was not now going to be met. We would have to await an announcement by the government. *Municipal Engineering* (25 September 1979), p. 743.

7. The National Water Council's intentions have been set out in a statement called *River Water Quality, the Next Stage. Review of Discharge Consent Conditions* (National Water Council, London, 1978).

8. C.D. Andrews, 'The Mosaic that Turned into a Unified Industry', *Water* (March 1979), pp. 24-8.

9. Department of the Environment, *Report of a River Pollution Survey of England and Wales*, 3 vols (HMSO, London, 1971, 1972, 1979). The National Water Council has since updated this classification.

10. The first programme was agreed in the Council Declaration of 22 November 1973, published in Official Journal No. C112 of 20 December 1973. The second programme is set out in supplement 6/76 of the Bulletin of the European Communities, and was agreed by EEC Environment Ministers on 9 December 1976, and published in OJ No. C139 of 13 June 1977. See also Chapter 3, p. 41.

11. Commission of the European Communities, *The European Community's Environmental Policy* (Luxembourg, 1977), p. 25.

12. Ibid., p. 9 and OJ No. C112 of 20 December 1973. See also S.P. Johnson, *The Pollution Control Policy of the European Communities* (Graham and Trotman, London, 1979), and H. Thomas, 'The Environment', *New Europe* (Autumn 1975), pp. 49-58 for further discussion. Nigel Haigh has argued that the Commission thought environmental issues should be included in its activity, but because of uncertainty about the authority for this in the Treaty being sufficient, it arranged for the summit to put a gloss on Article 2. See N. Haigh, 'The Community's Environment' in R. Manley (ed.), *Creating a Caring Community* (Fabian Tract no. 461, London, April 1979), pp. 16-19.

13. Source: *The European Community's Environmental Policy*, Annex 1, pp. 28-31.

14. The Official Journal is published in two series of volumes: 'C' and 'L' by the Office for Official Publications of the European Communities, Luxembourg, and is available from national stationery offices (e.g. HMSO). Series 'C' contains all communications other than legislation. Series 'L' contains legislation only.

15. The presidency rotates alphabetically through the members, at six-monthly intervals. Starting with Belgium in January 1973 the first cycle of the nine ended with the UK's turn in January 1977. The second cycle ends similarly with the UK's turn in July 1981.

16. The House of Commons Select Committee system was changed in 1979 – see Chapter 1, p. 16 and n. 10. The Lords Committee divisions are noted in HL (251) 1974-75, para. 4. In the current session the committee was appointed again: House of Lords, vol. 400 col. 231-3, 22 May 1979.

17. Second Special Report from the European Secondary Legislation Committee, 1974, HC 258 ii 20 August 1974.

18. House of Lords, 1974-5, HL 251. Second Special Report from the Select Committee, 24 June 1975, para. 18.

19. Second Report by the Select Committee on Procedures for Scrutiny of Proposals for European Instruments. House of Lords, 1972-3, HL 194, paras. 132-5.

20. See for example the House of Commons debate on 3 November 1975 (vol. 899, col. 27-108) and the House of Lords debate on 22 July 1975 (vol. 363, col. 274-313).

21. See House of Lords, 1977-8, HL 256-1. 44th Report of Select Committee on European Communities. *Relations between the United Kingdom Parliament and the European Parliament after Direct Elections* (July 1978).

22. See Department of the Environment, *Pollution Control in Great Britain: How it Works*, Pollution Paper no. 9 (HMSO, London, 1978), para. 8.

23. M. Carpentier, 'A Review of the Scope and Progress of the Commission's Programme to Date', *The European Community's Environment Policy* (National Council for Social Service, London, 1977), p. 7.

24. A. Lyall, 'The UK Approach to Pollution Control in Relation to Commission Policy', *The European Community's Environmental Policy*, p. 20.

25. R. Sandbrook and A. Sors, *Evaluation of the Current Environmental Action Programme of the European Community – a Discussion Paper*, undated (International Institute for Environment and Development + The Monitoring and Assessment Research Centre), pp. 3-4. See also: *The European Community's Environmental Policy*, p. 12.

26. Commission of the European Communities, *State of the Environment – First Report 1977* (EEC, Luxembourg, 1977), p. 25.

27. OJ No. C.67, 22 March 1975, p. 1.

28. OJ Vol. 18, No. C.128, 9 June 1975.

29. European Parliament, *Working Documents 1975-6*, Document J3/75 (12 May 1975).

30. Rt. Hon. Sir Derek Walker-Smith b. 1910 MP (Cons) East Hertfordshire. Minister of Health 1957-60. Member of European Parliament, 1973-9.

31. Carlo Scarascia Mugnozza: Commissioner and Vice President of the Commission of the European Communities 1973-7, responsible for Environmental Protection.

32. Lord Nicholas Bethell b. 1938 freelance writer, Conservative Whip (House of Lords) 1970-1, Member of European Parliament, 1975-9. Elected MEP (Conservative) London North West 1979.

33. Peter Kirk b. 1928, d. 1977 MP (Cons) Gravesend 1955-64 and Saffron Walden 1965-77. Parliamentary Under-Secretary of State, Ministry of Defence 1970-4. Member and leader of Conservative delegation to European Parliament 1973-7.

34. Pierre Rene Giraud b. 1913 Member of French Senate since 1968. Member of European Parliament and leader of Socialist Group in 1975.

35. James Spicer b. 1925 farmer, MP (Cons) Dorset West. Member of European Parliament 1975-8.

36. House of Commons, 1974-5, HC 45 xviii 29 April 1975.

37. Rt. Hon. Dennis Howell b. 1923. MP (Lab) Birmingham Small Heath 1961- Minister of State, Ministry of Housing and Local Government, 1969-70. Opposition spokesman for local government and sport 1970-4. Minister of State, Department of the Environment 1974-9.

38. House of Commons, 1974-5, HC 87 viii 1 July 1975. *Minutes of Evidence taken before the Select Committee on European Secondary Legislation.*

39. Ibid.

40. Julius Silverman b. 1905. MP (Lab) Birmingham Erdington, 1945-55 and 1974- and Birmingham Aston 1955-74.

41. House of Commons, 1974-5, HC 87 viii 1 July 1975.

42. House of Commons, 1974-5, HC 45 xxvii. *Twenty-seventh Report from the Select Committee*, 8 July 1975.

43. House of Lords, 1974-5, HL 298 i. *Minutes of Evidence taken before the European Communities Committee* (Sub-Committee F), 19 June 1975.

44. S. McQuillin, Principal DoE, ibid.

45. House of Lords, 1974-5, HL 298. *Thirtieth Report from the Select Committee of the House of Lords on the European Communities*, 29 July 1975, p. 4.

46. House of Commons, 1974-5, HC 45 xxxiii. *Thirty-third Report from the Select Committee*, 16 September 1975.

47. House of Lords, 1974-5, vol. 364, col. 721-65, 13 October 1975.
48. Lady Alma Birk. Life peer since 1967. Journalist, Parliamentary Under-Secretary of State, Department of the Environment 1974-9.
49. House of Lords, 1974-5, vol. 364, col. 755.
50. Ibid., col. 757.
51. Department of the Environment, *Implementation of the EEC Directive on the Quality of Bathing Water*, note by the Department of the Environment, March 1977.
52. These were not published.
53. Wessex Water Authority. *The Wessex Plan 1979-84*, Appendix I, p. 119 (published January 1979).
54. Rt. Hon. Peter Shore b. 1924 MP (Lab) Stepney 1964-74, Tower Hamlets 1974-   Secretary of State for Economic Affairs 1967-9. Opposition spokesman on Europe 1971-4. Secretary of State for Trade 1974-6. Secretary of State for the Environment 1976-9. Opposition spokesman on foreign affairs 1979- .
55. Department of the Environment, *Advice on the Implementation in England and Wales of the EEC Directive on the Quality of Bathing Water*, DoE, 9 July 1979.
56. Bathing beaches which had more than 1,500 bathers per mile and those with more than 750 bathers per mile had to be identified. Those in the former category had to be designated, those less than 750 were not to be designated, and those between the two figures were discussed with the local authorities to consider whether designation should be made.
57. The Minister's reply was also published in a press notice from the Department of the Environment: *Bathing Waters Identified*, Press Notice no. 578 (14 December 1979). The beaches concerned are at Bournemouth, Bridlington, Christchurch, Margate, Newquay, Paignton, Penzance, Poole, Ryde, St Ives, Sandown, Scarborough, Southend-on-Sea, Swanage, Torquay, Weston-super-Mare and Weymouth.
58. Medical Research Council Memorandum No. 37, *Sewage Contamination of Bathing Beaches in England and Wales* (HMSO, London, 1959).
59. *Water Pollution Control*, vol. 78, no. 2 (1979), p. 211.
60. V.J. Cabelli, 'Evaluation of Recreational Water Quality', in A. James and L. Evison (eds.), *Biological Indicators of Water Quality* (John Wiley, New York, 1979).
61. *Water Pollution Control*, vol. 78, no. 2 (1979), p. 211.
62. Department of the Environment, *Report of the Coastal Pollution Research Committee of the Water Pollution Research Laboratory* (HMSO, London, 1975), p. 3.
63. W.F. Ridley, 'Wastewater—the Convenience that is Still Taken for Granted', *Water* (July 1978), p. 26.
64. Ian Percival b. 1921 MP (Cons) Southport 1959- .
65. House of Commons, 1974-5, HC 87 viii. *Minutes of Evidence taken before the Select Committee on European Secondary Legislation*, 1 July 1975.
66. Commission of the European Communities, *State of the Environment—First Report EEC, 1977* (Luxembourg, 1977), p. 25.
67. See note 63.
68. Department of the Environment, *Implementation of the EEC Directive on the Quality of Bathing Water*, note by the Department of the Environment, March 1977, para. 23.
69. A.L.H. Gameson, 'EEC Directive on Quality of Bathing Water', *Water Pollution Control*, vol. 78, no. 2 (1979), p. 208.
70. Mr R. Saxon, Wessex Water Authority, in personal interview with author.
71. *Water Pollution Control*, vol. 78, no. 2 (1979), p. 212.
72. Quoted in 'Britannia Waives the Rules', *World Water* (June 1978), p. 26.
73. House of Lords, 1974-5, vol. 364, 13 October 1975, col. 729.
74. See Chapter 3, note 21.

75. Ibid.

76. A.L.H. Gameson, 'EEC Rules UK OK?', *Surveyor* (21 September 1978), p. 10.

77. See Renshaw's remarks in *Water Pollution Control*, vol. 78, no. 2 (1979), p. 195.

78. Water Research Centre, 'Notes on Water Research', *Bacterial Pollution of Bathing Beaches*, no. 10 (June 1977), p. iv.

79. House of Lords, 1974-5, HL 291 i. *Minutes of Evidence taken before the European Communities Committee Sub-Committee*, 19 June 1975, para. 23.

80. D.C. Renshaw, 'How and Why Legislation is Produced', *Water Pollution Control*, vol. 78, no. 2 (1979), p. 181.

81. Ibid., p. 182.

82. Gameson, 'EEC Directive on Quality of Bathing Water', pp. 209-10.

83. Renshaw, 'How and Why Legislation is Produced', p. 181.

84. See House of Commons, 1975-6, HC 336. First Special Report, 15 March 1976.

85. Mr R. Saxon, Wessex Water Authority, in personal interview with author.

86. Actual costs will depend on the size, length and situation of the outfall. But of the 25 identified bathing areas it seems that about 7 may not be up to the required standard. Of these, some have remedial works already planned as part of the water authorities' existing capital programmes.

87. National Water Council, *Water Industry Review 1978*, para. 43.

88. See for example the views of Mr Toms of Wessex Water Authority and Mr Willis of Severn Trent Water Authority, quoted in *Municipal Engineering*, 17 July 1979.

89. House of Commons, 1977-8, HC 128, para. 1068. See also 'Eureau – Finding a Common Approach to European Problems', *World Water* (April 1979), pp. 24-5.

6 NOISE ABATEMENT ZONES

Noise Nuisances and Control

Unlike pollution of the land, water and atmosphere, noise has only recently been acknowledged as a form of environmental pollution. Because it cannot be seen, and its effects are often transitory, and people's responses are so varied, attempts to define and control noise pollution have so far been comparatively modest.

'Noise' describes the undesired effects of a sound.[1] At relatively low levels noise is an unwanted disturbance, intrusion and interference. As levels increase these effects are magnified until eventually pain and damaged hearing may be produced. Noise is measured in decibels (dB), modified to take account of the response of the ear to differing frequencies (dBA) such that an increase of 10 dBA corresponds approximately to a subjective effect of doubling the loudness. Table 6.1 shows some approximate levels.

Table 6.1: Approximate Noise Levels

Source	Sound Level in dB(A)
Threshold of hearing	Zero
Rustle of leaf	10
Still day in country away from traffic	20
Quiet whisper	30
Background noise in public library	40
Quiet office	50
Ordinary conversation	60
Private car from pavement	70
Ringing alarm clock at 2-3 ft	80
Heavy goods vehicle from pavement	90
Pneumatic drill from 5 metres	100
Typical discotheque	105
Threshold of pain	130

Source: *Digest of Environmental Pollution Statistics*, no. 1 (1978) (DoE/HMSO, London, 1978).

The most significant sources of noise nuisance are usually categorised into four groups:

1. Road traffic
2. Aircraft
3. Neighbourhood (including industrial, entertainment and environmental noise)
4. Occupational

Traffic noise disturbs the largest number of people for the longest period. Its most annoying features are its general level and its variations— variations due to changes in volume of traffic at different times of the day and as individual vehicles pass. (In some cases frequency is important too, e.g. diesel engine exhaust arising from buses.) Traffic noise has been steadily increasing over recent decades: future projections for the UK suggest that between 1975 and 1985 the number of city dwellers exposed to high levels of traffic noise will increase by 600,000.[2] Aircraft noise suddenly became a nuisance with the introduction of the jet engine and it now affects urban as well as rural areas. The annoyance it causes is a function of the number of aircraft heard and their peak noise levels. Over two and a half million people are estimated to live and work within ten miles of an airport, where the noise nuisance is extensive and often intolerable.[3]

Neighbourhood noise covers several types of noise from stationary sources such as schools, factories, workshops, homes, places of entertainment, road works, construction sites and so on. It is much harder to quantify general levels of exposure and annoyance, partly because the individual sources of noise may be produced unpredictably (e.g. use of powered equipment such as lawn mowers, power tools or noisy parties) and partly, again, because individual tolerance of this type of nuisance is so varied.

Occupational noise from high-speed machinery and other equipment can present a serious risk of hearing loss or damage. Between half a million and one million people are probably exposed to this at work,[4] and many more are subjected to considerable annoyance. The problem is to improve design and use of quieter machines. The technology exists, but industry has not seemed sufficiently interested in protecting workers to date; nor have many workers responded to the advice of wearing protective equipment, perhaps because they find it interferes unacceptably with the social conditions at work.

As the Noise Advisory Council panel commented, 'although the four [types of noise] differ in certain respects they have much in common. They are all the products of an industrial civilisation; they all represent an increasing intrusion into the everyday lives of people throughout the country; but most important they are the product of ignorance and inertia in the past.'[5]

The first general Act of Parliament specifically to cover neighbourhood noise was the Noise Abatement Act 1960 (although similar local provisions had been made by several local authorities since the 1930s and the Public Health Act 1936 created a broad framework). It gave local authorities a duty to inspect their districts for nuisances and require abatement of any that were found. Their powers were extended by the Public Health (Recurring Nuisances) Act 1969 which also enabled them to prohibit the nuisances recurring. But, in the view of the DoE, 'the legislation was very restrictive. Procedures tended to be complicated and to work in favour of the noise maker and the penalties were small. Moreover it was difficult for local authorities to tackle some of the most serious noise problems, particularly since they could only act after the noise had been made.'[6] Separate legislation to control road traffic, aircraft and occupational noise began to be introduced during the 1970s, but local authorities were still unable to do anything to achieve overall reductions in environmental noise levels.

The Noise Advisory Council was set up in 1970 to advise the Secretary of State for the Environment on progress in preventing and abating noise.[7] It is chaired by a minister and works through a number of working groups to investigate detailed issues. Its membership includes scientists, other specialists and some lay people, and its reports are published. It is similar to the Clean Air Council which was established under the 1956 Clean Air Act to advise ministers on air pollution control.[8]

A working party set up by the Noise Advisory Council to report on the 1960 Noise Abatement Act confirmed these shortcomings and recommended that the existing nuisance provisions should be reinforced, and additional powers created to prevent new sources of noise disturbing established residential areas, and controlling noise levels in particular areas.[9] Other working parties of the Noise Advisory Council reported on aircraft and traffic noise,[10] but the next major step was not taken until the Control of Pollution Act 1974 was passed. Part III deals with noise and, again only relates to neighbourhood noise. The Departments of Transport, Trade and Employment are still responsible for legislation covering the other aspects, so there is not yet an integrated approach. However, in Sections 60-1, Part III does deal in important ways with noise from building sites and road works, and Section 68 covers noise from plant or machinery.

A major innovation of Part III concerns powers to set up noise abatement zones, and this is the subject of the case material discussed later in the chapter. Most of the other provisions deal with control of statutory nuisances and when Part III of the Control of Pollution Act was brought into force on 1 January 1976 in England and Wales it thereby replaced the equivalent provisions of the Noise Abatement Act 1960 which was repealed.[11] A related piece of legislation, the Noise Insulation Regulations 1973, made under powers in the Land Compensation Act 1973, permitted highway authorities to give grants to insulate dwellings against increased traffic noise from new or improved roads, and in 1973 a circular from the DoE, *Planning and Noise* strongly urged local authorities not to permit new residential developments in areas subjected to high noise levels, or to allow new commercial or industrial developments that might increase the noise exposure of existing residential areas.[12]

In 1974 a further report from the Noise Advisory Council reviewed the likely evolution of noise problems in the short term, and made specific recommendations for steps to prevent noise disturbance in each of the four categories. But it also commented that 'the constraints which can be foreseen in the immediate future are not technological. The key to any significant advance in the control and abatement of these major forms of noise nuisance is a demonstration of the political will at all levels throughout the country to tackle the problem.'[13] One of its suggestions was that a Quiet Town Experiment should be set up in an urban area where the local authority, industry and private individuals should be invited to co-operate voluntarily in an effort to see how far the ambient noise level of a town could be reduced. This was done in Darlington, and the results are currently being evaluated.[14]

Further initiatives to promote noise control have come from the European Community which has adopted several proposals relating to sound levels and exhaust systems of motor vehicles, construction machinery and plant noise and aircraft.[15] From the OECD there has recently been published a report, *Reducing Noise in OECD Countries*, which identified 15 action proposals for noise abatement policies, although acknowledging the difficulty of effective enforcement. It is difficult to be sure why exactly noise has found a place on the agenda of pollution control nevertheless, although it may be, as the OECD observes, because 'Today noise is the problem ranked highest by people in numerous surveys concerning the undesirable aspects of living conditions. It is also a problem that can be expected to persist and grow

unless strong and effective noise abatement policies are adopted.'[16] More
will be said of this later in the chapter.

Noise Abatement Zones

Sections 63 to 67 and Schedule 1 to the Control of Pollution Act contain
powers under which local authorities may create noise abatement zones
(NAZs) and have been chosen for the case study of this aspect of
pollution control for two main reasons. First, it is a substantial innovation
of policy and therefore particularly interesting to observe. Second, it is
one of the few significant parts of the Control of Pollution Act that has
been in force for some time.

The idea of controlling aspects of neighbourhood noise in this way
originated in the evidence submitted by the Association of Public Health
Inspectors (now the Environmental Health Officers Association) to the
Noise Advisory Council's working group on the Noise Abatement Act in
1971.[17] This drew the parallel with air pollution where, before the Clean
Air Act was introduced in 1956, local authorities were only able to
reduce emissions of smoke from individual premises by using the statutory
nuisance procedures under the public health legislation. They could do
little to 'reduce the general level of air pollution created collectively
where a multitude of chimney stacks were not causing a nuisance'.[18] But
the Clean Air Act empowered local authorities to declare smoke control
areas within which smoke emission could be broadly prohibited. The
evidence therefore proposed that local authorities should be given
powers 'to make orders declaring noise control areas and in these areas
they should have special powers to procure the reduction of noise'.[19]
The scheme then outlined impressed the working group although it
agreed with the Confederation of British Industry that the analogy
between smoke and noise control was imperfect. It nevertheless
recommended that these kinds of special control areas should be
introduced to supplement the nuisance provisions.[20] The Control of
Pollution Act adopted most of the working party's suggestions and since
January 1976 all district councils in England and Wales have been able
to designate noise abatement zones within their areas. The procedure,
explained in DoE Circular 2/76 is[21] that the authority, through its
environmental health staff, can select neighbourhoods where it would
be desirable to protect residents from an increase in noise levels. Designating such areas noise abatement zones commits the authority to measuring
noise from all premises, within specified classes, setting up a noise level

register (Section 64) and monitoring noise levels in the zone. Noise abatement orders made for each designated zone have to be confirmed by the Secretary of State for the Environment before they become operational (Section 63 and Schedule I).[22] And any owners and occupiers affected by the order can object to the Secretary of State who may hold a local enquiry to take further evidence. Once the noise abatement order has been confirmed, however, the local authority has a duty to monitor the noise levels around the classified premises. These are the typical, current levels at the time of measuring, and they are recorded in a register. Owners and occupiers must be informed by the local authority of the register entry details. If the levels are found to be exceeded without prior consent, then a statutory offence will have been committed which can be heard in a magistrates court (Section 65).

In addition a local authority can require noise from premises within a NAZ to be reduced if it appears 'that a reduction in the level is practicable at reasonable cost and would afford public benefit'. This is achieved by serving noise reduction notices on owners or occupiers of premises specifying the level of noise to be achieved within a certain time (Section 66). Appeal arrangements exist, but if (after the noise reduction scheme has been introduced) the reduced levels are being exceeded, the responsible people will be liable to prosecution (Section 65). Local authorities may also set noise levels for new or converted premises being constructed within NAZs which the occupiers will be required to comply with (Section 67).

For all premises affected by NAZs, prosecution is possible if the registered noise levels are exceeded, although in the case of prosecutions concerning Section 66 (which covers reductions in noise levels) the defence of 'best practicable means' is available. This means that if the defendant can prove he had used the best practicable means for preventing or counteracting the noise he will not be guilty of committing an offence. This defence is not available to defendants prosecuted under Section 65 (covering compliance with noise levels specified in the register under the original noise abatement order) although it is to defendants whose premises are covered by the NAZ by virtue of being converted or newly built within it and who have applied to the local authority for a predetermined noise level. Indeed the magistrates court can, in convicting a person of failing to comply with the registered noise level, order necessary work to be done to prevent recurrence either by the person concerned or the local authority itself.

These are the legal arrangements for establishing and managing NAZs. But within them there are important considerations about the noise levels to be set, the premises to be controlled, the methods of measuring sound levels, and the longer-term evaluation of the effectiveness of NAZs. First, it appears that there is more than one view about the purpose or objective of NAZs. The Noise Advisory Council defined this as being 'to reduce (or perhaps in some cases hold steady) the ambient noise level'.[23] The DoE declared the aim was 'to secure a positive reduction of noise levels'.[24] However a leaflet put out jointly by the Noise Advisory Council and the Central Office of Information in 1975 explained that the purpose of NAZs was to achieve the long-term control of noise particularly from fixed industrial premises. This leaflet runs through the steps taken by local authorities to establish NAZs and states that the power to reduce noise levels (Section 65 of the Act) 'is the key to the long-term effectiveness of NAZs'.[25]

It therefore appears that there are distinct short- and long-term objectives contained within the NAZs powers. In the short term, the designation of zones can hold steady noise levels from classified premises. In the long term, reduced levels can be set, though whether the overall amount of noise or maximum levels are reduced is still uncertain. This uncertainty relates to two factors: (1) the practicality of implementing NAZs; and (2) the effect of other kinds of noise (traffic, aircraft) not controlled by local authorities.

Looking at the practicalities, the most obvious problem is to measure noise levels accurately. Although very sophisticated meters exist and are widely in use, the readings they give are inevitably influenced by several factors including wind and weather, choice of monitoring points, time of day or night and levels of background noise. This is recognised in the standards by specifying that a number of readings should be taken on the same spot to give the Leq, which is effectively an 'average' noise level. Nevertheless the problem of obtaining reliable and repeatable sets of readings is troublesome.[26]

Another practical problem for local authorities is to select the premises that ought to be controlled within the NAZs. Circular 2/76 suggests that they classify types of premises as follows:

Industrial (factories, workshops)
Commercial (warehouses, offices, shops, hotels, garages)
Entertainment
Agricultural
Transport (stations, depots)
Public Utility (water works, power stations)
Domestic premises are excluded on the grounds that those sources of

noise are best dealt with under the nuisance provisions of Part III.

The advice is that only those premises where noise control is possible and would be beneficial should be covered by the noise abatement order.[27] The Act requires the order to state the classes of premises to which it will apply and within that the local authority measures the typical noise levels for each individual premises – these levels are recorded in the register. The local authorities have some degree of freedom in monitoring but they are also subject to a number of restrictions. A NAZ can be part or all of the authority's area and the fact that orders have to be confirmed by the Secretary of State has so far ensured that some degree of comparability across the country is maintained for comparable areas. The assumption is that mixed residential and industrial areas would be selected for NAZs as a priority.

Having established one or more zones in its area the local authority is then obliged to monitor how well the levels are being complied with. No new resources have been allocated for this to local authorities, so existing staff and equipment have to be specially deployed. One Chief Environmental Health Officer who is also a member of the Noise Advisory Council has said, 'I wonder how far NAZs are just concerned with cosmetic effects and not actively being monitored.'[28] The implication here is that having established NAZs in terms of completing all the paper work, the local authorities may not feel prompted to do much more if there are other demands on their time. He went on: 'most local authorities are heavily involved with noise control as part of development control, and since there is such pressure on resources, I doubt whether NAZs are going to be useful'.

A less critical view comes from Newcastle upon Tyne where the Environmental Health Department has already introduced two NAZs. They did encounter a number of practical difficulties – confirmation of the order by the Secretary of State took longer than they had expected; monitoring arrangements were complicated to arrange with occupiers of premises; and also the more information they gained about each source the harder they found it to know what to put in the register. Subsequently the preparation of register entries with maps of monitoring points was a time-consuming job, but 'at least there is no closely defined time schedule which has to be adhered to and which could create complications'.[29]

At the time of writing (December 1979) 24 NAZs had been confirmed in England, and 10 more were with the DoE, all of them accompanied by objections. According to the DoE it was taking their three-person section less than six months to confirm an order where there were no objections, and longer of course if there were. Objections are usually one of two kinds—either the occupier of the premises maintains the type of noise being produced is beyond further control by him (e.g. a launderette) or that the local authority already has sufficient powers under nuisance and planning legislation to control the noise in question so a NAZ is unlikely to be appropriate. So far all objections have been overruled although six have involved local enquiries. In the DoE's view, written objections are more suitable than enquiries, since they usually relate to individual occupiers' problems or opinions rather than to the community as a whole.[30]

A unique survey of NAZs was conducted by Dr Mulholland of Aston University in 1978. He found that 7 per cent of local authorities claimed to be setting up at least one NAZ, and 25 NAZs were in the process of being established. A further 25 per cent of authorities were 'thinking about' setting up a NAZ although that was (for most of them) all they were doing actively. Of the NAZs in progress the survey showed tremendous variety of detail: areas ranged from 6 acres to 6 sq miles; some contained only one factory while others covered hundreds of premises. The measuring times selected only in a few cases broke the 24-hour period down into 'working time', 'evening', 'night'. All the zones contained industrial or commercial premises—except in one solitary case where a mixed residential site was mentioned. Authorities' estimates of the time taken to set the zones up were also varied—6 months, 1 man-year, 100 man-hours, for example—reflecting the variety between zones.[31]

There are few published accounts yet of the experiences of local authorities or occupiers of premises or residents with NAZs.[32] For Newcastle upon Tyne, at least, their first zone has proved something of a success. Four factories within it were previously the sources of 80 to 100 complaints annually. But since the zone has been in operation only one has been received.[33]

When the Noise Advisory Council proposed that NAZs should become a device for noise control they acknowledged the difficulty of assessing neighbourhood noise problems (or evaluating measures taken to reduce them) on the basis of available statistical information which is, generally, the numbers of complaints of noise nuisance received by local authorities. Indeed the Wilson Committee (established in 1960 to report on the problem of noise) had already observed: 'many people who are annoyed do not complain for one reason or another, although they may be disturbed as much as those who do complain. Nor is there any means of assessing the seriousness of a complaint or the weight which should be attached to complaints from representative bodies compared with those from individuals.'[34]

It seems that in about half of all complaints the existence of a noise nuisance is confirmed by investigation, and that over 90 per cent of all confirmed nuisances are dealt with informally. Very few cases go to court because local authorities prefer the informal approach; also they are often unable to pin responsibility for the disturbance on a particular source, or frequently cannot be confident that adequate technical evidence would be available to justify legal proceedings. So the strengthening of the nuisance provisions together with the NAZs does in this context suggest that numbers of complaints or court cases will not be all that helpful in evaluating the success of the new measures.

Before the Control of Pollution Act was in force, environmental health officers knew that their noise control policies were resulting in 'the expenditure annually of hundreds of thousands of pounds on the installation of industrial plant and equipment to reduce the noise level from machinery from industrial processes'.[35] This was expected to continue as NAZs were progressively introduced, and conforms with the often quoted principles of noise control:

1. Reduction of the noise at source (by replacing the noisy machine or modifying it to produce less noise);
2. Acoustic insulation and sound absorption (by using materials and structures around the source that will prevent as much noise escaping);
3. Isolation (by preventing transmission of noise and vibration from noise source).[36]

In commending NAZs as a policy device the DoE recognises that local authorities must 'take into account local conditions and circumstances, the limitations of current technical knowledge and the financial implications'.[37]

Analysis

Although the results of NAZs so far are scanty, it is possible to draw attention to a number of features influencing their effectiveness. These will be considered in turn and are:

1. The consequences of introducing discretionary powers.
2. The connection with planning legislation.

3. The relative priority of controlling noise.

Discretionary Powers

It has already been mentioned that the timing of introducing different sections of the Control of Pollution Act has been in the main related to the financial consequences of the provisions. Part III (Noise) was amongst the first batch to become operational, on 1 January 1976 and the sections relating to NAZs are entirely discretionary in the sense that local authorities are free to use them or not as they choose. This is expressed in the Act in these words: 'It shall be the duty of every local authority to cause its area to be inspected from time to time . . . to decide how to exercise its powers concerning noise abatement zones.'[38]

The Noise Advisory Council examined the alternative of imposing 'a general duty on the citizen not to impose unnecessary noise on his neighbours'. This could try to get round the difficulty of proving a nuisance existed or having to set up special areas of control such as NAZs, by making it a general obligation to use the best practicable means to minimise the emission of noise. But this would in turn impose problems of enforcement partly 'because it would require business to treat as a prime economic cost what has hitherto been no more than a contingent liability'; but also because enforcement by the courts would 'introduce a substantial new element of uncertainty into the calculations of every industrial and commercial concern in the country'. So the Council recommended that the statutory declaration of such a general duty would give the stamp of parliamentary authority to the growing recognition of quiet as a social good, although its direct enforcement would be neither practicable nor in all cases desirable.[39]

Another aspect of the discretionary nature of the NAZ power is that the local authorities who opt to set up NAZs are not bound to follow specific national standards. In the DoE's words, 'the Act deliberately avoids laying down any kind of environmental standard to be applied nationally and it gives no indication of what local authorities might regard as acceptable. Noise has always been regarded as a local phenomenon and one which should be dealt with locally. Standards which might be too stringent in one situation might not be sufficiently stringent in another.'[40]

Although this statement reaffirms the general direction of the UK approach to pollution control (which relies on maintaining quality standards that vary according to the use to which that part of the natural environment is put),[41] it is not the only statement relevant here. One

striking feature of the work on noise is the existence of quite advanced
knowledge and technology to control noise coupled with much less
understanding of the *effects* of noise. As a result, the adequacy of any
noise standards that may be set is likely to continue to be debatable. But
a number of very definite standards do already exist and are commonly
used, particularly relating to traffic and aircraft noise. The Motor
Vehicles (Construction and Use) Regulations 1973[42] specify maximum
permitted noise levels for different types of motor vehicles—e.g. 89 dBA
for heavy goods, 85 dBA for passenger vehicles carrying more than
twelve passengers and 84 dBA for motor cars. These regulations are
examples of standards 'laid down on the basis of technical and/or
economic feasibility after relevant lobbying—there is no other stated
rationale'.[43]

The Noise Insulation Regulations of 1973 state that sound insulation
must be provided for owners of buildings the facades of which are
exposed to 68 dBA or more measured on the L_{10} index resulting from
new or altered road construction.[44] The Noise Advisory Council suggested
that to achieve acceptable levels of indoor noise, a maximum of 70 dBA
on the L_{10} index could be taken as an external traffic limit, this being
'the limit of the acceptable rather than a standard of what is desirable'.[45]
And the DoE's circular on planning and noise says: 'wherever an authority can, without sacrificing other important objectives, adopt as their
noise criteria a substantially lower value on the L_{10} scale than 70 dBA
they should do so'.[46]

Aircraft noise is described in terms of the Noise and Number Index
(NNI)[47] and on that basis, examples of levels are shown in Table 6.2.
The DoE circular, *Planning and Noise*,[48] set out criteria for local authorities to use in considering whether to allow developments at sites exposed
to certain levels of aircraft noise, e.g. at 60 NNI and above only factories
and warehouses should be permitted. Between 50 and 59 NNI offices
might also be allowed and at 40 to 49 NNI so perhaps could schools,
although sound insulation would be essential. Only at levels of 35 to 39
NNI ought planning permission for dwellings not be refused on grounds
of noise alone.

These examples show how extensively national emission standards
are in fact iterated, even if they are not all mandatory. Although local
discretion is acknowledged therefore, it is obliged to operate within a
network of guidelines and recommended levels, and so is considerably
qualified.

Table 6.2: Noise and Number Index Levels

Level	Average Reaction
0	not noticeable
20	noticeable
35	intrusive
45	annoying
60	very annoying
70	unbearable

Source: Open University.

Planning Legislation

The influence of planning legislation on noise control has already been referred to in the case material. Through their responsibility for development control, local authorities are able to prevent new uses of land (for housing, school, roads, etc.) from creating unduly high exposure to noise in certain instances. This contrasts with the powers available under the public health legislation and Control of Pollution Act to deal with noise problems arising from existing uses. The planning departments of local authorities tend to collaborate with their colleagues in the environmental health departments over the noise implications of planning applications, and it was to this that Mr Barnett referred.[49]

Confusion between the provisions of the planning legislation on the one hand, and those concerning NAZs on the other, arises because Sections 63 to 67 of the Control of Pollution Act cover new as well as existing uses of land. Section 67 in particular refers to the obligations of occupiers of new premises to adhere to specific noise levels if their premises fall within a NAZ. The Newcastle upon Tyne Environmental Health Officer commented that as far as his NAZs were concerned there were few advantages to be gained from Section 67 because wider powers were available through planning controls.[50] Furthermore, the main theme of central government advice to planning authorities in this context is 'where at all possible ambient noise levels should not be increased' and this is a central aim of NAZs. The planning circulars go further than the NAZ advice has done so far in saying that 'where existing levels are already likely to be high, . . . the ambient level affecting existing residential and other noise sensitive developments should not exceed a corrected noise level of 75 dBA by day or 65 dBA by night'.[51]

The fact that the two areas of policy (development control and noise control) overlap is in itself desirable so that consistent action may be taken within a local authority. But in the context of the case study the fact that there may be uncertainty over which powers to invoke to achieve a certain noise control may indicate why some local authorities are not apparently active in using their NAZ powers.[52] The more familiar planning powers may continue to be used in preference because they are more familiar, or because they have proved effective in the past. It could seem unduly complicated to use the NAZ powers also because occupiers of premises are not likely to be familiar with their rights or obligations if they are affected by a noise abatement or reduction order, and they could reasonably expect the local authority to explain this to them (this was done in the Newcastle upon Tyne example). Furthermore, the obligation to maintain publicly accessible registers of noise levels may not be attractive to local authorities if they fear overzealous citizens might use the information to call for more extensive or active monitoring of neighbourhood noise levels. These are some of the reasons why the existence of similar (though not identical) noise control powers under planning legislation may be confusing and may account for the relatively slow introduction of NAZs so far.

The Priority of Noise Control

As with other forms of pollution control, measures to abate noise, if they are to be successful, require compromises to be reached between different interests. But unlike other forms of pollution control, the benefits of containing or reducing noise are much harder to demonstrate in terms of health or money than are the benefits of protecting water and land or reducing smoke in the air. Although hearing can be damaged or lost completely as a result of exposure to very high sound levels, the physiological effects of noise are still not well documented or proven. The long-term consequences of exposure to noise, particularly amongst workers operating high-speed machinery, are still, perhaps surprisingly, not surveyed.[53] Few if any working days are lost as a direct result of noise-induced hearing problems.

Yet noise controls are a significant element of expenditure, particularly if the premises concerned were not originally designed with acoustic factors in mind. The cost of silencers, machine mountings, insulating materials in houses and sound barriers for roads and runways may be a considerable element in a local authority's budget. So from a naive perspective it could be said that noise costs nothing while noise controls cost a lot, with little benefits to show in economic terms if noise is controlled. This could be one reason why noise controls generally have had so little impact. One minister expressed the problem of neighbourhood noise in this way: 'noise can be an irritant and a nuisance. Wherever possible it ought to be diminished. I am sure that almost everybody would agree about that. The trouble is that certain sorts of noise can give positive pleasure to some people while annoying—even in a sense invading the privacy of—others.'[54]

The difficulty of establishing maximum levels within NAZs that are 'right' in any objective sense is obvious. Local authorities tend to choose levels that refer to existing general DoE guidelines, and that they can expect occupiers of premises to agree to without too much fuss. But it must be remembered that it was the local authorities' technical staff—environmental health officers—who urged the government, through the Noise Advisory Council to give them these powers. They must therefore believe that noise control can be improved with the device of NAZs. Whether faster progress on introducing NAZs could or should have been made by now is also hard to assess. As with other areas of local government activity the effects of reorganisation coupled with uncertain financial resources have encouraged a cautious approach, particularly to new responsibilities. Some authorities would certainly claim that this explains why they have not yet got any NAZs.[55] Others may feel that neighbourhood noise is less of a priority than other problems—e.g. smoke control or housing conditions. But observers have certainly pointed to the slowness with which NAZs have been established, particularly in comparison with the rate at which smoke control orders were made after the Clean Air Act was passed.[56]

Notes

1. The Open University, 'Environmental Control and Public Health PT272 Units 11-12', *The Control of the Acoustic Environment* (The Open University Press, Milton Keynes, 1975), p. 11.

2. OECD, *Reducing Noise in OECD Countries* (OECD, Paris, 1978).

3. Noise Advisory Council, *Noise in the Next Ten Years* (HMSO, London, 1974), para. 26.

4. Ibid., para. 45.

5. Ibid., para. 50.

6. Department of the Environment, *Pollution Control in Great Britain: How it Works*, Pollution Paper no. 9 (HMSO, London, 1978), para. 288.

7. Its terms of reference are 'to keep under review the progress made generally in preventing and abating the generation of noise; to make recommendations to Ministers with responsibility in this field; and to advise on such matters as they may refer to the council'. In September 1979 the government announced its intention to review the existence of several 'quangos' and the Noise Advisory Council was one of those but it has now officially been 'spared'.

8. Unlike the Clean Air Council though, the Noise Advisory Council is non-statutory. But see also Chapter 7, note 4.

9. Noise Advisory Council, *Neighbourhood Noise* (HMSO, London, 1971).

10. Noise Advisory Council, *Aircraft Noise: Flight Routeing near Airports* (HMSO, London, 1971); *Aircraft Noise: should the Noise and Number Index be Revised?* (HMSO, London, 1972); *Concorde Noise Levels* (HMSO, London, 1977); *Traffic Noise, the Vehicle Regulations and their Enforcement* (HMSO, London, 1972), etc.

11. These sections of the Act were brought into force by Statutory Instrument 1975 No. 2118. *Control of Pollution Act 1974 (Commencement No. 4) Order 1975*, 10 December 1975.

12. Department of the Environment, Circular 10/73, *Planning and Noise*, 19 January 1973.

13. Noise Advisory Council, *Noise in the Next Ten Years* (HMSO, London, 1974), para. 51.

14. See: *The Problem of Noise and the Quiet Town Experiment*, Report of seminar held in Darlington 5-7 September 1978, organised and published by Traffic Engineering and Control, 29 Newman Street, London W1; and W.C.B. Robson, *Darlington: the World's First Quiet Town* (District Councils Review, April 1979), pp. 86-7.

15. See: OJ L66 of 12 March 1977, OJ C82 of 14 April 1975, OJ C54 of 8 March 1976, OJ C126 of 9 June 1976, COM (76) 646.

16. OECD, *The State of the Environment in OECD Member Countries* (OECD, Paris, 1979), p. 118. But political scientists might offer another explanation: see for example, G. Tullock, *The Vote Motive* (Institute of Economic Affairs, 1976), Hobart Paper No. 9.

17. Appendix C, Memorandum by Association of Public Health Inspectors on Noise Control Areas. Noise Advisory Council, *Neighbourhood Noise* (HMSO, London, 1971), pp. 72-6.

18. Ibid., para. 5.

19. Ibid., para. 8.

20. Ibid., paras 17-25, pp. 3-5.

21. Department of the Environment, Circular 2/76, *Control of Pollution Act 1974 Implementation of Part III – Noise*, 27 February 1976.

22. But some of these powers may be repealed, as suggested in the government's White Paper: Department of the Environment, *Central Government Controls over Local Authorities*, Cmnd. 7634 (HMSO, London, 1979).

23. Noise Advisory Council, *Neighbourhood Noise* (HMSO, London, 1971), para. 165.

24. Department of the Environment, *Pollution Control in Great Britain: How it Works*, Pollution Paper no. 9 (HMSO, London, 1978), para. 306.

25. Noise Advisory Council, *Bothered by Noise? How the Law can Help You* (HMSO, London, 1975). Cresswell states in personal communication to author: 'few people would deny that in general terms, noise levels are increasing but whether this is primarily due to traffic, industry, individual habits, etc., it is impossible to be certain. However, to many people, rightly or wrongly, the introduction of NAZ provides an opportunity to halt this increase. It has to be looked at in conjunction with other measures . . .'

26. The Control of Noise (Measurement and Registers) Regulations 1976 S.1.1976 No. 37 prescribe the methods of measurement and manner of calculation. See also C. Cresswell, 'Neighbourhood Noise Levels – Newcastle's Experience and Some Future Problems', *Municipal Engineering* (31 July 1979), p. 569.

27. Department of the Environment, Circular 2/76, Appendix 2, paras 2-3.

28. D. Barnett, at seminar 'Implementing the Control of Pollution Act', SAUS, Bristol, May 1979.

29. C. Cresswell, 'Hushing Things up in Newcastle upon Tyne', *Municipal Engineering* (10 April 1979), p. 256.

30. The written objections procedure is non-statutory and has been adopted when the Secretary of State chose not to hold an enquiry, and when there is one objector who does not want a hearing.

31. K.A. Mulholland, 'Local Environmental Health Officers and Noise', *Environmental Health* (April 1979), pp. 74-6.

32. According to the Chairman of Darlington's Quiet Town Experiment Management Committee: 'in fact local authorities generally do not seem to be taking up the opportunities afforded them under the Control of Pollution Act for designating noise abatement zones' (*The Problem of Noise and the Quiet Town Experiment*, note 14).

33. Cresswell, 'Hushing Things up in Newcastle upon Tyne', and updated in personal communication with author.

34. Office of the Minister for Science: Committee on the Problem of Noise, *Final Report* (Chairman Sir Alan Wilson), Cmnd. 2056 (HMSO, London, 1963), para. 37.

35. *Neighbourhood Noise*, paras 85-6. But according to Cresswell 'The amount of additional money spent to reduce noise on construction sites as a result of our efforts with the Control of Pollution Act in comparison is phenomenal' (personal communication with author).

36. Circular 2/76.

37. Department of the Environment, *Pollution Control in Great Britain: How it Works*, Pollution Paper no. 9 (HMSO, London, 1978), para. 306.

38. Control of Pollution Act 1974 s.57.

39. Noise Advisory Council, *Neighbourhood Noise* (HMSO, London, 1971), para. 145-7; see also Chapter 10, note 24.

40. Pollution Paper no. 9, para. 307.

41. See Chapter 5, p. 93.

42. Statutory Instrument 1973 No. 24, *Motor Vehicles (Construction and Use) Regulations 1973.*

43. Open University, *Control of the Acoustic Environment*, p. 40.

44. Statutory Instrument 1973 No. 1363, *The Noise Insulation Regulations 1973.*

45. Quoted in DoE Circular 10/73, para. 7.

46. Ibid.

47. Ibid.

48. DoE Circular 10/73, Appendix 2.

49. See p. 125.

50. Cresswell, personal communication. But he adds that 'sometimes one gets a change of use which does not require planning control and yet may bring a more noisy activity into an area – here the NAZ is useful as the new occupier has to emit no more noise than the previous occupier' (personal communication with author).

51. Department of the Environment Circular 10/73.

52. In the DoE's view, NAZs and Circular 10/73 share the common aim of avoiding increases in ambient noise levels, but uncertainty over whether planning or NAZ powers should be used is not a reason for not making a noise abatement order.

53. Open University, *Control of the Acoustic Environment*, p. 13.

54. D. Howell, in 'Foreword', Noise Advisory Council, *Noise in the Next Ten Years* (HMSO, London, 1974), p. v.

55. See 'Not so Softly, Softly', *Municipal Engineering* (18 March 1977), p. 363.

56. Cresswell observes: 'Beaver, in his 1954 Report, said we could overcome the problem of pollution by smoke within 15 years. 25 years later there are still numerous large urban areas with acute smoke pollution and nothing has been done. For every Newcastle there is a Durham and Berwick. There is still a long way to go

nationally to achieve smoke control targets . . .' (personal communication to author). Another observer has suggested that slow progress with NAZs may be being caused by some local authorities which have perhaps bitten off more than they can chew, and by others who do not realise that they need bite very little (i.e. a zone can be as small and limited in scope as the local authority thinks fit).

7   IDENTIFYING INDUSTRIAL AIR POLLUTION

Air Pollution Control

The control of industrial air pollution in the UK is now well over 100
years old, and as such is probably the most advanced body of legislation
covering pollution control in this or comparable countries. In contrast,
the control of domestic air pollution is more recent, but nevertheless has
achieved significant improvements to the quality of the atmosphere,
particularly in towns and built-up areas.[1]

The first step to control industrial emissions was taken in 1863 when
the Alkali Works, Etc. Act was passed for a trial period of five years in
order to reduce the damage being done by acid fumes from alkali works
to crops and vegetation, and household fittings and materials. The Act
was subsequently extended by a series of measures to cover other
chemical processes, and consolidated in the 1906 Alkali, Etc. Works
Regulation Act. This provided that:

(a)   all works operating scheduled processes must be registered
      annually; and
(b)   must use the best practicable means 'for preventing the escape of
      noxious or offensive gases and for rendering such gases harmless
      and inoffensive';
(c)   the best practicable means must be maintained in good and
      efficient working order and must always be in use;
(d)   for a few scheduled processes, statutory limits on the emissions of
      acid gases are specified.

The Alkali, Etc. Acts are enforced by HM Alkali and Clean Air
Inspectorate (HMIPI in Scotland), which is a central government agency
within the Health and Safety Executive. It works through 15 regional
divisions and their supporting technical and administrative staff. The
agency is small (about 40 inspectors) and it has to control about 60
processes which involve some 2,200 works and 3,700 operations
registered under the Act.[2]

For some processes 'presumptive limits' are set by the Inspectorate.
These specify an emission standard which, if complied with, can be
taken as presumptive evidence that the best practicable means requirement
is being met. These limits are altered from time to time as new techniques

136

for control are developed, after discussions between industry and the Inspectorate, whereas the statutory emission standard can only be changed through legislation. Other industrial emissions that do not fall within the scope of the Alkali Acts are subject to the Public Health Acts and Clean Air Acts which are enforced by local authorities.

The Public Health Acts 1936, 1961 and 1969 empower district councils to stop industrial emissions (other than smoke, grit or dust) if they can be shown to have caused a hazard or a nuisance. These statutory nuisance procedures are lengthy but failure to comply can result in conviction and fines of up to £400. Under the Clean Air Acts of 1956 and 1968, emissions of smoke, grit and dust from any trade or industrial premises, from any chimney or railway engine or vessel in an inland port in excess of specified limits are an offence. In practice these powers are used to restrict emissions from combustion processes (i.e. furnaces, boilers) rather than to prevent them absolutely. Local authorities can also make smoke control orders to prohibit emissions of smoke from domestic premises particularly, and grants are available to householders who have to change their method of cooking or heating as a result. This legislation also permits local authorities to regulate the height of chimneys so that ground level concentrations of gases or particles will not be a health hazard or nuisance.

The Control of Pollution Act adds relatively minor powers on to these substantial foundations. Part IV of the Act which covers air pollution was brought into force on 1 January 1976.[3] There are two groups of new powers: Sections 75 to 77 empower the Secretary of State to regulate the content of fuel for motor vehicles, furnaces and engines, thus complementing the other powers to control pollution from motor vehicles under the Road Traffic Act 1972 which specify standards of manufacture, maintenance and use. Sections 79 to 83 deal with information about air pollution. This second group gives local authorities discretionary power to monitor industrial emissions more extensively than before and to publicise their findings after consultations with local interests. These powers are the subject of the case study that follows. (In addition Section 78 makes cable burning a new statutory offence.) Finally, the Health and Safety at Work Act 1974 must be mentioned since it contains a section permitting the Health and Safety Commission to control emissions from registered processes. This section is being used progressively to repeal and replace the Alkali Acts.

To summarise the arrangements flowing from this legislation, the Alkali Inspectorate is responsible for controlling emissions from certain more hazardous and complex chemical processes, while local authorities are responsible for controlling emissions from combustion processes in industry, domestic smoke and emissions giving rise to other statutory nuisances, e.g. smells. The Alkali Inspectorate is an agency of central government with wide discretionary powers of interpretation and enforcement. Local authorities, specifically the environmental health departments of district (and London Borough) councils, have discretionary use of extensive powers concerning smoke control. Two important national bodies have a role in influencing clean air policy: the Clean Air Council and the Royal Commission on Environmental Pollution. The Clean Air Council was established (actually there is one for England and Wales and another for Scotland) by the Clean Air Act 1956 to keep under review the progress made in abating air pollution, and to obtain specialist advice about preventing air pollution. Its 30 members are appointed by the Secretary of State for the Environment and include MPs, civil servants and air pollution experts. It advises the Secretary of State, and publishes reports from time to time.[4]

The standing Royal Commission on Environmental Pollution was established in 1970 to advise on a whole range of pollution issues,[5] and it has paid particular attention to questions of air pollution. Its second report raised the problem of secrecy about industrial emissions, and its fifth report suggested a basic reorganisation of administrative controls and the creation of a new National Pollution Inspectorate.[6] These will be referred to in the next section since they form part of the case study material.

Finally here it should be noted that in an area of policy as old and as extensive as air pollution control, public opinion has come to play a significant part. Through voluntary organisations such as the National Society for Clean Air, pressure has been put on government to promote change—and the NSCA was behind the 1956 Clean Air Act.[7] Other interested organisations such as Social Audit Limited have drawn attention to the problems of industrial emissions as far as workers and neighbourhoods are concerned, while *ad hoc* local groups may be formed to complain about hazards being caused in a particular district. Journalists have in one or two notable cases done a lot to inform public opinion about policies and problems.[8]

The UK approach to atmospheric pollution control is often described as 'pragmatic', and Lord Ashby (former chairman of the Royal Commission on Environmental Pollution) has identified five reasons for the success of this approach:[9]

1. Measures for control are firmly tied to the capacity of science and

technology to make them effective at reasonable cost.

2. The policy is not one of prevention, it is one of abatement.
3. The policy recognises that the cost of abating pollution may exceed the cost of damage done by pollution.
4. The policy is flexible.
5. The tradition of securing the confidence and co-operation of industrialists whose works are open to inspection has been established.

Lord Ashby raises two questions relevant to future progress in controlling air pollution that concern the case study that follows: will the public continue to allow the experts to make political decisions on their behalf without themselves participating, and can the existing pattern of control be extended to other and much more difficult political decisions where science and social values have to be integrated?

Public Information about Industrial Emissions

This case study focuses on Sections 79 to 83 of the Control of Pollution Act, and asks what benefits are being created by these provisions in relation to information about industrial emissions. To summarise briefly Sections 79 to 83, local authorities have since 1 January 1976 been able to undertake or fund research into problems of air pollution and publish this information. They can arrange with occupiers of industrial premises to measure and record emissions (Section 79). This may be done in a variety of ways, one of which is to issue a notice concerning emissions over not more than twelve months from particular chimneys or outlets (Section 80). Failure to comply with a notice is a statutory offence with a maximum fine of £400, although trade secrets may be protected, and works covered by the Alkali Acts are only obliged to supply the same type of information they already give to the Alkali Inspectorate; an appeals procedure exists, involving the Secretary of State (Section 81).[10] Information obtained as a result of Section 80 notices or the local authorities' general powers (Section 79) must be published in registers accessible to the public so that information relating to particular premises can be identified. Also the local authorities must, if they decide to use these powers, establish a local consultative committee where representatives of industry, amenity groups and others with an interest in air pollution can discuss a programme of action and gauge the strength of local opinion. The Secretary of State has the power to prescribe how and to what extent local authorities may seek and publish information under Sections 79 and 80 (Section 82). Lastly, the Secretary of State can require local authorities to obtain and provide him with information he may specifically ask them for (Section 83).[11]

So far, the details of these sections of the Act have been expanded through three sets of regulations and two circulars.[12] In addition, the Clean Air Council has published a leaflet called *Air Pollution Information: Your Rights and Obligations.*[13]

The importance of these provisions is that they add significantly to the information that may be collected and made known to the public. Particularly in connection with works covered by Alkali Acts, a lot of concern has arisen from the secrecy that was maintained between the Alkali Inspectorate and the firms concerned. The Royal Commission on Environmental Pollution drew attention to this in its second report. It observed that confidentiality about industrial emissions was largely unjustified on the grounds of protecting trade secrets. Its only value was to protect industry against the risk of common law actions or against misconceived or ill-informed allegations that the environment was being dangerously polluted.

The Royal Commission thought it was in the public interest that information about emissions should be available not just to the official authorities but to research workers and others who could make use of it to improve the environment. Public confidence would be strengthened if 'this needless cloak of secrecy were withdrawn'. The Royal Commission urged the DoE to devise measures that could increase the availability and flow of information on the production and disposal of industrial wastes 'to persons of responsibility' who could use it for the ultimate benefit of the environment, and it suggested MPs, research workers and 'persons with similar interests in pollution' might be eligible here.[14]

The DoE's response was to appoint a working party consisting of members of the Clean Air Council and a CBI representative. This group, chaired by Admiral P.G. Sharp (Director of the National Society for Clean Air), reported in 1973,[15] recommending that more information should indeed be released to the public, although this would need to be done by 'persons of responsibility'. The model they chose was that of local liaison committees which the Alkali Inspectorate had established in some places where the most contentious works were situated, in cooperation with local authorities. The Sharp Report suggested that district councils should set up committees with a duty and power to collect and consider information about industrial emissions, to publish annual (and also at their discretion, special) reports summarising and interpreting this information to the public, and send copies of their reports to the Secretary of State. The Sharp Committee recommended that this system should be flexible enough to meet varying local conditions.

The Sharp Committee's recommendations were the basis of Section 79 and the DoE suggested that these new consultative committees should be set up and involved before any programme of measurements or service of notices was started.[16] It is interesting to note that this guidance, together with the regulations prescribing what information local authorities could obtain and assess, were only issued in February 1977, over a year after the relevant parts of the Act had become operational.[17] There is consequently very little evidence yet to hand about the effect these new powers are having. A handful of consultative committees have been set up, but no reports have been published by them, nor have any Section 80 notices been issued.[18]

This does not mean that local authorities are inactive so far as monitoring industrial emissions is concerned. Many of them already had informal arrangements for doing this before Part IV of the Control of Pollution Act was brought in. Some were involved with the Alkali Inspectorate in monitoring the effects of emissions from scheduled works. Others, with industrial complexes in their areas that had been the subject of public complaint, had sought to find better ways of preventing nuisances occurring in co-operation with local groups. In Bristol City Council's case the industrial estate at Avonmouth/Severnside has proved a troublesome source of air pollution problems for many years. For example in 1972 the government called for a special enquiry into lead emissions from a lead and zinc smelter owned by Rio Tinto Zinc, following objections from workers about lead poisoning. The smelter was closed down while in-house investigations were conducted. The council decided to carry out a survey of blood lead levels in children, and identified those with unsatisfactory levels. The smelter problem continued for some time, and others have also arisen from the industrial complex. To quote one official:

in the past 12 months my department has had to respond to at least a dozen major chemical emergency problems outside working hours. In the first three months of 1978 there were five chemical incidents of significance which involved the department: a major hydrofluoric acid fume emission, a hydrochloric acid leak, an ammonia leak from a rail tanker and a major explosion at a fluoro-analine plant. All occurred in the Avonmouth area.[19]

With this level of risk the local authority could not afford to delay setting up local arrangements for solving these problems in collaboration with industry. So the council's Public Protection Committee receives a report of air pollution monitoring every six months and a Technical Committee (joint membership from the council and local industry) reviews the previous 18 months' work and decides what information to make publicly available.[20] The programme of surveys being carried out by the Environmental Health Department therefore identifies the materials handled, together with emissions and waste by-products, and environmental impact assessments are also conducted. 'Overall', the official said, 'the cost of both routine and special studies on atmospheric pollution carried out by my department amounts to a few pence per head of the population per annum.'[21]

But Bristol City Council may not be a typical example. As the Royal Commission on Environmental Pollution observed in its fifth report:

> the differing levels of competence of local authority officers have
> been very evident to us from the visits we have made. No doubt it
> is generally true that local authorities facing more difficult problems
> have better qualified staff but this is certainly not always true. We
> have been struck too by the range in understanding and concern of
> elected members with regard to air pollution matters. In some places
> we have seen energetic and well-informed environmental health com-
> mittees, alive to their responsibility and providing support and policy
> guidance for technically able and enterprising environmental health
> officers. In some districts the opposite has been apparent with
> evidence of confusion about responsibilities and powers and bitter
> public complaint about emissions from unregistered works.[22]

Analysis

Progress on Sections 79 to 83 has undoubtedly been slow although the time period is perhaps too short to make a fair judgement (i.e. 2½ years after the regulations were made). There are a number of factors which could help to explain the fate of these provisions to make public information about industrial emissions more available and these will be considered in turn:

1. the public demand for this is less urgent;
2. the information is already available;

3. local authorities are not being sufficiently encouraged;
4. other aspects of air pollution are considered to be of greater significance.

Public Demand

It is quite clear that in the early 1970s a number of powerful expressions
of public opinion were the reason for the Royal Commission and the
Sharp Committee's consideration of the public information issue that
culminated in Sections 78 to 83 of the Control of Pollution Act. Some
of this pressure was generated by local people exposed to hazards, and
reflected in numerous press reports and articles at the time.[23] A further
expression of concern is found in a study of the Alkali Inspectorate
published in 1974.[24] This criticised the Inspectorate's secretiveness, and
challenged justifications that it made arguing that information about
emissions would be meaningless to the lay person, would risk disclosure
of trade secrets to competitors, might deliberately be abused by
'extremists in the environmental movement', and would harm the trust
that existed between the Inspectorate and industry. The Inspectorate's
record of enforcement of the policy has been criticised too since the
number of prosecutions following infractions have been very few. The
Inspectorate argues that it should not give information to the public
about a registered works unless it has the firm's permission to do so, and
this stance has been backed with statutory force by the Health and
Safety at Work Act 1974 (although the Alkali Acts contain no comparable provision).[25]

Once the Sharp Committee had come down in favour of improving
public information about industrial emission, the battle had, technically,
been won, because the government was then prepared to accept the
need to provide for this in legislation. The timescale of subsequent events
therefore suggests that public pressure has declined considerably since
the passing of the Control of Pollution Act, as if the fact that the Act
has been made is more important than the actual use of specific powers
it contains.

January 1976 was the earliest date for any substantial progress to
introducing the Act for reasons that have already been discussed. But
the first set of regulations relevant to this aspect[26] only activated the
general powers contained in Sections 79 to 83. The Secretary of State's
job of prescribing how local authorities should collect and publish
information was not done until a year later when further relevant
regulations were issued, together with an explanatory circular.[27] It

is arguable that if public feeling was still running generally as high as it was in the early 1970s this rate of activity (which has to date produced very little evident change) would have been unacceptable. It is as if the arrival of Sections 79 to 83 on the statute book was the major victory for national environmental groups and informants of public opinion. Local perceptions are harder to judge, although it would seem probable that feelings will rise and be voiced wherever hazards are evident, irrespective of the Act. Major disasters (such as those at Seveso or Flixborough)[28] will in any case provoke a reaction. What is less clear is whether ongoing discussions between the Alkali Inspectorate, local authority, local industry and local people are now seen as a worthwhile device for providing information to the public at all.

Information Already Available

Some people argue that Sections 79 to 83 are superfluous anyway, since the objective of gathering and publishing information about industrial emissions is already achieved by informal means. The liaison committees created in some places by the Alkali Inspectorate are quoted as one example. Authorities such as Bristol City Council argue that their own system (described above) is another means. The Chief Environmental Health Officer explained:

> if there had been pollution problems, local authorities probably had ways of finding this out and collaborating with industry. This is the case in Bristol, therefore we want to avoid additional consultations and meetings if we are not going to get much out of them . . . that is why the Control of Pollution Act powers are not being used extensively.[29]

The Royal Commission did not agree with this analysis though. It deplored the fact that the Alkali Inspectorate was, under the Health and Safety at Work Act, prevented from making public disclosures about emissions from registered works, calling this a 'retrogressive step', but it welcomed Sections 79 to 83 which would remove the worst effects of this. However, in stating that 'the public should have the right to know the state of the air they breathe and the amounts of pollution by both registered and non-registered industry',[30] the Commission felt these powers did not go far enough. Specifically:

> the controlling authorities should also be able to collect and release such information themselves and we recommend that the existing bar

on the Alkali Inspectorate doing so should be removed . . . the
consents issued for all works, scheduled or non-scheduled should
also be kept by the local authority concerned on a publicly available
register, preferably on the same register as the emission data.[31]

Social Audit Ltd amplifies the argument in its recent publication *The
Social Audit Pollution Handbook*, drawing attention to the fact that if
local authorities choose to use their powers under Sections 79 to 83 they
are obliged to keep a public register. If they prefer to find out about
industrial emissions through informal arrangements, there is no statutory
obligation on them to publish the information. So although facts and
figures may be available within the authorities for any of their own
liaison committees, no outsider will have rights of access unless the
powers under Sections 79 to 83 have explicitly been used. The conclusion must be that although a number of local authorities may already
be working with local and industrial interests along the lines provided
for by Sections 79 to 83, through informal means, the statutory right to
see the information is not safeguarded unless the Act is invoked.[32] Where
the public demand for this right is substantial is difficult to judge
(although sales of Social Audit's book and another handbook for the
public *–Polluters Pay* – from Friends of the Earth suggest a considerable
level of interest).[33] Although in the Royal Commission's view not only
is the release of this information important, but more of it (i.e. that
currently protected by the Health and Safety at Work Act) should be
publicly available as a right.[34]

Local Authorities not Encouraged

Another reason why local authorities have been relatively slow to
respond to Sections 79 to 83 could be that there has been insufficient
encouragement from central government. The powers are of course
entirely discretionary, and no obligation to exercise them exists. In its
circulars to local authorities about these matters the DoE has itself
suggested a cautious approach:

in the light of continuing restraints on local authority expenditure it
will be difficult for authorities who wish to make use of the powers
to find the necessary resources from within their existing budgets.[35]

Furthermore, there has not yet been a government response to the Royal
Commission's fifth report, which apart from the recommendations about
reducing secrecy over industrial emissions, proposes a restructuring of

the administration of pollution control through a new National Pollution Inspectorate. The report is an authoritative review and the fact that there has been no response yet, even though it was published in 1976, must be discouraging to those local authorities (and others) who would like to see a firm central lead on reforms maintained.

Private industry is on the whole unlikely to put pressure on local authorities to disclose more information to the public. One CBI spokesman called Part IV of the Control of Pollution Act 'a sop to Tinker and Bugler' (Jon Tinker and Jeremy Bugler are journalists who had campaigned actively for a policy of more disclosure).[36] A trade union representative commenting on recent problems at Avonmouth was quoted as saying:

> we are not trying to close the chemical industry down. What goes on here is vital for the country . . . as well as being a major employment area for our members. But the chemical industry is paranoid about being over-regulated and misrepresented, so they operate in considerable secrecy.[37]

There is therefore a general impression that only the more adventurous local authorities will take on Sections 79 to 83, and this will be despite rather than because of any support they receive from central government. Industry's lack of enthusiasm for the provisions would weigh significantly with the government, partly because bodies such as the Chemical Industries Association put a lot of trouble and effort into lobbying MPs and departments about their view, but also because it might be argued that focusing on an area's air pollution problems could be a disincentive to industry to invest in jobs and plant there. The Royal Commission made this point when it said:

> local pressure to attract and retain industry so as to improve local employment prospects and rate revenue may be such that any industry, no matter how polluting, is welcomed, and that steps to control pollution are not taken if there is any risk that the industry might move elsewhere.[38]

This dilemma between jobs and pollution control is likely to influence the vigour of central government's advice to local authorities, especially in the current climate of concern over high rates of unemployment, coupled with a commitment to reduce public expenditure.

Air Pollution Priorities

Part IV is acknowledged to be the least important part of the Control of Pollution Act, in terms of the innovations or changes of major significance that it contains. But within the provisions of Part IV, Sections 79 to 83 are arguably less important than those concerning the content of petrol, diesel and other fuels. The Secretary of State's powers to regulate the content of petrol are particularly topical, as EEC legislation is progressively reducing the permissible levels of lead.[39] Lead pollution from heavy traffic is currently also being studied in large towns by a survey for the DoE of blood lead levels in adults and children.[40]

Other aspects of air pollution, particularly the risk of contamination from radioactivity, appear to have become much more of a preoccupation in the last few years. Indeed, the Royal Commission's sixth report, *Nuclear Power and the Environment*,[41] dealt with this and other aspects of the problem, and it was promptly taken up by the government which published a White Paper in May 1977 accepting many of the recommendations.[42]

So it may be unrealistic to expect a high level of activity on public information about industrial emissions in general, although where a hazard or problem exists locally, the conditions may favour more disclosure. The extra expenditure required by Sections 79 to 83 need not be high, so the 'financial deterrent' argument is not particularly persuasive. It is more likely that other priorities present themselves to all interested parties (central and local government, environmentalists and the media and industry) thus for the time being keeping Sections 79 to 83 in the background of implementation. The Open University thought that 'the key to continued improvement of air policy in the future lies, as it has done in the past, in an informed, vocal and responsive body of public opinion which is able to maintain pressure on those who make decisions'.[43]

Notes

1. The OECD observed. 'One of the main aims of pollution abatement policies has been to reduce the exposure of the population to high concentrations of sulphur dioxide. With few exceptions this has been achieved and in many cities where concentrations of sulphur dioxide were high, they have now declined.' OECD, *The State of the Environment in Member Countries* (OECD, Paris, 1979).
2. Department of the Environment, *Pollution Control in Great Britain: How it Works*, Pollution Paper no. 9 (HMSO, London, 1978), para. 21.
3. See Department of the Environment Circular 7/76, *Control of Pollution Act 1974 (Commencement Order No. 4). Part IV — Pollution of the Atmosphere*

(12 January 1976).

4. In September 1979 the Secretary of State for the Environment announced the government's intention to abolish the Clean Air Council (along with over 50 other 'quangos').

5. See Chapter 3, n. 43.

6. Royal Commission on Environmental Pollution, *Fifth Report: Air Pollution Control: an Integrated Approach*, Cmnd. 6371 (HMSO, London, 1976).

7. The objects of NSCA are 'to promote and create, by publicity and education, an informed public opinion on the value and importance of clean air and to initiate, promote and encourage the investigation and research into all forms of atmospheric pollution in order to achieve its reduction or prevention'. NSCA publishes a quarterly journal *Clean Air*, and annual *Clean Air Year Book*, and holds an annual conference. For an account of NSCA's role in the passing of the 1956 Clean Air Act, see R. Parker, 'The Struggle for Clean Air', in Hall, Land, Parker and Webb, *Change, Choice and Conflict in Social Policy* (Heinemann, London, 1975); and J.B. Sanderson's study in R. Kimber and J.J. Richardson (eds.), *Campaigning for the Environment* (Routledge and Kegan Paul, London, 1974).

8. Kimber and Richardson (ibid., pp. 1-2) observe that the International Press Cuttings Bureau filed 330 cuttings per month on air pollution in 1968, and 660 per month in 1971. For all aspects of pollution the Bureau filed cuttings in 1972 at the rate of over 1,400 per month.

9. Lord Ashby, 'The Politics of Noxious Vapours', *Clean Air* (Winter 1979), pp. 9-15. See also the forthcoming report of a seminar on regulatory and planning controls in air pollution from the University of Manchester Pollution Research Unit, held in September 1978.

10. In the DoE's publication, *Central Government Controls over Local Authorities*, Cmnd. 7634 (HMSO, London, September 1979), these provisions are identified for repeal.

11. Ibid.

12. Statutory Instruments SI 1977 No. 17, *Control of Atmospheric Pollution (Appeals) Regulations 1977*; SI 1977 No. 18, *Control of Atmospheric Pollution (Exempted Premises) Regulations 1977*; SI 1977 No. 19, *Control of Atmospheric Pollution (Research and Publicity) Regulations 1977*–all of which came into operation on 7 February 1977. Also DoE Circular 7/76 and DoE Circular 2/77, *Control of Pollution Act 1974. Part IV – Pollution of the Atmosphere* (19 January 1977).

13. Clean Air Council, *Air Pollution Information: Your Rights and Obligations* (HMSO, London, 1977).

14. Royal Commission on Environmental Pollution, *Second Report: Three Issues in Industrial Pollution*, Cmnd. 4894 (HMSO, London, 1972), paras 3-10.

15. Clean Air Council, *Information about Industrial Emissions to the Atmosphere: Report by a Working Party of the Council* (Chairman Rear Admiral P.G. Sharp) (HMSO, London, 1973).

16. In Circular 2/77 – see note 12.

17. The Commencement No. 4 order became effective on 1 January 1976: see note 3.

18. Consultative committees are beginning to operate in Walsall and Coventry. Elsewhere activity may also be underway, but no evidence is yet available.

19. E. Robson, 'Clean Air Bristol Fashion', *Surveyor* (5 October 1979), p. 11.

20. D. Barnett, Chief Environmental Health Officer, at seminar: Implementing the Control of Pollution Act, Bristol, SAUS, May 1979. Of course, this committee is not a statutory committee and has no power to issue notices under Section 80 nor is it obliged to disclose information it would have been able to obtain if the Control of Pollution Act powers had been employed. See note 32 for further reference to this.

21. Robson, 'Clean Air Bristol Fashion'.

22. Royal Commission on Environmental Pollution, *Fifth Report*, para. 134.

23. See note 8.

24. M. Frankel, 'The Alkali Inspectorate: The Control of Air Pollution', *London*

Social Audit, A Special Report, vol. 1, no. 4 (1974), and see also a special report prepared for the United Nations Conference in 1972 in Stockholm, where the authors observed '[The Alkali Inspectorate] functions in a climate of varying pressures from public opinion, industry and government. In view of the substantial increase over the last few years in public interest in pollution, it may well be that the Alkali Inspectorate should consider taking the public more into its confidence in future.' DoE, *Pollution: Nuisance or Nemesis* (HMSO, London, 1972), para. 137.

25. Health and Safety at Work etc. Act 1974, s.28(2).

26. See note 3.

27. See note 12.

28. Where accidental leakages of highly toxic chemicals into the air contaminated surrounding areas and caused serious damage to health.

29. D. Barnett, at seminar May 1979. See also note 20 above. This interpretation contrasts interestingly with the classic American study by Matthew Crenson: *The Un-politics of Air Pollution: a Study of Non-decision-making in the Cities* (The Johns Hopkins Press, Baltimore, 1971).

30. Royal Commission on Environmental Pollution, *Fifth Report*, para. 235.

31. Ibid., para. 236.

32. M. Frankel, *The Social Audit Pollution Handbook: How to Assess Environmental and Workplace Pollution* (Macmillan, London, 1978), pp. 67-9. This method (by which local authorities can avoid implementing the specific powers and duties in the Act) has led some observers to feel that the Act will prove unworkable here. They feel it should not be necessary anyway if there was a real commitment to making the information public. In comparison with the powers to disclose information about industrial effluents to water contained in Part II of the Act, these Part IV provisions can be said to do far less.

33. R. Macrory and B. Zaba, *Polluters Pay, the Control of Pollution Act Explained* (Friends of the Earth, London, 1978).

34. Royal Commission on Environmental Pollution, *Fifth Report*, paras 122-4.

35. DoE Circular 2/77, para. 2.

36. Said by R. Martindale, Senior Technical Adviser, CBI at seminar: Implementing the Control of Pollution Act, SAUS, Bristol, May 1974. See also note 8 above.

37. R. Vallance, Divisional Officer for ASTMS, quoted in 'Chemical Leaks Formula for Disaster, say Scientists', *Guardian*, 30 July 1979.

38. Royal Commission on Environmental Pollution, *Fifth Report*, para. 135.

39. See OJ C151 of 7 July 1975. OJ L105 of 28 April 1977, and OJ L197 of 22 July 1978.

40. See T. Fishlock, 'What is Lead in Petrol Doing to Us?', *The Times*, 25 July 1978; and *Municipal Engineering*, 23 February 1979.

41. Royal Commission on Environmental Pollution, *Sixth Report: Nuclear Power and the Environment*, Cmnd. 6618 (HMSO, London, 1976).

42. Department of the Environment, *Nuclear Power and the Environment, the Government's Response to the Sixth Report of the Royal Commission on Environmental Pollution*, Cmnd. 6820 (HMSO, London, 1977).

43. The Open University, 'Environmental Control and Public Health PT272 Unit 15', *Air Pollution Control* (The Open University Press, Milton Keynes, 1975), p. 74.

Part Three

THE PROCESS OF IMPLEMENTATION

8 THE FRAMEWORK FOR IMPLEMENTATION

In this third and final part of the book, the evidence presented in the four case studies will be put to work to clarify the problems of implementing pollution control policies. Two concepts will be used to help in this exercise. The first, *instruments for policy*, refers to the people, organisations and devices through which policies are expressed. The second, *enforcement*, covers the powers available to observe and influence the implementation of policies. They will be the focus of the case study analysis and follow in Chapters 9 and 10.

That will lead into the concluding observations on the two themes of the book—pollution control and policy implementation—in Chapters 11 and 12. It is therefore sensible to preface the four analytic chapters with a statement of the relevant issues illustrated by the case studies, and that is the aim of this chapter. Its purpose is to act as a bridge between the rather detailed technical features of the case studies and the more general theoretical aspects of the four final chapters. It is also designed to clarify those features of the case studies that could occur in studies of other public policies.

This framework therefore has been developed both to compare and contrast the specific case material and to apply more widely to other policy studies.

The three categories in this framework define the different types of factor relevant to analysis of the policy studies—*technical* (in the case of pollution this relates to the effect of pollutants on life and natural resources); *administrative* (including the statutory mechanisms for introducing and implementing the policy); and *interorganisational* (dealing with the relationships between those parties with an interest in the policy). The 13 subdivisions amplify these categories, and can be used as an analytic and descriptive framework for public policy studies generally. The four pollution cases of this present study are now set out according to the framework. Figure 8.1 covers the technical and administrative factors, while Figure 8.2 covers the interorganisational factors.

To illustrate how the framework has been used in the figures, look along the line for Factor 1: *Nature of the problem* in Figure 8.1. This identifies the specific *technical* subject matter of the four case studies in Chapters 4-7. It could just as well describe technical problems in economic policy, defence policy, education policy, and so on. Factor 2

TECHNICAL FACTORS	1. Nature of the problem
	2. Severity of problem
	3. State of technical knowledge
	4. Application of technical knowledge to the problem
ADMINISTRATIVE FACTORS	5. Statutory expression of policy
	6. Instruments for policy
	7. Framework within which policy belongs
	8. Timetable of introducing policy
	9. Financial and resource costs
	10. Enforcement
INTERORGANISATIONAL FACTORS	11. Interested organisations
	12. Organisations' roles
	13. Relations between organisations

looks at the *Severity of the problem* in terms of the technically relevant criteria — in the case of environmental pollution these are the risks to life and amenity. For education problems though, the technically relevant criteria might be concerned with literacy or educational achievement. The line for Factor 3 — *State of technical knowledge* — summarises the level of knowledge relative to the problem, and is judged in terms of the evidence that causal relationships can be described and that the problem can be recognised and quantified according to the relevant technical parameters. Thus, toxic wastes are still not yet categorically defined and their effects on the environment are only partly understood. Equally, the consequences of neighbourhood noise exposure of different levels are not yet technically quantified, nor are there sufficiently clear indications of the importance of neighbourhood noise as a form of pollution when compared with transport noise or construction site noise. Air pollution, despite its long history as a subject for public policy, is still, in *technical* terms, incompletely understood in the sense of the effects on human, plant and animal life of such pollutants as lead, sulphur and cadmium. However, water pollution by untreated sewage is fairly well understood, and the differential contributions of sunshine, tides, winds and temperature to diluting and dispersing the pollution have been spelt out.

Figure 8.1: Case Study Comparisons: Technical and Administrative Factors

	Toxic Waste	Bathing Water	Noise Abatement	Air Information
Technical				
1. Nature of problem	contamination of water and land	contamination of water	neighbourhood noise	pollution of atmosphere
2. Severity of problem	high risk to life	spoils amenity; no health risk	minor health risk	occasionally a severe risk to life
3. State of technical knowledge	insufficient	sufficient	insufficient	insufficient
4. Application of technical knowledge to problem	satisfactory	not always reliable	satisfactory	insufficient
Administrative				
5. Statutory expression of policy	s1 + 2 + 17: binding on WDAs	s32 + 41: binding on WAs	s63-7 + Schedule 1: discretionary on LAs	s79-83: discretionary on LAs
6. Instruments for policy	consignment note system; site licences & public registers	S/S approval for WA emission stds; public registers	S/S approval for NAZs; public registers	local committees; publication of information by LAs
7. Framework within which policy belongs	Deposit of Poisonous Waste Act 1972	EEC Environmental Action Programme	Public Health Acts + NAC report	Public Health & Alkali Acts + CAC report
8. Timetable of introducing policy	consultations in progress: date of intro ?1980	preparations in progress; Dec 1979 intro for 1986 target	in force since Jan 1976	in force since Jan 1976
9. Financial and resource costs	staff activity; transport; sites	staff deployment; treatment plant	staff deployment; noise control plant	staff deployment
10. Enforcement	litigation by WDAs; sanctions	litigation by public + ?EEC sanctions	litigation by LAs; noise reduction orders	litigation?

Figure 8.2: Case Study Comparisons: Interorganisational Factors

	Government Bodies				District			Advisory Bodies		Private Sector			Public	
	Interna-tional	Central	Regional	County	Plann-ing	Envr. Health	Tourism	Technical	Policy/Admin	Trade Assn	Employers Assn	Individual Firms	Groups	Indivs.
Toxic Waste	EEC a	DOE se	WA ie	WDA i	i			HAS a	WMAC a	CIA a / NADWC ia	CBI a	i		e
Bathing Water	EEC se	DOE ie	WA ie				i					i		e
Noise Abatement		DOE si				i			NAC a		CBI a	.		e
Air Information		DOE s / AI i			a	ie			RCEP CAC / a	CBI a		i	ie	ie

11. Interested Organisations

AI	Alkali Inspectorate
CAC	Clean Air Council
CBI	Confederation of British Industry
CIA	Chemical Industries Association
DOE	Department of the Environment
EEC	European Economic Community
HAS	Harwell Advisory Service
NAC	Noise Advisory Council
NAWDC	Nat. Assn of Waste Disposal Contractors
NWC	National Water Council
RCEP	Royal Commission on Environmental Pollution
WA	Water Authorities
WDA	Waste Disposal Authorities
WMAC	Waste Management Advisory Council
WRC	Water Research Centre

12. Organisational Roles

s	start/initiate
i	implement
e	enforce
a	advise

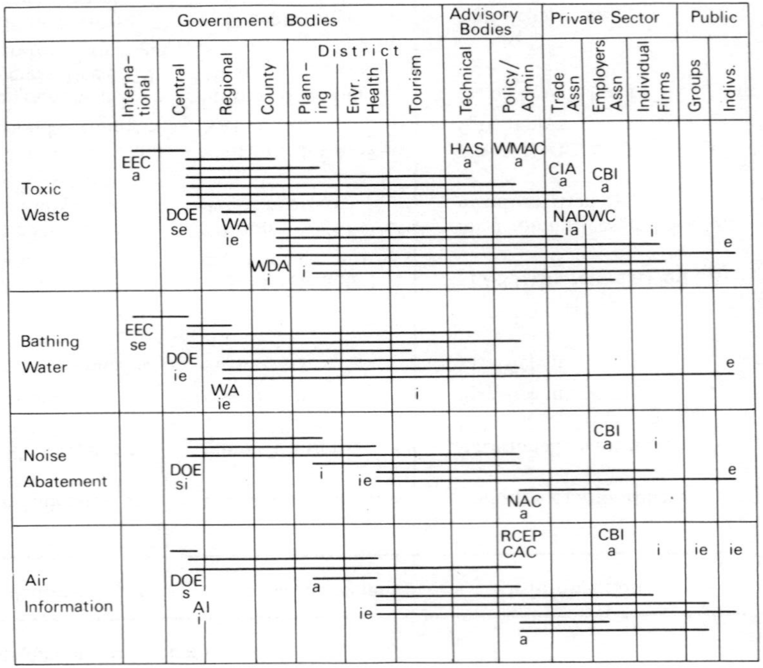

Factor 4 identifies the *Application of technical knowledge to the problem* and for the four pollution studies Figure 8.1 shows that the existing level of technical knowledge is on the whole satisfactorily applied in the case of noise and waste (i.e. noise meters are used to measure noise levels in noise abatement zones, and those toxic substances that are known about are generally covered by the Deposit of Poisonous Waste Act 1972 and will be by the Section 17 regulations). But for water and air the full extent of technical knowledge is not always applied (i.e. samples of bathing water tend not to be suitable for accurate analysis if transported a long way from the point of collection because their composition changes with time and alterations in temperature, etc.; air pollution monitoring is not practised as regularly or as comprehensively as it could be).

Factors 3 and 4 could equally well be used to describe problems of health policy where cause and effect of different illnesses may be known and applied, or in housing policy, to quote another area, where for example the technical knowledge of the causes of homelessness can be described and applied to the problem by the relevant agencies in a way that can be set out.

These technical factors contrast with the *administrative* ones that make up the next part of the framework in Figure 8.1. Some of these six (Factors 5-10) will be discussed much more fully in the chapters that follow. However, from the pollution examples set out in Figure 8.1 it can be seen that Factor 5 —*Statutory expression of policy* —gives a reference pointer to the relevant piece of legislation and some indication of its degree of administrative force. For other examples there might not of course always be a statutory expression of policy. Factor 6, *Instruments for policy*, shows the form of expression, the people, organisations and devices through which the policy relevant to the problem in question is expressed. For toxic waste these are the paper-work systems managed by the waste disposal authorities, but involving the producers and disposers of waste and the water authorities; while in the air pollution example the instrument is the local consultative committee. Chapter 9 discusses this further.

Factor 7, *Framework within which policy belongs*, identifies the antecedents and origins of the particular policy area and shows for example, the contribution of European environmental policy to the bathing water case, whereas the other three cases have not shown such clear international administrative connections. Factors 8 and 9, *Time-table for introducing policy* and *Financial and resource costs*, are further important dimensions of the *administrative* description and understanding of the problem in question, and set out in this way help to identify recurring as well as unique themes. Factor 10, *Enforcement*, is discussed more fully in Chapter 10, and it refers to the powers available to monitor and influence the implementation of policies by describing the scope for administrative action.

Moving on now to the third group of factors—the *interorganisational* factors—they are set out in Figure 8.2. For this group there are three important aspects to the framework (Factors 11-13). Factor 11 is the *Interested organisations* for the issue in question. Another way of saying this is that it lists the *dramatis personae* for the subject. In Figure 8.2 they are set down together for the four pollution examples. Factor 12 describes the commonly occurring *Organisational roles* that the bodies identified in Factor 11 tend to play in the policy process. Four have been named and are set out in Factor 12; start/initiate, implement, enforce and advise. Clearly such a typology does not do justice to the overlapping and blurring of roles that actually occurs. But in the interests of clarifying what is happening in the policy system for a given issue, it can be very helpful to sort out the predominant or usual role that an organisation adopts.

Then Factor 13, *Relations between organisations*, can be set out using the symbols shown in Factors 11 and 12, to demonstrate some of the complexity and extent of the interrelationships. The diagram in Figure 8.2 compares the four pollution cases, showing across the top the categories of organisations involved. Thus for example, both the toxic waste and bathing water studies show there to be a relationship between the EEC and the Department of the Environment but for the former the EEC is mainly in an advisory role, indicating to the DoE what substances should be included in regulations, whereas for the latter the EEC has been responsible for initiating the policy to control bathing water quality and is the organisation responsible for monitoring member-states' performance to see that they comply with the terms of the directive.

Also, for all four studies the figure shows the importance of the public's role in enforcement: the provision of a lot of information in public registers for the first time coupled with the right to take legal action where it appears standards are not adhered to, places a significant amount of power in the hands of the general public. The figure does not allow for judgements to be made readily about the effectiveness of the organisational roles. Rather it maps out the possible combinations and opportunities for action. The organisational types across the top of the figure will apply to other areas of policy too and are not specific to pollution alone. Most other public policies involve central and local government agencies of one kind or another, together with technical and administrative advisory bodies, and groups and individuals from both public and private sectors.

From this indication of the way the framework has been used in the four pollution cases it can be seen that the framework acts as an aid to describing and identifying the important features of the policy process. Of course there are drawbacks to such an abbreviated framework because a lot of detail cannot be accurately represented. The framework should therefore not be expected to do more than aid thought about a given policy area and system. It is one means to the end of analysing public policies, and can benefit discussion through the possibility it provides of comparing and contrasting different aspects.

9 INSTRUMENTS FOR POLICY

This chapter is concerned with the first of two concepts central to the analysis of policy implementation. It deals with instruments for policy, and is followed in Chapter 10 by an examination of the concept of enforcement. Instruments for policy are laws, people, organisations and other devices through which policies are expressed. The way these instruments are applied and their effects monitored constitutes the enforcement concept.

The purpose of making this distinction is to clarify the description and understanding of policies. Earlier chapters have already made the case for separating out various phases or dimensions in the total policy process: how policy is thought up, given expression, put into action and observed or controlled in action.[1] It was also emphasised that these elements have to be seen as distinct yet interacting, for the purposes of analysis. Equally, in isolating the 'instruments for policy' concept it has to be acknowledged that in the day-to-day circumstances in which a policy operates, the distinction may not be as apparent or as clearly defined as the following remarks might imply.

Nevertheless it is easily established that the instruments for policy in any particular area are not necessarily nor automatically determined by the policy itself. The objectives and intentions of policies can often be expressed in alternative ways through alternative instruments. The choice of instrument is therefore a matter of interest and relevance to policy studies. The choice may or may not be arbitrary — it may or may not be made in the knowledge that predictable consequences can follow from that choice.[2]

It is reasonable to assume that the less this aspect of the policy process is left to chance, the less likely there are to be unforeseen difficulties in implementation arising from this specific aspect. This statement can be supported by quoting some examples. For instance, in the case of disposal of solid toxic waste, one vital element is the consignment note instrument which will give expression to Section 17 of the Control of Pollution Act.[3] When this instrument is brought into statutory operation, all loads of wastes governed by the policy will be able to be tracked from their point of production to point of disposal; and the loads will be destined for appropriately licensed sites. In the area of water pollution control, the EEC directive on bathing water quality is given expression in the

UK through the instrument of designating beaches, and monitoring water quality there under the provisions of the directive.[4] The policy to control neighbourhood noise is given expression through the instrument of noise abatement zones.[5] This enables local authorities to identify geographical areas within their districts where the policy can be applied. For air pollution control, those local authorities which opt to obtain information about industrial air emissions can give expression to Section 79 of the Control of Pollution Act through the instrument of notices which can be served on the polluters, and which obliges the local authority to arrange for the information thus obtained to be publicised.[6]

In each case the instrument is a device or mechanism enabling the policy to be expressed. Its form and nature take account of the individuals and organisations that will be involved in operating it, although this is not equally developed. For example the consignment note system is intended to replace the notification system established by the Deposit of Poisonous Waste Act 1972.[7] It is an instrument that positively identifies those substances that fall within its scope, whereas the old notification instrument has worked by listing categories of waste that are exempted from its coverage. This has left an area of uncertainty, in which waste producers, unsure whether certain substances have been within or outside the control policy, have submitted loads to the notification system (with all the administrative inconvenience and cost this entails) 'to be on the safe side'.[8] Waste disposal authorities have consequentially been swamped, in some cases, with notifications which, in their view, have been unnecessary and unwelcome. They have assumed the policy was not meant to control toxic waste disposal to that extent, but rather that it was meant to eliminate irresponsible tipping of genuinely hazardous loads. But unable to offer waste producers the degree of re-assurance that loads precisely did or did not require to be notified, the result has been the overloading of the system together with a shortage of authorities prepared to accept notifiable wastes in their areas.[9] The new consignment note instrument has been adopted with just this kind of historical evidence available. Yet some parties (such as the Confederation of British Industry) fear that it will harm rather than improve opportunities for responsible disposal of toxic wastes by adding to the administrative costs without effectively preventing illegal or irresponsible tipping. On the other hand the Department of the Environment (whose job it is to design and introduce the instrument itself) has claimed that the new instrument will reduce uncertainty by positively identifying the substances it will control, and thus give producers as well as waste disposal authorities a more predictable and manageable admin-

istrative burden. The instrument will require consignments of these specified wastes to be followed 'from the cradle to the grave', thus—in the DoE's view—reducing the opportunities for illegal tipping to go on unnoticed, and reducing the administrative costs of the policy.[10]

It should be emphasised that the choice and design of the instrument is not always made by the organisations that will bear the responsibility for operating it. Thus the Section 17 consignment note instrument is being formulated by the Wastes Division of the DoE (in consultation with those interested parties that the DoE chooses to consult), although its day-to-day operation will not rest with the DoE, but with the waste disposal authorities, the waste producers and the disposal contractors.

This is not an uncommon arrangement. Indeed the EEC Bathing Water Directive is an instrument of Community policy, developed within the institutions of the Community and in consultation with member states. Yet the form of expression is specified by the directive even though no individuals or organisations of the Community will be directly concerned with operating it on a day-to-day basis. Hence the displeasure of the British representatives and officials with the Articles concerning methods of monitoring and analysing water quality, given the prevailing British view that these methods are inappropriate for achieving the desired controls.[11] But the organisations involved locally with the operation of the instrument—the water authorities which oversee designated bathing beaches—are not opposed to the objectives of the policy. They have willingly agreed that improvements in bathing water quality are in many cases desirable and attainable. If the choice of instrument was theirs, however, methods of monitoring and analysing water quality as well as the timetable for achievement of the policy objectives would be substantially modified.[12]

In the case of noise abatement zones an existing type of instrument has been applied to a new objective. The aim of the policy is to control and reduce neighbourhood noise levels, and this is a relatively unfamiliar area for policies to address.[13] The device concerns imposing controls over specified geographical areas, and as such it is a familiar type of instrument, often seen in planning and housing policy (e.g. housing action areas, conservation areas) and particularly in air pollution control (e.g. smoke control areas). Since local authorities are already familiar with these instruments for areas it may have been thought that this would be the most practical way to require them to operate the new policies for noise.[14]

But for the industrial air pollution example, the instrument chosen involves a combination of old and new models. Serving a notice on an

individual or organisation to produce a certain response is a well-established instrument (e.g. abatement notices)[15] but requiring the authority to then publish this information is less familiar to the authorities. The chosen instrument is a local consultative committee that can help with the selection and presentation of material and this was derived (by the Sharp Report) from the liaison committees established in some places by the Alkali Inspectorate.[16] The evidence quoted in the case study drew attention to the uncertainty that this instrument seems to have promoted: most authorities have not used it at all, and some have criticised it for being a superfluous device to achieve the goal of improving publicly available information.

These quotations from the case material already draw attention to a number of important aspects of the 'instruments for policy' concept. One is that the instrument can be designed taking into account the organisations and individuals whose job it will be to operate it. Secondly the instrument can draw on examples of instruments that are already tried in other or related policy areas, or can try a new form of expression, perhaps derived from elsewhere in that policy area. A third feature is that the instrument can build in different degrees of power and force. So, for example, the noise and air cases are both optional areas for policy activity, although once the relevant parties have decided to use the available powers, they are controlled by the policy instruments in the ways they can use them. This means that the regulations and procedures specified by the instruments (e.g. Schedule 1 to the Control of Pollution Act which deals with noise abatement zones) are ineffective or irrelevant in operational terms unless the given organisation has opted to implement the policy. In contrast, exemption from the provisions of the Bathing Water Directive appears to be available to water authorities only in special circumstances which must be notified in advance to the EEC Commission by the national government.[17] For toxic waste disposal, no exemption at all is anticipated from the coverage of the Section 17 consignment note system.

This continuum is obviously important because the greater the degree of control built into the instrument, the greater the design problems may be in the early stages (this has certainly been true for Section 17 where the DoE has admitted it is unsure exactly what details to include in the instrument in order to achieve the apparently simple objective).[18] The more flexible or optional the instruments' expressions of policy are, perhaps the easier the design can be. But this observation brings into focus the very important interorganisational relationships on which policy instruments have a bearing.

Earlier chapters have described the different categories of authorities that get involved in policy implementation—these include central, regional and local government agencies, private industry, professional bodies, local consumer or public pressure groups, policy advisory bodies and individuals, international government agencies and policy advisory groups.[19] Not all are necessarily always involved—a lot depends on the substance of the policy as well as the nature of the instruments. As an OECD report on water pollution policy has observed: 'the instruments seem bound to be subordinated to the organisations, yet their mere existence steers the organisations along special courses, ending even in the establishment of new organisations'.[20]

So to illustrate this in one respect, the fact that the Control of Pollution Act 1974 contains several sections which assist the public to obtain more information about pollution and the steps being taken to control it inevitably suggests that individual or organised members of the public will be involved in matters of detail expressed through instruments. This is not the case, for example, in certain instances of industrial legislation where other conditions (e.g. the protection of trade secrets) are held to be particularly important. The public interest is assumed to be a far lesser priority and the general public is consequently far less involved in the details as expressed through instruments of industrial policy. Two particularly important features of pollution control policy are the relationships between central and local government, and the relationships between government and non-government bodies. These are also important in other policy areas where one sector of power or activity wishes to control those in its environment, and where consent to activate and respond to such controls is unpredictable.[21]

Taking the bathing water example, the central-local government relations aspect becomes very clear. The material in Chapter 5 provides evidence that the DoE has changed its style of dealing with the water authorities between 1975 and 1979 as work on the directive has progressed.[22] Initially the DoE saw an important feature of its role being to *reassure* water authorities that they would not be required to authorise bathing as certain other EEC member-states do. Then it had to instruct water authorities about the information they should collect on its behalf in order to assess the quality of bathing water. Later the DoE tried to *devolve* the decision about beach designation entirely to the water authorities, but they objected that this would place them in an untenable position with the local tourist authorities. So then there had to be further *advice* from the Department to the water authorities although this was abruptly halted when the Minister's wish to halt progress was conveyed. Following the change of government in 1979 the DoE had again to *advise* water authorities generally on the timetable for bringing Part II of the Act into force as well as letting them know specifically what should be done about the Bathing Water Directive.

This summary, although it leaves out a lot of detail, shows the water authorities to be typically in a passive, responsive position as far as this policy is concerned. The DoE emerges as the active interpreter of the policy and controller over action at the local level. This predominantly 'top-down' style is very familiar in analyses of policy,[23] and it highlights the structural and organisational features of the policy process that favour it. Thus local agencies such as the water authorities are explicitly limited in the extent of their powers, relative to central government. One instrument which gives expression to this arrangement is the Water Act 1973. Section 1(1) gives the duty of promoting a national policy for water to ministers. Section 5 gives ministers the power to give directions of a general character to water authorities as to the exercise of their functions, in so far as this appears to ministers to effect the execution of the national policy for water.[24]

Furthermore, advisory bodies may be interposed between the central and local government agencies. In this case it is the National Water Council that takes such a position. It can be said to separate further the local authorities from the powers of policy expression and interpretation since part of its role, as defined in the Water Act, is to advise the ministers and the water authorities, and to promote and assist the efficient performance by water authorities of their functions.[25]

But as a contrast, the 'bottom-up' style of policy can be seen in the case of noise abatement zones. Pressure was put on the government by non-government bodies (such as the Noise Abatement Society and the Association of Public Health Inspectors) to acknowledge the problem of neighbourhood noise. The process by which this resulted in Sections 63-7 of the Control of Pollution Act has been described in Chapter 6.[26] It places central government in the more passive, responsive position relative to the local authorities who are enabled to activate, introduce and maintain controls over neighbourhood noise with very little interference from central government. It is true that central government has made statutory regulations and issued guidance on several details of the policy, and that it currently has the power (although not so far used) to refuse to approve a local authority's noise abatement order. But the predominant style of this policy and the instruments that give expression to it emphasise the autonomy of the local authorities and the relatively low-key role of the central government department.

These examples have to be seen in the broader context of the relations between different government agencies that prevail. The county and district councils have 'limited legislative powers delegated to them by Parliament, and specified executive powers likewise granted by Parliament'.[27] Any local authority legislation either requires approval by the relevant central government minister or parliamentary approval, depending on its standing. But close financial control is also exercised by central over local government, and this may be used to influence policy matters, in addition to the guidance issued through circulars. These foundations of central-local government relations have been maintained and built upon by successive pieces of legislation and by long-standing customary practices so that any policy with a bearing on these organisations will be forced to interact with the conditions that obtain.[28] It need not necessarily be one way only through – some policies will take aspects of central-local government relations into new realms or along unknown paths. But the weight and tone of tradition is strong and is an important factor in the present discussion since it shapes the expectations that individuals and organisations have of what is possible and what may be desirable.[29]

Another way of demonstrating the instruments for policy concept is to identify in general terms the devices that are known. These include:

Act of Parliament	
By-law	
Subordinate Instrument	
Circular	
Letter	
Directive	WRITTEN INSTRUMENTS
Consultative Document	
Code of Practice	
British Standard	
Emission Standard	
Quality and Objective	
Best Practicable Means	
Advisory Committee	
Technical Committee	
Committee of Enquiry	INSTRUMENTS INVOLVING
Royal Commission	INDIVIDUALS
Speech	

Grant
Compensation
Charge   ⎤
Polluter Pays Principle ⎦   ECONOMIC INSTRUMENTS

Each of these instruments offers a different way of expressing a
policy. Often more than one is used in combination. Some instruments
(e.g. the written ones) can exist without there necessarily having to be
continuous action. Others do not exist at all unless individuals take
action. Some instruments have a built-in timescale (e.g. commencement
orders, which are a kind of statutory instrument and define the dates
from when sections of an Act may be deemed to be in force). Others are
valid at any time they are used (e.g. a minister may make a speech or
announcement expressing a policy almost whenever he likes). Working
through the list with pollution policy examples, these and other features
of the instruments will be described.

The *Act of Parliament* instrument is very familiar. It can only be
initiated directly by parliamentary action (publishing a Bill) and can
only be achieved by parliamentary action (debate and votes). But the
process can be influenced by outside organisations and events to a considerable degree (well illustrated by the Deposit of Poisonous Waste Act
1972).[30] Some Acts need further expression before their provisions can
be activated (e.g. the Control of Pollution Act — when it received Royal
Assent in 1974 it was completely dormant, and only brought to life by
a sequence of commencements and other statutory orders).[31] Some
Acts, even though they are dormant, can promote action in anticipation
(e.g. the preparatory work of the water authorities and NWC even though
key sections of Part II of the Control of Pollution Act are still
dormant).[32]

By-laws are usually made by local government agencies such as county
and district councils, and water authorities. They can only concern
matters directly under the agency's control. They need not necessarily
follow a preordained form although they often do. The instrument is a
device for permitting individual and differential action by the agencies
concerned and therefore is a symbol of their scope to act autonomously.

Subordinate instruments are usually, but not always, statutory
instruments, which means that they have to be published. Orders, rules,
regulations, etc., whether statutory instruments or not, may be subject
to no parliamentary procedure. But if the instrument is of much
importance then the Act under which it is made usually provides that it
comes into effect automatically unless annulled by Parliament or that it

does not come into effect until it has been approved by Parliament.[33]
Two significant points here are:

(a)   that subordinate instruments cannot be amended in the course
of their passage through Parliament;

(b)   subordinate instruments cannot contain anything they are not
authorised to contain by the enactment that confers the power.

Thus the power of the Secretary of State to make regulations concerning atmospheric pollution from motor fuel are contained in Section 75
of the Control of Pollution Act.[34]

Circulars are literally 'communications of which copies are sent to
several persons'.[35] They are a common device through which government departments express instructions, information or request action
from other agencies. In the DoE's case, circulars are numbered in sequence
each year (e.g. the tenth circular issued in 1979 was identified as 10/79),
and sent by post to the local authorities, water authorities or other organisations. The specialist press almost always receive copies of each circular.
The contents can vary greatly as can the length. Some may be just one
or two paragraphs, for example informing recipients that a report of
interest has been published (e.g. Circular 26/71 announced the publication
of the Sumner Report on refuse disposal).[36] Others may be the size of
a pamphlet, containing detailed instructions and information (e.g.
Circular 55/76 on the licensing of waste disposal facilities).[37]

The *letter* is a more selective and private version of a circular. The
government department uses this device to communicate more confident-
ial information or instructions, usually to senior officials of the relevant
agencies. Copies will not necessarily go to the press although within the
receiving agency the contents may be quite widely circulated. Letters
often concern more sensitive policy issues where co-operative action or
unwelcome news has to be discussed. An example of this was the letter
from a DoE official to water authorities[38] in 1978 informing them of
the Secretary of State's wish that they should agree designations locally
with the district councils.

Directives as dealt with here are a device for the expression of
European Community policy. They originate in the institutions of the
Community, but, once agreed by the Council of Ministers, have binding
force on member states. Precisely, directives are binding as regards the
results to be achieved although they leave the method and means of
implementation to the discretion of the national authority.[39] Thus the
Bathing Water Directive is an expression of a certain aspect of the EEC's

Environmental Action Programme. To be implemented fully in the UK it requires the water authorities to exercise certain of their powers as contained in Part II of the Control of Pollution Act 1974. Some directives require member-states to introduce new legislation specially. Others can be accommodated by administrative action within existing legislation. Directives often specify times for achievement by member states of successive stages of the policy. They represent, therefore, a device of remote control, building in a considerable amount of national discretion but aiming at overall obedience by incorporating several rules and instructions of considerable detail. They emphasise the power of the policy-making body – the European Community – while implicitly exploiting the consent of the member states to pursue common policy objectives.

Consultative documents are expressions of policy intentions which invite the recipients to comment, criticise and suggest alternatives. Usually issued by government departments,[40] consultative documents set out a number of proposals or objectives together with supporting arguments. Within a certain time recipients may send back their views, although there is no absolute guarantee that these will be adopted. In the DoE's case it often consults not only individual local authorities, but their representative associations too. Thus the Associations of County Councils, Metropolitan Authorities and District Councils are frequently engaged in replying to consultative documents, drawing on the views of their members more or less directly. When used, this instrument acknowledges more of a partnership or joint approach to formulating policy, since it implies that influence is possible and is invited. It acknowledges that policies can benefit from being constructed from a range of viewpoints and amongst organisations with different objectives.

Codes of practice offer an instrument for expressing the practical aspects of a particular policy.[41] They may be agreed within and/or between organisations and they have the effect of describing how action under a particular policy is expected to happen. Codes of practice do not necessarily have legally binding force on the organisations that acknowledge them. But they are a powerful constraint, providing moral, if not legal, pressure to conform. None of the four case studies directly involves a code of practice although the Secretary of State has powers to promote codes of practice for minimising noise.[42] Under the Health and Safety at Work Act 1974, factory inspectors can use the general requirements of the Act to protect people by reference to the 'Code of practice for reducing the exposure of employed persons to noise', which gives guidance on exposure levels regarded as presenting a serious risk of hearing damage and on action which should be taken.[43]

British Standards are national quality standards for industrial and consumer products, prepared and published by the British Standards Institution. This is an independent body financed by voluntary subscriptions, an annual government grant, sales of publications and fees for testing and certification. British Standards are issued for voluntary adoption, but in a number of cases legislation can require compliance. The provisions for controlling noise nuisance rely on British Standard 4142: 1967,[44] which lays down methods for measuring the relevant noise levels and for assessing whether a noise of a given level and character will, in given circumstances, be likely to give rise to complaint. BS: 5228[45] is identified in a statutory instrument concerning noise controls for machinery used on construction sites under Section 60 of the Control of Pollution Act, and other regulations concerning motor fuel content covered also specify a British Standard.

Emission standards and *quality objectives* are distinct but related types of instrument with particular relevance to pollution policy. *Emission standards* set levels of pollutants or nuisances not to be exceeded in emissions. They usually apply to liquid or gaseous discharges, although restrictions on the disposal of solid wastes, occupational noise emissions and radioactivity are a similar type of control. A *quality objective* for a medium (air, land or water) is a requirement for:

> a degree of quality in that medium to be attained through an environmental specification, which is to be fulfilled at a given time and place, now or in the future. It can be short or long term, be national or reflect specific regional and local conditions; and it can take account of the use to which the medium is to be put.[46]

The implementation of quality objectives necessarily implies use of the emission standard instrument, since individual discharges have to be tailored to achieve the quality objective set for the medium.[47] Thus in the consents set by the water authorities for industrial and other discharges into rivers, emission standards specifying content, concentration, volume and temperature are calculated, taking into account the further polluting load that the river will have to bear, its natural capacity to dilute and disperse the pollutants, and the other uses to which the river will be put. By way of contrast, air pollution controls in the UK rely on emission standards only, with industrial polluters being subject to individual controls for their particular plant or factory. The choice of instrument has been a matter of controversy, both within the UK and between the UK and its European neighbours—as the case study material has indicated.

Another form of quality objective achieved via emission standards is shown in the site licences issued under Sections 3-11 of the Control of Pollution Act. These specify the wastes and the manner of their disposal that may be permitted on a given site, and the licence conditions have to be set taking account of the pollution risks from that use of the site that may effect the land, water and air in its environment.

Best practicable means or bpm is a variation on the theme of code of practice or emission standards/quality objectives. It is based on the principle that as technology improves, the controls on industry are made more stringent, so that the improvements will be applied to produce cleaner discharges. Used particularly in industrial air pollution control under the Alkali Acts, the instrument is employed by the Alkali Inspectorate to promote technical improvements, while taking account of the costs borne by the polluter and the community for given levels of pollution control. Absolute or improved standards may not necessarily be desirable if the cost of introducing them is unfair or unreasonable in commercial terms. This pragmatic approach is adopted in the belief that uniform controls (such as national quality objectives) do not maximise the benefit for a given expenditure. But as Chapter 7 indicated, the bpm instrument has given rise to considerable debate about the effectiveness of controls.[48] Chapter 6 also illustrated the use of bpm as a legitimate defence against certain noise nuisance offences.[49]

Instruments involving individuals form the next group of devices for expressing policy, and they are contrasted with the previous sorts of written instruments notably because of the greater degree of variation and idiosyncracy they exhibit. Whereas most of the written instruments permit only a limited amount of influence from interested parties before being set down in their final form, these instruments expressed through the action of individuals are far more flexible, unpredictable, open to pressure from interested parties. Examples are advisory committees (e.g. the Clean Air Council), technical committees (e.g. the Working Party on Refuse Disposal, Standing Technical Committee on Synthetic Detergents), Royal Commissions (e.g. the Royal Commission on Environmental Pollution), Committees of Enquiry (e.g. the enquiry into the behaviour of hazardous wastes in landfill sites, 1978), local enquiries (e.g. those concerning the use of sites at Pitsea for toxic liquid waste disposal, called by local authorities and the Secretary of State), and speeches (e.g. the Minister of State's announcement about implementation of the remaining sections of the Control of Pollution Act, made in April 1978). They are all devices for the expression of policy because the individuals concerned are permitted and expected to make assessments in the light of their knowledge and experience. This differs from the more specific and uniform expressions of policy contained in such instruments as codes of practice or emission standards, where the requirements of the policy are relatively unambiguous. In the case of a local enquiry or one of the committees being used to work on an issue, the actual outcome will be one of very many possible outcomes: it will be a function of the forces brought to bear on the deliberations of the individuals. Representations from interested parties, pressures of time or money, the weight of tradition and custom, the enthusiasm or demand for innovation—these are some of the forces that will determine the expression of policy that emerges in each case.

The choice of this sort of instrument is therefore important where a special degree of expertise or authority is required to give weight to the expression of policy, and where a certain degree of opposition to the policy from interested parties is anticipated. In a field such as pollution control such instruments are particularly useful where technical or scientific problems have got to be reconciled with social or administrative actions.[50]

Economic instruments form the third group of devices through which policies can be expressed, and they are based on the notion that costs and benefits of policies can be distributed differentially between interested parties. In the pollution sphere examples of economic instruments are:

grants (e.g. gifts of limited amounts of money to householders who need to change their heating or cooking systems in order to use smokeless fuels in a smoke control area);

compensation (e.g. to occupiers of premises that need to install insulating devices as a result of nearby road developments creating increased noise);

charges (e.g. payable by industrial waste producers to local authorities who arrange in return to collect or dispose of their waste).

In addition to these devices which have a wide application in several spheres of policy there is an additional economic instrument of special importance. Known as the 'polluter pays principle', it holds that the costs of pollution abatement measures should be borne by polluters, not governments—and it was agreed in 1972 by the member governments of the OECD. Its purpose is to prevent difficulties that would have arisen (in

trade terms) if some countries had decided to have costs borne by
polluters and therefore consumers, while others arranged to have them
borne by governments and thus by taxpayers.[51]

The principle has broadly been adhered to since it was agreed, and the
EEC has endorsed it too since the basis of many Community policies
rests on the need to harmonise conditions of competition between member-
states.[52] This has an influence on the pollution policies of the UK to the
extent that nothing in the domestic policies—their expression or enforcement—should violate the objectives of the polluter-pays principle.
Economic instruments, then, offer an indirect way of expressing pollution
control policies by focusing on the cost and benefits of abatement. The
instruments offer incentives or discouragement to follow certain courses
of action, and when employed in conjunction with one or both of the
categories of instrument already described, provide a powerful vehicle
for articulating the intentions and objectives of policies.[53]

Linking the description of policy instruments to the discussion earlier
in this chapter about interorganisational relationships, it is now reasonable
to argue that the effect of choice of instrument on these relationships is
significant. Similarly the nature of the interorganisational relationships
will affect the choice of policy instrument in important ways. Therefore
for those involved in the policy process—whether the substance of the
policies concerns pollution or any other issue—there is benefit to be
gained from clarifying the instruments and interorganisational relationships in which the policy must find expression. The interactions may be
complex and unpredictable, but that makes it no less important to
clarify what conditions obtain. It was claimed earlier that the less this
aspect of the policy process is left to chance, then the less likely it will
be that unwanted implementation problems will arise. The next chapter
will deal with evidence to support this claim.

Notes

1. See Chapter 1, p. 15, and Chapter 2, p. 23 for example. Others have agreed
on this point. For example, OECD identified 'administrative, regulatory, technical
and economic' instruments used by member-states in water pollution control and
suggested 'management objectives are achieved by co-ordinated operation of these
instruments'. OECD, *Water Management Policies and Instruments* (OECD, Paris,
1977), p. 150. Majone has observed two categories of instrument for pollution
control policies: administrative and market oriented. He argues that the significant
choice to be made is 'not among abstractly considered policy instruments but
among institutionally determined ways of operating them'. G. Majone, 'Choice
among Policy Instruments for Pollution Control', *Policy Analysis* (Autumn 1976),
p. 592.

2. For example, a DoE official claimed 'We apply a complete range of control mechanisms, . . . choosing carefully the instrument most appropriate to the need.' A. Lyall, 'The UK Approach to Pollution Control in Relation to Commission Policy' in *The European Community's Environment Policy* (National Council for Social Service, London, 1977), p. 20. OECD suggests 'member states have . . . their own social, institutional legal and economic backgrounds which explain their preference for a particular instrument'. *Water Management Policies*, p. 155.

3. See Chapter 4, p. 59.

4. See Chapter 5, p. 101.

5. See Chapter 6, p. 122.

6. See Chapter 7, p. 139.

7. See Chapter 4, p. 58.

8. See Chapter 4, p. 58.

9. See Chapter 4, p. 68.

10. See Chapter 4, p. 59.

11. See Chapter 5, pp. 97 and 106.

12. See Chapter 5, pp. 101-2.

13. See Chapter 6, p. 123.

14. The Association of Public Health Inspectors claimed 'this type of approach has been used with great success in dealing with air pollution'. Noise Advisory Council, *Neighbourhood Noise* (HMSO, London, 1971), Appendix C, para. 5, p. 72. See also C.S. Kerse, *The Law Relating to Noise* (Oyez, London, 1975), p. 49, for a discussion of zoning policy.

15. Under the Public Health Act 1936, local authorities can take action to stop statutory nuisances (i.e. injuries to public health). The procedure first involves service of an abatement notice. If this is disregarded, the person responsible may be brought to court, for a legal remedy. See J. McLoughlin, *The Law and Practice Relating to Pollution Control in the United Kingdom* (Graham and Trotman, London, 1976), p. 33.

16. See Chapter 7, p. 140.

17. See Department of the Environment, *Implementation of the EEC Directive on the Quality of Bathing Water*, Note by the Department of the Environment, March 1977, and Article 8 of the Directive. OJ No. L31 of 5 February 1976.

18. Anthony Fagin, Waste Division, DoE, in personal interview with author. Indeed, the Secretary of State's power to make regulations includes power to vary and revoke them.

19. See diagrams in Chapter 8.

20. OECD, *Water Management Policies*, p. 11.

21. Gunn has observed: 'it is now relatively rare for implementation of a public programme to involve only a government department on one hand and a group of affected citizens on the other. Instead there is likely to be an intervening network of local authorities, boards and commissions, voluntary associations and organised groups.' L.A. Gunn, 'Why is Implementation so Difficult?', *Management Services in Government* (November 1978), p. 172.

22. See Chapter 5, pp. 101-3.

23. See Chapter 1, p. 19.

24. Indeed, a body corporate such as a water authority is always limited in the extent of its powers because it has no powers other than those conferred by the Act or other instrument under which it is established.

25. McLoughlin, *Law and Practice Relating to Pollution Control*, p. 97.

26. See Chapter 6, p. 122.

27. McLoughlin, *Law and Practice Relating to Pollution Control*, p. 5.

28. See toxic waste case in Chapter 4 where the reason for delay in introducing specific controls was given as the wish to introduce more comprehensive measures once local government reorganisation had been achieved. In the event though, the problem was too urgent, so the Deposit of Poisonous Waste Act was introduced as an 'interim' measure. However, it is still in force several years later.

29. The position is exemplified in a recent government document which states: 'Democratically elected local authorities are wholly responsible bodies who must be free to get on with the tasks entrusted to them by Parliament without constant interference in matters of detail by the Government of the day. On the other hand, there are certain national policies which it is the Government's duty to pursue even though they may be administered locally . . . It would be inappropriate therefore to abandon all control over local government; to do so would be an abdication of the government's proper role.' Department of the Environment, *Central Government Controls Over Local Authorities*, Cmnd. 7634 (HMSO, London, 1979).

30. See Chapter 4, n. 15.

31. See diagrams in Chapter 3.

32. See Chapter 5, p. 101.

33. Subordinate legislation is classified according to the process adopted in implementing the law-making powers:

1. Orders in council give statutory effect to a cabinet decision by being expressed as a solemn order of the Privy Council.
2. Regulations have to be published as do orders, and they are numbered consecutively in the year of issue. They have to be subject to some form of parliamentary scrutiny. Scrutiny takes several forms:
   (a) laid before parliament
   (b) subject to annulment in either house within 40 days of being laid (this is achieved via prayers which are considered in the House of Commons after 10 p.m.)
   (c) subject to affirmative approval
   (d) draft orders may be subject to affirmative or negative approval
   (e) 28-day orders expire unless approved by a resolution of each House within 28 days of being laid. See J.F. Garner, *Administrative Law*, See J.F. Garner, *Administrative Law,* 5th edn (Butterworths, London, 1979), and D. Foulkes, *Introduction to Administrative Law*, 4th edn (Butterworths, London, 1976).

34. Statutory Instruments SI 1976 No. 1988 gives expression to the Minister's power.

35. D. Foulkes, *Introduction to Administrative Law*, 4th edn (Butterworths, London, 1976).

36. Department of the Environment Circular 26/71, *Report of the Working Party of Refuse Disposal.*

37. Department of the Environment Circular 55/76, *Control of Pollution Act 1974, Part I – (Waste on Land) Disposal Licences.*

38. See Chapter 5, p. 103.

39. The term 'directive' has no such precise meaning in English administrative law since it can include a range of statutory instructions, whereas the European Community usage is precise. Another Community instrument is the regulation, which has direct effect under the EEC Treaty.

40. But other bodies such as voluntary organisations, appointed committees, etc., could also do this.

41. 'These are on the borderland of law and administration.' Foulkes, *Administrative Law.*

42. Control of Pollution Act 1974, Section 71.

43. Department of the Environment, *Pollution Control in Great Britain: How it Works*, Pollution Paper no. 9 (HMSO, London, 1978), para. 303.

44. British Standard 4142: 1967, *Method of Rating Industrial Noise Affecting Mixed Residential and Industrial Areas.*

45. British Standard 5228: 1975, *Code of Practice for Noise Control on Construction and Demolition Sites.*

46. A. Lyall, 'UK Approach to Pollution Control', p. 19.

47. See Chapter 5, p. 86.

48. See the definition of bpm in Section 72 of the Control of Pollution Act

1974. The Open University sees it this way: 'we avoid giving the potential polluter a licence to pollute the air up to a level defined by [air quality] standards. Instead at all times the polluter is required to use the best practicable means . . . to minimise air pollution . . . opponents of this philosophy argue that there is insufficient incentive for those producing air-polluting wastes to find better ways of preventing their continued discharge. 'Environmental Control and Public Health, PT272 Unit 15', *Air Pollution Control* (The Open University Press, Milton Keynes, 1977), p. 73.

49. See Chapter 6, p. 123.

50. But examples from other public policy areas are just as evident – e.g. the Layfield Committee on local government finance, the Top Salaries Review Body, Sir Alan Marre's enquiry into compensation for thalidomide victims, the Royal Commission on Legal Services, the Roskill enquiry for the third London airport, etc.

51. OECD, *The State of the Environment in OECD Member Countries* (OECD, Paris, 1979).

52. The incorporation of the polluter pays principle in the communities' environment programme is described in S. Johnson, *The Pollution Control Policy of the European Communities* (Graham and Trotman, London, 1979), pp. 113-15.

53. For further discussion of charging policies see: A. Marin, 'Pollution Control: Economists' Views', *Three Banks Review*, no. 121 (March 1979), pp. 21-41 and G. Majone, 'Choice Among Policy Instruments for Pollution Control', *Policy Analysis* (Autumn 1976), pp. 589-614.

10 THE ENFORCEMENT OF POLICY

The concept of enforcement covers the ways in which instruments for policy may be applied and their effects monitored. There are several practical aspects of enforcement, dealing with different types of power: legal action and penalties imposed through the legal system are one important example. The use of sanctions, incentives and discretion are further examples. In all cases it is important to clarify the purpose and locus of the enforcement powers, and their strength and effectiveness in the policy process.

Again, this rather artificial distinction of elements of a concept is worked through for the purpose of analysis—although in the day-to-day operation of policies these features may seem much less clear or apparent. The advantage of spelling out the concepts in an abstract way is to identify which elements are significant and may be employed more purposefully as a result, when practical applications are required.

Legal Enforcement

Legal action is given power through common and criminal law. Although these channels may be distinct (i.e. common law can provide individuals with defined rights enforceable by civil actions such as trespass or compensation; criminal law can enable the provisions of Acts of Parliament and other statutes to be enforced), they are also often interdependent. For example, there are criminal offences at common law (e.g. it is an offence at common law to attempt to commit a statutory offence under the Control of Pollution Act) and there are also numerous statutes which confer rights that are enforceable by civil action. There can be no offence at common law that is not affected by some statutory provision as to, for example, mode of trial or penalties or jurisdiction. On the other hand, no statute can contain the last word on any given topic. As a simple illustration the rules by which judges interpret Acts of Parliament have been developed at common law.[1]

A legal expert in the field of pollution control, J. McLoughlin, has called for consistency between civil and criminal remedies for pollution offences.[2] But others suggest that, in the case of negligence, for example, it is more important that the law of negligence should be consistent than

that the law of negligence so far as it relates to pollution should be consistent with the criminal law as to pollution.

These views are offered, not to argue the specific points, but to show
the complex legal context within which enforcement of one sort of
policy—pollution control policy—finds itself. There are three classes of
government function: legislative, executive and judicial, and it has been
held conventionally according to democratic principles that these
functions should be separated to preserve the liberty of individuals
rather than vested in any one organisation or person of government. But
as subordinate legislation is used more and more and the executive is
given increasing powers of adjudication, this doctrine of separation of
powers is less relevant. The consequence is that pinpointing the locus of
power and the controls over exercise of power (with which the concept
of enforcement is closely concerned) becomes a complicated exercise.[3]

Taking civil proceedings first, these now represent the less significant
aspect of legal action as far as pollution policy is concerned. Nevertheless,
trespass, negligence and private nuisance actions are available and sometimes used by individuals to sue if these kinds of infringements have
been imposed on their legitimate rights. There is difficulty for special
interest groups (such as environmentalists opposed to pollution) taking
common law actions because the law does not recognise their collective
or corporate legal standing to sue — the action can only be brought by
an individual whose recognised interests have been offended against. In
addition, a polluter who wishes to protect himself against such civil
actions can buy the relevant rights (e.g. purchasing surrounding land and
leasing it with clauses restricting the use of the land or the activities of
the leasee). So common law still offers important if minor opportunities
to enforce pollution policies, in so far as they impinge on the rights of
individuals.

More importantly, though, criminal proceedings can be used to
defend and enforce policies that are expressed through statutes. Taking
the Control of Pollution Act as an example, there are numerous sections
specifying the penalties that can be imposed by the courts if offences
are committed. In Section 17 fines of not more than £400 on summary
conviction or two years imprisonment and a fine on indictment are
specified for offences against the provisions controlling the disposal of
special wastes. In relation to water pollution, Section 31 sets out precisely what would constitute a person's guilt under the Act and again
specifies the maximum limits for fines and/or terms of imprisonment
that may be imposed. The noise control provisions of the Act set out in
Sections 57-9 the arrangements under which summary proceedings may

be invoked by local authorities and occupiers of premises when a statutory nuisance exists. For prevention of atmospheric pollution the Act gives the Secretary of State powers to specify the manner and methods by which local authorities can use their statutory powers to obtain information about industrial emissions; and if polluters are served with a notice by local authorities under Section 80, the Secretary of State has powers to consider appeals and these are made explicit in Section 81 of the Act.

These four examples represent only a small indication of the range and detail of provision for enforcing policies through legal actions. In Part V of the Act, Sections 85-8 deal exclusively with the legal proceedings and Schedule 2 lists the alterations to penalties in other statutes that the Act introduces: these are further instances of the importance given to the relevant powers of legal enforcement the statute bestows.

But care should be taken to recognise that enforcement powers are not an automatic guide to enforcement action. This is where discretion comes in, since legal and other enforcement powers are all susceptible to variations of interpretation and different levels of activity. Not only may legal remedies often not be sought by individuals and organisations even when they are specially available, but courts and other enforcement agencies may opt not to use their powers as extensively or vigorously as the rules permit. The use of discretion is a vital component in the implementation process, and has of course already attracted considerable attention from observers.[4]

In relation to the Control of Pollution Act 1974, there has been little evidence of legal action to enforce its provisions, and it is difficult to determine how far this implies the use of discretion by individuals and authorities, or (more probably) whether too little of the Act has been in legal force for sufficient time for such actions to be selected. It clearly does take some time for authorities to become familiar with the provisions of new legislation and to identify the most suitable vehicle in each instance for the exercise of power. But two examples may be typical. First, in the area of waste disposal, one local authority official when asked whether he would use legal means to enforce the site licensing provisions on a private tip operator who had disobeyed certain rules about the disposal of toxic waste there said, 'No, that would be far too cumbersome a business, and too expensive for my authority. I can do much better by simply threatening to withdraw the chap's licence if he doesn't fall into line. That way he is forced to mend his ways or go out of business.'[5] In the second example, an environmental health officer quoted the case of a major nationalised industry with a factory in his

district which had, after encountering some pollution problems, installed
a fume arrestment plant at a cost of £6½ million over five years. Its
running costs are £1,000 per day. Yet if it had not installed this plant it
could easily have afforded to continue illegal fume emissions since the
maximum daily fine that could be imposed is £100 per day.[6] The
environmental health officer and the waste disposal official both describe
instances where the legal remedy falls short of the necessary force
needed by them to ensure that pollution control policies are effective. In
one case the procedural side of bringing a legal action appears to be the
deterrent. In the other case the penalty imposed on the offender may
be too slight to force him to change his actions.

Other problems with the use of the legal remedies have been identified
too. The technical or scientific nature of some pollution offences can
present problems of adjudication—as one environmental health officer
put it: 'The idea that magistrates or judges are competent in this subject
is ridiculous. Some stipendiary magistrates may get better with
experience, but the record is not good. In the High Court, calling technical expert witnesses may actually be a disadvantage because they tend
to confuse the judges.'

Nevertheless, the level of penalties that may be imposed on offenders
by the courts is considered important by legislators. A common cause of
approval for the Control of Pollution Bill and its predecessor in Parliament
was the higher level of penalties contained in it.[7] The belief that being
able to impose higher penalties will improve the enforcement of policies
is widely held. As the journal *Municipal Engineering* stated: 'The
opportunity now exists for waste disposal authorities to prosecute
operators quickly for breach of site licence conditions . . . The way is
therefore open for the strength of the county councils to be felt, and it
does not need many examples of fines and repeated fines to put the
industry on its toes.'[8]

Writing of over ten years' experience of the Noise Abatement Act
1960, the Noise Advisory Council commented, 'We consider that the
effectiveness as a deterrent of the current nuisance provisions is prejudiced
by the inadequacy of the maximum penalties which it is open to the courts
to impose'; and in calling for these to be set at a 'realistic' level the
Council suggested '£200 for default in complying with a notice, £500 for
failure to comply with a court order and £50 per day for continuance of
that failure after conviction'.[9]

Writing in 1972, another observer thought that the maximum fines of
£100 for pollution offences should be increased 100 times: 'Apart from
making pollution control equipment much easier for a works manager to

justify economically to his head office, heavy fines would bring down much heavier publicity upon companies that transgressed.'[10]

But there is no consensus about the true enforcement value of legal penalties. On the one hand, the Department of the Environment claims that the maximum fine of £400 and/or six months imprisonment on summary conviction and five years imprisonment and/or maximum fine on indictment under the 1972 Deposit of Poisonous Waste Act represent 'heavy penalties' which seek to 'instil a sense of responsibility in those concerned with waste disposal'.[11] In the parliamentary debate on the Bill it was similarly said that the penalties were 'designed to outweigh the undoubted profits which had hitherto accrued from illegal tipping'.[12]

But on the other hand evidence of penalties imposed by the courts for Deposit of Poisonous Waste Act offences gives a different impression. In 1976 E. Felton and Partners of Sandwich, a timber treatment firm, were fined £150 plus £25 costs after pleading guilty to tipping chrome/copper arsenate solution in a ditch. The tipping had gone on for 15 years but the magistrate was reported to have refused to accept that the offence had been committed intentionally by the company. That case represented the county council's first prosecution under the Act.[13]

In 1977 Aqua Descaling Co. Ltd was fined £2,000 plus £500 costs and Metro Waste Disposal Company Ltd was fined £2,250 plus £500 costs by Wolverhampton Crown Court for offences under the Deposit of Poisonous Waste and Control of Pollution Acts. (Both companies had the same registered address in Bilston.) But a former director of Metro received a two-year suspension of a twelve-month sentence and £400 fine for charges relating to unlawful tipping at two sites in Wolverhampton. Furthermore, two years earlier in 1975 Aqua was fined £250 plus £500 costs at Wolverhampton Magistrates Court under the Deposit of Poisonous Waste Act. In 1975 and 1976 Metro received fines of £50 plus £10 costs and was charged with the same penalties for three further offences.[14]

So these examples sit uncomfortably alongside the claims of those who advocate the practical value of penalties. Further evidence comes from the Keep Britain Tidy Group which calculated that 'Although the maximum fine under the Litter Acts is £100, the average fine during 1977 was £15.15'.[15]

Across the whole range of pollution offences, not only do reports of court hearings suggest that authorities use this device relatively infrequently but also that even if prosecutions are successfully brought, the enforcement value of the penalties is doubtful, particularly since they are often well below the maximum allowed. Evidence that known offences are ignored by the enforcement authorities is hard to come by. Evidence that non-legal actions are taken to enforce policies is more readily available. Persuasion, discussion, support and co-operation are the sorts of terms many interested parties prefer to use in describing how they go about improving adherence to policies. The case study material has illustrated this in several instances, where the activities of firms and individuals need to be constrained by public authorities in the interests of pollution control.[16]

But for the purpose of understanding how successfully, how effectively the policies are enforced, we also need more objective evidence of the success rate of informal techniques, and not surprisingly this is hard to pin down. One area where such a debate has been quite controversial concerns the role of the Alkali Inspectorate in enforcing the provisions of the Alkali Acts. This was raised in Chapter 7,[17] and a further aspect of it is particularly relevant here. The Inspectorate is a small group with a big task to do. It copes by vesting its Inspectors with a lot of discretion to interpret and enforce the Acts on the basis of the 'best-practicable-means' instrument. Certain protection from publicity of Inspectors' activities with firms is legally backed, and they also have the power to prosecute factories and works.[18] McLoughlin quotes figures from the Chief Alkali Inspector's Annual Report showing that the numbers of complaints about scheduled works exceeded 200 in 1971 and 300 in 1972. He says: 'It is therefore doubtful if the number of infractions recorded (28 and 58 respectively) is realistic.'[19] He also observes: 'enforcement is by advice and persuasion rather than coercion . . . the use of extra-legal pressures, especially when applied behind closed doors, is open to criticism on the grounds that the person under pressure does not have the advantage of the safeguards normally given to a citizen who finds himself opposed by a powerful public authority.'[20] On the other hand, 'the alkali inspector is not responsible to the local community. He is subject to control by the Secretary of State, who in turn is responsible to Parliament. Inspectors are responsive to publicity and pressure on a national scale, but far less responsive to local opinion. For this reason some authorities would like to see control of smoke, grit and dust from scheduled works transferred to them.'[21]

Hill and Mason's study found that 'the Alkali Inspectorate considers its major function to be the *education of industry* rather than the enforcement of standards and thus the solution of problems in *co-operation* with industry . . . such an approach is far removed from the punitive nature of law enforcement which applies in criminal law, and, being couched in the professional language of the industrial chemist or fuel technologist, and surrounded by a veil of secrecy designed to protect trade secrets, is a very covert process'.[22]

Ogus and Richardson also recognised the importance of the relationship between 'the formal definitions of unlawful conduct and the *de facto* standards adopted by the agencies who are responsible for enforcing them'. They suggest 'what we must be prepared to consider within the context of a general discussion of standard-setting are deliberate attempts by the legislature to apply *formal* obstacles to the prosecution process as a method of establishing standards which otherwise are not made explicit'.[23] This raises the question of control over enforcement that can be obtained by the way in which the policy instrument is formulated. Many observers have from time to time suggested that imposing a general duty on individuals not to cause pollution would provide a more comprehensive and flexible legal framework for policies than current arrangements permit.[24] They could cite the Alkali Acts as examples where the formal obstacles to enforcement built in to the legislation operate against the interests of those whom the Act is meant to serve.[25] This casts doubt on the purity of the legislature's intentions, and could imply undue pressure has been brought to bear, or that the public interest is not as sacred as we have been led to believe.[26]

Either way, the valuable message for this discussion of enforcement is that examination of the instrument agencies use for enforcement may be a significant factor in explaining how successful they are at enforcing the policies in question. This is a separate, but related, issue to that of the discretion that legal and other agencies can employ in acting on the powers that they possess under statutes. It concerns the formal, structural impediments to enforcement rather than the informal, discretionary variations that are possible.

Sanctions and Incentives

As the quote concerning site licences indicated,[27] the threat of removing a private contractor's licence to continue his business was perceived as a useful tool to ensure obedience. These sorts of sanctions are often available and form a common style in interorganisational relations. They may not be explicit—much depends on the particular policy in question. For example in Part II of the Control of Pollution Act, the right of the public to obtain information about water authorities' own discharges, coupled with their right to prosecute the authority if it breaches its own consent conditions appears to be acting as a powerful incentive to water authorities to improve their sewage treatment. The water authorities have said the idea of being subject to public prosecution is disagreeable to them and they have suggested it opens the door to malicious environmentalists who want to make life difficult for the authorities.[28] Nevertheless, in anticipation of the introduction of these sections of the Act, many authorities have as a priority been concentrating on bringing their sewage effluents into line with expected consent conditions. A strong incentive is at work.

Positive reasons can be advanced for favouring enforcement through sanctions and incentives. Particularly in cases where absolute standards are difficult to identify and apply, the more pragmatic responses that these informal enforcement devices provoke may in effect be more useful. As M.J. Hill has observed:

> Legislators are concerned to prevent *dangerous* driving, to ensure that food is *pure*, and that factories are *safe*. The provision of clear cut rules to define what is safe or dangerous, pure or polluted, is often difficult. It may be that legislators need the help of the experts who are to enforce the law to provide some specific rules. In this sense discretion may be limited at a later date when experience of enforcement enables explicit rules to be devised.[29]

Notes

1. For further discussion see, for example, P.S. James, *Introduction to English Law*, 9th edn (Butterworths, London, 1976).

2. J. McLoughlin, *The Law Relating to Pollution* (Manchester University Press, Manchester, 1972).

3. Hill draws attention to 'the many ways in which the activities of the State impinge upon the public . . .' and the 'kinds of relationship between the individual and the State which have developed as the State has increasingly tried to control its citizens, to provide benefits and services for them, and to plan on their behalf'. M.J. Hill, *The State, Administration and the Individual* (Fontana, London, 1976), p. 11.

4. See M.J. Hill, *Varieties of Discretion: their Characteristics and the Scope for their Control*, Public Administration Bulletin (December 1975), pp. 72-84 for a review of various approaches.

5. Glyn Perry, Chairman, South-West and South Wales group, ISWM, in personal interview with the author.

6. R.I. Burrows, Environmental Health Officer Sheffield, at seminar Implementing the Control of Pollution Act, SAUS, Bristol, 1979.

7. See for example Lord Ashby's remarks, House of Lords, vol. 347, col. 35.

8. *Municipal Engineering* (5 June 1979), pp. 12-13.

9. Noise Advisory Council, *Neighbourhood Noise* (HMSO, London, 1971), para. 190.

10. J. Bugler, *Polluting Britain* (Penguin, Harmondsworth, 1972), p. 172.

11. Department of the Environment, *Pollution Control in Great Britain: How*

it Works, Pollution Paper no. 9 (HMSO, London, 1978), para. 173. However, the Criminal Law Act 1977 has provided, generally speaking, that the penalty on summary conviction of an offence triable either summarily or on indictment is £1,000 (or such greater sum as may be substituted for it to take account of inflation).

12. Rt. Hon. Peter Walker MP, Secretary of State for the Environment, House of Commons, 3 March 1972, cols. 909-10.

13. *Municipal Engineering* (28 May 1976), p. 824.

14. *Municipal Engineering* (8 November 1977), p. 1048.

15. Keep Britain Tidy Group, *Annual Report 1978* (Brighton, 1979), p. 18.

16. See Chapter 8 Figure 8.2, p. 156.

17. See Chapter 7, p. 140.

18. J. McLoughlin, *The Law and Practice relating to Pollution Control in the United Kingdom* (Graham and Trotman, London, 1976), p. 70.

19. Ibid., p. 65.

20. Ibid., pp. 56-7.

21. Ibid., p. 71.

22. M.J. Hill and C. Mason, *Pollution Control – Implementation and Norm-setting* (SAUS, Bristol, 1979), mimeo, p. 21.

23. G.M. Richardson and A.I. Ogus, 'The Regulatory Approach to Environmental Control', paper presented at CES Conference on Urban Law, Queen's College, Oxford, June 1978, p. 3.

24. For example, Lady White raised this in connection with the Protection of the Environment Bill when she said 'Nowhere is there any general declaration of a general duty to avoid pollution or to take this into account in decisions reached by public bodies.' House of Lords, 27 November 1973, vol. 347, col. 21. See also Chapter 6, p. 128.

25. 'pollution control involves many difficult and debatable decisions, and governments and others in authority are unlikely always to judge correctly.' Department of the Environment, *Pollution: Nuisance or Nemesis* (HMSO, London, 1972), para. 295.

26. However, others could argue that as far as criminal law is concerned, a general duty not to cause pollution would simply be unenforceable, unless it went on to say precisely what kinds of conduct were to give rise to criminal liability. If, however, the provision of a general duty required the consent of the Director of Public Prosecution to a prosecution this would not be an obstruction to the enforcement of the law since the provision is intended to restrain unsuccessful prosecutions.

27. See p. 179 above.

28. See Chapter 5, p. 112.

29. Hill, *Varieties of Discretion*, p. 75.

11 IMPROVING POLLUTION CONTROL

In 1979 the OECD published a report analysing the progress made by member countries in meeting the 'heavy pressures imposed on the environment' by the expansion of human activity in the decade which ended in 1975. The report found that 'evidence of the damage it was causing heightened public awareness of the environment and led to strenuous demands for a better environment. Governments reacted by passing laws and setting up new institutions to control pollution, manage natural resources and improve towns as places in which to live.'[1]

Some progress has been made, but not equally in each member country. Overall though, the cost has only been moderate: 'National resources allocated to pollution abatement were nowhere estimated to be higher than 1.7% of gross domestic product in the mid-seventies.'[2] Table 11.1 shows some of the areas of success and of deterioration.

Table 11.1: Success and Deterioration in Pollution Control

	Areas of Success	Areas of Deterioration
WATER	reduced pollution by solids and biodegradable oxidisable matter	increasing concern over drinking water; more widespread lake pollution
AIR	reduced pollution by sulphur dioxide particles, and improved control over carbon monoxide	concern over photochemical oxidants and nitrogen oxide emissions
NOISE	–	more pervasive and unaltered greater numbers exposed to levels interfering with their daily life
LAND	reduced flows of persistent chemicals (DDT, PCBs etc)	–

But the OECD report also points to some new challenges to emerge from the experience of recent years:

1. Action on a limited set of pollutants has led to identification of a wider range of potentially damaging substances.
2. Emissions from point sources (e.g. chimneys, sewage outfalls) have often dropped but those from diffused sources are increasing.

186

3. Although concentrations of pollutants at one place have often been reduced, some (e.g. sulphur compounds transported long distances in the air) are now affecting much wider areas.
4. Although human exposure to intense short-term loads of pollution has generally decreased, long-term exposure that may give rise to genetic changes, cancer and congenital abnormalities is requiring increasing attention.
5. More accidents involving toxic substances have been occurring (including oil spills at sea), causing increasing environmental damage and economic losses.

But the OECD report warns its member governments that

> further increases in incomes, mobility and trends to suburban expansion, second homes and more spread out forms of industrial production . . . are likely to add to demands for land and energy. Such changes coupled with higher levels of education can in turn be expected to increase public support for environmental measures. Thus it will not be enough to go on applying effort where it has been successful and intensifying it where it has not. Future efforts will have to be set in the context of social and economic change . . .[3]

These observations and forecasts have interesting implications for the future of the Control of Pollution Act and related pollution control policies. The purpose of this chapter is to draw together the observations of reports such as the OECD's quoted above with the insights available from the earlier chapters on instruments for policy and enforcement. In other words, this chapter will place the practical aspects of developing and implementing pollution control policies in the theoretical context of the systems and processes that have been outlined.

As far as the Control of Pollution Act 1974 is concerned, the time-scale for making all its provisions available remains uncertain at the time of writing (Winter 1979). The major determining factor is claimed to be the public expenditure consequences of the provisions. In addition, the rate at which work under already activated sections of the legislation proceeds is also strongly influenced by the burden of expenditure or other demands on resources that the relevant agencies perceive them to make. In very simple terms then, it could be said that pollution control policy implementation is a function of public expenditure policy. But that does not necessarily explain why relatively uncostly aspects of the policies may still be neglected or alternative ways of facilitating and financing the policies may not be explored.

Taking the four case studies, they illustrate these features quite well. First, for toxic wastes, the preparations for introducing regulations under Section 17 to replace the Deposit of Poisonous Waste Act 1972 do not appear to have faltered. Consultations with interested parties about the consignment note system have happened broadly according to the plan the DoE set itself. Administrative problems have not arisen. But difficulties over the scientific and technical descriptions for toxic wastes have emerged and are taking time to deal with. The regulations may not be ready therefore early in 1980 as the DoE suggested originally. Public expenditure consequences for the deposit of toxic wastes on land are significant, but they are not new. Money and resources already have to be devoted by the central and local agencies concerned, under the 1972 Act's rules. Indeed, it is hoped by the DoE that the administrative costs of the new system to private industry as well as public agencies will be more economic than at present. So the policy for handling toxic waste disposal is being formulated according to plan, and cannot be assessed much more because it has yet to be put into practice. Observations about the policy instrument, enforcement and effectiveness are impossible to make, except by way of speculation at this stage, which would not be particularly helpful.

The second case involves the EEC Bathing Water Directive, and this became rather a cliff-hanger. The requirement contained in the directive, that member states should report by December 1979 about steps taken to introduce the measures nationally, was only just complied with by the UK. Potentially, the public expenditure consequences of this policy are considerable, not only because water authorities might need to invest substantial resources in improvements to sewage treatment plants if they are to meet the more stringent quality standards required by the directive, but also because the timescale for achieving the standards is set at 1985. This is sooner than the water authorities would like, in the context of shortage of funds, given their own chosen priorities to improve river quality and control industrial pollution, which might have to be postponed.

If the UK government had decided not to act promptly on the directive, that could have been interpreted as the subjugation of pollution control policy to public expenditure policy. But other explanations could also be advanced. The negotiations amongst national governments and between them and the EEC institutions have been shown to concern matters other than the substance of the policies in question. The Bathing Water Directive could have been used as ammunition to further other ends, or (as it now appears) it may be made to play the role of sacrificial victim in the pursuit of a 'higher' policy intention (such as the pursuit of EEC agreement that the UK's budget contribution should be reduced). So implementation of the policy has already shown itself to be vulnerable in the UK, but what longer-term consequences this will have are difficult to predict. Certainly the instruments for policy have been shown by the UK interests to have several features (e.g. the designation of beaches, the methods of measuring and monitoring water quality) that can be fundamentally criticised for offering undue obstacles to the achievement of the desired ends. In addition, enforcement of the policy has been shown to be susceptible to pressure from other relevant interests (e.g. the local tourist authorities, environmentalists). But equally, it could be argued that the policy instruments are as subject to criticism as this because of the inadequacy of UK representatives in promoting and protecting UK interests during the course of negotiations over the directive.

In the background too is the fact that Part II of the Control of Pollution Act is still not in force, and until it is, the legal powers of the water authorities and their responsibilities in relation to the directive are less than absolutely clear. Whatever else could be said to complicate the implementation of this policy, it is also evident that the lack of a really strong will or lobby amongst the agencies concerned to ensure predictable progress is a significant determinant. The fact that in the UK, neither bathing water quality nor enthusiastic involvement in EEC policies are a matter of general public priority is in part an explanation of the patchy implementation. Together with the other features just mentioned, there seems little reason to anticipate much enthusiastic action on this particular policy beyond that legally required.

Moving on to the third case, noise abatement zones show more evidence of implementation and for obvious reasons. Not only have the relevant sections of the Control of Pollution Act been in force since 1976, but the chosen instrument is familiar and acceptable to the enforcement agencies.[4] As the study has shown, noise abatement zones are gradually being set up. Their public expenditure consequences are not considerable, so this tends to confirm the interpretation of pollution control policy as a function of public expenditure policy.[5]

What is less clear is whether the implementation of the NAZ policy could or should have been different and whether or not that would have made it a better or more effective policy. Obviously progress at introducing the NAZs could be quicker and more widespread. But the discretionary nature of the instrument obscures the interpretations that could be made about the rate of progress. Unlike the Bathing Water Directive, there is consent among the interested parties for the desirability and importance of noise control policies. But like the toxic wastes case, the policy has possibly unwelcome consequences for the private sector polluters if, as a result, they become subject to greater control or interference by public sector agencies. Also, the technical features of the problem are relevant for enforcement since incentives offered by obtaining noise control do not appear to be strong. In other words the benefits of noise control are not directly experienced by the enforcement agencies, thus offering little incentive to do more. The bodies bearing the burden of action (e.g. firms that have to install noise insulation plant) also do not benefit directly—indeed they suffer directly by having to pay for the insulation. Whether they or the enforcement agency are influenced by the indirect benefits they receive (e.g. fewer complaints from residents, workers and residents less troubled by noise) is difficult to establish, and this is a particular quality of noise—that its polluting effects are difficult to identify precisely.

The last case concerns information about industrial air pollution, and this contradicts the public expenditure arguments. To introduce the policy, neither public nor private sector agencies would be involved in significantly new or increased expenditure. Yet progress has undoubtedly been minimal, even though the provisions have been in force for some time. Against this it can be said that the discretionary nature of the instrument (as for NAZs) makes it hard to establish what is a 'fast' or 'slow' rate of progress. But even so there is little in the policy instrument or the enforcement arrangements to deter implementation. Nor is technical complexity the issue. After all, the policy simply concerns release of certain information to the public.

A more likely explanation for the pattern of implementation concerns the interorganisational relationships. This policy shows particularly well the complexity of relations not only between public sector agencies (the DoE, local authorities, the Alkali Inspectorate) but also how private sector firms and public environmentalist groups become involved. Although the policy instrument itself appears sensible (local committees with representatives from each of the relevant interests), the consequences of the policy seem unwelcome. Not only may there be reluctance by firms to disclose what pollution they are producing. There may be unwillingness by local authorities to get involved if they think this will force them to be more vigilant. Or in some cases the Alkali Inspectorate's position may be perceived as being too powerful to welcome this kind of alternative approach.[6] In other places environmentalist groups or the general public may be less interested in exercising their rights to become involved in implementing the policy than in knowing that the rights have been established.[7]

These are just some of the speculative ideas about why the policy has seen little action. The other important one was mentioned in Chapter 7 itself and it is that perhaps the policy can be regarded as effective just because it exists, rather than because it is the subject of active efforts. Such an argument stresses the importance of policy formulation in the process, indicating that the particular achievement is to get the policy agreed.[8] If that is true, then even if little more evidence of the use of powers in Sections 79-83 appears, the policy may be judged to be effective because the principles it sets out, the rights it creates, the framework of interorganisational relationships it acknowledges, is the achievement. Enforcement becomes insignificant.

The case study material can be used to point out other aspects of the future for pollution control policies. For example, the importance of relations between central and local government agencies should not be underestimated. In particular, a general election followed by a change of government can suddenly bring about new priorities, and alter expectations. The 1979 election replaced the Labour Government with a new Conservative one, pledged to cut public expenditure, reduce bureaucracy and red tape, and encourage individual effort and enterprise. It quickly announced proposals to loosen the controls central government has over local government's actions, and listed several provisions of the Control of Pollution Act which would be repealed (these are mainly concerned with approving actions or confirming decisions).[9] It also decided to delay further the implementation of sections of the Act still waiting to become operational (e.g. the litter control powers, Sections 12-14 and Section Section 1 concerning local authorities' overall duty to control the disposal of waste).[10]

It has reserved its position on the introduction of Part II even though water authorities had been working to the December 1979 deadline set by the previous government, with only a few months in hand. These changes can increase or decrease confidence amongst local agencies; on the one hand they may welcome a government that seems prepared to take strong and decisive actions. On the other hand they may resent the alterations in expectations that such central actions may impose. In some cases local agencies may feel their longer experience of the policy problems puts them in a better position to determine the best way forward than the central agencies—which may be far more influenced by questions of short-term political expediency.

It is certainly clear that pollution control policies are no more immune from party political pressures or motives of expediency than any other area of public policy. Despite the large measure of agreement about the importance of protecting the environment, progress to date suggests that future policies will continue to be used within the policy system as vehicles of the power relationship between central and local government.[11] Rates of progress, selection of priorities, levels of interest and enthusiasm can all be expected to reflect the central-local relations obtaining. The same can be said of relations between public sector agencies and the private commercial and industrial sector.

The case studies have shown how important this dimension is, given the fact that so much pollution is produced by private firms, and the public sector agencies then try to impose controls. The picture of industry as a selfish, heartless giant interested only in making the most profit for the least outlay, unconcerned about damage to the environment or poor working and living conditions still persists in some people's minds. Despite the recognition that the benefits of industrial enterprise are shared indirectly by the whole community, the suspicion in which industry is held by certain public sector agencies cannot be overlooked. To some extent this is justified by the careless opportunism of a small number of firms who really do disregard the public interest and behave irresponsibly. But most industries have woken up to their obligations in this respect and try to impose and maintain acceptable standards.

This does not mean that the problems will disappear. Even if all sections of industry were environmentally conscious and worked to high standards of practice, that would not eliminate the tensions between the public and private sectors. Their priorities are bound to differ. Their short- and long-term objectives may well be in conflict. Their preferred methods of working towards objectives may well not coincide. These are just some of the reasons why pollution control policies in the future should expect to run into problems where public-private sector relations are concerned. But that is not to say steps cannot be taken to anticipate or reduce these problems.

In terms both of instruments for policy and enforcement, several lessons are clear. Consultations and the exchange of information between the two sectors have shown themselves to be valuable, particularly because they can improve trust. Explicit instruments with less discretionary elements are welcomed by industry when it fears unfair treatment. Flexible instruments though are preferred so that changes can be made where experience indicates the sense of this. Government agencies generally resent industry's assumptions that policy formulation in a sphere such as pollution can be quick and decisive. Local government though welcomes instruments that are simple to introduce and operate. Enforcement certainly could be improved if agencies were determined to do this (perhaps because of greater public pressure), and if there were fewer avoidable obstacles. For example, it is clear that not only are the maximum permitted penalties for pollution offences rarely imposed by the courts, but in some cases these are insufficient to deter the offender. That suggests not only some failure on the part of the judiciary to comprehend the consequences of their actions (i.e. to reduce enforcement agencies' faith in the effectiveness of legal remedies), but also that Parliament needs better advice on setting penalties that take account of offenders' differential ability to pay. It seems wasteful of public and private sector agencies' time if the methods of enforcement prove incapable of upholding policies and deterring or punishing offenders.

The role of public opinion is of course another vital influence on future pollution control policies. The case material and earlier chapters have shown how the very fact that environmental pollution became a policy issue owes much to the expressions of concern from individuals and organisations representing the general public.[12] The Control of Pollution Act itself could be said to be a monument to the public conscience of society in so far as it embodies the framework for policies that can reflect public demands for protection of the environment.[13] But public opinion is a fickle thing to rely on. It is susceptible to fashion, whim, persuasion, manipulation and apathy. During the 1960s and 1970s as far as pollution is concerned public opinion has grown and declined in vigour. Today in the UK, more members of the public now recognise the significance of pollution — awareness has increased. But amongst the vociferous and organised groups within the community, action has changed from being a concerted attack on international policies and priorities to a variety of more local and specialised endeavours, concerning discrete neighbourhood problems.[14] Another feature of groups of environmentalists is that their scientific and technical expertise is increasing. The recent handbooks produced by Social Audit and Friends of the Earth[15] are widely acknowledged to be well informed and proficient in assisting the public to understanding recent legislation and exercising their rights under it. In a related field, the part played by Friends of the Earth in the Windscale Enquiry was as sophisticated as any of the other interests represented.[16] So the charge of ignorance or amateurism can no longer be made against these organisations. Nor is it possible easily to dismiss the protests of residents' and community groups which can be expected when plans for waste disposal sites, factories, quarries, manufacturing plants and other land-use developments are brought before local authorities and planning enquiries.

But for the short-term future it seems that the fire has gone out of broadly-based initiatives or campaigns that challenge broad policies on a national or international scale. Public opinion is less interested, too, in lending continuous support to problems of long standing, such as litter abatement or river pollution. The sorts of issues that do now seem to be attracting public support concern specific pollutants (e.g. lead, oil, noise from a new airport) or specific vulnerable targets (e.g. whales, seals) and the whole question of pollution in the form of radioactivity resulting from the use of nuclear energy for power is of very topical concern.[17]

However, each of these trends could easily alter, and the unpredict-ability of public opinion is the point to note for future pollution control policies. Even so, it will continue to be important to distinguish between the role of public opinion locally, in response to specific policies or developments, and the broader national or international issues that may attract public attention. In both instances the force of public opinion is a factor in the implementation of policies, positively (as in the bathing water case, where potential public involvement has acted as an incentive on the water authorities to pursue certain objectives) and negatively (as in the industrial air pollution case, where the lack of public pressure seems to explain the lack of action). In all this, the role of the media cannot be ignored although it too is difficult to pin down precisely. The case studies have shown the low level of coverage (in quantity or quality) by newspapers, magazines, radio and television for the continuing policy issues raised by the Control of Pollution Act. Media interest is more readily attracted for the dramatic one-off incidents that arise, although in such cases it can be extremely powerful as a force in the policy system. The circumstances in which the Deposit of Poisonous Waste Act came to be passed bear testimony to this.[18]

The specialist technical press do of course keep a more consistent eye on pollution policies and can be relied upon not to miss major developments. However these journals do little to relate pollution to the broader economic and social context, and so tend to emphasise the insularity of professional and specialist readers' attitudes. In so far as these people are a force in the policy process, it matters how free they are to adapt to change or welcome alternative approaches to the achieve-ment of policy objectives. The toxic waste study showed how entrenched the attitudes of local authority waste disposal staff had become over the years. Their specialist journals and professional bodies could not be said to be challenging out-of-date attitudes all that vigorously.[19] Equally the bathing water study showed how professionals concerned with water quality found the activities of the politicians and bureaucrats in the EEC incomprehensible in terms of choice of policy instruments.[20] In both cases the media could have done more to show these interests in their practical context, and to question long-held prejudices. For example, the EEC directive needs to be seen as much a product of the international political bargaining process as it is a means to improve bathing water quality. Equally the fact that private waste disposal contractors are a legitimate and necessary part of the scene needs to be willingly acknowledged if local authorities want these firms to collaborate.

It is in the area of attitudes and perceptions that the media play their most important part, even though they do have a job to do in presenting information. This is not, naturally, peculiar to the pollution field.[21] But in speculating about the conditions in which future pollution policies will be implemented, it seems clear that both national and local specialist and generalist media could be used far more by all the interested parties to manipulate attitudes and inform perceptions. Instead of regarding the media as a necessary but rather unwelcome feature, each party could increase its efforts to employ media support at different stages in the policy process. The opportunities are there, at least for as long as the people and organisations in the media remain open to suggestion and welcome outside guidance.

Something that is, however, distinctive about pollution is that its effects ignore national or administrative boundaries. Therefore the policy system needs to find ways of ensuring that control policies are at the least not invalidated by neighbours' policies, and at best, designed to complement and enhance them. Thus the activities of the EEC, OECD and United Nations in this field are all concerned to improve international collaboration, and this can be expected to continue. Not only are valuable rewards available as a result for economic policies (e.g. the continuing prominence given to harmonisation of international trade competition), but strategic interests seem also to be served (e.g. by strengthening the bonds between member states of the EEC and thereby upholding shared policies in other areas such as defence or *détente*).[22] The EEC's Environmental Action Programme is a much more adventurous and forward-looking package of objectives than any single member state can claim to have. The OECD studies on environmental policies have also provided a more thorough and objective basis for evaluation of policies than individual countries could achieve. It therefore seems likely that initiatives will come increasingly from international organisations to control pollution and to harmonise policies, particularly those dealing with widespread hazards (e.g. lead, radioactivity) or where policies with significant economic consequences (e.g. elimination of certain processes or substances because of their risk) are called for.

Another feature of the national-international dimension is that comparisons of different policy instruments or enforcement arrangements can be made. This is not necessarily as useful as it might be because the reasons why one scheme works or does not work in one country may not apply in another place — or they may not have been correctly identified in the first place. A useful example here is the Environmental Protection Agency (EPA) set up in the United States in 1970 as a specialist agent to enforce policies made by Congress to control pollution. The EPA has often been cited in the UK and elsewhere in Europe as the sort of device that is needed to ensure pollution control progresses satisfactorily.[23] On the face of it the arguments are persuasive. The EPA's efforts are concentrated on the policy area in question. It is staffed by a mixture of specialists and administrators so that the necessary knowledge and skills are available. It has a sizeable budget.[24] Yet a recent report on its activities painted a disturbing picture: 'EPA has set permanent standards for exposure and effluent limits for only four hazardous air pollutants and six toxic water pollutants in the eight years it has been in existence.' As far as its responsibilities for enforcing the 1977 Toxic Substances Control Act are concerned, 'Bureaucratic delay and inertia are permanent features of the process: pressure from affected industries is constantly applied: the statutes are often unworkable from the start. As a result, prompt regulatory action is virtually non existent, and when action does occur it is usually at the prodding of outside citizen groups.' The EPA appears to have been taking a passive role 'acting as judge and not prosecutor in environmental protection'. The report's author therefore concludes: 'The agency is impelled to act only by the deadlines that Congress has imposed in legislation, as well as by the threat of lawsuits to enforce the deadlines. If no outside lawsuit is initiated, time has a way of slipping past.' The fact that EPA officials actually welcome this prodding from environmentalists is shown by grants of over $100,000 which it has given to at least two such organisations. Enforcement of the policies is therefore much less effective than it was intended to be, and the role of the EPA has become much more passive:

Instead of acting themselves according to an ethic of environmental protection, the regulators are typically acted upon by outsiders performing their tasks for them, shielding them from political troubles by forcing adherence to the laws through litigation. In this view, enforcement is a term most relevant to the bureaucrats, not industry, to do what they are supposed to. Long accused of chronic indecisiveness, the chief characteristics of the EPA . . . may better be termed chronic avoidance.[25]

The example of the EPA has been quoted at some length because it illustrates so powerfully the elements of failure of policy implementation when errors of policy-making are made. These will be returned to in the final chapter. What the EPA case also shows for future pollution control policies is that no matter how pressing or how important or how welcome certain policy objectives are, the instruments and enforcement agencies, the interorganisational relations and the climate of public opinion will determine the effectiveness with which that policy is implemented. So even if a specialist agency seems a good idea, it will not necessarily work, even if some of the problems encountered in the USA are avoided. Pollution charges are another instrument being considered in a number of places, and the experience of Holland and Germany is often quoted here. Although it is undoubtedly useful to examine alternatives, applications from one set of conditions into another need to be made less simplistically than has often been the case, if unnecessary difficulties are to be avoided.

Notes

1. OECD, *The State of the Environment in Member Countries* (OECD, Paris, 1979), p. 140.
2. Ibid., p. 141.
3. Ibid., p. 142.
4. See Chapter 9, p. 162.
5. The reason given by the DoE for being able to implement the noise abatement zone provisions early on was that they were discretionary and would not involve significant public expenditure. *Pollution Control in Great Britain: How it Works*, Pollution Paper no. 9 (HMSO, London, 1978), Annex B, para. 1, p. 94.
6. This is the implication in the guidance produced by Friends of the Earth: R. Macrory and B. Zaba, *Polluters Pay: The Control of Pollution Act explained* (DoE, London, 1978), pp. 67-8.
7. This would confirm Richardson and Jordan's observation that 'Once a decision is reached, once a policy is announced, once an Act is passed, there is a tendency for the issue concerned to leave the political agenda. In the eye of the public "informed" by the media, "the problem" has been "dealt with". There is little concern about what actually *happens* after that point.' J.J. Richardson and A.G. Jordan, *Governing Under Pressure* (Martin Robertson, London, 1979), p. 143. See also A. Downs, 'Up and Down with Ecology'.
8. According to J.F. Garner, for example, 'Much has been achieved merely by

the passing of the Act of 1974 . . .'. *Local Government Chronicle* (13 January 1978), p. 33. Richardson and Jordan quote J.E.S. Hayward's view that the test of a good policy has become whether it is *agreed*, not whether it is likely to succeed by some objectively defined criteria. J.J. Richardson and A.G. Jordan, *Governing Under Pressure*, p. 175.

9. Department of the Environment, *Central Government Controls Over Local Authorities*, Cmnd. 7634 (HMSO, London, September 1979).

10. DoE Press Release, *Waste Control Plans Deferred: Overriding Priority for Public Expenditure Restraint* (17 September 1979).

11. According to Stanyer and Smith there are four strong pressures towards central intervention in local government affairs: (A) the demand for honest and efficient government, and (B) for equality between areas; (C) geographical mobility and the growth of mass media provokes impatience with variations; and (D) there are intrinsically regional and national aspects of service provision. In contrast they describe four factors promoting local autonomy: (E) statutes allocating local powers; (F) popular elections; (G) independent powers of taxation; and (H) territorial responsibilities. They conclude: 'Local authorities are autonomous but not sovereign; the centre is powerful but not omnipotent.' J. Stanyer and B. Smith, *Administering Britain* (Fontana, London, 1976), p. 128.

12. See Chapter 3, pp. 29-30 and the case studies.

13. According to Garner, the Act 'was greeted by many as a great step forward in the war against the pollution of the environment caused by our highly industrialised society . . . Clearly it was a step forward of importance, if only because it recognised that legislative and administrative measures are essential if the war is to be won.' J. Garner, 'Control of Pollution', *Local Government Chronicle* (13 January 1978), p. 32.

14. In general though 'the danger of entrusting the environment to the mandate of public opinion is that most people ascribe a higher priority to the present than to the future'. Department of the Environment, *Pollution: Nuisance or Nemesis?* (HMSO, London, 1972), para. 288.

15. M. Frankel, *The Social Audit Pollution Handbook* (Macmillan, London, 1978) and R. Macrory and B. Zaba, *Polluters Pay* (Friends of the Earth, London, 1978). Referring to these the Deputy Director General of the National Water Council commented 'Anyone who has studied [the books] will appreciate that there are well-informed critics around who are likely to make effective use of this information.' D.L. Walker, *The Need to Review Consents*, Paper given at conference on the *Implications of the Control of Pollution Act 1974 Part II* (Oyez International Business Communications Ltd, London, December 1978).

16. And Friends of the Earth 'emerged as the cardinal adversary in these hearings'. *New Scientist*, quoted in 'Who's Who in the Environment. 2', *ENDS Report* (19 February 1979), pp. 10-14.

17. Garner, 'Control of Pollution', observed 'Much of the enthusiasm for action which was noticeable in the early 1970s seems to have in some measure evaporated'. See also A. Downs, 'Up and Down with Ecology'.

18. See Chapter 4, pp. 56-7.

19. See Chapter 4, p. 77.

20. See Chapter 5, p. 108.

21. But the case has been very clearly made in connection with pollution: 'The press, television and other mass media have a special responsibility. The task of translating into everyday language the subtle behaviour of pollutants in the environment, or of explaining the advantages of sophisticated and flexible control systems over simple emission limits, is a daunting one indeed. So far a relatively small number of specialist writers, journalists and TV and radio producers have responded to this challenge with sensitivity, imagination and responsibility.' Department of the Environment, *Pollution: Nuisance or Nemesis* (HMSO, London, 1972), para. 295. Much of the same could be said for several other public policy areas.

22. Writing about the European Communities' environment programme, Thomas observed it to be 'a question of politics as well as of science. For one thing it enters into virtually every other area of Community policy. The Environmental Protection Service must be deeply concerned with agriculture, industry, transport, urban development, to name only the most immediately obvious.' H. Thomas, 'The Environment', *New Europe* (Autumn 1975), p. 58.

23. One such reference was made by Lady White in criticising the Protection of the Environment Bill, House of Lords, vol. 347, col. 21, 27 November 1973.

24. W.D. Ruckleshaus, 'The Role of the Environmental Protection Agency', *Environmental Affairs* (November 1971), pp. 528-33.

25. R.J. Smith, 'Toxic Substances: EPA and OSHA are Reluctant Regulators', *Science*, vol. 203 (5 January 1979), pp. 28-32.

12 CONCLUSION: EFFECTIVE PUBLIC POLICY

Uncertainty about the benefits of public policy and the effectiveness of the policy-making process have caused increasing interest in implementation. Two routes have been followed here in studying these aspects: evidence from one area of public policy has been examined to highlight relevant characteristics; and aspects of implementation itself have been scrutinised to explore their relevance to the overall process.

Chapter 11 drew together the evidence in order to permit practical observations to be made about future implementation of pollution policies. This chapter is devoted to looking more widely at the whole sphere of public policy generally, in order to clarify the insights that the study has made it possible to assert. The focus is still a practical one though, in the sense that the value of policy analyses such as this should principally be to inform those concerned, whether as practition-

Figure 12.1: Some Important Features of Public Policy Implementation

---

1. Timescale for introducing legal powers
2. Public policy as a function of public expenditure policy
3. Opportunity cost of alternative priorities
4. Policy as a 'sacrificial victim'
5. Value of outside pressure on implementing agencies
6. Consequences of instruments with different discretionary levels
7. Uncertain benefits from action
8. Policy formulation as an end in itself
9. Stability of interorganisational relationships
10. Elements of surprise and power after change of government
11. Images as determinants in interorganisational dealings
12. Value of consultation
13. Possibilities of improving instrument design
14. Learning from enforcement experience
15. Role of public opinion in agenda-setting
16. Recognising trends in different interest groups' perceptions
17. Role of media in informing attitudes and perceptions
18. Benefits of international policy-making
19. Value of international comparisons

---

ers or observers, with the real forces and dimensions that are relevant. But the underlying assumption of this chapter is that the factors to be discussed are relevant to all kinds of public policy whatever the specific subject. These factors are inherent in public policy-making and, therefore, relevant (though in differing proportions) to any example that is put into focus for study.

Figure 12.1 sets out those factors that have been derived from preceding chapters and are generally relevant – they are not set out in any particular order of priority because, as the study has shown, this will vary from case to case. They will be discussed in turn and in a concise form, so that the sequence of points can be easily recognised. It would be possible to say much more about each one, drawing on evidence from earlier chapters and elsewhere in the literature. But in the interests of presenting the collectivity of points briefly and more immediately, this sort of detail has been kept to the very minimum.

The list is by no means exhaustive, but deals with the factors that have been discussed (sometimes more than once) in the earlier chapters.

1. The timescale for introducing legal powers can be selected to suit a number of objectives. The spectrum runs all the way from establishing enabling powers in advance of a specific policy even being articulated, to holding the policy in abeyance indefinitely by deliberately not introducing the necessary legal powers to make it operational. Staggered or phased introduction of legal powers can help to control the expenditure consequences of the policy. It can also allow time for further consultation to iron out persisting difficulties. It can be used to wear down opposition, or to improve details of application. It can be used to dovetail the implementation of policies from different but connected policy areas. International considerations may require or merit a different timescale than a state acting alone might otherwise adopt. These are some of the consequences.

But the important lesson for implementation from this factor is that it gives the central government agency a strong instrument with which to control action. Anything concerning statutory powers has to be agreed by the central institutions of the legislature, and, therefore, an important amount of power is retained at the centre, with the consequent limitations on peripheral exercise of discretion.

2. Public policy can be argued to be a function of public expenditure policy. Certainly in terms of the definition given earlier for public policy, it is intimately related to the use of government money and resources.

The particular force of this factor emerges when agencies need to find arguments to support their inaction or non-decision. The phenomenon is not confined to central agencies — local ones too adopt this rationale, and it is very evident at times of economic difficulty. But not only may the supremacy of public expenditure policy be used to justify implementation activity, it can also come to govern the expectations that other interested parties may have of what is possible. It can reduce pressure or soften opposition by appealing to a wider concern — drawing attention to the economic context within which the particular policy falls.

Although the validity of this factor may be open to challenge, the evidence clearly shows how powerfully it can be used at different points in the policy process to justify a particular approach to implementation.[1]

3. The opportunity cost of alternative priorities needs to be carefully assessed by implementing agencies. This factor draws attention not only to the financial implications of a given policy choice but to the relevance of political or social features too. Thus a lot of energy can be wasted in overcoming opposition to a particular policy because it has been made too high a priority. Equally if an issue is not yet or no longer regarded by interested parties as a high priority, effort put into its implementation may produce disappointing rewards.

In recognising the importance of interorganisational relationships as a feature of implementation this priority factor can be vital to the fate of a policy initiative.

4. Policies can act as 'sacrificial victims' sometimes when, important though they may be, they can be manipulated to serve 'higher' policy intentions. This factor highlights the elements of bargaining and negotiation that often arise in policy implementation. Where issues are contentious or threatening, the ability to deal or barter with policies gives agencies greater flexibility in exerting their power. Again, this factor is not confined to use by central government. It occurs throughout the implementation process where different interest groups need a symbolic way of recognising differential status and power. And where relatively unimportant issues can be given greater value by being used as a form of 'currency' in the policy system.

5. The value of outside pressure on implementing agencies can present a range of possibilities. For those large bureaucratic institutions which inevitably tend towards inertia, outside pressure may be necessary for any action at all on implementing policies to occur. But it may represent for other agencies a troublesome interference with their own chosen methods of getting action. Outside pressure can be encouraged directly, for example through the design of policy instruments that invite active involvement from pressure groups. Or it can be discouraged by curtailing access to information and influence that outside groups are permitted to enjoy.

The evidence shows that definitions of 'outside' pressure may be difficult to make given, in public policy-making, the frequently complex array of interested parties. But this factor can probably be particularly useful when direct pressure (say from the local onto central agencies) runs the risk of creating a bad impression. By permitting forceful pressure groups to take this on, apparently independently, the relative strength of the agencies can be more apparently defined.

6. *Instruments with different levels of discretion* built in to them are available. The possibilities are numercus, running from totally specific and obligatory varieties, to those enabling entire freedom of choice to the implementing agencies. The obvious importance of this factor is that it can permit differential rates and styles of implementation to suit differing local circumstances. It can delegate responsibility away from central agencies where this would be an inappropriate focus. It can improve interorganisational relationships by reducing the amount of central direction and enhancing local autonomy.

But different intentions (in policy terms) need differing amounts of uniformity in implementation. If a national service or standard is the objective of the policy, much discretion in the instrument may undermine this.

7. *Uncertainty about the benefits of action* will often introduce difficulties in assessing implementation. Where the policy cannot, in other words, be proved conclusively to have produced a given result (either because several other possible causal factors exist, or because several other possible causal factors exist, or because the result itself is hard to measure) there is likely to be confusion amongst the interested parties. This factor may well be beyond the control of those involved in the policy system, perhaps because scientific or technical knowledge is insufficient at that point in time. Or the effects of other contextual factors may be such as to obscure the performance of the policy in question.

This factor therefore needs to be identified or eliminated when

assessing implementation. It does commonly occur, although its importance can be exaggerated by parties wishing to delay or confuse further
action.

8. Policy formulation can be an end in itself. In such cases the level of
resulting action may be non-existent or very low. This reflects, in terms
of interorganisational relationships, the symbolic value that policies can
take on. It also undermines the view that policy implementation is
synonymous with action. So before paying undue attention to the kinds
of policy instruments or the methods of enforcement associated with a
policy that has seen little action, it is always worth checking what the
formulation of the policy has involved. Particularly where strongly vested
interests or fundamental shifts of power are concerned, this factor may
be relevant. But against that, it is also worth saying that policy implementation can be wrongly assessed if it is done prematurely. Some policies are
bound by their nature to take a long time to produce observable results.
In such cases a diagnosis of inaction may be faulty, if it is made
unreasonably soon.

It should be recognised that this feature—the symbolic value of
policies and politics and the consequences for action—has been the
subject of significant study, particularly by political scientists. They
have drawn attention to the importance of ambiguity in certain settings
and emphasised the relevance of these very real influences on the policy-
making process.[2] From that position it would be mistaken to suggest
that if all the constraints on implementation were laid bare, then
implementation would necessarily occur more readily or more easily.

9. The stability of interorganisational relationships is a significant
determinant of implementation, often where the value of maintaining
the *status quo* in these terms is greater than the perceived benefits of a
policy that may challenge it. So the comfort of predictable relations may
work against some policies unless there is something in the choice of
instruments or enforcement that can compensate the agencies concerned.
Conversely though, the degree of trust that may have grown out of
well-founded interrelationships can smooth the passage of an otherwise
difficult policy. The lesson for implementation from this factor, therefore, is that in pursuing implementation, the value of stability for each
party must be judged and weighed against the support or disruption of
it that the policy is likely to produce. This can be complex, but the
evidence shows that many pitfalls can be avoided by giving appropriate
attention to this factor at the design stage.

10. After a change of government the evidence shows that central government's relationships with its associated agencies can be radically altered. And this fact can be used to considerable advantage by those who wish to adopt new positions or consolidate existing ones. Those central agencies for example that wish to pull more power back into the centre can do this by making a lot of strong policy statements early on, and using suitable controlling instruments to express these intentions. On the other hand, those local agencies or other interested parties that wish to bend the new government to their way of thinking will take a lot of trouble to bombard the government with advice, information and other vehicles of pressure.

Above all, the election of a new government gives relationships, and assumptions about power, the chance to be realigned and this can have beneficial or damaging effects on particular policies. Although the actual consequences may be difficult to predict, much can be done in anticipation to maximise the desired consequences, as the evidence shows.

11. The images held by one agency of another can have a significant effect on the progress of implementation. These images often concern the quantity of influence or degree of strength that one party assumes another to have. Where the parties are opposed, such stereotypes can develop into caricatures that no longer identify the true position. And as a result, stances of action or inaction can be quite wrongly selected and lead to conflict or confusion that is really avoidable.

The evidence shows that in terms of implementation, understanding what these images contain and clarifying how extensively they are believed can do much to concentrate the energies of those concerned on real rather than imaginary problems. This factor occurs commonly in public policy implementation and is often evident where public and private sector agencies are both concerned.

12. The value of consultation is explicitly recognised in much policy-making now. Especially where the issues tackled by the policy are less than clear cut, or where instruments and enforcement may be difficult to keep simple, consultation with interested parties features prominently. At least it serves to acknowledge the difficulties and emphasise the collective involvement in formulation and implementation. It can lengthen the time before action can occur but this is often a price worth paying when a greater degree of support and consent for the policy may be obtained. On the other hand, consultation can sometimes be used as a sop by those agencies who wish to diffuse opposition by appearing to consider other points of view when their real intention is to ignore contrary positions, or delay meaningful action indefinitely.

In terms of maximising the effective implementation of policies then this factor has to be carefully judged. It is too simple to assume either that some policies do not require consultation or that others need a lot of it. In most areas of public policy, objectives can be defined and arrived at in alternative ways. So the degree of consultation should be explicitly chosen to benefit the timescale of the policy and the sensitivity of its instruments as closely as possible.

13. The design of instruments has already been argued to be of great significance. Not only do some instruments have built-in consequences for interpretation and action, which need to be recognised. But some instruments when put to work in combinations can enhance implement-ation while others can hamper it unnecessarily. The evidence illustrated something of the variety of instruments that are available and suggested that the choice could often be more carefully made to ensure desired outcomes. The decision to adopt a certain instrument just because it is familiar may not always be satisfactory. Equally, designing new and possibly confusing instruments can be wasteful if existing ones can be adapted to do the required job.

In so far as implementation goes, the benefits of choosing instruments may well have been overlooked. It should be noted too that organisations and individuals can act as instruments quite forcefully as well as the more obvious written devices. The concept of instruments for policy can be used to great effect in distinguishing which implementation features of a particular policy may merit further attention.

14. Experience of enforcement in practice can help considerably in clarifying the opportunities that exist to ensure acceptable policy implementation. The evidence drew attention to apparent lack of feed-back between the various agencies concerned with legal enforcement. As a consequence many policies are difficult if not impossible to enforce, and their effect may thereby be diminished. But it is also possible that obstacles can be put in the way of effective enforcement if an interested party wishes the policy limited success.

In general though, public policies often appear to fall short of their potential, and this may be attributed to other reasons (e.g. technical complexity, strong opposition), whereas in fact it may be that the vehicles for enforcement are inappropriate or unnecessarily encumbered.

15. The role of public opinion in agenda-setting is obviously an important factor, not least because public policies are an attempt to serve the public interest. Public opinion on some issues may be ahead of that of government agencies while on other issues government may lead. But the evidence suggested that central and local agencies are considerably influenced by their assumption of the public view on a particular issue, and will often gear their level and style of activity to the public response they anticipate. This has advantages if it keeps otherwise complacent agencies 'on their toes'. But it can act against improvements if public opinion is uncertain, divided or inaudible on certain issues and, therefore, does not exist as a force in the system.

For implementation then a judgement has to be made about the effort to be put into informing public opinion where it is ill informed, or countering it when it may be forcing unwelcome or inadvisable actions on implementing agencies. The fact that public opinion can lead and follow, that it can change unpredictably and drop old interests to nurture new ones needs to be acknowledged.

16. Trends in different interest groups' perceptions (i.e. not just in fashions of public opinion) also need to be recognised. There are quite discernible shifts in the perceived priorities of different agencies over time, and these can inform whether and how they will become involved in developments in policy. The currency of particular concepts (e.g. consumerism, growth) can be quite evident and may do much to determine the passage of certain policies. This draws attention to the 'packaging' of a policy – the words used to describe it, the instruments chosen to express it, and so on. These factors can be manipulated to good effect (and not necessarily subversively) by those parties who are sensitive to them. In so far as the implementation of public policies may principally involve changes in attitudes, this obviously becomes significant.

17. The role of the media in forming attitudes and perceptions is usually powerful, and often underestimated. But it does not always act positively. Many areas of public policy are treated less thoroughly and enthusiastically than they might be because they are poorly understood except by a small number of specialists. Yet the media's ability to handle complex issues, particularly if they do not necessarily involve 'newsworthy' elements, is quite undependable. As a result, not only professional attitudes but the general public's perceptions may remain apathetic or misinformed in areas where their active involvement is needed to improve action.

The evidence has shown several instances where implementation could be understood and modified considerably if greater attention was paid to this factor. The lesson is that the media (generalist as well as specialist) need to be recognised as belonging within the policy system as an integral component, rather than as disinterested or unwelcome observers.

18. The benefits of international policy-making on domestic policy are an interesting factor emerging from the study. While the processes may be lengthy and comparatively cumbersome, given the need to reach agreement between many different views, the advantages seem to be that more radical or novel objectives can be identified. The evidence illustrates the possibility of making international policy a regular influence in this way on domestic activity. However, this can produce unwelcome consequences, particularly if national or local priorities are unduly distorted, or if too much power is perceived to be lost by the agencies concerned.

But for many areas of policy, where problems may appear intractable, the wider forum and context seems able to produce new and welcome alternatives. The implementation consequences can also be complex though, involving instruments and methods of enforcement that may conflict with national custom and practice. So a balance needs to be found, by selecting which policies are appropriate for international action, and also recognising the consequences of widening the practical context for implementation.

19. International comparisons are often made in trying to improve policy formulation — obviously the challenges facing governments are broadly similar in the advanced Western societies. So it is tempting to compare instruments and enforcement, to contrast structural and financial arrangements, and above all to compare performance. The evidence showed that this can be very helpful in assessing national achievements against a wider context. But it can also lead to inappropriate policy action where comparisons have been made too mechanistically or by mistaken analysis of cause and effect. These benefits and pitfalls have, therefore, to be balanced if appropriate solutions to problems are to be chosen.

Notes

1. This factor merits fuller discussion than it has been possible to present, and it is worthy of detailed study and consideration.
2. See: M. Edelman, *Politics as Symbolic Action* (Markham Publishing Co., Chicago, 1971); and Dilys M. Hill, 'Political Ambiguity and Policy: the Case of Welfare', *Social and Economic Administration*, vol. 12, no. 2 (Summer 1978).

INDEX

DAT

The Search for Non-Newtonian Gravity

Ephraim Fischbach   Carrick L. Talmadge

The Search for
Non-Newtonian Gravity

With 58 Illustrations

Ephraim Fischbach
Carrick L. Talmadge
Department of Physics
Purdue University
1396 Physics Building
West Lafayette, IN 47907-1396
USA

Library of Congress Cataloging-in-Publication Data
Fischbach, Ephraim.
    The search for non-Newtonian gravity / Ephraim Fischbach, Carrick
L. Talmadge
        p.   cm.
    Includes bibliographical references and index.
    ISBN 0-387-98490-9 (alk. paper)
    1. Gravitation.   I. Talmadge, Carrick L.   II. Title.
QC178.F53   1998
531'.14—dc21   98-13181

Printed on acid-free paper.

Production managed by Timothy Taylor; manufacturing supervised by Jeffrey Taub.
Camera-ready copy prepared from the authors' LaTeX files.
Printed and bound by Maple-Vail Book Manufacturing Group, York, PA.
Printed in the United States of America.

9 8 7 6 5 4 3 2 1

ISBN 0-387-98490-9 Springer-Verlag New York Berlin Heidelberg   SPIN 10670124

To Janie and Nita for their unending patience and good humor.

Preface

The past several years have witnessed a resurgence of interest in experimental tests of gravity, particularly in the possibility of deviations from the predictions of classical (Newtonian) gravity. This interest was stimulated on the theoretical side by the work of a number of authors who demonstrated that various models suggested the existence of new, relatively weak, intermediate-range forces coexisting with gravity. The resulting net interaction would behave like a modified form of Newtonian gravity whose characteristic signature could include possible deviations from the expected inverse-square law, and a possible violation of the weak equivalence principle (WEP).

These ideas provided part of the stimulus for experimental studies undertaken in the 1970's and 1980's to search for deviations from the inverse-square law. The experimental efforts, which are described in detail in the text, eventually led in 1986 to a reanalysis of the classic Eötvös experiment, which had been designed to compare the accelerations of different pairs of materials to the Earth. It was observed that the Eötvös results suggested that all objects do not necessarily fall at the same rate and, additionally, could be interpreted as hinting at the presence of a new intermediate-range (or "macroscopic") force. The indication in the Eötvös data of an apparent violation of the Weak Equivalence Principle, and the concomitant suggestion of a possible new "fifth force" in nature, encouraged a large number of groups to undertake new tests of both the inverse-square law and WEP.

To date, after more than a decade of experiments, there is no compelling evidence for any deviations from the predictions of Newtonian gravity, or for the presence of a "fifth force." Nonetheless these experiments, which use a variety of imaginative technologies, are likely to continue for the simple reason that most are far from their ultimate limits of sensitivity. Ironically, during the very period when experimentalists were failing to find any evidence for new macroscopic forces, theorists were busy formulating numerous models in which such forces arose naturally. It thus appears that there will be continuing interest in the possibility of new macroscopic forces in the foreseeable future, and hence in tests of Newtonian gravity.

The object of the present book is to describe in detail the ideas that underlie searches for deviations from the predictions of Newtonian gravity. We have focused our attention on macroscopic tests, since the question of gravitational effects in quantum systems would warrant a separate work. Our book is aimed at introducing the subject to graduate students who are interested in studying this question either experimentally or theoretically. To achieve this aim, we have combined a historical development with very detailed technical discussions of the theoretical ideas and experimental results. It is our hope that a student interested in this field will find our book a helpful guide in getting started.

While our book was being written, an excellent history of the searches for a "fifth force" was published by Franklin [FRANKLIN, 1993]. The existence of Franklin's book has allowed us to abbreviate our own historical treatment, and to thus focus our efforts on the *technical questions* which are our primary concern. It is our hope that these books, when read together, will present a fairly complete description of the development of this field. There are, in addition, a number of more popular articles which help to round out the picture, including [SCHWARZSCHILD, 1986, 1988; SCHECTER, 1987; BOSLOUGH, 1989; WILL, 1990]. Additional material can be found in the extensive bibliography contained at the end of this book, as well as in a longer bibliography prepared in conjunction with the present book [FISCHBACH, 1992B].

As we have already noted, our main focus in this book will be on technical questions, both experimental and theoretical. We assume that the reader will have a background in electromagnetism at the level of Jackson's *Classical Electrodynamics* [JACKSON, 1975], in mechanics at the level of Goldstein's *Classical Mechanics* [GOLDSTEIN, 1980], and in relativistic quantum mechanics at the level of Sakurai's *Advanced Quantum Mechanics* [SAKURAI, 1967]. Otherwise we have attempted to make this book self-contained. A number of very helpful technical discussions have appeared recently, including [COOK, 1987, 1988; GILLIES, 1987, 1990, 1992; WILL, 1987, 1993; ADELBERGER, 1991C; FUJII, 1991B; FISCHBACH, 1992A; CHEN, 1993; CIUFOLINI, 1995].

Structure of the Book

After a brief introduction in Chapter 1 to the topic of non-Newtonian gravitation, we provide a detailed study in Chapter 2 of the phenomenology of non-Newtonian interactions. In Chapters 3 and 4 we discuss various paradigms for testing for the presence of violations of the inverse-square law and for violations of the weak equivalence principle. We follow this with a discussion in Chapter 5 of the constraints on the differences in the rate of free-fall of matter versus antimatter. In Chapter 6, we discuss constraints on interactions that couple to the neutral kaon system, and consider in Chapter 7 constraints on spin-dependent interactions. Chapter 8 provides an overview of the current status (April, 1998) of searches for non-Newtonian interactions. A comprehensive bibliography with approximately 450 entries is also provided. Finally, we have included three appendices: In Appendix A we discuss in more technical detail the effects of gravity gradients on torsion balances; in Appendix B we consider the issue of possible effects on Cavendish measurements of the Newtonian constant G from putative non-Newtonian interactions; and in Appendix C we present an isostatic model of the Earth's gravity field, which is relevant for various geophysical experiments.

We have also provided extensive cross-references to the various topics presented in this book. In addition to a table of contents (pages xi–xii) and the list of tables (page $xiii$) and list of figures (pages xv–$xvii$), we have also provided an author index (pages 287–295) and a separate subject index (pages 297–305). The author index was generated using all authors whose names appeared in the bibliography. For each author, the author's name is listed together with each page number on which a publication is cited that includes that author's name in the respective bibliographic entry. In entries with more than five names, only the first author was listed, and for this reason, some contributing author names may not be listed in the author index. In cited references, the letters "pc" denote a private communication.

Acknowledgments

We have benefited enormously from numerous discussions with many of our colleagues on various issues that have come up, and we especially wish to thank the following individuals for their help:

Eric Adelberger, Sam Aronson, Jeno Barnothy, David Bartlett, Anna Marie Bizzeti-Sona, Pier Giorgio Bizzeti, Paul Boynton, Gabriel Chardin, Hai-Yang Cheng, Ramanath Cowsik, Thibault Damour, Robert Dicke, Donald Eckhardt, Francis Everitt, Orrin Fackler, William Fairbank, Jim Faller, Allan Franklin, Richard Feynman, Yasunori Fujii, George Gillies, Jens Gundlach, Jim Hartle, Mark Haugan, Wick Haxton, Blaine Heckel, Richard Hughes, Boris Kayser, Peter Kiràly, Dennis Krause, Kazuaki Kuroda, Harry Kloor, Gabriel Luther, George Marx, John Moffat, Michael Moore, Riley Newman, Peter Nelson, Wei-Tou Ni, Anna Nobili, Ken Nordtvedt, Ho Jung Paik, Roberto Peccei, Terry Quinn, Fred Raab, Anestis Romaides, Roger Sands, Clive Speake, Frank Stacey, Christopher Stubbs, Joe Sucher, Daniel Sudarsky, Aaron Szafer, Dubravko Tadíc, Peter Thieberger, Jim Thomas, Gary Tuck, Jean Trân Thanh Vân, Christoph Wetterich, Bruce Winstein, Paul Worden, and Clifford Will.

We wish to extend a special thanks to Jean Trân Than Vân and Orrin Fackler for regularly incorporating sessions on non-Newtonian gravity and the "fifth force" into the January Moriond Workshops. These have provided an invaluable opportunity for workers in the field to exchange ideas and results. We also wish to specifically thank George Gillies, Dennis Krause, and Julie Schwan for helping compile the bibliography [FISCHBACH, 1992B] which was used extensively throughout this book.

Finally we are deeply indebted to Maria Taylor for guiding this book to completion, to Nancy M. Schnepp for her tireless efforts in typing the manuscript, and to Heather Jones and David Schleef for critically reading the manuscript.

Table of Contents

List of Tables

List of Figures

CHAPTER 1

Introduction

There has been renewed interest in recent years in the possibility of deviations from the predictions of Newton's "inverse-square" ($1/r^2$) law of universal gravitation: For two point masses m_i and m_j located a distance r apart, the magnitude of the force that one exerts on the other is given by

$$F = \frac{G_N m_i m_j}{r^2}, \tag{1.1}$$

where $G_N = (6.67259 \pm 0.00085) \times 10^{-11}\,\mathrm{m^3\,kg^{-1}\,s^{-2}}$ is Newton's gravitational constant. This interest stems from a number of sources, which include the following: Equation (1.1) is the expression one recovers by starting from Einstein's theory of General Relativity (GR) and passing to the limit of nonrelativistic velocities and weak fields. Hence GR shares with Newtonian gravity the feature, contained in Eq. (1.1), that the acceleration of a test mass (say m_i) is independent of m_i (both its magnitude and chemical composition). As an experimental statement this is often referred to as the *universality of free-fall* (UFF), and tests of UFF have recently gained increased prominence, as we describe below. In GR the fact that all objects fall at the same rate in the same gravitational field is elevated to a fundamental assumption known as the *equivalence principle* [WEINBERG, 1972; MISNER, 1973; WILL, 1993; CIUFOLINI, 1995]. Although it is beyond the scope of the present book to discuss the various forms of the equivalence principle and their implications, suffice it to say that a breakdown of UFF (and hence of the equivalence principle) would pose a challenge for both GR and Newtonian gravity.

This leads to a second reason for the renewed interest in Newtonian gravity. Various theoretical attempts to construct a unified theory of elementary particle physics naturally predict the existence of new forces whose effects extend over macroscopic distances. (See [FISCHBACH, 1992B] for a bibliography of such theories.) Although these new forces simulate the effects of gravity in some ways, they are usually not described by an inverse-square law, and generally do not obey the UFF. Hence the presence of such a force coexisting with gravity could be detected in principle by apparent deviations from either the inverse-square law and/or UFF in "gravitational" experiments. In principle, by studying such deviations (e.g., the dependence of the accelerations of different materials on their chemical composition), one could determine what interaction was producing these effects. Hence a strong theoretical motivation for studying deviations from Newtonian gravity is to probe for new fundamental forces in nature. It should be emphasized that we are *not* concerned with the well-known deviations from Newtonian gravity in strong gravitational fields or in relativistic systems, which are described by GR. Our focus will be exclusively on possible anomalies that arise in systems that *should* be described by Newtonian physics.

It is worth noting at this point that by attributing any possible break-down of UFF to a new interaction, we are in effect assuming that the gravitational interaction itself always respects UFF, as embodied in the equivalence principle. As a practical matter it seems likely that one could formulate a new interaction to account for whatever violations of UFF might be seen, and hence the validity of the equivalence principle and GR would be ensured even if a deviation from UFF were observed experimentally. Although this view is widely accepted among workers in the field, it is nonetheless commonplace for some researchers to characterize their experiments as tests of the equivalence principle, rather than as a search for a new force. We note in passing that any indication that the "gravitational" interaction has a finite range could be interpreted as evidence for a new force. This is a consequence of the fact that a relativistic theory with massive gravitons does not reduce to General Relativity as the graviton mass goes to zero, but rather to a linear combination of scalar and tensor fields [VAN DAM, 1970; ZAKHAROV, 1970; BOULWARE, 1972; GOLDHABER, 1974].

Since one of the primary motivations for the current interest in non-Newtonian gravity is as a probe for new long-range forces, we turn next to address the question of why certain classes of theories predict the existence of additional gravity-like interactions. Although many such specific models have been constructed over the years, those in which gravity is unified with other forces tend to be formulated along the following lines: We begin by observing that there are two natural mass scales in elementary particle physics, defined by $m_N \cong 1\,\mathrm{GeV}/c^2$ and $M_{\mathrm{Planck}} = (\hbar c/G_N)^{1/2} \cong 10^{19}\,\mathrm{GeV}/c^2$, where m_N is the nucleon mass, $\hbar$ is Planck's constant, and c is the speed of light. (In this book we will often use "natural" units where $\hbar = c = 1$ where appropriate.) The ratio of these scales, $m_N/M_{\mathrm{Planck}} \equiv (f^2/\hbar c)^{1/2} \cong 10^{-19}$, introduces a new small dimensionless constant into physics. In the models of interest this constant has a dynamical significance, since it determines the coupling strength of a new field to matter, just as the electric charge e ($e^2/\hbar c \equiv \alpha_{\mathrm{em}} \cong 1/137$) determines the strength of the coupling of photons to charged matter. The analog of α_{em} for this new force would be $f^2/\hbar c \cong 10^{-38}$, which corresponds to a force of gravitational strength ($f^2/Gm_N^2 = 1$). The second observation is that in the theories under consideration the product

$$\mu \equiv (f^2/\hbar c)m_N \cong 10^{-10} \, \text{eV}/c^2 \qquad (1.2)$$

determines the mass of a new field. The Compton wavelength ("range") λ associated with this field (which characterizes the distance over which the corresponding force acts) would then be

$$\lambda = \hbar/\mu c \cong 2000 \, \text{m}. \qquad (1.3)$$

This combination of parameters ($f^2/\hbar c \cong 10^{-38}$ and $\lambda \cong 2000\,\text{m}$) could thus describe a new intermediate-range field of gravitational strength.

It follows from the preceding discussion that in searching for new weak forces (via deviations from the inverse-square law or UFF), we are studying the implications of a broad class of theories, which may be referred to generically as "fifth force" theories. (The name "fifth force," as used in the present context, did not enter the literature until 1986. The specific model to which that name originally applied [FISCHBACH, 1986A] is an example of such a theory. Throughout this book we will use "fifth force" generically to characterize a theory broadly described by Eqs. (1.2)–(1.4), and the subscript "5" on a parameter will denote a quantity associated with such a theory.) From a historical point of view the theory (or model) which provided much of the impetus for the current interest in testing Newtonian gravity is due to Fujii [1971]. In addition to formulating a specific theory along the lines discussed above, Fujii noted that this new interaction coexisting with gravity would lead to a modified Newtonian potential $V(r)$ having the form

$$V(r) = -G_\infty \frac{m_i m_j}{r}(1 + \alpha e^{-r/\lambda}), \qquad (1.4)$$

where α and λ are two fundamental constants. (The derivation of Eq. (1.4) is presented in detail in Chapter 2.) G_∞ is the value of the Newtonian constant that describes the interaction of m_i and m_j as $r \to \infty$, and is in principle different from the effective gravitational constant G_0 at laboratory distances $(r/\lambda \ll 1)$,

$$G_0 = G_\infty(1 + \alpha). \qquad (1.5)$$

Since the Newtonian constant G_N appearing in Eq. (1.1) is in fact obtained from laboratory measurements, we can identify G_N and G_0, and hence we will use either notation as appropriate. However, the specific prediction of Fujii's paper was that $\alpha = 1/3$, and hence that G_0 and G_∞ would differ by a factor of 4/3 for λ in the range $10 - 1000\,\text{m}$. The fact that a difference this large between G_0 and G_∞ could have been compatible with then-existing data, is a measure of how little was known about Newtonian gravity over the distance scale $10-1000\,\text{m}$, a region sometimes known as the "geophysical window."

The work of Fujii and others at the same time [WAGONER, 1970; O'HANLON, 1972] stimulated a number of analyses aimed at establishing whether the same Newtonian constant describes gravitational interactions over different distance scales. Using various astrophysical and geophysical arguments, Mikkelsen and Newman [MIKKELSEN, 1977] claimed that G_0 and G_∞ could differ from each other by $\sim 40\%$, which is a large enough uncertainty to accommodate Fujii's value $\alpha = 1/3$. Other considerations based on stellar structure [SUGIMOTO, 1972; BLINNIKOV, 1978; HUT, 1981] suggested that this difference could be no more than 10–15%, but even a discrepancy of this magnitude would have been quite significant. (More recent astrophysical constraints on G_0/G_∞, and on the existence of new forces, are discussed in Section 8.3.

In the 1970's and early 1980's interest in the possibility of non-Newtonian gravity was further stimulated by claims of experimental evidence for deviations from the inverse-square law, first by Long [1974] and later by Stacey and collaborators [STACEY, 1981, 1987A; HOLDING, 1986]. To understand the relationship between these experiments and other tests of the inverse-square law, it is important to appreciate that any experiment is sensitive only to values of λ roughly comparable to the dimensions of the experimental system that is being used (see Section 3.1). That this is the case will become evident from the exclusion plots that we will present in Chapter 3, and is in part a consequence of the fact that the effects of the term proportional to α in Eq. (1.4) decrease exponentially for $r \gg \lambda$. It follows from this discussion that the very precise agreement between the predictions of Newtonian gravity and observation for planetary motion does not preclude the existence of large non-Newtonian effects over smaller distance scales. We will expand on this discussion below and in Chapter 3.

The preceding discussion serves as an introduction to the work of Long [1974, 1980A], who called attention to evidence in the literature for a possible dependence of the Newtonian constant on the separation of the test masses in laboratory-scale experiments. Long himself performed a laboratory experiment in which he presented direct evidence for such a variation over distances of ~ 4–$30\,\mathrm{cm}$ [LONG, 1976]. Long's work provided the impetus for a number of other tests of the inverse-square law, none of which supported his results [PANOV, 1979; YU, 1979; HIRAKAWA, 1980; SPERO, 1980; CHAN, 1982; OGAWA, 1982; HOSKINS, 1985; KURODA, 1985; FISCHBACH, 1992A,B].

During this period there was, however, one experiment which did see evidence for a deviation from the inverse-square law, namely the geophysical determination of the gravitational constant by Stacey and coworkers [STACEY, 1981, 1987A,B; HOLDING, 1986]. Stacey et al. revived the Airy method for measuring G_N over a scale of hundreds of meters, which we describe in detail in Chapter 3. Although the apparent anomalies found by

Stacey et al. were eventually accounted for in terms of conventional gravitational interactions, the work of Stacey and collaborators played an important role in motivating the reanalysis of the Eötvös experiment by Fischbach et al. in 1986.

The experimental efforts of the 1970's and 1980's aimed at finding evidence for new macroscopic forces were paralleled by theoretical efforts to understand what characteristics such forces might possess. In addition to the seminal work by Fujii and others which we have previously described, arguments based on supergravity, advanced by Scherk [1979A,B], suggested the possibility of "antigravity," which would be a long-range repulsive component to gravity. During this period an important phenomenological analysis was carried out by Gibbons and Whiting (GW) [GIBBONS, 1981], who analyzed gravity data over all available length scales to constrain possible unification theories. The analysis by GW underscored the point we have made earlier to the effect that precise experiments over one length scale do not necessarily constrain gravity over another scale (see Chapter 3). In addition to the experimental data we have already discussed, GW included the results obtained by Rapp [1974, 1977] from a comparison of satellite and terrestrial determinations of the acceleration of gravity at the surface of the Earth. Rapp's analysis, and its subsequent refinement [RAPP, 1987], provide stringent constraints on possible deviations from Newtonian gravity over distance scales up to $\sim 10^8$ m. GW noted, however, that as stringent as these constraints were, they did not severely test Newtonian gravity over the $10-1000$ m distance scale that we characterize as the "geophysical window." This comprises the values of λ which are larger than those that can be tightly constrained by laboratory experiments, but smaller than those for which satellite data provide the best constraints. In this regime, various geophysical experiments provide the most sensitive limits but, prior to the recent resurgence of interest in these questions, the existing limits were very weak. In fact the best limit on α for λ in the range of 10 m [YU, 1979] was compatible with $\alpha \cong 0.1$. Thus, almost 300 years following the publication of Newton's *Principia* in 1687, his law of gravitation could have been wrong by $\sim 10\%$ and still been consistent with then-existing data.

The GW analysis played an important role in motivating the subsequent analysis of [FISCHBACH, 1986A], by showing that the claimed effects of Stacey et al. were not necessarily in conflict with other more precise data. Motivated by Stacey et al. and by other results (see below), Fischbach et al. set out to inquire whether a new force whose strength α and range λ were compatible with the Stacey data would have shown up elsewhere. In addition to revisiting the systems previously considered by GW, these authors reanalyzed the classic experiment of Eötvös, Pekár, and Fekete (EPF) [EÖTVÖS, 1922, 1953], which GW had not included in their analysis. The reason for this omission is that, unlike the other experiments considered by

GW, the EPF experiment is a test of UFF, and not of the inverse-square law. As such it could be described by a potential such as Eq. (1.4), but only if α were *composition dependent*. Thus to discuss the EPF experiment and other tests of UFF, one must go beyond the parametrization in Eq. (1.4), which is also the starting point for the GW analysis. The formalism for doing this is presented in Chapter 2. Upon reanalyzing the EPF experiment, Fischbach et al. found evidence in the EPF data that the accelerations of the test samples depended on their chemical compositions, and that this dependence fitted a pattern consistent with the presence of a new intermediate-range force. (Throughout this book the term "long-range" will generally refer to a $1/r^2$ force like gravity. We will mostly be concerned with "intermediate-range" forces, such as that described by the term proportional to α in Eq. (1.4).) The work of Fischbach et al. provided renewed impetus for the current efforts to re-examine the experimental support for Newtonian gravity, and especially for tests of UFF. Before describing the EPF experiment, we review the considerations that led to the reanalysis of the EPF data. This history, and subsequent developments, are described in an excellent book by Franklin [1993], to which the interested reader should refer for additional details.

Another thread in the string of arguments that ultimately led to the reanalysis of the EPF experiment began in 1964 with the discovery of the CP-violating decay mode $K_L^0 \to \pi^+\pi^-$ [CHRISTENSON, 1964]. C denotes charge conjugation, P is parity and, by virtue of the famous CPT theorem, CP violation is loosely equivalent to a violation of time-reversal symmetry T. Two of the very first efforts to explain this decay attributed the observed CP violation to the presence of a new long-range force of galactic origin [BELL, 1964; BERNSTEIN, 1964]. If the "charge" to which the new field coupled was "hypercharge," $Y = B + S$ (B is baryon number and S is strangeness), then both the normal matter in the galaxy and the K-mesons (kaons) in the experiment would have a net Y, and hence could interact with each other. The violation of CP would then arise from the assumption (which is supported experimentally) that our galaxy is composed mostly of "matter" with relatively little "antimatter." As a result, the strength of the net interaction of our galaxy with the K^0 and $\bar{K}^0$ components of K_L^0 via the hypercharge field would be different, and this asymmetry would then lead to the observed decay mode, $K_L^0 \to \pi^+\pi^-$ [GOOD, 1961].

This theory made a very specific prediction, which eventually led to its rejection. In the rest frame of the moving K^0 and $\bar{K}^0$, the strength of the hypercharge field would appear to increase with increasing kaon energy as a result of the Lorentz transformation. (See Chapter 5 for detailed discussions.) Hence the magnitude of the CP-violating effect would depend on the laboratory energy at which a particular experiment was carried out, contrary to what was actually observed. This characteristic prediction assumed that the hypercharge field has spin-parity $J^P = 1^-$ in analogy to the electromagnetic interaction. One could escape from the implications of the experimental results by assuming that the hypercharge field was a scalar ($J^P = 0^+$), but this alternative was unattractive for other reasons. There was an additional argument against the hypercharge-field hypothesis which is sometimes known as the "Weinberg catastrophe" [WEINBERG, 1964]. If γ_Y denotes the quantum of the putative hypercharge field, then kaon decays should occur in which a physical γ_Y appears in the final state. What Weinberg showed was that for very light γ_Y (corresponding to a field extending over galactic distances) the decay rate for a mode such as $K^+ \to \pi^+\pi^0\gamma_Y$ would significantly exceed the experimentally known decay rate of K^+ into all modes (i.e., the inverse of its lifetime). At first sight this may seem surprising, given that γ_Y couples so weakly to kaons. A detailed discussion of how this comes about is presented in Chapter 5, where this question is re-examined in the context of the fifth-force hypothesis. Other constraints on the coupling of various long-range fields were discussed somewhat later by Nachtmann [1969].

Interest in the coupling of new intermediate-range fields to kaons revived in 1982 with the publication of a series of papers by Aronson and coworkers who reported an apparent anomalous energy dependence of various parameters of the K^0-$\bar{K}^0$ system [ARONSON, 1982, 1983A,B]. Aronson et al. analyzed data taken at Fermilab from a series of kaon regeneration experiments using hydrogen and carbon targets (e.g., $K_L^0 p \to K_S^0 p$) to determine the kaon parameters in the energy range $30-130\,\text{GeV}$. The specific parameters they studied were the K_L^0-K_S^0 mass difference $\Delta m = m_L - m_S$, the K_S^0 lifetime τ_S, as well as the magnitude and phase of the CP-violating parameter η_{+-} defined by

$$\eta_{+-} = \frac{Amplitude\ (K_L^0 \to \pi^+\pi^-)}{Amplitude\ (K_S^0 \to \pi^+\pi^-)} \equiv |\eta_{+-}|e^{i\phi_{+-}}. \tag{1.6}$$

As we have previously noted, these parameters should not depend on the kaon laboratory velocity (or energy) when measured in the rest frame of the kaons, in accordance with the principle of relativity. Although previous experiments had seen no evidence for any energy dependence at energies up to $5\,\text{GeV}$, the regeneration data indicated a small but detectable energy dependence at the higher (Fermilab) energies. Such an effect can arise from a force whose range is comparable to $\gamma(\hbar/\Delta mc) = \gamma(5.6\,\text{cm})$, where $\gamma = E_K/m_K c^2$ is the usual relativistic factor [FISCHBACH, 1982]. Aronson et al. developed a phenomenological framework to describe such effects [ARONSON, 1983B], which they then used to determine the energy dependence of the kaon parameters in various theoretical models.

The suggestion of anomalies in both the kaon data of Aronson et al. and in the geophysical data of Stacey et al., each of which could be ascribed to a new coupling, led to the question of whether both could originate from the *same* mechanism. The necessarily crude modeling of the local environment in each experiment allowed for enough uncertainty to conclude that this could indeed be the case. Moreover, if this were the case then the effects of such a coupling would show up in only a limited number of other systems, including the original EPF experiment [FISCHBACH, 1986A]. This conclusion emerged from a plot of the constraint curves in the α-λ plane arising from each of the above systems. If one assumed that EPF had seen an effect at their upper level of sensitivity ($\Delta\kappa = 1 \times 10^{-9}$ in their notation), and likewise for the K^0-$\bar{K}^0$ and geophysical data, then these curves suggested that a common value of α and λ could describe all three systems. By implication, the suggestion of an anomaly in the K^0-$\bar{K}^0$ and geophysical data raised the possibility that an anomaly could have been detected in the EPF experiment. The interested reader can find a more detailed discussion of these curves and their significance in [FISCHBACH, 1986C] and in [SCHWARZSCHILD, 1986, 1988; WILL, 1990].

As we have already noted, the reanalysis of the EPF experiment [FISCH-BACH, 1986A] found evidence for a new intermediate-range force whose strength and range were very roughly compatible with expectations based on the α-λ constraint curves. Initially, however, there was a question concerning the *sign* of the various effects [HAYASHI, 1986; THODBERG, 1986]. The geophysical results of Stacey et al. indicated the presence of a new *repulsive* force, which would arise from an intermediate-range *vector* field, as we discuss in Chapter 2. Similarly the K^0-$\bar{K}^0$ data of Aronson et al. necessitated a coupling which distinguished between K^0 and its antiparticle $\bar{K}^0$. As we discuss in Chapter 5, this again would require a new *vector* field. For the results of the EPF experiment to be compatible with both the geophysical and K^0-$\bar{K}^0$ data, it would thus be necessary for the EPF acceleration differences to arise from a *repulsive* force. This was in fact claimed to be the case in the original paper by Fischbach and coworkers [FISCHBACH, 1986A]. However, Thodberg [1986] pointed out a sign error in [FISCHBACH, 1986A] which, when corrected, appeared to imply that the EPF data now suggested a new *attractive* force. The sign issue was resolved when a number of different authors observed that for a force with the range that was being postulated, $\lambda \approx 200\,\mathrm{m}$, local horizontal mass inhomogeneities (e.g., buildings or mountains) could be the dominant source in the EPF experiment [BIZZETI, 1986; FISCHBACH, 1986B,C; MILGROM, 1986; TALMADGE, 1986; THIEBERGER, 1986]. Moreover, it was noted that a feature such as a hole (e.g., an excavated building basement) behaves as a source of opposite sign. In fact estimates of the effect of the basement at what is thought to be the site of the EPF experiment [TALMADGE, 1986; BOD, 1991] suggested that the basement might be the dominant effect if the putative fifth force had a range of approximately $200\,\mathrm{m}$. The net conclusion from these considerations was that the signal for a new force suggested by the EPF data could have been compatible with a repulsive vector force, as required by both the geophysical and K^0-$\bar{K}^0$ data.

From the present vantage point these considerations are of historic interest only, since there is at present no convincing evidence for a new intermediate-range force. However, given the significance of such experiments as probes for new forces, it is likely that tests of both the inverse-square law and UFF will continue for some time to come. This is especially true given the large number of theoretical models which predict such effects. For some representative examples see [BARR, 1986; BARS, 1986; CARLSON, 1987; CHANG, 1990; CHO, 1990, 1991; COHEN, 1990; CVETIČ, 1989; DE SABBATA, 1990; DONOGHUE, 1994; ELLIS, 1987, 1989; FAYET, 1986A,B, 1989, 1990; FISCHBACH, 1991B; FUJII, 1971, 1972, 1974, 1975, 1986, 1988, 1991A,B; GASPERINI, 1989B; HILL, 1988; IVANOV, 1989; KASTENING, 1989; MOFFAT, 1987, 1988, 1989; NUSSINOV, 1986; PECCEI, 1987; PECHLANER, 1966].

CHAPTER 2

Phenomenological Description of Non-Newtonian Gravity

2.1 Introduction

In searching for possible deviations from the predictions of Newtonian gravity (or from its generalization—Einstein's General Relativity), we will presume that these arise from a hypothetical new force such as the putative "fifth force," as discussed in Chapter 1. If any such deviations are eventually established experimentally, it will require further experimental and theoretical work to decide whether they can be understood instead in terms of some generalized theory of gravity such as "supersymmetry" or "supergravity," as some authors have suggested [ZACHOS, 1978; SCHERK, 1979A,B; FAYET, 1986A,B; GOLDMAN, 1986]. For present purposes, it is sufficient to characterize the experimental predictions of any specific theory in terms of relatively simple phenomenological potentials, as we describe below. We can then use experiments to fix the parameters of these potentials, while leaving for later the problem of deriving these parameters from a fundamental theory.

To illustrate how one can formulate a phenomenological theory of a new intermediate-range (i.e., macroscopic) force, we consider the interaction between two point masses mediated by a new field (i.e., particle) called the "hyperphoton." The strength of the interaction between these point masses will be determined by the quantity of some generalized point charge Q_5 that they carry, in units of a fundamental charge f (the analog of the electric charge e). Hence the first question that must be addressed in formulating a model is what Q_5 depends on. For ordinary matter, Q_5 can be chosen to be a linear combination of proton number (Z), neutron number (N), and electron (or lepton) number (L). With few exceptions, searches for new macroscopic forces are carried out with electrically neutral bulk matter, since the presence of charges would give rise to serious background problems from electromagnetic interactions. For neutral matter $Z = L$, and thus we can choose either of two linear combinations of the above charges to express Q_5.

The most common parametrizations used in the literature are:

$$Q_5 = B \cos \theta_5 + I_z \sin \theta_5, \tag{2.1.1a}$$

$$Q_5 = B \cos \bar{\theta}_5 + L \sin \bar{\theta}_5, \quad (-90° < \bar{\theta}_5 \leq 90°), \tag{2.1.1b}$$

$$B = N + Z, \quad I_z = N - Z = B - 2L. \tag{2.1.1c}$$

For a coupling to pure baryon number (B), $\sin \theta_5 = \sin \bar{\theta}_5 = 0$ and $Q_5 = B$. However, for a coupling to pure isospin, $\theta_5 = 90°$ in Eq. (2.1.1a), but $\bar{\theta}_5 = \tan^{-1}(-2) \cong -63°$ in Eq. (2.1.1b). Hence for an isospin coupling $Q_5 = I_z$ in Eq. (2.1.1a), but $Q_5 = (B - 2L) \cos \theta_5 = (B - 2L)/\sqrt{5}$ in Eq. (2.1.1b). Since the product of charges of the source and detector enters into the expression for the force on a test object, it follows that the charges defined in Eqs. (2.1.1a) and (2.1.1b) differ from each other by a normalization factor of $\cos^2 \bar{\theta}_5 = 1/5$. This is important to bear in mind when comparing the limits obtained by different groups on the strength of a possible coupling to isospin. We note in passing that in some models (such as that of [PECCEI, 1987]), Q_5 can also depend on the mass M. This typically occurs when the putative force arises from a new spin-0 (scalar) field, and leads to a somewhat different phenomenology than would be the case if the non-Newtonian coupling to mass were added in separately.

2.1.1 Modification of Newton's Law of Gravity

The next ingredient needed to formulate a model is the functional dependence of the potential energy $V(\vec{r})$ on the separation $r = |\vec{r}_i - \vec{r}_j|$ of the two objects. For both Newton's law and Coulomb's law, $V \propto 1/r$, which is a consequence of the fact that the fields which transmit these forces are presumed in both cases to be massless. However, since there is no compelling reason to assume that the fields which transmit a possible new force are also massless, we consider the more general case of a field with mass m_5, whose spin and parity (J^P) are in the "normal" parity series, $J^P = 0^+$, 1^-, or 2^+. (These are the only possible spins that we need to consider at present. In practice, phenomenological theories with fields $J > 2$ can lead to various inconsistencies.) We further note that the exchange of quanta in the abnormal parity series $(J^P = 0^-, 1^+, 2^-, \ldots)$ would give rise to a *spin-dependent* force at the nuclear or atomic level. Such a force would be detectable in experiments using macroscopic sources and test masses only if these had a net polarization. The possibility of a spin-dependent fifth-force arising from the exchange of light $J^P = 1^+$ quanta has been considered in [NI, 1977; FAYET, 1986A,B]. A number of experiments employing test masses which could detect such a force (or one arising from the exchange of a light $J^P = 0^+$ axion), have been carried out recently [ANSEL'M, 1982; NEWMAN, 1987; VOROBYOV, 1988; HSIEH, 1989; CHOU, 1990; NI, 1990; RITTER, 1990; BOBRAKOV, 1991; SU, 1994]. We will return in Chapter 6 to discuss such experiments in greater detail.

For the normal parity series, the free-space potential $\phi(\vec{r})$ that is produced by a static source has the same form for $J = 0$, 1, or 2, and is a solution of the time-independent Klein-Gordon equation (with $\hbar = c = 1$)

$$(\nabla^2 + m_5^2)\phi(\vec{r}) = 0. \tag{2.1.2}$$

We note that Eq. (2.1.2) is the generalization of Laplace's equation $\nabla^2\phi(r) = 0$, which describes the massless electromagnetic and gravitational fields. It is easy to verify by direct substitution that the solution to Eq. (2.1.2) for a point source is the familiar Yukawa potential,

$$\phi(\vec{r}) = \text{constant} \times \frac{e^{-r/\lambda}}{r}, \tag{2.1.3}$$

where $r = |\vec{r}|$, and where $\lambda = \hbar/m_5c$ ($= 1/m_5$ in natural units) is the Compton wavelength of the exchanged field. The quantity λ appearing in Eq. (2.1.3) is called the *range* of the Yukawa potential, and it characterizes the distance scale beyond which the effects of $\phi(\vec{r})$ start to become unimportant. For electromagnetism and gravity the analogs of m_5 are zero ($\lambda \to \infty$), and hence these fields are described as having infinite range. We can now combine Eqs. (2.1.1)–(2.1.3) to write the expression for the potential energy $V_5(r) = fQ_{5i}\phi_j(\vec{r})$ of a point mass i in the field of a point source j:

$$V_5(r) = \pm f^2 Q_{5i} Q_{5j} \frac{e^{-r/\lambda}}{r}. \tag{2.1.4}$$

Before discussing the overall sign of V_5, we note that Eq. (2.1.4), which forms the basis of much of the ensuing discussion, is the fifth-force analog of Coulomb's law,

$$V_{em}(r) = e^2 \frac{Q_i Q_j}{r}, \tag{2.1.5}$$

where Q_i and Q_j are the electromagnetic charges. We see from the preceding discussion that in the simple theory defined by Eqs. (2.1.1) and (2.1.4), V_5 is characterized by three parameters: 1) the range λ, 2) the overall strength f, and 3) the mixing angle θ_5 which specifies the charge Q_5.

We now return to the question of the sign of V_5 in Eq. (2.1.4), which is not determined by our considerations up to this point. This sign is fixed when $V_5(r)$ is calculated by field-theoretic methods, and the result is that the exchange of scalar ($J = 0$) or tensor ($J = 2$) fields leads to an *attractive* potential between like charges (corresponding to a negative sign in Eq. (2.1.4)), whereas vector ($J = 1$) exchange gives a *repulsive* interaction, just as for electromagnetism [BARKER, 1966; JAGANNATHAN, 1986; FEYNMAN, 1995]. For unlike charges, all three of these interactions lead to an attractive potential. If the charge in Eqs. (2.1.1) is B, then a *vector* exchange will always be repulsive for matter-matter interactions, since $B = +1$ for both neutrons and protons. However, the coupling between a macroscopic source and an *antiproton* would then be attractive, and this observation forms the basis of a current experiment to search for a vector field by comparing the gravitational accelerations of $\bar{p}$ and p [GOLDMAN, 1982; DYER, 1989; HOLZSCHEITER, 1990]. On the other hand, if the charge is I_z, then the interactions between samples of ordinary matter can be either attractive or repulsive, since proton-rich materials (e.g., H_2O) have $I_z < 0$, whereas $I_z > 0$ for neutron-rich (i.e., most other) substances. We see from this discussion that the combination of various possible exchanged fields ($J = 0, 1, 2$), and charges (B, I_z, or some other value of θ_5), produces a wide variety of possible forms for the putative fifth-force potential V_5.

We conclude the present discussion by commenting on the two expressions for I_z in Eq. (2.1.1c). For ordinary bulk matter $I_z = (N - Z) = (B - 2L)$, so that one can use $N - Z$ and $B - 2L$ interchangeably. (Note that the sign of $I_z = N - Z$ is in accord with the usual nuclear physics convention, which is opposite in sign to the particle physics convention.) However, $N - Z$ and $B - 2L$ can be physically different in some situations. Consider the case of a coupling of the fifth-force field to the K^0-$\bar{K}^0$ system, which is discussed in Chapters 1 and 5. Both B and L (and hence $B - 2L$) are zero for K^0, $\bar{K}^0$, K_L, or K_S. Hence if the relevant charge were really $B - 2L$ (or any other linear combination of B and L), we would expect no couplings to any neutral kaons. On the other hand, if the relevant charge is I_z, then $I_z = -\frac{1}{2}$ for K^0 (and $+\frac{1}{2}$ for $\bar{K}^0$), and so a coupling to K^0 and $\bar{K}^0$ might take place. Moreover, even for ordinary matter there might be a difference between $(N - Z)$ and $(B - 2L)$. This could occur if there were significant "screening" or "shielding" effects associated with a possible fifth-force coupling to L, but which would not be relevant for couplings to N or Z [FISCHBACH, 1988; WATANABE, 1988].

As we have noted previously, apparent deviations from the predictions of Newtonian gravity will arise whenever both $V_5(r)$ in Eq. (2.1.4) and the Newtonian potential energy $V_N(r)$ can contribute to a given process. In practice this will occur whenever $r \lesssim \lambda$, where r is the characteristic separation of the source and test objects. Under these conditions the total potential energy describing the interaction of i and j is given by

$$V(r) = V_N(r) + V_5(r)$$

$$= -G_\infty \frac{m_i m_j}{r} + f^2 \frac{Q_{5i} Q_{5j}}{r} e^{-r/\lambda}$$

$$= -G_\infty \frac{m_i m_j}{r} \left(1 - \frac{f^2 Q_{5i} Q_{5j}}{G_\infty m_i m_j} e^{-r/\lambda}\right)$$

$$\equiv -G_\infty \frac{m_i m_j}{r} \left(1 + \alpha_{ij} e^{-r/\lambda}\right). \tag{2.1.6}$$

It is convenient to simplify α_{ij} by expressing all masses in terms of $m_H \equiv$

$m(_1H^1) = (1.00782519 \pm 0.00000008)u$, so that $m_i = \mu_i m_H$, etc. This gives

$$\alpha_{ij} = -\frac{Q_{5i}}{\mu_i}\frac{Q_{5j}}{\mu_j}\xi \equiv q_{5i}q_{5j}\xi \; ; \quad \xi = \frac{f^2}{G_\infty m_H^2}. \tag{2.1.7}$$

The constant ξ plays an important role in the search for possible new long-range forces. First it represents a new fundamental constant in nature, and secondly, it directly measures the strength of a putative new force relative to gravity. In the form of Eq. (2.1.6) the effect of $V_5(r)$ appears as a modification of the Newtonian interaction. However, the modified coupling *destroys the universality of the effective gravitational interaction*, by introducing terms proportional to α_{ij} which explicitly depend on the chemical compositions of the interacting objects.

We can use Eq. (2.1.6) to characterize the two major classes of fifth-force experiments, which are the searches for *composition-independent* and *composition-dependent* deviations from Newtonian gravity. *Composition-independent* searches for non-Newtonian gravity look for deviations from the inverse-square law arising from the presence in $V(r)$ of the term proportional to $e^{-r/\lambda}$ in Eq. (2.1.6). These experiments can be viewed as tests of the constancy (with respect to r) of the Newtonian constant G or, in a popular oxymoronic construction, as searches for a "variable Newtonian constant." To explain what is meant by a "variable Newtonian constant," let us temporarily suppress the dependence of α_{ij} on i, j (since we are not interested in the composition dependence in these experiments). Then we may write $V(r)$ in Eq. (2.1.6) as

$$V(r) = -\frac{G_\infty m_i m_j}{r}\left(1 + \alpha e^{-r/\lambda}\right). \tag{2.1.8}$$

Differentiating Eq. (2.1.8), the force $\vec{F}(r) = -\vec{\nabla}V(r)$ is

$$\vec{F}(r) = -G_\infty \frac{m_i m_j}{r^2}\hat{r}\left[1 + \alpha e^{-r/\lambda}\left(1 + r/\lambda\right)\right] \equiv -G(r)\frac{m_i m_j}{r^2}\hat{r}, \tag{2.1.9}$$

with
$$G(r) = G_\infty\left[1 + \alpha e^{-r/\lambda}\left(1 + r/\lambda\right)\right]. \tag{2.1.10}$$

We see from Eqs. (2.1.9) and (2.1.10) that the effect of the non-Newtonian term proportional to α can be viewed as converting the Newtonian constant G_∞ into a function $G(r)$. Hence the results of searches for non-Newtonian contributions $\propto e^{-r/\lambda}$ are often expressed in terms of the deviations of $G(r)/G_\infty$ from unity as a function of r. For laboratory experiments, where $r/\lambda \ll 1$ can be presumed to hold,

$$G(r) \cong G(0) \equiv G_0 = G_\infty[1 + \alpha], \tag{2.1.11}$$

so that G_0 is the usual laboratory value, as we noted in Chapter 1. By contrast, for satellite measurements or planetary motion, where $r/\lambda \gg 1$,

$$G(r) \cong G(\infty) \equiv G_\infty. \tag{2.1.12}$$

It follows from Eqs. (2.1.9)–(2.1.12) that the usual $1/r^2$ force law pertains over distance scales that are either much smaller or much larger than λ, albeit with different values of $G(r)$. Observing such a difference between G_0 and G_∞ would, of course, be evidence for a new interaction. However, G_∞ always appears multiplied by some mass M which must itself be independently determined. One therefore requires an independent measurement of M, and we discuss in Chapter 3 how this can be done over several distance scales.

The second class of experiments are *composition-dependent* experiments, which focus on the fact that the "specific" charges q_{5i} and q_{5j} in α_{ij} are generally different from one material to another. Hence α_{ij} is generally different from α_{ik} if j and k are different materials, which means that $V(r)$ depends not only on the masses m_i, m_j but also on the compositions of i and j. More specifically, if i in Eq. (2.1.7) denotes the attracting body (e.g., the Earth) and j, j' represent the test masses whose accelerations to the Earth are being compared, then a composition-dependent experiment determines the quantity

$$\alpha_{ij} - \alpha_{ij'} = -\xi q_{5i}(q_{5j} - q_{5j'}) \equiv -\xi q_{5i}\Delta(q_5)_{j-j'}. \tag{2.1.13}$$

Composition-dependent experiments specifically look for an anomalous acceleration difference $\Delta\vec{a}$ between two samples of different chemical composition, which are being attracted to the same source. By way of illustration, we consider the case of the source being a point mass i. Using Eq. (2.1.9) then gives

$$\vec{a}_{ij} = \frac{\vec{F}_{5ij}}{m_j} = \xi q_{5i}q_{5j}\vec{\mathcal{F}}_i, \tag{2.1.14a}$$

$$\Delta\vec{a}_{j-j'} = \vec{a}_{ij} - \vec{a}_{ij'} = \xi q_{5i}\Delta(q_5)_{j-j'}\vec{\mathcal{F}}_i, \tag{2.1.14b}$$

$$\vec{\mathcal{F}}_i = \frac{\vec{F}_{5ij}}{\xi m_j q_{5i}q_{5j}}. \tag{2.1.14c}$$

$\vec{\mathcal{F}}_i = \vec{\mathcal{F}}_i(\vec{r})$ denotes the acceleration field which is the fifth-force analog of the gravitational field $\vec{g}(\vec{r})$. In practice, composition-dependent experiments usually test for a nonzero component of $\vec{a}_{ij}$ in some characteristic direction $\hat{n}$ defined by the particular experiment. (Galileo free-fall experiments, for instance, test for an anomalous acceleration difference along the direction of free fall.)

2.1.2 Effects of a Fifth Force in the Neutral Kaon System

As we noted in Chapter 1, the K^0-$\bar{K}^0$ system has historically played an important role in the search for new forces [GOOD, 1961; BELL, 1964; BERNSTEIN, 1964; NACHTMANN, 1969; THIRRING, 1972; ARONSON, 1982, 1983A,B; FISCHBACH, 1982; SUDARSKY, 1991]. The reason for this is that the physical eigenstates of the system, K_L and K_S, are very nearly degenerate in mass, so $\Delta m = m_L - m_S = (3.521 \pm 0.014) \times 10^{-6} \, \text{eV}/c^2$, which is comparable in magnitude to the Lamb shift, $\Delta E(2S-2P) = 4.4 \times 10^{-6} \, \text{eV}$. In many theoretical expressions, the quantity of interest is not just Δm by itself, but rather $\Delta m/m = (7.075 \pm 0.029) \times 10^{-15}$, where $m = (m_L + m_S)/2 = m(K^0)$. These numbers suggest (correctly, as we shall see) that the K^0-$\bar{K}^0$ system could detect the presence of a weak external force, provided it coupled to kaons in an appropriate way.

In Chapter 5 we discuss in greater detail the effects of an external field on the K^0-$\bar{K}^0$ system, and for present purposes we can summarize that discussion as follows: Suppose that the charges Q_{5i} and Q_{5j} in Eq. (2.1.4) were given by $Q_5 = Y = B + S$, where Y is hypercharge, B is baryon number, and S is strangeness. Since $Y = +1(-1)$ for $K^0(\bar{K}^0)$, it follows that K^0 and $\bar{K}^0$ can both couple to ordinary matter, which also has a nonzero value of Y. (The same argument would also apply to the third component of isospin, I_z.) Since the coupling has opposite signs for K^0 and $\bar{K}^0$, this leads to an apparent violation of CP or CPT symmetry. Among other consequences, kaon decays which are ordinarily forbidden by CP (such as $K_L \to 2\pi$) would then be allowed [GOOD, 1961]. Another manifestation of the presence of an external field would be an apparent violation of Lorentz invariance. Intuitively this could come about because the (static) sources of these fields define a preferred frame with respect to which the kaons are moving with differing velocities. More specifically, if $V_5(r)$ in Eq. (2.1.4) is the time component A_0 of a 4-vector (as would be the case in electromagnetism), then the potential A_0' "seen" by a moving kaon in its proper frame would be (see [JACKSON, 1975], page 518),

$$A_0'(x') = \gamma A_0(x). \tag{2.1.15}$$

Here $\gamma = [1 - (v/c)^2]^{-1/2}$ is the usual Lorentz factor (expressed in terms of the velocity v), and $x_\mu' = \Lambda_{\mu\nu}(\gamma)x_\nu$, where $\Lambda_{\mu\nu}(\gamma)$ describes the Lorentz boost. The presence of a contribution from A_0' modifies the fundamental parameters of the K^0-$\bar{K}^0$ system in a calculable way [BELL, 1964; BERNSTEIN, 1964; NACHTMANN, 1969; ARONSON, 1982; FISCHBACH, 1982; SUDARSKY, 1991]. Thus, for example, the presence of A_0' in Eq. (2.1.15) would modify the K_L-K_S mass difference so as to make Δm depend on the laboratory velocity of the kaons. A detailed discussion of such effects is presented in Chapter 5.

2.1.3 Searches for the Quanta of the Fifth Force

If evidence for a new force were to be found, then it would be natural to ask whether the presumed quantum of this field (γ_Y) can be seen directly. Initially this would appear to be a hopeless task, since the coupling strength of matter to this field is almost certainly much weaker than gravity, whose quanta (gravitons) have not yet been detected. Stated in this way, the problem of detecting γ_Y is actually more formidable, since even classical gravitational radiation (which is the coherent effect of *many* quanta) has not yet been detected in the laboratory. How then can one hope to detect γ_Y?

The answer is that it may in fact be possible to detect both classical fifth-force radiation and the individual quanta γ_Y if γ_Y couples to matter in an appropriate way. Let us first consider the possibility of classical fifth-force radiation, under the assumption that the charge Q_5 in Eqs. (2.1.1) has a component proportional to B. It follows that a neutron star in a binary system, such as PSR 1913+16 [TAYLOR, 1989], can be a source of fifth-force radiation, in the same way that it is a source of gravitational radiation. In fact the strongest evidence at present for the existence of gravitational radiation comes from the agreement between theory and observation for the rate of decay of the pulsar orbit ($\dot{P}$) [TAYLOR, 1991]. This agreement, now approximately at the 10^{-3} level, sets limits on other possible contributions to $\dot{P}$, such as would arise from fifth-force radiation [KRAUSE, 1994]. These limits can be quite stringent, since the pulsar can lose energy through *dipole* fifth-force radiation, whereas the lowest multipole for gravitational radiation is quadrupole. Radiation from PSR 1913+16 is discussed in more detail in Chapter 4.

We turn next to the possibility of detecting the individual quanta γ_Y of a possible fifth force, which could arise from the decays of various elementary particles. Consider, for example, the channel

$$K^+ \rightarrow \pi^+ \gamma_Y. \tag{2.1.16}$$

Since this is a 2-body decay, π^+ is produced with a characteristic 3-momentum p ($p = 227\,\mathrm{MeV}/c$) in the kaon rest frame. Noting that γ_Y would not register on any detector, the signal for this decay would be a pion of the appropriate momentum unaccompanied by any other detected particles. The reader may wonder at this point how the γ_Y decay rate can be sufficiently large to be of interest, when the coupling of γ_Y to ordinary matter is so small that γ_Y cannot be sensed by any detector. The answer lies in a phenomenon known as the "Weinberg catastrophe" [WEINBERG, 1964], wherein the *emission* of γ_Y in strangeness-violating decays is enhanced by a factor of order $(m_K^2 - m_\pi^2)/m_5^2 \approx 10^{35}$, relative to a typical *absorption* amplitude where strangeness is conserved. The phenomenology of such decays is discussed in greater detail in Chapter 5.

2.1.4 Finite-Size Effects for non-Newtonian Forces

In addition to the signals for non-Newtonian forces that we have considered thus far, there are effects which depend specifically on the finite size of the source and/or test masses (compared to the range λ for a Yukawa term). These effects, which were first discussed in the present context by Stacey [STACEY, PC; FISCHBACH, 1988B, 1990], make the non-Newtonian force appear to be composition dependent, even when the underlying potential in Eq. (2.1.8) contains no explicit dependence on the composition of the test masses.

As we demonstrate explicitly in Section 2.4, the finite-size effect arises from the circumstance that for any non-Newtonian potential, such as $V_5(r)$ in Eq. (2.1.6), $\nabla^2 V_5(r) \neq 0$. This means that the interaction energy W of a finite test mass with a point source can contain a term of the form

$$W = \int d^3 r \rho(\vec{r}) |\vec{r}|^2 \nabla^2 V_5(r) + \cdots, \qquad (2.1.17)$$

which depends on the mass distribution $\rho(\vec{r})$ of test mass. Since the integral in Eq. (2.1.17) will generally not be the same for two samples which have a common mass but different compositions, it follows that the coupling of these samples to V_5 will depend *implicitly* on composition through $\rho(\vec{r})$. One of the consequences of the finite-size effect is the recognition that *any* non-Newtonian force will lead to apparent composition-dependent deviations from Newtonian gravity. We refer the reader to Section 2.4 for a more detailed discussion.

2.2 Details of the Non-Newtonian Charge

As noted in the previous section, the non-Newtonian coupling strength for two interacting point masses can be assumed to depend on some linear combination of the known charges: baryon number (B), lepton number (L), and isospin (I_z), as given in Eq. (2.1.1). The charge Q_5 can also depend on the mass M in some theories where the new force arises from the exchange of a scalar field. Let us consider the simple case where Q_5 is given by the expression in Eq. (2.1.1a). We noted in Eq. (2.1.7) that the experimentally interesting quantity is actually the specific charge $q_{5i} = Q_{5i}/\mu_i$ where

$$q_5 = \frac{Q_5}{\mu_5} = \left(\frac{B}{\mu}\right) \cos \theta_5 + \left(\frac{I_z}{\mu}\right) \sin \theta_5. \qquad (2.2.1)$$

For an element such as Al, which is composed entirely of a single stable isotope, B/μ and I_z/μ can be obtained trivially. However, for most other elements (and all compounds) care must be taken to weight the individual values of B, I_z, and μ according to the composition of the material when finding the effective values of B/μ and I_z/μ.

For illustrative purposes let us consider the calculation of B/μ for the case of an element composed of two isotopes 1 and 2 with baryon numbers $B_{1,2}$ and masses $m_{1,2}$, and define $q_{1,2} = B_{1,2}m_{\rm H}$, where $m_{\rm H} = m({}_1{\rm H}^1)$. If we assume that the test sample consists of $n_1(n_2)$ atoms of isotope 1(2), then from the definition of $\vec{\mathcal{F}}$ the net acceleration of the sample is given by

$$\vec{a} = \frac{\text{total force}}{\text{total mass}} = \frac{(n_1 q_1 + n_2 q_2)\,\vec{\mathcal{F}}}{n_1 m_1 + n_2 m_2}$$

$$= \frac{n_1 B_1 + n_2 B_2}{n_1 m_1 + n_2 m_2}\, m_{\rm H}\, \vec{\mathcal{F}}$$

$$= \frac{n_1 B_1 + n_2 B_2}{n_1 \mu_1 + n_2 \mu_2}\, \vec{\mathcal{F}}. \tag{2.2.2}$$

For a single isotope the coefficient of $\vec{\mathcal{F}}$ is evidently B_1/μ_1, and from (2.2.2) we see that this generalizes to

$$\frac{B_1}{\mu_1} \longrightarrow \frac{B}{\mu} = \frac{\displaystyle\sum_{k=1}^{2} n_k B_k}{\displaystyle\sum_{k=1}^{2} n_k \mu_k}. \tag{2.2.3}$$

We can replace the n_k by the isotopic abundances r_k, with $0 < r_k \le 1$, so that finally

$$\frac{B}{\mu} = \frac{\displaystyle\sum_{k=1}^{2} r_k B_k}{\displaystyle\sum_{k=1}^{2} r_k \mu_k}, \tag{2.2.4}$$

where the summation extends over all isotopes. Evidently, the result in Eq. (2.2.4) applies *mutatis mutandis* to the calculation of I_z/μ. It may be necessary in computing B, I_z, or μ to rescale the quoted values of r_k so as to properly enforce the normalization condition

$$\sum_k r_k = 1. \tag{2.2.5}$$

In practice since B/μ is nearly unity for all substances, for purposes of evaluating $\Delta(B/\mu)$, (B_i/μ_i), and (B_j/μ_j) should each be calculated to at least six (and preferably seven) significant figures. By contrast, the variations in I_z/μ (or L/μ) are much greater, and it is sufficient to calculate each of these to five significant figures. Although μ_k (and obviously B_k and I_{zk}) are known with great precision for all of the necessary isotopes, the same is not always the case for r_k. Nonetheless we can show that any uncertainty δr_k in r_k leads to an uncertainty in B/μ or I_z/μ which is too small to be of any concern.

Consider first the case of B/μ. We use the fact that the B_k are known exactly, and that the uncertainty in the μ_k are negligible, to write

$$\delta B = \delta \sum_k r_k B_k = \sum_k \delta r_k B_k,$$

$$\delta \mu = \delta \sum_k r_k \mu_k = \sum_k (\delta r_k \mu_k + r_k \delta \mu_k) \cong \sum_k \delta r_k \mu_k.$$

(2.2.6)

Returning to Eq. (2.2.4), the error $\delta(B/\mu)$ is given by

$$\delta \left(\frac{B}{\mu} \right) = \frac{\delta B}{\mu} - \frac{B \delta \mu}{\mu^2}.$$

(2.2.7)

Combining Eqs. (2.2.6) and (2.2.7), we find for the error in B/μ (for a single determination of the various quantities)

$$\delta \left(\frac{B}{\mu} \right) = \sum_k \frac{\mu_k}{\mu} \delta r_k \left(\frac{B_k}{\mu_k} - \frac{B}{\mu} \right).$$

(2.2.8)

Squaring Eq. (2.2.8), averaging over a large number of determinations, and identifying $\langle r_k^2 \rangle$ with $\sigma_{r_k}^2$ gives

$$\left\langle \left[\delta \left(\frac{B}{\mu} \right) \right]^2 \right\rangle = \sum_k \left(\frac{\mu_k}{\mu} \right)^2 \sigma_{r_k}^2 \left(\frac{B_k}{\mu_k} - \frac{B}{\mu} \right)^2$$

$$+ 2 \sum_k \sum_\ell \frac{\mu_k}{\mu} \frac{\mu_\ell}{\mu} \sigma_{r_k} \sigma_{r_l} \rho_{k\ell} \left(\frac{B_k}{\mu_k} - \frac{B}{\mu} \right) \left(\frac{B_\ell}{\mu_\ell} - \frac{B}{\mu} \right), \quad (2.2.9a)$$

$$\rho_{k\ell} \equiv \frac{1}{\sigma_{r_k} \sigma_{r_\ell}} \langle \delta r_k \delta r_\ell \rangle.$$

(2.2.9b)

Here $\rho_{k\ell}$ is defined to be the correlation coefficient between δr_k and δr_ℓ, and is constrained by its definition [Eq. (2.2.9b)] so that $-1 \leq \rho_{k\ell} \leq 1$. We note that all of the factors in the cross terms in Eq. (2.2.9b) are positive definite, except for $\rho_{k\ell}$ and the differences between B_k/μ_k or B_ℓ/μ_ℓ versus B/μ. An upper limit on the sum over all terms in Eq. (2.2.9) can then be set as follows: We choose the values of $\rho_{k\ell} = \pm 1$ such that the product of

$\rho_{k\ell}(B_k/\mu_k - B/\mu)(B_\ell/\mu_\ell)$ is always positive. This is equivalent to setting $\rho_{k\ell} = 1$ and taking the absolute values of the terms involving B/μ. With the identification of $\langle[\delta(B/\mu)]^2\rangle$ with $\sigma^2_{(B/\mu)}$ we get

$$\sigma_{(B/\mu)} \le \sum_k \left(\frac{\mu_k}{\mu}\right)\sigma_{r_k}\left|\frac{B_k}{\mu_k} - \frac{B}{\mu}\right|. \qquad (2.2.10)$$

We see from Eq. (2.2.10) that the uncertainty $\sigma_{(B/\mu)}$ in B/μ is *smaller* than one might naively infer from the individual uncertainties σ_{r_k}, because the latter multiply factors such as $|B_k/\mu_k - B/\mu|$ which are themselves quite small. This result is intuitively reasonable, since the uncertainties σ_{r_k} in the individual abundances would evidently have no effect whatsoever if all the isotopes of a given element had the same value of B/μ. As it is, they have *nearly* the same value of B/μ, which is why $\sigma_{(B/\mu)}$ is relatively small. The preceding considerations apply *mutatis mutandis* to the calculation of the uncertainty $\sigma_{(I_z/\mu)}$ in I_z/μ: On the one hand the individual factors $|I_{z_k}/\mu_k - I_z/\mu|$ are larger than for the case of B/μ, but by the same token the values of I_z/μ for individual elements need not be determined as precisely, since $\Delta(I_z/\mu)$ for typical materials is usually larger than 10^{-2}. It follows that when we plot any experimental data against calculated values of $\Delta(B/\mu)$ or $\Delta(I_z/\mu)$, the latter can be treated as if they were exact for our purposes. For a numerical example of the application of Eq. (2.2.10) see [FISCHBACH, 1988B]. The values of B/μ, L/μ, and I_z/μ for the first 92 elements of the periodic table are shown in Table 2.1.

The preceding discussion can be generalized in a straightforward manner to apply to compounds, alloys and mixtures. The content of Eq. (2.2.4) is that when dealing with a collection of isotopes, B, I_z, and μ get replaced by their respective weighted averages

$$B \to \sum_k r_k B_k,$$

$$I_z \to \sum_k r_k I_{zk}, \qquad (2.2.11)$$

$$\mu \to \sum_k r_k \mu_k.$$

These results can then be generalized to compounds and alloys, in an obvious way, so that for water we have, for example,

$$\left(\frac{B}{\mu}\right)_{H_2O} = \frac{\frac{2}{3}B_{\text{hydrogen}} + \frac{1}{3}B_{\text{oxygen}}}{\frac{2}{3}\mu_{\text{hydrogen}} + \frac{1}{3}\mu_{\text{oxygen}}}. \qquad (2.2.12)$$

Equation (2.2.4) may also be recast into a form which is more convenient when the content of each substance is known as a fraction by *weight* (as is typically the case for solutions and alloys), rather than by number. We define w_k to be the fraction by weight of the substance k, μ_k to be its mean molecular weight normalized to that of $_1\mathrm{H}^1$, B_k its mean baryon number, I_z its mean isospin, n_k to be the numbers of moles of the substance, and m to be the total mass of the sample. Since $n_k = w_k m/(\mu_k m_\mathrm{H})$, we can write

$$\frac{B}{\mu} = \frac{\sum_k n_k B_k}{\sum_k n_k \mu_k} = \frac{\sum_k w_k (B_k/\mu_k)}{\sum_k w_k}. \qquad (2.2.13)$$

Since $\sum_k w_k = 1$, we find

$$\frac{B}{\mu} \cong \sum_k w_k \left(\frac{B_k}{\mu_k} \right), \qquad (2.2.14)$$

and similarly

$$\frac{I_z}{\mu} \cong \sum_k w_k \left(\frac{I_{zk}}{\mu_k} \right). \qquad (2.2.15)$$

Eqs. (2.2.4), (2.2.12), (2.2.14), and (2.2.15) are the basic results needed to calculate the effective values of B/μ and I_z/μ for any substance consisting of a collection of individual isotopes. Eqs. (2.2.14) and (2.2.15) are particularly useful since the constituents of various materials are often expressed in terms of percentages by weight.

It is instructive to plot B/μ as a function of atomic number Z for the elements in the periodic table, and this is shown in Fig. 2.1. B/μ is characterized by the fact that elements on either side of Fe can have the same values of this charge. For this reason the phenomenology of a theory based on a coupling to B is somewhat different from that of a coupling to other charges, e.g., L or I_z, as can be seen from the plots of L/μ and I_z/μ in Fig. 2.2. The fact that B/μ is not a monotonic function of Z played a role in the early discussion of a possible fifth force for the following reasons: As we have noted, the original EPF data showed that the observed anomalous acceleration differences Δa_{i-j} correlated with the differences $\Delta(B/\mu)_{i-j}$ for samples i and j, and thus suggested that these differences could have arisen from a new force coupling to B. However, there are many other possible explanations for the nonzero values of Δa_{i-j}, which do not involve new physics. These include various thermal effects [CHU, 1986; FISCHBACH, 1986D] and the possibility of unaccounted-for gravity gradients. What is significant is that these classical explanations characteristically lead to acceleration anomalies Δa_{i-j} which depend on such classical quantities as $\Delta \rho_{i-j}$, where $\rho_i(\rho_j)$ is the density of sample $i(j)$. Since both of these quantities are (at least approximately) monotonic functions of Z, it is not surprising that explanations of

Table 2.1: Average values of B/μ, L/μ, and I_z/μ for the first 92 elements of the periodic table, calculated using [CONDON, 1967].

Element	Z	B	μ	B/μ	L/μ	I_z/μ
Hydrogen	1	1.000149	1.000149	1.000000	0.99985	-0.99970
Helium	2	3.999999	3.971524	1.007170	0.50359	-0.00000
Lithium	3	6.924368	6.886418	1.005511	0.43564	0.13423
Beryllium	4	9.000000	8.942211	1.006462	0.44732	0.11183
Boron	5	10.803900	10.729954	1.006892	0.46599	0.07492
Carbon	6	12.011070	11.917848	1.007822	0.50345	0.00093
Nitrogen	7	14.003663	13.897972	1.007605	0.50367	0.00026
Oxygen	8	16.004452	15.875151	1.008145	0.50393	0.00028
Fluorine	9	19.000000	18.850893	1.007910	0.47743	0.05305
Neon	10	20.178975	20.014707	1.008207	0.49963	0.00894
Sodium	11	23.000000	22.811268	1.008274	0.48222	0.04384
Magnesium	12	24.324700	24.120799	1.008453	0.49750	0.01346
Aluminum	13	27.000000	26.772043	1.008515	0.48558	0.03735
Silicon	14	28.108800	27.867542	1.008657	0.50238	0.00390
Phosphorus	15	31.000000	30.733271	1.008679	0.48807	0.03254
Sulfur	16	32.092550	31.815478	1.008709	0.50290	0.00291
Chlorine	17	35.484585	35.177450	1.008731	0.48326	0.04220
Argon	18	39.985260	39.637491	1.008774	0.45412	0.10054
Potassium	19	39.137729	38.797711	1.008764	0.48972	0.02932
Calcium	20	40.114544	39.765762	1.008771	0.50295	0.00288
Scandium	21	45.000000	44.606862	1.008813	0.47078	0.06725
Titanium	22	47.930500	47.507173	1.008911	0.46309	0.08273
Vanadium	23	50.997600	50.546037	1.008934	0.45503	0.09887
Chromium	24	52.055700	51.592706	1.008974	0.46518	0.07861
Manganese	25	55.000000	54.511488	1.008962	0.45862	0.09172
Iron	26	55.912100	55.413691	1.008994	0.46920	0.07060
Cobalt	27	59.000000	58.475607	1.008968	0.46173	0.08551
Nickel	28	58.771192	58.249142	1.008962	0.48069	0.04757
Copper	29	63.616522	63.052162	1.008951	0.45994	0.08908
Zinc	30	65.459500	64.879191	1.008944	0.46240	0.08415
Gallium	31	69.792000	69.175916	1.008906	0.44813	0.11264
Germanium	32	72.708329	72.066646	1.008904	0.44403	0.12084
Arsenic	33	75.000000	74.339873	1.008880	0.44391	0.12107
Selenium	34	79.073000	78.376964	1.008881	0.43380	0.14128
Bromine	35	79.986272	79.283191	1.008868	0.44146	0.12596
Krypton	36	83.888664	83.150023	1.008883	0.43295	0.14298
Rubidium	37	85.557000	84.804461	1.008874	0.43630	0.13628
Strontium	38	87.710200	86.936180	1.008903	0.43710	0.13470
Yttrium	39	89.000000	88.215568	1.008892	0.44210	0.12470
Zirconium	40	91.318500	90.515443	1.008872	0.44191	0.12504

Table 2.1: Continued

Element	Z	B	μ	B/μ	L/μ	I_z/μ
Niobium	41	93.000000	92.185017	1.008841	0.44476	0.11933
Molybdenum	42	95.983800	95.145077	1.008815	0.44143	0.12595
Technetium*	43	96.500000	95.659403	1.008787	0.44951	0.10976
Ruthenium	44	101.161332	100.281750	1.008771	0.43876	0.13124
Rhodium	45	103.000000	102.106508	1.008751	0.44072	0.12732
Palladium	46	106.526447	105.604293	1.008732	0.43559	0.13756
Silver	47	107.963410	107.030804	1.008713	0.43913	0.13046
Cadmium	48	112.519800	111.550455	1.008690	0.43030	0.14809
Indium	49	114.914400	113.926782	1.008669	0.43010	0.14847
Tin	50	118.831400	117.811918	1.008653	0.42441	0.15984
Antimony	51	121.855000	120.813596	1.008620	0.42214	0.16434
Tellurium	52	127.723077	126.636871	1.008577	0.41062	0.18733
Iodine	53	127.000000	125.919129	1.008584	0.42091	0.16677
Xenon	54	131.387191	130.272668	1.008555	0.41452	0.17953
Cesium	55	133.000000	131.873420	1.008543	0.41707	0.17441
Barium	56	137.422188	136.260951	1.008522	0.41098	0.18657
Lanthanum	57	138.999110	137.826730	1.008506	0.41356	0.18138
Cerium	58	140.208695	139.026596	1.008503	0.41719	0.17413
Praseodymium	59	141.000000	139.813529	1.008486	0.42199	0.16451
Neodymium	60	144.329900	143.121049	1.008446	0.41923	0.17000
Promethium*	61	147.870700	146.639848	1.008394	0.41599	0.17642
Samarium	62	150.445200	149.195972	1.008373	0.41556	0.17725
Europium	63	152.043600	150.784255	1.008352	0.41782	0.17272
Gadolinium	64	157.331900	156.034982	1.008312	0.41016	0.18798
Terbium	65	159.000000	157.691386	1.008299	0.41220	0.18390
Dysprosium	66	162.571887	161.238121	1.008272	0.40933	0.18961
Holmium	67	165.000000	163.649830	1.008250	0.40941	0.18943
Erbium	68	167.329413	165.962758	1.008235	0.40973	0.18877
Thulium	69	169.000000	167.622567	1.008217	0.41164	0.18494
Ytterbium	70	173.098255	171.692889	1.008185	0.40770	0.19278
Lutetium	71	175.025900	173.608076	1.008167	0.40897	0.19023
Hafnium	72	178.546045	177.105160	1.008136	0.40654	0.19506
Tantalum	73	180.999877	179.542926	1.008115	0.40659	0.19494
Tungsten	74	183.890595	182.414337	1.008093	0.40567	0.19675
Rhenium	75	186.258600	184.767563	1.008070	0.40592	0.19624
Osmium	76	190.278986	188.761165	1.008041	0.40263	0.20279
Iridium	77	192.254000	190.723678	1.008024	0.40373	0.20057
Platinum	78	195.116262	193.565933	1.008009	0.40296	0.20208
Gold	79	197.000000	195.437208	1.007996	0.40422	0.19955
Mercury	80	200.627522	199.039464	1.007979	0.40193	0.20412

*no stable isotopes

Table 2.1: Continued

Element	Z	B	μ	B/μ	L/μ	I_z/μ
Thallium	81	204.410000	202.796901	1.007954	0.39941	0.20913
Lead	82	207.242649	205.609783	1.007942	0.39881	0.21031
Bismuth	83	209.000000	207.357780	1.007920	0.40027	0.20737
Polonium*	84	211.051854	209.400963	1.007884	0.40114	0.20559
Astatine*	85	210.933333	209.284384	1.007879	0.40615	0.19559
Radon*	86	215.179134	213.507617	1.007829	0.40280	0.20224
Francium*	87	218.300000	216.613331	1.007787	0.40164	0.20451
Radium*	88	222.200000	220.490628	1.007753	0.39911	0.20953
Actinium*	89	226.610000	224.877486	1.007704	0.39577	0.21616
Thorium*	90	228.000000	226.258236	1.007698	0.39778	0.21215
Protactinium*	91	230.910000	229.152770	1.007668	0.39711	0.21344
Uranium	92	237.978161	236.180722	1.007610	0.38953	0.22855

*no stable isotopes

the EPF data based on correlations with $\Delta\rho_{i-j}$ or $\Delta(1/\rho)_{i-j}$ have not been successful, given that $\Delta(B/\mu)_{i-j}$ is not monotonic and does work. At the present time these considerations are mostly of historical interest, since the recent repetitions of the EPF experiment have to date found no convincing evidence for deviations from Newtonian gravity.

It is worth noting that composition-dependent anomalies in Eötvös-type experiments can arise which depend on charges other than B or L. An example is the model of Lorentz noninvariance studied in [FISCHBACH, 1985] in which the charge is proportional to the weak binding energy per unit mass (B_w/M), which is given by

$$\frac{B_w}{M} \cong \left(1.705\frac{Z}{B} - 1.673\frac{Z^2}{B^2} \right). \tag{2.2.16}$$

Another example is an anomalous coupling to neutrino-exchange forces, which we discuss in Section 2.7 below. However, for most of the models which have been put forward recently it is sufficient to consider the generalized charge q_5 in Eqs. (2.1.1), which is a linear combination of B/μ and I_z/μ. We see from Eqs. (2.1.13) and (2.1.14) that since the acceleration difference $\Delta\vec{a}_{j-j'}$ of two test masses j and j' toward a common source i is proportional to the product $S = q_{5i}(\theta_5)\ \Delta[q_5(\theta_5)]_{j-j'}$, $\Delta\vec{a}_{j-j'}$ can vanish for those values of θ_5 where either $q_{5i}(\theta_5) = 0$ and/or $\Delta[q_5(\theta_5)]_{j-j'} = 0$.

The quantity S, which is sometimes referred to as the "Adelberger sensitivity function," was introduced in [ADELBERGER, 1987] as a means of

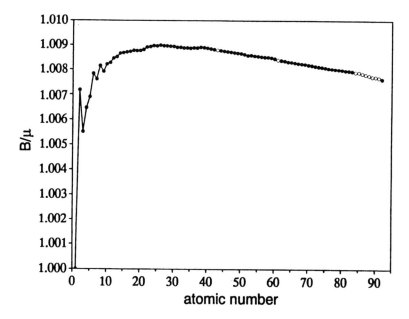

Figure 2.1: Plot of B/μ versus atomic number, where B denotes the baryon number, μ the mass in units of $m({}_1H^1)$, and where the average over isotopes is evaluated using Eq. (2.2.4). For elements with no stable isotopes, the value of the longest-lived isotope is plotted. Elements with at least one stable isotope are plotted using a filled circle, and elements which have no stable isotopes are plotted using an open circle.

graphically displaying the value(s) of θ_5 where various experiments lose sensitivity. Let us simplify our notation by defining $q_{5i}(\theta_5) \equiv q_s$, where "s" denotes the "source," and $\Delta[q_5(\theta_5)]_{j-j'} = (\Delta q)_d$, where "d" denotes the masses which constitute the "detector." Since the signal in any experiment is proportional to

$$\xi S = \xi q_s (\Delta q)_d, \qquad (2.2.17)$$

it follows that whenever q_s or $(\Delta q)_d$ vanishes, ξ can be arbitrarily large and still be compatible with any experimental signal or limit. In practical terms what this means is that when the results of a given experiment are represented as a plot of ξ as a function of θ_5 (for a fixed value of λ), $\xi(\theta_5)$ will have two poles corresponding to the values of θ_5 where

$$q_5 = q_5(\theta_5) = 0, \qquad (2.2.18a)$$
$$(\Delta q)_d = (\Delta q(\theta_5))_d = 0. \qquad (2.2.18b)$$

Such a plot is given in Fig. 1 of [ADELBERGER, 1987]. The loss of experimental sensitivity at these values of θ_5 can be seen by noting that all values

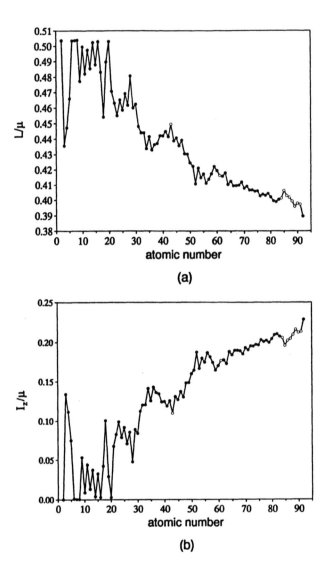

Figure 2.2: Plot of (a) L/μ and (b) I_z/μ versus atomic number for all elements except hydrogen, where L is lepton number, $I_z = N - Z$ is isospin, and μ is the mass in units of $m(_1H^1)$. For elements with no stable isotopes, the value of the longest-lived isotope is plotted. Elements with at least one stable isotope are plotted using a filled circle, and elements which have no stable isotopes are plotted using an open circle.

of θ_5 below the indicated curve are compatible with the given data.

Although it might appear at first sight that the vanishing of q_s or $(\Delta q)_d$ for a given experiment would be accidental, this is not necessarily the case. Let us first consider the situation with respect to q_s. It has been noted in [ADELBERGER, 1987] and in [TALMADGE, 1987A] that for values of $\sin\theta_5$ near unity in Eq. (2.2.1), the coupling is predominantly to I_z, and for most terrestrial sources the average value of I_z, $\langle I_z \rangle$, is close to zero. This is true for SiO$_2$, which is the most common constituent of ordinary rocks, and also for CaCO$_3$. More generally, typical rocks consist mostly of light elements (such as Si and O) which have equal numbers of protons and neutrons. By contrast, ores from which elements such as Fe, Au, U, and other metals are extracted are neutron rich. Hence if there existed an intermediate-range force in nature which coupled to isospin [see Eq. (2.2.1)], then q_s would in fact be zero for most geophysical sources (mountains, cliffs, etc.). Indeed the difference in the value of q_s from one site to another could depend on relatively small quantities of other minerals (with nonzero $\langle I_z \rangle$) present in the rocks. For this reason various experiments which have used geophysical sources to set limits on the strength ξ_I of a coupling to I_z have gone to some lengths to determine the chemical composition of their source [ADELBERGER, 1987; BOYNTON, 1987; FITCH, 1988; KURODA, 1990]. The uncertainty in determining q_5 for geophysical sources can be circumvented by using as a source either water [BENNETT, 1989], lead bricks [ADELBERGER, 1987; SPEAKE, 1988; STUBBS, 1989A; COWSIK, 1988, 1990; NELSON, 1990; GUNDLACH, 1997], or some other laboratory source [AKASAKA, 1989]. These experiments, which we discuss in greater detail in Chapter 4, set stringent limits on ξ_I, at least in the framework of the conventional Yukawa model that we have developed thus far. However, in the exponential model discussed in Section 2.5 below, laboratory experiments become relatively insensitive, and the limits on ξ_I are weaker. To summarize, q_s may indeed vanish for geophysical sources, and hence this possibility should be considered when setting limits on $\xi = \xi(\theta_5)$.

We consider next the other possibility in Eq. (2.2.18), which is that $(\Delta q)_d$ may vanish for the specific pair of materials which comprise the detector in a given experiment. Since

$$(\Delta q)_d = \Delta(B/\mu)\cos\theta_5 + \Delta(I_z/\mu)\sin\theta_5, \qquad (2.2.19)$$

it follows that $(\Delta q)_d = 0$ when

$$\tan\theta_5 = \frac{-\Delta(B/\mu)}{\Delta(I_z/\mu)}. \qquad (2.2.20)$$

Evidently there is always some value of θ_5 for which $(\Delta q)_d$ would vanish for a specific pair of materials (with particular values of $\Delta(B/\mu)$ and $\Delta(I_z/\mu)$). However, since θ_5 is presumably some fundamental constant of the theory,

$(\Delta q)_d$ will not in general vanish for another pair of materials with different values of $\Delta(B/\mu)$ and $\Delta(I_z/\mu)$. Adelberger et al., [ADELBERGER, 1987] carried out the first (modern) experiment in which the accelerations of *two pairs* of samples were compared, specifically Al-Be and Cu-Be. Their (null) result was (and still is) strong evidence against the existence of a composition-dependent intermediate-range force, because it definitively ruled out the possibility that Δq_d was accidentally zero in their original experiment [STUBBS, 1987].

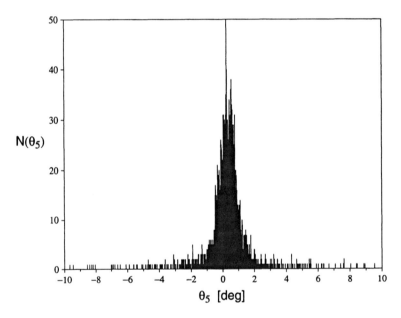

Figure 2.3: Histogram of values of θ_5 (in degrees) at which $\Delta q(\theta_5) = 0$ for all of the natural elements. The vertical axis gives the number of pairs $N(\theta_5)$ which vanish in a given interval of θ_5, as determined by Eq. (2.2.20). See the text for further discussion.

We have calculated $\Delta q_d(\theta_5)$ for the $92 \times 91/2 = 4186$ pairs that can be formed using the first 92 elements of the periodic table, and found the value of θ_5 for which each individual Δq_d vanishes. Shown in Fig. 2.3 is a histogram giving the number of pairs which vanish in a given interval of θ_5 as a function of θ_5. It is evident from the figure that many pairs vanish near $\sin\theta_5 \cong 0$, although one must hasten to add that the difference between $\sin\theta_5 = 0$ and $\sin\theta_5 \cong 0$ can be quite important, for reasons to be discussed below. It is easy to see from Eq. (2.2.20) why Δq_d vanishes for many pairs near $\sin\theta_5 = 0$. For most materials $\Delta(I_z/\mu) \gg \Delta(B/\mu)$, from which it follows that $|\sin\theta_5| \cong |\tan\theta_5| \ll 1$. As a side comment we observe that the envelope of the histogram has an approximately Gaussian or Lorentzian shape. If approximated as a Gaussian, it has a maximum at $\theta_5 = 0.320°$, and a full width at half maximum of $\sigma_\theta = 0.707°$.

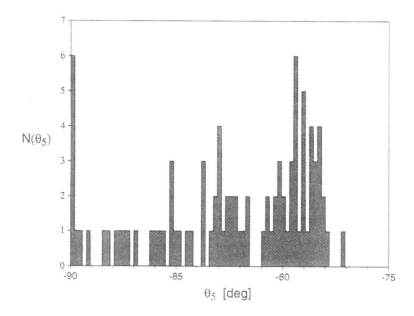

Figure 2.4: Histogram of values of θ_5 (in degrees) at which $q_s(\theta_5) = 0$ for all of the natural elements.

We have also determined the values of θ_5 for which q_s vanishes, and a histogram of these values is shown in Fig. 2.4. From this figure, we see that most elements have a vanishing q_s near $\cos\theta_5 \cong 0$. Again it is possible to understand from the definition of q_s why this occurs:

$$q_s = 0 = \left(\frac{B}{\mu}\right)_s \cos\theta_5 + \left(\frac{I_z}{\mu}\right)_s \sin\theta_5 \Longrightarrow \tan\theta_5 = -\frac{(B/\mu)_s}{(I_z/\mu)_s}. \qquad (2.2.21)$$

We note that $(B/\mu)_s \geq 1$ for all of the natural elements, while from Fig. 2.2b we see that for all of the elements except hydrogen, $0.25 > (I_z/\mu)_s \gtrsim 0$. For these elements, we therefore have $-90° \leq \theta_5 \lesssim -75°$, and $0.26 \gtrsim \cos\theta_5 \gtrsim 0$.

From the above discussion, we see that values of $\sin\theta_5 \cong 0$ result in experiments in which Δq_d tends to be suppressed, whereas values of $\cos\theta_5 \cong 0$ result in experiments in which q_s tends to be suppressed. For exploring the region near $\sin\theta_5 \cong 0$, the choice of which materials to use for the detector becomes critical, and for exploring the region near $\cos\theta_5 \cong 0$, the choice of the source becomes important.

2.3 Phenomenology of Extended Sources

2.3.1 General Formalism

Thus far we have considered only point-like sources interacting with a point-like test object. In this section, we generalize the phenomenology to include extended sources interacting with a point-like test object. Following the notation introduced in Section 2.1, we write the potential energy between two point masses m_i and m_j as

$$V_{5ij}(\vec{r}) \equiv V_{ij}(\vec{r}) = \xi G_\infty m_i m_j q_i(\theta_5) q_j(\theta_5) \frac{e^{-r/\lambda}}{r}, \qquad (2.3.1)$$

where $\vec{r}_i$ and $\vec{r}_j$ are the positions of two point-like masses, and $\vec{r} = r\hat{r} = \vec{r}_i - \vec{r}_j$, as shown in Fig. 2.5 below. To simplify our notation, we drop the subscript "5" (which labels fifth-force quantities) when no confusion would occur.

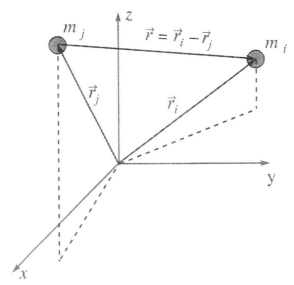

Figure 2.5: Definition of parameters for the interaction of two point-like masses.

As before, the non-Newtonian force on object j due to object i will then be

$$\vec{F}_{ij}(\vec{r}) = \xi G_\infty m_i m_j\, q_i(\theta_5) q_j(\theta_5) \left(1 + \frac{r}{\lambda}\right) \frac{e^{-r/\lambda}}{r^2} \hat{r}, \qquad (2.3.2)$$

and the acceleration of object i toward object j is

$$\vec{a}_{ij}(\vec{r}) = \frac{1}{m_i}\vec{F}_{ij} = \hat{r}\xi G_\infty m_j q_i(\theta_5)q_j(\theta_5)\left(1+\frac{r}{\lambda}\right)\frac{e^{-r/\lambda}}{r^2}. \qquad (2.3.3)$$

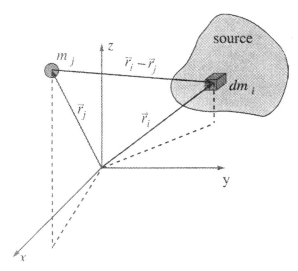

Figure 2.6: Definition of parameters for the interaction of a point-like mass with an extended source.

We can generalize Eqs. (2.3.1)–(2.3.3) by replacing the source mass m_i by dm_i, and then integrating over dm_i, using the notation of Fig. 2.6. We then find from Eq. (2.3.1)

$$V_{ij}(\vec{r}_j) = \xi G_\infty m_j q_j(\theta_5)\int dm_i \, q_i(\vec{r},\theta_5)\frac{e^{-|\vec{r}_i-\vec{r}_j|/\lambda}}{|\vec{r}_i-\vec{r}_j|}. \qquad (2.3.4)$$

The integral in the above expression depends in a complicated fashion on θ_5 and λ. In many cases, however, this expression can be simplified by separating out the dominant dependence on θ_5 and λ:

$$V_{ij}(\vec{r}_j) = \xi G_\infty m_j q_j(\theta_5)\,\bar{q}_i(\theta_5)\,\mathcal{V}_i(\vec{r}_j,\lambda;\theta_5), \qquad (2.3.5)$$

$$\mathcal{V}_i(\vec{r}_j,\lambda;\theta_5) = \int dm_i \, w_i(\vec{r}_i,\theta_5)\frac{e^{-|\vec{r}_i-\vec{r}_j|/\lambda}}{|\vec{r}_i-\vec{r}_j|}, \qquad (2.3.6)$$

$$\bar{q}_i(\theta_5) = \frac{\displaystyle\int dm_i \, q_i(\vec{r},\theta_5)}{\displaystyle\int dm_i}, \qquad (2.3.7)$$

$$w_i(\vec{r},\theta_5) = \frac{q_i(\vec{r},\theta_5)}{\bar{q}_i(\theta_5)}. \qquad (2.3.8)$$

Here $\bar{q}_i(\theta_5)\mathcal{V}_i(\vec{r}_j, \lambda; \theta_5) = \Phi(\vec{r}_j, \lambda; \theta_5)$ is the Yukawa potential due to the extended source i. (The indices i and j will normally be suppressed when there is no possibility of confusion.) Equations (2.3.5)–(2.3.8) have been written in such a fashion as to place the entire dependence on λ in $\mathcal{V}(\vec{r}, \lambda; \theta_5)$, and the predominant dependence on θ_5 for many distributions in $\bar{q}(\theta_5)$. This leaves $\mathcal{V}(\vec{r}, \lambda; \theta_5)$ depending only weakly on θ_5.*

The non-Newtonian force $\vec{F}_{ji}(\vec{r}_j)$ on object j due to an extended source i can be written in a similar fashion:

$$\vec{F}_{ji}(\vec{r}_j) = \xi G_\infty m_j q_j(\theta_5)$$
$$\times \int dm_i \, q_i(\vec{r}_i, \theta_5) \, (\vec{r}_j - \vec{r}_i) \left(1 + \frac{|\vec{r}_i - \vec{r}_j|}{\lambda}\right) \frac{e^{-|\vec{r}_i - \vec{r}_j|/\lambda}}{|\vec{r}_i - \vec{r}_j|^3}. \quad (2.3.9)$$

Separating out the dominant dependence on θ_5 and λ gives

$$\vec{F}_{ji}(\vec{r}_j) = \xi m_j \, \bar{q}_i(\theta_5) q_j(\theta_5) \vec{\mathcal{F}}(\vec{r}_j, \lambda; \theta_5), \quad (2.3.10)$$

$$\vec{\mathcal{F}}_i(\vec{r}_j, \lambda; \theta_5) = -\vec{\nabla} \mathcal{V}_i(\vec{r}, \lambda) \quad (2.3.11)$$

$$= G_\infty \int dm_i \, w_i(\vec{r}_i, \theta_5) \, (\vec{r}_j - \vec{r}_i) \left(1 + \frac{|\vec{r}_i - \vec{r}_j|}{\lambda}\right) \frac{e^{-|\vec{r}_i - \vec{r}_j|/\lambda}}{|\vec{r}_i - \vec{r}_j|^3}, \quad (2.3.12)$$

where $\bar{q}(\theta_5)\vec{\mathcal{F}}(\vec{r}, \lambda; \theta_5)$ is the non-Newtonian field strength due to the extended source i. Finally, the acceleration of particle j due to the configuration i will be

$$\vec{a}_{ji}(\vec{r}_j) \equiv \frac{\vec{F}_{ji}(\vec{r})}{m_j} = \xi \, \bar{q}_i(\theta_5) q_j(\theta_5) \vec{\mathcal{F}}(\vec{r}_j, \lambda; \theta_5), \quad (2.3.13)$$

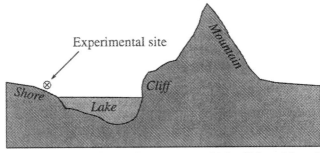

Figure 2.7: Example of a configuration in which $\bar{q}(\theta_5)$ could vanish due to cancellations among the different source contributions.

---

* Since quantities such as $\mathcal{V}(\vec{r}, \lambda; \theta_5)$ are expected to depend only weakly on θ_5, we have used a semicolon to distinguish this parameter from the other parameters. The dependence on θ_5 will usually be suppressed.

Equations (2.3.6) and (2.3.12) are not completely general, since they assume that $\bar{q}(\theta_5)$ for the source does not vanish, and hence that $w(\vec{r}, \theta_5)$ remains finite. This might not be the case for the configuration shown in Fig. 2.7. If we were to model this site as being dominantly the lake and the mountain, there could very well be values of θ_5 for which $\bar{q}(\theta_5)$ vanishes.

The preceding formalism can deal with such a scenario by writing $\vec{\mathcal{F}}(\vec{r}, \lambda; \theta_5)$ as a sum of two contributions, one arising from the lake, and the other from the mountain. Assuming that each of these sources is homogeneous, we now have $w_{\text{lake}}(\vec{r}, \theta_5) = w_{\text{mountain}}(\vec{r}, \theta_5) = 1$, and the acceleration on a test object j will be given by

$$\vec{a}_{j,\text{total}}(\vec{r}) = \xi \, \bar{q}_{\text{lake}}(\theta_5) q_j(\theta_5) \vec{\mathcal{F}}_{\text{lake}}(\vec{r}_j, \lambda; \theta_5)$$
$$+ \xi \, \bar{q}_{\text{mountain}}(\theta_5) q_j(\theta_5) \vec{\mathcal{F}}_{\text{mountain}}(\vec{r}_j, \lambda; \theta_5), \quad (2.3.14)$$

which is well defined for all values of θ_5. Similarly, for a heterogeneous source composed of N individual homogeneous sources, we write the *total* Yukawa field strength as

$$\vec{\mathcal{F}}_{\text{total}}(\vec{r}_j, \lambda; \theta_5) = \sum_{i=0}^{N} \vec{\mathcal{F}}_i(\vec{r}_j, \lambda; \theta_5), \quad (2.3.15)$$

where $\vec{\mathcal{F}}_i(\vec{r}_j, \lambda; \theta_5)$ is given by Eq. (2.3.12). Finally, the total acceleration of object j toward this heterogeneous source is

$$\vec{a}_{j,\text{total}}(\vec{r}) = \sum_{i=0}^{N} \xi \, \bar{q}_i(\theta_5) q_j(\theta_5) \vec{\mathcal{F}}_i(\vec{r}_j, \lambda; \theta_5). \quad (2.3.16)$$

2.3.2 Closed-Form Solutions

Starting from Eqs. (2.3.6) and (2.3.12), we next derive the results for various mass distributions. In obtaining these results, it is useful to note for that for $\rho(\vec{r}) = \text{constant}$, $w(\vec{r}', \theta) \equiv 1$. Working in Cartesian coordinates, we can write

$$\vec{\mathcal{F}}_{\text{extended}}(\vec{r}, \lambda; \theta_5) \equiv -\vec{\nabla}_{\vec{r}} \, V_{\text{extended}}(\vec{r}, \lambda) \quad (2.3.17a)$$

$$= G_\infty \rho \int_V d^3x' \, \vec{\nabla}_{\vec{r}'} \left[\frac{e^{-|\vec{r}-\vec{r}'|/\lambda}}{|\vec{r} - \vec{r}'|} \right] \quad (2.3.17b)$$

$$= G_\infty \rho \int_S d^2x' \, \hat{n}' \left[\frac{e^{-|\vec{r}-\vec{r}'|/\lambda}}{|\vec{r} - \vec{r}'|} \right], \quad (2.3.17c)$$

which follows from the divergence theorem. Here V and S are, respectively, the volume and surface of the configuration to be integrated over, and $\hat{n}'$ is the outwardly pointing normal to the surface.

(1) *Infinite half-space.* We first calculate the non-Newtonian potential $\mathcal{V}(\vec{r}, \lambda)$ and field strength $\vec{\mathcal{F}}(\vec{r}, \lambda)$ at a point z above a mass distribution extending from $-\infty < x < +\infty$, $-\infty < y < +\infty$, and $-\infty < z \leq 0$. From Eq. (2.3.6), we have in polar coordinates

$$\mathcal{V}(\vec{r}, \lambda) = \rho G_\infty \int_0^{2\pi} d\phi' \int_{-\infty}^0 dz' \int_0^\infty dr'\, r' \frac{e^{-\sqrt{r'^2+(z-z')^2}/\lambda}}{\sqrt{r'^2+(z-z')^2}}$$

$$= 2\pi \rho G_\infty \int_{-\infty}^0 dz' \int_0^\infty dr'\, r' \frac{e^{-\sqrt{r'^2+(z-z')^2}/\lambda}}{\sqrt{r'^2+(z-z')^2}}. \qquad (2.3.18)$$

Using the substitution $u(r') = \sqrt{r'^2+(z-z')^2}$, so $u\,du = r'dr'$, we obtain

$$\mathcal{V}(\vec{r}, \lambda) = 2\pi \rho G_\infty \lambda \int_{-\infty}^0 dz'\, e^{-|z-z'|/\lambda}, \qquad (2.3.19)$$

$$= 2\pi \rho G_\infty \lambda^2 \times \begin{cases} e^{-z/\lambda} & (z \geq 0), \\ 2 - e^{+z/\lambda} & (z \leq 0). \end{cases} \qquad (2.3.20)$$

From Eq. (2.3.17a), we then find

$$\vec{\mathcal{F}}(\vec{r}, \lambda) = \hat{z}\, 2\pi \rho \lambda G_\infty e^{-|z|/\lambda}. \qquad (2.3.21)$$

The results of Eqs. (2.3.20) and (2.3.21) are displayed in Fig. 2.8.

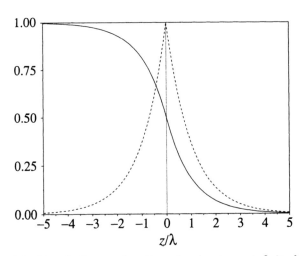

Figure 2.8: $\mathcal{V}$ and $\mathcal{F}_z$ as a function of z due to an infinite half-space mass distribution, as explained in the text. Here $\mathcal{V}$ (solid curve) and $\mathcal{F}_z$ (dashed curve) are normalized to their respective maximum values.

(2) *Spherical shell.* We determine the potential and field strength of a spherical shell of radius R and mass M. For this case, the density $\rho(\vec{r}) = \sigma\delta(r-R)$, where $\sigma = M/4\pi R^2$ is the surface density of the shell, and $\delta(x)$ is the usual Dirac delta function. We then have

$$
\mathcal{V}(\vec{r}, \lambda) = \sigma G_\infty \int_0^{2\pi} d\phi' \int_0^\pi d\theta' \sin\theta' \int_0^\infty dr' r'^2 \delta(r' - R)
$$
$$
\times \frac{e^{-\sqrt{r'^2 + r^2 - 2r'r\cos\theta'}/\lambda}}{\sqrt{r'^2 + r^2 - 2r'r\cos\theta'}}
$$
$$
= 2\pi\sigma G_\infty r^2 \int_0^\pi d\theta' \sin\theta' \frac{e^{-\sqrt{r^2 + R^2 - 2rR\cos\theta'}/\lambda}}{\sqrt{r^2 + R^2 - 2rR\cos\theta'}}. \qquad (2.3.22)
$$

Making the substitution $u(\theta') = \sqrt{r^2 + R^2 - 2rR\cos\theta'}$, this becomes

$$
\mathcal{V}(\vec{r}, \lambda) = \frac{2\pi\sigma G_\infty R\lambda}{r} \left[e^{-|r-R|\lambda} - e^{-(r+R)/\lambda} \right],
$$
$$
= \frac{G_\infty M}{r} \left(\frac{\lambda}{R}\right) \frac{1}{2} \left[e^{-|r-R|\lambda} - e^{-(r+R)/\lambda} \right], \qquad (2.3.23)
$$

which reduces to

$$
\mathcal{V}(\vec{r}, \lambda) = G_\infty M \times
\begin{cases}
\dfrac{e^{-r/\lambda}}{r} \dfrac{\sinh(R/\lambda)}{R/\lambda} & (r \geq R), \\[2ex]
\dfrac{e^{-R/\lambda}}{R} \dfrac{\sinh(r/\lambda)}{r/\lambda} & (r \leq R).
\end{cases} \qquad (2.3.24)
$$

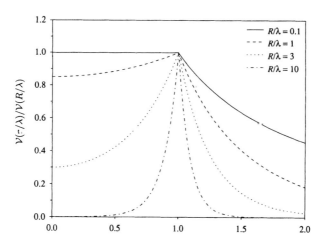

Figure 2.9: $\mathcal{V}(r/\lambda)/\mathcal{V}(R/\lambda)$ for a spherical shell of radius R for various choices of R/λ.

The results of these calculations are displayed in Fig. 2.9. We note that for $\lambda \to \infty$ (and hence for $R/\lambda \to 0$), $\mathcal{V}(\vec{r}, \lambda)$ approaches the expression expected from a simple $1/r$ potential: $\mathcal{V} = constant$ inside the shell, and falls off as $1/r$ outside the shell. Also, for $\lambda \to 0$, $\mathcal{V} \to 0$ except near $r = R$, as expected. The field strength can be derived from Eq. (2.3.24) by employing Eq. (2.3.17a) as before. The radial component of $\vec{\mathcal{F}}$ is given by

$$\mathcal{F}(\vec{r}, \lambda) = G_\infty M \times \begin{cases} \left(1 + \frac{r}{\lambda}\right) \frac{e^{-r/\lambda}}{r^2} \frac{\sinh(R/\lambda)}{R/\lambda} & (r \geq R), \\ -\frac{e^{-R/\lambda}}{R} \cdot \frac{1}{r^2} \left[\frac{r}{\lambda} \cosh\left(\frac{r}{\lambda}\right) - \sinh\left(\frac{r}{\lambda}\right)\right] & (r \leq R). \end{cases} \quad (2.3.25)$$

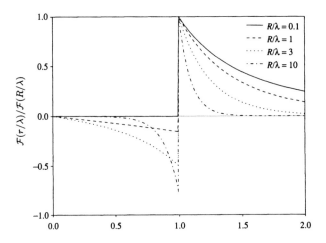

Figure 2.10: $\mathcal{F}(r/\lambda)/\mathcal{F}(R/\lambda)$ for a spherical shell of radius R for various choices of R/λ.

We note that $\mathcal{F}(\vec{r}, \lambda)$, which is displayed in Fig. 2.10, again has the expected limiting results for both small and large λ.

(3) *Uniform sphere.* We consider the case of a sphere of uniform density ρ and radius R. (For a previous derivation, see [FISCHBACH, 1986E].) We have

$$\mathcal{V}(\vec{r}, \lambda) = \rho G_\infty \int_0^{2\pi} d\phi' \int_0^\pi d\theta' \sin\theta' \int_0^R dr' r'^2$$
$$\times \frac{e^{-\sqrt{r'^2 + r^2 - 2r'r\cos\theta'}/\lambda}}{\sqrt{r'^2 + r^2 - 2r'r\cos\theta'}}$$
$$= 2\pi \rho G_\infty \int_0^R dr' r'^2 \int_0^\pi d\theta' \sin\theta' \frac{e^{-\sqrt{r'^2 + r^2 - 2r'r\cos\theta'}/\lambda}}{\sqrt{r'^2 + r^2 - 2r'r\cos\theta'}}. \quad (2.3.26)$$

Making the substitution $u(\theta') = \sqrt{r'^2 + r^2 - 2r'r\cos\theta'}$, this becomes

$$\mathcal{V}(\vec{r}, \lambda) = \frac{2\pi\rho G_\infty \lambda}{r} \int_0^R dr'\, r' \left[e^{-|r'-r|/\lambda} - e^{-(r'+r)/\lambda} \right], \tag{2.3.27}$$

$$= G_\infty M \times \begin{cases} \dfrac{e^{-r/\lambda}}{r} \Phi_s\left(\dfrac{R}{\lambda}\right) & (r \geq R), \\[2mm] \dfrac{r}{2R^3}\dfrac{6\lambda^2}{r^2}\left[1 - \left(1+\dfrac{R}{\lambda}\right)e^{-R/\lambda}\dfrac{\sinh(r/\lambda)}{r/\lambda}\right] & (r \leq R), \end{cases} \tag{2.3.28}$$

where

$$\Phi_s(x) \equiv \frac{3}{x^3}\left[x\cosh x - \sinh x\right]. \tag{2.3.29}$$

For future reference, $\Phi_s(x)$ has the limits

$$\Phi_s(x) = 1 + \frac{x^2}{10} + \frac{x^4}{280} + \cdots, \qquad (x \ll 1), \tag{2.3.30a}$$

$$\Phi_s(x) \cong \frac{3e^x}{2x^2}, \qquad (x \gg 1). \tag{2.3.30b}$$

Combining Eqs. (2.3.17a) and (2.3.28), we find for the radial component of the field strength

$$\mathcal{F}(\vec{r}, \lambda) = G_\infty M \times \begin{cases} \left(1+\dfrac{r}{\lambda}\right)\dfrac{e^{-r/\lambda}}{r^2}\Phi_s\left(\dfrac{R}{\lambda}\right) & (r \geq R), \\[2mm] \dfrac{r}{R^3}\Phi_s\left(\dfrac{r}{\lambda}\right)\left(1+\dfrac{R}{\lambda}\right)e^{-R/\lambda} & (r \leq R). \end{cases} \tag{2.3.31}$$

(4) *Simple Earth model.* Lastly, we consider a model of the Earth with mass $M_\oplus$, radius $R_\oplus$, and average density $\rho_\oplus$. We divide the Earth, which is assumed to be non-rotating and to have spherical symmetry, into an interior region (i.e., mantle plus core) and a crustal region. The interior region is assumed to extend from the center of the Earth to a radius R_i from the center, and the crustal region from R_i to $R_\oplus$. For simplicity each region is assumed to have constant density, with the interior region having a density ρ_i and the crustal region having a density $\bar{\rho}$. We then have

$$\mathcal{V}_\oplus(\vec{r}, \lambda) = \frac{\bar{\rho}}{\rho_\oplus}\mathcal{V}_{\text{sphere}}\left(\frac{r}{\lambda}, \frac{R_\oplus}{\lambda}\right) + \left[\frac{\rho_i}{\rho_\oplus} - \frac{\bar{\rho}}{\rho_\oplus}\right]\mathcal{V}_{\text{sphere}}\left(\frac{r}{\lambda}, \frac{R_i}{\lambda}\right), \tag{2.3.32}$$

$$\vec{\mathcal{F}}_\oplus(\vec{r}, \lambda) = \frac{\bar{\rho}}{\rho_\oplus}\vec{\mathcal{F}}_{\text{sphere}}\left(\frac{r}{\lambda}, \frac{R_\oplus}{\lambda}\right) + \left[\frac{\rho_i}{\rho_\oplus} - \frac{\bar{\rho}}{\rho_\oplus}\right]\vec{\mathcal{F}}_{\text{sphere}}\left(\frac{r}{\lambda}, \frac{R_i}{\lambda}\right), \tag{2.3.33}$$

where $\mathcal{V}_{\text{sphere}}(x, y)$ and $\vec{\mathcal{F}}_{\text{sphere}}(x, y)$ are the functions given by Eqs. (2.3.28) and (2.3.31). As a practical matter, for $R_\oplus/\lambda \gg 1$ we can ignore the respective contributions from $\mathcal{V}_{\text{sphere}}(r/\lambda, R_i/\lambda)$ and $\vec{\mathcal{F}}_{\text{sphere}}(r/\lambda, R_i/\lambda)$. This is because all experiments in the foreseeable future will be taking place in a region for which $r \gtrsim R_\oplus$, and for this region $\mathcal{V}_{\text{sphere}}(r/\lambda, R_i/\lambda) \ll$

$V_{\text{sphere}}(r/\lambda, R_\oplus/\lambda)$ and $|\vec{\mathcal{F}}_{\text{sphere}}(r/\lambda, R_i/\lambda)| \ll |\vec{\mathcal{F}}_{\text{sphere}}(r/\lambda, R_\oplus/\lambda)|$. In this limit, for $r \geq R_\oplus$,

$$V_\oplus(\vec{r}, \lambda) = \frac{G_\infty M_\oplus}{r} \left\{ \frac{\bar{\rho}}{\rho_\oplus} e^{-r/\lambda} \Phi_s \left(\frac{R_\oplus}{\lambda} \right) \right\},$$

$$\vec{\mathcal{F}}_\oplus(\vec{r}, \lambda) = \hat{r}_5 \frac{G_\infty M_\oplus}{r^2} \left\{ \frac{\bar{\rho}}{\rho_\oplus} (1 + \frac{r}{\lambda}) e^{-r/\lambda} \Phi_s \left(\frac{R_\oplus}{\lambda} \right) \right\}.$$

$$(2.3.34)$$

Similarly, for $r \leq R_\oplus$ and $\lambda \ll (R_\oplus - r)$

$$V_\oplus(\vec{r}, \lambda) = \frac{G_\infty M_\oplus r^2}{2 R_\oplus^3} \left\{ \frac{\bar{\rho}}{\rho_\oplus} \frac{6\lambda^2}{r^2} \times \left[1 - \left(1 + \frac{R_\oplus}{\lambda} \right) e^{-R_\oplus/\lambda} \frac{\sinh(r/\lambda)}{r/\lambda} \right] \right\},$$

$$\vec{\mathcal{F}}_\oplus(\vec{r}, \lambda) = \hat{r}_5 \frac{G_\infty M_\oplus r}{R_\oplus^3} \left\{ \frac{\bar{\rho}}{\rho_\oplus} \left(1 + \frac{R_\oplus}{\lambda} \right) e^{-R_\oplus/\lambda} \Phi_s \left(\frac{r}{\lambda} \right) \right\}.$$

$$(2.3.35)$$

Here $\hat{r}_5$ is the unit vector normal to the surface of the Earth, so that $\hat{r}_5 = \hat{r}$ for the case of a spherical Earth. The terms in curly brackets are the modifications to $V_\oplus(\vec{r}, \lambda)$ and $\vec{\mathcal{F}}_\oplus(\vec{r}, \lambda)$ arising from the short-range nature of the force, and the ratio $\bar{\rho}/\rho_\oplus$ accounts for the fact that only local matter will contribute meaningfully for $\lambda \ll R_\oplus$. A limit that is of particular interest arises when $r = R_\oplus + z$, with $z \ll R_\oplus$. We find for $z > 0$

$$V_\oplus(z, \lambda) \cong 2\pi \bar{\rho} G_\infty \lambda^2 \frac{e^{-z/\lambda}}{1 + z/R_\oplus} \left(1 - \frac{\lambda}{R_\oplus} \right)$$

$$\cong 2\pi \bar{\rho} G_\infty \lambda^2 e^{-z/\lambda} \left[1 - \frac{(z + \lambda)}{R_\oplus} \right], \tag{2.3.36}$$

$$\vec{\mathcal{F}}_\oplus(z, \lambda) \cong \hat{r}_5 2\pi \bar{\rho} G_\infty \lambda \left(\frac{\lambda}{R_\oplus} \right) \left(1 - \frac{\lambda}{R_\oplus} \right) \left(1 + \frac{R_\oplus}{\lambda} + \frac{z}{\lambda} \right) \frac{e^{-z/\lambda}}{(1 + z/R_\oplus)^2}$$

$$\cong \hat{r}_5 2\pi \bar{\rho} G_\infty \lambda e^{-z/\lambda} \left[1 - \frac{z}{R_\oplus} \right], \tag{2.3.37}$$

where we have used

$$e^{-r/\lambda} \Phi_s(R_\oplus/\lambda) \longrightarrow \frac{3}{2} \frac{\lambda^2}{R_\oplus^2} e^{-z/\lambda} \left(1 - \frac{\lambda}{R_\oplus} \right), \qquad (\lambda \ll R_\oplus). \tag{2.3.38}$$

Similarly, for $z < 0$, we find

$$V_\oplus(z, \lambda) \cong 4\pi \bar{\rho} G_\infty \lambda^2 \left[1 - \frac{1}{2} e^{z/\lambda} \frac{R_\oplus + \lambda}{R_\oplus + z} \right]$$

$$\cong 4\pi \bar{\rho} G_\infty \lambda^2 \left\{ 1 - \frac{1}{2} e^{-|z|/\lambda} \left[1 + \frac{(|z| + \lambda)}{R_\oplus} \right] \right\}, \tag{2.3.39}$$

$$\vec{\mathcal{F}}_\oplus(z, \lambda) \cong \hat{r}_5 2\pi \bar{\rho} G_\infty \left(\frac{\lambda}{R_\oplus + z} \right)^2 \left(1 + \frac{R_\oplus}{\lambda} \right) \left(1 - \frac{\lambda}{R_\oplus + z} \right) (R_\oplus + z) e^{z/\lambda}$$

$$\cong \hat{r}_5 2\pi \bar{\rho} G_\infty \lambda e^{-|z|/\lambda} \left[1 + \frac{|z|}{R_\oplus} \right]. \tag{2.3.40}$$

It is instructive to compare the potential energy and force on a test particle of mass m_i and charge $q_i(\theta_5)$ from this Yukawa-type interaction to the ordinary Newtonian $1/r^2$ interaction. For a Newtonian interaction at the surface of the Earth, we have

$$V_N \cong \frac{GM_\oplus m_i}{R} = \frac{4}{3}\pi\rho_\oplus m_i G_\infty R_\oplus^2, \tag{2.3.41}$$

$$F_N \cong \frac{GM_\oplus m_i}{R^2} = \frac{4}{3}\pi\rho_\oplus m_i G_\infty R_\oplus, \tag{2.3.42}$$

and, from Eqs. (2.3.36) and (2.3.37), the corresponding expressions for the Yukawa interaction at the surface of the Earth are

$$V_Y \cong 2\pi\bar{q}(\theta_5)q_i(\theta_5)\bar{\rho}G_\infty\xi\lambda^2, \tag{2.3.43}$$

$$F_Y \cong 2\pi\bar{q}(\theta_5)q_i(\theta_5)\bar{\rho}G_\infty\xi\lambda. \tag{2.3.44}$$

Combining these equations gives

$$\frac{V_Y}{V_N} \cong \frac{3}{2}\frac{\bar{\rho}}{\rho_\oplus}\frac{\lambda^2}{R_\oplus^2}\xi\bar{q}(\theta_5)q_i(\theta_5), \tag{2.3.45}$$

$$\frac{F_Y}{F_N} \cong \frac{3}{2}\frac{\bar{\rho}}{\rho_\oplus}\frac{\lambda}{R_\oplus}\xi\bar{q}(\theta_5)q_i(\theta_5). \tag{2.3.46}$$

As an example, if $\xi = 0.01$, $\lambda = 100\,\text{m}$, and $\bar{q}(\theta_5), q_i(\theta_5) \approx 1$, then

$$\frac{V_Y}{V_N} \cong \frac{3}{2} \times \frac{1}{2} \times \left[\frac{100\,\text{m}}{6.4 \times 10^6\,\text{m}}\right]^2 \times 0.01 \approx 1.8 \times 10^{-12}, \tag{2.3.47a}$$

$$\frac{F_Y}{F_N} \cong \frac{3}{2} \times \frac{1}{2} \times \left[\frac{100\,\text{m}}{6.4 \times 10^6\,\text{m}}\right] \times 0.01 \approx 1.2 \times 10^{-7}. \tag{2.3.47b}$$

These results show that even for ξ as large as 0.01, the magnitude of the putative fifth force will be small compared to the usual Newtonian "background." This is one indication of why experiments to search for new intermediate-range forces are so difficult: Not only are these forces intrinsically weaker than gravity (i.e., $\xi \ll 1$), but their contributions are further suppressed (when λ is not infinite) since only part of the matter in a source can contribute in general.

2.4 Derivation of the Finite-Size Effect

As noted in Section 2.1, an apparent composition-dependent acceleration difference between two test masses can arise even when the underlying interaction is not explicitly composition dependent. To understand the origin of this "finite-size effect," consider the interaction energy W of a test object whose charge distribution is $\rho(\vec{r})$, with the potential $\Phi(\vec{r})$ of an external field,

$$W = \int d^3r \rho(\vec{r}) \Phi(\vec{r}). \tag{2.4.1}$$

$\Phi(\vec{r})$ can be expanded about the center of mass of the test object ($\vec{r} = 0$) and, retaining the first few terms, we have

$$W = \int d^3r \rho(\vec{r}) \left[\Phi(0) + \vec{r} \cdot \vec{\nabla}\Phi(0) + \frac{1}{2}\sum_{i,j} x_i x_j \partial_i \partial_j \Phi(0) + \cdots \right], \tag{2.4.2}$$

where $\partial_i \equiv \partial/\partial x_i$, and $(\vec{r})_i = x_i$. If $\Phi(\vec{r})$ arises from a massless field (so that $\nabla^2\Phi(\vec{r}) = 0$), then the usual multipole expansion for W is obtained by adding to Eq. (2.4.2) the term $-\frac{1}{6}|\vec{r}|^2\delta_{ij}\nabla^2\Phi(0)$. This allows the third term in Eq. (2.4.2) to be expressed in terms of the quadrupole moment tensor Q_{ij},

$$Q_{ij} = \frac{1}{6}\int d^3r \rho(\vec{r})\left(3x_i x_j - |\vec{r}|^2\delta_{ij}\right). \tag{2.4.3}$$

However, in searching for deviations from Newtonian gravity we are probing specifically for interactions for which $\nabla^2\Phi(\vec{r}) \neq 0$. It follows that if we wish to expand W in terms of the same multipole moments that arise in the massless case, then we must add back the term proportional to $\nabla^2\Phi(0)$, so that the leading rotationally-invariant contribution to W now has the form

$$W = \int d^3r \rho(\vec{r})\left[1 + \frac{1}{6}|\vec{r}|^2\nabla^2 + \cdots\right]\Phi(0). \tag{2.4.4}$$

Since the term proportional to $|\vec{r}|^2$ is independent of the orientation of the test object, it will behave as an additional contribution to its mass. To see what effect this term has, consider the case where $\Phi(\vec{r})$ is given by a Yukawa,

$$\Phi(\vec{r}) = \frac{\alpha GM}{|\vec{r} - \vec{r}'|}\exp(-|\vec{r} - \vec{r}'|/\lambda), \tag{2.4.5}$$

corresponding to a point source of mass M and strength αG located at $\vec{r}'$. Since $\Phi(\vec{r})$ is a solution of the time-independent Klein-Gordon equation, it follows that

$$\nabla^2\Phi(\vec{r}) = (1/\lambda^2)\Phi(\vec{r}), \tag{2.4.6}$$

and hence

$$W = \int d^3r \rho(\vec{r}) \left[1 + \frac{1}{6} \frac{|\vec{r}|^2}{\lambda^2} + \cdots \right] \Phi(0) = m \left[1 + \frac{1}{6} \frac{\langle R^2 \rangle}{\lambda^2} \right] \Phi(0) + \cdots.$$
(2.4.7)

Here m is the mass of the test object, $\langle R^2 \rangle \equiv (1/m) \int d^3r \rho(r) |\vec{r}|^2$ is its mean-square-charge radius, and $\cdots$ denotes the remaining terms from Eq. (2.4.2), which depend on higher derivatives of $\Phi(\vec{r})$. We see from Eq. (2.4.7) that for a Yukawa potential the leading correction to the standard multipole formula, arising from the fact that λ is finite, has the effect of multiplying the (inertial) mass m by the expression in square brackets in Eq. (2.4.7). As we now show, this correction leads to an apparent violation of the equivalence principle.

Let $\vec{F}_1$ denote the total force acting on a test mass m_1 in the combined presence of the Earth's acceleration field $\vec{g}(\vec{r})$ and $\vec{\nabla}\Phi(\vec{r})$,

$$\vec{F}_1 = m_1 \vec{g} - m_1(1 + \kappa_1) \vec{\nabla}\Phi,$$
(2.4.8)

where $\kappa_1 = \langle R^2 \rangle_1 / 6\lambda^2$. The acceleration difference of objects 1 and 2 along the direction $\hat{n}$, $\Delta a = (\vec{a}_1 - \vec{a}_2) \cdot \hat{n}$, is then given by

$$\frac{\Delta a}{\vec{a} \cdot \hat{n}} = \Delta\kappa \left(-\frac{\vec{\nabla}\Phi \cdot \hat{n}}{\vec{g} \cdot \hat{n}} \right),$$
(2.4.9)

where $\Delta\kappa = \kappa_1 - \kappa_2$, and $\vec{a} = (\vec{a}_1 + \vec{a}_2)/2$. It follows from Eq. (2.4.9) that two objects with different values of $\langle R^2 \rangle$ will experience different accelerations in the presence of Φ, *irrespective of whether or not they have the same composition*. $\Delta\kappa$ will almost always be different from zero in an Eötvös experiment, where the accelerations of two objects having the same mass but different compositions are compared. For the current generation of Eötvös experiments, where test samples have not only the same mass but the same external dimensions as well, $\rho(\vec{r})$ must be different for the two test masses, and hence $\Delta\kappa$ is necessarily different from zero.

The finite-size contribution in Eq. (2.4.4), which applies to any matter distribution $\rho(\vec{r})$ interacting with an arbitrary potential $\Phi(\vec{r})$, generalizes a result originally derived by Stacey [STACEY, PC] for a spherical mass in the field of a point Yukawa source. To establish the connection between Eq. (2.4.4) and Stacey's work, we consider (as he did) the experiment of Thieberger [1987A] in which the differential acceleration between a spherical copper shell and the water it displaced was measured. For a uniform sphere of radius R_2 we have

$$\langle R^2 \rangle = \frac{3}{5} R_2^2,$$
(2.4.10)

while for a shell with outer (inner) radius $R_2(R_1)$ the corresponding result is

$$\langle R^2 \rangle = \frac{3}{5} \frac{(R_2^5 - R_1^5)}{(R_2^3 - R_1^3)}.$$
(2.4.11)

From Eqs. (2.4.10), (2.4.11), and (2.4.7), we find immediately that the (anomalous) acceleration difference between the shell and the water sphere is proportional to

$$\Delta\kappa = \kappa_{\text{sphere}} - \kappa_{\text{shell}} = \frac{-R_1^3}{10\lambda^2 R_2} \frac{(1 - R_1^2/R_2^2)}{(1 - R_1^3/R_2^3)}, \qquad (2.4.12)$$

which is what Stacey found. In addition to generalizing Stacey's result, Eq. (2.4.4) also demonstrates that the leading non-Newtonian corrections to the multipole formula can be obtained *directly*, without having to start from an exact analytic result as Stacey did. This means that the non-Newtonian contribution can be calculated simply for test masses of arbitrary shape, where an analytic expression would be difficult (if not impossible) to come by.

It follows from the preceding discussion that any experiment which measures the acceleration of a test object i will be sensitive at some level to the finite-size anomaly κ_i. This effect will be the dominant signal for a non-Newtonian force when the mean-square charge radius $\langle R^2 \rangle$ of an object is comparable to the distance scale over which the non-Newtonian potential is varying, which for a Yukawa occurs when $\langle R^2 \rangle^{1/2} \approx \lambda$. This observation suggests that the finite-size effect may offer a practical means of adapting Eötvös experiments to carry out high-precision searches for composition-independent non-Newtonian gravity over distances of several centimeters, which is the characteristic size of the masses that are typically used. More significantly, by appropriately redesigning the test masses, it may be possible to achieve a far greater sensitivity to composition-independent short-range forces than is currently possible by other means.

2.5 Non-Yukawa Forms of the Non-Newtonian Interaction

Up to this point, our analysis of non-Newtonian effects has been based on the assumption that the functional form of the non-Newtonian potential $V_5(r)$ is given by the Yukawa expression in Eq. (2.1.4). As we explained in the course of arriving at this expression, a Yukawa is the natural form for a new force which arises from exchange of a *single* new quantum of mass m_5. However, there is no compelling reason why a putative new force should have this simple form, and proposed alternatives to the simple Yukawa have included the possibility of several Yukawas (with different ranges), as well as non-Yukawa forces. The latter can arise from modified gravitational theories in which the non-Newtonian behavior is due to the presence of antisymmetric terms in the metric tensor $g_{\mu\nu}(x)$ [Moffat, 1987]. In Moffat's theory, the new force varies as $1/r^5$, rather than as a Yukawa, and so acts as a force with a longer range than would be the case for a Yukawa. Such theories tend to be somewhat specialized, and hence the interested reader should refer to the original papers for further discussion. Another example is provided by the force arising from the exchange of massless neutrino-antineutrino ($\nu\bar{\nu}$) pairs, which is discussed in Section 2.7. In this case the force between two heavy fermions (electrons, protons, or neutrons) due to $\nu\bar{\nu}$ exchange falls off as $1/r^6$.

By contrast, theories with two or more Yukawas are straightforward extensions of the model leading to $V_5(r)$ in Eq. (2.1.4), and have been extensively studied in the literature [GOLDMAN, 1986; TALMADGE, 1987B; STUBBS, 1988B, 1989B; TALMADGE, 1989A; FISCHBACH, 1991]. Apart from the obvious benefit of increasing the number of theoretical parameters available to accommodate experiments, such theories are of interest in the case when the various Yukawa components cancel against one another. For the case of two Yukawas a cancellation between the vector and scalar contributions (which generally have opposite signs) is quite natural, and this possibility is of interest for various proposed experiments on antimatter [GOLDMAN, 1986], as we discuss in Chapter 5. To appreciate why, consider the sum of two Yukawa couplings, each having the form given in Eq. (2.1.4),

$$V_5(r) = +f_V^2 Q_{5i}^V Q_{5j}^V \frac{e^{-r/\lambda_V}}{r} - f_S^2 Q_{5i}^S Q_{5j}^S \frac{e^{-r/\lambda_S}}{r}, \qquad (2.5.1)$$

where the subscripts (or superscripts) V and S refer to the vector and scalar contributions respectively. Note that the signs in Eq. (2.5.1) are those appropriate to the case where both i and j are test masses of ordinary matter. Suppose, however, that we replace j with a test mass composed of antimatter (e.g., $\bar{p}$). Since the sign of the vector contribution will change, whereas the scalar contribution remains unaffected [GOLDMAN, 1986], it follows that the contributions in Eq. (2.5.1) will add instead of canceling. In an extreme case when $f_V^2 \approx f_S^2$ and $\lambda_V \approx \lambda_S$, the strength of the matter-antimatter coupling can be significantly greater than that for the normal matter-matter interaction. This forms part of the motivation for searching for a possible difference in the gravitational accelerations of p and $\bar{p}$ toward the Earth [GOLDMAN, 1982, 1986, 1987, 1988; NIETO, 1988; HOLZSCHEITER, 1990, 1991]. Unfortunately, it is difficult to predict with any certainty the magnitude of the expected $p - \bar{p}$ acceleration difference, since this would require a detailed dynamical model of $f_{V,S}$ and $\lambda_{V,S}$ which we do not as yet possess. One can, however, set theoretical limits on the possible acceleration differences of particles and antiparticles by noting that if such differences existed, they would lead to a nonzero signal in Eötvös-type experiments [SCHIFF, 1960]. This question is discussed in more detail in Chapter 5.

The case of two (nearly) canceling Yukawa potentials is also of interest for matter-matter interactions, since the interpretation of searches for non-Newtonian gravity can be quite different in this situation from what it would be for a single Yukawa. A particularly interesting limiting case occurs when the two Yukawas can be represented by a single exponential, as discussed in [TALMADGE, 1989A; FISCHBACH, 1991]. To understand how an exponential can arise, we set $Q_5^V = Q_5^S = Q$ in Eq. (2.5.1) and generalize the notation so that $f_v \to f_a$, $f_s \to f_b$, $\lambda_v \to \lambda_a$, and $\lambda_s \to \lambda_b$, where a and b denote any two fields. It is straightforward to show that if the masses $m_{a,b} = 1/\lambda_{a,b}$, and coupling constants $f_{a,b}$, are related via

$$m_a = m_b \left[1 + \mathcal{O}(\varepsilon)\right], \qquad f_a = f_b \left[1 + \mathcal{O}(\delta\varepsilon)\right], \qquad (2.5.2)$$

where $\varepsilon, \delta \ll 1$, then the leading contribution to the potential $V_5(r)$ has the form of an exponential,

$$V_5 \equiv V_E(r) \cong f_b^2 Q_1 Q_2 \left[\left(\frac{\Delta\lambda}{\lambda}\right) \frac{e^{-r/\lambda}}{\lambda}\right], \qquad (2.5.3a)$$

$$\vec{F}_E(r) = -\vec{\nabla} V_E(r) = f^2 Q_1 Q_2 \left[\left(\frac{\Delta\lambda}{\lambda}\right) \frac{e^{-r/\lambda}}{\lambda^2}\hat{r}\right], \qquad (2.5.3b)$$

$$\vec{a}_E = \frac{\vec{F}_E(r)}{m_1} \equiv \xi \left(\frac{\Delta\lambda}{\lambda}\right) \left(\frac{Q_1}{\mu_1}\right) \left(\frac{Q_2}{\mu_2}\right) \vec{F}_E(r, \lambda). \qquad (2.5.3c)$$

Here $\Delta\lambda = \lambda_a - \lambda_b$ and $\lambda = (\lambda_a + \lambda_b)/2$. A more complete expression for the expansion of $V_5(r)$ in terms of various small quantities is given in the Appendix of [FISCHBACH, 1991], which also discusses models in which the necessary starting point in Eq. (2.5.2) could hold.

We now demonstrate how the exponential potential can lead to a rather different phenomenology from that expected from a single Yukawa potential. Combining Eq. (2.5.3) with the Newtonian potential, we can write an expression for the total potential in a form analogous to Eq. (2.1.8), but with $G(r)$ now having the form

$$G(r) \equiv G_E(r) = G_\infty \left\{1 - \xi \left(\frac{\Delta\lambda}{\lambda}\right) \left(\frac{Q_1}{\mu_1}\right) \left(\frac{Q_2}{\mu_2}\right) \left(\frac{r}{\lambda}\right)^2 e^{-r/\lambda}\right\}, \qquad (2.5.4)$$

where $\xi = f_b^2/G_\infty m_H^2$. Comparing Eq. (2.5.4) with the analogous Yukawa expression in Eq. (2.1.10), we see that for both the exponential and Yukawa cases the non-Newtonian effects vanish as $r \to \infty$, due to the presence of the exponential. This is, of course, what we expect from any finite-range force. What is new in the exponential case is that *the non-Newtonian effects also vanish as $r \to 0$*, owing to the presence of the factor $(r/\lambda)^2$. This behavior of $G_E(r)$ contrasts markedly with that of $G_Y(r)$, for which

$$G_Y(0) = G_\infty \left[1 - \xi \left(\frac{Q_1}{\mu_1}\right) \left(\frac{Q_2}{\mu_2}\right)\right]. \qquad (2.5.5)$$

The fact that $G_Y(0) \neq G_\infty$ is the basis of a number of high-sensitivity laboratory experiments designed to search for both composition-independent and composition-dependent deviations from Newtonian gravity, as we discuss in more detail in Chapters 3 and 4. However, we see from Eq. (2.5.4) that for the exponential model such experiments are greatly reduced in sensitivity. As an illustration consider a laboratory experiment which uses as its source a sphere of radius $R = 1$ m. In such an experiment the deviations of $G_E(r)$ from G_∞ would be proportional to $(R/\lambda)^2$, and for a "typical" value of λ, $\lambda = 10^3$ m, $(R/\lambda)^2$ would then be $\mathcal{O}(10^{-6})$. Since the constraints on a coupling to I_z come primarily from laboratory experiments, it follows that in the exponential model such couplings would not be significantly constrained, which would change the existing phenomenology considerably.

One can understand the behavior of $G_E(r)$ near $r = 0$ in the following way: From Eq. (2.5.3) we see that when $r \ll \lambda$, $\vec{F}_E$ is proportional to $1/\lambda^2$ rather than $1/r^2$ as is the case for the Yukawa force. This means that in the exponential model, test masses act *as if* they are a fixed distance λ apart (when $r \ll \lambda$), even though their actual separation is r. Hence even though $\vec{F}_E(r)$ is nonzero at $r = 0$, it is suppressed relative to the Newtonian contribution by a factor of $(r/\lambda)^2$, since the Newtonian contribution is increasing as $1/r^2$ in the limit $r \to 0$.

For experiments utilizing geophysical sources the forces arising from the exponential and Yukawa potentials can be obtained by directly integrating the two-body expressions for $\vec{F}_E(r)$ in Eq. (2.5.3) and $\vec{F}_Y(r) = \vec{F}(r)$ in Eq. (2.1.9). However, if the field strength $\vec{\mathcal{F}}_Y(r, \lambda)$ for the Yukawa model is already known, then $\vec{\mathcal{F}}_E(r, \lambda)$ can be obtained directly by noting that the exponential model is the limiting case of two Yukawas. Hence, with $\varepsilon \equiv \Delta\lambda/\lambda \ll 1$,

$$
\begin{aligned}
\vec{F}_E(r, \lambda) &= \vec{F}_Y(r, \lambda + \Delta\lambda) - \vec{F}_Y(r, \lambda) \\
&= \xi q_1 q_2 \left\{ \vec{\mathcal{F}}_Y(r, \lambda + \Delta\lambda) - \vec{\mathcal{F}}_Y(r, \lambda) \right\} \\
&\cong \xi q_1 q_2 \, \Delta\lambda \frac{\partial \vec{\mathcal{F}}_Y(r, \lambda)}{\partial \lambda} = \xi q_1 q_2 \left(\frac{\Delta\lambda}{\lambda}\right) \lambda \frac{\partial \vec{\mathcal{F}}_Y(r, \lambda)}{\partial \lambda} \\
&= \xi \epsilon q_1 q_2 \left[\lambda \frac{\partial \vec{\mathcal{F}}_Y(r, \lambda)}{\partial \lambda} \right],
\end{aligned}
\tag{2.5.6}
$$

and thus

$$
\vec{\mathcal{F}}_E(r, \lambda) = \lambda \frac{\partial \vec{\mathcal{F}}_Y(r, \lambda)}{\partial \lambda}.
\tag{2.5.7}
$$

This result was used in [FISCHBACH, 1991] to compare $\vec{F}_E(r, \lambda)$ and $\vec{F}_Y(r, \lambda)$ for two interesting geophysical sites, namely the locations of the experiments of Adelberger et al. (e.g., [ADELBERGER, 1990]) in Seattle, and that of

Boynton et al. [BOYNTON, 1987] near Mt. Index, Washington. To describe the topography of each site, the surface terrain surrounding each experiment was modeled in a series of grids of different scales, covering an area of approximately $30\,\text{km} \times 30\,\text{km}$ at each site. The results demonstrate that $|\vec{F}| = \sqrt{F_{\text{North}}^2 + F_{\text{East}}^2}$ at each site can look quite different depending on whether it is being evaluated in the Yukawa or exponential models. Similar comparisons of the exponential and Yukawa models have been carried out by Bizzeti et al. [BIZZETI, 1989] using the results of their floating ball experiment at Vallambrosa, Italy (see Section 4.5 below), and also by Kuroda and Mio [KURODA, 1990] for their free-fall experiment (see Section 4.3 below). As is evident from the preceding discussion, by interpreting the results of a given experiment in terms of both the exponential and Yukawa models, one can constrain an even broader class of theoretical models, specifically those which postulate the existence of two (nearly) canceling Yukawas.

Models of non-Newtonian dynamics assuming both Yukawa and non-Yukawa forms for a new interaction have also been applied on larger scales to understand the observed "rotation curves" in galaxies. The rotation curves are plots of the velocity v of a star as a function of its distance r from the center of the galaxy. Assuming Newtonian dynamics, we would expect that the acceleration v^2/r of a star about the galactic center should be given by [OLIVE, 1996]

$$v^2/r = G_0 M(r)/r^2, \tag{2.5.8}$$

where $M(r)$ is the mass interior to r. If most of the mass were concentrated inside a radius R (as is the case for the visible matter), then for a star located at $r > R$ we would expect

$$v^2 \approx GM(R)/r = \text{constant}/r, \tag{2.5.9}$$

which contrasts with the observed behavior, $v^2 \approx$ constant. The observations could be explained if additional nonluminous (i.e., "dark") matter were present for $r > R$, which is one indication of the presence of "missing mass" in the Universe. However, another possibility is that Newtonian dynamics are wrong, and this can come about through either a modification of the inverse-square law of gravitation, or via a modification of the second law of motion ($F = ma$). The latter possibility has been put forward by Milgrom [1983A,B,C], who proposed replacing the second law by

$$F = ma\,\mu(a/a_0), \tag{2.5.10}$$

where $\mu(a/a_0)$ is a function of a, and a_0 is a small constant acceleration. To agree with classical physics, $\mu(a/a_0)$ must be such that $\mu(a/a_0) = 1$ when $a \gg a_0$, but to explain galactic dynamics Milgrom assumes that $\mu(a/a_0) = a/a_0$ when $a \ll a_0$. The interested reader should consult the above references and [BEKENSTEIN, 1984] for further details of this model.

From the present point of view the more natural approach to explain the observed galactic rotation curves is via a modification of the inverse-square law over galactic distances [FINZI, 1963; TOHLINE, 1983; SANDERS, 1984, 1986A,B; KUHN, 1987; FRIEMAN, 1991; ECKHARDT, 1992, 1993; MANNHEIM, 1997]. To understand how such an approach can work consider the model of Kuhn and Kruglyak [TOHLINE, 1983; KUHN, 1987] in which the Newtonian force law is modified to read

$$F(r) = G_0 m_1 m_2 / r^2 + G_1 m_1 m_2 / r, \qquad (2.5.11)$$

where G_1 is a new phenomenological constant. If the magnitude of G_1 were such that this term dominated the Newtonian term proportional to G_0 over galactic distance scales, then the approximate constancy of v^2 as a function of r would follow immediately. Kuhn and Kruglyak demonstrate that a $1/r$ force can in fact account for various observational data over different distance scales. This is an interesting result, notwithstanding the fact that a $1/r$ force would imply a logarithmic potential, for which there is little theoretical motivation.

Alternative functional forms for the non-Newtonian interaction which have a stronger theoretical basis have also been considered by some authors [SANDERS, 1984, 1986A,B; ECKHARDT, 1992, 1993; MANNHEIM, 1997]. Sanders has considered the implications for galactic dynamics of a simple Yukawa modification, such as Eq. (2.1.8). Although it is not evident that a new interaction for which there is an associated length scale λ can reproduce the rotation curves for galaxies of different mass and size, Sanders shows that this can in fact be done for a range of galactic sizes. Eckhardt [1992, 1993] has applied the exponential potential to the study of galactic dynamics. He demonstrates that for an appropriate choice of the strength and range of an exponential potential, the exponential force can dominate over the conventional Newtonian force. He then proceeds to show that if this is the case, then the "anomalous" galactic rotation curves can be understood without having to introduce additional "dark matter." Irrespective of whether the specific model advanced by Eckhardt proves to be successful, it amply demonstrates that an exponential potential could play a role in some physical systems.

We conclude this discussion on a somewhat philosophical note by observing that scenarios in which non-Newtonian dynamics are invoked to explain galactic rotation curves are no more speculative at present than "dark matter" models. Many such models assume the existence of matter not present in the Standard Model of particle physics, just as models invoking non-Newtonian dynamics assume the existence of new forces. Since each scenario leads to characteristic experimental predictions, understanding galactic rotation curves will likely depend on the accumulation of new data.

2.6 Lorentz-Noninvariance and the Eötvös Experiment

A question that is closely related to the existence of new forces is the possibility of a breakdown of Lorentz invariance. In physical terms this could come about if there were a preferred coordinate system in the universe, e.g., that defined by the 3 K cosmic black-body radiation, whose existence influenced local experiments. Recently there has been renewed interest in this question, motivated both by advances in experimental techniques [HUGHES, 1960; DREVER, 1961; PRESTAGE, 1985; LAMOREAUX, 1986, 1989; CHUPP, 1989] and by various theoretical ideas [HAUGAN, 1979, 1987; FISCHBACH, 1985; GABRIEL, 1990; WILL, 1993]. We include a brief discussion of Lorentz-noninvariance and its experimental consequences, because some of these are similar to those expected from the existence of new forces.

One can understand some of the connections between Lorentz noninvariance and the existence of new forces in the following way: For a test object moving in a (static) force field, the sources of this force define a preferred frame, namely, that in which the sources are at rest. As explained in Section 2.1.2, this is the motivation behind the searches for an anomalous velocity dependence of the K^0-$\bar{K}^0$ parameters. It is interesting to observe that anomalous velocity-dependent effects, arising from a breakdown of Lorentz invariance, can also show up in the Eötvös experiment, as was first noted by Haugan [HAUGAN, 1979; FISCHBACH, 1985]. Consider the energy E of some nucleus of mass M falling in a gravitational field,

$$E = Mc^2 + \frac{1}{2}M|\vec{v}|^2 + Mgz + \Delta Mc^2 \left(C + \frac{1}{2}D\frac{|\vec{v}|^2}{c^2} \right), \qquad (2.6.1)$$

where we have reinstated factors of c. In a typical situation C and D are model-dependent constants, and ΔMc^2 is a particular contribution to the binding energy of the nucleus, e.g., from the electromagnetic interaction or the weak interaction. More generally E can depend on tensor quantities such as $v_i v_j$, where v_i ($i = 1, 2, 3$) is a component of $\vec{v}$, but for present purposes we restrict our attention to the expression in Eq. (2.6.1) above. Assuming energy conservation, we can equate the expressions for E at two different heights z_1 and z_2 to give

$$\frac{1}{2}Mc^2 \left(1 + D\frac{\Delta M}{M} \right) \left| \frac{\vec{v}_1}{c} \right|^2 + Mgz_1 = \frac{1}{2}Mc^2 \left(1 + D\frac{\Delta M}{M} \right) \left| \frac{\vec{v}_2}{c} \right|^2 + Mgz_2.$$
$$(2.6.2)$$

In the nonrelativistic regime we can write

$$z = v_0 t + \frac{1}{2}at^2,$$
$$v = v_0 + at, \qquad (2.6.3)$$

and we can further take $v_0 = 0$ without loss of generality. Combining Eqs. (2.6.2) and (2.6.3), we find

$$a = \frac{-g}{1 + D\frac{\Delta M}{M}}. \qquad (2.6.4)$$

It follows from Eq. (2.6.4) that the accelerations of test samples of different chemical composition are not the same, because the factor $\Delta M/M$ varies from one substance to another. For example, in the model discussed in [FISCHBACH, 1985] $\Delta M/M \sim B_w/M$, where B_w is the weak interaction contribution to M given in Eq. (2.2.16). We conclude from this discussion that a violation of Lorentz invariance can manifest itself in the Eötvös experiment as a composition-dependent anomalous acceleration.

2.7 Neutrino-Exchange Forces

In considering the possibility of new intermediate-range or long-range forces, our attention has focused thus far on the existence of corresponding new bosonic fields as the mediators of such forces. It is well known, however, that a long-range force between fermions can also arise from the exchange of neutrino-antineutrino (ν-$\bar{\nu}$) pairs, as shown in Fig. 2.11 [FEINBERG, 1968, 1989; HSU, 1994; FISCHBACH, 1995, 1996A] In this section we review the phenomenology of such forces.

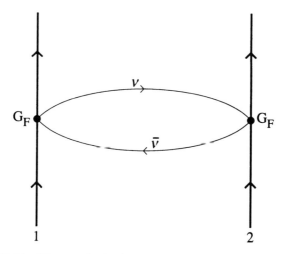

Figure 2.11: The two-body force between fermions arising from the exchange of a ν-$\bar{\nu}$ pair. The heavy lines denote the external fermions, and the lighter lines represent the exchanged neutrinos.

Since neutrinos exist, and are presumed to be massless, a neutrino-exchange force *must* be present at some level. Hence this force represents at least one example of a new long-range interaction that coexists with gravity and electromagnetism. Moreover, since the strength of the ν-$\bar{\nu}$ force between any two fermions depends on the product of their weak charges (which are different for p, n, and e), the neutrino-exchange force between two test masses will necessarily depend on their chemical compositions. The phenomenology of such a force is more complicated than what would be expected from a picture in which one simply viewed each new boson as a neutrino-antineutrino bound state. Historically this force has been thought to be unobservably small, which explains why relatively little attention has been devoted to this question until recently. In what follows we show, however, that neutrino-exchange forces may have observable effects [FISCHBACH, 1995, 1996A].

The first correct calculation of the ν-$\bar{\nu}$-exchange potential was carried out by Feinberg and Sucher (FS) [FEINBERG, 1968, 1989], to whom the interested reader should refer for earlier literature on the subject. Some of this literature deals with the issue of whether the gravitational interaction could originate from neutrino-exchange forces, a question raised by Feynman [1995]. However, the results of FS, and subsequent work by Hartle [1970, 1971, 1972], make this seem very unlikely. Feinberg and Sucher found for the potential energy of interaction of two electrons arising from ν-$\bar{\nu}$ exchange

$$V_{ee}^{(2)}(r) = \frac{G_F^2}{4\pi^3 r^5} \otimes \begin{cases} 1 & \text{four-fermion theory,} \\ (2\sin^2\theta_W + 1/2)^2 & \text{Standard Model.} \end{cases} \quad (2.7.1)$$

In Eq. (2.7.1) $r = |\vec{r}_1 - \vec{r}_2|$ is the separation of the two electrons, $G_F \cong (1.16639 \pm 0.00002) \times 10^{-5} \, \text{GeV}^{-2}$ is the Fermi decay constant, and $\sin^2\theta_W = 0.2325 \pm 0.0008$. The FS result in Eq. (2.7.1) has been confirmed recently by Hsu and Sikivie [HSU, 1994]. We note that since $(2\sin^2\theta_W + 1/2)^2 = 0.9312$, the overall strength of $V_{ee}^{(2)}(r)$ between electrons is essentially the same in the original four-fermion theory (where only charged currents are present) and in the Standard Model (neutral and charged currents). Inserting the values of the various numerical constants in Eq. (2.7.1), we have

$$V_{ee}^{(2)}(r) = 3 \times 10^{-82} \frac{\text{eV}}{(r/1\text{m})^5}, \quad (2.7.2)$$

$$\left| \vec{F}_{ee}^{(2)}(r) \right| = \left| \vec{\nabla} V_{ee}^{(2)}(r) \right| = \frac{2 \times 10^{-100}}{(r/1\,\text{m})^6} \, \text{Newtons.} \quad (2.7.3)$$

To appreciate how weak the ν-$\bar{\nu}$-exchange force is, we compare it to the gravitational force $|\vec{F}_g(r)|$ between two electrons at a nominal separation of $1000\,\text{m}$,

$$\frac{|\vec{F}_{ee}^{(2)}(r = 1000\,\text{m})|}{|\vec{F}_g(r = 1000\,\text{m})|} = 4 \times 10^{-42}. \quad (2.7.4)$$

We see that at a typical macroscopic separation of $1\,\text{km}$, the ν-$\bar{\nu}$-exchange force is completely negligible compared to gravity, itself the weakest of the known forces. However, since $|\vec{F}_{ee}^{(2)}(r)|$ increases more rapidly than $|\vec{F}_g(r)|$ as r decreases, there will be some value of r where $|\vec{F}_{ee}^{(2)}|$ overtakes $|\vec{F}_g(r)|$, and this happens when $r \cong 5 \times 10^{-8}\,\text{m}$. Even so $\vec{F}_{ee}^{(2)}$ is still not directly detectable, since for a value of r this small (or smaller), the electromagnetic force between the electrons will dominate over both $\vec{F}_{ee}^{(2)}$ and $\vec{F}_g$. It thus appears that there is no distance scale over which $\vec{F}_{ee}^{(2)}$ leads to observable effects [FISCHBACH, 1995, 1996A].

Notwithstanding the implications of the preceding discussion, it has been argued recently [FISCHBACH, 1995, 1996A] that neutrino-exchange forces may in fact lead to detectable effects. This could happen through either (or both) of two mechanisms. The first possibility is that the 2-body force shown in Fig. 2.11 may be detectable in an Eötvös-type experiment if gravity couples anomalously to neutrinos. The second is that many-body effects could be inherently large enough to have observable consequences. We proceed to discuss both of these possibilities below [WILL, 1993; FISCHBACH, 1995].

We consider first the possibility that a violation of the weak equivalence principle (WEP) could arise from an anomalous coupling of gravity to neutrinos. Let $W^{(2)}$ denote the contribution to the mass-energy of a nucleus arising from $V_{ee}^{(2)}(r)$ in Eq. (2.7.1). Then an anomalous coupling of gravity to neutrinos would lead to a difference between the (passive) gravitational mass (m_G) of a sample i and its inertial mass (m_I) [WILL, 1993; FISCHBACH, 1995],

$$(m_G)_i = (m_I)_i + \eta_{\nu\bar{\nu}} W_i^{(2)}/c^2. \qquad (2.7.5)$$

Here $\eta_{\nu\bar{\nu}}$ is a dimensionless constant whose magnitude reflects the strength of the violation of the WEP. Since the gravitational acceleration of sample i is $\vec{a}_i = (m_G/m_I)_i(-\vec{\nabla}V_g)$, where V_g is the Newtonian potential, an experimental test of the WEP sets a limit on the difference between the accelerations of a selected pair of samples,

$$\frac{a_1 - a_2}{g} = \eta_{\nu\bar{\nu}}\left[\left(\frac{W^{(2)}}{m_I c^2}\right)_1 - \left(\frac{W^{(2)}}{m_I c^2}\right)_2\right], \qquad (2.7.6)$$

with $g \equiv |-\vec{\nabla}V_g|$. When combined with a calculation of $W^{(2)}$, this experimental limit implies a constraint on the magnitude of $\eta_{\nu\bar{\nu}}$, and hence on the nature of the coupling between gravity and matter.

The first estimates of weak contributions to the nuclear binding energy were made by Nordtvedt [NORDTVEDT, 1972], and by Haugan and Will [HAUGAN, 1976; LOBOV, 1990; FISCHBACH, 1996B], who calculated the $\mathcal{O}(G_F)$ effects arising from $W^{\pm}$ and Z^0 exchange. Our focus here is the $\mathcal{O}(G_F^2)$ contribution $W^{(2)}$ arising from the ν-$\bar{\nu}$-exchange diagram in Fig. 2.11, which would lead to a violation of the WEP if gravity coupled anomalously to neutrinos. Since $W^{(2)}$ can be viewed as the weak analog of the Coulomb energy W_C of a nucleus, it can be calculated in the same way from the fundamental 2-body potential. For both the Coulomb potential and $V_{ee}^{(2)}(r)$ in Eq. (2.7.1), we can utilize the fact that these are long-range interactions to obtain the corresponding contributions to the mass-energy of a nucleus semi-classically, by approximating the nucleus as a spherical matter and charge distribution.

Consider the function $\mathcal{P}(r)$ which gives the normalized probability density for finding two points randomly chosen in a sphere to be a distance $r = r_{12}$ apart. The average value $\langle g \rangle$ of any function $g(r)$ taken over a spherical volume is then given by

$$\langle g \rangle = \int_0^{2R} dr \mathcal{P}(r) g(r). \tag{2.7.7}$$

The functional form of $\mathcal{P}(r)$ has been obtained by a number of authors [OVERHAUSER, 1952; SANTALÓ, 1976] and is given by

$$\mathcal{P}(r) = \frac{3r^2}{R^3} - \frac{9}{4}\frac{r^3}{R^4} + \frac{3}{16}\frac{r^5}{R^6}. \tag{2.7.8}$$

For the Coulomb interaction we wish to calculate $W_C = \langle e^2/r \rangle$ using Eq. (2.7.7). We find

$$W_C = e^2 \langle 1/r \rangle = e^2 \int_0^{2R} dr \left(\frac{3r^2}{R^3} - \frac{9r^3}{4R^4} + \frac{3r^5}{16R^6} \right) \frac{1}{r} = \frac{6}{5}\frac{e^2}{R}. \tag{2.7.9}$$

The result in Eq. (2.7.9) gives the Coulomb energy for a single pair of charges spread out through a spherical volume, and for a nucleus containing Z charges there are $Z(Z-1)/2$ such pairs. Hence the final expression for the Coulomb energy W_C is given by

$$W_C = \frac{1}{2}Z(Z-1)\frac{6}{5}\frac{e^2}{R} = \frac{3}{5}Z(Z-1)\frac{e^2}{R}, \tag{2.7.10}$$

which is the standard result [BOHR, 1969].

The ν-$\bar{\nu}$-exchange contribution can be calculated in an identical manner, the only difference being that the nucleon-nucleon hard core radius r_c must be included explicitly. The dominant contribution arises from neutrino exchange between two neutrons and is given by [FISCHBACH, 1995]

$$\langle V^{(2)}(r) \rangle = \int_{r_c}^{2R} dr \mathcal{P}(r) \left(\frac{\kappa_n}{r^5} \right) = \frac{3\kappa_n}{2R^3 r_c^2} \bar{\xi}(B), \tag{2.7.11a}$$

where $\kappa_n = G_F^2 a_n^2 / 4\pi^3$, $a_n = -1/2$, and

$$\bar{\xi}(B) = 1 - \frac{0.593}{B^{1/3}} + \frac{0.117}{B^{2/3}} - \frac{0.008}{B}. \tag{2.7.11b}$$

In analogy to the Coulomb case, the final expression for $W^{(2)}$ is then obtained by multiplying the result in Eq. (2.7.11) by $N(N-1)/2$, where N is the number of neutrons, which gives

$$W^{(2)} = \frac{3}{16\pi^3} \frac{(G_F a_n)^2}{\hbar c} \frac{N(N-1)}{R^3 r_c^2} \bar{\xi}(B), \tag{2.7.12}$$

where a factor of $\hbar c$ has been reinstated.

We proceed to evaluate $W^{(2)}$ for a nucleus with N neutrons and Z protons, with $N + Z = B$. The hard-core radius r_c is taken to be [BOHR, 1969], $r_c = 0.49 \times 10^{-13}$cm, and for R we use [BOHR, 1969] $R \simeq 1.24 \times 10^{-13}cm\cdot B^{1/3}$. It is convenient to express the inertial mass M of a nucleus in atomic mass units (amu) so that for any nucleus, $M = \mu \times 1$ amu. $W^{(2)}/Mc^2$ in Eq. (2.7.6) can then be written in the form [FISCHBACH, 1995]

$$\frac{W^{(2)}}{Mc^2} = 1.4 \times 10^{-16} \frac{N(N-1)}{B\mu} \bar{\xi}(B). \tag{2.7.13}$$

Combining the previous results, we find

$$\frac{\Delta a}{g} \equiv \frac{a_1 - a_2}{g}$$

$$= \eta_{\nu\bar{\nu}}(1.4 \times 10^{-16}) \left[\frac{N_1(N_1-1)}{B_1\mu_1} \bar{\xi}(B_1) - \frac{N_2(N_2-1)}{B_2\mu_2} \bar{\xi}(B_2) \right]. \tag{2.7.14}$$

The sensitivity of existing or proposed experiments to $\nu\bar{\nu}$-exchange can be estimated by considering as an example the samples used in the experiment of Roll, Krotkov, and Dicke [ROLL, 1964], which were Al and Au:

$$_{13}\text{Al}^{27} \Rightarrow \frac{N(N-1)}{B\mu} \bar{\xi}(B) = 0.204,$$

$$_{79}\text{Au}^{179} \Rightarrow \frac{N(N-1)}{B\mu} \bar{\xi}(B) = 0.321. \tag{2.7.15}$$

Combining Eqs. (2.7.14) and (2.7.15), we then have

$$\frac{\Delta a}{g} = 1.7 \times 10^{-17} \eta_{\nu\bar{\nu}}. \tag{2.7.16}$$

For a nominal value $\eta_{\nu\bar{\nu}} = 1$, the fractional acceleration difference is then $\Delta a/g \cong 10^{-17}$, which is well below the sensitivity limit of current laboratory experiments, as we discuss in Chapter 4. However, this sensitivity level may be achieved by the proposed STEP (Satellite Test of the Equivalence Principle) experiment, which is considered in more detail in Chapter 4.

Since the proposed STEP experiment is designed to achieve a sensitivity $\Delta a/g \simeq 10^{-17}$, it follows from Eq. (2.7.15) that STEP will be able to set a nontrivial limit on $\eta_{\nu\bar{\nu}}$,

$$|\eta_{\nu_i\bar{\nu}_i}| \lesssim 0.60, \qquad (2.7.17)$$

for each neutrino species i. If there is a universal breakdown of the WEP for all neutrinos, characterized by a common value of $\eta_{\nu\bar{\nu}}$, then in this case the indicated level of sensitivity in the STEP experiment would lead to

$$|\eta_{\nu\bar{\nu}}| \lesssim 0.20. \qquad (2.7.18)$$

Given a limit such as in Eq. (2.7.17) or (2.7.18), one can in principle work backwards in any detailed theory of WEP violation to infer a constraint on the anomalous coupling of gravity to any of the neutrinos $\nu_e, \bar{\nu}_e, \nu_\mu, \bar{\nu}_\mu, \nu_\tau$, and $\bar{\nu}_\tau$.

We turn next to a discussion of many-body interactions arising from neutrino exchange. Following Primakoff and Holstein (PH) [PRIMAKOFF, 1939], we note that when the interactions of particles (e.g., neutrons in the present case) are described by means of static potentials, as in Eq. (2.7.1), then relativistic invariance requires that all possible many-body interactions be included along with the 2-body interaction. Ordinarily many-body effects are relatively small in both electromagnetic and strong interactions, for reasons originally discussed by PH. However, the considerations that apply to these interactions do not necessarily apply to the interactions arising from neutrino exchange, and hence we examine these effects in more detail.

Table 2.2: Summary of the necessary conditions for the existence of a large neutrino-exchange many-body effect. For each interaction, "Yes" indicates that the condition is met, and "No" indicates that it is not. Among known interactions only neutrino exchange meets all three conditions. See text and [FISCHBACH, 1996A] for further details.

Condition	Strong	E&M	Weak[a]	Gravity	ν-Exchange
Long-range	No	Yes	No	Yes	Yes
Bulk matter "charge"	Yes	No	Yes	Yes	Yes
Large coupling strength	Yes	Yes	Yes	No	Yes

[a] Z^0-Exchange

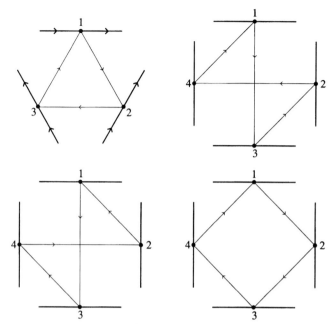

Figure 2.12: Three-body and four-body forces arising from the exchange of ν-$\bar\nu$ pairs. See text for further discussion.

Many-body interactions arising from neutrino exchange have been considered by a number of authors, including Feynman [1995]. Hartle [1970] employed a phenomenological 4-fermion coupling to evaluate the $\mathcal{O}(G_F^4)$ contribution corresponding to the 4-body diagrams in Fig. 2.12. We discuss below the possibility that a large energy-density can arise in some circumstances from many-body effects, and hence we begin by asking why such effects play an important role for neutrino exchange, but are relatively unimportant in most other circumstances. The explanation can be found in Table 2.2, which compares neutrino exchange to other known forces with respect to three conditions which determine when many-body effects become significant. As was first noted by PH, the net contribution from a k-body amplitude ($k = 2, 3, \ldots$) is proportional to the binomial coefficient $\binom{N}{k} = N!/k!(N-k)!$, which counts the number of k-body interactions that exist among a collection of N particles. The binomial coefficient can provide a substantial enhancement factor if a large number of particles interact with sufficient strength in a small volume [CHANMUGAM, 1970]. The conditions necessary to achieve this are summarized in Table 2.2, from which one can see that only neutrino-exchange forces can be expected to produce large many-body effects [FISCHBACH, 1996A]. To understand quantitatively how such effects can give rise to a large energy-density, we follow the discussion of Feinberg and Sucher [FEINBERG, 1968], who note that the functional form of $V_{ee}^{(2)}(r)$ can be inferred on dimensional grounds. Since the Standard Model is renormalizable, the only dimensional factors upon which the static spin-independent potential can depend are G_F and r. Evidently the exchange of a single ν-$\bar{\nu}$ pair must be proportional to G_F^2, from which it follows that $V_{ee}^{(2)} \propto G_F^2/r^5$, in agreement with Eq. (2.7.1). An analogous argument shows that for $k \geq 3$ the k-body neutrino-exchange energy $W^{(k)}$ for a spherical collection of N interacting particles must be proportional to $(G_F^k/R^{2k+1})\begin{pmatrix} N \\ k \end{pmatrix}$, where R is the radius of the matter distribution, which is assumed for present purposes to have a uniform density. Since $\begin{pmatrix} N \\ k \end{pmatrix} \simeq N^k/k!$ for $k \ll N$, it follows that

$$W^{(k)} \sim \frac{1}{k!}\frac{1}{R}\left(\frac{G_F N}{R^2}\right)^k. \qquad (2.7.19)$$

For a typical nucleus $G_F N/R^2 = \mathcal{O}(10^{-6})$, from which we conclude that many-body effects in nuclei are indeed negligible. However, for a typical neutron star $G_F N/R^2 = \mathcal{O}(10^{13})$, and hence it follows from Eq. (2.7.19) that for $k \ll N$ higher order many-body interactions make increasingly larger contributions to $W^{(k)}$. As we discuss below, many-body effects could be sufficiently large to have observable consequences.

The many-body neutrino-exchange potentials can be obtained by adapting a formula due to Schwinger [1954]:

$$W = \frac{i}{2\pi}Tr\left\{\int_{-\infty}^{\infty} dE \ln\left[1 + \frac{G_F a_n}{\sqrt{2}} N_\mu \gamma_\mu (1+\gamma_5) S_F^{(0)}(E)\right]\right\}. \qquad (2.7.20)$$

Here $W = \sum_k W^{(k)}$ is the static weak interaction energy of the constituent neutrons in a neutron star, for example, which are described by the vector number current $N_\mu = i\bar{\Psi}\gamma_\mu\Psi$, $a_n = -1/2$, and $S_F^{(0)}(E)$ is the free Feynman propagator for the neutrino at a fixed energy E. A derivation of Eq. (2.7.20) due to Hartle is presented in Appendix B of [FISCHBACH, 1996A]. When the expression for W is expanded as a perturbation series in powers of G_F, the term proportional to G_F^k gives rise to the k-body contribution, and this derives from diagrams where k neutrons are attached to a neutrino loop as in Fig. 2.12. The k vertices represent in configuration space the coordinates $\vec{r}_i (i = 1, 2, ..., k)$ of the k particles, which are connected by k legs representing the $k(k-1)/2$ variables $r_{ij} = |\vec{r}_i - \vec{r}_j|$. There are $(k-1)!/2$ topologically distinct diagrams and, as in the case of Furry's theorem, both senses of the neutrino-loop momentum must be included for each diagram.

It can be shown that only even-k potentials contribute for a spherically symmetric neutron star [FISCHBACH, 1996A], and the general k-body potential $V^{(k)}$ can be derived in a straightforward manner from the Schwinger formula given by Eq. (2.7.19). The k-body potentials are integrated over a spherical volume representing a neutron star of radius R to obtain W. When the contributions from the $(k-1)!/2$ topologically distinct diagrams and the combinatoric factor $\binom{N}{k}$ are included, the total 0-derivative contribution W_0 to W can be approximated by [FISCHBACH, 1996A]

$$|W_0| \sim \frac{4}{RN} \left(\frac{G_F |a_n| N}{2\pi \sqrt{2} e^2 R^2} \right)^N . \tag{2.7.21}$$

In Eq. (2.7.21), $\ln e = 1$, and various smaller contributions have been neglected. Eq. (2.7.21) is the direct many-body analog for neutrino exchange of the 2-body Coulomb energy W_C in Eq. (2.7.10).

For illustrative purposes we evaluate W_0 for a typical neutron star, which is taken to be the observed pulsar in the Hulse-Taylor binary system PSR 1913+16 [TAYLOR, 1989], whose mass is $M_1 = (1.4411 \pm 0.0007) M_\odot$. Hence we adopt for the mass M of a typical neutron star the value $M = 1.4 M_\odot = 2.8 \times 10^{33}$ g, which then gives $N = 1.7 \times 10^{57}$. The radius R of the neutron star can be inferred in various models, and we assume a nominal value $R = 10\,\text{km} \equiv R_{10}$, which corresponds to a mass density $\rho_m = 6.7 \times 10^{14}\,\text{g cm}^{-3}$, and a number density $\rho = 4.0 \times 10^{38}\,\text{cm}^{-3}$. Using these values, it follows that $|W_0|/M \gg 1$ for a neutron star, and it can be shown that the same conclusion holds if we include the effects of varying densities, ellipticities, etc. Since this result is unphysical, it could be a signal for a breakdown in perturbation theory in higher orders, along the lines discussed recently by various authors [CORNWALL, 1990; GOLDBERG, 1990; ZAKHAROV, 1991]. However, an alternative possibility is that perturbation theory remains valid, but that neutrinos have a small mass m_ν. In such a case the quantity in parentheses in Eq. (2.7.21) would acquire an additional factor $\exp(-m_\nu R)$, which causes the ν-$\bar{\nu}$-exchange force to "saturate" as in the case of the strong interaction in nuclei. $|W_0|$ in Eq. (2.7.21) will then have a physically acceptable value whenever

$$m_\nu \gtrsim \frac{2}{3e^3} \frac{G_F}{\sqrt{2}} |a_n| \frac{\rho}{c^2} = 0.4\,\text{eV}/c^2. \tag{2.7.22}$$

This value of m_ν is sufficiently close to the current bound $m_\nu \lesssim 10\,\text{eV}/c^2$ [PDG, 1996] to suggest that a "fifth force" arising from neutrino exchange could lead to detectable effects.

To summarize this discussion, we have shown that neutrino exchange gives rise to a long-range "fifth force" which might possibly have observable experimental consequences. Most importantly, an anomalous coupling of gravity to neutrinos could be detected as a violation of the weak equivalence principle at the level of sensitivity of the proposed STEP experiment. In addition, many-body forces could be detected either through a breakdown of perturbation theory, or by leading to constraints on neutrino masses. We note in passing that a long-range force can also arise from the exchange of a *single* neutrino (rather than a ν-$\bar{\nu}$ pair) if this takes place in the presence of a background neutrino sea [HOROWITZ, 1993].

While on the subject of a possible anomalous coupling of gravity to neutrinos, we briefly discuss several other related papers. There are a number of different issues associated with neutrinos beginning with the same question addressed by the STEP experiment: Do neutrinos couple to gravity with the same strength that other matter does? This has been considered by several authors who have analyzed supernova SN1987A to infer constraints on neutrino couplings [KRAUSS, 1988; LONGO, 1988; FIORENTINI, 1989; MALANEY, 1995]. The idea behind these analyses begins with the assumption that the observed light and detected neutrinos from the supernova were emitted at approximately the same time. Since the light and the neutrinos traveled approximately 1.6×10^5 ly before reaching the Earth, the fact that they arrived within a few hours of each other suggests that gravity couples to light and to neutrinos with approximately the same strength.

As is well known, light reaching the Earth from a distant star is deflected by the gravitational field of the Sun [WILL, 1993]. For grazing incidence the gravitational deflection $\delta\phi$ is given to lowest order in the gravitational coupling by

$$\delta\phi = \frac{1}{2}(1+\gamma)(1.75 \text{ arcsec}), \qquad (2.7.23)$$

where γ is one of the so-called "parametrized-post-Newtonian" (PPN) parameters, and is equal to unity in General Relativity. The fact that γ is experimentally equal to unity to a high precision [WILL, 1993] can be used to constrain α in Eq. (2.1.8), as shown by Riveros and Vucetich [RIVEROS, 1986]. Similarly, a constraint on α over a distance scale of ~ 23 m can be inferred from the agreement between theory and experiment for the gravitational red shift, as measured by the Mössbauer effect [CRANSHAW, 1988].

Another effect arising from the presence of matter is the "Shapiro time-delay" δt, which represents the additional time that a light wave (or neutrino) requires to traverse a given path when matter is present [WILL, 1993]. Since δt is also proportional to $(1+\gamma)$, comparing the arrival times of photons and neutrinos from SN1987A allows a limit to be set on the difference $(\gamma_\gamma - \gamma_\nu)$, where γ_γ and γ_ν are the PPN parameters for photons and neutrinos respectively. There is some uncertainty in the results due to the uncertainty in the gravitational potential of the galaxy at large distances, but both [LONGO, 1988] and [KRAUSS, 1988] quote limits of order

$$|\gamma_\gamma - \gamma_\nu| \lesssim \mathcal{O}(10^{-3}). \qquad (2.7.24)$$

Data from SN1987A can also be used to probe for a spin-1 fifth force coupling to neutrinos [FIORENTINI, 1989]. The basis of such an analysis is that for relativistic particles such as neutrinos, the strength of the fifth force coupling depends on the energy of the particle. Since the detected neutrinos were not monoenergetic, one can use this argument to set limits on fifth force couplings under a variety of assumptions. The interested reader should consult the above reference and [LONGO, 1988] for further details.

A similar discussion can be used to directly compare the universality of the gravitational couplings to ν_e and $\bar{\nu}_e$, under the assumption that both $\nu_e e$ scattering and $\bar{\nu}_e p$ scattering were detected for the SN1987A neutrinos [PAKVASA, 1989]. Data on the spread of the arrival times of neutrinos can then be used to set a limit,

$$|\gamma_{\nu_e} - \gamma_{\bar{\nu}_e}| < 10^{-6}. \tag{2.7.25}$$

In the same spirit one can also ask whether gravity couples universally to the three neutrino flavors ν_e, ν_μ, ν_τ and their antiparticles [GASPERINI, 1988, 1989A; HALPRIN, 1991, 1996; BUTLER, 1993; PANTALEONE, 1993; MINAKATA, 1995]. A fractional difference of order 10^{-14} in the strength of the gravitational coupling to ν_e and ν_μ could make the gravitational contribution to the conversion of ν_e to ν_μ comparable to the weak interaction effect arising from the Mikheyev-Smirnov-Wolfenstein (MSW) mechanism [WOLFENSTEIN, 1978; MIKHEYEV, 1985].

2.8 Graphical Representation of Experimental Constraints

If we return to the simple Yukawa potential in Eq. (2.1.8), we see that this model is characterized by the two parameters α and λ, which give the strength (relative to gravity) and the range of the force. In the framework of this model, the results of any experimental search for non-Newtonian gravity can be used to set limits on how large α can be for a given assumed value of λ. A typical set of such curves is shown in Fig. 2.13, which is adapted from [TALMADGE, 1988], and these curves are interpreted as follows:

a) The results of a composition-independent experiment which finds no evidence for deviations from Newtonian gravity are represented by a single curve $\alpha = \alpha(\lambda)$ in the α-λ plane. Values of (α, λ) *above* the curves (the shaded region) are excluded by that experiment at the 2σ level, while those below the curve are allowed. (Here and throughout this book, we use the convention of plotting exclusion curves at the 2σ level.) Clearly the more stringent the limit set by a given experiment, the lower will be the corresponding curve. We note in passing that some care must be taken in comparing different results quoted in the literature, since the corresponding

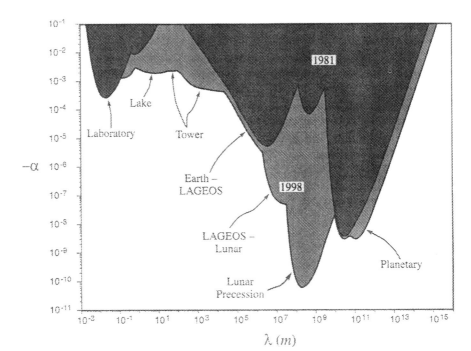

Figure 2.13: Constraints on the coupling constant α as a function of the range λ from composition-independent experiments. The dark shaded area indicates the status as of 1981, and the lighter region gives the current limits. Note that only the most sensitive results are exhibited in each regime in λ, and that all limits are quoted at the 2σ level. For references to the earlier experiments which contribute to the curves, see [TALMADGE, 1988] and [DERUJULA, 1986].

limits are variously quoted at the 1σ, 2σ, or 3σ level. [Recall that a 1σ (i.e., 1 standard deviation) signal has a probability of $\sim 32\%$ of being consistent with zero (i.e., no effect), and that the probabilities for 2σ and 3σ are 5% and 0.3% respectively.]

b) For a composition-independent experiment which claims to detect evidence for non-Newtonian gravity, the signal would be represented by the region between two curves in the α-λ plane, as in the Stacey data shown in Fig. 1 of [TALMADGE, 1988].

c) For composition-dependent experiments α is replaced by the difference $(\alpha_{ij} - \alpha_{ij'})$ in Eq. (2.1.13), which describes the acceleration difference of samples j and j' to the source i. From Eq. (2.1.13) we see that this introduces in addition to the coupling strength ξ, the mixing angle θ_5, which determines the specific charge q_5 (see Eqs. (2.1.1) and (2.1.7)). Hence the simplest composition-dependent model is determined by the 3 parameters ξ,

θ_5, and λ. For this reason the constraints implied by a given experiment are shown as plots of ξ versus θ_5 (for fixed λ), or as ξ versus λ (for fixed θ_5). The latter representation is useful when comparing the experimental constraints for some popular choice for the charge, such as $Q = I_z$ which corresponds to $\theta_5 = 90°$ in Eq. (2.1.1).

Exactly what level of significance constitutes a "signal" is a matter of taste, convention, and argument. Almost everybody would agree that a careful experiment which detects, say, a 5σ effect (e.g., $\alpha = (5 \pm 1) \times 10^{-6}$) should be taken seriously. By contrast, a result such as $\alpha = (1 \pm 1) \times 10^{-6}$ is clearly not evidence for a signal. Questions typically arise in interpreting a result like $\alpha = (2 \pm 1) \times 10^{-6}$. On the one hand, with 1σ constraints, this can be viewed as a very weak signal ($1 \times 10^{-6} \lesssim \alpha \lesssim 3 \times 10^{-6}$). More conservatively, however, if we use 2σ constraints, this result is consistent with zero ($0 \times 10^{-6} \lesssim \alpha \lesssim 4 \times 10^{-6}$). An unambiguous result such as $\alpha = (5 \pm 1) \times 10^{-6}$ can be graphically represented by *two* curves in the α-λ plane, which give the bounds on α at the desired confidence level (e.g., 1σ, 2σ, ...). At the 2σ level the preceding result corresponds to $3 \times 10^{-6} \leq \alpha \leq 7 \times 10^{-6}$, and would be represented by the region between the curves corresponding to $\alpha = 3 \times 10^{-6}$ and $\alpha = 7 \times 10^{-6}$.

CHAPTER 3

Searches for
Composition-Independent Effects

3.1 Introduction

As we noted in Chapter 1, the possibility of a short-range modification to Newtonian gravity was first raised in a seminal paper by Fujii [1971], who proposed a new interaction mediated by a hypothetical field called the *dilaton*. For two masses i and j, this interaction would give rise to an effective gravitational interaction of the form

$$V(r) \cong -\frac{3}{4}\frac{G_\infty m_i m_j}{r}\left(1 + \frac{1}{3}e^{-r/\lambda}\right).$$

(3.1.1)

As in Eq. (1.4), G_∞ denotes the value of the Newtonian constant in the limit $r \to \infty$, and λ is the range of the new force, which Fujii suggested was approximately $10\,\mathrm{m} \lesssim \lambda \lesssim 1\,\mathrm{km}$. Motivated in part by Fujii's work, Long [1974] examined various laboratory determinations of the Newtonian constant of gravitation G_N and concluded that there existed a systematic dependence of G_N on the separation r of the test masses. Long also performed his own experiment explicitly searching for a deviation of gravity from the inverse-square law. As shown in Fig. 3.1, Long's experiment [1976] involved comparing the measured torque τ_{near} exerted on a 60 g tantalum sphere by a 1.225 kg tantalum ring separated by a distance of 4.48 cm, to the torque τ_{far} exerted on the tantalum sphere by a 57.6 kg brass ring separated by a distance of 29.9 cm. In terms of the quantity measured in this experiment,

$$\Delta_\tau = \frac{\tau_{\mathrm{far}} - \tau_{\mathrm{near}}}{\tau_{\mathrm{near}}},$$

(3.1.2)

the net discrepancy observed was

$$\begin{aligned}
\delta(\Delta_\tau) &= \Delta_\tau(\text{experiment}) - \Delta_\tau(\text{theory}) \\
&= (0.04174 \pm 0.00044) - (0.003807 \pm 0.00051) \\
&\cong +0.00367 \pm 0.00067,
\end{aligned}$$

(3.1.3)

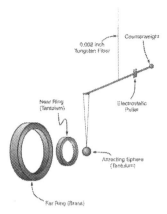

Figure 3.1: Schematic diagram of the apparatus used in the experiment of Long [1976]. The torque on the attracting sphere to, alternately, the "near ring" and the "far ring" was measured using the electrostatic puller shown in the figure. The puller was designed to maintain the pendant in a stationary position, which allowed the torque to be determined from the experimentally measured balance voltage.

which corresponded nominally to a 5.5σ systematic effect. Although more recent work [LONG, 1988] has suggested that the observed discrepancy was due to a tilt of the laboratory floor during his experiment, the effect of Long's work at the time was to stimulate interest in this question by a number of other groups, for instance Riley Newman and coworkers.

As we discussed in Chapter 1, the theoretical work of Fujii laid the foundation for much of the phenomenology of non-Newtonian interactions, which was later further developed by various authors including Mikkelsen and Newman [MIKKELSEN, 1977], Scherk [1979A,B], and Gibbons and Whiting [GIBBONS, 1981]. Fujii's work, and the early experimental results of Long, served as the principal stimuli for many of the modern tests of the inverse-square law which were to follow. In particular the geophysical research of Stacey and colleagues (see Section 3.4) can be directly traced to the contention by Fujii that the Newtonian gravitational constant could differ by as much as 33% over geophysical scales compared to the laboratory value. Similarly, the tantalizing evidence obtained by Long prompted numerous laboratory tests of the inverse-square law.

Modern tests of the inverse-square law may generally be separated into two classes:
1) Experiments involving a direct measurement of the magnitude of $G(r)$, which involve a comparison to preexisting laboratory Cavendish measurements of G.
2) Experiments directly measuring a variation of $G(r)$ with r.

As will be discussed below, experiments such as the geophysical mea-

surements of Stacey and Earth-Lunar-satellite studies of Rapp [1987] fall
under class (1), whereas laboratory experiments and astrophysical tests fall
under class (2). It is also possible for an experiment to be sensitive to deviations arising from both (1) and (2), as in the ocean experiment of Zumberge
et al. [1991].

Experiments which fall under either class (1) or (2) give rise to constraints which have the important property that their maximum sensitivity
occurs for values of λ comparable to the distance scale of the experiment. To
illustrate this point, we consider the variation $\Delta G(r)$ in $G(r)$ between two observations made at spatial separations r_1 and r_2. If we define $r_a = (r_1 + r_2)/2$
and $\delta r = (r_1 - r_2)/2$, then from Eq. (2.1.10)

$$\Delta G(r) \equiv G(r_1) - G(r_2)$$

$$= -G_\infty \xi \left[\left(1 + \frac{(r_a + \delta r)}{\lambda} \right) e^{-(r_a + \delta r)/\lambda} - \left(1 + \frac{(r_a - \delta r)}{\lambda} \right) e^{-(r_a - \delta r)/\lambda} \right]$$

$$= 2G_\infty \xi e^{-r_a/\lambda} \left[\left(1 + \frac{r_a}{\lambda} \right) \sinh \left(\frac{\delta r}{\lambda} \right) - \left(\frac{\delta r}{\lambda} \right) \cosh \left(\frac{\delta r}{\lambda} \right) \right]. \qquad (3.1.4)$$

In the limit $\delta r \ll \lambda$, Eq. (3.1.4) becomes

$$\Delta G(r) \cong 2G_\infty \xi e^{-r_a/\lambda} \left(\frac{r_a}{\lambda} \right) \left(\frac{\delta r}{\lambda} \right). \qquad (3.1.5)$$

Thus for experiments whose distance scales are small compared to the range
of the force, any variation in $G(r)$ will be reduced by a factor of r_a/λ. As
an example, consider a typical laboratory experiment for which $r_a = 0.2\,\text{m}$
and $\delta r = 0.1\,\text{m}$. The fractional variation in G would only be of order 10^{-8}
for $\xi = 0.01$ and $\lambda = 200\,\text{m}$, which is much smaller than current laboratory
sensitivities. We can further ask for the value of (r_a/λ) for which $\Delta G(r)$ is
most sensitive to δr (i.e., for which $\partial^2 \Delta G / \partial r_a \, \partial(\delta r) = 0$). We find

$$\left(\frac{r_a}{\lambda} \right) \cong \frac{\cosh \left(\frac{\delta r}{\lambda} \right) + \left(\frac{\delta r}{\lambda} \right) \sinh \left(\frac{\delta r}{\lambda} \right)}{\cosh \left(\frac{\delta r}{\lambda} \right)}, \qquad (3.1.6)$$

which for $\delta r \lesssim \lambda$ gives the expected result that the maximum sensitivity
occurs when $r_a \sim \lambda$. A specific example of this discussion is given in Section 3.8 when we consider the constraints implied by planetary precession.

3.2 Laboratory Cavendish Tests of the Inverse-Square Law

3.2.1 Introduction

Laboratory Cavendish experiments involve measuring the gravitationally induced torque on the proof mass of a torsion balance arising from source masses at two or more fixed positions from the balance (see Fig. 3.2). In principle, one could measure the gravitationally induced torque between the proof mass and a single source mass at a single separation distance, and compare this answer to that predicted from using Newton's second law. There are, however, several systematic effects which make this seemingly simple experiment more complicated in practice, as we now discuss.

The dominant issue facing most tests of Newton's second law concerns the determination of Newton's constant $G = (6.67259 \pm 0.00085) \times 10^{-11} \, \mathrm{N \, m^2 \, kg^{-2}}$ [LUTHER, 1982], which is known to a precision of only about 127 ppm. This fundamentally limits the accuracy of any single experimental comparison of theory and experiment to a level of only 10^{-4}, a result which is not of sufficient precision to be useful.

A second issue is that an accurate comparison to the standard value of G requires that the masses be accurately calibrated to an existing mass standard. However, absolute accuracy in mass measurements is a tedious and challenging metrological problem, and makes this experiment much more demanding than a multiple separation experiment. A single separation experiment would result in a new and independent measurement of G. The ultimate comparison in such an experiment would then be between the new measured value of G and the standard laboratory value.

Consequently, inverse-square law tests usually determine the ratio between the torques measured at different separations between the torsion balance proof mass and the test masses. By taking this ratio, we eliminate the need to know the precise values of either G or the proof mass. To reduce possible systematics associated with the torsion constant of the fiber, the test masses are chosen so that the net torques for both separations are approximately equal.

3.2.2 Model Calculation

As an illustration of the principles behind inverse-square tests, we consider the simple configuration illustrated by Fig. 3.2. In this illustration, M_1 and M_2 lie along a common line passing through one of the proof masses m of the torsion pendant (i.e., the torsion rod containing the test bodies of mass m). Considering only the case where the torsion rod is perpendicular to this line, the gravitational torque τ_i exerted on the pendant from a mass

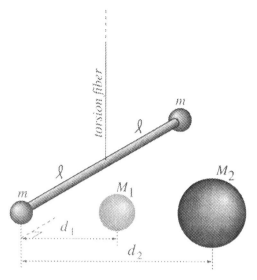

Figure 3.2: Example of an experimental configuration for the laboratory Cavendish test of the inverse-square law. Here we assume that all test bodies are spherical and homogeneous, and that the mass of the torsion rod is negligible. We also assume that the two proof masses m are at an equal distance ℓ from the suspension point of the pendant.

M_i $(i = 1, 2)$ is

$$\tau_{i,t} = G_\infty m M_i \ell \left[\frac{1}{d_i^2} - \frac{d_i}{r_i^3} \right], \qquad (3.2.1)$$

$$r_i \equiv \sqrt{d_i^2 + 4\ell^2}, \qquad (3.2.2)$$

where the subscript t refers to the theoretically expected value. The predicted relative difference in the induced torque normalized to τ_1 is then

$$\Delta_t \equiv \frac{\tau_{2,t} - \tau_{1,t}}{\tau_{1,t}}, \qquad (3.2.3)$$

and Eq. (3.2.3) represents the theoretical prediction if gravitation were purely $1/r^2$.

Experimental and theoretical quantities are generally expressed as fractional differences, as in Eq. (3.2.3), because this removes the dependence of the experiment on the laboratory value of G, and as well allows one to take measurements of relative mass (that is, not calibrated to an absolute mass standard). This approach is very important, because otherwise factors such as the absolute accuracy of the mass measurement, or uncertainty in the laboratory value of G, might be the limiting constraints on the accuracy of the experiment.

Substituting Eq. (3.2.1) into (3.2.3) gives

$$\Delta_t = \left(\frac{M_2}{M_1}\right) \cdot \left(\frac{d_1}{d_2}\right)^2 \cdot \left[\frac{1 - (d_2/r_2)^3}{1 - (d_1/r_1)^3}\right] - 1. \qquad (3.2.4)$$

In the presence of a non-Newtonian force, Eq. (3.2.1) is modified so that

$$\tau_{i,m} = G_\infty m M_i \ell \left[\frac{1 - \xi\beta(d_i/\lambda)}{d_i^2} - \frac{[1 - \xi\beta(r_i/\lambda)]d_i}{r_i^3}\right], \qquad (3.2.5)$$

$$\beta(x) \equiv (1 + x)\exp(-x), \qquad (3.2.6)$$

where $\tau_{i,m}$ represents the measured torque exerted on the torsion pendant. In obtaining Eq. (3.2.5), we have assumed that the radii of the various test masses are small compared to λ. If we do not make this assumption, then it would be necessary to incorporate the higher order multipole moments of the gravitational attraction between the test and the proof masses.

Normalizing the measured torque difference to $\tau_{i,m}$ then gives

$$\Delta_m \equiv \frac{\tau_{2,m} - \tau_{1,m}}{\tau_{1,m}}. \qquad (3.2.7)$$

Substituting Eq. (3.2.5) into Eq. (3.2.7) then gives

$$\Delta_m = \left(\frac{M_2}{M_1}\right) \cdot \left(\frac{d_1}{d_2}\right)^2 \cdot \left[\frac{1 - \xi\gamma_2}{1 - \xi\gamma_1}\right] - 1, \qquad (3.2.8)$$

where

$$\gamma_i \equiv \frac{\beta(d_i/\lambda) - (d_i/r_i)^3 \beta(r_i/\lambda)}{1 - (d_i/r_i)^3}. \qquad (3.2.9)$$

Combining Eqs. (3.2.4) and (3.2.8) leads to

$$(1 + \Delta_m) = (1 + \Delta_t) \cdot \left[\frac{1 + \xi\gamma_2}{1 + \xi\gamma_1}\right], \qquad (3.2.10)$$

and solving for ξ, we find

$$\xi = \frac{-(\Delta_m - \Delta_t)}{(\gamma_2 - \gamma_1) - (\gamma_2\Delta_t - \gamma_1\Delta_m)}. \qquad (3.2.11)$$

Finally, letting

$$\gamma_a = \frac{1}{2}(\gamma_1 + \gamma_2), \qquad (3.2.12a)$$

$$\delta\gamma = \gamma_2 - \gamma_1, \qquad (3.2.12b)$$

$$\mathcal{D} \equiv \Delta_m - \Delta_t, \qquad (3.2.12c)$$

$$\mathcal{M} \equiv 1 + \frac{1}{2}(\Delta_m + \Delta_t), \qquad (3.2.12d)$$

gives

$$\xi = \frac{-\mathcal{D}}{\mathcal{M}\delta\gamma - \mathcal{D}\gamma_a}. \tag{3.2.13}$$

An important limiting case arises when $d_i \gg \ell$, that is, when the distances at which the measurements take place are large compared to the size of the torsion pendant. A naive approach to this problem is to let

$$\tau_{i,t} \to G_\infty m M_i \ell \left[\frac{1}{d_i^2}\right], \tag{3.2.14}$$

$$\tau_{i,m} \to G_\infty m M_i \ell \left[\frac{1 - \xi\beta(d_i/\lambda)}{d_i^2}\right]. \tag{3.2.15}$$

Substituting these expressions into Eqs. (3.2.3) and (3.2.7), we find

$$\gamma_i \to \beta_i \equiv \beta(d_i/\lambda), \tag{3.2.16}$$

with Eqs. (3.2.12a-d) being otherwise unchanged, so that

$$\xi = \frac{-\mathcal{D}}{\mathcal{M}(\beta_2 - \beta_1) - \mathcal{D}(\beta_1 + \beta_2)/2}. \tag{3.2.17}$$

This level of approximation, however, does not give the correct limiting behavior for ξ as a function of λ, as we discuss below.

In order to compare the constraints from Eq. (3.2.13) to its approximation Eq. (3.2.17), we generate constraint curves using the following realistic experimental configuration:

$$M_1 = 0.25\,\text{kg}, \; M_2 = 1.0\,\text{kg}, \; d_1 = 1\,\text{m}, \; d_2 = 2\,\text{m}, \; \ell = 20\,\text{cm}. \tag{3.2.18}$$

For this configuration, we have approximately

$$\tau_{1,t} \approx 1.332 \times 10^{-13}\,\text{N m}, \tag{3.2.19a}$$

$$\tau_{2,t} \approx 3.812 \times 10^{-13}\,\text{N m}, \tag{3.2.19b}$$

$$\Delta_t \approx 1.862. \tag{3.2.19c}$$

Figure 3.3 displays what the numerical results would look like for the configuration described by Eqs. (3.2.18) and (3.2.19). As we discussed in the introduction, there are two important distance scales in this experiment, the mean distance of the masses from the proof mass r_a, and the distance separating the two masses δr. The value of r_a determines the value of λ to which the experiment is most sensitive, whereas the mass separation δr governs the size of the region in λ for which the constraint curve remains near its minimum value (i.e., gives the most stringent constraint).

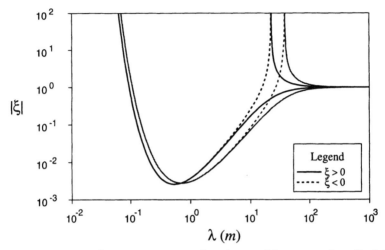

Figure 3.3: Constraint curves for the model system described by Eqs. (3.2.16) and (3.2.17) (black lines). Shown for comparison are the results from the approximate formula in Eq. (3.2.17) (light gray lines). The area above each curve is excluded by experiment at the 2σ level.

We note that $\beta_i \ll 1$ for $\lambda \ll r_a$, which implies that $|\xi| \to \infty$. The fact that there is no limit on $|\xi|$ can be understood by noting that when $\lambda \ll r_a$, the range of the putative fifth force is too short for the proof mass m to be significantly influenced by M_1 or M_2. A more interesting limit occurs when $\lambda \gg r_a$, for which $\beta_i \to 1$. In this limit, we expect from Eq. (3.2.13) that $\xi \to +1$, which is a consequence of $\lim_{\lambda \to \infty} \gamma_i \to 1$. It can be shown that the limit $\xi \to 1$ for $\lambda \to \infty$ is present *only* if measurements are made at two mass separations. Experiments such as Hoskins et al. [HOSKINS, 1985] and Panov and Frontov [PANOV, 1979] will not exhibit this limit, but rather $|\xi| \to \infty$ for $\lambda \to \infty$.

In an actual experiment, Δ_t will not be precisely known, since the quantities given in Eq. (3.2.18) will have uncertainties associated with them. In typical laboratory experiments, most quantities can be determined to at best 0.01%. Thus, the eventual limiting precision of the experiment is determined by the precision with which the test samples can be fabricated, and the precision to which the mass configuration is actually known.

3.2.3 Experimental Review

As noted in the chapter introduction, the claim of an anomaly by Long [1976] stimulated a flurry of laboratory experiments. In the end, all of these newer experiments, which were often carried out in more controlled environments, strongly contradicted Long's results. In spite of eventually being shown wrong, Long's work made an important contribution to gravity research, because it pointed toward a need to better understand Newtonian gravity on the laboratory scale (0.001−10 m), and thus led to a substantial improvement of our understanding of Newtonian gravity.

We summarize below some of the inverse-square experiments which followed Long's original work:

1) Yu et al. [YU, 1979] performed an experiment which used a gravimeter to measure the acceleration of gravity g in the vicinity of an oil tank. In 2 m intervals over a distance 2−8 m from the tank, they compared the measured accelerations when the tank was full versus empty. Due to uncertainties arising, for example, from tilt effects induced by the filled oil tank, this experiment was only able to set a limit $\xi \lesssim 0.1$ for $\lambda \lesssim$ 10 m. At the time this experiment was performed, and for several years afterwords, this was the most sensitive limit on ξ for $\lambda \approx 10$ m. Thus, more than 300 years following the publication of Newton's *Principia*, it would have been possible for Newton's inverse-square law of gravity to be wrong by as much as $\sim 10\%$ at separations ~ 10 m, and yet still appear compatible with the existing experiments.

2) V. I. Panov and V. N. Frontov [PANOV, 1979] performed an important larger scale laboratory experiment, in which they compared the torque induced on a balance over mass separations from 0.4 m to 10 m. This experiment remains the most sensitive laboratory experiment over distance scales $\lambda \gtrsim 2$ m.

3) R. Newman and collaborators carried out an extensive series of precise measurements [SPERO, 1980; HOSKINS, 1985] that currently represent the most precise constraints on Yukawa fields over laboratory scales. These experiments will be discussed in detail in the following subsections.

4) A group led by K. Tsubono [OGAWA, 1982; MIO, 1986, 1987] has performed a series of dynamical measurements using a mass dipole and a gravity-wave antenna. Although these experiments perform inverse-square tests on a laboratory scale, we defer discussion of this class of experiments to Section 3.10, and restrict our discussion to Cavendish-type experiments below.

5) H. J. Paik and coworkers [CHAN, 1982; MOODY, 1993] have developed a new type of instrument which directly measures the Laplacian of the gravitational potential. Since $\nabla^2(1/r) = 0$ in free space (where the mass sources vanish), any deviation from a zero value is a signal for a gravitational potential that is not exactly $1/r$, and hence for a violation of the inverse-square law. Again, we reserve full treatment of this class of experiments to Section 3.3 below.

6) Y. T. Chen, A. H. Cook, and A. J. F. Metherell [CHEN, 1984] performed a series of precise measurements involving a comparison of the torques for mass separations of 5.0−9.1 cm (non-null measurement), and

for 12.0−19.6 cm (null measurement). These authors were able to set a 2σ limit of $\xi \lesssim 10^{-3}$ for $\lambda \sim 1 - 5$ cm.

We note from Fig. 2.13 that the limits on the validity of the inverse-square law are relatively poor over very short distance scales, e.g., in the sub-centimeter regime. There are several reasons for this, including the obvious fact that over short distance scales the test masses themselves must be small, which means that any signal would also be relatively small. In addition, the effects of various electromagnetic backgrounds become comparatively more important for the same reason. A number of authors have attempted to extract limits over very short distances scales, and we briefly review some of this work below.

One experimental system which naturally probes relatively small (but nonetheless macroscopic) distances is the Casimir effect [CASIMIR, 1948; ITZYKSON, 1980; LAMOREAUX, 1997]. It is well known that two parallel plates separated by a distance a experience an attractive force due to vacuum fluctuations. The force per unit area is then given by

$$\frac{F(a)}{A} = \frac{\pi^2}{240}\frac{\hbar c}{a^4} = \frac{0.013}{a^4} \text{ dyne cm}^{-2}, \qquad (3.2.20)$$

where the plate spacing a is measured in microns (10^{-6} m). Notwithstanding the weakness of the "Casimir force," even for reasonably small plate separations, its presence has been confirmed for various geometries, where expressions analogous to Eq. (3.2.20) hold [ELIZALDE, 1991; LAMOREAUX, 1997]. However, a quantitative comparison of theory and experiment for small separations is complicated by the presence of conventional "retardation" forces, such as van der Waals forces [SPRUCH, 1986]. Nonetheless, some quantitative limits on the presence of additional new forces can be inferred from such experiments, and these have been considered by Mostepanenko et al. [MOSTEPANENKO, 1987A,B, 1988, 1989, 1993; BORDAG, 1994]. The interested reader should consult these references for additional details, particularly the last one, which contains a summary of the limits arising from a number of different experiments. Other references to proposed experiments over short distance scales include [MITROFANOV, 1988; PRICE, 1988]. To date no direct experimental results have been reported for these distance scales.

In the following sections, we will obtain approximate constraints from a number of the most sensitive experiments. It should be emphasized that "most sensitive" is necessarily a model-dependent statement. For instance, static measurements, such as Spero et al. [SPERO, 1980] were initially criticized by Long [1980A,B] on the basis that they did not test his predicted vacuum polarization effect (see Section 3.2.5 below). Furthermore, almost all of the experimental designs incorporate unique features that could potentially make them relatively more sensitive to some models of non-Newtonian gravity, and less sensitive to others.

3.2.4 Experiment of Long

Although it is a virtual certainty at this point in time that the results of Long's 1976 experiment are wrong, his experiment is nonetheless of interest for both experimental and theoretical reasons. On the experimental side, Long employed a configuration of test masses different from that used in any other experiment. This is related to the theoretical motivation for his work: Long conjectured [1980] that there might exist a gravitational analog of vacuum polarization in electromagnetism, which leads to the Uehling effect [UEHLING, 1935; CHEN, 1989]. Since vacuum polarization introduces a logarithmic modification of Coulomb's law [GELL-MANN, 1954], Long suggested that there might exist an analogous logarithmic modification of Newton's inverse-square law. He further argued that such a modification might not show up in various null experiments (which his was not), because in a null experiment there would be no "polarizing gravitational field" present near the test masses.

It must be emphasized that the theoretical underpinnings for Long's conjectures are tenuous at best. This is in part because vacuum polarization depends on the existence of positive and negative charge, for which there is no gravitational analog. However, Long's work helped to stimulate Newman and collaborators to carry out a series of experiments which established unambiguously that Long's experimental results were unsupportable. In addition, his suggestion of a logarithmic modification of the Newtonian potential, although theoretically unattractive, does serve to underscore the point made earlier that the relative sensitivities of different experiments depend on what model is used to describe the non-Newtonian interaction. From this point of view, our parametrization of $V(r)$ in Eq. (1.4) is merely the simplest plausible theoretical description, but is by no means the only possibility.

The configuration for Long's experiment [1976] is shown in Fig. 3.1. This experiment involved the comparison of the torque generated on a torsion balance by a "near" ring composed of tantalum and a "far" ring composed of copper. The experimental quantities are shown in Table 3.1 below:

Table 3.1: Experimental parameters and their values for Long [1976].

Description	"near" ring	"far" ring
mass separation	$r_1 = 0.0448 \, \text{m}$	$r_2 = 0.299 \, \text{m}$
ring mass	$M_1 = 1.225271 \, \text{kg}$	$m_2 = 57.58083 \, \text{kg}$
inner radius	$R_{i,1} = 0.027513 \, \text{m}$	$R_{i,2} = 0.045536 \, \text{m}$
outer radius	$R_{o,1} = 0.045536 \, \text{m}$	$R_{o,2} = 0.27112 \, \text{m}$
thickness	$t_1 = 0.017765 \, \text{m}$	$t_2 = 0.07633 \, \text{m}$

Long calculated the experimental quantity $\Delta = (\tau_2 - \tau_1)/\tau_1$, with τ_i representing the torque measured on the torsion balance from the near ring ($i = 1$) and the far ring ($i = 2$). As we noted earlier, forming such a ratio cancels the factor of G_∞, making the experimentally reported measurements independent of this poorly determined constant. Long reported a theoretically calculated value of

$$\Delta_t = 0.003807 \pm 0.0005, \qquad (3.2.21)$$

to be compared with an experimentally measured value of

$$\Delta_m = 0.004174 \pm 0.0004. \qquad (3.2.22)$$

He concluded that the statistically significant difference

$$\Delta_{\text{Long}} = \Delta_m - \Delta_T \cong +0.00367 \pm 0.00064 \qquad (3.2.23)$$

was consistent with an anomalous dependence of the laboratory value of G on the separation of the test masses [LONG, 1976]. As we have already noted, such an effect could arise in his model via a vacuum polarization effect [LONG, 1974, 1980].

For present purposes we wish to model Long's experimental results using the Yukawa parametrization in Eq. (1.4). To do so, we make the simplifying assumption that we need only consider interactions between the test rings and the proof mass of the torsion pendulum, so that interactions between the rings and the remaining portion of the torsion pendulum can be neglected. In this case, the quantity Δ can be rewritten as $\Delta = (a_2 - a_1)/a_1$, where a_i represents the acceleration of the proof mass toward the ring i. In calculating the theoretically expected value Δ_T, we consider only *Newtonian* contributions to the net acceleration:

$$a_{T,i} = g_i. \qquad (3.2.24)$$

Here g_i represents the gravitational acceleration of the (spherical) proof mass toward the ring i. In calculating the experimentally measured value Δ_m, we must include both the Newtonian and the (putative) Yukawa contributions

$$a_{E,i} = g_i - q_i \xi \mathcal{F}_i, \qquad (3.2.25)$$

where q_i is the normalized non-Newtonian charge.

Since the proof mass lies along the axis of rotation of the ring (see Fig. 3.1), the corresponding expression for g_i is relatively simple:

$$g_i = g(M_i, r_i, R_{1,i}, R_{2,i}, t_i) = \frac{2G_\infty M_i}{t_i(R_{2,i}^2 - R_{1,i}^2)} \times$$

$$\left[\sqrt{R_{2,i}^2 + (r_i + t_i/2)^2} + \sqrt{R_{1,i}^2 + (r_i - t_i/2)^2} \right.$$

$$\left. - \sqrt{R_{2,i}^2 + (r_i - t_i/2)^2} - \sqrt{R_{1,i}^2 + (r_i + t_i/2)^2} \right]. \quad (3.2.26)$$

Here M_i is the mass of the ith ring, r_i is the separation between this ring and the torsion pendant, $R_{1,i}$ ($R_{2,i}$) is the inner (outer) radius of the ring, and t_i is its thickness. Along the axis of symmetry, the corresponding Yukawa field also has a simple form:

$$\mathcal{F}_i = g(M_i, r_i, R_{1,i}, R_{2,i}, t_i, \lambda) = \frac{2G_\infty M_i \lambda}{t_i(R_{2,i}^2 - R_{1,i}^2)} \times$$

$$\left[\exp\left\{ -\frac{\sqrt{R_{2,i}^2 + (r_i - t_i/2)^2}}{\lambda} \right\} + \exp\left\{ -\frac{\sqrt{R_{1,i}^2 + (r_i + t_i/2)^2}}{\lambda} \right\} \right.$$

$$\left. - \exp\left\{ -\frac{\sqrt{R_{2,i}^2 + (r_i + t_i/2)^2}}{\lambda} \right\} - \exp\left\{ -\frac{\sqrt{R_{1,i}^2 + (r_i - t_i/2)^2}}{\lambda} \right\} \right]. \quad (3.2.27)$$

The constraint relation for this experiment is obtained by combining Eqs. (3.2.23)–(3.2.25):

$$\Delta_{\text{Long}} = \frac{(g_2 - q_2 \xi \mathcal{F}_2) - (g_1 - q_1 \xi \mathcal{F}_1)}{g_1 - q_1 \xi \mathcal{F}_1} - \left(\frac{g_2 - g_1}{g_1} \right). \quad (3.2.28)$$

Solving for ξ gives

$$\xi = \frac{g_1^2 \Delta_{\text{Long}}}{g_1 q_2 \mathcal{F}_2 - g_2 q_1 \mathcal{F}_1 - g_1 q_1 \mathcal{F}_1 \Delta_{\text{Long}}}. \quad (3.2.29)$$

Figure 3.4 exhibits the results of applying this constraint relation to Long's experimental data at the 2σ level, under the assumption that $q_i = 1$.

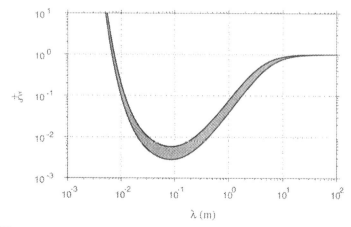

Figure 3.4: Constraints on values of ξ and λ from the experiment of Long [1976]. The shaded region indicates those values of ξ and λ which are consistent at the 2 standard deviation (2σ) level with the reported results from this experiment.

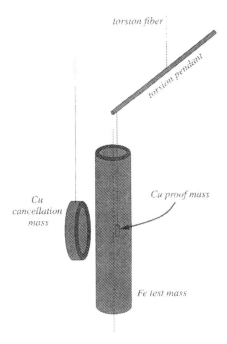

Figure 3.5: Illustration of the experimental apparatus for the laboratory experiment of Spero et al. [1980].

3.2.5 Constraint from Spero et al.

As we have already noted, Long's results motivated Riley Newman and coworkers to undertake a series of experiments to test the inverse-square law over laboratory distances. The first of these was [SPERO, 1980], which is illustrated in Fig. 3.5. The idea behind this null experiment is that if $V(r)$ has the expected $1/r$ behavior, then the force on a proof mass inside a long cylinder is *almost* zero (see discussion below). Hence if the Fe cylinder is moved relative to the proof mass, which is part of a torsion balance, there should be no torque on the balance (except for small calculable "end effects" from the cylinder). In the Spero experiment the proof mass was a small Cu cylinder, which was hung near the center of a hollow cylindrical Fe test mass. The null character of the experiment was further improved by the inclusion of a Cu cancellation mass on the opposite side of the Fe test mass to the small Cu cylinder (see Fig. 3.5). This cancellation mass was moved together with the Fe cylinder so as to nearly cancel the gravitational forces due to the end effects of the Fe cylinder. The experimental values reported in [SPERO, 1980] are presented in Table 3.2 below.

The authors found for the difference $\Delta\tau$ between the experimental (mea-

Table 3.2: Experimental parameters and their values for Spero et al. [SPERO, 1980].

Description	Measured Value
test body inner radius	$R_1 = 3\,\text{cm}$
test body outer radius	$R_2 = 4\,\text{cm}$
test body length	$L = 60\,\text{cm}$
proof body mass	$m = 10.44\,\text{kg}$
proof body radius	$r = 0.4\,\text{cm}$
proof body length	$L = 4.4\,\text{cm}$
length of torsion pendant	$2\ell = 60\,\text{cm}$

sured) and theoretical (gravitational) torques,

$$\Delta\tau \equiv \tau_{\text{E}} - \tau_{\text{T}} = (+0.02 \pm 0.14) \times 10^{-13}\,\text{N}\,\text{m}. \qquad (3.2.30)$$

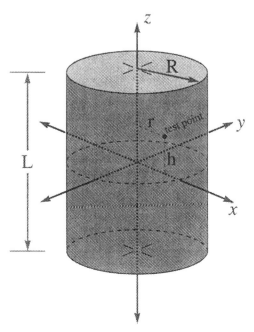

Figure 3.6: Explanation of the notation used in the analysis of the Spero et al. experiment.

To extract the constraint on ξ and λ, we assume a point-like proof mass, in which case the non-Newtonian torque on the test mass due to the hollow cylinder is given by

$$\vec{\tau} = \hat{z}\,\xi q_{\text{Fe}} q_{\text{Cu}} m\ell\,\mathcal{F}_{\text{test}}. \tag{3.2.31}$$

Here q_{Cu} and q_{Fe} are the normalized "charges" for Cu and Fe, as defined in Eq. (2.2.1), and $\mathcal{F}_{\text{test}}$ is the non-Newtonian field strength due to the cylindrical test mass. We obtain a constraint on ξ as a function of λ by combining Eqs. (3.2.30) and (3.2.31):

$$\xi = \frac{\Delta\tau}{q_{\text{Fe}} q_{\text{Cu}} m\ell\,\mathcal{F}_{\text{test}}}. \tag{3.2.32}$$

The field strength for the test mass can be approximated by writing

$$\mathcal{F}_{\text{test}} = \mathcal{F}(R_2) - \mathcal{F}(R_1), \tag{3.2.33}$$

where $\mathcal{F}(R_2) - \mathcal{F}(R_1)$ is the field strength for a solid cylinder of length L and inner radius R_1 and outer radius R_2. The field strength $\mathcal{F}(R)$ for a solid cylinder of length L and radius R is given by

$$\mathcal{F}(R) = \rho G_\infty \int_{-L/2-h}^{+L/2-h} dz \int_0^{2\pi} d\varphi \cos\varphi\, \frac{\exp\left\{-\sqrt{r^2 + R^2 - 2rR\cos\varphi + z^2}/\lambda\right\}}{\sqrt{r^2 + R^2 - 2rR\cos\varphi + z^2}}. \tag{3.2.34}$$

Letting

$$a(\varphi) \equiv \sqrt{r^2 + R^2 - 2rR\cos\varphi}, \tag{3.2.35}$$

this becomes

$$\mathcal{F}(R) = \rho G_\infty \int_{-L/2-h}^{+L/2-h} dz \int_0^{2\pi} d\varphi \cos\varphi\, \frac{\exp\left\{-\sqrt{a^2(\varphi) + z^2}/\lambda\right\}}{\sqrt{a^2(\varphi) + z^2}}. \tag{3.2.36}$$

(For conciseness we temporarily suppress the dependence of $a(\varphi)$ on φ.) The integration with respect to z can be performed by letting

$$z^2 + a^2 = a^2 \cosh^2 t, \tag{3.2.37}$$

so

$$z' = a \sinh t, \tag{3.2.38}$$

and

$$dz' = a \cosh t\, dt. \tag{3.2.39}$$

Substituting Eqs. (3.2.37)–(3.2.39) into Eq. (3.2.34) gives

$$\mathcal{F}(R) = \rho G_\infty \int_0^{2\pi} d\varphi \cos\varphi \left[\int_0^{\zeta_a} dz + \int_0^{\zeta_b} dz \right] e^{-(a/\lambda)\cosh t}, \tag{3.2.40}$$

where

$$\cosh \zeta_a = \sqrt{1 + (L/2 + h)^2/a^2},$$
$$\cosh \zeta_b = \sqrt{1 + (L/2 - h)^2/a^2}. \tag{3.2.41}$$

We define

$$k_0(x, y) \equiv \int_0^{\cosh y + 1} dt \, e^{x \cosh t}, \tag{3.2.42}$$

where the function $k_0(x, y)$ is related to the modified Bessel function of the third kind $K_0(x)$. In particular, $k_0(x, y) \to K_0(x)$ as $y \to \infty$. Combining Eq.(3.2.42) with Eq. (3.2.40) gives

$$\mathcal{F}(R) = \rho G_\infty \int_0^{2\pi} d\varphi \cos \varphi \, (k_0[a(\varphi)/\lambda, y_a(\varphi)] + k_0[a(\varphi)/\lambda, y_b(\varphi)]), \tag{3.2.43}$$

with

$$y_a(\varphi) = \sqrt{1 + (L/2 + h)^2/a^2(\varphi)} - 1,$$
$$y_b(\varphi) = \sqrt{1 + (L/2 - h)^2/a^2(\varphi)} - 1. \tag{3.2.44}$$

The function $k_0(x, y)$ can be evaluated analytically by employing the close relationship of this function to $K_0(x)$.

Figure 3.7 exhibits the results of applying the constraint relation in Eq. (3.2.31) to the experiment of Spero et al. at the 2σ level. These results were obtained under the assumption that $q_i = 1$.

We conclude this section by citing an experiment which is similar to that of Spero et al., although less precise [LIU, 1983]. In this experiment, the test masses are suspended from a torsion fiber so as to hang inside a *horizontal* cylinder. When $G(r)$ in Eq. (2.1.10) is parametrized in the form

$$G(r) = G_0 \left[1 + \epsilon \ln(r/1 \, \text{cm}) \right], \tag{3.2.45}$$

to follow the parametrization suggested by Long [1974], Liu et al. found

$$\epsilon = (8.5 \pm 13.6) \times 10^{-3}. \tag{3.2.46}$$

3.2.6 Constraint from Hoskins et al.

As we noted previously, Long [1980, 1981] observed that since the experiment of Spero et al. [1980] was a null-test (in the sense that the gravitational acceleration felt by the test masses was almost zero), it might not be sensitive to the type of vacuum polarization effect suggested previously by Long. This motivated Newman and coworkers to perform a new non-null experiment [HOSKINS, 1985], which is illustrated in Fig. 3.8. The experimental configuration of Hoskins et al. consisted of two "far" masses riding on carts

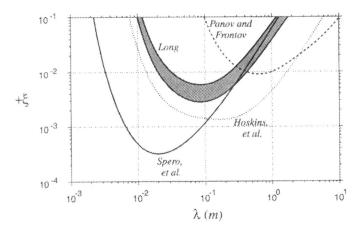

Figure 3.7: Constraints on values of ξ and λ from the experiments of Long [1976]; Panov and Frontov [PANOV, 1979]; Spero et al. [SPERO, 1980]; and Hoskins et al. [HOSKINS, 1985]. We have chosen to display Long's original experiment and those laboratory experiments which set the most stringent constraints on $+\xi$ as a function of λ. The interested reader is directed to Hoskins et al. [HOSKINS, 1985] for a more complete review of the experiments available at that time. Notice that the more recent experiments exclude the result of Long [1976].

to a maximum distance of 105 cm from the axis of a torsion pendulum, plus a "near" mass suspended only 5 cm from one end of the torsion pendulum.

The objective of the experiment was to measure the ratio of the torques $\mathcal{R} = \tau_{105}/\tau_5$, where τ_{105} was the torque from the far masses and τ_5 was the torque from the near mass. The deviation of the measured value $\mathcal{R}_m$ from the theoretical value $\mathcal{R}_t$ was used to test for any possible discrepancy from Newtonian physics:

$$\delta_{\text{Hoskins}} = \frac{\mathcal{R}_m}{\mathcal{R}_t} - 1. \tag{3.2.47}$$

The summary of this experiment presented below is based on the much more detailed description found in [HOSKINS, 1985]. The experimental configuration and protocol were carefully designed in order to reduce the sensitivity of his apparatus to alignment errors in the orientation of the torsion bar, the bearing track, the position of the near mass, etc. For example:

(1) The near mass was transported between two lateral positions an equal distance from the end of the torsion bar. The resulting torque change in alternating between these two configurations was sensitive to the lateral position uncertainty of the near mass only in second order. The locations of the near mass in its two positions were carefully controlled by a precision spacer bar (see Fig. 3.8). Also, the position of the near mass

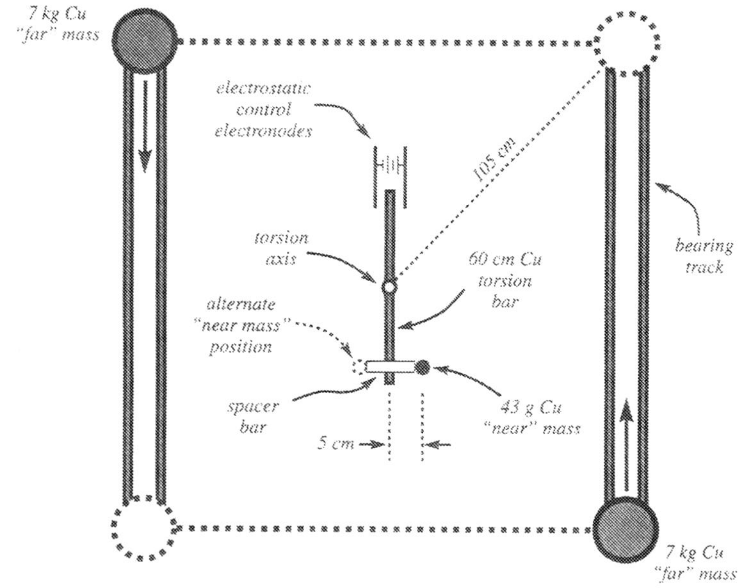

Figure 3.8: Illustration of the experimental apparatus and layout for the laboratory experiment of Hoskins et al. [1985].

along the torsion bar was chosen to maximize the torque produced on the balance by the near mass. This reduced the sensitivity of the torque measurements to positional errors in either the vertical direction or in the position of the test mass along the torsion bar.

(2) The rectangular configuration of the far masses, and the fact that they were moved in opposite directions, helped to reduce the sensitivity of the experiment to the placement and orientation of the torsion axis relative to these masses.

(3) The orientation of the torsion bar was read out using an optical lever, and the change of this orientation with time was used as a feedback control to dampen the torsional modes of the pendulum using the electrostatic plates shown in Fig. 3.8. The gain on the feedback loop was adjusted to nearly critically damp the pendulum torsional mode.

The possibility of an unconscious bias on the part of the experimentalists was reduced by intentionally concealing from them the exact value of the near mass and its dimensions until the group was ready to report a result. Since the mass (in particular) was known to only 1%, the approximate values used for the near mass parameters were *guaranteed* to generate an apparent anomalous effect. Any efforts on the part of the experimentists to "reduce" this anomalous effect to zero would thus result in an anomaly in the final result, once the true values for the mass and dimensions of the near mass were inserted in the experimental analysis. Hoskins et al. obtained a value of $\delta_{\text{Hoskins}} = (-2 \pm 7) \times 10^{-4}$ after the "correct" values for these parameters were incorporated. Further minor refinement of some of the systematics, as well as correction for a nonlinear effect discussed in [HOSKINS, 1985] led to the final quoted value of

$$\delta_{\text{Hoskins}} = (+1.2 \pm 7) \times 10^{-4}. \tag{3.2.48}$$

We conclude this section with a discussion of an approximate constraint on Yukawa forces implied by this experiment. We can write approximately

$$\mathcal{R}_m = \mathcal{R}_t \frac{1 - \xi\beta(r_{105}/\lambda)}{1 - \xi\beta(r_5/\lambda)}, \tag{3.2.49}$$

where $\beta(x)$ is given by Eq. (3.2.6), $r_5 = (4.7901 \pm 0.0004)\,\text{cm}$, and $r_{105} = (105.016 \pm 0.008)\,\text{cm}$. Solving for ξ in Eq. (3.2.49) and using Eq. (3.2.47) gives

$$\xi \cong \frac{\delta_{\text{Hoskins}}}{\beta(r_5/\lambda)\delta_{\text{Hoskins}} + \beta(r_5/\lambda) - \beta(r_{105}/\lambda)}. \tag{3.2.50}$$

Fig. 3.7 displays the approximate constraint arising from Eqs. (3.2.48) and (3.2.50).

As we noted at the beginning of this subsection, one motivation for the experiment of Hoskins et al. was to exclude the type of vacuum polarization mechanism proposed by Long. Another experiment carried out for a similar reason during the same period is that of Milyukov [1985], which looked for the spatial variation of $G(r)$ over the distance scale $11-21$ cm. As in the case of Hoskins et al., this is not a null experiment, and hence is not subject to the criticism raised by Long against Spero et al. Milyukov's apparatus was a torsion balance of the type used to measure G_0, which measures the oscillation frequency of two smaller test masses in the presence of two larger source masses. Milyukov found

$$G(r_2)/G(r_1) = 1.00062 \pm 0.00069, \tag{3.2.51}$$

where $r_1 = 11$ cm and $r_2 = 21$ cm, which is compatible with $G(r) = $ constant. Since Milyukov's experiment is more sensitive than Long's, this result directly contradicts [LONG, 1976], and Long's proposed logarithmic potential

An experiment having some conceptual similarities to that of Hoskins et al. is that of Schurr et al. [SCHURR, 1991]. In this experiment the gravitational force exerted by a laboratory mass on a Fabry-Perot microwave resonator is measured. The results agreed with the $1/r^2$ law to within $\cong 10^{-3}$.

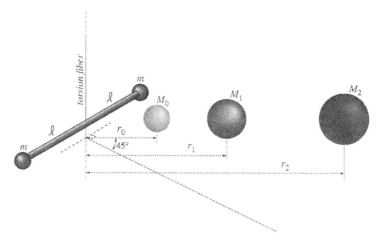

Figure 3.9: Illustration of the experimental apparatus for the laboratory experiment of Panov and Frontov [PANOV, 1979].

3.2.7 Constraint from Panov and Frontov

The experiment of Panov and Frontov (PF) [1979] was one of the earliest tests of the inverse-square law to follow Long's announced result. This experiment is distinguished from other laboratory experiments by the large distance scales (0.3–10 m) over which the measurements were performed, and also because it is one of only a few Cavendish experiments to make measurements at more than two mass separations. Because of the relatively large distance scales, this experiment was able to set precise constraints for larger values of λ than other experiments of this class.

The experimental configuration employed by PF is shown in Fig. 3.9. Note that the test masses are positioned at a 45° angle from the normal to the torsion bar. Measurements were carried out at the three separations shown. In the discussion which follows, the indices $i = 0, 1, 2$ will refer to the three locations of the masses M_0, M_1, and M_2 at the locations r_0, r_1, and r_2 respectively. The gravitational torque on the balance from location i at the assumed angle ϕ is approximately

$$\tau_i = \tau(r_i) = G_\infty M_i m\ell \left[\frac{r_i \sin\phi}{(r_i^2 + \ell^2 - 2r\ell\cos\phi)^{3/2}} \right.$$
$$\left. - \frac{r_i \sin\phi}{(r_i^2 + \ell^2 + 2r\ell\cos\phi)^{3/2}} \right], \quad (3.2.52)$$

where $\ell \cong 20\,\text{cm}$ and $m \cong 10\,\text{g}$. For $\ell/r_i \ll 1$, this reduces to

$$\tau_i \cong \frac{3G_\infty M_i m\ell^2 \sin 2\phi}{r_i^3}. \quad (3.2.53)$$

PF rewrote this equation as

$$\tau_i \cong \frac{3G_\infty M_i m C_i \ell^2 \sin 2\phi}{r_i^3}, \tag{3.2.54}$$

where the constants $C_i \cong 1$ are geometrical factors that account for deviations of each mass configuration from the ideal form assumed in obtaining Eq. (3.2.53). In the presence of a Yukawa force, $G_\infty \to G(r_i)$, and we have

$$\tau_i \cong \frac{3G(r_i) M_i m C_i \ell^2 \sin 2\phi}{r_i^3}. \tag{3.2.55}$$

To avoid having to know the overall normalization, PF formed the ratios

$$A_i \equiv \frac{C_0 M_0}{C_i M_i} \cdot \left(\frac{\Delta V_i}{\Delta V_0}\right) \left(\frac{r_i}{r_0}\right)^3 = \frac{G(r_i)}{G(r_0)} = \frac{1 - \xi\beta(r_i/\lambda)}{1 - \xi\beta(r_0/\lambda)}. \tag{3.2.56}$$

Here $V_i = k_{\mathrm{pf}}\tau_i$ is the voltage read-out corresponding to the torque τ_i exerted on the torsion pendulum, k_{pf} is the normalization constant relating V_i and τ_i, and $\beta(x)$ is the usual exponential factor given by Eq. (3.2.6). Table 3.3 displays the experimental parameters and measured results from this experiment.

Table 3.3: Experimental parameters for Panov and Frontov [PANOV, 1979], as explained in the text.

i	M_i (kg)	r_i (cm)	$\frac{C_i}{C_0}$	ΔV_i (mV)	Δv_i $\left(\frac{\mathrm{mVcm}^3}{\mathrm{kg}}\right)$	A_i
0	0.2013	42.06	1.000	302.1	1.1182	1.000
	±0.0001	±0.05	±0.000	±0.8	±0.0033	±0.000
1	56.66	295.8	1.367	335.2	1.1201	1.003
	±0.02	±0.3	±0.001	±1.0	±0.0036	±0.006
2	594.9	984.0	1.472	102.4	1.1141	0.998
	±0.5	±2.5	±0.002	±1.0	±0.0114	±0.013

We note that it is unnecessary to determine the normalization factor k_{pf}, since we can write

$$G(r_i) = \tilde{G} \cdot \hat{G}(r_i), \tag{3.2.57}$$

$$\tilde{G} \equiv G \cdot k_{\mathrm{pf}} \cdot 3m\ell^2, \tag{3.2.58}$$

$$\hat{G}(r_i) = 1 - \xi\beta(r_i). \tag{3.2.59}$$

This allows us to write

$$\Delta V_i = \tilde{G}\left(\frac{M_i \mathcal{C}_i}{r_i^3}\right)\hat{G}(r_i), \tag{3.2.60}$$

or equivalently

$$\Delta v_i \equiv \Delta V_i\left(\frac{r_i^3}{M_i \mathcal{C}_i}\right). \tag{3.2.61}$$

Δv_i has the interesting property that in the absence of a violation of the inverse-square law, $\Delta v_i \to 1$. Note that in calculating the quantities Δv_i, it is necessary to incorporate all of the sources of experimental error, including the metrological errors in r_i, M_i, and $\mathcal{C}_i$.

In order to obtain a constraint relation among the three separations r_0, r_1, and r_2, we form the χ^2 function

$$\chi^2 = \sum_{i=0}^{2}\frac{[\Delta v_i - \tilde{G}(1 - \xi\beta(r_i))]^2}{\sigma_i^2}, \tag{3.2.62}$$

where $\sigma_i = \sigma[\Delta v_i^2]$ is the uncertainty in the quantity Δv_i. Equation (3.2.62) contains two unknowns that must be solved for, $\xi\tilde{G}$ and $\tilde{G}$. Applying the least-squares-fit procedure, we differentiate Eq. (3.2.62) with respect to each of these parameters to obtain

$$\frac{\partial\chi^2}{\partial\tilde{G}} = -2\sum_{i=0}^{2}\frac{\Delta v_i - \tilde{G} + \xi\tilde{G}\beta(r_i)}{\sigma_i^2} = 0, \tag{3.2.63}$$

$$\frac{\partial\chi^2}{\partial(\xi\tilde{G})} = 2\sum_{i=0}^{2}\frac{\Delta v_i\beta(r_i) - \tilde{G}\beta(r_i) + \xi\tilde{G}\beta(r_i)^2}{\sigma_i^2} = 0. \tag{3.2.64}$$

Solving for $\xi\tilde{G}$ and $\tilde{G}$ in Eqs. (3.2.63) and (3.2.64) gives

$$\xi\tilde{G} = \frac{\sum\dfrac{\Delta v_i}{\sigma_i^2}\sum\dfrac{\beta(r_i)}{\sigma_i^2} - \sum\dfrac{\Delta v_i\beta(r_i)}{\sigma_i^2}\sum\dfrac{1}{\sigma_i^2}}{\sum\dfrac{1}{\sigma_i^2}\sum\dfrac{\beta(r_i)}{\sigma_i^2} - \left(\sum\dfrac{\beta(r_i)}{\sigma_i^2}\right)^2}, \tag{3.2.65}$$

$$\tilde{G} = \frac{\sum\dfrac{\Delta v_i}{\sigma_i^2}\sum\dfrac{\beta(r_i)^2}{\sigma_i^2} - \sum\dfrac{\Delta v_i\beta(r_i)}{\sigma_i^2}\sum\dfrac{\beta(r_i)}{\sigma_i^2}}{\sum\dfrac{1}{\sigma_i^2}\sum\dfrac{\beta(r_i)}{\sigma_i^2} - \left(\sum\dfrac{\beta(r_i)}{\sigma_i^2}\right)^2}. \tag{3.2.66}$$

It is a trivial matter to solve these two equations for ξ:

$$\xi = \frac{\sum \frac{\Delta v_i}{\sigma_i^2} \sum \frac{\beta(r_i)}{\sigma_i^2} - \sum \frac{\Delta v_i \beta(r_i)}{\sigma_i^2} \sum \frac{1}{\sigma_i^2}}{\sum \frac{\Delta v_i}{\sigma_i^2} \sum \frac{\beta(r_i)^2}{\sigma_i^2} - \sum \frac{\Delta v_i \beta(r_i)}{\sigma_i^2} \sum \frac{\beta(r_i)}{\sigma_i^2}}. \qquad (3.2.67)$$

We observe that in taking the Newtonian limit ($\Delta v_i \to 1$) in Eqs. (3.2.66) and (3.2.67), $\tilde{G} \to 1$ and $\xi \to 0$, as we would expect.

Figure 3.7 displays the results obtained by combining the constraint in Eq. (3.2.67) and the 2σ values from Table 3.3. We see from this figure that the PF experiment remains the most sensitive laboratory constraint on Yukawa forces over distance scales on the order of a few meters.

3.3   Tests of Laplace's Equation

As we noted in Section 3.2.3, the potential $\mathcal{V}_N(\vec{r}) = \text{constant}/r$ has the property that its Laplacian vanishes identically outside a matter source:

$$\nabla^2 \mathcal{V}_N(\vec{r}) = 0. \qquad (3.3.1)$$

Conversely, $\mathcal{V}_N(\vec{r}) \propto 1/r$ is the unique potential compatible with Eq. (3.3.1), provided that we restrict our attention to potentials which vanish at infinity. It follows that an experimental measurement of the Laplacian $\nabla^2 \mathcal{V}(\vec{r})$ in the vicinity of a matter source is also a direct test of whether $\mathcal{V}(\vec{r}) \propto 1/r$. In principle this is a null experiment, and hence should be capable of achieving greater sensitivity than some other experiments which directly measure $G(r)$.

The proposal to test Newton's law of gravity in this way was first put forward by Paik [1979], and has been pursued by his group for more than a decade. To understand how $\nabla^2 \mathcal{V}(\vec{r})$ can be measured experimentally, we note that the Newtonian acceleration $\vec{a}(\vec{r}) = -\vec{\nabla}\mathcal{V}(\vec{r})$ satisfies

$$\vec{\nabla} \cdot \vec{a}(\vec{r}) = 0, \qquad (3.3.2)$$

if $\nabla^2 \mathcal{V}(\vec{r}) = 0$. We can write Eq. (3.3.2) explicitly in the form

$$0 = \vec{\nabla} \cdot \vec{a}(\vec{r}) = \frac{\partial a_x(\vec{r})}{\partial x} + \frac{\partial a_y(\vec{r})}{\partial y} + \frac{\partial a_z(\vec{r})}{\partial z}$$
$$\cong \frac{\Delta a_x}{\Delta x} + \frac{\Delta a_y}{\Delta y} + \frac{\Delta a_z}{\Delta z}. \qquad (3.3.3)$$

In the form of Eq. (3.3.3) we see that $\nabla^2 \mathcal{V}(\vec{r}) = 0$ can be tested by simultaneously measuring the gravity gradients $\partial a_x/\partial x$, $\partial a_y/\partial y$, and $\partial a_z/\partial z$ arising from some chosen source along three mutually perpendicular directions. In practice this could be achieved by determining Δa_x over an appropriate distance scale Δx, and similarly for Δa_y and Δa_z. Although such an experiment may appear straightforward in principle, it is difficult in practice for a number of reasons. One is the challenge of ensuring that the three gradiometers which measure Δa_x, Δa_y, and Δa_z are in fact mutually perpendicular at a metrologically interesting level, since a misalignment of the three gradiometers could produce a spurious suggestion that $\nabla^2 \mathcal{V}(\vec{r}) \neq 0$. We will return to discuss some other sources of error below.

The Laplacian detector provides an interesting example of an experiment in which several different distance scales are relevant. To understand how this comes about we consider the example of a Yukawa potential arising from a source of mass M,

$$\mathcal{V}_Y(\vec{r}) = +\xi G_\infty M \frac{e^{-r/\lambda}}{r}. \tag{3.3.4}$$

Since a Yukawa function $\Phi(r) = \exp(-r/\lambda)/r$ is a solution of the time-independent Klein-Gordon equation,

$$[\nabla^2 - (1/\lambda)^2]\Phi(r) = 0, \tag{3.3.5}$$

it follows that

$$\nabla^2 \mathcal{V}_Y(\vec{r}) = \xi \frac{G_\infty M e^{-r/\lambda}}{\lambda^2 r} \cong \left(\frac{\Delta a_x}{\Delta x} + \frac{\Delta a_y}{\Delta y} + \frac{\Delta a_z}{\Delta z} \right), \tag{3.3.6}$$

where in the last step we have used Eq. (3.3.3). For a point source the three relevant distance scales are provided by λ, the distance r from the source to the detector, and the size of the detector as determined by Δx, Δy, and Δz. The interplay among these determines the sensitivity of this experiment, but in ways that are not always obvious. Consider, for example, a laboratory experiment where $r/\lambda \ll 1$ for some presumed value of λ. Under these conditions we find from Eq. (3.3.6)

$$\nabla^2 \mathcal{V}_Y(\vec{r}) \cong \frac{\xi G_\infty M}{\lambda^2 r}, \tag{3.3.7}$$

from which it would seem that ξ/λ^2 can be determined from a laboratory experiment even if $r/\lambda \ll 1$. If this were indeed the case, it would violate our intuition that laboratory experiments are only useful in setting limits on λ for values of λ comparable to the dimensions of the apparatus. However, a detailed analysis of the peak-to-peak signal for $\nabla^2 \mathcal{V}(\vec{r})$ by Chan and Paik [CHAN, 1984] shows that in fact laboratory experiments provide limited information on ξ when λ is large. The interested reader is referred to [CHAN, 1984] for additional details.

We turn next to a discussion of the experimental results obtained to date from this group. Although we have described the Laplacian detector as *simultaneously* measuring $\Delta a_x/\Delta x$, $\Delta a_y/\Delta y$, and $\Delta a_z/\Delta z$ along three mutually perpendicular directions by using three detectors, one can also carry out such an experiment by using a single detector which is sequentially oriented along three perpendicular directions. This methodology was employed in [CHAN, 1982] to set the first limits on $-\xi = \alpha = \alpha(\lambda)$ over laboratory distance scales. The sensitivity of the Laplacian detector is such that even with the inevitable errors that arise when the single detector was successively rotated into the three orientations, the limits on α that emerged were competitive with those obtained from other contemporary experiments. Specifically they found $\alpha = (2.4 \pm 3.6) \times 10^{-2}$ for $\lambda \cong 1$ m, which compared favorably with the limit obtained earlier by Panov and Frontov [PANOV, 1979].

More recently Moody and Paik have used a 3-axis gradiometer to obtain an improved bound on α for $\lambda = 1.5$ m [MOODY, 1993]. The source in their experiment was a (1498 ± 3) kg pendulum constrained to oscillate in a vertical plane, and which was composed of a spherical aluminum shell filled with lead. The gradiometer consisted of six superconducting accelerometers which were mounted on the six faces of a precision cube. The differential readings of each pair of accelerometers located on opposite faces comprised a single gradiometer, so that the whole apparatus consisted of three mutually perpendicular gradiometers. The cube containing the gradiometers was oriented in such a way that the vertical coincides with one diagonal. Thus rotating the cube by 120° about a diagonal allows the positions of the three axes relative to the source to be interchanged. In this way the combined output from each axis summed over the three configurations constituted a separate null test as in the original experiment of [CHAN, 1982]. Although data were obtained in this way for each of the three gradiometers, one of these evidenced some unexpected systematic effects, and so only two of the gradiometers were used to obtain the final result. Their most stringent limit on α, which corresponds to $\lambda = 1.5$ m, is

$$\alpha = (0.9 \pm 4.6) \times 10^{-4}. \tag{3.3.8}$$

This limit can be improved by reducing the random noise in the gradiometer, and also by use of an improved (null) source which is currently being designed.

3.4 Mine and Borehole Experiments

3.4.1 Historical Background

Following the suggestion of Fujii [1971] that a violation as large as $\xi = -1/3$ could exist for values of λ in the interval 10 m $\lesssim \lambda \lesssim 1000$ m, Frank Stacey, Gary Tuck and collaborators recognized that such a large

deviation from Newtonian gravity would lead to an anomalous free-air gravity gradient in measurements of gravity performed in mine shafts [STACEY,
1981, 1983, 1984, 1987A,B; HOLDING, 1984, 1986]. The technique they
employed was first suggested by Airy [1856] as a means of determining G,
and a schematic outline of the Airy method is shown in Fig. 3.10 for an
idealized model of a spherical nonrotating Earth [STACEY, 1984]. Suppose
we compare the acceleration $g(0)$ of a test mass at the surface of the Earth
with its acceleration $g(z)$ at a depth z below the surface. (The test mass
in each case is simply the proof mass in a standard gravimeter, usually of
the LaCoste-Romberg type.) It is straightforward to see that there are two
different effects which contribute to $\Delta g(z) \equiv g(z) - g(0)$, and that these
have opposite signs. The first is the *free-air gradient*, which represents the
increase in $g(z)$ arising from the circumstance that the test mass at z is only
a distance $(R - z)$ from the center of the inner mass, rather than at R as
would be the case at the surface (see Fig. 3.10). The second effect, known as
the *double-Bouguer term*, accounts for the fact that at a depth z, $g(z)$ will
decrease since the test object is now attracted to the center of the Earth by
a smaller total mass $(M - \Delta M)$. (Recall that if Newton's $1/r^2$ law of gravity
holds, then the shell of matter of thickness z does not contribute to $g(z)$.)
From Fig. 3.10 and the preceding discussion we see that in this simplified
model $\Delta g(z)$ is given by

$$\Delta g(z) = g(z) - g(0) = \frac{G(M - \Delta M)}{(R - z)^2} - \frac{GM}{R^2} \cong \frac{2g(0)z}{R} - 4\pi G\bar{\rho}z, \quad (3.4.1)$$

where $\bar{\rho}$ is the density of the material in the shell, and $g(0) = GM/R^2$. It
follows from Eq. (3.4.1) that G can be ascertained over geophysical scales
by a series of *local* measurements which determine $g(z)$, $g(0)$, and $\bar{\rho}$, and
this constitutes the Airy method. In practice Eq. (3.4.1) must be modified
to include the effects of the Earth's rotation and ellipticity, and a detailed
discussion of the method is given in Appendix C and also by [STACEY, 1984;
HOLDING, 1986; FISCHBACH, 1986E].

    Historically, this method had not been competitive with laboratory
Cavendish measurements of G, and it was not until the work of Fujii [1971],
O'Hanlon [1972], and others (e.g., Zachos [1978]; Scherk [1979A,B]; Gibbons and Whiting[1981]), that the importance of obtaining G over different
distance scales was recognized. In fact, the Airy method was often *inverted*,
and used (together with G_0) to estimate the value of $\bar{\rho}$, the local density of
material in a mine shaft. Such measurements of $\bar{\rho}$ have allowed geophysical
prospectors to single out locations within a mine for likely ore-bearing rock.

    This geophysical prospecting technique was the reason for the existence
of a database which could be used by Stacey et al. and others to search for
a possible deviation of G on geophysical scales from the laboratory value.

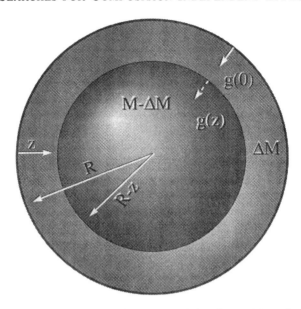

Figure 3.10: Sketch of the Airy method for determining the Newtonian gravitational constant. By comparing the acceleration $g(z)$ at a depth z with the value $g(0)$ at the surface, the shell of mass ΔM can be "weighed." See text, [STACEY, 1984], and Eq. (3.4.1) for details.

The original analysis of these data by Stacey and coworkers in fact found an anomalously high value of G, and suggested the need to repeat these measurements in a controlled environment. The best value obtained by Stacey et al. [HOLDING, 1986] was derived from a mine at Mt. Hilton in Australia: $G = (6.720 \pm 0.024) \times 10^{-11}\,\mathrm{N\,m^2\,kg^{-2}}$. This was larger than the laboratory value, $G = (6.67259 \pm 0.00085) \times 10^{-11}\,\mathrm{N\,m^2\,kg^{-2}}$, by approximately twice the maximum error admitted by Stacey et al. Interpreted in terms of a Yukawa force, their result corresponded to $\xi \sim +0.01$ and $\lambda \sim 200\,\mathrm{m}$. Their data are shown in Fig. 3.11 below.

The results of Stacey and coworkers were initially supported by the subsequent announcement of an apparent effect by Hsui [1987A], who analyzed data gathered previously from boreholes in Michigan. Hsui found $G = (6.672 \pm 0.004) \times 10^{-11}\,\mathrm{N\,m^2\,kg^{-2}}$, which was compatible with the value reported by Stacey et al., albeit with larger error bars. This experimental result, however, was marred by uncertainties in the mass determination over geophysical scales [HSUI, 1987A].

Most recently, a borehole experiment in the Greenland ice cap was performed by Ander et al. [1989A,B]. They reported an anomalous *low* value, $G \approx 6.646 \times 10^{-11}\,\mathrm{N\,m^2\,kg^{-2}}$, corresponding to $\xi \sim -0.03$. For comparison to the experiment of Stacey et al., their results are displayed in Fig. 3.11. The results of Ander et al. represented an effect three times larger than that

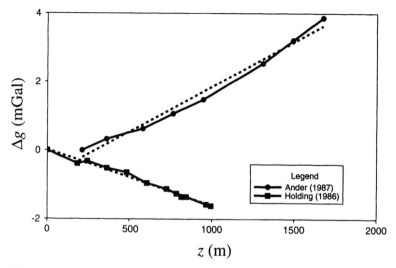

Figure 3.11: Measured anomalous gravity residuals for the experiments of Stacey et al. [HOLDING, 1986] and Ander et al. [1989A,B]. The dashed lines correspond to best fit values, with the slope for the Ander experiment (Greenland) being $d\Delta g/dz \cong +2.6 \times 10^{-8}\,\text{s}^{-2}$, and for the Holding experiment $d\Delta g/dz \cong -1.6 \times 10^{-8}\,\text{s}^{-2}$. Note that in using these gradients to obtain the corresponding values of G, one must include the fact that $\bar\rho \cong 1000\,\text{kg m}^{-3}$ at the Greenland ice cap, whereas $\bar\rho \cong 2750\,\text{kg m}^{-3}$ at the Hilton mine.

reported by Stacey et al. and with the *opposite* sign. However, these authors could not attribute their results unambiguously to non-Newtonian gravity. Specifically, it was shown that local concentrations of dense material, which could give rise to their reported gravity anomaly, could not be ruled out on the basis of the limited surface measurements that they were able to complete [ANDER, 1989A,B; PARKER, 1989; THOMAS, 1990].

3.4.2   The Effects of Terrain Bias

Notwithstanding the great care that was exercised by Stacey and coworkers in carrying out their mine experiment, a subtle effect of the local terrain was not fully accounted for, as was originally pointed out by Bartlett and Tew [BARTLETT, 1989A,B,C]. This effect, and a similar one for the tower experiments which we discuss below, resolved the discrepancy that existed between the experimental results and the predictions of Newtonian gravity. The end result is now *support* for Newtonian gravity from the mine and tower experiments, and this fills in part of the "geophysical window" ($\lambda \sim 10-10^3\,\text{m}$).

The effect pointed out by Bartlett and Tew (BT) arises from the circumstance that the Hilton mine effectively lies in a valley, with the mean elevation

of the terrain at a distance of 3 km from the mine being 24 m higher than at
the mine shaft itself. As BT note, the additional mass at a higher elevation
can be pictured as an extra ring which opposes the expected variation of $g(z)$
with depth. Not surprisingly this opposing ring would simulate the behavior expected from a new "antigravity" fifth force (see Eqs. (2.1.6)–(2.1.7)),
which is just the effect that Stacey and coworkers originally reported. It
should be noted that such an effect can be produced by inadvertently un-
dersampling the terrain at higher elevation when measuring gravity at the
surface, and this can come about if the higher terrain is less accessible than
that in the vicinity of the experiment. We will return to this discussion when
we consider the tower experiments in Section 3.7.

3.4.3 Yukawa Coupling in a Mine/Borehole Experiment

In this subsection we present the formalism for constraining ξ and λ using mine/borehole data. One of the interesting features of such experiments
is that they are only weakly sensitive to λ, and hence they lead to a determination of ξ which is almost independent of λ. We also demonstrate that
mine/borehole measurements can be interpreted as direct measurements of
G_∞.

In characterizing such experiments, we will allow for multiple Yukawa
components with coupling strengths ξ_k and ranges λ_k. We begin by noting
that the experimental input consists of data for the accelerations $g(z)$ at
various depths z below the surface, along with information on the local density $\bar{\rho}$. Consider the function $g(z, \xi_k)$, which is the acceleration that would
be measured at a depth z below the surface of the Earth in the combined
presence of gravity and a fifth force (characterized by the ξ_k). One can then
examine the functions

$$\Delta g(z, \xi_k) = g(z, \xi_k) - g(0, \xi_k), \tag{3.4.2}$$

$$\Delta g(z, 0) = g(z, 0) - g(0, 0), \tag{3.4.3}$$

which describe the difference in the local acceleration at the surface and at a
depth z, as would hold in the presence of a fifth force [Eq. (3.4.2)], or if only
Newtonian gravity were present [Eq. (3.4.3)]. The relevant experimental
quantity is the difference of these two functions, which is defined as the
gravity residual $\delta\Delta g(z)$:

$$\delta\Delta g(z) \equiv \Delta g(z, \xi_k) - \Delta g(z, 0). \tag{3.4.4}$$

Physically $\delta\Delta g(z)$ is just the difference of the local acceleration measured at
the surface and at a depth z, corrected for what one expects from Newtonian
gravity. If we consider the simplified model of a spherical nonrotating Earth
with constant local density $\bar{\rho}$, then if there were no fifth force ($\xi_k = 0$), G_∞

in Newton's law would have the value G_0 measured in the laboratory. Hence the expected value for $g(z) - g(0)$ would be

$$\Delta g(z,0) = 2g_0 \frac{z}{R_\oplus} - 4\pi G_0 \bar{\rho} z, \qquad (3.4.5)$$

where $g_0 = g(0)$ is the acceleration at $z = 0$, and where we assume that $z \ll R_\oplus$. As we noted earlier, the first term on the right-hand side of Eq. (3.4.5) is known as the *free-air gradient*, and describes the *increase* of $g(z,0)$ with depth as one comes closer to the center of mass of the Earth. The second term is known as the *double-Bouguer term*, and represents the *decrease* in $g(z,0)$ owing to the fact that in going from 0 to z one crosses a layer of matter with average density $\bar{\rho}$ and thickness z. (It is an interesting fact that these two terms very nearly cancel in practice, so that $g(z,0)$ varies relatively slowly with z near the Earth's surface, as can be seen from Fig. C.2 in Appendix C.) In the presence of a fifth force, which acts independently of gravity, there is an additional contribution proportional to the ξ_k so that the value of g_0 is given by

$$g_0 = \frac{G_0 M_\oplus}{\left(1 - \sum_j \xi_j\right) R_\oplus^2} - \frac{2\pi G_0 \bar{\rho}}{\left(1 - \sum_j \xi_j\right)} \sum_k \xi_k \lambda_k. \qquad (3.4.6)$$

Hence when $\xi_k \neq 0$, $\Delta g(z, \xi_k)$ is given by

$$\Delta g(z, \xi_k) = \left[\frac{2 G_0 M_\oplus z}{\left(1 - \sum_j \xi_j\right) R_\oplus^3} - \frac{4\pi G_0 \bar{\rho} z}{\left(1 - \sum_j \xi_j\right)} \right]$$
$$- \frac{2\pi G_0 \bar{\rho}}{\left(1 - \sum_j \xi_j\right)} \sum_k \xi_k \lambda_k \left(e^{-z/\lambda_k} - 1 \right). \qquad (3.4.7)$$

The expression in square brackets is the Newtonian contribution, and depends on ξ_k when expressed in terms of G_0. The remaining term is the direct contribution from the Yukawa interactions. Combining Eqs. (3.4.4)–(3.4.7), we obtain the expression for the gravity residual $\delta \Delta g(z)$ for the case $\lambda_k \ll R_\oplus$ (see [HOLDING, 1986] for an alternate derivation):

$$\delta \Delta g(z) = -\frac{4\pi G_0 \bar{\rho}}{\left(1 - \sum_j \xi_j\right)} \sum_k \xi_k \left[z + \frac{\lambda_k}{2} \left(e^{-z/\lambda_k} - 1 \right) \right]. \qquad (3.4.8)$$

It should be emphasized that the left-hand side of Eq. (3.4.8) is a directly measurable quantity. It is arrived at by first determining $[g(z) - g_0]$, and then correcting the values so obtained by subtracting the full Newtonian contribution (as given in Eqs. (2)–(5) of [HOLDING, 1986]), which includes the effects of the Earth's rotation, variable ellipticity, variable density, etc. (See also Appendix C.)

In principle the experimental values $\delta\Delta g(z)$ and $\bar{\rho}$ can be used to infer ξ_k and λ_k. In practice the information that can be extracted is limited by the lack of sensitivity to λ_k: For $z \ll \lambda_k$ the expression in square brackets in Eq. (3.4.8) is just $z/2$, whereas for $z \gg \lambda_k$ it is z. In either case only $\sum_k \xi_k/(1 - \sum_j \xi_j)$ can be determined from the slope $d(\delta\Delta g(z))/dz$, and if we assume that $\sum_k$ is dominated by a single constant ξ, then the slope directly determines ξ. This is the origin of one of the most interesting features of the geophysical data, namely, that $\xi/(1 - \xi)$ [or $\sum_k \xi_k/(1 - \sum_j \xi_j)$] can be determined independently of λ. Hence the "compensation" for not being able to determine λ is that the decoupling of ξ and λ in the geophysical data allows us to set limits on the characteristic strength f^2 of a putative fifth force through Eq. (3.4.8).

Since the decoupling of ξ and λ is so important a part of the geophysical analysis, it is useful to have a physical picture of how this comes about. It is easy to see that an observer located at a depth $z \gg \lambda$ experiences no effects due to a possible fifth force. This is because such an observer is effectively at the center of a sphere of radius $r \approx \lambda$, and so the effects of the matter with which he interacts via a putative fifth force cancel by spherical symmetry. Only when the observer is at a depth $z \lesssim \lambda$ is the spherical symmetry of the surrounding matter destroyed, and the effects of a fifth force start to show up. In particular an observer at the surface of the Earth interacts with a hemisphere of matter below him, and since the canceling upper hemisphere is absent, a net effect due to a fifth force results. Although measurements of $g(z)$ at depths $z \lesssim \lambda$ could thus tell us about λ, these are hard to carry out because weathering of the surface layers of the Earth leads to unreliable values for the densities $\bar{\rho}(z)$. For $z \gg \lambda$ the observer sees only the usual Newtonian gravitational interaction, whose strength is characterized by the constant $G_\infty = G_0/(1 + \alpha)$. In this case a measurement of $\Delta g(z)$ will give a result different from that expected only because G_∞ is different from G_0. Hence

$$\delta\Delta g(z) = \Delta g(z)|_{G=G_\infty} - \Delta g(z)|_{G=G_0}$$

$$\cong -4\pi\bar{\rho}z\left\{\frac{G_0}{1+\alpha} - G_0\right\}$$

$$= +4\pi G_0\bar{\rho}z\frac{\alpha}{1+\alpha}. \tag{3.4.9}$$

3.4.4 Role of the Earth Model

An important issue that must be raised is that in determining $\delta\Delta g(z)$, in principle one must have an accurate global model of how gravity varies with depth z, or an apparent anomalous gravity residual could result. A very important related issue is the effect of the variation in the ellipticity of the Earth with depth, and it was an issue that was ignored in the original calculation performed by Stacey et al. [STACEY, 1983]. As was first pointed out by Dahlen [1982], the naive assumption that the variation of the ellipticity with depth would play a significant role in the gradient $dg(z)/dz$ is not borne out by detailed calculations. Because of the importance of this question, it has been re-addressed in the context of a more comprehensive Earth model [TALMADGE, 1989B]. An adaptation of this analysis is presented in Appendix C.

3.5 Ocean Experiments

3.5.1 Introduction

One of the principal difficulties in the mine/borehole experiments is determining the local density $\bar{\rho}$ in Eq. (3.4.8). In fact it is likely that the anomalies reported by both Ander et al. and Hsui resulted from local mass concentrations which were not properly accounted for. As has been often noted, mines are located where they are precisely because of the presence of pockets of ore, and hence it is not surprising that determining $\bar{\rho}$ accurately in such an environment might be difficult.

One way of circumventing such problems is to carry out a similar experiment in a lake, or beneath the ocean, where $\bar{\rho}$ is much better known. This advantage is offset somewhat by the fact that $\bar{\rho}$ is smaller than in a mine or borehole, and hence the "signal" is correspondingly smaller. To date one ocean experiment and several lake experiments have been carried out. We begin in this section with a description of the ocean experiment, followed in the next section by a discussion of the lake experiments.

The ocean experiment of Zumberge et al. [ZUMBERGE, 1991] forms a natural bridge between mine/borehole experiments and the lake experiments. It is similar in principle to the mine/borehole experiments, except that the medium is salt water, whose density is more homogeneous and better known. However, in contrast to (most of) the lake experiments, where gravity is measured as a function of the (time-varying) water level, here the gravity measurements are made as a function of depth in an (almost) static medium. To obtain these measurements Zumberge et al. used a submersible (Sea Cliff) and a research submarine (Dolphin), as well as a remotely operated gravity meter on the ocean bottom.

Notwithstanding the fact that the ocean itself is more homogeneous than the regions in which mines and boreholes are typically located, regional density variations in the soil beneath the ocean are important. This is because such variations can create gravity gradients which could simulate the signal expected from a non-Newtonian force. Both the terrain-corrected gravity measured at various depths by the Dolphin, and the ocean-surface data, showed a relatively featureless gravity field in the region of the survey. This was true despite the fact that the variation in the actual underwater topography would have implied much larger variations in the gravity field. As noted by Zumberge et al., the explanation of why the gravity field was nonetheless relatively flat lies in the phenomenon of "isostasy" or "isostatic compensation" [STACEY, 1984; VANÍČEK, 1986]. While surveying the Himalayas in the 1850's, Pratt and Airy showed that the additional gravitational force expected from the mass of a mountain was compensated for by the mountain's "roots," which consist of relatively low-density material extending to great depths. In effect mountains are regions of lower density "floating" on higher density material. Zumberge et al. developed a model incorporating isostatic compensation to apply various corrections to their data.

To understand how all the measurements fit together, it is helpful at this stage to return to the simple Earth model in Eq. (3.4.1),

$$
\begin{aligned}
\Delta g(z) &= g(z) - g(0) \cong 2\gamma z - 4\pi G \bar{\rho} z, \\
\gamma &\equiv 2g(0)/R_\oplus \cong 309 \ \mu\mathrm{Gal\,m}^{-1},
\end{aligned}
\tag{3.5.1}
$$

where $1\,\mu\mathrm{Gal} = 10^{-8}\,\mathrm{m\,s}^{-2}$. In practice both γ and $\bar{\rho}$ themselves depend on z, and when the measured values of $\gamma(z), \bar{\rho}(z)$, and $\Delta g(z)$ are inserted into Eq. (3.5.1), one can solve for G, which is the object of the experiment. To determine $\gamma(z)$, one must know z along the surface, and this can be obtained by radar altimetry using satellites. Vertical coordinates can be referenced to the geoid or to the ellipsoid which approximates the shape of the Earth. (The geoid is a theoretical construct representing the gravitational equipotential surface that best conforms to mean sea level.)

In addition to determining $\gamma(z)$, one must also know $\bar{\rho}(z)$. The premise of carrying out an ocean experiment is that the local density $\bar{\rho}(z)$ is better known and less variable than for a comparable mine/borehole experiment. Nonetheless $\bar{\rho}(z)$ does vary with z, and the ultimate precision to which G can be measured is governed by how well $\bar{\rho}(z)$ can be determined. The density can be inferred from an equation of state for sea water which uses as input the conductivity, temperature, and salinity of the sea water. Zumberge et al. found that the density varied between $1023.6\,\mathrm{kg\,m}^{-3}$ (near the surface) and $1050.5\,\mathrm{kg\,m}^{-3}$ at a depth of $5000\,\mathrm{m}$.

There are numerous corrections to the raw data which the authors describe in some detail. Their final result for the Newtonian gravitational constant is

$$
G = (6.677 \pm 0.013) \times 10^{-11}\,\mathrm{N\,m}^2\,\mathrm{kg}^{-2},
\tag{3.5.2}
$$

which agrees with the laboratory value to within the quoted errors.

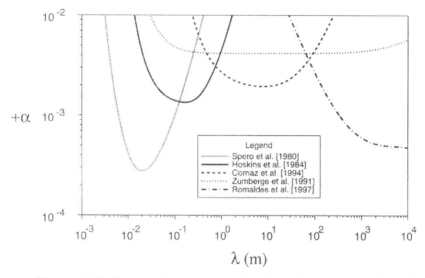

Figure 3.12: Constraints on $+\alpha$ as a function of λ in the "geophysical window." As can be seen from the figure, the constraints from the ocean experiment [ZUMBERGE, 1991] have been superseded by more recent results from lake experiments [CORNAZ, 1994; HUBLER, 1995] and tower experiments [ROMAIDES, 1997].

The result in Eq. (3.5.2) can be used to constrain ξ or α as a function of λ by combining that result with the laboratory value. Since G is determined to be a constant over a distance scale ranging from a few centimeters to $5000\,\mathrm{m}$, the resulting constraint would be an approximately horizontal line in the α-λ plane. However, as shown in Fig. 3.12, the most recent lake and tower results, along with the earlier laboratory experiments, provide more stringent constraints over the same distance scales. The ocean experiment is nonetheless of interest because it confirms the other results by an entirely different set of measurements.

3.5.2   Theoretical Formalism

We now turn to the question of how one takes the experimental results from an ocean-based experiment and converts these into an experimental constraint on α versus λ. We proceed by considering the difference in the gravitational acceleration measured at the surface of the ocean ($z = 0$) and the acceleration at a depth $z = R_\oplus - r$, where r is the distance from the point of comparison to the geophysical center of the Earth (see Fig. 3.10).

As discussed in Section 3.4, the acceleration difference arising entirely from Newtonian mechanics $\Delta g_N(z)$ is just (see Eq. (3.4.5))

$$\Delta g_N(z) \cong \frac{2g_N(0)z}{R_\oplus} - 4\pi G_\infty \bar{\rho} z, \tag{3.5.3}$$

where $\bar{\rho} \cong 1.037\,\mathrm{g\,cm^{-3}}$ is the average density of ocean water. Additionally, the measured gravitational acceleration difference $\Delta g_m(z)$, accounting for a possible non-Newtonian force, would be

$$\Delta g_m(z) \cong \frac{2g_N(0)z}{R_\oplus} - 4\pi G_\infty \bar{\rho} z + \alpha[\mathcal{F}_\oplus(z, \lambda) - \mathcal{F}_\oplus(0, \lambda)]. \tag{3.5.4}$$

Here $\mathcal{F}_\oplus(z, \lambda)$ is the magnitude of the non-Newtonian acceleration field as a function of depth z. Section 2.3 gives a sufficiently detailed model of $\mathcal{F}_\oplus(z, \lambda)$ for the purposes of this treatment.

Finally, the extrapolated gravitational acceleration $\Delta g_e(z)$ is determined by measuring the gravitational acceleration $g_m(0)$ at the surface of the ocean, and then using Eq. (3.5.3) to extrapolate what the value should be at depth z. We first note that

$$g_m(0) = \frac{G_\infty M_\oplus}{R_\oplus^2} + \alpha \mathcal{F}_\oplus(R_\oplus, \lambda). \tag{3.5.5}$$

Since G_∞ is not an experimentally measured quantity, we replace it with the Cavendish laboratory value G_c, where

$$G_\infty = \frac{G_c}{1 + \alpha \Phi_c(\lambda)} \tag{3.5.6}$$

and $\Phi_c(\lambda)$ is given by Eq. (B.2.4) in Appendix B. Note that G_c should be distinguished from $G_0 \equiv G(0)$, which strictly speaking is the value of $G(r)$ for $r \to 0$. Including the effect of $G_c \neq G_0$ gives rise to a short-distance cut-off on the constraint from ocean experiments as λ approaches the scale of the laboratory experiments. This is a result of the limit $G_c \to G_\infty$ for λ small compared to the laboratory scale. This consideration was not important for mine experiments, since sizable unaccounted-for mass inhomogeneities are present at depths close to the surface of the Earth. (Hence it would be an error to attempt to use the measured gravitational residuals to set limits on non-Newtonian forces over very short distance scales.) However, we know *ab initio* that ocean water is very close to being uniform in density, so this issue is not relevant for ocean experiments.

From Eq. (3.5.3) we have

$$\Delta g_e(z) = \frac{2g_m(0)z}{R_\oplus} - 4\pi \bar{\rho} G_c z, \tag{3.5.7}$$

and applying Eq. (3.5.5) gives

$$\Delta g_e = \frac{2g_N(0)z}{R_\oplus} + \frac{2\alpha \mathcal{F}_\oplus(z,\lambda)}{R_\oplus} - 4\pi\bar{\rho}G_c z. \tag{3.5.8}$$

Similarly, combining Eq. (3.5.6) and Eq. (3.5.4) gives

$$\Delta g_m(z) \cong \frac{2g_N(0)z}{R_\oplus} - \frac{4\pi G_c \bar{\rho} z}{1 + \alpha\Phi_c(\lambda)}$$
$$+ \alpha \left[\mathcal{F}_\oplus(z,\lambda) - \mathcal{F}_\oplus(0,\lambda)\left(1 - \frac{2z}{R_\oplus}\right) \right]. \tag{3.5.9}$$

A final correction involves noting that the field strength $\mathcal{F}_\oplus(0,\lambda)$ is normalized by $\mu_\oplus \equiv G_\infty M_\oplus$. Again, $\mu_\oplus$ is not measured directly, but rather is inferred from satellite measurements. The best current value of $\mu_\oplus$ comes from the LAGEOS satellite measurements [RAPP, 1987], so that we have

$$(\mu_\oplus)_\infty = \frac{(\mu_\oplus)_L}{1 + \alpha\Phi_L(\lambda)}, \tag{3.5.10}$$

$$\Phi_L(\lambda) \equiv \left(1 + \frac{R_L}{\lambda}\right)e^{-R_L/\lambda}\Phi_\oplus(R_\oplus;\lambda). \tag{3.5.11}$$

Here $(\mu_\oplus)_\infty$ is the value of $\mu_\oplus$ measured at ∞, and $(\mu_\oplus)_L$ is the value of $\mu_\oplus$ measured at $r = R_L$, the mean radius of the LAGEOS satellite orbit. Also $\Phi_\oplus(R_\oplus;\lambda) \approx \bar{\rho}/\rho_\oplus\Phi_s(R_\oplus/\lambda)$ is the Yukawa form factor for the Earth and is given approximately by the value for a sphere, normalized to the mass density of ocean water. We thus have

$$\mathcal{F}_\oplus(z,\lambda) \rightarrow \frac{\mathcal{F}_\oplus(z,\lambda)}{1 + \alpha\Phi_L(\lambda)}, \tag{3.5.12}$$

which provides a cutoff in sensitivity of the ocean experiment for $\lambda \gtrsim R_\oplus$. Making this final correction gives

$$\delta\Delta g_m(z) \cong 4\pi G_c \bar{\rho} z \frac{\alpha\Phi_c(\lambda)}{1 + \alpha\Phi_c(\lambda)}$$
$$+ \frac{\alpha}{1 + \alpha\Phi_L(\lambda)}\left[\mathcal{F}_\oplus(z,\lambda) - \mathcal{F}_\oplus(0,\lambda)\left(1 - \frac{2z}{R_\oplus}\right)\right]. \tag{3.5.13}$$

Combining Eq. (3.5.13) with the results from Zumberge et al. [ZUMBERGE, 1991] gives the constraint curve shown in Fig. 3.12.

3.6 Lake Experiments

3.6.1 Introduction

The first of the lake experiments was carried out by Stacey and coworkers at the Splityard Creek reservoir near Brisbane, Australia [MOORE, 1988A,B; TUCK, 1988]. A small lake above the reservoir was under construction in a quarry at the time this experiment was being considered. It was arranged that a tower to house the experiment be built in the quarry before the quarry was flooded to form a storage reservoir for surplus hydroelectric power. The experiment then consisted of comparing the weights of two 10 kg stainless-steel masses which were suspended in evacuated tubes, and arranged so that one was always below the low water level while the other was above the high water level. After correcting for various systematic effects the value of G they obtained was

$$G = 6.689(7) \times 10^{-11} \, \mathrm{N \, m^2 \, kg^{-2}}, \tag{3.6.1}$$

which agrees within errors with the laboratory value G_0. This experiment measures the gravitational attraction of the two test masses to the water in the lake, which is on average at a distance of 22 m from the test masses. Hence the constraint implied by Eq. (3.6.1) on ξ corresponds to $\lambda \cong 22 \, \mathrm{m}$.

The second lake experiment [MÜLLER, 1989, 1990] took place at the Hornberg lake reservoir in Germany. In contrast to the Splityard Creek experiment, which used a specially constructed balance to measure the change in gravity due to the changing water level, this experiment utilized several LaCoste-Romberg gravimeters. Their readings were correlated with the water level data, which typically varied by $5 - 22 \, \mathrm{m}$ over a day. These data were then used to predict the changing signal that would be expected assuming Newtonian gravity to be correct. They find for G

$$(G - G_0)/G_0 = (0.25 \pm 0.4)\%, \tag{3.6.2}$$

which reflects agreement with the Newtonian value. The constraint implied by Eq. (3.6.2) corresponds to an average mass separation of $40-70 \, \mathrm{m}$ between the water and the gravimeters.

An experiment similar in design to that of Müller et al. has been carried out by Oldham, Lowes, and Edge at the Ffestiniog pumped-storage power station in North Wales [OLDHAM, 1991, 1993]. As in the Hornberg experiment, Oldham et al. employed LaCoste-Romberg gravimeters: An "upper" gravimeter located 3 m above the highest water level in the reservoir, and a "lower" gravimeter located 3 m below the lowest water level. The authors note that the location of the two gravimeters made it possible to subtract out various perturbing effects which would be common to both sites, such as the Earth's tides. As in the other experiments, the data consisted of correlating the gravity measurements on the two gravimeters with the water level in the lake. The data were then compared with the predictions of Newtonian gravity over the effective distances which could be probed by the two gravimeters, which were 26 m, 36 m, and 94 m. The results of this experiment can be interpreted as setting a limit on the quantity $\delta \equiv (G_{obs} - G_{lab})/G_{lab}$, where G_{lab} can be identified with the accepted laboratory value G_N in Eq. (1.1), and G_{obs} is what is measured in the experiment. They find a value $\delta = (1 \pm 2) \times 10^{-3}$, which indicates that there is no evidence for a new intermediate-range coupling for distance scales of order 26–94 m.

We mention in passing another lake experiment for which preliminary results have been reported. This is the experiment of Hipkin and Steinberger [HIPKIN, 1990]. Rather than measuring the gravitational attraction that a *varying* mass of water exerts on one or two *fixed* gravimeters, they measure the force exerted by a fixed body of water at 21 sites surrounding the Megget Water Reservoir in Scotland. In contrast to the other lake experiments, where the time-varying signal allowed various background contributions to be subtracted out, the Megget experiment required detailed modeling of the background gravity. Unfortunately their modeling proved problematic, and this illustrates the practical importance of having a time-varying signal which allows background effects to be subtracted. We return to this point in Section 4.3 below.

The lake experiments of Cornaz et al. [CORNAZ, 1991, 1994; HUBLER, 1995] took place at Gigerwald Lake, which is a pumped storage reservoir in eastern Switzerland. The design of this experiment is similar to that of Splityard Creek, in that both experiments utilize a single balance to compare the weights of two stainless-steel test masses, one of which is always below the water level and the other above it. Figure 2 of [CORNAZ, 1994] shows how closely the weight difference correlates with the water level as the latter varies in response to demand for electrical power. After correcting for a number of small effects, their final value for the Newtonian constant was

$$G = (6.669 \pm 0.005) \times 10^{-11} \, \text{N} \, \text{m}^2 \, \text{kg}^{-2}, \qquad (3.6.3)$$

which is in excellent agreement with the laboratory value G_0. This constraint corresponds to an effective interaction distance of 112 m. A similar null result was found for an interaction distance of 88 m.

To summarize, the lake experiments discussed above determine an effective value of the Newtonian constant G over a distance scale of ~ 10–100 m, and all find results in agreement with the laboratory value G_0. However, the most recent experiment which we describe below appears to disagree with the earlier experiments, as we now discuss.

Results from a recent lake experiment [ACHILLI, 1997] point to a possible discrepancy between the new experimental results and the predictions of Newtonian gravity. The experiment was carried out at the Brasimone-Suviana lake site, where water is pumped up from Suviana to Brasimone and then released (back to Suviana) when additional electric power is needed. As in other similar experiments, a gravimeter was used to "weigh" the mass of water pumped between Suviana and Brasimone. Their results can then be used to determine the Newtonian constant $(G_N)_{lake}$ at an effective distance $< r_{\text{eff}} >= 47$ m. Achilli et al. find

$$\frac{G_N(\text{lake})}{G_0} = 1.0127 \pm 0.0013. \tag{3.6.4}$$

Taken at face value this represents a discrepancy of more than 9σ with the predictions of Newtonian gravity. Additionally this result also appears to conflict with the results of [CORNAZ, 1994] and [HUBLER, 1995] discussed above, although this experiment covered a somewhat different distance scale ($\langle r_{\text{eff}} \rangle = 112$ m).

The experiment of Achilli et al. employed only one gravimeter (a potential drawback), although theirs was a very sensitive superconducting gravimeter. Their claimed sensitivity of 10 nGal should be compared to an expected signal of ≈ 280 μGal arising from the variation of the water level. The authors carried out a very careful analysis which accounted for changes in the water density with location, time, and temperature, and which corrected as well for effects of air temperature, relative humidity, and atmospheric pressure, among other factors. The interested reader should consult this reference for an excellent discussion of how these effects were dealt with.

There is, however, one systematic effect which requires further exploration, and this is the seepage of water from the lake through micro-fissures in the material enclosing the lake [HAGIWARA, PC; FUJII, PC]. Estimates from lakes in Japan where measurements have been made suggest that seepage may be a more significant problem then has been generally recognized [HAGIWARA, PC]. Since this observation would apply to all the other lake experiments as well, there remains a possibility that after properly correcting for seepage effects the earlier (null) experiments would now evidence deviations from Newtonian gravity [HAGIWARA, PC]. Clearly additional work is needed to better understand various systematic effects in the lake experiments. We have elected not to modify Fig. (2.13) to include the recent results of Achilli et al. given these uncertainties, despite the great care taken in carrying out the latter experiment.

3.6.2 Theoretical Formalism

For simplicity, we take the location of the measurement to be at the center of a circular-cylindrical slab of water of radius "a" and height "h," and we view the experiment as measuring the change in the vertical component of gravity upon adding and subtracting a measured height of water to/from this cylinder. The result of this analysis is given in Eq. (3.6.12), and can be arrived at in several steps.

(i) *Evaluation of the Newtonian acceleration g_z*

We have

$$g_z(z) = -\rho G_\infty \int_0^{2\pi} d\theta \int_0^a r dr \int_0^h \frac{(z+z')dz'}{(r^2 + (z+z')^2)^{3/2}}$$

$$= +2\pi\rho G_\infty \int_0^a \frac{rdr}{\sqrt{r^2 + (z+z')^2}}\Bigg|_0^h , \tag{3.6.5}$$

which reduces to

$$g_z(z) = +2\pi\rho G_\infty \left[\sqrt{a^2 + (z+h)^2} - \sqrt{a^2 + z^2} - |z+h| + |z| \right]. \tag{3.6.6}$$

(ii) *Evaluation of the acceleration $\mathcal{F}(z)$ due to a Yukawa potential*

We have:

$$\mathcal{F}(z) = \rho G_\infty \int_0^{2\pi} d\theta \int_0^a r\, dr \int_0^h \frac{(z+z')dz'}{(r^2 + (z+z')^2)^{3/2}}$$

$$\times \left[1 + \sqrt{r^2 + (z+z')^2}/\lambda \right] e^{-\sqrt{r^2 + (z+z')^2}/\lambda}$$

$$= 2\pi\rho G_\infty \int_0^a \frac{rdr}{\sqrt{r^2 + (z+z')^2}} e^{-\sqrt{r^2 + (z+z')^2}/\lambda}\Bigg|_0^h , \tag{3.6.7}$$

from which we obtain

$$\mathcal{F}(z) = +2\pi\rho G_\infty \lambda$$

$$\times \left[e^{-|z|/\lambda} - e^{-|z+h|/\lambda} - e^{-\sqrt{a^2+z^2}/\lambda} + e^{-\sqrt{a^2+(z+h)^2}/\lambda} \right]. \tag{3.6.8}$$

(iii) *Derivation of the anomalous acceleration difference Δa*

The net measured acceleration $g_m(z)$ at any point is given by

$$g_m(z) = 2\pi\rho G_\infty \left[\sqrt{a^2 + (z+h)^2} - \sqrt{a^2 + z^2} - |z+h| + |z| \right]$$

$$+ 2\pi\rho G_\infty \sum_i \xi_i \lambda_i \left[e^{-|z|/\lambda} - e^{-|z+h|/\lambda} \right.$$

$$\left. - e^{-\sqrt{a^2+z^2}/\lambda} + e^{-\sqrt{a^2+(z+h)^2}/\lambda} \right]. \tag{3.6.9}$$

Similarly, the extrapolated acceleration (i.e., the acceleration inferred by extrapolating from $z = 0$ assuming Newtonian gravity) is given by

$$g_e(z) = 2\pi\rho G_0 \left[\sqrt{a^2 + (z+h)^2} - \sqrt{a^2 + z^2} - |z+h| + |z| \right], \tag{3.6.10}$$

$$G_0 = G_\infty \left[1 - \sum_i \xi_i \right]. \tag{3.6.11}$$

Thus, the anomalous acceleration difference $\Delta g(z) \equiv g_m(z) - g_e(z)$ is

$$\Delta g(z) = -\frac{2\pi\rho G_0}{1 - \sum_i \xi_i} \sum_i \xi_i \left[\sqrt{a^2 + (z+h)^2} - \sqrt{a^2 + z^2} - |z+h| + |z| \right]$$

$$+ \frac{2\pi\rho G_0}{1 - \sum_i \xi_i} \sum_i \xi_i \lambda_i \left[e^{-|z|/\lambda} - e^{-|z+h|/\lambda} \right.$$

$$\left. - e^{-\sqrt{a^2+z^2}/\lambda} + e^{-\sqrt{a^2+(z+h)^2}/\lambda} \right]. \tag{3.6.12}$$

Finally, the above equation can be rewritten in a somewhat more compact form,

$$\frac{\Delta g(z)}{g_e(z)} = \left(\frac{1}{1 - \sum_i \xi_i} \right) \sum_i \xi_i \left[1 - \frac{\mathcal{F}_i(z)}{g_e(z)} \right]. \tag{3.6.13}$$

We note in passing that $\mathcal{F}_i/g_e \to +1$ as $\lambda \to \infty$, so that $\Delta g(z)/g_e \to 0$ in this limit, as expected.

3.7 Tower Gravity Experiments

3.7.1 Introduction

Among the most interesting new experiments to emerge in the post-1986 era were those measuring the acceleration of gravity $g(z)$ as a function of the height z up a tall tower. The idea behind these experiments is straightforward: If the inverse-square law is correct, then $g(z)$ can be predicted from a knowledge of $g(\vec{r})$ at the surface, and this can then be compared to the value $g_0(z)$ actually observed on the tower. Any discrepancy between $g_0(z)$ and the theoretical value $g_t(z)$ could be interpreted as evidence for a deviation from the inverse-square law. For example, in the presence of a single new Yukawa field with coupling strength α and range λ, as in Eq. (2.1.8), we would find (for a spherical nonrotating Earth),

$$g_0(z) - g_t(z) = 2\pi\rho G_0\alpha\lambda(e^{-z/\lambda} - 1), \qquad (3.7.1)$$

where $\rho = 2670 \, \text{kg m}^{-3}$ is the mean terrain density. In practice such experiments can be thought of as proceeding in the following three steps (although not necessarily in this sequence!): 1) $g(\vec{r})$ is measured on the surface in the region surrounding the tower. In principle $g(\vec{r})$ must be known everywhere over the surface, but in practice direct measurements are made only in the immediate vicinity of the tower, usually out to a radius of several kilometers in all directions. Beyond that distance, archived data and models of the Earth can be used. 2) A model is developed, assuming Newtonian gravity, which uses the measured surface gravity to determine what $g_t(z)$ is. 3) Actual measurements are made on the tower to obtain $g_0(z)$, from which the difference $\Delta g(z) = g_0(z) - g_t(z)$ can be computed. Since towers are available which are as tall as $\sim 600 \, \text{m}$, such measurements serve to probe the region in the geophysical window near $\lambda = 1 \, \text{km}$.

The technique for carrying out such measurements was pioneered by Donald Eckhardt and collaborators at the Air Force Geophysical Laboratory (now Phillips Laboratory) at Hanscom AFB in Massachusetts. Prior to their work the main impediment to such an experiment was thought to be the difficulty of measuring $g_0(z)$ on the tower, due to swaying of the tower in the wind. It is now recognized that towers are available which are sufficiently stable (for wind speeds $\lesssim 5 \, \text{km/hr}$) to permit $g_0(z)$ to be determined. Eckhardt and collaborators first used this technique on the 610 m WTVD television tower in Garner, North Carolina [ECKHARDT, 1988], and found a discrepancy of $(-500 \pm 35) \, \mu\text{Gal}$ between $g_0(z)$ and $g_t(z)$ at $z = 562.24 \, \text{m}$. The negative sign corresponds to the effect expected from a new *attractive* non-Newtonian force, which Eckhardt and coworkers termed the "sixth force." As noted in Section 3.4.2, however, Bartlett and Tew subsequently pointed out that the surface gravity data base used by Eckhardt et al. (which had been compiled by the Defense Mapping Agency) could have been biased because the terrain at higher elevation was oversampled relative to that at lower elevation [BARTLETT, 1989B].

"Terrain bias" can occur because low-lying terrain is often relatively inaccessible, as would be the case if a stream were running through the region. Since the gravimeters used in such experiments are expensive, it is not surprising that fewer measurements would be made, for instance, at the edge of a body of water than at a nearby road running above the water. A difference of 1 m between the average elevation of the actual topography and that of the sampled points would lead to a discrepancy of $\sim 309\,\mu$Gal, which is comparable to the magnitude of the effect observed by Eckhardt et al. These authors subsequently re-examined their results in light of the work of Bartlett and Tew, and now find a result consistent with Newtonian gravity [JEKELI, 1990]. More recently this group has performed another tower experiment, using the 610 m WABG television tower in Inverness, Mississippi [ROMAIDES, 1994, 1997]. The WABG tower was chosen, in part, because it is located in the Mississippi delta region where, because of the flatness of the terrain, terrain-bias problems would be minimal. The maximum discrepancy $\Delta g(z)$, which is $(+32 \pm 32)\,\mu$Gal at $z = 569$ m, confirms the validity of the $1/r^2$ law over this distance scale [ROMAIDES, 1994, 1997].

This conclusion is supported by two other tower experiments carried out during the same period. Speake et al. [SPEAKE, 1990] used the 300 m NOAA meteorological tower in Erie, Colorado. These authors devoted considerable effort to understanding how tower motion affects the performance of the LaCoste-Romberg gravimeters used in these experiments. Their careful analysis supported the claim by Eckhardt et al. that $g(z)$ could be measured on towers with sufficient precision to allow a meaningful test of Newtonian gravity. The results of Speake et al. are in complete agreement with the predictions of Newtonian gravity to within their experimental error.

The third tower experiment utilized the 465 m BREN tower at Jackass Flats, Nevada [THOMAS, 1989; KAMMERAAD, 1990]. This tower was originally built to support a reactor, which has since been removed. By arranging to take measurements on their tower at sunrise, the authors were able to ensure that the wind speeds were below 5 km/hr. As in the previous experiments, the authors combined their own measurements of gravity near the tower with archived data, which in their case extended out to 300 km. Kammeraad et al. consider in detail the effects of correlations on their final results, and the interested reader should consult the above references for further discussion. The BREN tower results are in agreement with the predictions of Newtonian gravity: At the maximum height, $z = 454.86$ m, the authors find $\Delta g(z) = (-60 \pm 95)\,\mu$Gal.

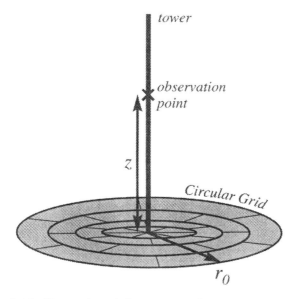

Figure 3.13: Illustration of the geometry for tower experiments. The gravitational acceleration g at some height z is compared to that extrapolated using surface measurements obtained in a circular grid of radius r_0 about the tower.

3.7.2 Theoretical Formalism

We conclude with a discussion of some of the technical modeling considerations that enter into the calculation of $g_t(z)$. To calculate $g_t(z)$, one begins by measuring the gravitational acceleration on a circular grid extending out to some radius r_0, as shown in Fig. 3.13. For purposes of extrapolation, a reference spherical Earth model with radius $R_\oplus$ is used in which ϕ and θ are, respectively, the local azimuthal and polar angles describing the location of each gravity measurement $g_t(z, \theta, \phi)$. Deviations of a particular measurement in z from the reference Earth model are accounted for by subtracting a contribution γz, where $\gamma = dg/dz$ is the local value of the free-air gradient. After this correction each measured value of gravity $g_0(0, \theta, \phi)$ is then reduced to a value near zero by subtracting the value $g_t(0, \theta, \phi)$ that a standard Earth model would predict for that location. This leaves a measured gravity residual,

$$\Delta g_0(0, \theta, \phi) \equiv g_0(z, \theta, \phi) - \gamma z - g_t(0, \theta, \phi). \tag{3.7.2}$$

This correction also accounts for the terrain outside of the radius r_0 which has not been measured: If the Earth model accurately describes the global behavior of $g(0, \theta, \phi)$, then there will be no error associated with collecting gravity measurements only over a localized region of the Earth's surface. From Laplace's equation for a spherical mass distribution, we know that $(R_\oplus + z)g(R_\oplus + z)$ represents a solution for the region exterior to the mass, so we can extrapolate the surface gravitational residual measurements using Poisson's integral (see [JACKSON, 1975], page 63),

$$
\Delta g_t(z) = \frac{1}{4\pi} \frac{R_\oplus^2 [(R_\oplus + z)^2 - R_\oplus^2]}{(R_\oplus + z)}
$$

$$
\times \int_0^{2\pi} d\phi \int_0^{\theta_0} d\theta \sin\theta \frac{\Delta g_0(0, \theta, \phi)}{[R_\oplus^2 + (R_\oplus + z)^2 - 2R_\oplus(R_\oplus + z)\cos\theta]^{3/2}}, \quad (3.7.3)
$$

where $\tan\theta_0 = r_0/R_\oplus$. Defining the average value $\langle \Delta g_0 \rangle$ in the obvious fashion, this equation becomes

$$
\Delta g_t(z) = \frac{1}{2} \frac{R_\oplus^2 (z^2 + 2R_\oplus z)}{(R_\oplus + z)} \langle \Delta g_0 \rangle \left[\frac{1}{R_\oplus(R_\oplus + z)} \right]
$$

$$
\times \left[\frac{1}{z} - \frac{1}{\sqrt{R_\oplus^2 + (R_\oplus + z)^2 - 2R_\oplus(R_\oplus + z)\cos\theta_0}} \right]. \quad (3.7.4)
$$

Writing $\cos\theta_0 \cong 1 - r_0^2/2R_\oplus^2$, we have

$$
R_\oplus^2 + (R_\oplus + z)^2 - 2R_\oplus(R_\oplus + z)\cos\theta_0 \cong r_0^2(1 + z/R_\oplus) + z^2. \quad (3.7.5)
$$

Since $z \ll r_0 \ll R_\oplus$, we can expand Eq. (3.7.4) to find

$$
\Delta g_t(z) \cong \langle \Delta g_0 \rangle \left[1 - \left(\frac{3}{2R_\oplus} + \frac{1}{r_0} \right) z + \frac{2}{R_\oplus} \left(\frac{1}{R_\oplus} + \frac{1}{r_0} \right) z^2 \right]. \quad (3.7.6)
$$

If we assume that there are no local mass concentrations, then

$$
g_0(z, \theta, \phi) \cong \frac{G_\infty M_\oplus}{(R_\oplus + z)^2} \left[1 - \frac{3J_2 R_\oplus^2}{(R_\oplus + z)^2} P_2(\sin\Theta) \right]
$$

$$
- \omega^2(R_\oplus + z)\cos^2\Theta + \alpha \mathcal{F}(R_\oplus + z, \lambda), \quad (3.7.7)
$$

where $P_2(\sin\Theta)$ is the second Legendre polynomial, J_2 is the quadrupole moment of the Earth, ω is its angular velocity, $\mathcal{F}(r, \lambda)$ is the vertical component of the non-Newtonian acceleration field due to the Earth, and $\Theta \cong \theta \sin\phi + \theta_{\text{lat}}$, where θ_{lat} is the geocentric latitude of the experiment. In the global gravity model for the Earth (the so-called *reference* Earth model), $g_t(z, \theta, \phi)$ may be written approximately as

$$
g_t(z, \theta, \phi) = \frac{G_{\text{ref}} M_\oplus}{(R_\oplus + z)^2} \left[1 - \frac{3J_2 R_\oplus^2}{(R_\oplus + z)^2} P_2(\sin\Theta) \right]
$$

$$
- \omega^2(R_\oplus + z)\cos^2\Theta, \quad (3.7.8)
$$

with

$$\frac{G_{\mathrm{ref}} M_{\oplus}}{R_{\mathrm{ref}}^2} \approx \frac{G_{\infty} M_{\oplus}}{R_{\mathrm{ref}}^2} + \alpha \mathcal{F}(R_{\mathrm{ref}}, \lambda). \tag{3.7.9}$$

Combining Eqs. (3.7.7), (3.7.8), and (3.7.9), we then have

$$\Delta g_0(z, \theta, \phi) = \Delta g_0(z)$$

$$= \alpha \left[\mathcal{F}(R_{\oplus} + z, \lambda) - \frac{R_{\mathrm{ref}}^2}{(R_{\oplus} + z)^2} \mathcal{F}(R_{\mathrm{ref}}, \lambda) \right]. \tag{3.7.10}$$

Inserting Eq. (3.7.10) into Eq. (3.7.6) then gives

$$\Delta g_t(z) \cong \alpha \left[\mathcal{F}(R_{\oplus}, \lambda) - \frac{R_{\mathrm{ref}}^2}{R^2} \mathcal{F}(R_{\mathrm{ref}}, \lambda) \right]$$

$$\times \left[1 - \left(\frac{3}{2R_{\oplus}} + \frac{1}{r_0} \right) z + \frac{2}{R_{\oplus}} \left(\frac{1}{R_{\oplus}} + \frac{1}{r_0} \right) z^2 \right]. \tag{3.7.11}$$

Noting that $\mathcal{F}(r, \lambda)$ is calculated in our case relative to R_{ref}, it follows that

$$\mathcal{F}(r, \lambda) = [1 + \alpha (1 + R_{\mathrm{ref}}/\lambda) \exp(-R_{\mathrm{ref}}/\lambda)]^{-1} \mathcal{F}_{\mathrm{calc}}(r, \lambda)$$

$$\cong \mathcal{F}_{\mathrm{calc}}(r, \lambda). \tag{3.7.12}$$

Hence we finally have

$$\delta \Delta g \equiv \Delta g_0(z) - \Delta g_t(z)$$

$$= \alpha \left\{ \left[\mathcal{F}_{\mathrm{calc}}(R_{\oplus} + z, \lambda) - \frac{R_{\mathrm{ref}}^2}{(R_{\oplus} + z)^2} \mathcal{F}_{\mathrm{calc}}(R_{\mathrm{ref}}, \lambda) \right] \right.$$

$$- \left[\mathcal{F}_{\mathrm{calc}}(R_{\oplus}, \lambda) - \frac{R_{\mathrm{ref}}^2}{R_{\oplus}^2} \mathcal{F}_{\mathrm{calc}}(R_{\mathrm{ref}}, \lambda) \right]$$

$$\left. \times \left[1 - \left(\frac{3}{2R_{\oplus}} + \frac{1}{r_0} \right) z + \frac{2}{R_{\oplus}} \left(\frac{1}{R_{\oplus}} + \frac{1}{r_0} \right) z^2 \right] \right\}. \tag{3.7.13}$$

3.8   Planetary Constraints

It is certainly fair to say that, from a historical point of view, our belief
in the validity of Newtonian gravity rests heavily on its successes in describing planetary motion. Perhaps foremost among these successes was the
prediction of the existence of Neptune by Adams and Leverrier in 1845 [NEW-
MAN, 1955], and its subsequent discovery. (In light of the present discussion,
it is interesting to note that one of the alternatives considered by Airy to
the existence of a new planet was a breakdown of the $1/r^2$ law [NEWMAN,

1955].) When Newtonian gravity failed to account for some aspect of planetary motion, as in the case of the precession of the perihelion of Mercury, this
foreshadowed the dramatic new physics to arise from General Relativity. In
the same vein we show below that any *additional* precession (over and above
that predicted by General Relativity) could be interpreted as evidence for
a new intermediate-range force. As we also discuss, a second signal for the
existence of a new coupling would be evidence that the product $G(a_P)M_\odot$
is not a constant, where $G(a_P)$ is the effective Newtonian "constant" $G(r)$
defined in Eq. (2.1.10) evaluated at the position of the semimajor axis a_P of
each planet from the Sun.

To proceed we follow the discussion of [TALMADGE, 1988] and consider
the differential equation for the orbit $u = u(\theta)$ of a planet about the Sun,
where $u = 1/r$ and r is the distance to the Sun. For the motion of a planet
of mass m under the influence of a central force $\vec{F}(r) = \hat{r}F(r)$, $u(\theta)$ is a
solution of [SYMON, 1971]

$$\frac{d^2u}{d\theta^2} + u = -\frac{m^2}{L^2u^2}F(1/u), \qquad (3.8.1)$$

where $L = |\vec{r} \times m\vec{v}| = mr^2\dot{\theta}$ is the (conserved) orbital angular momentum,
and $\dot{\theta} = d\theta/dt$ is the angular velocity. For motion under the influence of a $1/r$
potential, $\vec{F} = -m\mu_\odot\hat{r}/r^2$, where $\mu_\odot \equiv G_\infty M_\odot$, and $F(1/u) = -m\mu_\odot u^2$.
Eq. (3.8.1) then becomes

$$\frac{d^2u}{d\theta^2} + u = \frac{m^3\mu_\odot}{L^2} = \text{constant}, \qquad (3.8.2)$$

the solution of which is

$$u(\theta) = u_P + u_\varepsilon \cos(\theta - \theta_0), \qquad (3.8.3a)$$

$$u_P = \frac{m^3\mu_\odot}{L^2} \equiv 1/p, \qquad (3.8.3b)$$

$$p = a_P(1 - \varepsilon^2), \qquad \varepsilon = u_\varepsilon/u_P. \qquad (3.8.3c)$$

Note that ε is the usual planetary eccentricity, and θ_0 determines the orientation of the orbit.

We turn next to consider the modifications in the differential equation (3.8.1) and its solution Eq. (3.8.3) that arise in the presence of a non-
Newtonian coupling. It is sufficient to consider the modification of the usual
$1/r^2$ force law for planetary motion in the presence of a single Yukawa, and
from Eq. (2.1.9), we find

$$\vec{F}(r) = -\hat{r}G_\infty\frac{M_\odot m}{2r^2}[1 + \alpha(1 + r/\lambda)e^{-r/\lambda}] \equiv -\frac{m\mu_\odot(r)\hat{r}}{r^2}. \qquad (3.8.4)$$

From the general discussion in Chapter 2 we recall that if the distance r of a planet from the Sun was either much larger or much smaller than λ, then $\vec{F}(r)$ would look like a $1/r^2$ force with an effective Newtonian constant given by G_∞ or $G_0 = G_\infty(1 + \alpha)$ respectively. As we have noted, distinguishing between the constants G_∞ and G_0 would be extremely difficult, and hence the interesting regime in the α-λ plot is near $\lambda \cong a_P$, where a_P is the semimajor axis for the motion of the Pth planet.

In the presence of the additional non-Newtonian contribution given in Eq. (3.8.4) above, the differential equation for u becomes

$$\frac{d^2u}{d\theta^2} + u = G_\infty \frac{M_\odot m^2}{L^2}\left[1 + \alpha\left(1 + \frac{1}{\lambda u}\right)e^{-1/\lambda u}\right] \equiv B(u). \qquad (3.8.5)$$

If we assume that $\alpha \ll 1$, then the solution for u should lie near the unperturbed (i.e., $\alpha = 0$) value, $u_0 = 1/p_0$, and for this reason it is convenient to expand $B(u)$ in a Taylor series about u_0. From Eq. (3.8.3c) we can also write $p_0 \approx a_{P0}$, where a_{P0} is the unperturbed semimajor axis, since the ε^2 correction is of higher order for the major planets for which precise astronometric data are available. Letting $u_{P0} \equiv 1/a_{P0}$, we find

$$B(u) = B(u_{P0}) + (u - u_{P0})\left[\frac{dB(u)}{du}\bigg|_{u=u_{P0}}\right] + \dots$$

$$\cong B\left(\frac{1}{a_{P0}}\right) + \left(u - \frac{1}{a_{P0}}\right)\left[\alpha\left(\frac{a_{P0}}{\lambda}\right)^2\right]e^{-a_{P0}/\lambda}, \qquad (3.8.6)$$

where, as before, the subscript 0 denotes the value corresponding to $\alpha = 0$. The differential equation for u now assumes the form

$$\frac{d^2u}{d\theta^2} + u\left[1 - \alpha\left(\frac{a_{P0}^2}{\lambda^2}\right)e^{-a_{P0}/\lambda}\right] = u_P, \qquad (3.8.7a)$$

$$u_P \equiv \frac{1}{p} = \frac{1}{p_0}\left[1 + \alpha e^{-a_{P0}/\lambda}\left(1 + \frac{a_{P0}}{\lambda} - \frac{a_{P0}^2}{\lambda^2}\right)\right]. \qquad (3.8.7b)$$

We see from Eq. (3.8.7b) that the effect of $\alpha \neq 0$ is to modify the coefficient ω^2 of u, which determines the precession rate of the planet. In addition $\alpha \neq 0$ modifies the value of u_P, as is seen in Eq. (3.8.7b). The solution to (3.8.7a) is

$$u(\theta) = u_P + u_e \cos\omega(\theta - \theta_0), \qquad (3.8.8)$$

where u_e determines the eccentricity of motion of the planet as before. Substituting Eq. (3.8.8) into (3.8.7a), we find for ω

$$\omega = \left[1 - \alpha(a_{P0}^2/\lambda^2)e^{-a_{P0}/\lambda}\right]^{1/2} \cong 1 - (\alpha/2)(a_P^2/\lambda^2)e^{-a_P/\lambda}, \qquad (3.8.9)$$

where we have written $a_{P0} \cong a_P$ to $\mathcal{O}(\alpha)$. It is easy to show that $\omega \neq 1$ leads to a precession of the perihelion of the planet. From Eq. (3.8.8) and (3.8.9) we see that the planet will be at its perihelion when

$$\omega(\theta - \theta_n) = 2\pi n \equiv \omega\theta_n, \qquad (3.8.10)$$

where n is an integer. Hence

$$\theta_n = 2\pi n/\omega, \qquad (3.8.11)$$

so that, in the approximation of neglecting terms $\mathcal{O}(\varepsilon^2)$, the precession angle $\delta\phi_a$ is given by

$$\delta\phi_a \equiv (\theta_{n+1} - \theta_n) - 2\pi = \frac{2\pi}{\omega} - 2\pi \cong +\pi\alpha(a_P/\lambda)^2 e^{-a_P/\lambda}. \qquad (3.8.12)$$

The sign in Eq. (3.8.12) is such that for $\alpha > 0$ the precession of the perihelion is in the same direction as the planet's motion. We note that for a fixed value of α, the maximum sensitivity to a new force is achieved when $a_P/\lambda = 2$, and that the sensitivity vanishes for both $a_P/\lambda \to 0$ and $a_P/\lambda \to \infty$. This provides a nice demonstration of the point we have made in Section 3.1 that experimental systems are typically most sensitive to values of λ which are comparable to the natural scale (here given by a_P) of the system.

We consider next the constraints that are implied by the constancy of $G(a_P)M_\odot$, where $G(a_P)$ is the effective Newtonian "constant" of gravitation evaluated at the distance a_P of the Pth planet from the Sun. Evidently, for values of λ comparable to a_P, $G(a_P)$ will differ in a nontrivial way from G_∞, and hence its variation from one planet to another should be detectable. As above, our discussion is based on [TALMADGE, 1988].

We begin by writing Kepler's third law in the form

$$a_P^3 = \mu_\odot(a_P)\left(\frac{T_P}{2\pi}\right)^2, \qquad (3.8.13)$$

where T_P is the period and a_P is the physically measured semimajor axis of the orbit of planet P. In the absence of any non-Newtonian forces, $\mu_\odot = G_\infty M_\odot = constant$, and in principle the value of this constant can be determined by measuring a_P and T_P for each planet. Since T_P has been known much more accurately than a_P until very recently, what has been done is to define μ_0 to have the constant value

$$\mu_\odot(r) \equiv \mu_\odot(a_\oplus) \equiv \kappa^2, \qquad (3.8.14)$$

where $\kappa = 0.01720209895 \, \text{AU}^{3/2} \, \text{day}^{-1}$ is Gauss' constant expressed in terms of the astronomical unit (AU), with $1 \, \text{AU} \cong 1.495979 \times 10^8 \, \text{km}$. If the period

T_P is the only precisely measured quantity, then the best that can be done is to use T_P and the defined value of $\mu_\odot$ to derive a "semimajor axis parameter" $\tilde{a}_P^3$ by writing

$$\tilde{a}_P^3 = \mu_\odot(a_\oplus)(T_P/2\pi)^2. \qquad (3.8.15)$$

In effect this procedure expresses the semimajor axis $\tilde{a}_P$ in terms of a standard distance, which is $1\,\mathrm{AU}$. However, for several planets (Mercury, Venus, Mars, and Jupiter) range data are also available from a combination of radar, spacecraft tracking to a planetary orbiter, lander, or a flyby of the planet. Ranging to these planets determines their absolute distances from the Earth in kilometers, and hence these data eventually lead to a measurement of the AU in kilometers.

Suppose now that $\mu_\odot = G(r)M_\odot$ is not a constant, but depends on r through $G(r)$. Then $\mu_\odot(a_P)$ for the above planets will differ from $\mu_\odot(a_\oplus)$, and hence a_P and $\tilde{a}_P$ will also be different, as can be seen from Eqs. (3.8.13) and (3.8.15). Their ratio is

$$\frac{a_P}{\tilde{a}_P}\left[\frac{\mu_\odot(a_P)}{\mu_\odot(a_\oplus)}\right]^{1/3} = \left[\frac{\mu_\odot(a_P)}{\kappa^2}\right]^{1/3} \equiv 1 + \eta_P. \qquad (3.8.16)$$

The signal for $G(r) \neq constant$ is thus a nonzero value of η_P, which reflects a disparity in the way that the AU would be converted to kilometers for each of the different planets.

The results of [TALMADGE, 1988] shown in Fig. 2.13 are adapted from that paper. We see that over distances of order $1\,\mathrm{AU} \cong 1.5 \times 10^{11}\,\mathrm{m}$, there is no evidence for any deviations from the predictions of Newtonian gravity. The maximum value of α compatible with the planetary data is of order 10^{-9}. Not surprisingly, these limits rapidly decrease in sensitivity for values of λ either larger or smaller than $\approx 1\,\mathrm{AU}$. For further discussion of this analysis the interested reader is referred to [TALMADGE, 1988].

3.9   Constraints from the Earth-LAGEOS-Lunar System

3.9.1   Introduction

An important set of data that significantly constrain non-Newtonian gravity are the measurements of Newtonian gravity at the surface of the Earth [RAPP, 1987], at the height of the LAGEOS satellite orbiting the Earth [SMITH, 1985], and via measurements inferred from lunar laser range-finding [DICKEY, 1994].

Surface measurements of equatorial gravity normally involve determining the average acceleration of gravity g, after correcting for various gravitational anomalies. These include the flattening of the figure of the Earth due to its rotation and the differences in height of particular measurements above the geoid, as well as latitude corrections to individual measurements. Rapp [1987] found the mean surface value of g to be

$$g_{\text{terr}}(R_\oplus) = (9.7803243 \pm 0.0000005)\,\text{m}\,\text{s}^{-2}, \qquad (3.9.1)$$

where $g_{\text{terr}}(r)$ refers to the acceleration field of the Earth inferred from terrestrial experiments, and $R_\oplus = (6.3781362 \pm 0.0000001) \times 10^6$ m is the average radius of the Earth about its equator.

Gravity measurements from satellite [SMITH, 1985] and lunar ranging [DICKEY, 1994] give rise to a determination of $\mu_\oplus(r) = G(r)M_\oplus$. Smith et al. [1985] find for the LAGEOS ranging measurements

$$\mu_\oplus(r_{\text{sat}}) = (3.98600436 \pm 0.00000002) \times 10^{14}\,\text{m}^3\,\text{s}^{-2}, \qquad (3.9.2)$$

where the subscript "sat" denotes the value inferred at the average distance $r_{\text{sat}} \cong 1.2271 \times 10^7$ m of the LAGEOS satellite from the Earth. Using primarily laser ranging to the corner cube retro-reflectors placed on the Moon by the Apollo 14 and Apollo 15 space flights, Dickey et al. [1994] find

$$\mu_\oplus(r_L) = (3.98600443 \pm 0.00000006) \times 10^{14}\,\text{m}^3\,\text{s}^{-2}, \qquad (3.9.3)$$

where $r_L \cong (3.88401 \pm 0.0001) \times 10^8$ m is the mean radius of the Moon's orbit.

Since the value of $M_\oplus$ is highly uncertain, direct comparison of the value of $G(r)$ inferred from a given measurement to that obtained in a laboratory Cavendish measurement of $G(r)$ would not give meaningful limits.* Instead, these separate data sets are combined with one another using ratios of quantities so as to cancel out the contribution from $M_\oplus$.

3.9.2 Earth-LAGEOS Measurements

If we let $g_{\text{sat}}(r)$ refer to the Earth's acceleration field inferred from satellite measurements, then we can write

$$\eta \equiv \frac{\Delta g(R_\oplus)}{g_{\text{sat}}(R_\oplus)} = \frac{g_{\text{terr}}(R_\oplus) - g_{\text{sat}}(R_\oplus)}{g_{\text{sat}}(R_\oplus)}. \qquad (3.9.4)$$

As usual, we calculate the value of η inferred by assuming Newtonian physics (the so-called "extrapolated value"), and compare it to the value expected when an additional non-Newtonian component of strength α and range λ is

---

* Care must be taken not to attempt to set limits based upon values for the mass of the Earth quoted in geophysics textbooks, since these are derived by dividing $\mu_\oplus$ from space-based measurements by the value of G determined in the laboratory.

present (the "calculated value"). Notice that an extrapolation is necessary in this case, because the two experiments do not measure the same experimental quantity.

Using the value of $\mu_\oplus(r_{\text{sat}})$ from Eq. (3.9.2), the value for the radius of the Earth given above, and including angular velocity and flattening corrections, Rapp [1987] finds

$$g_{\text{sat}}(R_\oplus) = (9.7803278 \pm 0.0000020)\,\text{m}\,\text{s}^{-2}. \qquad (3.9.5)$$

Combining this equation with Eqs. (3.9.1) and (3.9.4), we find

$$\eta_{\text{ext}} = (-2 \pm 5) \times 10^{-7}, \qquad (3.9.6)$$

where the subscript *ext* refers to the "extrapolated" value of η. For an acceleration field that strictly obeys an inverse-square law, η should be zero. We next calculate the value of η expected for a deviation from the inverse-square law introduced by a nonzero value of α and λ. Letting $g_\oplus(r)$ be the "true" acceleration field felt by a particular test mass, we have

$$g_\oplus(r) = g_N(r) + \alpha \mathcal{F}_\oplus(r, \lambda), \qquad (3.9.7)$$

$$g_N(r) \equiv \frac{G_\infty M_\oplus}{r^2}. \qquad (3.9.8)$$

We then have

$$g_{\text{sat}}(R_\oplus) = \frac{\mu_\oplus(r_{\text{sat}})}{R_\oplus^2} = g_\oplus(r_{\text{sat}}) \times \left(\frac{r_{\text{sat}}}{R_\oplus}\right)^2$$

$$= [g_N(r_{\text{sat}}) + \alpha F_\oplus(r_{\text{sat}}, \lambda)] \times \left(\frac{r_{\text{sat}}}{R_\oplus}\right)^2. \qquad (3.9.9)$$

Similarly,

$$g_{\text{torr}}(R_\oplus) = g_N(R_\oplus) + \alpha \mathcal{F}_\oplus(R_\oplus, \lambda). \qquad (3.9.10)$$

Inserting Eqs. (3.9.9) and (3.9.10) into Eq. (3.9.4) gives

$$\eta_{\text{calc}} = \alpha \left[\frac{R_\oplus^2 \mathcal{F}_\oplus(R_\oplus, \lambda) - r_{\text{sat}}^2 \mathcal{F}_\oplus(r_{\text{sat}}, \lambda)}{\mu_\oplus(r_{\text{sat}})} \right], \qquad (3.9.11)$$

where the subscript *calc* refers to the calculated value of η. Combining Eqs. (3.9.6) and (3.9.11) leads to the Earth-LAGEOS constraint shown in Fig. 2.13. We also note that in the limit $\alpha \to 0$, $\eta_{\text{calc}} \to 0$, as expected.

3.9.3 LAGEOS-Lunar Measurements

A similar constraint can be placed on α and λ by comparing the inferred values of $\mu_\oplus$ measured at Earth-satellite distances as compared to Earth-lunar distance scales. As with Earth-satellite measurements, the technique is to form a combination of terms in which the uncertain value of $M_\oplus$ cancels out. In this case, we write

$$\eta' \equiv \frac{\mu_\oplus(r_{\rm sat}) - \mu_\oplus(r_L)}{[\mu_\oplus(r_{\rm sat}) + \mu_\oplus(r_L)]/2}. \tag{3.9.12}$$

From Eqs. (3.9.2) and (3.9.3), we have

$$\eta'_{\rm meas} = (-1.8 \pm 1.6) \times 10^{-8}, \tag{3.9.13}$$

where the subscript "meas" refers to the measured value of η'.

We next calculate the expected value of η' in the presence of a non-Newtonian force. Over these distance scales, for a point particle, we can write (see, e.g., Eq. (2.3.31))

$$g_\oplus(r_{\rm sat}) \cong g_N(r_{\rm sat}) \left[1 + \alpha \left(1 + \frac{r_{\rm sat}}{\lambda} \right) \Phi_s \left(\frac{R_\oplus}{\lambda} \right) e^{-r_{\rm sat}/\lambda} \right], \tag{3.9.14}$$

where $\Phi_s(x)$ is given by Eq. (2.3.29). Since the Moon is an extended object, an additional form factor must be included to account for its finite size. Approximating the Moon as a sphere of radius $R_L = 1.738 \times 10^6$ m, we include the form factor $\Phi_s(R_L/\lambda)$ to obtain

$$g_\oplus(r_L) \cong g_N(r_L) \left[1 + \alpha \left(1 + \frac{r_L}{\lambda} \right) \Phi_s \left(\frac{R_\oplus}{\lambda} \right) \Phi_s \left(\frac{R_L}{\lambda} \right) e^{-r_L/\lambda} \right]. \tag{3.9.15}$$

From Eq. (3.9.9), we have $\mu_\oplus(r) = r^2 g_\oplus(r)$, so

$$\eta'_{\rm calc} = \alpha \times$$
$$\left[\frac{\left(1 + \frac{r_{\rm sat}}{\lambda}\right) \Phi_s \left(\frac{R_\oplus}{\lambda}\right) e^{-r_{\rm sat}/\lambda} - \left(1 + \frac{r_L}{\lambda}\right) \Phi_s \left(\frac{R_\oplus}{\lambda}\right) \Phi_s \left(\frac{R_L}{\lambda}\right) e^{-r_L/\lambda}}{1 - \alpha \left[\left(1 + \frac{r_{\rm sat}}{\lambda}\right) \Phi_s \left(\frac{R_\oplus}{\lambda}\right) e^{-r_{\rm sat}/\lambda} + \left(1 + \frac{r_L}{\lambda}\right) \Phi_s \left(\frac{R_\oplus}{\lambda}\right) \Phi_s \left(\frac{R_L}{\lambda}\right) e^{-r_L/\lambda} \right]} \right]. \tag{3.9.16}$$

Combining Eqs. (3.9.13) with (3.9.16) gives rise to the LAGEOS-lunar constraint shown in Fig. 2.13.

3.9.4 Lunar Precession Measurements

A constraint can be placed on α and λ by using the measured anomalous precession $\delta\phi_a$ of the Moon's orbit about the Earth, together with Eq. (3.8.12). From Dickey et al. [DICKEY, 1994], we infer

$$(\delta\phi_a)_{\rm Moon} = (+2.1 \pm 3.3) \times 10^{-12}\,{\rm rad\,s}^{-1}. \tag{3.9.17}$$

Using this, together with the appropriate lunar orbital parameters ($\mu \cong 3.98 \times 10^{14}\,{\rm m}^3\,{\rm s}^{-2}$, $a \cong 3.844 \times 10^8$ m, and $\varepsilon \cong 0.0549$), we obtain the lunar precession constraint shown in Fig. 2.13.

3.10 Experiments Using Gravity-Wave Detectors

In searching for deviations from the predictions of Newtonian gravity arising from a putative non-Newtonian interaction, one must be able to detect extremely weak signals. Since attempts to detect gravitational radiation also anticipate very weak signals, it is not surprising that several groups have adapted the technology of gravity-wave detectors to carry out fifth-force experiments. In this section we describe several such experiments.

It must be emphasized at the outset that the motivation for using gravity-wave detectors to search for non-Newtonian gravity has nothing to do with the detection of either gravitational radiation, or radiation from a possible non-Newtonian field. At present such radiation can only be detected in systems such as the Hulse-Taylor binary PSR 1913+16, as we discuss in more detail in Section 4.7. Rather, the detectors merely sense the change in the force arising from the changing position of a rotating source, and this can be used to set limits on both composition-independent and composition-dependent non-Newtonian forces.

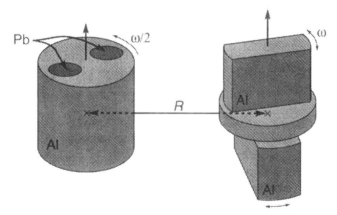

Figure 3.14: Schematic diagram of the apparatus of Kuroda and Hirakawa [1985]. A rotor containing two lead masses rotating at a frequency $\omega/2$ will excite the torsional mode of the detector at a frequency ω. The signal is measured as a function of the separation R between the rotor and the detector.

One of the earliest such experiments was that of Hirakawa et al. [HIRAKAWA, 1980] in which a 44 kg steel bar rotating at 30.3 Hz was used to excite a 1400 kg Al quadrupole antenna having a resonant frequency of 60.5 Hz. By measuring the response of the detector as the distance between the rotating bar and the detector was varied, the $1/r^2$ force law could be tested at distances up to 4.2 m. If the results of this experiment, which had an accuracy of $\sim 3\%$, are used to parametrize the gravitational potential $V(r)$ as $V(r) \sim 1/r^{1+\delta}$, then this experiment gives $\delta = 0.000 \pm 0.053$ for $4.3\,\mathrm{m} \gtrsim r \gtrsim 2.2\,\mathrm{m}$. A similar technique was employed by Ogawa et al. [OGAWA, 1982] to test the $1/r^2$ force law over the distance scale $10.7\,\mathrm{m} \gtrsim r \gtrsim 2.6\,\mathrm{m}$. Using the same parametrization as before, these authors found $\delta = (2.1 \pm 6.2) \times 10^{-3}$.

The latest in the series of such experiments by the Tokyo group is that of Kuroda and Hirakawa [KURODA, 1985], which is shown in Fig. 3.14. These authors used as a source a rotor consisting of two Pb cylinders, each of mass $0.49\,\mathrm{kg}$, which were fitted into an Al supporting cylinder. Two detectors were used which covered the distances 0.1–$0.15\,\mathrm{m}$ and 0.15–$0.30\,\mathrm{m}$ respectively. Both were torsional antennas, and had resonant frequencies of $96\,\mathrm{Hz}$ and $61\,\mathrm{Hz}$ respectively. When parametrized in terms of δ, their results give

$$\delta = (-0.7 \pm 2.9) \times 10^{-3}, \tag{3.10.1}$$

and when expressed in terms of the usual non-Newtonian potential $V(r)$ in Eq. (1.4), they yield

$$\alpha < 1.4 \times 10^{-2}, \tag{3.10.2}$$

for $\lambda = 0.1\,\mathrm{m}$. Interestingly, this experiment can also be used to measure the Newtonian constant G in absolute terms. They find

$$G = (6.70 \pm 0.02) \times 10^{-11}\,\mathrm{N\,m^2\,kg^{-2}}, \tag{3.10.3}$$

in agreement with the laboratory value.

A similar experiment has been initiated by a group at CERN [ASTONE, 1991]. The detector is a gravity-wave antenna consisting of a $2270\,\mathrm{kg}$ cylindrical Al bar $60\,\mathrm{cm}$ in diameter and $297\,\mathrm{cm}$ long with a resonant frequency of $916\,\mathrm{Hz}$. The source in this experiment was an $8.75\,\mathrm{kg}$ rotating Al cylinder from which two vertical slices were removed so as to produce a mass quadrupole. When rotated at $448\,\mathrm{Hz}$, which is approximately half the resonant frequency of the antenna, the quadrupole-quadrupole interaction of the source and detector will drive the antenna at a frequency close to its resonant frequency. In this way the inherently weak time-varying gravitational force exerted on the antenna by the source can be amplified to a level that can (hopefully) be detected. The results quoted by [ASTONE, 1991] serve as an absolute calibration of the detector, since the quadrupole signal can be exactly calculated using Newtonian gravity.

The CERN experiment can become a fifth-force experiment by operating in either of two modes: A test for *composition-dependent* non-Newtonian interactions can be carried out by replacing the quadrupole source by a composition dipole, which would be two half cylinders of different materials joined along the symmetry axis. This existing apparatus can also be used to carry out a test of the inverse-square law by varying the distance of the source from the detector. Assuming Newtonian gravity, the variation of the strength of the signal with this distance can be computed, and then compared to experiment. The advantage of carrying out such an experiment dynamically (rather than statically) is that this produces a time-dependent signal which can be more easily distinguished from background noise than in the static case. Specifically, the gravitational fields due to surrounding matter become relatively less important. In addition, it is easier to amplify (and hence extract) a time-varying signal in the presence of background noise than it is for a constant signal. To date this experiment has not been developed to the point of producing actual constraints on possible non-Newtonian interactions.

CHAPTER 4

Searches for
Composition-Dependent Effects

4.1 Introduction

As we discussed in Chapters 1 and 2, composition-dependent effects are
those (apparently) gravitational effects which depend on the chemical composition of the test masses. A simple example would be a difference in the
accelerations of two dissimilar objects dropped from the same height, an
experiment Galileo is reputed to have carried out. We noted in Chapter 1
that any such difference could be ascribed to the presence of a new force
rather than to gravity, but for most experimental purposes we can describe
the relevant experiments without reference to any specific theoretical picture.
(Theory *is* important, however, when comparing the *sensitivities* of different
experiments, since such comparisons necessarily involve assumptions about
the relative sizes and charges of different sources and detectors. This, in
turn, introduces model-dependent assumptions about the form on the non-
Newtonian force.) Interest in such experiments has greatly increased in recent years, and a number of imaginative techniques have been developed to
search for such composition-dependent effects. In anticipation of the ensuing
discussion, we summarize some of the main conclusions that have emerged
to date.

1) Torsion balances have thus far proved to have the greatest *intrinsic*
   sensitivity to composition-dependent effects, in the sense that they can
   detect the smallest acceleration differences Δa_{ij} between two samples i
   and j.

2) Although Galileo (free-fall) experiments have less intrinsic sensitivity,
   they may provide important theoretical constraints for some values of
   λ. Unlike torsion balance experiments, which are only sensitive to the
   component of the non-Newtonian field $\vec{\mathcal{F}}$ perpendicular to the torsion
   fiber (which may be only a small fraction $\mathcal{F}_\perp$ of the total field strength),
   Galileo experiments are sensitive to the entire field strength $|\vec{\mathcal{F}}|$. (See
   Section 4.3 below.)

3) Floating-ball experiments can also be quite sensitive, and could be the method of choice if water is one of the test samples.

4) Taken together, the results of many experiments strongly support the principle of universality of free-fall and, by implication, provide no evidence for a new intermediate-range composition-dependent force.

In the following sections we consider these experiments one at a time.

4.2 Torsion Balance Experiments

4.2.1 Historical Background

In the current generation of experiments, torsion balances provide some of the most stringent limits on possible composition-dependent non-Newtonian forces—limits which are rivaled only by Galileo-type experiments over ranges approaching the radius of the Earth. The modern interpretation of what is measured in these experiments is somewhat different from the historical interpretation, which regarded these experiments as testing the equivalence of passive gravitational and inertial mass (i.e., the "weak equivalence principle" or WEP). This modern-day perspective can be traced back to a paper by Lee and Yang [LEE, 1955], which pointed out that an apparent violation of the WEP can arise from a hitherto undiscovered new force coupling to objects in a composition-dependent fashion. This observation of Lee and Yang eventually led to the reanalysis [FISCHBACH, 1986A] of the classic experiment by Eötvös, Pekár, and Fekete (EPF) [EÖTVÖS, 1922, 1953], which in turn has helped to stimulate the current interest in searches for new intermediate-range forces.

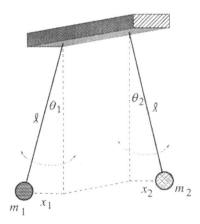

Figure 4.1: Newton's pendulum experiment.

We next review the evolution of WEP tests, in order to provide the background for understanding modern torsion balance experiments. The first significant experimental test of the WEP was performed by Newton (see [NEWTON, 1960]), who measured the differential periods between two pendulums as shown in Fig. 4.1. To understand the theory of this experiment, we begin by writing down the equation of motion for a single pendulum of length ℓ (neglecting friction),

$$m_I \ell \ddot{\theta} + m_G g \sin \theta = 0, \tag{4.2.1}$$

where m_I is the inertial mass and m_G is the passive gravitational mass. Assuming $|\theta| \ll 1$, we can write $\sin \theta \approx x/\ell$, and therefore

$$\ddot{x} + \left(\frac{m_G}{m_I} \frac{g}{\ell} \right) x = 0. \tag{4.2.2}$$

We see from this equation that the period T is given by

$$T = 2\pi \sqrt{\frac{\ell}{(1 + \kappa)g}}, \tag{4.2.3}$$

where

$$\frac{m_G}{m_I} \equiv 1 + \kappa. \tag{4.2.4}$$

In this notation, κ parametrizes the degree of the violation of the WEP, and is defined to be zero if the WEP is exactly obeyed.

In Newton's experiment, the two pendulums were constructed of different materials and were adjusted so as to have the same length ℓ. Thus, if the WEP was valid, the pendulums should also have had the same period T. The fractional period difference $\Delta T_{1-2}/T$ of the two pendulums was measured from their beat frequency, and this was used to set a limit on the value of $\Delta \kappa_{1-2} \equiv \kappa_1 - \kappa_2$. Assuming that κ is small, we find from Eqs. (4.2.3) and (4.2.4)

$$\Delta \kappa_{1-2} \approx -\frac{2\Delta T_{1-2}}{T}. \tag{4.2.5}$$

Using this technique, Newton obtained a limit on $\Delta \kappa$ of

$$|\Delta \kappa| \lesssim \frac{1}{1000}, \tag{4.2.6}$$

and, in a repeat of this experiment, Bessel found [EÖTVÖS, 1909]

$$|\Delta \kappa| \lesssim \frac{1}{60\,000}. \tag{4.2.7}$$

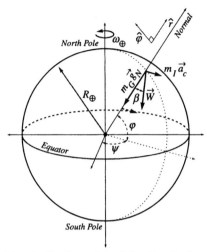

Figure 4.2: Highly idealized model of the Earth showing the direction of the weight of an object $\vec{W}$ as a function of latitude φ. The Earth is assumed to be a perfectly rigid sphere rotating at an angular velocity $\omega_\oplus$. Here $m_G \vec{g}_N$ is the Newtonian gravitational force due to the Earth, and $m_I \vec{a}_c$ is the centrifugal force. A more detailed model of the Earth is presented in Appendix C.

A second technique for measuring $\Delta\kappa$ was developed by Guyòt [EÖTVÖS, 1909], who noted that the angle β that a suspended mass (pendant) at rest makes with respect to some arbitrary reference system could depend on its composition if the WEP were violated. To see this, we examine the model of the Earth shown in Fig. 4.2, which vectorially displays the dependence of the weight $\vec{W}$ upon latitude φ. We have from Fig. 4.2

$$\vec{W} = \vec{g}_N + \vec{a}_c, \tag{4.2.8}$$

where $\vec{g}_N$ is the ordinary Newtonian gravitational acceleration given by

$$\vec{g}_N = -\frac{GM_\oplus}{R_\oplus^2}\hat{r}, \tag{4.2.9}$$

and $\vec{a}_c$ is the centrifugal acceleration at the latitude φ given by

$$\vec{a}_c = \omega_\oplus^2 R_\oplus \cos\varphi \left(\cos\varphi\,\hat{r} - \sin\varphi\,\hat{\varphi}\right). \tag{4.2.10}$$

From Fig. 4.3 we see that

$$\tan\beta = \frac{m_I a_c \sin\varphi}{m_G g_N - m_I a_c \cos\varphi}, \tag{4.2.11}$$

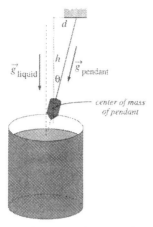

Figure 4.3: Guyòt's pendant experiment. A mass is suspended over a pool of mercury in such a way that $\vec{g}(\text{liquid})$ and $\vec{g}(\text{pendant})$ can be compared. See text for details.

or

$$\beta \cong (1 - \kappa)\frac{\omega_\oplus^2 R_\oplus^3}{GM_\oplus} \sin\varphi\cos\varphi \cong \frac{1}{289}(1 - \kappa)\sin\varphi\cos\varphi, \qquad (4.2.12)$$

where we have assumed that $a_c \ll g_N$, and $\kappa \ll 1$. We note that the angle β lies entirely in the north–south direction.

To obtain limits on $\Delta\beta \equiv \beta_1 - \beta_2$ for various pairs of materials (and thus limits on $\Delta\kappa$), Guyòt compared the deviation from vertical as defined by the normal to a mercury surface with that defined by a pendant at rest, as shown in Fig. 4.3. From the measured deviation $\Delta\beta$, one can directly obtain a value for $\Delta\kappa$ given by

$$\Delta\kappa \cong - \left[\frac{GM_\oplus}{\omega_\oplus^2 R_\oplus^3 \sin\varphi\cos\varphi}\right] \Delta\beta. \qquad (4.2.13)$$

In fact Guyòt obtained a nonzero value, $\Delta\beta \approx 8 \times 10^{-5}\,\text{rad}$, in a set of measurements carried out in the Pantheon in Paris [EÖTVÖS, 1909]. This implies that $\Delta\kappa \cong 0.02$, which is very large compared to the limits set by previous experiments. However, in a later series of measurements Guyòt was able to convince himself that the deviations he had measured were the result of air currents due to convection [EÖTVÖS, 1953].

Although the method employed by Guyòt was ultimately unsuccessful, it appears to have been the motivation for the torsion balance experiment designed by Eötvös. For purposes of illustration, we will initially consider an Eötvös experiment in which two masses (of different chemical composition) are attached to the ends of a bar which is suspended by a torsion fiber (wire), as shown in Fig. 4.4. In its simplest form the experiment is performed by

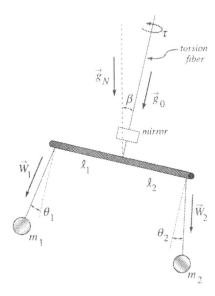

Figure 4.4: The Eötvös torsion balance weak equivalence principle test. Here $\vec{g}_0$ is the local acceleration of gravity along the direction of the torsion fiber, and θ_1 and θ_2 are the deviations from the local vertical defined by $\vec{g}_0$.

hanging the bar east–west, measuring the torque on the fiber, and then remeasuring the torque after rotating the apparatus by 180°. If there is a difference in the rate at which the two test masses would fall toward the Earth, then in principle this will show up as a difference in these two torques, as we now show.

We first examine the effect of a WEP violation of the type parametrized by Eq. (4.2.4) due to a spherical Earth, which we assume to have a radially-symmetric density distribution. From Figs. 4.2 and 4.4, the net force $\vec{T}_{\text{net}} = \vec{W}_1 + \vec{W}_2$ exerted by the fiber on the bar in Fig. 4.4 is

$$\vec{T}_{\text{net}} = -(m_1 + m_2)a_c \sin\varphi\hat{r} + \{[m_1(1 + \kappa_1) + m_2(1 + \kappa_2)]g_N \\ - (m_1 + m_2)a_c \cos\varphi\}\,\hat{\varphi}, \tag{4.2.14}$$

where the coordinate system is as shown in Figs. 4.2 and 4.5. The suspension wire (assumed to be massless) will be parallel to $\vec{T}_{\text{net}}$, and hence the angle β that the suspension wire will make with respect to $\vec{g}_N$ is given by

$$\tan\beta = \frac{(m_1 + m_2)a_c \sin\varphi}{[m_1(1 + \kappa_1) + m_2(1 + \kappa_2)]g_N - (m_1 + m_2)a_c \cos\varphi}$$
$$\approx \frac{a_c \sin\varphi}{g_N}. \tag{4.2.15}$$

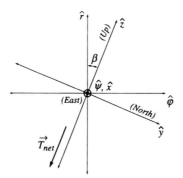

Figure 4.5: Local coordinate system for the Eötvös balance. Here $\hat{x}$ points east (out of the page), $\hat{y}$ points north, and $\hat{z}$ points upwards along the torsion fiber.

Note that the angle β defines "true vertical" for this configuration of masses, and that in general $\vec{W}_1$ and $\vec{W}_2$ will not be parallel to $\vec{T}_{\rm net}$. We define an "apparatus" coordinate frame, in which $\hat{x}$ is directed along the torsion bar pointing toward mass m_2, $\hat{y}$ is the normal to the mirror attached to the torsion wire, and $\hat{z}$ is the axis of rotation of the torsion balance. Then

$$\hat{x} = \hat{\psi},$$
$$\hat{y} = \cos\beta\,\hat{\theta} + \sin\beta\,\hat{r},$$
$$\hat{z} = -\sin\beta\,\hat{\theta} + \cos\beta\,\hat{r}. \tag{4.2.16}$$

The net gravitational torque on the fiber is given by

$$\vec{\tau}_{\rm net} = [(m_1\ell_1(1+\kappa_1) - m_2\ell_2(1+\kappa_2))g_N - (m_1\ell_1 - m_2\ell_2)a_c\cos\varphi]\,\hat{y}$$
$$+ (m_1\ell_1 - m_2\ell_2)a_c\sin\varphi\,\hat{z}, \tag{4.2.17}$$

and the balance condition (i.e., that there is no net torque about the $\hat{y}$ axis) implies

$$m_2\ell_2 = m_1\ell_1 \frac{(1+\kappa_1)g_N\cos\beta - a_c\cos(\varphi+\beta)}{(1+\kappa_2)g_N\cos\beta - a_c\cos(\varphi+\beta)}$$
$$\cong m_1\ell_1\left[1 + \mathcal{O}((1+\kappa_1) - (1+\kappa_2))\right]. \tag{4.2.18}$$

From Eq. (4.2.15) we see that $a_c\sin\varphi \cong g_N\tan\beta \cong g_N\sin\beta$ (since β is small), and hence by combining Eqs. (4.2.17) and (4.2.18) we find for the net torque on the fiber

$$\Delta\tau \equiv \hat{z}\cdot\vec{\tau}_{\rm net} \cong -m_1\ell_1\Delta\kappa g_N\sin\beta, \tag{4.2.19}$$

where $\Delta\kappa \equiv \kappa_1 - \kappa_2$. Eq. (4.2.19) gives the standard Eötvös result relating the torque about the fiber axis to the WEP-violating parameter $\Delta\kappa$. The results of this seminal experiment will be presented in the next section.

In its original conception, the Eötvös torsion balance experiment was a test of the principle of equivalence. It is interesting to note that in the period (circa 1910) when the experiment was actually completed, there was no theory which would lead to a non-null result, other than a fundamental breakdown of the principle of equivalence. Indeed, even concepts such as baryon number or isospin did not and could not exist until the neutron was discovered in 1932 by Chadwick. It was not until 1955, when Lee and Yang [LEE, 1955] proposed a long-range coupling to baryon number, that any detailed model even existed which predicted a specific composition dependence for any effect that could be observed in the Eötvös experiment. It is nonetheless instructive to interpret the Eötvös parameter $\Delta\kappa$ in terms of a more modern framework. We begin by noting that the anomalous torque is

$$\vec{\tau}_{\text{net}} = \vec{r} \times \vec{F}_{\text{net}} = \ell_1 \hat{x} \times m_1 \vec{a}_1 - \ell_2 \hat{x} \times m_2 \vec{a}_2 = m_1 \ell_1 (\hat{x} \times \Delta\vec{a}), \quad (4.2.20)$$

where $\Delta\vec{a}$ is the anomalous acceleration difference between the test masses 1 and 2, as discussed above. The net torque difference is then given by

$$\Delta\tau = \hat{z} \cdot \vec{\tau}_{\text{net}} = m_1 \ell_1 \Delta a_y \equiv m_1 \ell_1 \Delta a_\perp. \quad (4.2.21)$$

Combining this result with Eq. (4.2.19), we find

$$\Delta\kappa = \frac{-\Delta a_\perp}{g_N \sin\beta}. \quad (4.2.22)$$

For an intermediate-range force such as that discussed in Section 2.1, this becomes

$$\Delta\kappa = -\xi q_s \Delta q \frac{\mathcal{F}_\perp}{g_N \sin\beta}. \quad (4.2.23)$$

Eq. (4.2.23) gives the specific relationship between the values of $\Delta\kappa$ reported by Eötvös and the parameters of the more fundamental theory outlined in Chapter 2 (see Eq. (2.2.17) for example).

4.2.2 The Eötvös Experiment

a. *Introduction*

In 1889, Eötvös used a torsion balance to test the equivalence principle to a sensitivity level of one part in 20,000,000—an improvement in the limit set by Bessel by a factor of ~ 300 [EÖTVÖS, 1889]. In 1922, the results of an improved version of this experiment were published by Eötvös, Pekár, and Fekete (EPF) [EÖTVÖS, 1922]. These results were based on a series of experiments carried out between 1904 and 1909, and an essay based on this work won the Benecke Foundation prize [SCHINDEL, 1986; ILLY, 1989] for the year 1909, which was awarded by the philosophy faculty of the University of Göttingen. Prior to the publication of [EÖTVÖS, 1922], the details of the EPF experiment went unreported except for a brief summary of the limits they had set on $\Delta\kappa$: In a 1909 paper [EÖTVÖS, 1909] dealing with measurements of gravity gradients, Eötvös quoted the limit $\Delta\kappa < 10^{-8}$, and the citation [SCHINDEL, 1986] for the Benecke Foundation prize gives $\Delta\kappa < 5 \times 10^{-9}$. In the introductory paragraph of [EÖTVÖS, 1922], EPF attribute the delay in writing up their results to a desire to redo the original experiment with a more sensitive apparatus. Although such an apparatus was built, it was diverted to other purposes and the original experiments were never repeated. The advent of Einstein's theory of General Relativity in 1916 seems to have provided the impetus for publishing their results, which constituted at their time the best experimental test of the equivalence principle. Most of the text of [EÖTVÖS, 1922] was apparently written by Pekár [BARNOTHY, PC], as Eötvös died on 8 April 1919. His death came several weeks before the solar eclipse of 29 May 1919, during which Dyson, Eddington, and Davidson [DYSON, 1920] confirmed Einstein's prediction for the gravitational deflection of light, and three years before the final publication of the classic EPF paper.

Although most of the EPF observations compared the accelerations of different materials toward the Earth, they also measured the accelerations of magnalium (a magnesium-aluminum alloy) and platinum toward the Sun, and concluded that $\Delta\kappa$ for these materials was no larger than 6×10^{-9} (no errors are quoted for this result). EPF also noted that in some sense the measurements toward the Earth and Sun complemented each other. From a modern perspective, it is well understood how these two experiments complement each other: In the framework of intermediate-range interactions, it is possible to construct models for which a violation of the equivalence principle could be observed in measurements made relative to the Earth, but not to the Sun (e.g., a single Yukawa model with an appropriate value of λ can achieve this). It is also possible, however, to construct models in which *no observable violation* would be seen in measurements toward the Earth, but yet effects could be detected in measurements toward the Sun. This could occur, for example, in exponential models of the type considered in [FISCHBACH, 1991].

b. *The Apparatus*

In this section we describe the EPF apparatus and methodology in more detail. Although this experiment is of interest largely for historical reasons, its methodology serves as a springboard for the discussion of the current generation of experiments.

The torsion balances used by Eötvös, Pekár, and Fekete (EPF) in performing their experiments were originally designed to measure gravity gradients, and in fact a set of experiments was performed by Eötvös in the mountains of Hungary [EÖTVÖS, 1922] for the purpose of measuring gradients. In order to increase the sensitivity of the torsion balance to gravity gradients, the centers of mass of the test bodies used in the apparatus were separated by a vertical distance of about $\approx 50\,\mathrm{cm}$ (see Fig. 4.6). This had the unfortunate side effect of making Eötvös' apparatus significantly more sensitive to vertical gravity gradients than to anomalous accelerations. To reduce the effects of gravity gradients in their equivalence principle experiments, EPF reduced the vertical distance between the Pt standard and the test masses, and also combined the results of measurements made with the torsion balance oriented in different directions. The water-Cu comparison, for example, was carried out by measuring the difference in the deflection of the torsion bar when it was oriented north–south versus south–north (a quantity they called m) and east–west versus west–east (a quantity they called v). This was done for both water compared to Pt (where the Pt was loaded at the upper position of the torsion balance), and for Cu compared to Pt. The effects due to the gravity gradients could then be eliminated by taking the difference between the measurements of v or v/m for water-Pt and v' or v'/m' for Cu-Pt. A more detailed description of the formalism used by EPF to eliminate gravity gradients is given in Appendix A of [FISCHBACH, 1988B].

The central feature of the Eötvös torsion balances was a torsion arm consisting of a thin brass tube 40 cm long and 0.5 cm in diameter, which was suspended using measurement wires made of platinum and iridium. These wires were carefully annealed under a load, and claimed by EPF to be much superior to quartz fibers. A platinum cylinder weighing about 30 g was inserted into one end of the brass tube, and the test mass (which typically weighed 25.5 g) was hung about 21 cm below the torsion arm. The entire pendant was enclosed in a brass housing constructed such that it had, depending on the part of the housing, two or three concentric walls. The purpose of this design was to minimize the effects of thermal gradients. There were actually two instruments used in the experiments: One was a single torsion balance, and the other consisted of two torsion balances in tandem located on the same mount. In this arrangement each of the two balances was identical to the "single" balance, and the two balances were mounted so that the Pt standard masses were at opposite ends of the apparatus. For the purpose of thermal isolation, each apparatus was also enclosed in a large "tent" consisting of two layers of linen suspended on a frame, with the space between the two layers filled with sawdust. To further minimize thermal effects, the room was kept dark. Although not explicitly mentioned in the EPF paper, thermometers were affixed to various parts of the single- and double-arm torsion balances (see Fig. 4.6), which further indicates the attention paid by EPF to excluding thermal influences. (Some of the original balances are preserved in the museum of the Geophysical Observatory in Tihany, Hungary.)

As we have already noted, the design of the Eötvös balances made them

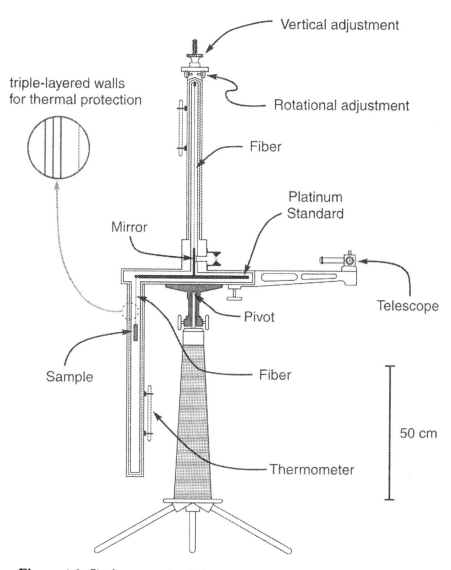

Figure 4.6: Single-arm torsion balance used by Eötvös, Pekár, and Fekete.

highly sensitive to gravity gradients. A consequence of this was that the apparatus was also sensitive to *changes* in the gravity gradients as might result, for example, from a change in the local water table. However, the presence of a person recording data was not a problem: Since the period of oscillation was typically 10–11 minutes, the response time of the system was much longer than the time necessary to make a single measurement. To minimize perturbations on the torsion balances, the observers ran to and from the apparatus [MARX, PC].

Table 4.1: Quoted measurements [EÖTVÖS, 1953] of $\Delta\kappa$ for each comparison made by EPF, and calculated values of $\Delta(B/\mu)$ and $\Delta(I_z/\mu)$ from [TALMADGE, 1987A; FISCHBACH, 1988B]. Here "brass-Pt" refers to the comparison of brass + RaBr$_2$ discussed in Eötvös [EÖTVÖS, 1953]. Note also that the misprint in the sign quoted by EPF for this datum has also been corrected. See [FISCHBACH, 1988B] for further details.

Samples compared	$10^9\Delta\kappa$	$10^5\Delta(B/\mu)$	$10^3\Delta(I_z/\mu)$
Magnalium-Pt	4 ± 1	$+50.0$	-167
Brass-Pt	1 ± 2	$+93.2$	-115
Cu-Pt	4 ± 2	$+94.2$	-113
Ag-Fe-SO$_4$	0 ± 2	0.0	0
CuSO$_4$ (dissolution)	2 ± 2	0.0	0
Snakewood-Pt	-1 ± 2	-50.9	-262
Asbestos-Cu	-3 ± 2	-74.0	-99
CuSO$_4\cdot$5H$_2$O-Cu	-5 ± 2	-85.7	-106
CuSO$_4$ (sol'n)-Cu	-7 ± 2	-146.3	-173
H$_2$O-Cu	-10 ± 2	-171.8	-201
Tallow-Cu	-6 ± 2	-203.1	-208

c. Experimental Results

Table 4.1 summarizes the results quoted by EPF [EÖTVÖS, 1953] along with the computed values of $\Delta(B/\mu)$ and $\Delta(I_z/\mu)$, which are based on the values quoted in [TALMADGE, 1987A; FISCHBACH, 1988B], which are reproduced in Table 2.1. In this table, "magnalium" refers to an alloy of approximately 90% Al and 10% Mg, "snakewood" is a South American heartwood (i.e., principally cellulose), and the measurement "Ag-Fe-SO$_4$" refers to the comparison of the reactants before and after the chemical reaction

$$Ag_2SO_4 + 2FeSO_4 \longrightarrow 2Ag + Fe_2(SO_4)_3. \qquad (4.2.24)$$

Also, "CuSO$_4$ (dissolution)" refers to a measurement of $\Delta\kappa$ for the dissolution of CuSO$_4$·5H$_2$O in water. A large amount of additional information regarding these measurements and the materials used has been presented elsewhere [EÖTVÖS, 1953; TALMADGE, 1987A; FISCHBACH, 1988B], and the interested reader is directed to these references.

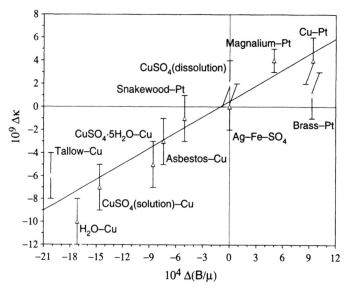

Figure 4.7: Plot of the data from Table 4.1 for calculated $\Delta(B/\mu)$ versus the quoted EPF values of $\Delta\kappa$. The solid line represents the result of fitting to all data points. The CuSO$_4$ (dissolution) point is represented by a circle to denote the fact that this result is quoted by EPF without any discussion. The tallow-Cu and brass-Pt points are represented by squares to highlight the uncertainties regarding these points that still remain.

Since $\Delta q = 0$ for Ag-Fe-SO$_4$ and for the dissolution of CuSO$_4$, $\Delta\kappa$ should be zero in both of these cases, as well. As expected, both measurements of $\Delta\kappa$ were consistent with zero. However, many of the other measurements of $\Delta\kappa$ gave statistically significant results: 4 of the remaining 9 measurements deviated from zero by 3 or more standard deviations, and all but two were more than one standard deviation (1σ) from zero. In the absence of any systematic effects, the probability of obtaining such a large excursion from $\Delta\kappa = 0$ is quite remote: We find for these nine points that the cumulative probability of obtaining a net excursion from $\Delta\kappa = 0$ this large or larger to be only about 1.4×10^{-12}.

From Eq. (4.2.23), for a coupling to baryon number we have

$$\Delta \kappa = \left[-\xi \left(\frac{B}{\mu} \right)_s \frac{\mathcal{F}_\perp}{g_N \sin \beta} \right] \Delta \left(\frac{B}{\mu} \right)_{1-2}. \qquad (4.2.25)$$

Figure 4.7 plots the data from Table 4.1 for $\Delta(B/\mu)$ versus $\Delta \kappa$.* The straight line represents a least-squares fit to these data, which gives

$$\Delta \kappa = \gamma \Delta \left(\frac{B}{\mu} \right) + \delta, \qquad (4.2.26a)$$

$$\gamma = (4.51 \pm 0.56) \times 10^{-6}, \qquad (4.2.26b)$$

$$\delta = (0.47 \pm 0.55) \times 10^{-9}, \qquad (4.2.26c)$$

$$\chi^2 = 10.4 \ (9 \text{ degrees of freedom}) \quad [\text{confidence level} = 29\%]. \qquad (4.2.26d)$$

The model given by Eq. (4.2.25) thus gives a satisfactory description of the EPF data. In particular, we note that the slope γ differs from zero by 8 standard deviations (8σ). Furthermore, the intercept δ is consistent with zero, as it should be if Eq. (4.2.25) holds. By way of contrast, a similar fit between ΔI_z and $\Delta \kappa$ yields $\chi^2 \cong 71$ for 9 degrees of freedom, which is clearly unacceptably high. A substantial amount of material has been published in [FISCHBACH, 1988B] regarding the compatibility of a coupling to baryon number, with the EPF data, and the interested reader is directed to this and related references for more details [HAYASHI, 1986, 1987A; KIM, 1986; NUSSINOV, 1986; VECSERNYÉS, 1987].

From a historical perspective the EPF data as summarized in Fig. 4.7 supported the suggestion that a new intermediate-range non-Newtonian force might be present in nature. This hint of a possible new force served in turn to motivate the new generation of Eötvös-type experiments, as we will discuss next. With few exceptions, these new experiments are all compatible with Newtonian gravity, and are in conflict with the results of the Eötvös experiment, as interpreted above.

4.2.3 Solar Equivalence Principle Experiments

As we have noted previously, one of the factors which limits the sensitivity of both the EPF experiment and its latter-day successors is the noise introduced when the torsion balance is rotated through 180°. Although a modulation of the signal is necessary in order to eliminate spurious disturbances, this can be achieved by having the *source* rotated, rather than the torsion balance detector. One way to achieve this is to use the Sun as a source, since its position relative to a torsion balance fixed in the laboratory

---

* This figure is an updated version of a figure first published in [FISCHBACH, 1986A].

varies throughout the day. We have previously noted that EPF themselves carried out a series of measurements earlier which compared the accelerations of their test masses toward the Sun, but these were of relatively poor quality. Solar equivalence principle tests were revived by the experiments of Roll, Krotkov, and Dicke (RKD) [DICKE, 1961; ROLL, 1964], and Braginskiĭ and Panov (BP) [BRAGINSKIĬ, 1971]. Subsequently a third such experiment was carried out by Keiser and Faller (KF) [KEISER, 1982] using a liquid-supported torsion balance. We describe these experiments in this section.

As implied by the preceding discussion, a signal for a WEP violation would be an acceleration difference of the test masses whose amplitude had a 24 hr periodicity. Unfortunately such a "signal" can also be misleading, since there are many possible conventional sources for signals with a 24 hr periodicity, such as various thermal effects. However, by controlling the thermal environment such effects can be suppressed, as can other potential sources of spurious signals. Another disadvantage of having the Sun as a source is that the Newtonian acceleration of the test masses produced by the Sun is only $0.6 \, \mathrm{cm\,s^{-2}}$. This compares to the effective acceleration $g_N \sin\beta$ in Eq. (4.2.19). From Eq. (4.2.12),

$$ g_N \sin\beta \cong g_N\beta \cong g_N \times \frac{1}{289}\left(\frac{1}{\sqrt{2}}\right)^2 \cong 1.67\,\mathrm{cm\,s^{-2}}, \qquad (4.2.27) $$

where we have used $\sin\varphi \cong \cos\varphi \cong 1/\sqrt{2}$ for the latitude of Budapest ($\cong 45°$). Hence the solar acceleration is only $\sim 3/8$ that of the centrifugal acceleration that drives the Eötvös experiment. As RKD show, however, this disadvantage is more than offset by the advantages discussed above.

The torsion balance used by RKD consisted of a triangular quartz frame (made of fused silica) suspended from a quartz torsion fiber. Solid cylindrical 30 g masses were suspended from each vertex, two being aluminum and one gold. In contrast to all of the recent (i.e., post-1986) Eötvös-type experiments, which have gone to great lengths to make the test masses look the same *externally*, the masses used by RKD had different external dimensions, reflecting the different densities of Al and Au. This made the RKD experiment more sensitive to some types of conventional disturbances (e.g., convection effects), a point which has been repeatedly emphasized by the Eöt-Wash collaboration (see Section 4.2.5). To minimize thermal effects, the apparatus was placed in an instrument pit 12 ft deep by 8 ft^2 located at the edge of the Princeton University campus. Elaborate measures were taken to control the thermal environment, and these are described in detail in [ROLL, 1964]. Another potential source of spurious signals is a magnetic impurity in the torsion balance, which could couple to a residual ambient magnetic field. The efforts employed by RKD to prevent such backgrounds are also detailed in [ROLL, 1964].

RKD expressed their result in terms of the parameter $\eta(A, B)$, which they define as

$$\eta(A, B) = \frac{[(m_G/m_I)_A - (m_G/m_I)_B]}{\frac{1}{2}[(m_G/m_I)_A + (m_G/m_I)_B]}, \tag{4.2.28}$$

where m_G and m_I are, as before, the passive gravitational mass and the inertial mass, respectively. Using Eq. (4.2.4), we then have

$$\eta(A, B) \cong \kappa_A - \kappa_B \equiv \Delta\kappa_{A-B}. \tag{4.2.29}$$

Their final result was

$$\eta(\mathrm{Au}, \mathrm{Al}) = (1.3 \pm 1.0) \times 10^{-11}, \tag{4.2.30}$$

which indicates agreement with the WEP. This result is often quoted as a 3σ limit,

$$|\eta(\mathrm{Au}, \mathrm{Al})| < 3 \times 10^{-11}. \tag{4.2.31}$$

From a historical point of view, the RKD experiment played an important role in motivating the reanalysis of the Eötvös experiment in [FISCHBACH, 1986A]. Not only does [ROLL, 1964] give a very detailed account of the principles underlying their own experiment, but it also presents an analysis of the original EPF experiment, as well as the subsequent experiment by Eötvös' student Renner [1935]. The analysis by RKD of the Renner experiment was especially significant [DICKE, 1961; ROLL, 1964], since Renner had claimed a greater sensitivity than that achieved earlier by EPF, and yet his results showed no evidence for the composition-dependent force suggested by the EPF data. However, in studying the Renner paper RKD found several inconsistencies, which are discussed in detail in both [ROLL, 1964] and [FISCHBACH, 1988B]. Renner himself confirmed to Dicke the difficulties noted by RKD [DICKE, PC], and the conclusion is that Renner's results cannot be relied upon with any degree of confidence. By contrast, these criticisms do not apply to the original EPF results, which appear to be internally consistent.

The experiment of Roll, Krotkov, and Dicke was followed by that of Braginskiĭ and Panov in 1971. BP claim that an acceleration as small as $\sim 1 \times 10^{-13}\,\mathrm{cm\,s^{-2}}$ should be detectable in principle before encountering background problems from Brownian motion. Their overall design is conceptually similar to that of RKD, with some exceptions. One is that their torsion pendant had a higher degree of symmetry than the triangular frame used by RKD, and its purpose was to reduce the effects of variable local gravity gradients. The pendant was an eight-pointed "star" from which four aluminum and four platinum masses (all equal) were suspended. As in the case of the RKD masses, no effort was made to ensure that the external dimensions of the test masses were the same by compensating for the different densities of Al and Pt. The result was that their masses had different geometrical cross sections, and this produced a correction due to radiometric pressure. The authors also discuss the effects of other perturbations, such as diurnal variations of the magnetic field in the laboratory, local perturbations of gravity gradients, variations of the laser light beam pressure used to monitor the torsion fiber, and seismic effects.

The final results of BP are expressed in terms of their parameter $\tilde{\Delta}$, which is approximately the negative of η defined in Eq. (4.2.28). BP quote

$$\eta(\text{Al}, \text{Pt}) \cong -\tilde{\Delta}(\text{Al}, \text{Pt}) = (+0.3 \pm 0.9) \times 10^{-12} \qquad (4.2.32)$$

at the 95% confidence level.

A third solar equivalence experiment has been carried out by Keiser and Faller [KEISER, 1982]. These authors measure the acceleration difference between copper and tungsten test masses using a liquid-supported torsion balance and find

$$\eta(\text{Cu}, \text{W}) = (0.6 \pm 4) \times 10^{-11}. \qquad (4.2.33)$$

Although this is somewhat less sensitive than the RKD or BP results, it uses a novel technology to which we return below when we discuss modern torsion balance experiments.

We conclude this discussion of pre-1986 equivalence principle tests by briefly considering the experiment of Kreuzer [1968]. Although conceived of as a test of the equality of active and passive gravitational mass [BONDI, 1957], it can be reinterpreted as a laboratory-scale test for a new composition-dependent force. The experiment consisted of measuring the torque on a Cavendish-type torsion balance exerted by a solid Teflon cylinder moving sinusoidally through a liquid mixture of trichloroethylene and dibromomethane. In effect the source is the Teflon cylinder and an equal volume of the liquid, and for present purposes it suffices to note that there would be no signal if the solid and liquid had the same chemical composition (e.g., ice in water). Any time-varying signal could be interpreted as evidence for an intermediate-range composition-dependent force [NEUFELD, 1986]. Kreuzer's result can be expressed in terms of the fractional density difference $\Delta\rho/\rho$ between the Teflon and the liquid it displaces at neutral buoyancy. If Newtonian physics holds, $\Delta\rho$ should vanish, and Kreuzer finds

$$\Delta\rho/\rho = (1.2 \pm 4.4) \times 10^{-5}. \qquad (4.2.34)$$

This result can be used in principle to set limits on the coupling to B or I_z, but the sensitivity of this experiment implied by Eq. (4.2.34) is considerably less than that of the more recent Eötvös-type experiments.

Kreuzer used this result to set a limit on the ratio of active and passive gravitational mass by noting that at neutral buoyancy the Teflon and the liquid have the same *passive* gravitational mass in the presence of the Earth's gravitational field. (Recall that at neutral buoyancy the *weight* of the Teflon is equal to the *weight* of the fluid it displaces.) If at neutral buoyancy the two equal weights influenced the torsion balance differently, we could conclude that the *active* gravitational masses of Teflon and the liquid (which are what influence the test masses in the balance) are unequal, even though the passive masses *are* equal.

Although the Kreuzer experiment can be interpreted as setting a limit on a laboratory-scale intermediate-range force, its stated objective was to compare active and passive gravitational mass, as we have noted. Another limit on the ratio of active and passive gravitational mass has been deduced by Bartlett and Van Buren (BVB) [BARTLETT, 1986] from a study of the Moon's orbit. Their work builds on an observation due to Bondi [1957] that Newton's third law would be violated if active and passive gravitational masses were unequal. BVB then argue that a 2 km offset between the geometric center of the Moon and its center of mass suggests an asymmetry in the distribution of Fe and Al in the Moon. Their limit then derives from the implication that if active and passive gravitational masses were not equal, the forces that the Fe and Al distributions exert on each other would also be unequal. This would induce a continuous increase in the angular velocity of the Moon about the Earth. Their final result is

$$(M/m)_{\text{Al}} - (M/m)_{\text{Fe}} \leq 4 \times 10^{-12}, \qquad (4.2.35)$$

where M and m are the active gravitational mass and the passive gravitational mass respectively.

An astrophysical limit on the equality of gravitational and inertial mass can also be inferred from lunar laser ranging, which allows the Earth-Moon distance to be measured as a function of time [NORDTVEDT, 1988]. The accelerations $\vec{a}_e$ and $\vec{a}_m$ of the Earth and Moon toward the Sun can be written as

$$\vec{a}_e = (m_G/m_I)_e \, \vec{g}_s \equiv (1 + \Delta_e)\vec{g}_s, \qquad (4.2.36)$$

$$\vec{a}_m = (m_G/m_I)_m \, \vec{g}_s \equiv (1 + \Delta_m)\vec{g}_s. \qquad (4.2.37)$$

Here $\vec{g}_s$ is the Sun's acceleration field at the Earth, and any WEP violation would be reflected by a nonzero difference $(\Delta_e - \Delta_m)$. The effect of a WEP violation would be to perturb the Earth-Moon distance by an amount $x(t)$ given by

$$x(t) = (1.83 \times 10^{12}\,\text{cm}) \times (\Delta_e - \Delta_m) \cos[(\omega - \Omega)t], \qquad (4.2.38)$$

where ω is the sidereal angular rate of the Moon around the Earth, and Ω is the Earth's sidereal rate around the Sun. The effect of $(\Delta_e - \Delta_m) \neq 0$ is thus to polarize the Earth-Moon orbit in a manner similar to the Nordtvedt effect [NORDTVEDT, 1968A,B]. From existing data Nordtvedt infers the limit

$$|\Delta_e - \Delta_m| \lesssim 5.5 \times 10^{-13}. \tag{4.2.39}$$

Since Δ_e and Δ_m are phenomenological parameters which depend on the detailed compositions of the Earth and the Moon, additional modeling is needed to relate this limit to that obtained from laboratory Eötvös experiments.

Nordtvedt makes the important point that the same lunar ranging data cannot be used to simultaneously test both universal free-fall (UFF) and post-Newtonian metric gravity, since a breakdown of either would have the same effect on $x(t)$. He then suggests that one approach could be to use improved laboratory Eötvös experiments to verify the validity of UFF to the necessary precision, in which case the lunar ranging data would become an unambiguous test of post-Newtonian metric gravity.

4.2.4 Modern Torsion Experiments

In the preceding section we derived the expression in Eq. (4.2.19) for the torque $\Delta\tau$ on the Eötvös balance in a manner quite similar to that given in the original EPF paper. In this section we present another derivation of this result which illustrates more clearly the principles behind the modern (i.e., post-1986) generation of torsion balance experiments. Before doing so, we reexamine the theory behind the Eötvös balance in the presence of an intermediate-range non-Newtonian force.

As we noted above, the design of the EPF experiment was motivated by an attempt to measure the difference between the (passive) gravitational mass m_G and the inertial mass m_I in Eq. (4.2.4). As is evident from that discussion, and particularly from Eq. (4.2.19), detecting $\Delta\tau \neq 0$ when $\kappa_1 \neq \kappa_2$ depends entirely on the fact that the centrifugal acceleration $\vec{a}_c$ is different from zero. Although $a_c \cong \omega^2 R_\oplus$ is nonzero, it is in fact small compared to g_N, which results in a suppression of the sensitivity of such experiments. Specifically, we see from Fig. 4.4 and Eqs. (4.2.12) and (4.2.15) that the angle β which measures the misalignment of $\vec{g}_N$ and $\vec{g}_0$ (due to $\vec{a}_c \neq 0$) is given by

$$\beta \cong \tan\beta = \frac{\omega_\oplus^2 R_\oplus}{g_N} \sin\varphi\cos\varphi \cong 1.7 \times 10^{-3}\,\text{rad}, \tag{4.2.40}$$

where we have assumed that $\varphi = 45°$ (Budapest corresponds to $\varphi \cong 47.5°$). Since $\varphi = 45°$ leads to the maximum value of β in Eq. (4.2.40), it follows that an Eötvös experiment aimed at detecting a difference between m_G and m_I is always suppressed by a factor of order 10^{-2}–10^{-3} compared to what

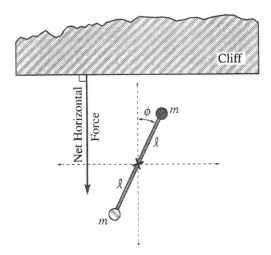

Figure 4.8: Overhead view of a torsion balance showing the angle of orientation relative to local topography.

would be the case if the misalignment between $\vec{g}_N$ and $\vec{g}_0$ were "maximal," as we now discuss.

Returning to Eq. (4.2.19), suppose that there exists another mechanism for an acceleration anomaly (in addition to that produced by $\kappa_1 \neq \kappa_2$), arising from a composition-dependent non-Newtonian force. (In this example, $\kappa_1 \neq \kappa_2$ might arise from a non-Newtonian coupling as well, but could also derive from a fundamental breakdown of the equivalence principle.) To be specific, consider the effect in the original Eötvös experiment of a local mass distribution to the north of the apparatus (see Fig. 4.8). We approximate this mass distribution by replacing it with a spherical mass distribution of mass M' and radius R' located a distance r to the north of the apparatus. From the preceding discussion, the Eötvös apparatus is normally oriented in the east–west direction, so that a non-Newtonian source situated to the north of the apparatus would exert the maximum possible torque. If we assume that this source couples to a test mass through a simple Yukawa whose charge is Q, then the additional force $\vec{F}'$ on an object of mass m is

$$
\begin{aligned}
\vec{F}' &= \left(\frac{Q}{\mu}\right) m\xi\vec{\mathcal{F}}' \\
&= \left(\frac{Q}{\mu}\right) m\xi g'(r) \left(1 + \frac{r}{\lambda}\right) e^{-r/\lambda} \Phi_s \left(\frac{R'}{\lambda}\right) (\cos\varphi'\hat{y} - \sin\varphi'\hat{z}), \quad (4.2.41)
\end{aligned}
$$

where $g'(r) \cong G_0 M'/r^2$, and $\vec{\mathcal{F}}'$ is as defined in Eq. (2.3.12). Here r is the distance from the center of inertia of the source to the center of inertia of the apparatus, $\Phi_s(x) = (3/x^3)(x\cosh x - \sinh x)$, and the primes refer to the local spherical source. The gravitational acceleration $\vec{g}'$ due to the spherical source is then

$$\vec{g}' = g'(r)(\cos \varphi' \hat{y} + \sin \varphi' \hat{z}). \tag{4.2.42}$$

Proceeding as before, we find that Eq. (4.2.19) generalizes to

$$\Delta \tau = \hat{z} \cdot \vec{\tau}_{\text{net}} = -m_1 \ell_1 [(\kappa_1 - \kappa_2) a_c \sin \varphi + (\kappa'_1 - \kappa'_2) g'(r) \cos(\varphi' + \beta)]. \tag{4.2.43}$$

Here

$$\kappa_i = 1 - \left(\frac{Q}{\mu}\right)_i \left(\frac{Q}{\mu}\right)_{\oplus} \frac{\mathcal{F}_{\oplus}}{g_N} \xi,$$

$$\kappa'_i = 1 - \left(\frac{Q}{\mu}\right)_i \left(\frac{Q}{\mu}\right)' \frac{\mathcal{F}'}{g'} \xi, \tag{4.2.44}$$

where $i = 1, 2$, and $\mathcal{F}_{\oplus}$, $\mathcal{F}'$ are the analogs of $\mathcal{F}$ in Eq. (2.3.12). Using

$$(\kappa_1 - \kappa_2) = -\frac{\mathcal{F}_{\oplus}}{g_N} \Delta \left(\frac{Q}{\mu}\right),$$

$$(\kappa'_2 - \kappa'_2) = -\frac{\mathcal{F}'}{g'} \Delta \left(\frac{Q}{\mu}\right), \tag{4.2.45}$$

$$\Delta \left(\frac{Q}{\mu}\right) \equiv \frac{Q_1}{\mu_1} - \frac{Q_2}{\mu_2},$$

Eq. (4.2.43) reduces to

$$\Delta \tau = m_1 \ell_1 \Delta \left(\frac{Q}{\mu}\right) [\mathcal{F}_{\oplus} \sin \beta + \mathcal{F}' \cos(\varphi' + \beta)]. \tag{4.2.46}$$

This result is easily checked by noting that the inertial and gravitational forces acting on the system can be simultaneously balanced if one assumes universality of free-fall and the equivalence of inertial and gravitational mass. The only effect of gravitation and the rotation of the Earth under these circumstances is to place the axis of rotation of the pendant at an angle β with respect to the direction of the acceleration of gravity. From Fig. 4.8, we see that the normal component to the axis of rotation of the non-Newtonian field $\mathcal{F}_{\perp}$ acting on a mass m is then

$$\mathcal{F}_{\perp} = \mathcal{F}_{\oplus} \sin \beta + \mathcal{F}' \cos(\varphi' + \beta), \tag{4.2.47}$$

from which Eq. (4.2.46) can be derived.

We now describe another way to understand how a torsion balance can be used to study intermediate-range non-Newtonian forces. This discussion will help clarify the relationship between the two primary variants of the Eötvös experiment currently in use, which are described in greater detail below. For pedagogical purposes we simplify the geometry of Fig. 4.4 by taking $\ell_1 = \ell_2 = \ell$ and $m_1 = m_2 = m$. We further assume that the pendant suspended from the fiber is oscillating in a horizontal plane in the vicinity of a vertical cliff, which is the presumed source of any non-Newtonian signal (see Fig. 4.8). The motion of the pendant is then described by the differential equation

$$I\ddot{\theta} + D\dot{\theta} + K\theta + \tau_0 \sin(\theta + \varphi) = 0, \qquad (4.2.48)$$

where θ is the angular displacement of the pendant from its equilibrium position, $I = 2m\ell^2$ is the moment of inertia of the pendant, D is the drag coefficient, K is the torsion constant of the fiber, and τ_0 is the magnitude of the maximum torque exerted by the external non-Newtonian field. The (constant) angle φ has been introduced to allow for the possibility that the pendant is oriented in such a way that the minimum restoring torque due to the fiber (which occurs at $\theta = 0$) does not coincide with the minimum restoring torque due to the external field (which occurs at $\theta = -\varphi$). Furthermore φ is defined in such a way that for $\varphi = 0$ the bar is aligned with the direction of the horizontal component of the external force due to the cliff. For small-amplitude oscillations ($\theta \ll 1$) we can write

$$\sin(\theta + \varphi) = \sin\theta \cos\varphi + \cos\theta \sin\varphi \cong \theta \cos\varphi + \sin\varphi, \qquad (4.2.49)$$

and hence Eq. (4.2.48) reduces to

$$I\ddot{\theta} + D\dot{\theta} + (K + \tau_0 \cos\varphi)\theta = -\tau_0 \sin\varphi. \qquad (4.2.50)$$

We see from Eq. (4.2.50) that the presence of an external non-Newtonian field ($\tau_0 \neq 0$) can be manifested in two distinct ways: a) $\tau_0 \cos\varphi$ acts like an additional contribution to the torsion constant, so that

$$K \rightarrow K_{\text{eff}}(\varphi) = K + \tau_0 \cos\varphi. \qquad (4.2.51)$$

Since the frequency ω of the oscillations is given by $\omega = [K_{\text{eff}}(\varphi)/I]^{1/2}$, assuming no damping for simplicity, it follows that one manifestation of the external field is via an apparent φ-dependence of the frequency $\omega = \omega(\varphi)$. b) A second manifestation is through the offset $\tau_0 \sin\varphi$, which has the effect of shifting the equilibrium position of the pendant from the value it would have when $\tau_0 = 0$.

To elaborate on the preceding discussion, we note that the solution to the differential equation (4.2.48) can be written in the form

$$\theta = Ae^{\gamma t} \sin\omega(t - t_0) + \theta_0, \qquad (4.2.52a)$$

$$\gamma = -\frac{D}{2I}, \qquad (4.2.52b)$$

$$\omega = \left[\frac{K + \tau_0 \cos\varphi}{I} - \frac{D^2}{4I^2}\right]^{1/2}, \qquad (4.2.52c)$$

$$\theta_0 = \frac{-\tau_0 \sin\varphi}{K + \tau_0 \cos\varphi}, \qquad (4.2.52d)$$

with t_0 and A being chosen so as to satisfy the initial boundary conditions. If we define

$$\omega_0 \equiv \left[\frac{K}{I} - \frac{D^2}{4I^2} \right]^{1/2}, \qquad (4.2.53)$$

then we can write

$$\omega = \omega(\varphi) \cong \omega_0 + \frac{\tau_0}{2I\omega_0} \cos \varphi. \qquad (4.2.54)$$

Note that the maximum and minimum values of ω occur when $\varphi = 0°$ and $180°$ respectively. Hence if we define $\Delta\omega = \omega(0°) - \omega(180°)$, then

$$\begin{aligned} \frac{\Delta\omega}{\omega_0} &\cong \frac{\tau_0}{I\omega_0^2} = \frac{m\ell\Delta(Q/\mu)_{1-2}}{I\omega_0^2} \xi\mathcal{F} \\ &= \frac{\Delta(Q/\mu)_{1-2}}{2\ell\omega_0^2} \xi\mathcal{F}, \end{aligned} \qquad (4.2.55)$$

where $\tau_0 = m\ell\xi\mathcal{F}\Delta(Q/\mu)_{1-2}$ for our simple torsion balance. As a numerical example we consider a pendant with $\ell = 5$ cm and with a period of oscillation of 10 minutes. If the two test masses are composed of Cu and Be respectively and $Q = B$, then Eq. (4.2.55) becomes

$$\frac{\Delta\omega}{\omega_0} \approx (230 \, \mathrm{m}^{-1} \mathrm{s}^2) \xi\mathcal{F}. \qquad (4.2.56)$$

For the nominal values $\xi = 10^{-4}$ and $\lambda = 200$ m the maximum value of $\mathcal{F}$ is given by $\mathcal{F}_\oplus$ in Eqs. (2.3.33) and (2.3.46), which is

$$\mathcal{F}_{\max} = \mathcal{F}_\oplus = 2.4 \times 10^{-9} g_N = 2.3 \times 10^{-8} \, \mathrm{m\,s}^{-2}. \qquad (4.2.57)$$

It follows from Eqs. (4.2.56) and (4.2.57) that the minimum sensitivity needed to detect $\mathcal{F}_{\max}$ under these assumptions is $\Delta\omega/\omega_0 \cong 5.3 \times 10^{-6}$, which is within the demonstrated sensitivity of the original experiment of Boynton et al. [BOYNTON, 1987] which used this technique, and well within current capabilities.

We turn next to describe the other class of Eötvös-type experiments, which involve measuring the shift θ_0 in the equilibrium position of a torsion balance, as the apparatus is rotated through $180°$. In this case we can simply carry through the result in Eq. (4.2.52d) to write

$$\theta_0(\varphi) \cong \frac{-\tau_0}{I\omega_0^2} \sin \varphi, \qquad (4.2.58)$$

where we have used $K \cong I\omega_0^2$. The maximum sensitivity to τ_0 and $\mathcal{F}$ is obtained when $\varphi = \pm 90°$, in which case the maximum difference in the deflection is

$$\Delta\theta_0 \cong \frac{2\tau_0}{I\omega_0^2} = \frac{2m\ell\Delta(Q/\mu)_{1-2}}{I\omega_0^2} \xi\mathcal{F} = \frac{\Delta(Q/\mu)_{1-2}\xi\mathcal{F}}{\ell\omega_0^2}. \qquad (4.2.59)$$

Assuming the same numerical values used to obtain Eq. (4.2.57), we find

$$\Delta\theta_0 \approx (460\,\mathrm{m}^{-1}\,\mathrm{s}^2)\xi\mathcal{F}. \tag{4.2.60}$$

Hence to achieve the same sensitivity to $\mathcal{F}_{\max}$ as the torsion pendulum experiment described above would require measuring the shift $\Delta\theta_0$ in the offset θ_0 to 1×10^{-5} radians. Again this is well within the capability of existing experiments, as we discuss in Section 4.2.6 below. We note in passing that since $\omega(\varphi)$ and $\theta_0(\varphi)$ depend on $\cos\varphi$ and $\sin\varphi$ respectively, the pendant orientations which give the maximum sensitivity for ω and θ_0 differ by $90°$.

4.2.5   The Eöt-Wash Experiments

The most extensive series of experiments to date searching for composition-dependent effects has been carried out by the "Eöt-Wash" collaboration, under the direction of Eric Adelberger. (The collaboration name is a play on the correct pronunciation of Eötvös, ["uht-vush"], by the University of Washington group). Excellent summaries of the Eöt-Wash experiments can be found in [ADELBERGER, 1990, 1991C; SU, 1994]

In terms of the formalism of Section 4.2.4, the Eöt-Wash experiments aim to measure θ_0, the shift in the equilibrium position of a composition dipole due to a hypothetical new force. This experiment is thus conceptually similar to the original EPF experiment, although it differs from EPF in a number of crucial ways, as can be seen from Figs. 4.6 and 4.9. We recall from Section 4.2.3 that in any torsion balance the masses must be rotated relative to the presumed source, so as to change their position as "seen" by the source. Among other things, this allows any possible non-Newtonian contribution to θ_0 to be distinguished from an effect such as an intrinsic twist of the torsion fiber which could also contribute to θ_0.

In the original EPF experiment the balance arm was rotated so that it was oriented during various runs east–west, west–east, north–south, and south–north. Inevitably the act of physically rotating the balance perturbs the torsion fiber, and the subtle stresses induced in this way are a major source of noise in such experiments. In fact the motivation for the previously discussed equivalence principle tests which used the Sun as a source [ROLL, 1964; BRAGINSKIĬ, 1971; KEISER, 1982], was to avoid the need to disturb the fiber, by having the balance remain stationary while the source moved relative to it over a 24 hr cycle. As we discuss in greater detail below, some modern experiments have used local sources (such as a mass of lead) in place of the Sun, and these were moved relative to the stationary fiber.

In the Eöt-Wash experiment (see Fig. 4.9) the apparatus is moved *continuously* relative to the source, by means of a high-precision turntable. This minimizes the stress on the fiber (compared to the EPF technique), and yet is competitive with the solar equivalence principle tests where the balance remains stationary. The reason for this is that the turntable period can be

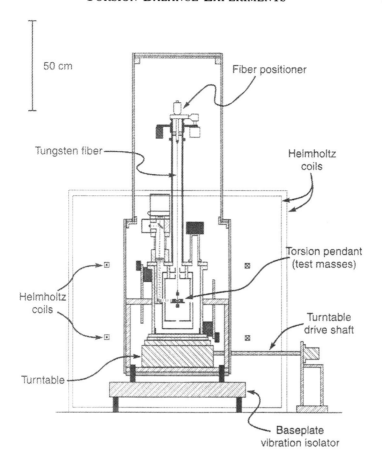

Figure 4.9: Diagram of the Eöt-Wash torsion balance of Adelberger et al. adapted from [ADELBERGER, 1990]. The experimental site is the Nuclear Physics Laboratory, located on a hillside at the University of Washington in Seattle.

set to be considerably shorter than the 24 hr period of the Sun. Since many sources of noise have a 24 hr periodicity, these would have a more pronounced effect on the solar experiments than on the Eöt-Wash experiment, which uses the Earth as its source. Moreover, the horizontal component of the centrifugal acceleration of the test masses at the surface of the Earth (due to its rotation) is approximately 3 times larger than the acceleration of the test masses produced by the Sun (see Eq. (4.2.10) and (4.2.27)).

The Eöt-Wash experiment departed from all previous tests of the equivalence principle in another significant way. To reduce or eliminate a variety of backgrounds (see below), the cylindrical masses comprising the composition dipole were constructed to have exactly the same external dimensions, as well as identical masses (see Fig. 4.10). To arrange for dissimilar materials with different densities (e.g., Be and Al) to have the same mass, the denser one was drilled out to form a hollow cylinder (with end caps) inside the original cylinder. The actual height (h) and diameter (d) of the cylinders were $h = (17.341 \pm 0.008)$ mm and $d = (19.977 \pm 0.008)$ mm. Following a suggestion of Fujii, this aspect ratio ($2h/d = \sqrt{3}$) was chosen to give each test mass vanishing mass quadrupole and octapole moments, which minimizes the coupling of the masses to the quadrupole and octapole components of the ambient gravity gradient. It should be emphasized, however, that there remain even larger gravitational multipole contributions which come from positioning the test masses in the tray that hangs from the torsion fiber. Finally the masses were plated with gold to prevent any buildup of static charges. At this stage the masses would appear identical for (almost) all conventional physics effects, but were obviously different in terms of their chemical composition as reflected in their values of Q/μ. (One classical difference between the masses was their respective moments of inertia: In principle the samples could be distinguished from one other by rolling them down an inclined plane.)

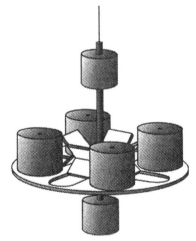

Figure 4.10: Pendant for the torsion balance of Adelberger et al. adapted from [ADELBERGER, 1990]. In contrast to the original Eötvös apparatus (shown in Fig. 4.6), the Eöt-Wash balance exhibits a very high degree of symmetry among the different test masses.

Why was so much effort expended to ensure that the samples would be almost indistinguishable classically? The answer lies in the recognition dating back to EPF that a number of classical effects can apply torques to the torsion balance which could simulate the signal expected from a non-Newtonian force. For example, the samples suspended from the torsion fiber could act as the vanes of a radiometer and cause a torque about the fiber. Additionally, a small temperature gradient can give rise to a very gentle "molecular breeze" acting on the samples. If these had different cross-sectional areas, then they would act as "sails" and again exert a torque on the fiber.

Such a mechanism was advanced by Chu and Dicke (CD) [CHU, 1986] as an explanation of the EPF data shown in Fig. 4.7. These authors note that the magnitude of the force on each test mass arising from convection currents should be approximately proportional to the cross-sectional area of each sample. Hence $\Delta\kappa$ for each pair should be proportional to the difference ΔS in the surface areas of the corresponding test masses, and various fits by the authors to the EPF data using this model suggest a possible correlation between $\Delta\kappa$ and ΔS. However, the CD explanation of the EPF data was criticized by Fischbach et al. on a number of grounds [FISCHBACH, 1986D]. Most significantly the CD model would require the presence of an undetected thermal gradient whose magnitude and direction remained constant over the approximately four year period during which the EPF experiment took place. This is highly unphysical, especially given the previously mentioned fact that EPF went to great lengths to monitor the temperature and to eliminate just such effects. The CD paper is nonetheless useful as a model of how thermal effects can simulate the composition-dependent signal arising from a new force. We note in passing that thermal gradients can produce spurious signals in other ways, such as by modifying the optical read-out systems or the electronics, or by causing the laboratory floor to tilt. For this reason, all searches for composition-dependent effects go to great lengths to control the thermal environment surrounding the apparatus.

To further understand some of the design features of the Eöt-Wash experiment (as well as other similar experiments), we proceed to discuss the effects of gravity gradients on this apparatus. Along with thermal effects, the gravitational torques exerted on the apparatus by the gradients $\partial g_i/\partial x_j$ of the gravitational field $\vec{g}(\vec{r})$ constitute the most serious sources of spurious signals in such an experiment. An extensive analysis of gravity-gradient effects is given in Appendix A, but for purposes of analyzing the Eöt-Wash experiment we follow the simplified discussion of [ADELBERGER, 1990]. Consider the gravitational torque $\tau_{\text{grav}}(\phi)$ acting on a simple two-mass pendant suspended from a fiber with torsion constant κ_f (see Fig. 4.9):

$$\tau_{\text{grav}}(\phi) = \kappa_f \bar{\theta}(\phi) = -4\pi i G \sum_{\ell=o}^{\infty} \frac{1}{2\ell+1} \sum_{m=-\ell}^{+\ell} m\bar{q}_{\ell m} Q_{\ell m} e^{-im\phi}. \qquad (4.2.61)$$

Here ϕ is the angle between the dipole and the extended source, $\bar{\theta}$ is the deflection of the fiber produced by τ_{grav}, and the tensors $\bar{q}_{\ell m}$ and $Q_{\ell m}$ describe the matter distribution in the detector pendant and the source respectively:

$$\bar{q}_{\ell m} = \int_{\text{det}} d^3 r \rho_{\text{det}}(\vec{r}) r^\ell Y_{\ell m}^*(\hat{r}), \tag{4.2.62}$$

$$Q_{\ell m} = \int_{\text{source}} d^3 r' \rho(\vec{r}\,')(r')^{-\ell-1} Y_{\ell m}(\hat{r}\,'). \tag{4.2.63}$$

In Eq. (4.2.62) $\rho_{\text{det}}(\vec{r})$ is the matter density (of the detector pendant), $Y_{\ell m}(\hat{r})$ are the usual spherical harmonics, and the integration is carried out in a body-fixed frame centered at the center of mass of the object suspended from the fiber. Similarly the integration in Eq. (4.2.63) is carried out in a frame fixed in the laboratory. Following [ADELBERGER, 1990], we note that since each term in Eq. (4.2.61) is proportional to the angular momentum component m, it follows that there is no contribution from the $m = 0$ moments. We also note from Eq. (4.2.61) that the $m = 1$ components vary as $e^{\pm i\phi}$, and hence these gravitational contributions must be suppressed because they can mimic the signal at 1ω expected from the putative fifth force. (A composition dipole produces a signal at 1ω, where ω is the rotation frequency of the can containing the apparatus, because the dipole returns its original position relative to the can once per revolution.) The lowest order source of a signal at 1ω is Q_{21} rather than Q_{11} (as might be naively expected), since the coefficient $\bar{q}_{11}$ of Q_{11} in Eq. (4.2.62) vanishes. This follows by noting that, at equilibrium (where the sum of the torques is zero), the center of mass of the pendant must lie below the suspension point, so that there can be no "dipole force."

Gravity gradient couplings can produce large torsional signals, although they do not necessarily give rise to 1ω signal components. Nonetheless, it should be pointed out that the presence of significant higher-order gradient couplings would give rise to a significantly increased noise level. The reason for this is that seismic noise produces fluctuations in the background gravity field, and the resulting variations in gravity gradients couple through the pendant's higher-order moments of inertia to give an elevated seismic noise level in the system. It should be emphasized that this effect will occur, *even in a vibrationally isolated system* (such as the Eöt-Wash apparatus), as long as significant gradient couplings are present. For this reason, a high degree of symmetry was built into the Eöt-Wash pendant (see Fig. 4.10), which not only reduced possible spurious 1ω signals, but also reduced the overall noise level of the system.

In this context, we comment briefly on the liquid-supported torsion balance (LSTB) of Faller et al. [FALLER, 1988]. These authors note that in a torsion balance the fiber plays a dual role, namely, supporting the pendant against gravity and applying the restoring torque on the pendant. By floating the test masses in a liquid (e.g., water or mercury), these roles can be separated and (perhaps) better optimized: The support role is evidently carried out by the liquid, while the restoring torque is supplied by electrodes attached to the masses. The relevance of this apparatus in the present context is that the LSTB has the disadvantage that the Q_{11} contribution does *not* vanish, which makes such a system more sensitive to gravity gradients than a torsion balance would be. Moreover, the LSTB proved to have another more serious problem, which was a sensitivity to convection currents in the liquid used to suspend the test masses. A similar experiment using liquid helium as the supporting fluid was attempted by Bartlett and coworkers [BARTLETT, PC], but ran into difficulties with helium leaks [TEW, 1989].

Returning to Eq. (4.2.61) above we note that a pendulum for which $\bar{q}_{\ell 1} \neq 0$ due to an imperfection could couple to the corresponding $Q_{\ell 1}$ moment of the ambient matter distribution to produce a "1ω signal." From the preceding discussion we see that such a signal would mimic that expected from a genuine fifth force, and so it is important to reduce or eliminate the $Q_{\ell 1}$ background to the extent possible. The dominant gravity-gradient term arises from Q_{21}, which is in general nonzero, and its effects on the Eöt-Wash pendant were canceled by means of a gradient "compensator" consisting of a rotatable mass distribution. A more detailed discussion of the compensator and its effects can be found in [ADELBERGER, 1990].

It is worth contrasting at this stage the fundamentally different ways in which the Eötvös and Eöt-Wash experiments dealt with gravity gradients. As we noted in Section 4.2.2, the torsion balance in the Eötvös experiment was specifically designed to be sensitive to gradients, and it was for this reason that the test masses were suspended below the platinum standard. Gradient effects were then eliminated by combining data with the apparatus in different orientations, as we have described previously. The Eötvös approach thus relied on "software" (i.e., a formalism), in contrast to the "hardware" approach used by all modern experiments, where both the test masses and the environment are designed to minimize such effects from the outset. This distinction between the two approaches might be significant if there existed a "gradient-type" new force which could pass through the Eötvös "software," but not through the "hardware" approach of modern experiments. If such a theory existed, it could conceivably explain why the Eötvös experiment saw evidence for a new force while modern torsion experiments do not. However, to date no such theory has been put forward.

We consider next various systematic effects in the Eöt-Wash experiments. As we will discuss, this group has found no evidence whatever for a non-Newtonian force, a conclusion which is now supported by almost every other experiment. For an experiment which sees no effect it is, of course, necessary to calibrate the apparatus to make sure that it *could* see an effect if one existed. Evidently such a calibration cannot be carried out with a nonexistent force, but it can be simulated by studying the response of the Eöt-Wash apparatus to the known effects of gravity gradients. The Eöt-

Wash collaboration carried out an extensive series of tests in which they deliberately applied a known gravitational hexadecapole torque to their pendulum [ADELBERGER, 1990]. Their experimental results are in excellent agreement with theoretical expectations, which strengthens the claims of the Eöt-Wash group that they would have seen a signal for a new force had one been present.

Such tests were important in the early period of research on the putative fifth force, since results from the first Eöt-Wash experiment [STUBBS, 1987] appeared shortly after the positive signal from Thieberger [1987A,B], which supported the suggestion from the EPF experiment for the existence of a new force. In that context, these checks and others served to convincingly rule out the possibility that the Eöt-Wash group had suppressed a genuine signal in the process of suppressing various sources of noise which would simulate a signal. Although it is less likely that a systematic effect would mask a signal than it is for such an effect to simulate a signal when none exists, it is nonetheless extremely important to understand all possible influences on the apparatus.

The Eöt-Wash group identified several sources of error in their most recent experiments: gravity gradients, linear tilt, magnetism, thermal effects which produce a 1ω signal, thermal gradients, and calibration drifts. Here a 1ω thermal effect refers to a temperature modulation of the apparatus at the same frequency ω as the rotating turntable. Such effects are important because the torsion constant of the fiber depends sensitively on temperature. To deal with such effects, the authors deliberately induced such "driving terms" (as they refer to them) and determined the sensitivity of their apparatus to each. This allowed them to either correct for the given effect, or else to place an upper limit on its contribution. It is clear that such tests are critical in understanding the apparatus, and the authors note that these tests consumed a significant fraction of their overall effort [SU, 1994]. The interested reader should consult [SU, 1994] for an excellent discussion of their treatment of systematic effects.

We turn next to a discussion of the Eöt-Wash results. The authors have extracted from their data limits on the differential acceleration of Be-Al and Be-Cu toward different possible sources, including the Earth, the Sun, the galaxy, and the cosmic microwave dipole. We present here some selected results from [SU, 1994] and their implications. For the differential acceleration in the Earth's field they find

$$\Delta a_\perp(\text{Be-Al}) = [(-2.3 \pm 4.6)\hat{E} + (-0.3 \pm 4.6)\hat{N}] \times 10^{-12}\,\text{cm}\,\text{s}^{-2},$$
$$\Delta a_\perp(\text{Be-Cu}) = [(-3.6 \pm 4.1)\hat{E} + (-3.2 \pm 4.1)\hat{N}] \times 10^{-12}\,\text{cm}\,\text{s}^{-2}, \quad (4.2.64)$$

where $\Delta a_\perp(\text{Be-Al})$ is the horizontal component of the acceleration difference between Be and Al (i.e., the component in the direction of their hillside), and $\hat{E}(\hat{N})$ is a unit vector in the east (north) direction. These results are obviously compatible with a null signal. The Eöt-Wash limits from [SU, 1994] on differential accelerations toward the Sun are

$$
\begin{aligned}
\Delta a^\odot(\text{Be-Al}) &= (+2.4 \pm 5.8) \times 10^{-12}\,\text{cm s}^{-2}, \\
\Delta a^*(\text{Be-Al}) &= (+2.6 \pm 5.8) \times 10^{-12}\,\text{cm s}^{-2}, \\
\Delta a^\odot(\text{Be-Cu}) &= (-3.0 \pm 3.6) \times 10^{-12}\,\text{cm s}^{-2}, \\
\Delta a^*(\text{Be-Cu}) &= (-3.4 \pm 3.6) \times 10^{-12}\,\text{cm s}^{-2}.
\end{aligned}
\tag{4.2.65}
$$

Here $\Delta a^\odot$ and Δa^* point toward the Sun and 90° away from the Sun, respectively.

It is interesting to compare the sensitivity of the Eöt-Wash limits as a test of UFF to those obtained earlier. This can be done in terms of the parameter η in Eq. (4.2.28), which measures the fractional acceleration difference $\Delta a/a$ of two test masses A and B:

$$
\eta(A, B) = \frac{\delta a}{a}(A\text{-}B) = \frac{[(m_G/m_I)_A - (m_G/m_I)_B]}{\frac{1}{2}[(m_G/m_I)_A + (m_G/m_I)_B]}.
\tag{4.2.66}
$$

[SU, 1994] quote

$$
\begin{aligned}
\eta(\text{Be-Al}) &= (-0.2 \pm 2.8) \times 10^{-12}, \\
\eta(\text{Be-Cu}) &= (-1.9 \pm 2.5) \times 10^{-12},
\end{aligned}
\tag{4.2.67}
$$

and these results compare to

$$
\begin{aligned}
\eta(\text{Au-Al}) &= (1.3 \pm 1.0) \times 10^{-11}, & &[\text{ROLL, 1964}] \\
\eta(\text{Pt-Al}) &= (-0.3 \pm 0.9) \times 10^{-12}, & &[\text{BRAGINSKIĬ, 1971}] \\
\eta(\text{Cu-W}) &= (0.6 \pm 4) \times 10^{-11}. & &[\text{KEISER, 1982}]
\end{aligned}
\tag{4.2.68}
$$

What is striking about these results is that the Eöt-Wash group achieve a sensitivity almost equal to the most sensitive of the three solar experiments (Braginskiĭ and Panov), despite the fact that the latter experiments do not move the test masses. It will be recalled that these experiments achieve their great sensitivity in part because they do not perturb the test masses or the torsion fiber by having to rotate the masses as EPF do. Rather, by measuring the acceleration of their test masses toward the Sun, they can modulate their signal with a 24 hr periodicity. It is thus a remarkable achievement that the Eöt-Wash collaboration can reach the same sensitivity by measuring the acceleration of their test masses toward the Earth, while rotating them *continuously*.

We consider next the earlier Eöt-Wash results on a coupling to I_z, which utilized a laboratory source [STUBBS, 1989A]. Following the report by Boynton et al. of an anomalous signal, interest in a possible coupling to I_z (rather than to B) increased, since only an I_z coupling appeared consistent with the Boynton data [BOYNTON, 1987]. However, these data had only limited sensitivity to I_z because, as noted earlier, most geophysical sources have $\langle I_z \rangle \cong 0$. Stubbs et al. observed that since Pb has a large neutron excess, a laboratory source of Pb could have a sufficiently large net I_z to set a limit on a coupling to I_z which would be comparable in sensitivity to that obtained from a geophysical source, at least for small values of λ. Their apparatus is as described earlier, except that now their source is 1288 kg of Pb. They find

$$\Delta a(\text{Be-Al}) = (-0.15 \pm 1.31) \times 10^{-10} \, \text{cm s}^{-2}, \qquad (4.2.69)$$

which gives

$$\xi_I = (0.14 \pm 1.24) \times 10^{-3}. \qquad (4.2.70)$$

The interested reader is referred to [TALMADGE, 1987B; HECKEL, 1989; STUBBS, 1989A,B] for further details.

We conclude this section with a discussion of the most recent Eöt-Wash results, which tested the equivalence principle over relatively short ranges [GUNDLACH, 1997]. As in the earlier equivalence principle tests, the experiment was designed to have the source move with respect to the torsion balance, thus providing a signal of known period which could be extracted from the data. In this experiment the source was 3 tons of ^{238}U in close proximity to a torsion balance utilizing Cu and a Pb alloy as test masses. One of the purposes of this experiment (called "Rot-Wash" by the authors) was to fill in the constraints on the coupling strengths ξ_B and ξ_I (corresponding to B and I respectively) for $10 \, \text{km} \leq \lambda \leq 1000 \, \text{km}$, where previous constraints were relatively weak. Prior to this experiment, the best constraints for $\lambda \approx 1000 \, \text{km}$ came from Galileo (free-fall) experiments, as we discuss in Section 4.3. However, the constraints implied by these experiments on ξ_B and ξ_I are somewhat difficult to infer, because the composition of the Earth over the relevant distance scales is uncertain. By contrast, the composition of the attracting ^{238}U mass is completely known, and since this experiment is extremely sensitive, it can constrain the same region in a $\xi - \lambda$ plot that the free-fall experiments do. As in other experiments by the Eöt-Wash group, the test masses were located in machined recesses on a Be tray, and this allowed the masses to be interchanged in such a way as to remove any systematic effects arising from imperfections in the system. The final result of Gundlach et al. for the acceleration difference between the Cu and Pb samples was

$$a(\text{Cu}) - a(\text{Pb}) = (-0.7 \pm 5.4 \pm 1.9) \times 10^{-13} \, \text{cm s}^{-2}, \qquad (4.2.71)$$

where the first error is statistical and the second is systematic. This result can then be used to set new limits on ξ_B and ξ_I, and these have been incorporated into Figs. 4.16 and 4.17. We note in passing that the increased sensitivity to ξ_I at larger values of λ arises in part because ^{238}U has a relatively large neutron excess, with $(N - Z)/(N + Z) = 0.23$ compared to ≈ 0 for the terrestrial sources that would dominate at large λ [GUNDLACH, 1997].

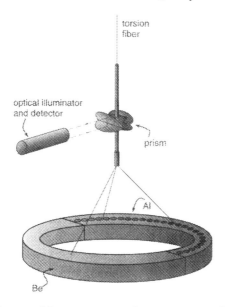

Figure 4.11: Pendant used in experiment of Boynton et al. [BOYNTON, 1987].

4.2.6   The Experiment of Boynton et al.

As we noted in Section 4.2.4, the experiment of Boynton et al., [BOYN-TON, 1987] (BCES) seeks to measure the shift $\Delta\omega$ (due to a presumed non-Newtonian force) in the frequency ω of a torsion pendulum oscillating in a horizontal plane. Since this is the only Eötvös-type experiment to date which uses this technique, we will study it in some detail. The heart of the experimental apparatus is the suspended pendant, which in the original experiment was a composition dipole composed of Al and Be formed by joining two half-rings as shown in Fig. 4.11. For illustrative purposes we will focus our discussion on the pendant used in the original published work of this group [BOYNTON, 1987]. With only slight modification this discussion can then be taken over to describe the improved pendant currently in use. The pendant was fabricated by starting with discs of Al and Be, and then removing the material inside the disc to form an 11.4 g ring of inside radius $R_1 = 3.97$ cm and outside radius $R_2 = 4.45$ cm. R_1, R_2 and the thickness were adjusted so that the cross-sectional area of the half-rings before they were joined was a square of area 0.48×0.48 cm^2. To minimize the effects of couplings to gravity gradients, it was important in constructing the ring to ensure that the masses of both halves were nearly equal. It was also desirable to arrange for the external dimensions of the two half-rings to be the same, so as to reduce the sensitivity of the pendant to various systematic perturbations such as thermal effects. Since Al has a greater density than Be, these two goals were achieved by drilling 24 equally spaced holes in the Al half-ring, as shown in Fig. 4.11. We note in passing that since the two half-rings have different mass distributions, they will in general have different values of the mean square radius $\langle R^2 \rangle$. For this reason, the construction of the pendant in the experiment of BCES allows their apparatus to be sensitive not only to composition-dependent forces, but to composition-independent forces as well, through the finite-size effect discussed in Section 2.4. (This applies as well to the Eöt-Wash experiments and to the other composition-dependent tests that we discuss.) The pendant, once assembled, was plated with gold to prevent static charges from building up, and was then suspended from a gold-plated tungsten fiber attached at three equally spaced points on the pendant. The torsion constant of the fiber and the design of the pendant were such that the period T was 975 s.

The experiments of BCES were carried out at the base of a 130 m nearly vertical wall on the southeast face of a 330 m high granite intrusion in the North Cascades mountain range, near the town of Index, Washington. The apparatus was located 4 m inside the cliff face in a blind tunnel which had been drilled to test mining equipment. While the apparatus was running, the entrance of the tunnel was sealed by a heavy door, and this provided a stable thermal environment for their experiment. This, along with extensive thermal shielding of the instrument, reduced the nominal temperature coefficient of the fractional frequency shift $(\Delta\omega/\omega)$ of the torsion fiber to 10^{-4} per °C change in the temperature.

As we discussed in the preceding section, the signal for a composition-dependent fifth force would be a dependence of the oscillation frequency on the equilibrium orientation of the pendant, which is determined by the orientation φ of the apparatus. To search for such an effect, Boynton et al. changed the equilibrium orientation of the dipole axis by 45° increments (so that data were taken at $0°, 45°, 90°, 135°, \ldots, 315°$) and then plotted their results as a function of φ in Eq. (4.2.54). From Eq. (4.2.54) we would expect to find a $\cos\varphi$ dependence for the fractional period shift $\Delta T(\varphi)/T_0$, and BCES found

$$[\Delta T(\varphi)/T_0] = -[\Delta\omega(\varphi)/\omega_0] = (-4.6 \pm 1.1) \times 10^{-6} \cos\varphi$$
$$+ (+0.1 \pm 1.2) \times 10^{-6} \sin\varphi. \quad (4.2.72)$$

This result corresponds to a 4.2σ deviation from a null measurement along the tunnel.

Gravity gradient couplings are the largest and most troublesome systematic contributions to $\Delta T(\varphi)$ in the BCES experiment. As we have

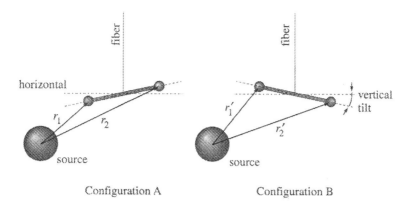

Configuration A   Configuration B

Figure 4.12: Schematic representation of a torsion balance with tilt present.

noted previously, this is because such couplings can produce via conventional physics a contribution to $\Delta T(\varphi)$ which mimics the signal expected from a non-Newtonian composition-dependent force. To understand how this can come about, we examine the gravitational forces on the *tilted* pendant shown in Fig. 4.12 in the presence of a nonuniform gravitational field. In practice any pendant will likely be tilted to some extent, in the sense that its mass distribution will not lie entirely in a horizontal plane. If this tilted mass distribution interacts with a gravitational field $\vec{g}(\vec{r})$, whose components $g_i(\vec{r})$ are such that $\partial g_i/\partial x_j \neq 0$ $(i,j = 1,2,3)$, then upon rotation of the pendant through $180°$ the forces on the pendant will not be the same as they were in the original orientation. This is illustrated in Fig. 4.12, from which we see that the gravitational torque on the pendant is greater in configuration A than in configuration B, since $|\vec{F}_1(\vec{r}_1)| > |\vec{F}_1(\vec{r}_1')|$ while at the same time $|\vec{F}_2(\vec{r}_2)| < |\vec{F}_2(\vec{r}_2')|$. Thus even for a pendant composed of two identical masses, there would be a net gravitational torque tending to rotate the pendant into a "preferred" position, exactly as if it were coupling to a composition-dependent non-Newtonian force.

The gravity gradient problem affects all torsion balance experiments, including the original EPF experiment. As we noted in Section 4.2.2, the EPF method of removing such effects involved combining different measurements in such a way that gravity gradients canceled out of the final result. By contrast, modern experiments have chosen to directly cancel the ambient gradients by use of compensating lead masses positioned close to the test objects, as in the Eöt-Wash experiments. The theory behind these techniques is discussed in detail in Appendix A.

The first experiment of the BCES collaboration (known as Index I), was followed by a similar experiment (Index II) using a ring composed of Cu and polyethylene $[(CH_2)_n]$. A flaw in the design of this pendant led to a subtle hydrodynamic effect which simulated the signal expected from a non-Newtonian force [BOYNTON, 1989]. To eliminate this effect, Boynton et al. redesigned the Cu-CH_2 dipole by hermetically sealing the test masses in a thin-walled Cu container. After some additional minor changes, including better temperature control, their experiment was rerun (Index III). In contrast to the case for Index I, the Index III results of Boynton et al. were consistent with no effect. They found for the coefficient of $\cos \varphi$ in $[\Delta T(\varphi)/T]$ (see Eq. (4.2.72)) the value $(-2.2 \pm 1.9) \times 10^{-7}$ [BOYNTON, 1990], which implies the following 2σ limits on couplings to B, $(B-L)$, and $(B-2L)$ respectively:

$$-3.2 \times 10^{-5} < \xi_B < 1.2 \times 10^{-4}$$
$$-2.6 \times 10^{-6} < \xi_{B-L} < 9.8 \times 10^{-6} \qquad (4.2.73)$$
$$-4.3 \times 10^{-5} < \xi_{B-2L} < 1.8 \times 10^{-4}$$

Since this experiment is roughly an order of magnitude more sensitive than Index I, and took place at the same site, it calls into question the 4.2σ effect found at Index I, which was probably due to an undetected magnetic impurity in the pendant [BOYNTON, PC].

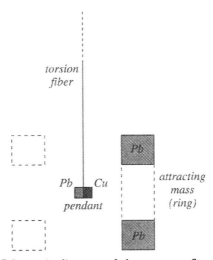

Figure 4.13: Schematic diagram of the mass configuration for the experiment of Nelson et al. [NELSON, 1988, 1990], showing both the Cu-Pb torsion pendant and the Pb attracting mass. The experiment consists of modulating the Pb source by moving it to the opposite side of the pendant. The torsion pendant is not shown to scale.

4.2.7 The Experiment of Nelson, Graham, and Newman

We turn next to the experiment of Nelson, Graham, and Newman (NGN) [NELSON, 1988, 1990], which is a search for a composition-dependent coupling to I_z using a laboratory source. As in the Eöt-Wash experiments [STUBBS, 1988A, 1989A], the source was taken to be Pb, which has a large neutron excess. To further increase the signal strength, the test masses forming the dipole pendant were Cu and Pb, which produce a relatively large value for $\Delta(I_z/\mu)$. The principle of their experiment is shown in Fig. 4.13. The external (attracting) Pb mass is a 321 kg ring whose outside and inside diameters were 60.8 cm and 29.5 cm respectively.

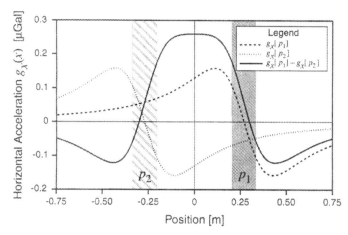

Figure 4.14: Plot of the induced horizontal acceleration $g_x(x)$ as a function of x, evaluated when the Pb attracting mass is at location p_1 ($g_x[p_1]$) versus when the ring is located at p_2 ($g_x[p_2]$). In this diagram, the pendant is at $x = 0$. Also shown is the differential acceleration ($g_x[p_1] - g_x[p_2]$). The two shaded regions correspond to values of x which are interior to the attracting ring, were it at the labeled position. We see from the solid line that ($g_x[p_1] - g_x[p_2]$) is nearly constant in the vicinity of $x = 0$. This minimizes the effects of small repositioning errors when the ring is moved from p_1 to p_2 and back.

The motivation for choosing a ring shape for the external mass can be understood from Fig. 4.14, which displays the acceleration field $g_x(x)$ arising from the attracting Pb ring. The results shown were obtained using only the lead component of the attracting masses, and do not include the Al cladding used in the construction of the attracting ring. (However, the general features of $g_x(x)$ would not be expected to change with the inclusion of the Al cladding. We would primarily expect an increase in magnitude of $g_x(x)$, since the cladding is placed symmetrically about the Pb masses.) As we have already discussed, a major source of problems in such experiments is a coupling to gravity gradients. NGN note that if the Pb-Cu composition dipole is placed on the ring axis at an appropriate distance from the center of the ring, then when the Pb ring is moved to a symmetric position on the opposite side of the dipole, the *change* in the gravitational field is spatially uniform to a high degree. (Specifically, all the spatial derivatives of the change in field vanish through third order.) Since the torsion balance only responds to a change in the field, the suppression of gravity gradients in the NGN experiment is similar to what would be seen if they had used an attracting mass which gave an extremely uniform gravitational field. For this reason first-order imperfections in either the dipole pendant or the ring produce only a second-order error due to gravity gradients. To further reduce couplings to gravity gradients, the Pb ring itself was carefully fabricated and tested to ensure homogeneity of the Pb.

In the Pb-Cu dipole pendant, the Pb was sandwiched between two identical pieces of Al, so that the dimensions and mass of the Pb-Al "sandwich" were the same as those of the Cu sample. The test masses were then placed in a hexagonal Cu tray, which was suspended in vacuum by a 93 cm long tungsten wire. The whole apparatus was contained in an unventilated subbasement chamber which was sealed with a Styrofoam roof plug for thermal stability. The apparatus was further shielded with thermal insulation, and magnetically shielded as well.

The signal in this experiment is the change $\Delta\theta(\psi)$ in the equilibrium angle θ of the pendant when the ring is transported from an angle ψ to an angle $\psi + 180°$:

$$\Delta\theta(\psi) = \theta(\psi) - \theta(\psi + 180°). \tag{4.2.74}$$

Here ψ is defined such that $\psi = 90°$ corresponds to the axis of the Pb ring coinciding with the diameter of the pendant which separates the two halves of the dipole. The specific signal for a non-Newtonian force is a variation of $\Delta\theta(\psi)$ with ψ given by

$$\Delta\theta(\psi) = A_5 \sin\psi, \tag{4.2.75}$$

where A_5 is a constant. One of the novel (and probably unique) features of the NGN experiment was their "blind" data analysis, which was carried out in the following way: Once their computer determines a value of $\Delta\theta(\psi)$, it returns the function $F(\psi)$ defined by

$$F(\psi) = \Delta\theta(\psi) + X \sin\psi, \tag{4.2.76}$$

where X is a constant known to the computer, but not to the experimentalists. Thus even if there were no new force, so that A_5 and $\Delta\theta(\psi)$ are both zero, $F(\psi)$ will simulate the effects of a fifth force if $X \neq 0$. All the checks that NGN carry out to exclude various systematics (see below) can be performed in the same way with $X \neq 0$, so that what is being determined is the sum $(A_5 + X)$. At the very end of the analysis X is revealed, and this determines A_5 in an unambiguous and unbiased way.

The authors carried out checks for various systematic effects, including magnetic couplings between the Pb ring and the dipole pendant, tilt effects, thermal effects, and gravitational gradient couplings, etc. The interested reader should refer to [NELSON, 1990] for further details. NGN see no evidence for a coupling to either I_z or B, and their respective limits are

$$\xi_I = (5.7 \pm 6.3) \times 10^{-5}, \qquad\qquad (4.2.77)$$

$$\xi_B = (-1.2 \pm 1.3) \times 10^{-3}. \qquad\qquad (4.2.78)$$

4.2.8 The TIFR Experiment

We turn next to the torsion balance experiment of Ramanath Cowsik and his group at the Tata Institute of Fundamental Research (TIFR) in Bombay, India [COWSIK, 1988, 1989A,B, 1990]. As in the Eöt-Wash experiments [STUBBS, 1989A; GUNDLACH, 1997], and the Irvine experiment [NELSON, 1988, 1990], this experiment tests for a possible new force coupling to $I_z = N - Z$, which uses a movable lead source. The composition dipole in this experiment is formed by joining two half-rings of Pb and Cu to form a single 1500 g ring, in a manner similar to the experiment of Boynton et al. [BOYNTON, 1987]. The novel feature of the TIFR experiment is that the Pb masses which provide the isospin source are moved in a circle about the suspension axis of the dipole at the resonant frequency of the balance. If there were an isospin coupling between the dipole and the Pb masses, moving the masses in this way would have the effect of resonantly increasing the torsional amplitude. This could be a significant help since, as noted by the authors, the horizontal component of the gravitational field (and by extension any new force field) produced by their source is $\sim 10^5$ smaller than what could be available at some geophysical sites.

As in the case of all other composition-dependent experiments, the TIFR experiment is sensitive to gravity gradients and thermal effects which could couple differently to the Pb and Cu half-rings. To minimize gradient couplings, grooves were cut in the Pb half to make the Pb mass distribution correspond more closely to that of the Cu. Thermal systematics were suppressed by carrying out the experiment at an isolated location in a specially constructed site located 25 m below ground level, and this limited temperature variations to less than $10^{-3}\,^\circ$C around the measurement frequency.

An important series of checks was carried out by orienting the external Pb masses (and the associated brass counterweights) in different positions relative to the composition dipole. These were called the "isospin mode" (where the effect on the masses arising from the putative force would have been maximal), the "90° mode" (where there should have been no torque), the "null mode" (where the Pb and brass masses were exchanged so as to again produce no torque), and the "free cycling" mode (during which the masses were stationary). By comparing their signals in these various modes, any genuine signal from a coupling to isospin could be extracted. Since the composition and geometry of the external Pb masses are known, limits on the coupling constant ξ_I for $Q_5 = I_z$ can be extracted. The TIFR group saw no evidence for a new force, and their 2σ bounds are

$$-2.3 \times 10^{-4} < \xi_I < +2.7 \times 10^{-5}. \tag{4.2.79}$$

4.2.9 The Experiment of Fitch, Isaila, and Palmer

As we have noted previously, the sensitivity of an Eötvös-type search for an intermediate-range force increases if the experiment is carried out in the vicinity of a source with a large horizontal field component, such as a vertical cliff. The floating-ball experiments, described in Section 4.5 below, and the BCES experiment [BOYNTON, 1987], are examples of experiments which have sought to maximize this effect. Another such experiment is that of Fitch, Isaila, and Palmer [FITCH, 1988], which was carried out at the Yellowstone Bighorn Research Association (YBRA) camp near Red Lodge, Montana. This site, on the slopes of Mt. Maurice, was chosen because the terrain has a significant tilt in different directions. Experiments carried out in different kinds of terrain are extremely important, given that we cannot at present exclude the possibility that the source of the systematic effect in the original EPF experiment had something to do with the site of their experiment. This applies not only to features such as the tilt of the terrain but, most importantly, to its chemical composition. Since $B/\mu \cong 1$ for any source, the chemical composition of a given site is relatively unimportant for purposes of setting limits on ξ_B. However, this is not true for a coupling to isospin, as we have noted previously. One advantage of the YBRA site is that the geology of the area is sufficiently well known, particularly as a function of distance from the apparatus, to allow I_z/μ for the source to be inferred.

This experiment employed three torsional balances, one of which was used to measure gravity gradients. The principal measurements were made with a toroidal pendant, one half of which was Cu and the other half polyethylene $[(CH_2)_n]$, which gives a large difference $\Delta(Q_5/\mu)$ for both $Q_5 = B$, and $Q_5 = I_z$. The results of this experiment, summarized in their Table III, are quite interesting, because they exhibit the fluctuations that can arise when working under field conditions. However, their weighted central values give a null result, and their weighted mean is

$$\Delta a(\text{Cu-CH}_2) = (0.30 \pm 0.49) \times 10^{-12} \, \text{cm s}^{-2}. \tag{4.2.80}$$

To convert this result into a limit on ξ_B or ξ_I as a function of λ requires, as usual, a detailed discussion of the local geology, which the authors present. The interested reader is referred to this paper for further details.

4.2.10 The Bennett Experiment

Bennett [1989] carried out an experiment which looked for an intermediate-range coupling to I_z between a Cu-Pb dipole pendant and the water contained in a large lock on the Snake River in eastern Washington. This experiment has the advantage of using a large source of known composition, which at the same time has a relatively large value of I_z/μ. Moreover, the source could be turned on or off within 12 min, and this provided an additional check on any possible signal. This interesting experiment combines some features of laboratory experiments with movable sources, such as [COWSIK, 1988, 1990; SPEAKE, 1988; STUBBS, 1989A; NELSON, 1988, 1990; GUNDLACH, 1997], and those which use geophysical sources. Although the lock fillings could not be controlled by the experimentalist, they happened sufficiently often to allow useful results to be obtained. Bennett found no evidence for any coupling to isospin, and two of his limits (as a function of λ) are

$$\xi_I = (+2.2 \pm 4.6) \times 10^{-3} \text{ for } \lambda = 10\,\text{m}, \tag{4.2.81}$$

$$\xi_I = (+0.5 \pm 1.0) \times 10^{-3} \text{ for } \lambda \geq 200\,\text{m}. \tag{4.2.82}$$

4.3 Galileo (Free-Fall) Experiments

As noted above, these experiments aim to repeat the experiment which Galileo is supposed to have carried out around 1590 using the famous leaning tower of Pisa. Actually the historical record suggests that if Galileo carried out any such experiment at all, it was not to compare objects of different composition, but rather objects of the same composition differing in size [DRAKE, 1978; FULIGNI, 1996]. In their original paper on the Eötvös experiment, Fischbach et al. [FISCHBACH, 1986A] noted that a metrologically interesting free-fall experiment might be feasible utilizing modern interferometric techniques.

Classically, one of the chief difficulties in Galileo free-fall experiments was the effect of air resistance on the falling bodies. Modern free-fall instruments compensate for this problem by utilizing a "drag-free" technology that was first developed for drag-free satellites (see Section 4.8). For absolute gravimeters, the drag-free system works by placing the "proof mass" inside of a larger chamber, which is then pumped to a near-vacuum state. The chamber and the proof mass are then dropped together, with the relative separation of the two falling bodies being measured by interferometric means. The outer chamber is controlled by a servo mechanism, which keeps the separation between the falling bodies constant. Since the air pressure in the evacuated chamber is very small, the effect of air resistance is negligible in these systems.

The first such experiment was carried out by Niebauer, McHugh, and Faller [NIEBAUER, 1987]. More recent experiments have been performed by Kuroda and Mio [KURODA, 1989, 1990], and by Carusotto et al. [CARUSOTTO, 1992], and we will return shortly to describe these experiments in more detail. To demonstrate that such experiments are sensitive enough to lead to useful constraints, we consider a simple estimate in which the Earth is modeled as a nonrotating spherical source with an average mass density $\rho_\oplus$, a local density $\bar{\rho}_\oplus$, and a local average charge $\bar{q}$. Then using Eq. (2.3.46) we can write for the acceleration difference between masses 1 and 2

$$\frac{\Delta a_{1-2}}{g_N} = \frac{a_1 - a_2}{g_N} = \frac{\left|\vec{\mathcal{F}}_\oplus\right|}{g_N}\xi\bar{q}\Delta q_{1-2} \cong \frac{3}{2}\frac{\bar{\rho}_\oplus}{\rho}\frac{\lambda}{R_\oplus}\xi\bar{q}\Delta q_{1-2}, \qquad (4.3.1)$$

where $g_N \cong 9.8\,\mathrm{m\,s^{-2}}$. Equation (4.3.1) can then be used to estimate the sensitivity of a free-fall experiment by inserting the nominal values $\lambda = 1000\,\mathrm{m}$, $\xi = 10^{-4}$, and $\bar{\rho}/\rho \cong 1/2$. This gives

$$\left|\frac{\Delta a_{1-2}}{g_N}\right| \cong \frac{3}{2} \times \frac{1}{2} \times \frac{1000\,\mathrm{m}}{6.4 \times 10^6\,\mathrm{m}} \times 10^{-4} \times \bar{q}\Delta q_{1-2}$$

$$\cong 1.2 \times 10^{-8}\bar{q}\Delta q_{1-2}, \qquad (4.3.2)$$

and

$$|\Delta a_{1-2}| \approx 1.1 \times 10^{-7}\bar{q}\Delta q_{1-2}\,\mathrm{m\,s^{-2}}. \qquad (4.3.3)$$

For typical laboratory materials the magnitude of the q-dependent factor in Eq. (4.3.3) is of order 10^{-3} assuming $q = B/\mu$, and hence

$$|\Delta a_{1-2}| \approx 1 \times 10^{-10}\,\mathrm{m\,s^{-2}}. \qquad (4.3.4)$$

If $|\Delta a_{1-2}|$ is determined by comparing the time difference $\Delta t_{1-2} = t_1 - t_2$ for 1 and 2 to fall through a common distance s, then

$$\left|\frac{\Delta t_{1-2}}{t}\right| \cong \frac{1}{2}\left|\frac{\Delta a_{1-2}}{g_N}\right| \approx 6 \times 10^{-10}, \qquad (4.3.5)$$

where $t = (t_1 + t_2)/2$. For $s = 1\,\mathrm{m}$, $t \cong 0.5\,\mathrm{s}$, and $\Delta t_{1-2} \approx 3 \times 10^{-10}\,\mathrm{s} = 300\,\mathrm{ps}$. In the experiment of Niebauer et al. [NIEBAUER, 1987], test masses of copper and depleted uranium were dropped in two separate absolute gravimeters, which were placed side-by-side over a common interferometer base. A corner cube retro-reflector was attached to each mass, and this allowed the relative positions of the test masses to be monitored interferometrically, as a function of time. As noted in Section 3.10, it is experimentally easier to measure a time-varying signal than a constant signal, and hence one test mass was released 25 ms before the other. This introduced at the start of the measurement a vertical separation Δx_0 of 3 mm, and a velocity difference Δv_0 of 25 cm s^{-1}. By continuously monitoring the positions of the test masses, one can determine the equation for the differential trajectory [NIEBAUER, 1987],

$$\Delta x = \Delta x_0 + \Delta v_0 t \left(\frac{1 + \gamma t^2}{6} \right) + \frac{1}{2} (\Delta a) t^2, \qquad (4.3.6)$$

by fitting for Δx_0, Δv_0, and the experimentally interesting quantity Δa. In Eq. (4.3.6) the term proportional to γ represents a correction due to the known vertical gravity gradient γ. Since the zero crossings of the fringes can be timed to ± 100 ps, which is comparable to the rough estimate for Δt_{1-2} given above, it is reasonable to expect an interesting limit for Δa_{1-2} from such an experiment.

Niebauer et al. discuss a number of conventional effects which can produce an apparent nonzero value of Δg, and which have nothing to do with a possible non-Newtonian force. In the presence of the vertical gravity gradient due to the Earth, the nonzero values of Δx_0 and Δv_0 result in a greater acceleration for the object dropped first. In addition, there is a horizontal gravity gradient which acts differently on the two test masses, which are separated in the horizontal direction by 20.3 cm. Furthermore, the test bodies do not remain at the same location over the duration of the experiment (as is the case for most other types of composition-dependent experiments.) Because of this, the effects of gravity gradients, stray magnetic fields, etc., tend to accumulate over the trajectories of the falling bodies, making Galileo experiments more sensitive to these systematics than is the case for other experiments.

The final result of Niebauer et al. is

$$\Delta a(\text{U-Cu}) = +(0.13 \pm 0.50) \times 10^{-8} \, \text{m s}^{-2}, \qquad (4.3.7)$$

where the overall sign corresponds to U having a greater acceleration. For a coupling to B the results in Eq. (4.3.7) lead to the limit

$$\xi_B \lambda = (-1.6 \pm 6.0) \, \text{m}. \qquad (4.3.8)$$

In a subsequent dropping experiment, Kuroda and Mio (KM) [KURODA, 1989, 1990] have attempted to circumvent the problems that arise from having two separate gravimeters sitting side-by-side. They have designed a series of composite test masses in which two objects differing in composition are arranged so that their centers of mass coincide to within 0.3 mm initially.

The separations of the two test masses can then be monitored interferometrically, as in the experiment of Niebauer, et al.. KM estimate that with their configuration of test masses gravity gradients will produce a negligible acceleration difference of $\sim 0.1\,\mu$Gal. On the other hand, because their test masses are so close to each other, their mutual gravitational attraction has to be taken into account, and KM estimate that this effect is of the order $0.3\,\mu$Gal for all pairs. Other effects such as residual gas pressure, adsorbed gasses, and electrostatic effects can also lead to small acceleration differences between the two components of the composite mass. Their final results for three pairs are

$$
\begin{aligned}
\text{Al-Be}: \quad & \Delta a = (+0.43 \pm 1.23) \times 10^{-8}\,\mathrm{m\,s}^{-2}, \\
\text{Al-Cu}: \quad & \Delta a = (-0.13 \pm 0.78) \times 10^{-8}\,\mathrm{m\,s}^{-2}, \qquad (4.3.9)\\
\text{Al-C}: \quad & \Delta a = (-0.18 \pm 1.38) \times 10^{-8}\,\mathrm{m\,s}^{-2},
\end{aligned}
$$

where the dominant source of their (1σ) statistical error comes from unexplained motion of the release mechanism. KM [1990] have used the experimental results in Eq. (4.3.9) to set limits on the strengths ξ_B and ξ_I for couplings to B and I_z as a function of λ, in both the exponential and Yukawa models. Although the limits on ξ_B are insensitive to detailed models of the Earth (which is the source in this experiment), the limits on ξ_I do depend on the composition of the various layers of the Earth. KM use a 3-layer model of the Earth to compute the constraints on ξ_I as well as on ξ_B. For ξ_B the KM 1σ results correspond to $|\xi_B\lambda| \lesssim 9\,\mathrm{m}$ in the Yukawa model, which is comparable to the limits from Niebauer et al. [NIEBAUER, 1987] given in Eq. (4.3.8) above. KM have also analyzed their results in terms of the exponential model discussed in Section 2.5 above. They verify the observation made in [FISCHBACH, 1991] that for sources whose dimensions are large compared to λ, the constraints implied by the exponential and Yukawa models are quite similar. For further details of the KM experiment, including an analysis of various experimental error sources, the interested reader is referred to the discussions in [KURODA, 1990].

A third free-fall experiment has been carried out recently at CERN by a CERN-Pisa collaboration [CAVASINNI, 1986; CARUSOTTO, 1992]. In this version of the experiment the test masses are two half-disks of dissimilar materials (e.g., Be and Cu) which are joined to form a single rigid disk. The composite disk is dropped, and its angular acceleration $\dot{\omega}$ is then monitored interferometrically, by means of two corner-cube reflectors mounted on opposite sides of the disk. The anomalous free-fall acceleration difference Δa is then related to $\dot{\omega}$ via

$$
\dot{\omega} = \frac{4}{3\pi}\frac{\Delta a}{R}, \qquad (4.3.10)
$$

where R is the radius of the disk. Among the various free-fall experiments this utilizes the largest free-fall path, which is approximately $8\,\mathrm{m}$.

In the absence of any composition-dependent forces there should be no torque on the disk, since both halves of the disk would look the same to a gravitational field. The disk geometry was chosen to minimize the influence from local gravity gradients, and the half-disks were fabricated to have very nearly the same mass and the same moments of inertia, etc.

Although this experiment is clever and simple in principle, in practice it is subject to a number of sources of systematic error, as are all other experiments. Here the major source of error is precession of the disk about the direction of the angular momentum, which can simulate the signal due to an external field. This effect can be compensated for by monitoring the components of the disk's angular velocity in the plane of the disk, and this procedure was checked using a homogeneous Al disk, for which no effect was expected or seen. Their final results are

$$\frac{\Delta a}{a}(\text{Al-Cu}) = (2.9 \pm 7.2) \times 10^{-10}, \qquad (4.3.11)$$

$$\Delta a = (0.28 \pm 0.71) \times 10^{-8} \, \text{m}\,\text{s}^{-2}. \qquad (4.3.12)$$

These results are comparable in sensitivity to those of Niebauer et al. in Eq. (4.3.7), and to Kuroda and Mio in Eq. (4.3.9).

We conclude this discussion by noting that all of these free-fall experiments are sensitive to values of λ up to $\lambda \approx R_\oplus$, and until recently free-fall experiments provided the best constraints for some values of λ. Torsion balance experiments are only sensitive to the component of the non-Newtonian field $\vec{\mathcal{F}}$ perpendicular to the torsion fiber (i.e., $\mathcal{F}_\perp$ in Eq. (4.2.47)), whose sources for small λ are nearby local features (e.g., cliff, mountain, etc.). For λ comparable to $R_\oplus$, $\mathcal{F}_\perp \sim \mathcal{F}_\oplus \sin\beta$. For intermediate ranges ($10^3\,\text{m} < \lambda < 10^6\,\text{m}$), the deformation of the Earth to an oblate spheroid becomes important and suppresses the $\sin\beta$ contribution. For these distance scales, the sources of $\mathcal{F}_\perp$ become uncertain, and the older torsion balance experiments were unable to set meaningful constraints. However, the results of Gundlach et al. [1997] described in Section 4.2.5 now provide more stringent constraints than the free-fall experiments in the region of the ξ-λ plane where both are relevant.

Looking to the future, free-fall experiments using even longer vertical paths may be possible with the "Bremen" drop tower [DITTUS, 1991; MAZILU, 1996]. This will allow experiments to be carried out under conditions of weightlessness which will persist up to 4.74 s during a fall of 110 m.

4.4 Beam Balance Experiments

As we have noted in the previous section, the Galileo (free-fall) experiments are of particular interest because the entire Earth can be the source of any non-Newtonian effect. This feature is shared (in principle at least) by the beam-balance weighing experiment of Speake and Quinn (SQ) [SPEAKE, 1986, 1988], which we now describe. The idea behind this experiment, which was carried out at the Bureau International des Poids et Mesures (BIPM) in Paris, is that in the presence of a composition-dependent non-Newtonian force, test objects having the same inertial mass will appear to have different weights. Hence if the weights of two objects could be compared on a balance before a putative non-Newtonian force was "turned on," then the weights would no longer be in balance afterwards. Of course the problem is that if any non-Newtonian force in fact exists, then it acts all the time, and cannot simply be turned on and off. However, what can be done experimentally is to position movable laboratory sources of different composition beneath the test masses which are being compared, so that by changing the sources the strength of any non-Newtonian force can be modulated. Thus by comparing the balance condition for two dissimilar test masses, the background contribution from the Earth can be removed, and any new force arising from the sources thereby isolated.

In their experiment, SQ compared the weights of 2.3 kg test masses of Pb, C, and Cu in the presence of a 1782 kg source which was either Pb or brass. One of the novel features of this experiment is an equal-arm beam-balance utilizing flexure strip pivots instead of the usual knife edges. The balance is maintained in a horizontal position by a servo system, which senses a current through appropriate coils placed above two small permanent magnets mounted on the balance beam. The weight difference between the test masses can then be calculated by monitoring the current needed to keep the balance horizontal.

By comparing the weight difference ΔW for a given pair of test masses with the sources (i.e., attracting masses) in one position to that with the sources interchanged, the contributions from Newtonian gravity can be subtracted out, at least in principle. Any residual effect could then be interpreted as new physics, since the conventional gravitational interaction should not depend on the chemical composition of the source below each test mass. In practice, however, a number of conventional effects can simulate a composition-dependent signal, just as in the case of other experiments.

To start with, there is a contribution from gravity gradients which arises from the circumstance that the matter distribution in the lead and brass sources was not the same: Owing to the greater density of lead, the source was constructed by interleaving lead bricks with layers of plywood to produce an object with the same exterior dimensions and total mass as the brass source. However, since the mass distribution in the lead source was not entirely homogeneous, there is a small correction which was estimated numerically. The construction of the sources also led to a more subtle systematic influence which arose from thermal effects: The upper layers of the brass were in much better thermal contact with the floor than was the lead mass, due to the insulation provided by the plywood. As a consequence, the brass source was slightly colder than the lead, and hence the rate at which the test masses outgassed in the presence of each source was different, due to this temperature difference. This led to an apparent dependence of ΔW on the composition of the source mass just as would arise from a composition-dependent non-Newtonian force. To minimize this problem, a temperature-stabilized copper plate was eventually inserted between the source and the test masses which further reduced the thermal influence of the sources on the balance.

By examining the results of various measurements, SQ set an upper limit (1σ) of 12×10^{-11} N on the magnitude of any composition-dependent non-Newtonian force. This corresponds to an apparent mass uncertainty of 1.2×10^{-8} g in comparing the 2.3 kg test masses, and hence to a relative uncertainty in weighing of 5×10^{-12}. When translated into a limit on the strength of a coupling to I_z, their results give for the corresponding coupling ξ_I

$$\xi_I = (0.8 \pm 2.0) \times 10^{-2}. \tag{4.4.1}$$

The pioneering experiment of Speake and Quinn is important for a number of reasons: In the first place it utilizes a unique technology that is quite different from that of other experiments, and hence provides an independent check on those experiments. Secondly, it demonstrates the precision that can be obtained in mass comparisons by means of this balance, and hence is of great inherent interest from a metrological point of view. Finally it shows via Eq. (4.4.1) above that other technologies, particularly torsion balance experiments, are intrinsically more sensitive to the extent that they lead to significantly more stringent limits on ξ_I.

4.5 Floating-Ball Experiments

4.5.1 Introduction

In contrast to most of the experiments discussed in the previous sub-sections, which are based on previously utilized technology, the floating-ball experiments described in this section are completely new. For this reason, and because one of the experiments has suggested possible evidence for a non-Newtonian force, we discuss this class of experiments in some detail.

The ideas behind the floating-ball accelerometer date back to the work of Rózsa and Sélenyi [ROZSA, 1931], but the first practical realization of such a device was due to Thieberger [1987A]. Subsequently a second version of such a differential accelerometer was developed by Bizzeti and coworkers [BIZZETI, 1989], and a third design for such an accelerometer has been proposed by Davisson [DAVISSON, PC]. To understand the principle behind these accelerometers, consider the forces acting on a hollow Cu sphere of mass M submerged in water, as in Thieberger's experiment (see Fig. 4.15). If Newtonian gravity were the only force acting on the sphere (and on the surrounding water), then by virtue of Archimedes' principle the sphere would be buoyed up by a force equal to the weight of the water displaced. Since the gravitational force $M\vec{g}$ and the opposing buoyant force $\vec{F}_b$ act along the same line, the density $\rho(\text{Cu})$ of the sphere can be adjusted to exactly equal that of the displaced water, in which case $\vec{F}_b + M\vec{g} = 0$ and the sphere would float in neutral equilibrium. Under these conditions, if the sphere starts out at rest, then it will remain at rest in the water.

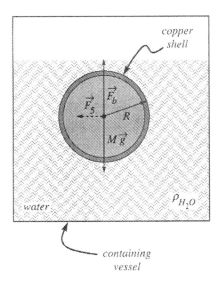

Figure 4.15: Schematic representation of Thieberger's floating-ball experiment.

Suppose that there exists in addition to gravity a new non-Newtonian *composition-dependent* intermediate-range force $\vec{F}_5$, as shown in Fig. 4.15. The fact that $\vec{F}_5$ is a force of finite range is crucial to this search for composition-dependent forces, since it prevents $\vec{F}_5$ and the Newtonian force $M\vec{g}$ from being parallel in general. This is because $\vec{g}$ arises from all the matter in the Earth (and includes as well the effects of the Earth's rotation), whereas $\vec{F}_5$ depends only on the "local" (i.e., nearby) matter distribution. [In some special circumstances $\vec{F}_5$ and $M\vec{g}$ can in fact be parallel: This could be the case for an experiment carried out over a frozen lake, where the surface of the ice (which determines $\vec{F}_5$) would itself be determined by $\vec{g}$.] If $\vec{F}_5$ and $M\vec{g}$ are not parallel, then the net force on the Cu shell is not in general parallel to that on the water it displaces, because $\vec{F}_5(\text{Cu}) \neq \vec{F}_5(\text{water})$. Since it is impossible to align two different *vectors* [$\vec{F}_{net}(Cu)$ and $\vec{F}_{net}(water)$] by adjusting a single *scalar* [$\rho(Cu)$], it follows that there will be a net unbalanced force $\Delta F = \left| \vec{F}_{net}(Cu) - \vec{F}_{net}(water) \right|$ acting on the Cu sphere. This force can then be determined by measuring the terminal velocity v of the moving sphere (of radius R) using Stokes' law [LANGLOIS, 1964]

$$\Delta F \cong 6\pi\eta Rv \left(1 + \frac{3}{8}\Re \right) = 6\pi\eta Rv + \frac{9}{4}\pi\rho_{water}R^2v^2, \qquad (4.5.1)$$

$$\Re = \frac{\rho_{water}vR}{\eta}, \qquad (4.5.2)$$

where η is the viscosity of the water, ρ is its density, and $\Re$ is the Reynolds number.

To derive the relation between ΔF and the fields $\vec{g}$ and $\vec{\mathcal{F}}$, we consider a simplified geometry in which the matter sources are the Earth and an idealized vertical cliff. If the normal to the Earth's surface points in the $+z$-direction, and the normal to the cliff face points in the $+y$-direction, then the dominant fields acting on the water and the Cu sphere in Thieberger's experiment are g_z, $\mathcal{F}_z$, g_y, and $\mathcal{F}_y$. Let N_1 ($1 \equiv$ Cu) denote the number of Cu atoms in the sphere, and N_2 ($2 \equiv$ water) denote the number of water molecules displaced by the sphere. The condition for equilibrium in the z-direction (in the approximation of uniform fields) is that the net force on the spherical masses 1 and 2 be the same. This gives

$$N_1\mu_1 g_z + q_1 q_S N_1\mu_1 \mathcal{F}_z = N_2\mu_2 g_z + q_2 q_S N_2\mu_2 \mathcal{F}_z, \qquad (4.5.3)$$

where $N_1\mu_1 = M_1$, etc.. The variables that can be controlled to achieve buoyancy are N_1 and N_2, which then determine the respective densities of the samples, given that they have the same overall volume. We find from Eq. (4.5.3)

$$\frac{N_2}{N_1} = \frac{\mu_1(g_z + q_1 q_S \mathcal{F}_z)}{\mu_2(g_z + q_2 q_S \mathcal{F}_z)}, \qquad (4.5.4)$$

which reduces to the familiar result $N_1\mu_1 = N_2\mu_2$ (i.e., $M_1 = M_2$) when $\mathcal{F}_z = 0$. However, since $\mathcal{F}_z/g_z \neq \mathcal{F}_y/g_y$ in general, the value of N_2/N_1 which makes the sphere buoyant in the z-direction will lead to an unbalanced force $\Delta F_y = F_y^{(1)} - F_y^{(2)}$ in the y-direction, where the superscripts refer to the ball and water as before. This can be calculated from Eq. (4.5.3) in an obvious way, by replacing g_z and $\mathcal{F}_z$ by g_y and $\mathcal{F}_y$ respectively:

$$\Delta F_y \cong M g_z q_S \Delta q_{1-2} \frac{[\mathcal{F}_y - g_y(\mathcal{F}_z/g_z)]}{[g_z + q_S q_2 \mathcal{F}_z]}, \qquad (4.5.5)$$

where M is the mass of the sphere. We see that, as expected, ΔF_y vanishes when $\Delta q_{1\text{-}2} = 0$, and also when

$$\frac{\mathcal{F}_y}{g_y} = \frac{\mathcal{F}_z}{g_z}, \qquad (4.5.6)$$

which is the condition that the gravitational and non-Newtonian equipotentials coincide. For an experiment conducted in the vicinity of a cliff, $\mathcal{F}_y \approx \mathcal{F}_z$ but $g_z \gg g_y$ so that Eq. (4.5.6) will not be satisfied. Under these conditions ΔF_y is given by [THIEBERGER, 1987A]

$$\Delta F_y \cong M q_S \Delta q_{1-2} \mathcal{F}_y. \qquad (4.5.7)$$

Combining Eqs. (4.5.1) and (4.5.7), we see that a measurement of the equilibrium velocity v leads to a determination of $\mathcal{F}_y$ and ultimately to a value for $\xi\lambda$, if we assume the typical Yukawa model of $\vec{\mathcal{F}}$.

4.5.2 The Thieberger Palisades Experiment

Although the general formalism leading up to Eq. (4.5.7) applies to all three of the floating-ball experiments that have been proposed to date, there are substantial differences among these experiments which have to do with such questions as how the spheres are made buoyant. In Thieberger's experiment a 4.925 kg Cu sphere with a diameter of 21.11 cm was floated in water cooled to $T \approx 4°C$, which is the temperature at which the density ρ_{water} is maximum. It follows from the fact that $\partial\rho_{water}/\partial T = 0$ at $T = 3.98°C$ that at this temperature the local water density is less sensitive to small temperature fluctuations. Since a variation in the local density can produce an unbalanced force on the sphere which could simulate the effect of an external fifth force, it is evidently important to minimize the sensitivity to temperature gradients. It should be noted that it is not as essential that T be fixed exactly at $T = 3.98°C$, as it is that the temperature be *uniform* over the entire volume of water. The actual temperature was maintained at $T = (4.0 \pm 0.2)°C$, and temperature differences across the tank were less than $5 \times 10^{-3}°C$. To guarantee that the Cu sphere (which has fixed dimensions) will float in the water at any T near 4°C (and thus at any water density near its maximum), the sphere in Thieberger's experiment was outfitted with a small pin which protruded from the water by a variable amount, and which thus served to "fine tune" the buoyancy condition. The sphere also incorporated several internal counterweights (whose total mass was ~ 200 g) which could be adjusted to balance the sphere so that its center of mass coincided with that of the displaced water to within 0.002 cm. This is sufficient to ensure that any couplings to gravity gradients would be small enough to be of no concern. To reduce any chemical reactions between the water and the Cu in the sphere, Thieberger used distilled water from which the dissolved O_2 was removed by exchange with N_2.

In addition to the problems that can arise from thermal effects, another source of possible spurious signals for a non-Newtonian force is electromagnetic effects. For example, ferromagnetic impurities in the Cu sphere could couple to the Earth's magnetic field and generate a force which might simulate the effect expected from a non-Newtonian force. To test for this possibility, and to calibrate his system, Thieberger applied a known non-uniform magnetic field to the apparatus. The gradient of such a field exerts a different force on the Cu and the water it displaces, owing to the different diamagnetic constants for Cu and water. Thieberger demonstrated that the measured terminal velocity of the Cu sphere agreed quite well with the values expected from Eq. (4.5.1), when the known electromagnetic contribution ΔF_{em} was used. From these measurements Thieberger estimated that a magnetic gradient of $10\,\mathrm{Gauss\,m^{-1}}$ would be required to produce the signal that he reported as possible evidence for a non-Newtonian force (see below). In fact a μ-metal shield was placed around the apparatus to exclude the Earth's magnetic field, and measurements inside the shield indicated that the residual field was less than $0.1\,\mathrm{Gauss}$. As we discuss below, these checks are important in Thieberger's case, since his is one of the few (remaining) experiments to claim a possible signal for a non-Newtonian force.

Thieberger carried out his experiment at a site atop the Palisades cliff in New Jersey $\sim 5\,\mathrm{m}$ from the edge [THIEBERGER, 1987A,B]. The cliff rises to a height of $161\,\mathrm{m}$ from the Hudson river below, and its face extends approximately north–south. The actual data collection in Thieberger's experiment involved photographing the position of the sphere with an automatic television camera, from which the horizontal coordinates $x(t)$ and $y(t)$ of the sphere could be determined. Thieberger found that the sphere exhibited a constant drift of $(4.7 \pm 0.2)\,\mathrm{mm\,hr^{-1}}$ in the y-direction, which is the direction approximately normal to the face of the cliff. It is important to bear in mind that when describing the source of a hypothetical finite-range force, the direction of the normal at some geophysical site will depend on the presumed range λ, which determines what matter in the (inhomogeneous) cliff can actually contribute to the experiment. In fact if Thieberger's claimed effect were correct, then we could constrain λ by requiring that both the direction and magnitude of the calculated acceleration $\vec{a}$ of the sphere agree with observations. We note in passing that there is a Coriolis correction that must be applied to Thieberger's experiment before $\hat{a}$ can be determined: Since the velocity $v = |\vec{v}|$ in Eq. (4.5.1) is different from zero, the sphere will experience an additional acceleration $\Delta \vec{a}_{Coriolis}$ given by [THIEBERGER, 1987B],

$$\Delta \vec{a}_{Coriolis} = -\hat{n} \times [(2\vec{v} \times \vec{\omega}) \times \hat{n}], \qquad (4.5.8)$$

where $\hat{n}$ is the unit vector along the local vertical, and $\vec{\omega}$ is the angular velocity of the Earth.

By combining Eq. (4.5.1) with his measured values for the x- and y-velocity components, Thieberger was able to infer the unbalanced force ΔF and the horizontal acceleration $|\vec{a}|$ of the sphere. He found

$$v_x = \dot{x}(t) = (0.6 \pm 0.2)\,\mathrm{mm\,hr^{-1}}, \qquad (4.5.9a)$$
$$v_y = \dot{y}(t) = (4.7 \pm 0.2)\,\mathrm{mm\,hr^{-1}}, \qquad (4.5.9b)$$

$$|\Delta \vec{F}| = (4.2 \pm 0.6) \, \text{dyne}, \qquad (4.5.9c)$$

$$|\Delta \vec{a}| = (8.5 \pm 1.3) \times 10^{-8} \, \text{cm s}^{-2}. \qquad (4.5.9d)$$

The errors in determining $|\Delta \vec{F}|$ and $|\Delta \vec{a}|$ arise from linearly combining the errors in $v_{x,y}$, estimated to be 5%, and an error of 10% in the applicability of Stoke's law in Eq. (4.5.1). Taken at face value, the results in Eqs. (4.5.9) suggest a 7σ signal for a non-Newtonian composition-dependent force. If these results are interpreted in terms of the single-component Yukawa potential of Eq. (2.1.6) with $Q = B$, then for λ much smaller than the cliff height,

$$\xi_B \lambda = +(1.2 \pm 0.4) \, \text{m}. \qquad (4.5.10)$$

Note that the error has increased in going from Eq. (4.5.9) to Eq. (4.5.10) because of the uncertainties associated with Thieberger's model of the Palisades cliff [this modeling is necessary to obtain the result in Eq. (4.5.10)].

For an experiment such as Thieberger's which claims a positive result, additional checks are obviously called for to ensure that the signal for a non-Newtonian force was not due to some conventional effect. One of the most important of these checks was a run Thieberger made with the entire apparatus rotated by 90° relative to its initial orientation. If the motion of the sphere was due to some imperfection in the apparatus (e.g., one wall being warmer than the others), then the direction of motion of the sphere would have been expected to remain fixed relative to the *apparatus*. In fact what Thieberger observed was that the direction of motion remained fixed relative to the *cliff*. This suggests that whatever the cause of the motion, it probably had something to do with the local environment, a conclusion which is obviously consistent with the presence of a new force. In another test Thieberger dropped the east side of his instrument by 4.6 mm, which tilts his apparatus by more than ten times the amount that might have been the case for the rest of the experiment. This test is important because in some experiments (e.g., torsion-balance experiments) the effect of a tilt could be to mimic an external non-Newtonian force. Thieberger detected no discernible sensitivity to tilt. Other tests are described in more detail in [THIEBERGER, 1987A,B].

We note in passing that one of the advantages of floating-ball accelerometers is that they are relatively portable. In fact Thieberger was able to capitalize on this by running at Brookhaven National Laboratory, using the beam dump at the Alternating Gradient Synchrotron (AGS) as a source.

Historically the Thieberger experiment was the first completed in the period following the reanalysis of the Eötvös experiment [FISCHBACH, 1986A], and as such was also the first experiment to apparently support the suggestion of a "fifth force." The results in Eq. (4.5.10) were also in qualitative agreement with the values of $\xi_B \cong -\alpha$ and λ extracted by Stacey et al. and quoted in [FISCHBACH, 1986A]:

$$\xi_B \cong 0.01, \tag{4.5.11a}$$

$$\lambda = (200 \pm 50)\,\text{m}, \tag{4.5.11b}$$

$$\xi_B \lambda \cong (2.0 \pm 0.5)\,\text{m}. \tag{4.5.11c}$$

Thieberger's experiment was quickly followed by the first of the "Eöt-Wash" torsion balance experiments [STUBBS, 1987], which saw no evidence for any non-Newtonian effects. From our present perspective the agreement between the results in Eqs. (4.5.10) and (4.5.11) is fortuitous, since the Stacey results were subsequently withdrawn [TUCK, PC]. Although this does not necessarily imply that Thieberger's results are wrong, the fact that the value of $\xi\lambda$ in Eq. (4.5.11c) is much larger than that allowed by other results is cause for concern. For example, the limits on $\xi_B\lambda$ inferred from torsion balance experiments of the Eöt-Wash collaboration [ADELBERGER, 1990, 1991C; SU, 1994] suggest that $\xi_B\lambda < 5 \times 10^{-4}\,\text{m}$ (2σ) for $10\,\text{m} < \lambda < 200\,\text{m}$. This represents a factor of 2400 in relative magnitude between Thieberger's central value and the more restrictive Eöt-Wash limits.

Several attempts to attribute Thieberger's results to thermal effects have thus far proven inconclusive [KIM, 1987; MARIS, 1988; KEYSER, 1989; THIEBERGER, 1988, 1989]. In principle, the question of whether Thieberger saw a genuine effect can only be determined by repeating this experiment. It must be emphasized, however, that no presently known model of non-Newtonian gravity is able to reconcile an effect as large as that reported by Thieberger, with the much more stringent limits from the modern torsion balance experiments.

4.5.3   The Bizzeti Vallambrosa Experiment

Bizzeti et al. [BIZZETI, 1989, 1990] have developed an alternative way of arranging for the test mass to be buoyant, which preserves the spherical symmetry of the floating object. Their test mass is a solid sphere of radius $R = 5\,\text{cm}$, composed mostly of NYLON 12, which is a hard plastic whose density is very nearly equal to that of the saline solution in which it floats. This solution is obtained by dissolving salts such as KBr and $MnSO_4$ in water, and varying the concentration of the salt so as to achieve a low density gradient in the vertical direction. This ensures the stability of the sphere in the vertical direction, and at the same time prevents thermal convection, which is one of the major sources of concern in such an experiment. In practice, the sphere is initially placed at the bottom of a glass vessel, and then equally thick layers of fluid (of different density) are introduced in such a way as to establish the needed gradient. This gradient (with the denser liquid at the bottom) decreased exponentially with time, with a time constant $\tau \cong 55$ days. This demonstrates that a usable density gradient can be maintained over a sufficiently long period to allow the necessary measurements to take place.

Bizzeti et al. carried out their measurements in Vallambrosa (which is near Florence, Italy), at a site on the side of a mountain 1032 m above sea level. The large horizontal component of any non-Newtonian force expected from the Vallambrosa site translates into a useful constraint on $|\sum \alpha_i \lambda_i|$ for ranges up to $\lambda \cong 10^4$ m. Bizzeti et al. find no evidence for motion of the sphere such as would be expected from an external non-Newtonian force. In their original published paper [BIZZETI, 1989], a limit is set on the horizontal velocity $\vec{v}$ of their sphere, $|\vec{v}| < 10 \, \mu\text{m} \, \text{hr}^{-1}$, which corresponds to an anomalous horizontal acceleration $|\Delta \vec{a}| < 2.4 \times 10^{-9}$ Gal from Eq. (4.5.5). The sensitivity of this experiment is reduced somewhat by virtue of the fact that for the sphere and the solution in which it floats, Δq_5 is very small for almost any choice of the specific charge $q_5(\theta_5)$ in Eq. (2.2.1). Nonetheless their experiment sets limits on $|\sum \alpha_i \lambda_i|$ which are in conflict with those of Thieberger [1987A,B]. If $q_5 = B/\mu$, for example, then Bizzeti et al. find $|\alpha \lambda| < 0.30$ m, whereas Thieberger's result (at $\lambda \sim 1$ km) is $|\alpha \lambda| \cong (3 \pm 1)$ m. As always, it is necessary to emphasize that the relative sensitivities of these experiments depend crucially on the underlying theoretical model, so that care must be taken not to read into the existing results more than can be justified theoretically.

Following the publication of their original results, Bizzeti et al. carried out a number of additional tests [BIZZETI, 1990] which, along with those published earlier, rule out various conventional explanations for their null result. In an experiment utilizing a floating-ball technology, a major source of concern is that a ball might get "trapped" in its initial location due to some combination of convective and/or gravity gradient effects. To demonstrate that this was not the case in their experiment, Bizzeti et al. performed the following tests:

a) To check the validity of Stokes' law, a paramagnetic solution containing $MnSO_4$ was used, and an external magnetic field was applied to the sphere. Since the solution was chosen to have a different magnetic susceptibility from that of the sphere, the effect of the field was to exert a known net force on the sphere which could then be used to check Stokes' law, as Thieberger had also done. Bizzeti et al. then verified that the terminal velocity v in Eq. (4.5.1) was proportional to the calculated force difference ΔF as expected.

b) As was already noted, one of the advantages of the floating-ball geometry is that the spherical symmetry of the test masses (i.e., the sphere and the fluid it displaces) makes this apparatus relatively insensitive to gravity gradients. In actual practice plastics like NYLON 12 do not in general have a spatially constant density, and neither does the fluid in Bizzeti's case. For this reason the vertical coordinates of the centers of mass of the solid and fluid (z_s and z_f respectively) do not coincide, and this can lead to a horizontal force in the presence of an appropriate gravity gradient. The components ΔF_x and ΔF_y of this force are given by

$$\Delta F_x \cong M \frac{\partial g_x}{\partial z} \Delta z = M \frac{\partial g_x}{\partial z} (z_s - z_f), \tag{4.5.12a}$$

$$\Delta F_y \cong M \frac{\partial g_y}{\partial z} \Delta z = M \frac{\partial g_y}{\partial z} (z_s - z_f), \tag{4.5.12b}$$

where M is the mass of the sphere (or of the displaced fluid), and $g_{x,y}$ are the $x-$ and $y-$components of the gravitational acceleration field due to the mountain. Bizzeti et al. estimated the components of the gravity gradient by directly measuring $\vec{g}$ using a LaCoste-Romberg gravimeter. In addition, they estimated $(z_s - z_f)$ using Thieberger's oscillation method [THIEBERGER, 1987A]. In a region of irregular topography such as Vallambrosa, one expects the gravity gradients to be relatively large and, not surprisingly, this is what Bizzeti et al. find

$$\begin{aligned}
\frac{\partial g_x}{\partial z} = \frac{\partial g_z}{\partial x} &= (-12.4 \pm 0.7)\,\mu\mathrm{Gal\,cm}^{-1}, \\
\frac{\partial g_y}{\partial z} = \frac{\partial g_z}{\partial y} &= (+21.9 \pm 0.5)\,\mu\mathrm{Gal\,cm}^{-1}.
\end{aligned} \tag{4.5.13}$$

We note in passing that since $\vec{g} = -\vec{\nabla}\phi$, where ϕ is the gravitational potential, it follows that

$$\frac{\partial g_x}{\partial z} = -\frac{\partial^2 \phi}{\partial x \partial z} \quad \text{and} \quad \frac{\partial g_y}{\partial z} = -\frac{\partial^2 \phi}{\partial y \partial z}, \tag{4.5.14}$$

and hence the partial derivatives in Eq. (4.5.13) above are equal as indicated. Thus even though the quantities which are directly needed are $\partial g_x/\partial z$ and $\partial g_y/\partial z$, the actual measurements are of $\partial g_z/\partial x$ and $\partial g_z/\partial y$ which are obtained by determining the vertical component of $\vec{g}$ in a horizontal region surrounding the experimental site. When Bizzeti et al. combine the results of Eq. (4.5.13) with their estimate of $|z_s - z_f| < 32.5\,\mu\mathrm{m}$, they find that the maximum acceleration $\Delta \vec{a}_{\mathrm{grad}}$ that can arise from gravity gradients is

$$|\Delta \vec{a}_{\mathrm{grad}}| < 0.8\,\mathrm{nGal} = 0.8 \times 10^{-9}\,\mathrm{cm\,s}^{-2}. \tag{4.5.15}$$

Since this is substantially smaller than their measured upper limit for a non-Newtonian force, $|\Delta \vec{a}| < 2.4\,\mathrm{nGal}$, it follows that that an anomalous non-Newtonian acceleration at the level of 2.4 nGal could not be "masked" by a gravity-gradient force acting in the opposite direction.

4.5.4 The Davisson Proposal

We conclude this section by describing the design for a third floating-ball experiment which has been proposed by Davisson [PC]. In this experiment a hollow sphere of the ceramic MACOR is machined to have a net density slightly *greater* than that of water at 4°C. When this sphere is placed in a large water-filled tank which is itself spherical, it will sink immediately to the bottom, coming to rest at a point below the center of the tank. By applying pressure to the water via a transducer attached to the tank, the density of the water can be made to increase slightly without at the same time affecting the MACOR sphere, which is much more rigid. When the density of the water is greater than that of the sphere, the sphere will rise and can be brought to rest at the center of the tank. The Davisson apparatus thus behaves as an "inverse Cartesian diver," so named to contrast its behavior with that of the familiar Cartesian diver which *sinks* when the external pressure is increased [SUTTON, 1938]. Once positioned at the center of the tank, the MACOR sphere will remain there in the absence of non-Newtonian forces, as discussed above.

The position of the sphere can then be monitored by a camera, as in the experiments of Thieberger and Bizzeti et al.. The design of Davisson's apparatus has the nice feature that it maximizes spherical symmetry of the apparatus (compared to the experiments of Thieberger and Bizzeti et al.), and hence minimizes the sensitivity of his experiment to gravity gradients.* Such an experiment would be sensitive to the charge difference Δq between the water and MACOR, which for most values of the mixing angle θ_5 in Eq. (2.1.1) is somewhere in between that expected for Cu-H_2O (Thieberger) or nylon-H_2O solution (Bizzeti et al.). Unfortunately the elegance of the Davisson design has not been demonstrated in a working model, since his experiment has not actually been carried to completion.

4.6 Experiments Using Gravity-Wave Detectors

As we noted in Section 3.10, the availability of sensitive gravity-wave detectors opens the possibility for using these detectors to search for deviations from the predictions of Newtonian gravity. Previously we described experiments to test the inverse-square law, and in the present section we consider the possibility of using gravity-wave detectors to search for composition-dependent forces.

---

* Another advantage of Davisson's design is that the sphere can be easily repositioned at the center of the tank by first releasing the pressure being applied by the transducer, which drops the sphere to the bottom, and then increasing it to move the sphere up.

Following Akasaka et al. [AKASAKA, 1989], we consider a schematic arrangement similar to that shown in Fig. 3.14, where the Pb is replaced by two samples (A and B) of different composition but with the same mass. If Newtonian gravity is correct, then the gravitational force on a detector depends only on the masses M_A and M_B of the spherical samples and on their respective distances from the detector. Each half-cycle the positions of A and B are interchanged, but the response of the detector would be the same as if both samples were A or both were B. It follows that in each complete rotor rotation, the detector experiences two maxima in the Newtonian force, and hence a rotor frequency ω induces a detector signal at 2ω. By contrast if A and B coupled to the detector via an additional non-Newtonian force, then a rotor frequency ω would give rise to a detector signal which was also at ω. Hence the signal for a non-Newtonian force would be a detector signal at the fundamental frequency ω of the rotor.

As in the case of the tests of the inverse-square law, it is important to emphasize that the gravity-wave detector is not being used to look for radiation from a new composition-dependent interaction. Rather, the purpose of the detector is merely to sense the changing ultra-weak force due to the putative new interaction. The purpose in having the rotor driven at ω is twofold: In the first place ω can be matched to the resonant frequency of the detector and, secondly, a time-varying field eliminates the influences from any static background.

Akasaka et al. [AKASAKA, 1989] describe two experiments (called I and II respectively) using different arrangements of sources and detectors. In experiment I, cylindrical 7.0 kg test masses of stainless steel and Pb are embedded in an aluminum rotor, which is driven at 31.6 Hz to produce the signal. The detector consists of two antennas of different composition (Al and brass), arranged perpendicular to each other, and located approximately 39 cm from the rotor. Early test results indicated that this experiment could set a limit on $|\xi_I|$ at the 10^{-2} level, which is interesting but not yet competitive with the results from torsion balance experiments.

In their experiment II, the rotor consisted of cylindrical test masses, embedded in an aluminum frame, each having a mass of 8.36 kg. The masses two of which were Zn and two of Sn—were arranged on the rotor in such a way that a rotor frequency of 30 Hz would produce a 60 Hz signal (the resonant frequency of the detector) for a hypothetical composition-dependent force, and a 120 Hz signal from conventional Newtonian gravity. As in experiment I, the detector was a composite-type torsional antenna, but in this arrangement the upper mass was polyethylene and the lower mass was an aluminum alloy. By arranging for the upper and lower masses to have the same orientation, the torsional mode of the detector can be made insensitive to the Newtonian contribution. The authors estimate that their experiment could set a 1σ limit, $|\xi_I| < 3 \times 10^{-4}$ in a 3 hour run. Unfortunately, neither of these experiments has obtained more recent results, so the ultimate capability of this technology has not yet been reached.

A second proposed experiment would employ the CERN gravity-wave detector [Astone, 1991], which we described in Section 3.10. In principle this detector can be used to search either for deviations from the inverse-square law or as a probe for a new composition-dependent force. As noted in Section 3.10, an actual test for composition-dependent forces has not been carried out as of this writing.

4.7 Multipole Radiation from Massive Fields

In discussing modern-day Eötvös experiments in the previous sections, we have noted the efforts that these experiments make to suppress the backgrounds from gravitational and electromagnetic effects. For example, most experimentalists arrange for the test masses whose accelerations are being compared to have the same external shapes and masses. (In the floating-ball experiments described in Section 4.5, both of these objectives are achieved automatically.) Another example of a system in which gravitational effects may be suppressed is the radiation of energy by a binary pulsar system. It is well known that the leading multipole for gravitational radiation is quadrupole, whereas it is monopole or dipole for scalar or vector fields respectively [Price, 1972a,b; Krause, 1994]. Since each successive multipole order is suppressed by a factor of order d/λ, where d is the characteristic dimension of the system and λ is the wavelength of the emitted radiation, emission of scalar or vector radiation may compete favorably with gravitational radiation in some systems. An example of such a system is the Hulse-Taylor pulsar PSR 1913+16, which provides the strongest evidence to date for the existence of gravitational radiation [Taylor, 1989]. In principle we could attribute any discrepancy between theory (i.e., General Relativity) and experiment to radiation of some hitherto unknown field. Hence a study of the radiation (gravitational and otherwise) arising from the orbital motion of the objects in a binary system can constrain the parameters which describe the coupling of a new field to matter [Li, 1986; Bertotti, 1991; Krause, 1994].

Our discussion and conventions follow [Krause, 1994], which also contains references to earlier related work. Consider first the radiation of the quanta from a massive vector field, which is described by the Maxwell-Proca equations [Krause, 1994]

$$\vec{\nabla} \cdot \vec{E} = 4\pi f_V \rho - \mu_5^2 A^0, \qquad (4.7.1a)$$

$$\vec{\nabla} \cdot \vec{B} = 0, \qquad (4.7.1b)$$

$$\vec{\nabla} \times \vec{E} = -\frac{1}{c}\frac{\partial \vec{B}}{\partial t}, \tag{4.7.1c}$$

$$\vec{\nabla} \times \vec{B} = \frac{4\pi f_V}{c}\vec{J} + \frac{1}{c}\frac{\partial \vec{E}}{\partial t} - \mu_5^2 \vec{A}. \tag{4.7.1d}$$

Here the vector field is described by a 4-vector $(\vec{A}, A^0)$ with

$$\vec{E} = -\frac{1}{c}\frac{\partial \vec{A}}{\partial t} - \vec{\nabla}A^0, \qquad \vec{B} = \vec{\nabla} \times \vec{A}. \tag{4.7.2}$$

The source of the field (whose mass is $\mu_5\hbar/c$) is the 4-vector $(\vec{J}, \rho)$, and the coupling strength to matter is f_V. We note from the Maxwell-Proca equations that when $\mu_5 \neq 0$, the potentials $\vec{A}$ and A^0 are physically observable, since they are directly related to $\vec{E}, \vec{B}, \vec{J}$, and ρ, which are measurable quantities. The derivation of the radiation fields in the massive case then parallels that in the massless case (electrodynamics), and for a periodic source we find for the time-averaged energy flow per unit solid angle

$$\left\langle \frac{d\dot{E}}{d\Omega} \right\rangle = \frac{1}{2\pi c}\sum_{n>n_0}\left\{\left(\frac{n^2\omega_0^2}{c^2}\right)\cdot\left[1 - \left(\frac{n_0}{n}\right)^2\right]^{1/2} \otimes\right.$$
$$\left. \left[|\hat{r} \times \vec{I}_n|^2 + \left(\frac{n_0}{n}\right)^2 |\hat{r} \cdot \vec{I}_n|^2\right]\right\}. \tag{4.7.3}$$

In Eq. (4.7.3) $\omega_0 \equiv 2\pi/T$ is the characteristic frequency of the system, expressed in terms of the period T, and $n_0 = \mu_5 c/\omega_0$. $\vec{I}_n$ is the source integral defined by

$$\vec{I}_n = f_V \int d^3x' e^{-ik_n\hat{r}\cdot\vec{x}'}\vec{J}_n(\vec{t}'), \tag{4.7.4}$$

where

$$k_n = \frac{n\omega_0}{c}\left[1 - \left(\frac{n_0}{n}\right)^2\right]^{1/2}, \tag{4.7.5}$$

$$\vec{J}(\vec{x}, t) = \sum_{n=-\infty}^{\infty}\vec{J}_n(\vec{x})e^{-in\omega_0 t}. \tag{4.7.6}$$

The presence of the factor $[1 - (n_0/n)^2]^{1/2}$ in Eqs. (4.7.3) and (4.7.5) has a simple interpretation: The minimum energy that a quantum can carry off corresponds to its rest mass energy, and hence ω_0 must be such that $n\omega_0 > \mu_5 c$ (i.e., $n_0 < n$) for radiation to take place. When this condition is not met, $\vec{I}_n$ is exponentially damped, which is what we expect.

Radiation of massive scalar quanta can be treated in a similar manner. In the metric conventions of [KRAUSE, 1994] a scalar field $\Phi(\vec{x}, t)$ satisfies the equation

$$\left[-\nabla^2 + \frac{\partial^2}{c^2 \partial t^2} + \mu_5^2 \right] \Phi(\vec{x}, t) = 4\pi f_S \rho(\vec{x}, t), \qquad (4.7.7)$$

where $\rho(\vec{x}, t)$ is the source of Φ, and $4\pi f_S$ is the scalar coupling constant. (The factor of 4π is purely conventional.) For a periodic source the time-averaged energy flow per unit solid angle is then given by

$$\left\langle \frac{d\dot{E}}{d\Omega} \right\rangle = \sum_{n > n_0} \frac{n^2 \omega_0^2}{2\pi c} \left[1 - \left(\frac{n_0}{n} \right)^2 \right]^{1/2} |I_n|^2, \qquad (4.7.8)$$

$$I_n = f_S \int d^3 x' e^{-i k_n \hat{r} \cdot \vec{x}'} \rho_n(\vec{x}'). \qquad (4.7.9)$$

I_n and ρ_n in Eq. (4.7.9) are the analogs of $\vec{I}_n$ and $\vec{J}_n$ in Eq. (4.7.4).

The expressions for $\langle d\dot{E}/d\Omega \rangle$ for the vector and scalar cases in Eqs. (4.7.3) and (4.7.8) respectively are exact, but somewhat cumbersome to use. As in the case of massless electrodynamics, it is convenient to carry out a multipole expansion of the radiation fields. As noted previously, the leading multipoles for scalar and vector fields are monopole and dipole respectively. However, if we assume that the scalar charge is conserved, then the leading scalar multipole is also dipole. In the dipole approximation $\langle d\dot{E}/d\Omega \rangle$ depends on the Fourier components $\vec{p}_n$ of the dipole moment $\vec{p}$. For a system of two bodies orbiting under the influence of an inverse-square force law, the $\vec{p}_n$ are proportional to

$$\Delta \left(\frac{Q}{m} \right) = \frac{Q_p}{m_p} - \frac{Q_c}{m_c}, \qquad (4.7.10)$$

where $Q_p (Q_c)$ is the charge of the pulsar (companion), and m_p (m_c) is the corresponding mass. The factor $\Delta(Q/m)$ is the same composition-dependent factor that arises in the various laboratory experiments described earlier in this chapter. Owing to the fact that the $\vec{p}_n$ (and hence $\langle d\dot{E}/d\Omega \rangle$) depend on $\Delta(Q/m)$, the predicted rate of energy loss due to the emission of radiation from some new field depends on the nature of the companion, given that the pulsar is presumed to be a rotating neutron star. The three most plausible candidates for the companion are another neutron star, a white dwarf, or a black hole, and since m_p and m_c are known, $\Delta(Q/m)$ can be calculated for any hypothesized charge Q.

Using the expressions for $\langle d\dot{E}/d\Omega \rangle$ in Eq. (4.7.3) and (4.7.8), we can find the integrated time-averaged radiated power

$$\langle \dot{E} \rangle = \int \langle d\dot{E}/d\Omega \rangle d\Omega, \qquad (4.7.11)$$

due to the orbital motion of the pulsar and its companion about their common center of mass. As energy is radiated (through gravitational or any other radiation), the orbital period P_b of the binary system decreases according to the formula

$$\frac{\dot{P}_b}{P_b} = -\frac{3}{2}\frac{\langle \dot{E}_{tot} \rangle}{E_{tot}}, \tag{4.7.12}$$

where E_{tot} is the total energy of the system. The interesting experimental quantity is δ_b, which measures the discrepancy between the value of $\dot{P}_b$ predicted by General Relativity (GR) and the experimental value [TAYLOR, 1993]

$$\frac{\dot{P}_b^{GR}}{\dot{P}_b^{expt}} \equiv 1 - \delta_b = 1 - (0.0032 \pm 0.0035). \tag{4.7.13}$$

Since $\delta_b \neq 0$ could be an indication of the emission of nongravitational radiation, we can use Eq. (4.7.13) to set limits on the coupling of new scalar or vector fields to matter.

The actual limits will depend on the charge Q and on the nature of the pulsar's companion in the binary system, as well as on the mass μ_5 of the quantum. Hence there are many possible cases that one can consider when setting limits on the coupling constants ξ_V and ξ_S defined by

$$\xi_{V,S} = \frac{f_{V,S}^2}{Gm_H^2}. \tag{4.7.14}$$

In Table 4.2 we display the constraints on $\xi_{V,S}$ for a coupling to baryon number B. $\Delta(Q/m)$ in Eq. (4.7.10) has been rewritten in terms of the usual quantity $\Delta(B/\mu)$, and we have assumed in all cases that the Compton wavelength of the quantum is much larger than the dimensions of the binary system, so that the quanta can be considered for these purposes to be "massless."

Table 4.2: Constraints on the coupling constants $\xi_{V,S}$ for the coupling of a massless vector (V) or scalar (S) quantum to baryon number B. Here $\xi_{V,S}$ are the maximum values allowed at the 2σ level using Eq. (4.7.13) as input. See text and [KRAUSE, 1994] for further discussion.

Companion	$\Delta(B/\mu)$	ξ_V	ξ_S
Neutron star	0.005	2.5×10^{-2}	1.3×10^{-2}
White dwarf	0.1	6.2×10^{-5}	3.1×10^{-5}
Black hole	1.1	5.1×10^{-7}	2.6×10^{-7}

Several interesting conclusions emerge from this table. As expected, $\Delta(B/\mu)$ is quite small if the companion is a neutron star, although it is nonzero [KRAUSE, 1994]. The largest $\Delta(B/\mu)$ occurs for a black hole, and consequently leads to the tightest constraints. However, the limits on ξ_V and ξ_S even in this case are still much less stringent than the results emerging from the modern Eötvös-type experiments, which typically give $\xi_{V,S} \lesssim 10^{-8} - 10^{-9}$. Nonetheless the radiation limits are interesting, because the data on PSR 1913+16 and other binary systems are constantly accumulating and improving.

4.8 The STEP Experiment

We conclude the discussion of composition-dependent experiments with a look to the future. From Section 4.2 we note that at present the most sensitive Earth-based torsion balance experiments can detect fractional acceleration differences of order $\delta a/a \approx 10^{-12}$. Although it is likely that this sensitivity will improve in the near future, it is also clear that seismic effects and other terrestrial noise sources will ultimately prove to be limiting factors.

Space-based experiments offer the possibility for carrying out an equivalence principle test to a sensitivity level $\delta a/a \approx 10^{-17}$ or better. One such experiment known as STEP (Satellite Test of the Equivalence Principle) has been the focus of considerable attention in both the United States and Europe [REINHARD, 1996]. Although different variants of STEP have been proposed in both the United States and Europe, we can illustrate the general features of space-based tests by examining the MiniSTEP experiment being developed at Stanford by Paul Worden and Francis Everitt [WORDEN, 1996]. Very roughly, the hoped-for improvement in sensitivity by a factor of order $10^5 - 10^6$ is achieved in the following way: To start with, the entire Earth acts as the source in a satellite experiment, since the test masses are in free-fall. This has the effect of replacing $\sin \beta$ in Eq. (4.2.19) by unity, which represents an enhancement by a factor ≈ 600 relative to a terrestrial experiment using an idealized spherical Earth as a source. Similarly, if we compare the STEP experiment to that of Roll, Krotkov, and Dicke [ROLL, 1964], where the acceleration of the test masses to the Sun is only $0.6\,\mathrm{cm\,s^{-2}}$, then there is an enhancement of order $980\,\mathrm{cm\,s^{-2}}/0.6\,\mathrm{cm\,s^{-2}} \approx 2,000$. It should be emphasized that these estimates assume that any WEP violation arises from a force whose range is at least comparable to $R_\oplus$. If the range is substantially shorter than this, the STEP experiment could be insensitive to a possible WEP violation. The remaining enhancement comes from a suppression of various noise sources that can be achieved by working in the relatively isolated environment of space. Among the more important terrestrial sources of noise are seismic effects, which can be reduced by a factor of order $10^4 - 10^5$ in a drag-free satellite (see discussion in Section 4.3 relating to drag-free systems). The space environment also makes cryogenic techniques more practicable, and this reduces sources of noise due to gas pressure effects.

The heart of the MiniSTEP experiment consists of 8 test masses arranged in 4 cryogenic differential accelerometers. Each accelerometer consists of a cylindrical outer mass of one material, and a cylindrical inner mass of a different material, which are free to move relative to each other on superconducting magnetic bearings. A typical pair of materials would be Be and Pt. If the two masses (each $\sim 200\,\text{g}$) fall in the Earth's field with the same acceleration, then the relative positions of these masses should remain fixed, and these are monitored by a SQUID (Superconducting Quantum Interference Device) position detector. Any relative motion of the two masses could be interpreted as evidence for a violation of the equivalence principle.

The differential accelerometers are located inside a drag-free satellite, which ensures that the external disturbances (e.g., air resistance, radiation pressure) acting on the satellite itself do not affect the free-fall motion of the test masses inside. A drag-free environment is achieved by accelerating the satellite as necessary by use of helium thrusters, to compensate for the external forces. The details of how this system would operate are described by Jafry [1996].

At present the MiniSTEP proposal, which is an American-European collaboration, has a good chance of being funded and of being launched around 2002 [EVERITT, PC]. If this experiment succeeds as planned, it should provide the most stringent limits available on possible violations of the WEP arising from a new force (or other mechanism) whose range is comparable to or larger than $R_\oplus$.

Another space-based experiment which can search for both composition-dependent and composition-independent deviations from Newtonian gravity is SEE (Satellite Energy Exchange). In this proposal by Sanders and collaborators at the University of Tennessee, the mutual perturbation of two free-floating co-orbiting satellites is analyzed. The SEE configuration allows both the inverse-square law and the WEP to be tested on several distance scales simultaneously, which provides a check against other results [SANDERS, 1992].

4.9 Summary

We summarize this chapter by presenting constraints on the coupling strength ξ as a function of λ. In Fig. 4.16, we present the constraint on ξ_B (coupling to baryon number), and in Fig. 4.17 the constraints on ξ_I (coupling to isospin). For each case, we exhibit only the envelope $\xi = \xi(\lambda)$ which is determined by the most sensitive experiments. With the exception of the regions denoted by "Solar Eötvös," and by "Laboratory Inverse-Square," all

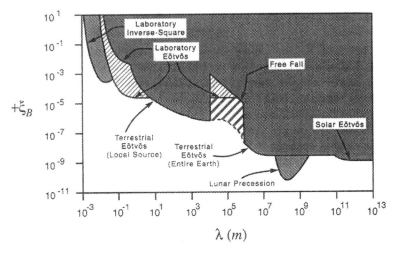

Figure 4.16: Constraints on the coupling constant ξ_B as a function of the range λ.

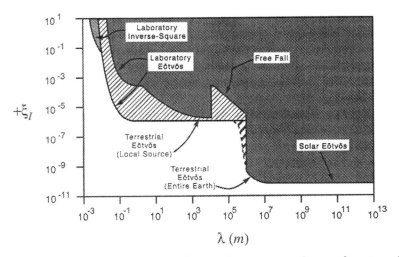

Figure 4.17: Constraints on the coupling constant ξ_I as a function of the range λ. See text for further discussion.

of the constraints shown have been obtained since 1986, and most of the results are from the Eöt-Wash experiments [ADELBERGER, 1990; SU, 1994; GUNDLACH, 1997].

The wide-diagonally shaded regions in Figs. 4.16 and 4.17 denote a regime (in λ) where the constraints on ξ_B and ξ_I are uncertain. This uncertainty is due to a lack of a sufficiently detailed model of the Earth for the corresponding values of λ. The narrow-diagonally shaded regions show the constraints from the recent experiment of Gundlach [1997].

For most values of λ, the constraints on ξ_I are approximately 10 times more sensitive than for ξ_B. This is due to the relative variation in the assumed charge for the non-Newtonian force: Typically $|\Delta(I_z/\mu)|(I_z/\mu)_{\text{source}} \sim 10|\Delta(B/\mu)|(B/\mu)_{\text{source}}$. The exception to this is in the range $10\,\text{m} \lesssim \lambda \lesssim 10^3\,\text{m}$, for which $(I_z/\mu)_{\text{source}} \approx 0$.

As was previously discussed in Section 2.2, for certain values of θ_5 the source charge q_5 vanishes. This is especially a problem for terrestrial experiments, because common minerals such as SiO_2 have a nearly vanishing isospin charge, $(I_z/\mu)_{SiO_2} = 0.00197$. Since the isospin of water is $(I_z/\mu)_{H_2O} = -0.11162$, it is easy to see that a very small quantity of water in the soil will tend to cause a complete cancellation of the isospin charge of surface rock. (q_{SiO_2} vanishes for $\theta_5 \cong -89.9°$.) For this reason, a number of composition-dependent experiments have been performed relative to Pb laboratory sources. (q_{Pb} vanishes for $\theta_5 \cong -78.2°$.) Figure 4.18 displays the most stringent limits for these "laboratory Eötvös" experiments. Notice that the composition-dependent tests in this figure ([ADELBERGER, 1990; NELSON, 1990; GUNDLACH, 1997]) lose sensitivity for certain values of θ_5 (as discussed in Section 2.2): Near $\theta_5 \approx -78°$, the source strength q_s vanishes for Pb, and near $\theta_5 \approx 0°$, the charge difference Δq_d of the composition dipole also vanishes. The inverse-square-law test of Spero et al. [SPERO, 1980] was performed using Cu test and attracting masses. Since it is strictly sensitive only to violations of the inverse-square law, one would expect a loss of sensitivity only when the test and/or source charge vanishes, which is what occurs in this case.

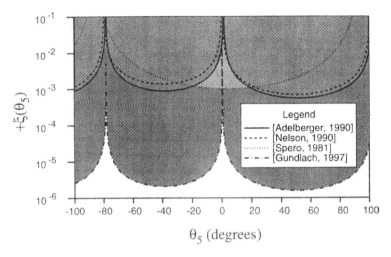

Figure 4.18: Constraints on the coupling constant ξ as a function of θ_5 for $\lambda = 0.1$ m.

CHAPTER 5

Gravitational Properties

of Antimatter

We have been concerned in the previous chapter with the detection of a non-Newtonian interaction via the composition-dependent acceleration differences that such a field would produce for two dissimilar samples of ordinary matter. However, a new intermediate-range force could also give rise to an acceleration difference between matter and antimatter, and hence it is of interest to explore what can be learned from antimatter experiments.

We have already noted in Section 2.1 that a theory of gravity arising from the exchange of any combination of $J = 2$ and $J = 0$ fields will have the property that the resulting potential is attractive for both matter-matter and matter-antimatter interactions. This holds in particular for Einstein's General Relativity, which can be derived from a field theory based on the exchange of $J = 2$ quanta [FEYNMAN, 1995]. By contrast, a force arising from the exchange of a vector $(J = 1)$ quantum has the opposite sign for matter-matter and matter-antimatter interactions. Hence one could in principle infer the presence of a non-Newtonian vector field by comparing the accelerations of e^+ and e^-, or p and $\bar{p}$, in the presence of the Earth's "gravitational" field. (Here we are again adopting the viewpoint that if any deviation were seen from what is expected on the basis of Newtonian or Einsteinian gravity, then it could eventually be attributed to the presence of a new interaction.)

Long before the suggestion of a possible "fifth force," various authors had raised the question of whether matter and antimatter behaved the same way in a gravitational field [MORRISON, 1957, 1958; SCHIFF, 1958, 1959, 1966; GOOD, 1961; FAIRBANK, 1974; SCHERK, 1979A,B; MACRAE, 1984]. Schiff's contribution was particularly important in the present context, since he demonstrated that one could infer from the Eötvös experiment that positrons do not fall "up" in a gravitational field. Schiff's argument depends on a generalization of the discussion starting from Eq. (2.7.5), which uses the Eötvös experiment to constrain how well different forms of energy obey the weak equivalence principle. We thus begin by reviewing this analysis [WAPSTRA, 1955; BOWLER, 1976; WILL, 1993], after which we will return to Schiff's argument.

Generalizing Eq. (2.7.5), we can write [WILL, 1993; FISCHBACH, 1995]

$$(m_G)_i = (m_I)_i + \eta_\alpha (E_\alpha)_i / c^2, \qquad (5.1)$$

where, as before, $(m_G)_i$ and $(m_I)_i$ are the (passive) gravitational mass, and the inertial mass, respectively, of a sample i. $(E_\alpha)_i$ is its type-α energy content (α = strong, electromagnetic, weak, ν-$\bar{\nu}$-exchange, ...), and η_α is a dimensionless constant whose magnitude reflects the strength of the violation of the weak equivalence principle induced by the coupling to type-α energy. Eq. (2.7.6) then generalizes to [FISCHBACH, 1995]

$$\frac{a_1 - a_2}{g} = \eta_\alpha \left[\left(\frac{E_\alpha}{m_I c^2} \right)_1 - \left(\frac{E_\alpha}{m_I c^2} \right)_2 \right]. \qquad (5.2)$$

Given an experimental limit on $(a_1 - a_2)$, one can infer a limit on η_α by calculating $(E_\alpha)_1$ and $(E_\alpha)_2$, as was done for $W^{(2)}$ in Eq. (2.7.12). For some forms of energy this is a straightforward calculation, as in the case of the Coulomb energy given in Eq. (2.7.10), but for other interactions some effort may be required. Detailed discussions of the resulting limits on different forms of energy are given in [BOWLER, 1976; WILL, 1993; SU, 1994].

We learn from the preceding discussion that the utility of Eötvös-type experiments in constraining the couplings of gravity to different types of energy stems in part from the fact that all forms of energy show up in some manner in a sample of bulk matter. The neutrino-exchange energy discussed in Section 2.7 illustrates how the coupling of gravity to neutrinos can be studied via the Eötvös experiment. Barring an accidental cancellation in Eq. (5.2) which would make the difference in square brackets vanish, one can similarly infer a limit on the parameter η_α for any type of energy E_α.

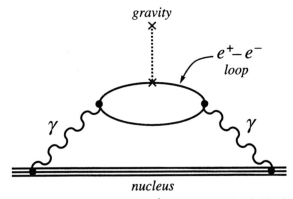

Figure 5.1: Coupling of gravity to e^+-e^- pairs in the field of a nucleus. The solid dots (•) denote the electromagnetic interaction.

The Schiff argument is similar to the discussion in Section 2.7, with an e^+-e^- pair replacing the ν-$\bar{\nu}$ pair. (In fact the discussion in Section 2.7 was modeled after Schiff's analysis.) As Schiff notes, e^+-e^- pairs are continually being created in a nucleus through a mechanism such as that shown in Fig. 5.1, and hence the nuclear wavefunction can be thought of as having an e^+-e^- component part of the time. It follows that if antimatter and matter accelerated differently in a gravitational field, then the antimatter component would give rise to an anomalous acceleration of a sample of ordinary bulk matter. By comparing the accelerations of different samples, the presence of an anomalous antimatter interaction could in principle be inferred from its characteristic dependence on chemical composition.

Schiff considers two alternatives to the conventional assumption that positrons and electrons behave identically in a gravitational field. These are that a) the gravitational rest mass of the positron is opposite in sign to that for an electron, but its kinetic energy behaves normally, and b) that the signs of both the positron rest mass and its kinetic energy are opposite to those for the electron. Schiff notes that case (b) produces the higher anomalous acceleration, so that it is sufficient to show that even case (a) is excluded with a high degree of confidence by the experimental data. One can anticipate the order of magnitude of E_{pair}, the e^+-e^- contribution to the energy of a nucleus (i.e., E_α when α arises from e^+-e^- pairs), by referring to the relevant Feynman diagram shown in Fig. 5.1. Since the amplitude for a nucleus producing a virtual photon is proportional to its charge Ze_0, where e_0 is the electric charge, we expect on dimensional grounds that

$$E_{\text{pair}} \approx m_e (Z\alpha_{\text{em}})^2, \tag{5.3}$$

where m_e is the electron (or positron) mass, and $\alpha_{\text{em}} \cong 1/137$ is the fine structure constant. The expression in Eq. (5.3) agrees with Schiff's detailed calculation up to a coefficient of order unity which depends on the nuclear charge distribution. If we take Eq. (5.3) to be exact, then we can combine this equation with the result for the fractional acceleration difference $\eta(\text{Be}, \text{Cu})$, where $\eta(\text{Be}, \text{Cu})$ is the experimental quantity defined in Eq. (49) of [SU, 1994]. We find

$$(3.3 \times 10^{-7}) |\eta_{\text{pair}}| \leq |(-1.9 \pm 2.5) \times 10^{-12}|, \tag{5.4}$$

and hence at the 1σ level,

$$|\eta_{\text{pair}}| \lesssim 1 \times 10^{-5}. \tag{5.5}$$

Despite various ambiguities in Schiff's calculation, this result represents a significant constraint on the gravitational acceleration of antimatter, and we will return to it below. Ericson and Richter [ERICSON, 1990] have used similar considerations to argue that the accelerations of antiprotons and protons are equal to $\sim (10^{-6}-10^{-7})$.

Interest in this question has continued, despite the apparently stringent limits implied by Schiff's work, and to understand more recent developments it is helpful to proceed chronologically. In the late 1960's Witteborn and Fairbank [WITTEBORN, 1967, 1968] set out to measure the gravitational acceleration of electrons as a prelude to the more challenging task of carrying out such a measurement for positrons. They never succeeded, and to this day no experiment has managed to directly measure the gravitational acceleration of any *charged* particle. (For neutrons see [COLELLA, 1975; SCHMIEDMAYER, 1989].)

An excellent discussion of the formidable difficulties that such experiments face is given in [DARLING, 1992], and center around the problem of eliminating various sources of background electromagnetic fields. We note that the presence of a single electric charge 5 meters away from an electron falling in the Earth's gravitational field would produce an acceleration equal to its gravitational acceleration. Even if stray charges can be eliminated, there are some internal sources of electric fields which would be difficult to eliminate, such as arise from Schiff-Barnhill effect [SCHIFF, 1966]. Consider an electron falling inside an evacuated metal tube. In the walls of the tube the electrons are in equilibrium, since there is no net current flowing in the tube. We see that the net force $\vec{F}_e$ on an electron with charge e_0 must be zero so that

$$\vec{F}_e = e_0\vec{\mathcal{E}} + m_e\vec{g} = 0, \tag{5.6}$$

where $\vec{\mathcal{E}}$ is the electric field that the electron "sees," and $\vec{g}$ is the Earth's gravitational field. It follows from Eq. (5.6) that there must be a gravity-induced electric field $\vec{\mathcal{E}}$ in the tube and, by continuity, just outside the walls as well. One can understand the origin of this field by viewing the metal tube as containing a free-electron gas, which "sags" under the influence of the Earth's gravitational field, just as the Earth's atmosphere does. This density variation as a function of height produces the field $\vec{\mathcal{E}}$ in (5.6),

$$\vec{\mathcal{E}} = -(m_e/e_0)\vec{g},$$
$$\mathcal{E} = |\vec{\mathcal{E}}| = 5.6 \times 10^{-11}\,\mathrm{V\,m^{-1}}. \tag{5.7}$$

In addition to the Schiff-Barnhill field, there is a field (of opposite sign) arising from the sagging of the positive ion lattice [DESSLER, 1968], and also local "patch effect" fields in the metal. At first sight the experimental result of Witteborn and Fairbank,

$$|\vec{a}_e| = |\vec{F}_e/m_e| < 0.09g, \tag{5.8}$$

seems compatible with the implication of the Schiff-Barnhill argument that $|\vec{a}_e| = 0$. However, the presence of the other fields (which can be even larger) makes the Schiff-Barnhill explanation of the Witteborn-Fairbank result less clear. It is fair to say that this remains an open question at present.

In 1982 Goldman and Nieto (GN) [GOLDMAN, 1982] made the interesting observation that although the Schiff-Barnhill field $\vec{\mathcal{E}}$ in Eq. (5.7) would completely offset the Earth's gravitational field for an electron, it would have a negligible effect on a more massive particle such as a proton (p) or antiproton ($\bar{p}$). Indeed, we see from Eq. (5.7) that the acceleration of p or $\bar{p}$ due to $\vec{\mathcal{E}}$ would be given by

$$|\vec{a}_p| = |e\vec{\mathcal{E}}/m_p| = (m_e/m_p)g \cong 0. \qquad (5.9)$$

To be sure, the Schiff-Barnhill field $\vec{\mathcal{E}}$ is not the only field acting on p or $\bar{p}$, but the implication of the GN observation is that whatever the source of the ambient electric field, its influence on p or $\bar{p}$ would be substantially less than for e^+ or e^-.

The GN paper, along with subsequent work by Goldman, Hughes, and Nieto (GHN) [GOLDMAN, 1986, 1987, 1988], helped to motivate an experiment to measure the gravitational acceleration of $\bar{p}$ using the Low Energy Antiproton Ring (LEAR) at CERN [HOLZSCHEITER, 1990, 1991]. In this experiment bunches of antiprotons from LEAR would be cooled to approximately $10\,\mathrm{K}$. The antiprotons would then be launched in the vertical direction, and the time it takes for them to reach the top of a drift tube of length L is then measured. In such an experiment there is a maximum time for any $\bar{p}$ to reach the top of the drift tube, which corresponds to $\bar{p}$ whose initial kinetic is exactly equal to $m_p g L$. (A $\bar{p}$ with more kinetic energy arrives in a shorter time, whereas one with less kinetic energy never makes it.) By measuring this maximum "cutoff" time, g can be determined for $\bar{p}$. The effects of stray electromagnetic fields can be accounted for by carrying out a similar measurement on H^-, which has the same charge as $\bar{p}$, nearly the same mass, but is composed of matter rather than antimatter. It was hoped that this experiment would achieve a 1% precision in determining $g_{\bar{p}}$. (However, the recent closing of LEAR leaves the status of this experiment uncertain.)

The advent of the "fifth force" hypothesis in 1986, along with the ensuing improvements in Eötvös-type experiments, reopened the question of whether a direct measurement of $g_{\bar{p}}$ provides information on new long-range fields that would not already be provided by the Eötvös experiments. The argument that antimatter experiments could indeed provide new information was put forward by GHN [GOLDMAN, 1987, 1988; NIETO, 1991] on the basis of the following simple model: In the presence of long-range scalar ($J = 0$), vector ($J = 1$), and tensor ($J = 2$) fields (with the latter being responsible for Newtonian gravity) the static potential $V(r)$ between two masses m_1 and

m_2 can be written as

$$V(r) = -\frac{Gm_1m_2}{r}(1 \mp ae^{-r/v} + be^{-r/s}). \tag{5.10}$$

In Eq. (5.10) the upper (lower) sign in the second term (which arises from vector exchange) corresponds to the case of like (opposite) charges for the test masses. The constants a and b (which are closely related to α_{ij} in Eq. (2.1.6)) give the strength of each interaction (relative to Newtonian gravity), and the parameters v and s (which have the dimensions of length) characterize the range of the vector and scalar forces respectively. GHN argue that if it were to happen that $v \approx s$ and $a \approx b$, then the non-Newtonian terms proportional to a and b could very nearly cancel for matter-matter interactions, but would add for matter-antimatter interactions (such as $\bar{p}$ falling in the field of the Earth). Thus the limits on α_{ij} (and hence on α or ξ) which follow from the experiments described in Chapters 3 and 4 might still allow a large matter-antimatter contribution from a new force, and this could show up in the proposed $\bar{p}$ experiment. The possibility of a near-cancellation of two Yukawa terms was discussed in Section 2.5, where it was noted that such a cancellation can lead to an effective exponential potential. This, in turn, would modify the strength of the source compared to what would be expected from a Yukawa potential.

In the present context, however, the relevant question is what effect such a cancellation would have on the strength of the *detector*, namely the two chemically different masses whose accelerations are being compared. This question has been addressed recently by Adelberger et al. [STUBBS, 1988B; ADELBERGER, 1991A,B; GOLDMAN, 1991; MORPURGO, 1991]. Adelberger et al. note that the constants a and b in Eq. (5.10) depend on the vector and scalar charges, q_V and q_S respectively, where q_V can be identified with q_5 in Eq. (2.2.1). The scalar charge q_S cannot generally be written in as simple a form as q_V, since scalar fields can couple to binding energy (whereas vector fields do not). As can be seen from the Coulomb energy W_C in Eq. (2.7.10), and the neutrino-exchange energy $W^{(2)}$ in Eq. (2.7.12), various forms of binding energy can depend in a complicated manner on the chemical compositions of the test samples. Hence the scalar charge q_S in any specific theory is likely to have a very different composition dependence from the vector charge q_V. For this reason it is very unlikely that the vector and scalar contributions in Eq. (5.10) will always cancel for all pairs of test masses. Since many pairs of test masses have been compared to date in various high-precision null experiments, it follows that a scenario involving a high degree of cancellation in matter-matter interactions is hard to justify.

Adelberger et al. quantify the above considerations by utilizing the observation we made previously that any difference in the acceleration of matter and antimatter to a source must be due to a vector interaction. If N_p and

$N_{\bar{p}}$ denote the numbers of protons and antiprotons in a test sample, then q_V can be expressed in the form

$$q_V = q_p(N_p - N_{\bar{p}}) + q_n(N_n - N_{\bar{n}}) + q_e(N_{e^-} - N_{e^+}), \qquad (5.11)$$

where q_p, q_n and q_e are constants, and $N_n, N_{\bar{n}}, N_{e^-}, N_{e^+}$ are defined in an obvious way. (Note that only the first-generation fermion contributions are included.) Adelberger et al. then proceed to demonstrate that both the LEAR $\bar{p}$ experiment and a Galileo free-fall experiment using ordinary matter (see Section 4.3) depend on the same two quantities $(q_p + q_e)$ and q_n. Since these quantities are already highly constrained by experiments using ordinary matter, the implication is that one is unlikely to detect an acceleration difference between p and $\bar{p}$ at the level of sensitivity that could have been expected in the LEAR $\bar{p}$ experiment.

Direct experiments on antimatter are nonetheless interesting, if for no other reason than to teach us how to handle e^+, $\bar{p}$, and possibly $\bar{n}$. Moreover, such experiments could conceivably uncover some exotic gravitational interaction involving antimatter, not anticipated in the usual formalisms. Some interesting speculations on a possible connection between antigravity and CP-violation have been advanced by Chardin [1990, 1992]. The general question of how the K^0-$\bar{K}^0$ system responds to the influence of external fields, and the implications for CP-violation, warrant a separate discussion, and are considered in detail in the next chapter. Further discussion of gravitational experiments utilizing antimatter are given in [BEVERINI, 1988; HUGHES, 1991, 1992].

CHAPTER 6

Effects of External Forces
in the Kaon System

6.1 Energy Dependence of the Kaon Parameters

As noted in Chapter 2, the K^0-$\bar{K}^0$ system can play the role of a sensitive detector for certain types of new forces, because of the naturally small mass scale provided by the K_L-K_S mass difference Δm. Not all forces which might exist can be detected in the K^0-$\bar{K}^0$ system, since (to a good approximation) kaons do not couple to certain "charges", including baryon number (B) and electric charge (Q). This point deserves some additional discussion: Although K^0 and $\bar{K}^0$ are bound states of charged quarks ($d\bar{s}$ and $\bar{d}s$ respectively), K^0 and $\bar{K}^0$ have no net electric charge, and hence they will not be influenced by a weak external electromagnetic field. Evidently a similar remark applies to a possible coupling to baryon number. It was for this reason that the source of the proposed "fifth force" was originally assumed to be the hypercharge $Y = B + S$, where S is strangeness, since this quantum number would couple to both kaons and ordinary matter.

To describe the effects of an external field which does couple to kaons, we follow the phenomenological treatment of Aronson, Bock, Cheng, and Fischbach (ABCF) [ARONSON, 1983A, 1983B]. This treatment is more general than the analysis given earlier by Nachtmann [1969], who considered the influence of particular choices of C-odd scalar, vector, and tensor fields on Δm and η_{+-}. For the fields he considers $|\eta_{+-}|$ is always proportional to γ^J, where $\gamma = E_K/m_K$ and $J = 0, 1$, or 2 for scalar, vector, or tensor fields respectively. This is not sufficiently general to describe some kaon data, which is part of the motivation for the ABCF analysis. We assume that in the absence of any external fields, the time evolution of the K^0-$\bar{K}^0$ wave function $\Psi(t)$ is given by

$$-\frac{\partial \Psi(t)}{\partial t} = iH_0\Psi(t), \qquad (6.1.1)$$

where H_0 is a 2×2 matrix, and we have set $\hbar = c = 1$. For some purposes it is convenient to express iH_0 in a number of equivalent forms:

$$iH_0 = \Gamma + iM = h_0 1 + h_x \sigma_x + h_y \sigma_y + h_z \sigma_z = \begin{pmatrix} id & p^2 \\ q^2 & i\bar{d} \end{pmatrix}. \qquad (6.1.2)$$

Here $\Gamma = \Gamma^\dagger$ and $M = M^\dagger$ are 2×2 matrices, the σ's are the Pauli matrices, and $h_0, h_x, ..., d, \bar{d}, p^2$, and q^2 are complex numbers which phenomenologically describe the various physical parameters of the K^0-$\bar{K}^0$ system. Specifically the eigenvalues $\lambda^\pm$ of iH_0 are given by

$$\lambda^\pm = \frac{i}{2}(d + \bar{d}) \pm \frac{1}{2}[4p^2 q^2 - (d - \bar{d})^2]^{1/2}, \qquad (6.1.3)$$

and the corresponding eigenvectors $\Psi^\pm$ are

$$\Psi^\pm = \begin{pmatrix} a^\pm \\ b^\pm \end{pmatrix}, \qquad (6.1.4)$$

$$\frac{a^\pm}{b^\pm} = \frac{p^2}{\lambda^\pm - id} = \frac{\lambda^\pm - i\bar{d}}{q^2}. \qquad (6.1.5)$$

As is well known, it was discovered in 1957 that parity (P) and charge-conjugation (C) were not separately conserved in weak interactions, but that their product CP was (at least at that time). By virtue of the well-known CPT theorem, any locally Lorentz-invariant Lagrangian must be invariant under the product CPT (taken in any order). The CPT theorem implies that the constraints following from CP are essentially equivalent to those of T, and for several years following 1957 it was believed that both CP and T were conserved by all known interactions. However, observation of the CP-violating decay mode $K_L \to \pi^+ \pi^-$ in 1964 [CHRISTENSON, 1964] not only challenged this assumption but also questioned whether the observed decay mode could be evidence for a new cosmological field [BELL, 1964; BERNSTEIN, 1964]. It is now generally believed that CP is indeed violated by some term in the total Hamiltonian, and is not due to an asymmetry produced by a new long-range force. Nonetheless the formalism that leads to this conclusion also indicates that the effects of any new force could show up at a lower level in the K^0-$\bar{K}^0$ system by modifying the intrinsic CP-violating K^0-$\bar{K}^0$ parameters, as we now discuss.

Returning to the eigenvectors $\Psi^\pm$ in Eq. (6.1.4), we note that the phases of $|K^0\rangle$ and $|\bar{K}^0\rangle$ can be chosen such that

$$CP|K^0\rangle = -|\bar{K}^0\rangle, \qquad (6.1.6)$$

from which it follows that the CP eigenfunctions $|K_1^0\rangle$ and $|K_2^0\rangle$ are given by

$$|K_1^0\rangle = \frac{1}{\sqrt{2}}(|K^0\rangle - |\bar{K}^0\rangle) = \frac{1}{\sqrt{2}}\begin{pmatrix} 1 \\ -1 \end{pmatrix} \qquad (CP = +1),$$

$$|K_2^0\rangle = \frac{1}{\sqrt{2}}(|K^0\rangle + |\bar{K}^0\rangle) = \frac{1}{\sqrt{2}}\begin{pmatrix} 1 \\ 1 \end{pmatrix} \qquad (CP = -1).$$

(6.1.7)

If CP is not conserved (but CPT is), then the eigenfunctions in Eq. (6.1.7) are replaced by

$$|K_1^0\rangle \rightarrow |K_S\rangle = (|p^2| + |q|^2)^{-1/2}(p|K^0\rangle - q|\bar{K}^0\rangle) \equiv \Psi^-,$$

$$|K_2^0\rangle \rightarrow |K_L\rangle = (|p^2| + |q|^2)^{-1/2}(p|K^0\rangle + q|\bar{K}^0\rangle) \equiv \Psi^+.$$

(6.1.8)

The time-evolution of the states $\Psi^\pm$ is given by

$$\Psi^+(t) = e^{-im_L t}e^{-\Gamma_L t/2}\Psi^+(0)$$

$$\Psi^-(t) = e^{-im_S t}e^{-\Gamma_S t/2}\Psi^-(0).$$

(6.1.9)

The preceding description accounts for the behavior of the K^0-$\bar{K}^0$ system in the absence of external fields. To incorporate the effects of an external field, we write

$$iH_0 = \Gamma + iM \rightarrow iH = \Gamma + iM + iF,$$

$$iF = u_0 1 + u_x \sigma_x + u_y \sigma_y + u_z \sigma_z.$$

(6.1.10)

The u's are complex functions of position and of $\gamma = E_K/m_K = (1-\beta^2)^{-1/2}$, where β is the kaon velocity. The reason for the γ-dependence (which is the characteristic signal for the presence of an external field) is that the strength of a field produced by charges that are at rest in the laboratory changes as a function of the kaon energy, when transformed to the kaon rest frame, where Eq. (6.1.1) holds. To illustrate how this γ-dependence comes about, consider the example of the original fifth force hypothesis in which it was assumed that the "charge" of the new field was the hypercharge $Y = B + S$. Since Y is nonzero for the Earth (which has a nonzero B) and for kaons (which have a nonzero S), the Earth (or any other macroscopic object) could influence the K^0-$\bar{K}^0$ system via a coupling to Y. If Y is described by a vector field $A_\mu(x)$, in analogy to electromagnetism, then the hypercharge potential A_0 due to the galaxy can be written as

$$A_0 = f^2 \frac{Y_G}{R_G},$$

(6.1.11)

where Y_G and R_G are the hypercharge and effective radius of the galaxy, and f is the coupling constant appearing in Eq. (2.1.6). Note that although A_0 is in principle a function of position, in practice the potential A_0 arising from the galaxy would be essentially constant for any experiment carried out on Earth. Since the Hamiltonian for the K^0-$\bar{K}^0$ system in Eqs. (6.1.1) and (6.1.10) is defined in the kaon rest frame, the expression for A_0 must be transformed to this frame. Under a Lorentz transformation (see [JACKSON, 1975], page 518),

$$A_0 \to A_0\gamma, \tag{6.1.12}$$

and since γ is greater than unity, the effect of the Lorentz transformation is to amplify A_0, and to thus make possible the detection of a relatively weak interaction. For a kaon with a laboratory energy of $100\,\text{GeV}$, $\gamma = E_K/m_K \cong 200$, and for $E_K = 1\,\text{TeV}$, $\gamma = 2000$. An interaction which couples to hypercharge, and which thus contributes with opposite signs to K^0 and $\bar{K}^0$, can be represented by the Hamiltonian in Eq. (6.1.10) with $u_z = \gamma A_0$. When this Hamiltonian is diagonalized, the K_L-K_S mass difference Δm (in the absence of any forces) is replaced by $(\Delta m)_u$, where [ARONSON, 1983B]

$$(\Delta m)^2_u = [(\Delta m)^4 + 4A_0^4\gamma^4]^{1/2} + 2A_0^2\gamma^2. \tag{6.1.13}$$

Similarly, the expression for η_{+-} in Eq. (1.6) becomes

$$\eta_{+-} \cong \frac{1}{2}(\epsilon + \epsilon') \to (\eta_{+-})_u \equiv |\eta_{+-}|_u e^{i(\phi_{+-})_u} \cong \frac{1}{2}(\epsilon + \epsilon') + \frac{1}{2\Delta m}A_0\gamma(1 - i), \tag{6.1.14}$$

where $\epsilon = p/q$, and ϵ' measures CP violation arising from the decay matrix. From Eqs. (6.1.13) and (6.1.14), we see that in the presence of an external hypercharge field Δm, $|\eta_{+-}|$, and ϕ_{+-} become γ-dependent, and it is straightforward to show that the same holds for Γ_L and Γ_S as well. Shortly after the discovery of CP violation the possibility was raised that the entire CP-violating effect was due to an external field [BELL, 1964; BERNSTEIN, 1964], which corresponds to setting $\epsilon = \epsilon' = 0$ in Eq. (6.1.14). It follows from Eq. (6.1.14) that if this were the case, then $|\eta_{+-}|_u$ would be directly proportional to γ, and that ϕ_{+-} would be $-45°$. Both of these predictions are in clear conflict with experiments, as was evident from even the earliest data. As we discuss below, existing data indicate that $|\eta_{+-}|$ is constant, and $\phi_{+-} \cong +45°$ for a range of values $350 \gtrsim \gamma \gtrsim 1$.

It follows from this discussion that the observed CP violation cannot be explained as arising entirely from an external vector hypercharge field, although such a field can represent part of the contribution to η_{+-}, as in Eq. (6.1.14). Such a possibility was raised by the experimental results of ABCF [ARONSON, 1982, 1983A, 1983B] who extracted from the first set of kaon data taken at Fermilab energies ($110 \gtrsim E_K \gtrsim 30\,\text{GeV}$) values of $\Delta m, \Gamma_S, |\eta_{+-}|$, and ϕ_{+-}. Any discrepancy between the ABCF results and the conventional low-energy values [PDG, 1982], taken at $E_K \cong 5\,\text{GeV}$, could be interpreted as evidence for an anomalous γ-dependence. In fact the

Table 6.1: Comparison of the ABCF and PDG results for the kaon parameters. PDG denotes the Particle Data Group values taken at $E_K \cong 5\,\text{GeV}$.

Parameter	ABCF (30-110 GeV)	PDG (5 GeV)
$10^{-10}\Delta m$ $(\hbar sec^{-1})$	0.482 ± 0.014	0.5349 ± 0.0022
$10^{10}\tau_S$ (sec)	0.905 ± 0.007	0.8923 ± 0.0022
$10^3 |\eta_{+-}|$	2.09 ± 0.02	2.274 ± 0.022
$\tan\phi_{+-}$	0.709 ± 0.102	0.986 ± 0.041

ABCF results did disagree with the low-energy values, as we summarize in Table 6.1.

As we have already discussed, the suggestion that the K^0-$\bar{K}^0$ parameters had an anomalous γ-dependence compatible with the presence of a new interaction was one of the motivations for the fifth force hypothesis. However, subsequent high-energy determinations of the kaon parameters have failed to support the ABCF results, or to find any evidence for an anomalous γ-dependence. Coupal et al. [COUPAL, 1985] measured $|\eta_{+-}|$ in the energy range $150 \geq E_K \geq 30\,\text{GeV}$ and found

$$|\eta_{+-}| = (2.28 \pm 0.06) \times 10^{-3}, \qquad (6.1.15)$$

which is consistent with the low-energy ($\sim 5\,\text{GeV}$) value quoted in Table 6.1. The K_S lifetime τ_S has been measured in a high-energy high-statistics experiment [GROSSMAN, 1987], which gives

$$\tau_S = (0.8920 \pm 0.0044)10^{-10}\,\text{s}, \qquad (6.1.16)$$

which is also in excellent agreement with the low-energy value. Carosi et al. [CAROSI, 1990] have reported high-energy determinations of ϕ_{+-} and ϕ_{00}, for $170 \gtrsim E_K \gtrsim 70\,\text{GeV}$. ($\eta_{00}$ and ϕ_{00} are the analogues for the $\pi^0\pi^0$ decay mode of η_{+-} and ϕ_{+-}.) They obtain

$$\begin{aligned} \phi_{+-} &= 46.9° \pm 1.4° \pm 0.7°, \\ \phi_{00} &= 47.1° \pm 2.1° \pm 1.0°, \end{aligned} \qquad (6.1.17)$$

where the first errors are statistical and the second systematic. Again these results are in good agreement with the corresponding low-energy values.

There have been three more recent experiments which have determined various parameters of the K^0-$\bar{K}^0$ system at high energies [BARR, 1993; GIBBONS, 1993A,B]. The most direct test of the original ABCF results come from [GIBBONS, 1993A] who measured Δm, τ_S, and ϕ_{+-} for kaons in the momentum range $(20-160)\,\mathrm{GeV}/c$. The results are

$$\Delta m = (0.5286 \pm 0.0028) \times 10^{10}\hbar\,\mathrm{s}^{-1}, \qquad (6.1.18\mathrm{a})$$

$$\tau_S = (0.8929 \pm 0.0016) \times 10^{-10}\,\mathrm{s}, \qquad (6.1.18\mathrm{b})$$

$$\phi_{+-} = 42.2^\circ \pm 1.4^\circ. \qquad (6.1.18\mathrm{c})$$

As noted by the authors, their determination of τ_S is in good agreement with the world average value, $\tau_S = (0.8922 \pm 0.0022) \times 10^{-10}\,\mathrm{s}^{-1}$, while their determination of Δm is $\sim 2\sigma$ below the current world average, $\Delta m = (0.5351 \pm 0.0024) \times 10^{-10}\hbar\,\mathrm{s}^{-1}$. This difference is not statistically significant, and in the context of the present discussion should not be interpreted as evidence for new couplings to kaons.

We can conclude from the preceding summary of recent experiments that there is no experimental support for the original ABCF results from any subsequent determination of any of the kaon parameters. Most likely this means that the original data contained a systematic effect of unknown origin which simulated the behavior expected from an external field. The fact that the magnitude of this effect was such as to suggest originally [FISCH-BACH, 1986A] that it could have been produced by the same mechanism that produced the Eötvös anomaly is then purely coincidental.

It is conceivable, of course, that the Fermilab experiments which provided the data for the ABCF analysis were configured differently from subsequent experiments, and in a way that could explain the data as a legitimate effect. One possibility has to do with the fact that in the original experiments the kaon beam was not parallel to the surface of the Earth, as was the case in all subsequent experiments. Rather, the target area was below ground level, and the beam entered the Earth at an angle of 7 mrad. This has as a consequence the fact that kaons of different energies would see a different matter distribution, owing to the effects of Lorentz transformations. For a field of the appropriate strength and range, such a mechanism might explain why energy-dependent effects could have been seen in the earlier kaon experiments, but not in the subsequent ones. This possibility is discussed in more detail in Chapter 8.

6.2 Decays into Hyperphotons

In their original paper reanalyzing the EPF experiment, Fischbach et al. noted that it might be possible to detect the quanta (hyperphotons) of the putative new force responsible for the EPF data, if this force coupled to kaons [FISCHBACH, 1986A]. At first sight such a possibility is difficult to understand, since we are considering the detection of the quanta of a force which couples to matter even more weakly than gravity. As is well known, classical gravitational radiation has not yet been detected in the laboratory, although its existence has been confirmed from observations on the binary pulsar 1913+16 [TAYLOR, 1989]. However, the presumed quanta of the gravitational field, gravitons, would be even more difficult to detect, and there are no prospects for doing so in the foreseeable future. Nonetheless, individual hyperphotons *can* be detected, even though gravitons cannot, because they couple to a charge (hypercharge) which is not conserved, as was first noted by Weinberg [1964]. Several groups have studied the decays $K^{\pm} \to \pi^{\pm} + \gamma_Y$ (where γ_Y is the hyperphoton) and have shown that the apparent absence of this decay mode leads to stringent constraints on the product $f^2\lambda^2$, where f is the coupling strength of hyperphotons to kaons and $\lambda = 1/m_Y = 1/m_5$ is the range of the putative new force expressed in terms of the hyperphoton mass m_Y [ARONSON, 1986, 1988; BOUCHIAT, 1986; FISCHBACH, 1986A; LUSIGNOLI, 1986; SUZUKI, 1986; GALIĆ, 1989; TRAMPETIĆ, 1989].

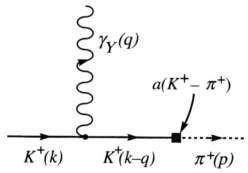

Figure 6.1: Pole-model diagram for $K^+ \to \pi^+ \gamma_Y$. The momenta of various particles are given in parentheses.

To understand how these constraints come about, we write the matrix element T for the decay $K^+(k) \to \pi^+(p)\gamma_Y(q)$ in the form (see Fig. 6.1),

$$T = \bar{f}\epsilon_{\mu}^{(m)}(q)M_{\mu}, \qquad (6.2.1)$$

where $\bar{f} = \sqrt{4\pi}f$ and $\epsilon_{\mu}^{(m)}$ is the polarization vector for the γ_Y emitted in the polarization state m. Since $\epsilon_{\mu}(q)$ satisfies $q \cdot \epsilon(q) = 0$, a term proportional to q_μ in Eq. (6.2.1) makes no contribution. When $|T|^2$ is calculated from M_μ, the sum over the polarization states of the emitted γ_Y gives rise to the expression

$$\sum_m \epsilon_\mu^{(m)*}(q)\epsilon_\nu^{(m)}(q) = \delta_{\mu\nu} + \frac{q_\mu q_\nu}{m_Y^2}. \tag{6.2.2}$$

If m_Y is the mass of the ultralight quantum of an intermediate-range field, then typically m_Y is quite small ($\lambda = 2\,\text{km} \Rightarrow m_Y = 1 \times 10^{-10}\,\text{eV}$), whereas q_μ is of order the K^+-π^+ mass difference, which is 354 MeV. It follows that the magnitude of the term proportional to $q_\mu q_\nu$ is of order

$$\left|\frac{q_\mu q_\nu}{m_Y^2}\right| \approx \frac{(354\,\text{MeV})^2}{(10^{-10}\,\text{eV})^2} \cong 1 \times 10^{37}, \tag{6.2.3}$$

and hence the presence of this term provides a large enhancement factor. It is this factor which allows a coupling to γ_Y to be detected through decays such as $K^\pm \to \pi^\pm \gamma_Y$, notwithstanding the fact that the coupling strength f in Eq. (6.2.1) is expected to be very small. The rate Γ for this decay can then be written in the form [ARONSON, 1986]

$$\Gamma(K^\pm \to \pi^\pm \gamma_Y) = \frac{|\vec{p}|}{2M_K^2}|a(K^\pm - \pi^\pm)|^2 \frac{f^2}{m_Y^2}, \tag{6.2.4}$$

where $|\vec{p}| = 227\,\text{MeV}$ is the $\pi^\pm$ momentum in the rest frame of the decaying $K^\pm$, and $a(K^\pm - \pi^\pm)$ is the weak hadronic amplitude shown in Fig. 6.1. We see from Eq. (6.2.4) that a limit on $f^2/m_Y^2 = f^2\lambda^2$ can be inferred by combining an experimental bound on $\Gamma(K^\pm \to \pi^\pm \gamma_Y)$ with a theoretical calculation of $a(K^\pm - \pi^\pm)$. The theoretical uncertainties surrounding the calculation of $\Gamma(K^\pm \to \pi^\pm \gamma_Y)$ obviously determine what bound can be set on the product $f^2\lambda^2$, given the experimental data that we discuss below. Several groups have calculated the branching ratio $B(K^+ \to \pi^+ \gamma_Y)$,

$$B(K^+ \to \pi^+ \gamma_Y) = \frac{\Gamma(K^+ \to \pi^+ \gamma_Y)}{\Gamma(K^+ \to all)}, \tag{6.2.5}$$

and $B(K^+ \to \pi^+ \gamma_Y)$ varies not only from one calculation to another, but also within a given calculation depending on the values used for certain parameters. Table 6.2 summarizes the results that have been obtained to date by various authors.

From the analysis of [ARONSON, 1988], we conclude that it would be difficult to account for the energy dependence of the K^0-$\bar{K}^0$ parameters inferred by ABCF (see Table 6.2) in terms of a single new vector field, in view of the stringent limits on $B(K^+ \to \pi^+ \gamma_Y)$. The most likely conclusion is that the ABCF data are wrong, which agrees with the implication to be

Table 6.2: Theoretical predictions for $B(K^\pm \to \pi^\pm \gamma_Y)$ in units of $10^{16}\,\text{eV}^2 f^2 \lambda^2$. The theoretical predictions are from [ARONSON, 1988], and the experimental data used to obtain the limits on ξ are from [ADLER, 1996], as described below. ξ is related to f^2 via $\xi = f^2/G_\infty m_H^2$.

Authors	$B(K^\pm \to \pi^\pm \gamma_Y)$	Limit on $\xi(\lambda^2/1\,\text{m}^2)$
Aronson et al. [1986]	6	5.3×10^{-2}
Bouchiat and Iliopoulos [1986]	403	9.4×10^{-4}
Galić [1989]		
Model A	320	1.0×10^{-3}
Model B	23	1.4×10^{-2}
Lusignoli and Pugliese [1986]	380	9.4×10^{-4}
Suzuki [1986]		
$(r = 1.5)$	56	6.1×10^{-3}
$(r = 12)$	444	7.9×10^{-4}

drawn from recent experiments, as we have already noted. However, should it turn out that these data are correct, for the reasons discussed above, then they could still be compatible with $B(K^+ \to \pi^+ \gamma_Y)$ in the framework of more exotic models.

Experimentally, since γ_Y couples very weakly to ordinary matter, it cannot be detected directly. However, the decays $K^\pm \to \pi^\pm \gamma_Y$ can still be detected because they would have a unique signature: In the rest frame of the decaying $K^\pm$ the signal would be a $\pi^\pm$ with a fixed 3-momentum, $|\vec{p}| = 227\,\text{MeV}$, and no other particles detected. This signal is the same as that for $K^\pm \to \pi^\pm \tilde{a}$ ($\tilde{a} = $ axion), and hence one can take over the limits from existing axion searches for the branching ratio $\Gamma(K^+ \to \pi^+ + \text{undetected neutrals})$. The limits on this branching ratio have improved steadily over the years [ADLER, 1996], and currently the best value is

$$B(K^+ \to \pi^+ X^0) < 5.2 \times 10^{-10}, \tag{6.2.6}$$

where X^0 is any undetected neutral particle such as γ_Y or $\tilde{a}$. This limit gives rise to the bounds on ξ in the third column of Table 6.2 when combined with the theoretical predictions given in the second column. For other discussions of constraints on a possible fifth force from rare decays, see [RIZZO, 1986; GOLDMAN, 1988; ALIEV, 1989], and summaries of rare kaon decays are given in [HAGELIN, 1989; PAVER, 1989].

CHAPTER 7

Spin-Dependent
Intermediate-Range Forces

As we have noted previously, the dominant effect arising from the exchange of a boson with spin-parity $J^P = 0^+, 1^-, 2^+, \ldots$ is a static spin-independent potential between fermions. By contrast, the exchange of $0^-, 1^+, \ldots$ bosons leads to spin-dependent potentials, and we proceed to discuss the phenomenology of such interactions in this section.

It should be observed at the outset that even the exchange of $J^P = 0^+, 1^-, 2^+, \ldots$ bosons leads to spin-dependent interactions between fermions, although these are not the dominant couplings in each case. In particular, spin-dependent terms are present in the gravitational interaction both at the macroscopic and microscopic levels. As an example, the Hamiltonian describing the motion of an electron in the Earth's gravitational field $\vec{g}$ contains the spin-dependent term [BARKER, 1966; FISCHBACH, 1981]

$$V_\sigma = \frac{3\hbar}{4m_e c^2}\vec{g}\cdot(\vec{\sigma}\times\vec{p}) = \frac{3}{2}\frac{G_N M_\oplus}{m_e c^2 r^3}\vec{S}\cdot\vec{L}. \qquad (7.1)$$

Here m_e is the electron mass, $\vec{p}$ is its momentum, $\vec{S} = (\hbar/2)\vec{\sigma}$ is the electron spin, r is the distance from the electron to the center of the (spherical) Earth, and $\vec{L}$ is the orbital angular momentum of the electron relative to the Earth. The term proportional to $\vec{S}\cdot\vec{L}$ would also describe the geodetic precession of a macroscopic object, such as an orbiting gyroscope. Moreover, if we took account of the Earth's spin $\vec{S}_\oplus$, then an additional coupling proportional to $\vec{S}\cdot\vec{S}_\oplus$ would arise, and this gives the Lense-Thirring precession ("dragging of inertial frames"). To date no spin-dependent gravitational interaction has ever been directly observed, but this should change in the near future when the Stanford Gravity Probe B experiment is launched [EVERITT, 1994]. The reason why such terms are difficult to detect is that they are suppressed relative to the familiar Newtonian interaction by factors such as $|\vec{p}/m_e c| \ll 1$, as can be seen from Eq. (7.1). However, should any long-range or intermediate-range spin-dependent interaction be observed experimentally, then we could distinguish between a gravitational effect and one arising from the exchange of some other field by utilizing the fact that the respective potentials are different, as we now discuss.

The simplest example of a nongravitational spin-dependent potential would be that arising from the exchange of a 0^- quantum, such as the hypothetical axion [FAYET, 1986A,B; CHENG, 1988]. For present purposes the axion can be thought of as a very light analog of π^0 with mass m_a, and hence the resulting interaction is described by the usual one-pion-exchange potential (OPEP) [BOHR, 1969]

$$V(r) = \frac{1}{3}\frac{g_a^2}{4\pi}\left(\frac{m_a}{2m_N}\right)^2\left[\vec{\sigma}_1 \cdot \vec{\sigma}_2 + \left(1 + \frac{3}{m_a r} + \frac{3}{m_a^2 r^2}\right)S_{12}\right]\frac{e^{-m_a r}}{r}, \quad (7.2)$$

$$S_{12} = [3(\vec{\sigma}_1 \cdot \hat{r})(\vec{\sigma}_2 \cdot \hat{r}) - \vec{\sigma}_1 \cdot \vec{\sigma}_2].$$

Here g_a is the axion-nucleon coupling constant defined by

$$-\mathcal{L} = ig_a\bar{\psi}(x)\gamma_5\psi(x)\phi_a(x), \quad (7.3)$$

where $\phi_a(x)$ is the field operator for the axion, and $\psi(x)$ is the operator for the fermion (e.g., nucleon) to which the axion is coupling. The OPEP plays a fundamental role in the physics of nuclei with spin, such as the deuteron. It follows from Eq. (7.2) that for an analogous long-range weak interaction to be detected between macroscopic bodies, it is necessary that these bodies themselves have a net spin polarization, and this poses a variety of experimental challenges, as we discuss below.

In practice it is usually assumed that m_a is small enough compared to the dimensions of the experimental apparatus that $\exp(-m_a r)$ can be approximated by unity. In the same approximation ($m_a \to 0$) the expression for $V(r)$ then reduces to

$$V(r) = -\frac{g_a^2}{4\pi}\left(\frac{1}{4m_N^2}\right)[\vec{\sigma}_1 \cdot \vec{\sigma}_2 - 3(\vec{\sigma}_1 \cdot \hat{r})(\vec{\sigma}_2 \cdot \hat{r})]\frac{1}{r^3}. \quad (7.4)$$

(A massless pseudoscalar Goldstone boson is sometimes referred to as an "arion" [ANSEL'M, 1982].) $V(r)$ in Eq. (7.4) has the form expected from the interaction of two magnetic dipoles, and hence it is conventional to parametrize $V(r)$ in terms of the magnetic moment of the electron μ_e,

$$V(r) = -\frac{\alpha_a\mu_e^2}{r^3}[\vec{\sigma}_1 \cdot \vec{\sigma}_2 - 3(\vec{\sigma}_1 \cdot \hat{r})(\vec{\sigma}_2 \cdot \hat{r})]. \quad (7.5)$$

Here α_a is a phenomenological constant which characterizes the strength of the new interaction (relative to electromagnetism), and the results of any experiment can be converted into an upper bound on α_a. From Eqs. (7.4) and (7.5) this bound can be translated into a bound on the fundamental coupling g_a via

$$|\alpha_a \mu_e^2| = \left| \frac{g_a^2}{16\pi m_N^2} \right|. \tag{7.6}$$

It is instructive to consider typical limits on α_a and g_a from such experiments before discussing the details of how these experiments are actually carried out. Consider first the experiment of Ritter et al. [RITTER, 1990] who measure the force between two specially prepared polarized samples. They find $|\alpha_a| < 9 \times 10^{-12}$, which translates into a limit

$$g_a^2/4\pi \lesssim 8 \times 10^{-13}. \tag{7.7}$$

It is interesting to compare this limit to that for the constant f defined in Eq. (2.1.6), which determines the strength of a hypothetical fifth force mediated by a vector ($J^P = 1^-$) particle. From [SU, 1994] we have, for $Q_5 = B$,

$$f^2/4\pi \lesssim 10^{-45}, \tag{7.8}$$

which is far more stringent than the limit on g_a in Eq. (7.7). It is surprising, at first sight, that there should be so large a difference in the limits on g_a and f, given that similar techniques (with roughly comparable intrinsic sensitivities) were being used in both experiments. (For example, both experiments use torsion fiber technology.) The explanation for this disparity comes in part from the factor $(m_a/2m_N)^2$ in Eq. (7.2), which arises because the axion is a pseudoscalar meson. For parity to be conserved, the axion must be emitted with nonzero orbital angular momentum relative to the initial and final fermions. This gives rise to an angular momentum barrier whose "memory" is $(m_a/2m_N)^2$. In the limit $m_a \to 0$, this factor is replaced by $(1/2m_N r)^2$, where r is the typical dimension of the experimental apparatus. For a nominal value $r = 1\,\text{m}$, this gives

$$(1/2m_N r)^2 \cong (1 \times 10^{-16})^2 = 10^{-32}, \tag{7.9}$$

and this is part of what is responsible for the reduced sensitivity to g_a.

From a practical point of view, the primary difficulty that any experiment encounters is that two polarized samples which can interact via a new weak force can also interact electromagnetically in general. Since the magnetic moment interaction in a typical experiment would be significantly stronger than any hypothesized new weak coupling, one is then faced with the task of extracting a very small signal from a very large background. The electromagnetic background can be substantially reduced, however, by working with special materials in which the net magnetic moment arising from the polarized spins is compensated by an opposing magnetic moment due to orbital motion of the electrons in the sample. This suppresses the unwanted electromagnetic background while at the same time leaving the putative new spin-spin force unaffected.

In the experiment of [RITTER, 1990] the material used for the polarized source is Dy_6Fe_{23}, and a discussion of the properties of this material and their samples is given in the above reference, and in [HSIEH, 1989]. The compensation factor (at room temperature) for each of the samples used is 62. This means that the net magnetic field produced by the polarized spins in each sample was 62 times smaller than would have been expected for a similar sample of spins without the compensating contribution from orbital angular momentum. It follows that for the interaction of two samples the net suppression of the electromagnetic interaction is of order $(62)^2 = 3800$. When this suppression is combined with the effects of using shielding, the product of the compensation and shielding factors is greater than 10^7 per test mass, or 10^{14} for the net electromagnetic interaction strength of the two samples. Of course, such a compensation can only be achieved in small test samples, and hence another limitation on the sensitivity of such experiments (relative to Eötvös-type experiments) is the size of the test samples.

A similar experiment has been carried out by Graham et al. [GRAHAM, 1987, 1989; NEWMAN, 1987], who use a different method for suppressing electromagnetic effects. In their experiment, Graham et al. use superconducting split toroids composed of $GdNi_5$ and $NdNi$ which produce a large net spin polarization at the interface between the half-tori, but only a small net magnetic moment. The force between a fixed toroid and a movable one is then measured by a torsion balance, and they find

$$\alpha_a = -(8.0 \pm 6.3 \pm 1.1) \times 10^{-11}, \tag{7.10}$$

where the first error is statistical and the second is systematic.

Other variants of this experiment have been carried out by Vorobyov and Gitarts (VG) [VOROBYOV, 1988], and by Bobrakov et al. [BOBRAKOV, 1991]. The VG experiment looked for the interaction between a Permalloy test sample, placed inside a superconducting shield, and permanent magnets located outside. The presumption is that the superconducting shield suppresses the electromagnetic interaction, but not the axionic interaction. These authors quote a limit, $|\alpha_a| < 5 \times 10^{-14}$, which is more stringent than the value 9×10^{-12} obtained by Ritter et al. However, the VG limit has been questioned by Ritter et al. on the grounds that it involves a large extrapolation in the behavior of the Permalloy sample as a function of the external field. For further discussion of this point the interested reader should refer to [RITTER, 1990].

To circumvent this criticism Chui and Ni (CN) [CHUI, 1993] carried out an experiment similar to VG, but substituting terbium fluoride (TbF_3) in place of Permalloy. In addition, CN used polarized Dy_6Fe_{23} as the external masses instead of the ferromagnetic masses employed by VG. The reason for choosing TbF$_3$ is that this is a paramagnetic salt and, in contrast to Permalloy, the behavior of such salts in the presence of small applied fields is well understood. For this reason, the quoted limit can be accepted with greater confidence, and is given by

$$\alpha_a = (2.7 \pm 2.4) \times 10^{-14}. \tag{7.11}$$

The potential in Eq. (7.2) arises from the Lagrangian in Eq. (7.3), which conserves all the discrete space-time symmetries C, P, CP, and T. However, another possibility is that the axionic interactions violate P and T [MOODY, 1984], in which case the axion (ϕ_a) could couple to a fermion (ψ) via

$$-\mathcal{L} = g'_a \bar{\psi}(x)\psi(x)\phi_a(x). \tag{7.12}$$

The exchange of such an axion, which couples at one vertex as in Eq. (7.12) and at the other as in Eq. (7.3), gives rise to what is sometimes termed a "monopole-dipole" interaction [MOODY, 1984], or a "mass-spin" interaction [JEN, 1992], between point masses 1 and 2,

$$V(r) = g'_1 g_2 \frac{\vec{\sigma}_2 \cdot \hat{r}}{8\pi M_2} \left(\frac{m_a}{r} + \frac{1}{r^2} \right) e^{-m_a r} + (1 \leftrightarrow 2), \tag{7.13}$$

where $(1 \leftrightarrow 2)$ denotes the term with the labels 1 and 2 interchanged. The operator $\vec{\sigma}_2 \cdot \hat{r}$ in Eq. (7.13) violates T, and this is the "memory" of the fact that the vertices proportional to g_a and g'_a imply opposite transformation properties for ϕ_a under CP and T. An interaction proportional to $\vec{\sigma} \cdot \hat{r}$ had been discussed earlier by Leitner and Okubo [LEITNER, 1964], O'Connell [1974], and Hari Dass [1976, 1977], in connection with the invariance of the gravitational interaction under discrete space-time symmetries.

An experiment for detecting such a force with a range 3–5 cm is discussed in [CHOU, 1990; JEN, 1992; PAN, 1992A,B]. The apparatus is essentially of the Cavendish-type where the external ("attracting") masses are spin-polarized Dy$_6$Fe$_{23}$. The experiment then consists of comparing the force on the unpolarized test masses exerted by the polarized masses when the spins of the latter point toward the test masses and away from them. Preliminary results indicate that the upper limit on the strength of such a mass-spin interaction is less than 1% that of the usual gravitational interaction.

An interesting variant of this experiment, which looks for an interaction proportional to $\vec{\sigma} \cdot \hat{r}$ over a larger distance scale, is that of [HSIEH, 1989]. This experiment compares the weight of a 45.6 g test mass of Dy$_6$Fe$_{23}$ when its polarization is "up" or "down" relative to the direction of the Earth's gravitational field. Such mass comparisons can be carried out quite precisely using commercially available balances, and they find for $\delta m = m_{\text{up}} - m_{\text{down}}$

$$\frac{\delta m}{m} = (1.1 \pm 7.8) \times 10^{-9}, \tag{7.14}$$

where $m = \frac{1}{2}(m_{\text{up}} + m_{\text{down}})$. Since there are on average 0.1 polarized electrons per atom in the test sample, the limit in Eq. (7.14) implies that the acceleration rate of an electron in the Earth's gravitational field is independent of its spin to within $\sim 1\%$. A similar test using nuclear polarized bodies has been discussed by Ni [1990].

We conclude this section with a discussion of several atomic physics resonance experiments, which have been used to set limits anomalous long-range (or intermediate-range) couplings to spin. The prototype of many of these are the Hughes-Drever (H-D) experiments [HUGHES, 1960; DREVER, 1961], variants of which have been performed more recently with higher sensitivity [PRESTAGE, 1985; LAMOREAUX, 1986, 1989; PHILLIPS, 1987; CHUPP, 1989; WINELAND, 1991; VENEMA, 1992]. These experiments, which were originally viewed as tests of Mach's principle, have been understood recently as tests of the isotropy of space or, more generally, of Lorentz invariance [HAUGAN, 1979, 1987].

To illustrate this technique and its implications, we consider the experiment of Wineland et al. [1991], which uses stored $^9\text{Be}^+$ ions. The authors study the hyperfine transition from the $^2S_{1/2}$ ground state $(F, m_F = 1, 0)$ to the state $(F, m_F = 1, -1)$ in a magnetic field $B \cong 0.8194\,\text{T}$. In the absence of any long range spin-dependent forces, the energy difference $\Delta E = 2\pi\hbar\nu_0$ between these two states would correspond to a frequency $\nu_0 \cong 303\,\text{MHz}$. In the presence of an intermediate-range or long-range spin-dependent interaction such as Eq. (7.13), one would expect ν_0 to depend in some way on the orientation of the spin $\vec{S}_A$ of Be. Since the orientation of $\vec{S}_A$ is determined by the applied magnetic field $\vec{B}_0$, the experiment looked for a change in the magnitude of ν_0 depending on whether $\vec{B}_0$ was parallel or antiparallel to the vertical direction in the laboratory. To search for a dipole-dipole interaction such as in Eq. (7.4), the relevant correlation depends on $\vec{S}_A \cdot \vec{S}_B$, where $\vec{S}_B$ was taken to be the direction of the electron spins in the iron pole faces of an electromagnet. No correlation was seen in either case, and for the dipole-dipole interaction their limit corresponds to

$$\alpha_a < 4.1 \times 10^{-11}. \tag{7.15}$$

CHAPTER 8

Epilogue

8.1 Status of Experiments Suggesting a Fifth Force

This chapter collects together a number of topics which have not been addressed previously. We begin by looking back at the experiments which claimed a signal for a fifth force and end with a look at some possible future experiments.

In the preceding chapters we have described many experimental searches for non-Newtonian gravity, including some which found evidence for deviations from the inverse-square law or UFF. It is safe to say that as of this writing (April, 1998), the widespread view among workers in the field is that there is no compelling evidence for any anomalies which could be interpreted as evidence for a new force. In this chapter we briefly summarize the status of each of the experiments or analyses in which an anomaly was reported.

(1) *Eötvös, Pekár, and Fekete* [1922, 1953] (Chapter 4): As we have discussed, the EPF data pointed to the existence of an intermediate-range composition-dependent fifth force. More recent experiments with much higher sensitivity have not seen evidence for such a force, and hence (by implication) suggest that the EPF results are wrong. However, numerous attempts to find significant flaws in the EPF experiment have failed, as have efforts to explain the EPF data in terms of conventional physics [CHU, 1986; FISCHBACH, 1988]. There remains a slight possibility that by virtue of its configuration and/or its location, the EPF experiment might have been sensitive to a new force to which other experiments were not.

In this connection we comment on an alternative model of the EPF results due to Hall et al. [HALL, 1991]. These authors note that the acceleration differences $\Delta\kappa$ measured by EPF correlate not only with $\Delta(B/\mu)$, but also with $\Delta(Q/\mu)$ where the charge Q is defined as follows:

$$Q = M\delta; \qquad \delta = \begin{cases} 1 & \text{for } J > 0, \\ 0 & \text{for } J = 0, \end{cases} \qquad (8.1)$$

where M is the mass of the nucleus and J is its nuclear spin. A plot of $\Delta\kappa$ versus $\Delta(Q/\mu)$ is shown in Fig. 8.1 based on the data given in Hall

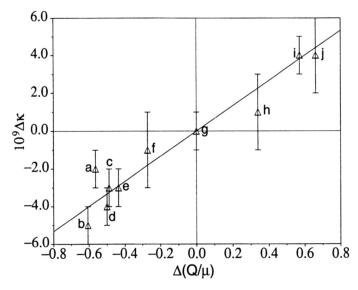

Figure 8.1: Plot of $\Delta(Q/\mu)$ obtained from Eq. (8.1) versus $\Delta\kappa$. See Hall et al. [HALL, 1991] for further details.

et al. [HALL, 1991]. Comparing this figure to Fig. 4.7, we see that the charge defined by Eq. (8.1) provides just as good a fit to the EPF data as does B, with $\chi^2 = 5.1$ (8 degrees of freedom) in the present case. The implication of this correlation is that the EPF results are somehow sensitive to the nuclear spin. However, since the EPF samples were not deliberately polarized, it is difficult to understand how any new force could in fact couple to nuclear spin, as is discussed in more detail in [HALL, 1991]. The analysis of Hall et al. adds one more element to the mystery which surrounds the origin and interpretation of the EPF results, since it raises the possibility that there could be other long-range forces with different characteristics that could account for the EPF data.

(2) *Long* [1976] (Chapter 3): This work was the motivation for the very careful laboratory experiments of Newman and collaborators, as well as other groups (see, for example, [HOSKINS, 1985]). None of the more recent experiments confirm Long's results. Subsequent analysis by Long himself suggests that he may have been seeing the effects of a tilt of the floor in his laboratory as his test masses were moved [LONG, PC].

(3) *Stacey and Tuck* [1981] (Chapter 3): This revival of the Airy method for measuring G_0/G_∞ by geophysical means initially found a result for G_∞ higher than the conventional laboratory value G_0. Following the analysis of terrain bias by Bartlett and Tew [BARTLETT, 1989A,B], Stacey et al. re-examined their data and concluded that the discrepancy between their value of G_∞ and G_0 was a consequence of having undersampled the local gravity

field at higher elevations [TUCK, PC].

(4) *Aronson et al.* [1982] (Chapter 5): This analysis by ABCF of earlier Fermilab data on kaon regeneration presented evidence for an anomalous energy dependence of the kaon parameters, such as could arise from an external hypercharge field. Since the effects reported by ABCF have not been seen in any subsequent experiments, we are led to conclude that the original data were probably biased by some unknown (but conventional) systematic effect. There is, however, a slight possibility that the results of ABCF are correct, notwithstanding the later experiments. This arises from the circumstance that these data came from experiments (E-82 and E-425) in which the kaon beam was not horizontal, but entered the ground at a laboratory angle $\theta_L = 8.25 \times 10^{-3}$rad (to a detector located below ground level). It is straightforward to show that θ_L is related to the angle θ_K seen by the kaons in their proper frame by

$$\tan \theta_K = \gamma \tan \theta_L, \tag{8.1.1}$$

where $\gamma = E_K/m_K$ is the usual relativistic factor. For a typical kaon momentum in those experiments, $p_K = 70\,\text{GeV}/c$, $\gamma \cong 140$ and hence $\theta_K \cong 49°$. It follows that the incident kaons in these experiments would have had a large component of momentum *perpendicular* to the Earth, which would not have been the case for the subsequent kaon experiments. As shown in [SUDARSKY, 1991], motion of a kaon beam perpendicular to a source of a hypercharge field can induce an additional γ-dependence in the kaon parameters. It is thus theoretically possible that the ABCF results are not in conflict with the subsequent experiments, and this could be checked in a number of obvious ways. Similar observations have been made independently by Chardin [CHARDIN, PC].

(5) *Thieberger* [1987A,B] (Chapter 4): In this experiment a hollow copper sphere floating in a tank of water was observed to move in a direction roughly perpendicular to the face of a cliff on which the apparatus was situated. Although the reported results were compatible with the original fifth-force hypothesis, the results of more sensitive torsion balance experiments carried out subsequently were not. As in the case of the original EPF experiment, the implication is that Thieberger's observations can be explained in terms of conventional physics, for example, as a convection effect. This is an important experiment, which should be repeated.

(6) *Hsui* [1987A,B] (Chapter 3): This is another determination of G_0/G_∞ using the Airy method, based on earlier data from a borehole in Michigan. The inferred value of G_0/G_∞ was roughly compatible with the original results of Stacey et al., but with larger errors. Since the original measurements were not taken with the present objectives in mind, it is likely that this determination of G_0/G_∞ suffered from the same terrain bias that Stacey et al. encountered. Moreover, a far more serious problem in Hsui's

analysis was the imprecise and very limited knowledge of the mass distribution in the region surrounding the borehole, which the author himself noted (see also [THOMAS, 1990]).

(7) *Boynton et al.* [BOYNTON, 1987] (Chapter 4): This torsion balance experiment detected a dependence of the oscillation frequency of a composition-dipole pendant on the orientation of the dipole relative to a cliff. A subsequent repetition of this experiment by the authors using an improved pendant and apparatus saw no effect. Despite efforts to shield the apparatus from stray magnetic fields, it is possible that the original effect was due to a small magnetic impurity in the pendant which coupled to a residual magnetic field [BOYNTON, PC].

(8) *Eckhardt et al.* [1988] (Chapter 3): This was the original WTVD tower experiment in North Carolina which saw evidence for an attractive ("sixth") force. As we have previously noted, the analysis of terrain bias by Bartlett and Tew [BARTLETT, 1989A,C] suggested that Eckhardt et al. may have undersampled the local gravity field in low-lying regions surrounding their tower. When the tower results were corrected for this effect, the predicted and observed gravitational accelerations on the tower agreed to within errors. A subsequent experiment by these authors on the WABG tower in Mississippi found agreement with Newtonian gravity [ROMAIDES, 1994, 1997], as did experiments on the Erie tower in Colorado [SPEAKE, 1990], and the BREN tower in Nevada [THOMAS, 1989; KAMMERAAD, 1990].

(9) *Ander et al.* [1989A,B] (Chapter 3): This was another version of the Airy method, which used a borehole in the Greenland ice cap, and observed an anomalous gravity gradient down the borehole. However, this effect could not be attributed unambiguously to a deviation from Newtonian gravity, since it could have also arisen from unexpected mass concentrations, etc., in the rock below the ice [PARKER, 1989; THOMAS, 1990].

8.2 Possibility of an Electromagnetic Fifth Force

Our focus in this book has been on possible new forces which, coexisting with gravity, would manifest themselves through apparent deviations from Newton's inverse-square law. It is natural to ask whether a similar analysis can be carried out for a hypothetical electromagnetic "fifth force," whose presence could be detected through apparent deviations from Coulomb's law. This question has been addressed by Bartlett and Lögl [BARTLETT, 1988], and subsequently in [KLOOR, 1994A,B] and [FISCHBACH, 1994]. Although there are obvious similarities between the gravitational and electromagnetic cases, there are also some significant differences. In part these have to do with the fact that over certain distance scales the relevant electromagnetic data come from systems where quantum mechanical effects are important, and this introduces issues that are not relevant for existing gravitational experiments. A more detailed consideration of the phenomenology of an electromagnetic fifth force is beyond the scope of the present work, and the interested reader should refer to the previous papers for further discussion.

8.3 Astrophysical Constraints on New Forces

As we noted in the Introduction, limits on non-Newtonian interactions can also be inferred from various astrophysical arguments such as the thermodynamics of white dwarfs [MEMBRADO, 1988A,B, 1990]. These authors note that in principle a Yukawa-like interaction can change the mass-radius relation for a white dwarf, although for the (small) values of α compatible with Fig. 2.13, the effects would not be detectable. However, the authors make the interesting observation that when $\alpha \neq 0$ the Chandrasekhar limit [CHANDRASEKHAR, 1957] on the maximum mass M_{ch} of a white dwarf, $M_{ch} > 1.46 M_\odot = 2.8535 \times 10^{33} g$, is replaced by a limiting minimum radius which depends on α. The interested reader should consult the above references for further details. A related analysis of the effects of intermediate-range forces on stellar structure has been carried out by Glass and Szamosi [GLASS, 1987, 1989]. Glass and Szamosi show that the effects of such forces are comparable to those arising from general relativistic effects for values of the strength and range compatible with the Eötvös experiment. Unfortunately, these effects are too small to lead to significant new constraints on ξ and λ.

In a similar spirit Gilliland and Däppen have inferred limits on possible new interactions from a study of solar structure [GILLILAND, 1987]. These authors note that for $\lambda \ll R_\odot$, gravitation can be treated as an exact inverse-square law for purposes of studying stellar evolution. The only effect of an additional Yukawa term, as in Eq. (2.1.8), would be to modify the effective Newtonian constant, as in Eq. (2.1.11):

$$G_\infty \rightarrow G_0 = G_\infty(1 + \alpha). \tag{8.3.1}$$

Since G_∞ appears in the combination $G_\infty M_\odot$, such a change has the effect of changing the value of $M_\odot$ that would be inferred from planetary motion (see Section 3.8). This in turn would modify the mean density and luminosity of the Sun, and hence $\alpha \neq 0$ could lead to detectable effects. However, for values of α and λ compatible with other experiments, the effects on solar structure and evolution would be masked by other theoretical uncertainties.

Similar considerations have been used by Grifols and Massó [GRIFOLS, 1986] to set limits on new forces coupling to baryon number or lepton number. These limits are derived by noting that energy would be transferred to the quanta of any new field in the core of stars. Since these quanta interact weakly with matter, this mechanism could significantly modify the stellar cooling rates. However, as noted by the authors, these limits on couplings to B and L are not as restrictive as those arising from Eötvös-type experiments.

Astrophysical limits can also be inferred by comparing theoretical predictions for the orbital precession in binary systems with observation [BURGESS, 1988; MALONEY, 1989]. These authors focus on apparent discrepancies between theory and observation for two systems, DI Her and AS Cam, and ask whether these could be a signal for a new non-Newtonian coupling. In the end the conclusion is that existing laboratory experiments set limits on ξ or $|\alpha|$ which are sufficient to rule out non-Newtonian gravity as an explanation of these discrepancies. Nonetheless, it is clear that these systems are quite sensitive to possible new forces, for reasons spelled out by Burgess and Cloutier: They observe that the interaction energy in General Relativity differs from the corresponding Newtonian law by velocity-dependent terms which are of order $v^2/c^2 \approx GM_\odot/R_\odot c^2 \ll 1$. This suppresses the contribution from General Relativity to orbital precession compared to that for a Yukawa interaction, since the latter exists even in the static limit, as shown in Section 3.8.

8.4 Future Space-Based Experiments

In addition to the STEP experiment discussed in Section 4.8, a number of other space-based experiments have been proposed to search for deviations from the predictions of Newtonian gravity [HAYASHI, 1987B; NOBILI, 1987, 1988, 1990, 1996; SILVERMAN, 1987; WILL, 1989; SPALLICCI, 1990; BRAMANTI, 1992; SANDERS, 1992; REINHARD, 1996]. These have in common the theme that space-based experiments can reduce various sources of noise that are present in terrestrial experiments. As an example we consider the proposal by Nobili and coworkers [NOBILI, 1987] to measure the Newtonian constant G in space by placing a small-scale planetary system in geosynchronous orbit. Since both the compositions of the orbiting masses and their relative separations can be controlled in such an experiment, one can in principle test simultaneously for composition-dependent and composition-independent non-Newtonian forces. Apart from the STEP experiment, none of the other space-based experiments have been fully pursued at this time. However, a number of imaginative proposals have been advanced, and the interested reader should consult the above references for further details.

Gravity-Gradient Couplings
to Torsion Pendants

A.1 Theoretical Formalism

In searching for a hypothetical fifth force using a torsion balance, care must be taken to distinguish between the genuine signals for such a force and those arising from conventional gravity gradients. Since gravity gradients can produce large signals with characteristics similar to those of a fifth force, almost all torsion balance experiments dating back to EPF have gone to some lengths to reduce or eliminate these spurious influences. In this appendix we describe in detail the coupling of gravity gradients to torsion balances and give numerical results for some of the actual experiments.

As before we denote the external gravitational field by $\vec{g}(\vec{r})$, where $\vec{r} \equiv x\,\hat{x} + y\,\hat{y} + z\,\hat{z}$ is the distance from the center of mass of the torsion balance to an infinitesimal mass point in the source. If $\vec{r}_0$ denotes the position of the center of mass of the torsion balance relative to the center of coordinates then the gravitational torque $\vec{\tau}$ will be given by

$$\vec{\tau} = \int \vec{r} \times [\vec{g}(\vec{r} - \vec{r}_0)dm(\vec{r})]. \qquad (A.1.1)$$

We can expand $\vec{g}$ in terms of $|\vec{r}|/|\vec{r}_0|$ to give

$$
\begin{aligned}
-\vec{g}(\vec{r} - \vec{r}_0) = &[V_x\hat{x} + V_y\hat{y} + V_z\hat{z}] + [(xV_{xx} + yV_{xy} + zV_{xz})\hat{x} \\
&+ (xV_{xy} + yV_{yy} + zV_{yz})\hat{y} + (xV_{xz} + yV_{yz} + zV_{zz})\hat{z}] \\
&+ \frac{1}{2}\Big[(x^2V_{xxx} + y^2V_{xyy} + z^2V_{xzz} + 2xyV_{xxy} + 2xzV_{xxz} + 2yzV_{xyz})\hat{x} \\
&+ (x^2V_{xxy} + y^2V_{yyy} + z^2V_{yzz} + 2xyV_{xyy} + 2xzV_{xyz} + 2yzV_{yyz})\hat{y} \\
&+ (x^2V_{xxz} + y^2V_{yyz} + z^2V_{zzz} + 2xyV_{xyz} + 2xzV_{xzz} + 2yzV_{yzz})\hat{z}\Big] \\
&+ \cdots
\end{aligned}
\qquad (A.1.2)
$$

Here we have defined $V(\vec{r})$ such that $\vec{g} = -\vec{\nabla}V$, with $V_x \equiv \partial V/\partial x$, etc. Inserting Eq. (A.1.2) into Eq. (A.1.1) gives

$$
\begin{aligned}
\vec{\tau} = m\Big\{ &(\ell_z V_y - \ell_y V_z)\hat{x} + (\ell_x V_z - \ell_z V_x)\hat{y} + (\ell_y V_x - \ell_x V_y)\hat{z}\Big\} \\
&+ \Big\{ [(I_{zz} - I_{yy})V_{yz} - I_{yz}(V_{zz} - V_{yy}) + I_{xz}V_{xy} - I_{xy}V_{xz}]\hat{x} \\
&\quad + [(I_{xx} - I_{zz})V_{xz} - I_{xz}(V_{xx} - V_{zz}) + I_{xy}V_{yz} - I_{yz}V_{xy}]\hat{y} \\
&\quad + [(I_{yy} - I_{xx})V_{xy} - I_{xy}(V_{yy} - V_{xx}) + I_{yz}V_{xz} - I_{xz}V_{yz}]\hat{z}\Big\} \\
&+ \Big\{ \tfrac{1}{2}[(Q_{zzz} - Q_{yyz})V_{yzz} - (Q_{yyy} - Q_{yzz})V_{yyz} - Q_{yzz}(V_{zzz} - V_{yyz}) \\
&\quad + Q_{yyz}(V_{yyy} - V_{yzz}) + 2(Q_{xzz} - Q_{xyy})V_{xyz} - 2Q_{xyz}(V_{xzz} - V_{xyy}) \\
&\quad + Q_{xxz}V_{xxy} - Q_{xxy}V_{xxz}]\hat{x} \\
&\quad + \tfrac{1}{2}[(Q_{xxx} - Q_{xzz})V_{xxz} - (Q_{zzz} - Q_{xxz})V_{xzz} - Q_{xxz}(V_{xxx} - V_{xzz}) \\
&\quad + Q_{xzz}(V_{zzz} - V_{xxz}) + 2(Q_{xxy} - Q_{yzz})V_{xyz} - 2Q_{xyz}(V_{xxy} - V_{yzz}) \\
&\quad + Q_{xyy}V_{yyz} - Q_{yyz}V_{xyy}]\hat{y} \\
&\quad + \tfrac{1}{2}[(Q_{yyy} - Q_{xxy})V_{xyy} - (Q_{xxx} - Q_{xyy})V_{xxy} - Q_{xyy}(V_{yyy} - V_{xxy}) \\
&\quad + Q_{xxy}(V_{xxx} - V_{xyy}) + 2(Q_{yyz} - Q_{xxz})V_{xyz} - 2Q_{xyz}(V_{yyz} - V_{xxz}) \\
&\quad + Q_{yzz}V_{xzz} - Q_{xzz}V_{yzz}]\hat{z}\Big\} \\
+ \cdots &
\end{aligned}
$$

$$\text{(A.1.3)}$$

In Eq. (A.1.3) we have defined

$$\ell_{x_i} \equiv \frac{1}{m}\int_{\text{pendant}} x_i\, dm, \tag{A.1.4a}$$

$$I_{x_i x_j} \equiv \int_{\text{pendant}} x_i x_j\, dm, \tag{A.1.4b}$$

$$Q_{x_i x_j x_k} \equiv \int_{\text{pendant}} x_i x_j x_k\, dm. \tag{A.1.4c}$$

It should be noted that if we demand that the first-order contributions to $\vec{\tau}$ vanish, i.e., $\tau_x^{(1)} = \tau_y^{(1)} = 0$, then $\tau_z^{(1)} = 0$ as well. This can be seen as follows:

$$\tau_x^{(1)} \equiv 0 \longrightarrow \ell_y = \frac{\ell_z V_y}{V_z}$$

$$\tau_y^{(1)} \equiv 0 \longrightarrow \ell_x = \frac{\ell_z V_x}{V_z}$$

hence,

$$\tau_z^{(1)} = \ell_y V_x - \ell_x V_y = \frac{\ell_z V_x V_y}{V_z} - \frac{\ell_z V_x V_y}{V_z} \equiv 0. \qquad (A.1.5)$$

When we include higher-order terms in this balance condition, the effect of any imbalance is of order V_x/V_z and V_y/V_z, which we take for these calculations to be negligible. Requiring that $\tau_x = \tau_y = 0$ then gives from Eq. (A.1.3)

$$\begin{aligned}
\vec{\tau} = \Big\{ &\big[(I_{yy} - I_{xx})V_{xy} - I_{xy}(V_{yy} - V_{xx}) + I_{yz}V_{xz} - I_{xz}V_{yz} \big] \\
&+ \frac{1}{2}\big[(Q_{yyy} - Q_{xxy})V_{xyy} - (Q_{xxx} - Q_{xyy})V_{xxy} \\
&\quad - Q_{xyy}(V_{yyy} - V_{xxy}) + Q_{xxy}(V_{xxx} - V_{xyy}) \\
&\quad + 2(Q_{yyz} - Q_{xxz})V_{xyz} - 2Q_{xyz}(V_{yyz} - V_{xxz}) \\
&\quad + Q_{yzz}V_{xzz} - Q_{xzz}V_{yzz} \big] + \cdots \Big\} \hat{z} \, .
\end{aligned} \qquad (A.1.6)$$

We can also write this expression in a form which is less symmetric, but perhaps more useful:

$$\begin{aligned}
\vec{\tau} = \Big\{ &\big[(I_{yy} - I_{xx})V_{xy} - I_{xy}(V_{yy} - V_{xx}) + I_{yz}V_{xz} - I_{xz}V_{yz} \big] \\
&+ \frac{1}{2}\big[Q_{yyy}V_{xyy} - Q_{xxx}V_{xxy} - Q_{xyy}(V_{yyy} - 2V_{xxy}) \\
&\quad + Q_{xxy}(V_{xxx} - 2V_{xyy}) + 2(Q_{yyz} - Q_{xxz})V_{xyz} \\
&\quad - 2Q_{xyz}(V_{yyz} - V_{xxz}) + Q_{yzz}V_{xzz} - Q_{xzz}V_{yzz} \big] \\
&+ \cdots \Big\} \hat{z} \, .
\end{aligned} \qquad (A.1.7)$$

$I_{x_i x_j}$ and $Q_{x_i x_j x_k}$ in Eq. (A.1.7) are, respectively, the components of the moment of inertia and quadrupole moment tensors relative to the external coordinate system (i.e., the coordinate system in which $V_{x_i x_j}$ and $V_{x_i x_j x_k}$ are measured). We can re-express these in terms of the body-fixed coordinate system of the pendant by rotating these quantities about the z-axis, using the definitions in Eqs. (A.1.4b,c), where

$$x \longrightarrow x\cos\theta - y\sin\theta, \qquad (A.1.8a)$$
$$y \longrightarrow x\sin\theta + y\cos\theta. \qquad (A.1.8b)$$

We will henceforth refer to the values for the I's and Q's defined in the external coordinate system as $I_{x_i x_j}(\theta)$ and $Q_{x_i x_j x_k}(\theta)$ to distinguish these from the quantities in the body-fixed coordinate system. We then have

$$I_{xx}(\theta) = I_{xx}\cos^2\theta + I_{yy}\sin^2\theta - I_{xy}\sin 2\theta, \qquad (A.1.9a)$$
$$I_{yy}(\theta) = I_{yy}\cos^2\theta + I_{xx}\sin^2\theta + I_{xy}\sin 2\theta, \qquad (A.1.9b)$$
$$I_{xy}(\theta) = I_{xy}\cos 2\theta + (I_{xx} - I_{yy})\sin 2\theta, \qquad (A.1.9c)$$
$$I_{xz}(\theta) = I_{xz}\cos\theta - I_{yz}\sin\theta, \qquad (A.1.9d)$$
$$I_{yz}(\theta) = I_{xz}\sin\theta + I_{yz}\cos\theta, \qquad (A.1.9e)$$
$$I_{zz}(\theta) = I_{zz}, \qquad (A.1.9f)$$

and

$$Q_{xxx}(\theta) = Q_{xxx}c^3 - 3Q_{xxy}c^2 s + 3Q_{xyy}cs^2 - Q_{yyy}s^3, \tag{A.1.10a}$$

$$Q_{xxy}(\theta) = Q_{xxx}c^2 s + Q_{xxy}(c^3 - 2cs^2) + Q_{xyy}(s^3 - 2c^2 s) + Q_{yyy}cs^2, \tag{A.1.10b}$$

$$Q_{xyy}(\theta) = Q_{xxx}cs^2 - Q_{xxy}(s^3 - 2c^2 s) + Q_{xyy}(c^3 - 2cs^2) - Q_{yyy}c^2 s, \tag{A.1.10c}$$

$$Q_{yyy}(\theta) = Q_{xxx}s^3 + 3Q_{xxy}cs^2 + 3Q_{xyy}c^2 s + c^3 Q_{yyy}, \tag{A.1.10d}$$

$$Q_{xxz}(\theta) = Q_{xxz}c^2 - Q_{xyz}2cs + Q_{yyz}s^2, \tag{A.1.10e}$$

$$Q_{xyz}(\theta) = (Q_{xxz} - Q_{yyz})cs + Q_{xyz}(c^2 - s^2), \tag{A.1.10f}$$

$$Q_{yyz}(\theta) = Q_{xxz}s^2 + Q_{xyz}2cs + Q_{yyz}c^2, \tag{A.1.10g}$$

$$Q_{xzz}(\theta) = Q_{xzz}c - Q_{yzz}s, \tag{A.1.10h}$$

$$Q_{yzz}(\theta) = Q_{xzz}s + Q_{yzz}c, \tag{A.1.10i}$$

$$Q_{zzz}(\theta) = Q_{zzz}, \tag{A.1.10j}$$

where $s \equiv \sin\theta$ and $c \equiv \cos\theta$ in Eqs. (A.1.10). Combining Eqs. (A.1.8)–(A.1.10) gives

$$
\begin{aligned}
\tau_z(\theta) = {}& [(I_{yy} - I_{xx})\cos 2\theta + 2I_{xy}\sin 2\theta]V_{xy} \\
& - [I_{xy}\cos 2\theta - \tfrac{1}{2}(I_{yy} - I_{xx})\sin 2\theta](V_{yy} - V_{xx}) \\
& + (I_{yz}\cos\theta + I_{xz}\sin\theta)V_{xz} - (I_{xz}\cos\theta - I_{yz}\sin\theta)V_{yz} \\
& + \tfrac{1}{8}[Q_{xxx}(s + s_3) + Q_{xxy}(c + 3c_3) + Q_{xyy}(s - 3s_3) + Q_{yyy}(c - c_3)]V_{xxx} \\
& + \tfrac{1}{8}[-Q_{xxx}(c + 3c_3) + Q_{xxy}(s + 9s_3) - Q_{xyy}(c - 9c_3) + Q_{yyy}(s - 3s_3)]V_{xxy} \\
& + \tfrac{1}{8}[Q_{xxx}(s - 3s_3) + Q_{xxy}(c - 9c_3) + Q_{xyy}(s + 9s_3) + Q_{yyy}(c + 3c_3)]V_{xyy} \\
& + \tfrac{1}{8}[-Q_{xxx}(c - c_3) + Q_{xxy}(s - 3s_3) - Q_{xyy}(c + 3c_3) + Q_{yyy}(s + s_3)]V_{yyy} \\
& + [(Q_{xxz} - Q_{yyz})\sin 2\theta + 2Q_{xyz}\cos 2\theta](V_{xxz} - V_{yyz}) \\
& + [(Q_{yyz} - Q_{xxz})\cos 2\theta + 2Q_{xyz}\sin 2\theta]V_{xyz} \\
& + \tfrac{1}{2}(Q_{yzz}\cos\theta + Q_{xzz}\sin\theta)V_{xzz} + \tfrac{1}{2}(Q_{xzz}\cos\theta - Q_{yzz}\sin\theta)V_{yzz} \\
& + \cdots
\end{aligned}
\tag{A.1.11}
$$

where $c_3 = \cos 3\theta$ and $s_3 = \sin 3\theta$. It is sometimes convenient to rewrite the previous expression as a Fourier series expansion by explicitly identifying the coefficients of $\sin n\theta$ and $\cos n\theta$:

$$
\begin{aligned}
\tau_z(\theta) \cong {}& \Big[I_{xz}V_{xz} + I_{yz}V_{yz} + \tfrac{1}{2}(Q_{xzz}V_{xzz} + Q_{yzz}V_{yzz}) \\
& + \tfrac{1}{8}(Q_{xxx} + Q_{xyy})(V_{xxx} + V_{xyy}) \\
& + \tfrac{1}{8}(Q_{xxy} + Q_{yyy})(V_{xxy} + V_{yyy}) \Big]\sin\theta
\end{aligned}
$$

$$+ \left[I_{yz}V_{xz} - I_{xz}V_{yz} + \frac{1}{2}(Q_{yzz}V_{xzz} - Q_{xzz}V_{yzz}) \right.$$

$$+ \frac{1}{8}(Q_{xxx} + Q_{xyy})(V_{xxx} + V_{xyy})$$

$$\left. + \frac{1}{8}(Q_{xxy} + Q_{yyy})(V_{xxy} + V_{yyy}) \right] \cos\theta$$

$$+ \left[I_{xy}V_{xy} + \frac{1}{2}(I_{yy} - I_{xx})(V_{yy} - V_{xx}) + 2Q_{xyz}V_{xyz} \right.$$

$$\left. + (Q_{yyz} - Q_{xxz})(V_{yyz} - V_{xxz}) \right] \sin 2\theta$$

$$+ \left[I_{xy}(V_{yy} - V_{xx}) - V_{xy}(I_{yy} - I_{xx}) \right.$$

$$\left. - 2Q_{xyz}(V_{yyz} - V_{xxz}) - V_{xyz}(Q_{yyz} - Q_{xxz}) \right] \cos 2\theta$$

$$+ \frac{1}{8} \left[(Q_{xxx} - 3Q_{xyy})(V_{xxx} - 3V_{xyy}) \right.$$

$$\left. + (Q_{yyy} - 3Q_{xxy})(V_{yyy} - 3V_{xxy}) \right] \sin 3\theta$$

$$+ \frac{1}{8} \left[(Q_{xxx} - 3Q_{xyy})(V_{yyy} - 3V_{xxy}) \right.$$

$$\left. - (Q_{yyy} - 3Q_{xxy})(V_{xxx} - 3V_{xyy}) \right] \cos 3\theta. \qquad \text{(A.1.12)}$$

A.2 Gravity Couplings to Various Experimental Systems

We consider in this section the coupling of the higher gravity multipoles to various experimental systems. To do so we introduce the generalized multipole tensor

$$\mathcal{M}_{npq} \equiv \int d^3x \, \rho(\vec{x}) x^n y^p z^q. \qquad \text{(A.2.1)}$$

In terms of this notation, for instance, $\mathcal{M}_{000}$ is simply the total mass of the pendant, $\mathcal{M}_{200}$ is the quadrupole moment I_{xx}, $\mathcal{M}_{111}$ is the octapole moment Q_{xyz}, etc. The utility of the definition of $\mathcal{M}_{npq}$ is that it allows us to express all of the multipole moments in terms of a single analytic expression. Additionally, this form is especially suited for generating the desired terms algebraically via software such as MATHEMATICA, or numerically via any standard numerical integration package.

A.2.1 The Eötvös Experiment

This experiment [EÖTVÖS, 1922, 1953] utilized a two-mass pendant, as described previously. In this arrangement, both masses were always cylinders, with the lower hanging mass being attached in such a way that the axis of symmetry of the cylinder was (nearly) parallel to the axis of the torsion fiber. The standard mass, however, was attached to the brass torsion bar such that its axis of symmetry was parallel to the brass torsion bar, which was itself perpendicular to the fiber. Letting quantities with the subscript "1" refer to the lower hanging mass, and "2" refer to the horizontal standard mass, we obtain for this system

$$
\mathcal{M}_{npq} = \rho_1 \int_0^{2\pi} d\phi \int_0^{R_1} dr\, r \int_{-L_1/2}^{L_1/2} dz\, (r\cos\phi + \ell_1)^n (r\sin\phi)^p (z+h)^q
$$
$$
+ \rho_2 \int_0^{2\pi} d\phi \int_0^{R_2} dr\, r \int_{-L_2/2}^{L_2/2} dz\, (z-\ell_2)^n (r\sin\phi)^p (r\cos\phi)^q. \quad \text{(A.2.2)}
$$

Evaluating the integrals in (A.2.2) we find

$$\mathcal{M}_{000} \equiv m_t = \rho_1 \pi R_1^2 L_1 + \rho_2 \pi R_2^2 L_2 = m_1 + m_2, \tag{A.2.3a}$$

$$\mathcal{M}_{100} \equiv m_t \ell_x = m_1 \ell_1 - m_2 \ell_2 \cong 0, \tag{A.2.3b}$$

$$\mathcal{M}_{010} \equiv m_t \ell_y = 0, \tag{A.2.3c}$$

$$\mathcal{M}_{001} \equiv m_t \ell_z = m_1 h, \tag{A.2.3d}$$

$$\mathcal{M}_{200} \equiv I_{xx} = m_1(\ell_1^2 + \tfrac{1}{4} R_1^2) + m_2(\ell_2^2 + \tfrac{1}{12} L_2^2), \tag{A.2.3e}$$

$$\mathcal{M}_{110} \equiv I_{xy} = 0, \tag{A.2.3f}$$

$$\mathcal{M}_{020} \equiv I_{yy} = \tfrac{1}{4} m_1 R_1^2 + \tfrac{1}{4} m_2 R_2^2, \tag{A.2.3g}$$

$$\mathcal{M}_{101} \equiv I_{xz} = m_1 \ell_1 h, \tag{A.2.3h}$$

$$\mathcal{M}_{011} \equiv I_{yz} = 0, \tag{A.2.3i}$$

$$\mathcal{M}_{002} \equiv I_{zz} = m_1(h^2 + \tfrac{1}{12} L_1^2) + \tfrac{1}{4} m_2 R_2^2, \tag{A.2.3j}$$

$$\mathcal{M}_{300} \equiv Q_{xxx} = m_1 \ell_1(\ell_1^2 + \tfrac{3}{4} R_1^2) - m_2 \ell_2(\ell_2^2 + \tfrac{1}{4} L_2^2), \tag{A.2.3k}$$

$$\mathcal{M}_{210} \equiv Q_{xxy} = 0, \tag{A.2.3l}$$

$$\mathcal{M}_{120} \equiv Q_{xyy} = \tfrac{1}{4} m_1 \ell_1 R_1^2 - \tfrac{1}{4} m_2 \ell_2 R_2^2, \tag{A.2.3m}$$

$$\mathcal{M}_{030} \equiv Q_{yyy} = 0, \tag{A.2.3n}$$

$$\mathcal{M}_{201} \equiv Q_{xxz} = m_1 h(\ell_1^2 + \tfrac{1}{4} R_1^2), \tag{A.2.3o}$$

$$\mathcal{M}_{111} \equiv Q_{xyz} = 0, \tag{A.2.3p}$$

$$\mathcal{M}_{021} \equiv Q_{yyz} = \tfrac{1}{4} m_1 h R_1^2, \tag{A.2.3q}$$

$$\mathcal{M}_{102} \equiv Q_{xzz} = \tfrac{1}{4} m_1 \ell_1(h^2 + \tfrac{1}{12} L_1^2) - \tfrac{1}{4} m_2 \ell_2 R_2^2, \tag{A.2.3r}$$

$$\mathcal{M}_{012} \equiv Q_{yzz} = 0, \tag{A.2.3s}$$

$$\mathcal{M}_{003} \equiv Q_{zzz} = m_1 h(h^2 + \tfrac{1}{4} L_1^2). \tag{A.2.3t}$$

We take as typical values from [EÖTVÖS, 1922], $m_1 \cong 25.4\,\mathrm{g}$, $m_2 \cong 30.0\,\mathrm{g}$, $\ell_1 = 20.0\,\mathrm{cm}$, $h \cong 21.2\,\mathrm{cm}$, $L_2 = 11.1\,\mathrm{cm}$, and $R_2 \cong 0.2\,\mathrm{cm}$. We also insert into Eq. (A.1.12) representative values for the various gravity gradients which are taken from our best model of the site of the Eötvös experiment [BOD, 1991]. We obtain for the net gravitational torque

$$\tau \cong -\Big\{ \left(0.378 + 0.478L_1^2 - 1.43R_1^2\right)\sin\theta$$
$$+ \left(1.33 + 1.42L_1^2 - 4.27R_1^2\right)\cos\theta$$
$$- 5.56\sin 2\theta - 0.0944\cos 2\theta$$
$$- 0.0290\sin 3\theta + 0.0780\cos 3\theta\Big\} \times 10^{-10}\,\mathrm{N\,m}. \qquad (A.2.4)$$

Here L_1 and R_1 are expressed in units of meters, and we have used the convention of EPF that a positive torque is one which would tend to rotate the torsion bar clockwise as viewed from above. Eq. (A.2.4) gives values for the experimental quantities v and m defined by EPF (see Section 4.2) which are roughly in the correct proportion to the values they actually obtained, although these values are too large by a factor of ~ 2.

The gravity-gradient contributions to τ in Eq. (A.2.4) are large compared to the limits quoted by EPF for the validity of the equivalence principle, or to the size of the claimed signal for the fifth force, as inferred by [FISCHBACH, 1986A]. This is, of course, not surprising, since the EPF apparatus was originally designed to measure gravity gradients, which was the purpose of the set of experiments performed by Eötvös in the mountains of Hungary [EÖTVÖS, 1953]. To cancel out the effects of gravity gradients, EPF combined the results of measurements made with the torsion balance oriented in different directions, as explained in Section 4.2.

The fact that the EPF experiment was as sensitive as it was to gravity gradients leads to the suggestion that perhaps the correlation in the EPF data suggesting a fifth force is actually due to some uncanceled gradient coupling. A model of this sort suggested by Stubbs has been analyzed by Talmadge [1987A], who shows (using the preceding analysis) that the gradient couplings are too small by roughly a factor of 10 to account for the EPF data.

A.2.2 The Eöt-Wash Experiment

In this section, we consider the coupling of gravity gradients to the pendant in the experiment of Stubbs et al. [STUBBS, 1987]. The pendant for this experiment consisted of two hollow Cu cylinders and two solid Be cylinders. All of the cylinders had a length $L = 1.908\,\mathrm{cm}$, radius $R = 0.9525\,\mathrm{cm}$, and mass $M = 10.04\,\mathrm{g}$. These were situated at the four corners of a square whose side was $S = 3.9\,\mathrm{cm}$, with the Cu masses being located at adjacent corners. In this discussion, we consider only the effects arising from the gravitational coupling of the compensating lead bricks to the difference in the density distribution between the two Cu masses and the two Be masses. We note that there will also be, for instance, effects due to the misalignment of the vertical positions of the centers of mass of the cylinders, which we are ignoring. For this mass configuration we then have

$$
\begin{aligned}
\mathcal{M}_{npq} = \\
\rho_{Be} & \int_0^{2\pi} d\phi \int_0^R dr\, r \int_{-L/2}^{L/2} dz\, (r\cos\phi - S/2)^n (r\sin\phi + S/2)^p (z - \delta z_1)^q \\
+ \rho_{Be} & \int_0^{2\pi} d\phi \int_0^R dr\, r \int_{-L/2}^{L/2} dz\, (r\cos\phi - S/2)^n (r\sin\phi - S/2)^p (z - \delta z_2)^q \\
+ \rho_{Cu} & \int_0^{2\pi} d\phi \int_0^R dr\, r \int_{-L/2}^{L/2} dz\, (r\cos\phi + S/2)^n (r\sin\phi - S/2)^p (z - \delta z_3)^q \\
- \rho_{Cu} & \int_0^{2\pi} d\phi \int_0^{R-t} dr\, r \int_{-L/2+t}^{L/2-t} dz\, (r\cos\phi + S/2)^n (r\sin\phi - S/2)^p (z - \delta z_3)^q \\
+ \rho_{Cu} & \int_0^{2\pi} d\phi \int_0^R dr\, r \int_{-L/2}^{L/2} dz\, (r\cos\phi + S/2)^n (r\sin\phi + S/2)^p (z - \delta z_4)^q \\
- \rho_{Cu} & \int_0^{2\pi} d\phi \int_0^{R-t} dr\, r \int_{-L/2+t}^{L/2-t} dz\, (r\cos\phi + S/2)^n (r\sin\phi + S/2)^p (z - \delta z_4)^q .
\end{aligned}
$$

$$(A.2.5)$$

In this equation δz_1, ..., δz_4 represent the errors in the vertical positioning of the centers of mass of the test bodies and, as mentioned above, will be taken to be zero for this analysis. Also, $t \cong 0.71$ mm represents the thickness of the Cu cylinders and their end caps (assumed for this analysis to be the same). The analytic forms of the various mass multipoles, which are somewhat involved, are not particularly useful in this case. For this reason, only the numerical results for the nonzero mass moments are quoted here:

$$I_{xx} = I_{yy} = 1.643 \times 10^{-5}\, \text{kg}\,\text{m}^2, \qquad (A.2.6a)$$

$$I_{zz} = 1.553 \times 10^{-6}\, \text{kg}\,\text{m}^2, \qquad (A.2.6b)$$

$$Q_{xxx} = 1.464 \times 10^{-8}\, \text{kg}\,\text{m}^3, \qquad (A.2.6c)$$

$$Q_{xyy} = 4.882 \times 10^{-9}\, \text{kg}\,\text{m}^3, \qquad (A.2.6d)$$

$$Q_{xzz} = 6.519 \times 10^{-9}\, \text{kg}\,\text{m}^3. \qquad (A.2.6e)$$

The configuration we use for the compensating lead bricks is that described by Stubbs et al. [1988A]. In the present analysis, the configuration was built up of two parallelepipeds whose centers of geometry were along the $+x$-axis, with the origin of coordinates at the center of mass of the pendant, and the $+z$-direction pointing upwards along the torsion fiber. Both parallelepipeds

Table A.1: Dimensions of the compensating masses in the experiment of Stubbs et al. [STUBBS, 1987, 1988A], as used for the analysis this appendix. The coordinate positions given are for the faces of each parallelepiped along the coordinate axis to which it is perpendicular. All dimensions are given in inches, and the parallelepipeds were composed of lead, for which $\rho_{Pb} \cong 11.35\,\mathrm{g\,cm^{-3}}$.

Paralellipiped	x_1	x_2	y_1	y_2	z_1	z_2
#1	+6.5	+14.5	−6.0	+6.0	+1.0	+5.0
#2	+7.0	+11.0	−4.0	+4.0	+5.0	+7.0

were so aligned that their faces were parallel to the coordinate planes, with the coordinate positions along the axis perpendicular to each face given in Table A.1.

For this configuration we find for the nonvanishing components of the various (relevant) gravitational gradients

$$g_x = +6.42 \times 10^{-8}\,\mathrm{m\,s^{-2}}, \tag{A.2.7a}$$

$$g_z = +2.31 \times 10^{-8}\,\mathrm{m\,s^{-2}}, \tag{A.2.7b}$$

$$V_{xx} = -3.75 \times 10^{-7}\,\mathrm{s^{-2}}, \tag{A.2.7c}$$

$$V_{yy} = +2.02 \times 10^{-7}\,\mathrm{s^{-2}}, \tag{A.2.7d}$$

$$V_{xz} = -2.80 \times 10^{-6}\,\mathrm{s^{-2}}, \tag{A.2.7e}$$

$$V_{xxx} = -2.80 \times 10^{-6}\,\mathrm{m^{-1}\,s^{-2}}, \tag{A.2.7f}$$

$$V_{xyy} = +1.65 \times 10^{-6}\,\mathrm{m^{-1}\,s^{-2}}, \tag{A.2.7g}$$

$$V_{xxz} = -2.91 \times 10^{-6}\,\mathrm{m^{-1}\,s^{-2}}, \tag{A.2.7h}$$

$$V_{yyz} = +0.63 \times 10^{-6}\,\mathrm{m^{-1}\,s^{-2}}, \tag{A.2.7i}$$

$$V_{xzz} = +1.15 \times 10^{-6}\,\mathrm{m^{-1}\,s^{-2}}, \tag{A.2.7j}$$

$$V_{zzz} = +2.29 \times 10^{-6}\,\mathrm{m^{-1}\,s^{-2}}. \tag{A.2.7k}$$

Substituting the results of Eqs. (A.2.6) and (A.2.7) into Eq. (A.1.12) gives

$$\tau(z) \cong 9.4 \times 10^{-16} \sin\theta\,\mathrm{N\,m}, \tag{A.2.8}$$

with all other terms being negligible. To make a connection between this result and the experiment of Stubbs et al. [STUBBS, 1987], we write

$$K = I\omega^2 = \frac{4\pi^2 I}{T^2}. \tag{A.2.9}$$

Since $T \cong 420\,\text{s}$ and $I \cong 3.28 \times 10^{-5}\,\text{kg}\,\text{m}^2$, for this experiment, we then have $K \cong 7.34 \times 10^{-9}\,\text{N}\,\text{m}$, and the implied net angular deflection is then $9.4 \times 10^{-16}/7.34 \times 10^{-9} \cong 0.13\,\mu\text{rad}$. Comparing this value to the quoted result of Stubbs et al. which is $0.53 \pm 0.59\,\mu\text{rad}$, we see that this particular systematic was not a problem for the Stubbs experiment.

Luther-Towler Cavendish Experiment

B.1 Theoretical Formalism

The classic experiment of Luther and Towler [LUTHER, 1982; BAGLEY, 1997] is among the most accurate measurements of G in the laboratory. Since this result is used in many other experiments, it is important to understand the relationship between the measured value $G_C = (6.6726 \pm 0.0005)\,\mathrm{N\,m^2\,kg^{-2}}$ and the Newtonian constant G_∞. The following discussion illuminates how one analyzes the effects of non-Newtonian gravity on various laboratory measurements, such as the determinations of G_C, which were carried out for purposes other than studying non-Newtonian gravity.

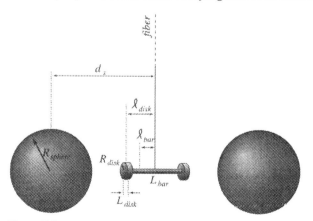

Figure B.1: Schematic diagram of apparatus used in the laboratory measurement of G by Luther and Towler [LUTHER, 1982].

The experimental arrangement for Luther and Towler is shown in Fig. B.1. The apparatus involved a small tungsten mass mounted in a dumbbell configuration suspended from a torsion fiber, and two large attracting masses also composed of tungsten. The experiment consisted of accurately constructing and measuring the mass configuration, and then comparing the predicted shift in frequency of the pendant for this configuration, with and without the attracting masses present, to the actual measured frequency shift of the system. The various dimensions and constants of the experiment are given in the Table B.1.

Table B.1: Physical constants for the experiment of Luther and Towler.

Constant	Description	Value
L_{disk}	length (thickness) of disk	0.0025472 m
ℓ_{disk}	lever arm of disk	0.0155472 m
R_{disk}	radius of disk	0.0035830 m
r_{disk}	separation distance between disk & sphere	0.0547501 m
L_{bar}	length of bar	0.0285472 m
ℓ_{bar}	lever arm of bar	0.0071368 m
R_{bar}	radius of bar	0.0005174 m
r_{bar}	separation distance between bar & sphere	0.0631605 m
R_{sphere}	radius of sphere	0.05082545 m
d_s	distance between sphere & center of pendant	0.07029727 m
m_{disk}	mass of disk	0.001983 kg
m_{bar}	mass of bar	0.0004633 kg
m_{sphere}	mass of sphere	10.490070 kg
ρ_{sphere}	inferred density of sphere	19074.2 kg/m^3

As discussed above, Luther and Towler measure the frequency shift resulting from the introduction of the spherical attracting masses. If we let I be the moment of inertia, D the drag coefficient, K the torsion constant for the torsion balance, and θ the angle between the torsion bar and the line connecting the centers of mass of the attracting spheres, then we can write from Eq. (4.2.50)

$$I\ddot{\theta} + D\dot{\theta} + K\theta = -\tau_m\theta, \tag{B.1.1}$$

where $\tau_m\theta$ is the torque produced for small deviations from $\theta = 0$. The presence of τ_m leads to a shift in frequency given by

$$\omega^2 = \omega_0^2 + \frac{\tau_m}{I}, \qquad \omega_0^2 \equiv \frac{K}{I} - \frac{D^2}{4I^2}. \tag{B.1.2}$$

In this case, τ_m is given by

$$\tau_m = m_{\text{sphere}} \ell_{\text{disk}} \left(g_{\text{disk}} - \xi \mathcal{F}_{\text{disk}} \, \Phi_{\text{sphere}} \right)$$
$$+ m_{\text{sphere}} \ell_{\text{bar}} \left(g_{\text{bar}} - \xi \mathcal{F}_{\text{bar}} \, \Phi_{\text{sphere}} \right), \tag{B.1.3}$$

where the various acceleration terms g_{disk}, g_{bar}, $\mathcal{F}_{\text{disk}}$, and $\mathcal{F}_{\text{bar}}$ are all calculated at $\theta = 0$, and

$$\Phi_{\text{sphere}} = \Phi(R_{\text{sphere}}/\lambda), \qquad \Phi(x) = \frac{3}{x^3}(x \cosh x - \sinh x). \tag{B.1.4}$$

The pendant configuration, which is composed of cylinders aligned along their axes relative to the center of mass of the sphere, is a particularly simple one in which to calculate both the gravitational and non-Newtonian torque contributions. The gravitational acceleration is given by

$$
\begin{aligned}
g_{\text{cyl}}\left(z; R, L\right) &= \rho G_\infty \int_{-L/2}^{+L/2} dz' \int_0^{2\pi} d\varphi' \int_0^R dr'\, r' \frac{\partial}{\partial z} \frac{1}{\sqrt{r'^2 + (z - z')^2}}, \\
&= -2\pi\rho G_\infty \int_0^R dr'\, r' \int_{-L/2}^{+L/2} dz' \frac{\partial}{\partial z'} \frac{1}{\sqrt{r'^2 + (z - z')^2}}, \\
&= -2\pi\rho G_\infty \int_0^R dr'\, r' \frac{1}{\sqrt{r'^2 + (z - z')^2}} \bigg|_{z'=-L/2}^{z'=+L/2}, \\
&= -2\pi\rho G_\infty \sqrt{r'^2 + (z - z')^2} \bigg|_{r'=0}^{r'=R} \bigg|_{z'=-L/2}^{z'=+L/2}, \\
&= -2\pi\rho G_\infty \left[\sqrt{R^2 + \left(z - \frac{L}{2}\right)^2} - \sqrt{R^2 + \left(z + \frac{L}{2}\right)^2} \right. \\
&\qquad\qquad \left. - \left|z - \frac{L}{2}\right| + \left|z + \frac{L}{2}\right| \right].
\end{aligned}
\tag{B.1.5}
$$

For $(z \gg R, L)$, this reduces to

$$
g_{\text{cyl}} \cong -M \frac{|z|}{z^3} \left[1 + \left(\frac{L^2 - 3R^2}{4z^2} \right) - \frac{5L^2 R^2}{8z^4} \right].
\tag{B.1.6}
$$

The acceleration field arising from a Yukawa potential can be found in a similar manner:

$$
\begin{aligned}
\mathcal{F}_{\text{cyl}}\left(z; R, L\right) &= -\rho G_\infty \int_{-L/2}^{+L/2} dz' \int_0^{2\pi} d\varphi' \int_0^R dr'\, r' \frac{\partial}{\partial z} \frac{e^{-\sqrt{r'^2 + (z - z')^2}/\lambda}}{\sqrt{r'^2 + (z - z')^2}}, \\
&= 2\pi\rho G_\infty \int_0^R dr'\, r' \int_{-L/2}^{+L/2} dz' \frac{\partial}{\partial z'} \frac{e^{-\sqrt{r'^2 + (z - z')^2}/\lambda}}{\sqrt{r'^2 + (z - z')^2}}, \\
&= 2\pi\lambda\rho G_\infty e^{-\sqrt{r'^2 + (z - z')^2}/\lambda} \bigg|_{r'=0}^{r'=R} \\
&= -2\pi\lambda\rho G_\infty \left[e^{-\sqrt{R^2 + (z - L/2)^2}/\lambda} - e^{-\sqrt{R^2 + (z + L/2)^2}/\lambda} \right. \\
&\qquad\qquad \left. - e^{-|z - L/2|/\lambda} + e^{-|z + L/2|/\lambda} \right].
\end{aligned}
\tag{B.1.7}
$$

Note that for $\lambda \to \infty$, $\mathcal{F}_{cyl} \to -g_{cyl}$ as expected. For the sake of notational simplicity, we define

$$\overline{g_{cyl}}(z; R, L) = \frac{1}{\rho G_\infty} g_{cyl}(z; R, L),$$
(B.1.8)

$$\overline{\mathcal{F}_{cyl}}(z; R, L) = \frac{1}{\rho G_\infty} \mathcal{F}_{cyl}(z; R, L).$$
(B.1.9)

The measured torque τ_m is then given by

$$\begin{aligned}
\tau_m = \; & m_{sphere} \, \ell_{disk} \, \rho G_\infty \left[\overline{g_{cyl}}\left(r_{disk} ; R_{disk} , L_{disk} \right)\right. \\
& - \xi \Phi_{sphere} \, \overline{\mathcal{F}_{cyl}}\left(r_{disk} ; R_{disk} , L_{disk} \right)\right] \\
& + m_{sphere} \, \ell_{bar} \, \rho G_\infty \left[\overline{g_{cyl}}\left(r_{bar} ; R_{bar} , L_{bar} /2\right)\right. \\
& \left. - \xi \Phi_{sphere} \, \overline{\mathcal{F}_{cyl}}\left(r_{bar} ; R_{bar} , L_{bar} /2\right)\right].
\end{aligned}$$
(B.1.10)

Similarly, the theoretical torque τ_t that would be expected in the absence of non-Newtonian gravity is

$$\begin{aligned}
\tau_t = \; & m_{sphere} \, \ell_{disk} \, \rho G_C \overline{g_{cyl}}\left(r_{disk} ; R_{disk} , L_{disk} \right) \\
& + m_{sphere} \, \ell_{bar} \, \rho G_C \overline{g_{cyl}}\left(r_{bar} ; R_{bar} , L_{bar} /2\right).
\end{aligned}$$
(B.1.11)

Equating Eqs. (B.1.10) and (B.1.11) gives

$$G_C = G_\infty \frac{\ell_{disk}\left(\overline{g_{disk}} - \xi \overline{\mathcal{F}_{disk}} \, \Phi_{sphere}\right) + \ell_{bar}\left(\overline{g_{bar}} - \xi \overline{\mathcal{F}_{bar}} \, \Phi_{sphere}\right)}{\ell_{disk} \, \overline{g_{disk}} + \ell_{bar} \, \overline{g_{bar}}},$$
(B.1.12)

$$\equiv G_\infty \left[1 - \xi \Phi_{sphere} \, \Phi_{pendant}\right],$$
(B.1.13)

$$\Phi_{pendant} = \frac{\ell_{disk} \, \overline{\mathcal{F}_{disk}} + \ell_{bar} \, \overline{\mathcal{F}_{bar}}}{\ell_{disk} \, \overline{g_{disk}} + \ell_{bar} \, \overline{g_{bar}}},$$
(B.1.14)

where

$$\overline{g_{bar}} = \overline{g_{cyl}}\left(r_{bar} ; R_{bar} , L_{bar} /2\right),$$
(B.1.15)

$$\overline{\mathcal{F}_{bar}} = \overline{\mathcal{F}_{cyl}}\left(r_{bar} ; R_{bar} , L_{bar} /2\right),$$
(B.1.16)

$$\overline{g_{disk}} = \overline{g_{cyl}}\left(r_{disk} ; R_{disk} , L_{disk} \right),$$
(B.1.17)

$$\overline{\mathcal{F}_{disk}} = \overline{\mathcal{F}_{cyl}}\left(r_{disk} ; R_{disk} , L_{disk} \right).$$
(B.1.18)

In terms of the quantities listed in Luther and Towler [1982],

$$R_{bar} = \frac{D_{bar}}{2},$$
(B.1.19)

$$\ell_{bar} = \frac{L_{disk}}{2} + \frac{L_{bar}}{2},$$
(B.1.20)

$$r_{bar} = d_s - \ell_{bar},$$
(B.1.21)

$$R_{\text{disk}} = \frac{D_{\text{disk}}}{2}, \tag{B.1.22}$$

$$\ell_{\text{disk}} = \frac{L_{\text{disk}}}{4}, \tag{B.1.23}$$

$$r_{\text{disk}} = d_s - \ell_{\text{disk}}, \tag{B.1.24}$$

$$R_{\text{sphere}} = \frac{D_{\text{sphere}}}{2}. \tag{B.1.25}$$

B.2   Discussion of Results

The operative equations in the previous section are Eqs. (B.1.13) and (B.1.14), which express the λ dependence of the laboratory measurement of G in terms of the Newtonian constant G_∞:

$$G_C(\lambda) = G_\infty \left[1 - \xi \Phi_{\text{sphere}}(\lambda) \Phi_{\text{pendant}}(\lambda)\right]. \tag{B.2.1}$$

It is useful to note that the "form factors" $\Phi_{\text{sphere}}(\lambda)$ and $\Phi_{\text{pendant}}(\lambda)$ factorize in this equation due to the presence of the spherical attracting mass. This result is easily shown to hold for the attraction of a spherical mass to any other mass of arbitrary shape.

To understand Eq. (B.2.1), we note that

$$G_0 = G_\infty(1 - \xi). \tag{B.2.2}$$

The constant G_0 has the interpretation of the effective value of G for distance scales which are small compared to λ. Although it is often assumed that λ is large compared to the scale of laboratory measurements of G, one must also allow for the possibility that λ is comparable to this scale as well. We can combine Eqs. (B.2.1) and (B.2.2) to write

$$G_C(\lambda) = G_\infty - (G_\infty - G_0)\Phi_{\text{sphere}}(\lambda)\Phi_{\text{pendant}}(\lambda), \tag{B.2.3}$$

or equivalently,

$$\Phi_c(\lambda) \equiv \Phi_{\text{sphere}}(\lambda)\Phi_{\text{pendant}}(\lambda) = \frac{G_\infty - G_C(\lambda)}{G_\infty - G_0} = \frac{\Delta G_C(\lambda)}{\Delta G_0}, \tag{B.2.4}$$

where $\Delta G_C(\lambda) = G_C(\lambda) - G_\infty$ and $\Delta G_0 = G_0 - G_\infty$. The product $\Phi_{\text{sphere}} \Phi_{\text{pendant}}$ can thus be interpreted as the fractional difference of the value of G_C between G_∞ and G_0. The fraction $\Delta G_C(\lambda)/\Delta G_0$ is exhibited in Fig. B.2 as a function of λ, in the model of Eq. (2.1.8).

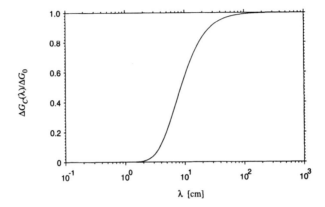

Figure B.2: The fractional difference $\Delta G_C(\lambda)/\Delta G_0$ as a function of λ plotted for the experiment of Luther and Towler. Note that for distances much less than a few centimeters, the expected value of $G_C(\lambda)$ would be very nearly that of G_∞, and it is only at distances larger than or comparable to one meter that $G_C(\lambda) \to G_0$.

APPENDIX C

The Earth's Gravity Field

C.1 Formulation of the Model

For a spherically symmetric nonrotating mass distribution, the local acceleration of gravity $g(z)$ may be written as

$$g(z) = \frac{GM(z)}{(R_\oplus - z)^2}, \tag{C.1.1}$$

where G is the Newtonian constant of gravity, $R_\oplus$ is the radius of the Earth, and $M(z)$ is the total mass inside the sphere of radius $(R_\oplus - z)$. Since in all of the geophysical experiments performed to date $z \ll R_\oplus$, we may expand Eq. (C.1.1) in small quantities to obtain [STACEY, 1977, 1983]

$$g(z) = g(0) + \frac{2g(0)}{R_\oplus} z - 4\pi G \int_0^z dz' \, \rho(z'), \tag{C.1.2}$$

where $\rho(z)$ is the local density as a function of depth. The above expression may be rewritten in the suggestive form

$$\Delta g(z) \equiv g(z) - g(0) = U(z) - 4\pi G X(z), \tag{C.1.3}$$

$$U(z) = \frac{2g(0)}{R_\oplus} z, \tag{C.1.4}$$

$$X(z) = \int_0^z dz' \, \rho(z'). \tag{C.1.5}$$

As discussed in Section 3.4, $U(z)$ characterizes the increase in $g(z)$ resulting from moving closer to the center of the Earth in the limit that $\rho(z) \to 0$ (i.e., the "free-air gradient" term), and $-4\pi G X(z)$ is the "double-Bouguer" term, which represents the decrease in $g(z)$ resulting from removing the mass above the sphere of radius $(R_\oplus - z)$.

Note: This appendix has been adapted from [TALMADGE, 1989B].

Stacey et al. [STACEY, 1983] introduced a refinement of the above model by including effects due to ellipticity and rotation. They assumed that the Earth could be modeled as an elliptically layered structure, with each ellipsoidal surface of constant density having the same ellipticity.

Under this assumption, only the mass interior to the ellipsoidal shell passing through the point z will contribute to the gravitational acceleration $g(z)$. The gravitational acceleration of the ellipsoidal body interior to z, including both Newtonian gravity and the centrifugal acceleration due to the rotation of the Earth, is then given to first order by the formula [STACEY, 1977]

$$g(z) = \frac{GM(z)}{(r_s - z)^2} - 3G\frac{C(z) - A(z)}{r^4}P_2(\sin^2\phi) - \omega^2 r \cos^2\phi, \qquad (C.1.6)$$

where

$$r_s \cong a\left[1 - \frac{1}{2}\left(\frac{a^2}{c^2} - 1\right)\sin^2\phi_s\right] + h, \qquad (C.1.7)$$

is the distance from the center of the Earth to the surface of the Earth at the latitude ϕ_s at which the experiment is being performed. In Eq. (C.1.6) $C(z)$ and $A(z)$ are the axial and equatorial moments of inertia of the interior ellipsoid, $P_2(x) = \frac{1}{2}(3x^2 - 1)$ is the usual second Legendre polynomial, and $\omega \cong 7.292115 \times 10^{-5}\,\mathrm{rad\,s^{-1}}$ is the angular rotation rate of the Earth. Keeping only terms of $\mathcal{O}(1)$ in small quantities, Stacey et al. [STACEY, 1983] found

$$U(z) \cong \frac{2g_s}{r_s}z\left[1 + \frac{3}{2}\frac{z}{r_s} - 3J_2P_2(\sin^2\phi_s)\right] + 3\omega^3 z\cos^2\phi_s, \qquad (C.1.8)$$

$$X(z) \cong \frac{c}{a}\left[1 + 2\frac{z}{r_s} + \frac{1}{2}\left(1 - \frac{c^2}{a^2}\right)\right]\int_0^z dz'\,\rho(z') - \frac{2}{r_s}\int_0^z dz'\,z'\rho(z'), \quad (C.1.9)$$

where the subscript s denotes surface values, a and c are respectively the equatorial and polar radii of the Earth, and h is the height above sea level of the surface of the Earth at (r_s, ϕ_s). Dahlen [1982] has noted that although Stacey et al. explicitly assumed a constant ellipticity with depth, which is clearly not the situation for the Earth, Eqs. (C.1.8) and (C.1.9) hold even when the effects from a variation of ellipticity with depth are included, provided one assumes that the Earth is in hydrostatic equilibrium.

Although the model of Stacey et al., when augmented by Dahlen's observation, appears to properly describe the effects of variable ellipticity, it would be useful to formulate an Earth model in which such effects were included from the outset. This would allow us to more easily examine certain questions such as i) the variation of $g(z)$ with depth, ii) the magnitude and orientation of a possible fifth force field of the Earth for large ranges ($\lambda \sim R_\oplus$), and iii) the validity of various simplifying assumptions that are usually made, such as the neglect of matter circulation, the neglect of distant topographic features, or the assumption of an oblate-spheroidally layered density distribution. This third point will be discussed in more detail below. We first enumerate the principal assumptions in this formulation:

1) The Earth can be represented by an oblate-spheroidally layered density distribution given by $\rho(r, \phi)$.

2) Surfaces of constant pseudo-potential V align with surfaces of constant density ρ and constant pressure P to first order in the oblateness f. This is equivalent to the assumption that the Earth is in hydrostatic equilibrium.

3) The angular velocity ω is constant throughout the Earth.

4) Nonradial accelerations are negligible (i.e., the effects of circulating matter in the mantle are small).

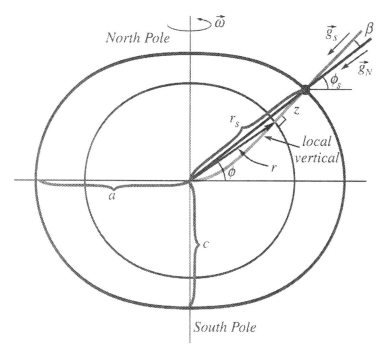

Figure C.1: Pictorial representation of the relevant parameters of an Earth model with variable ellipticity. For a definition of these parameters see Table C.1.

We may now introduce a new nonorthogonal coordinate system (u, ϕ, ψ), where the "oblate spheroidal radius" u is related to the radius r via

$$r = u \left[1 - \varepsilon(u) P_2(\sin \phi) \right]. \tag{C.1.10}$$

Table C.1: Table of notation used for calculating the Earth's gravity field. The equation numbers indicate where each quantity first appears in this appendix. The entries appear in alphabetical order.

Notation	Description	Equation
$\Delta M(z)$	mass difference $= M_s - M(z)$	(C.2.8)
$\Delta g(z)$	gravity difference $= g(z) - g_s$	(C.1.3)
ε	eccentricity of Earth's figure	(C.1.10)
η	normalized derivative of ε; $\eta \equiv \frac{r}{\varepsilon}\frac{d\varepsilon}{dr}$	(C.1.16)
$\rho(z)$	density as function of depth z	(C.1.2)
ϕ	geocentric latitude	(C.1.6)
ψ	longitude	(-)
ω	angular rotation rate of the Earth $\omega \cong 7.292115 \times 10^{-5}\,\mathrm{rad\,s^{-1}}$	(C.1.6)
A	equatorial moment of inertia	(C.1.6)
a	equatorial radius of the Earth $\cong 6\,378\,136\,\mathrm{m}$	(C.1.9)
C	axial moment of inertia	(C.1.6)
c	polar radius of the Earth $\cong 6\,356\,751\,\mathrm{m}$	(C.1.9)
f_s	oblateness of the Earth's figure $= 3\varepsilon/2$	(C.2.4)
f_0	centripetal acceleration scale parameter $= \omega^2 u_s^3/GM_s$	(C.1.25)
G	Newtonian constant of gravity	(C.1.1)
g	net gravitation acceleration	(C.1.1)
$g(0), g_s$	gravitational acceleration at surface	(C.1.2),(C.1.8)
J_2	quadrupole moment of the Earth $\cong 0.001082635$	(C.1.8)
$P_2(\sin\phi)$	second Legendre polynomial $= \frac{3}{2}\sin^2\phi - \frac{1}{2}$	(C.1.6)
r	distance to center of Earth	(C.1.6)
r_s, ϕ_s	radius, geocentric latitude of experiment on the Earth's surface	(C.1.8)
$M(z)$	Earth's mass at depth z	(C.1.1)
M_s	Earth's mass at the surface	(C.1.25)
$R_\oplus$	mean radius of Earth	(C.1.1)
$U(z)$	free-air gradient contribution to $\Delta g(z)$	(C.1.4)
u	oblate spheroidal radius defined by $r = u[1 - \varepsilon(u)P_2(\sin\phi)]$	(C.1.10)
$V(r, \phi)$	gravitational potential	(C.1.11)
$V_{\mathrm{eff}}(r, \phi)$	*effective* gravitational potential (Newtonian + rotational pseudopotential)	(C.1.19)
$X(z)$	double Bouguer contribution to $\Delta g(z)$	(C.1.5)
z	depth below surface	(C.1.1)

Here ϕ and ψ measure the geocentric latitude and longitude respectively, and $\varepsilon(u)$ is defined so that $\rho(r, \phi) = $ constant on surfaces of constant u. (See Fig. C.1 and Table C.1 for the definitions of various physical quantities.) Starting from Eq. (C.1.10), the Newtonian gravitational potential can be explicitly written as [JEFFREYS, 1970]

$$V_N(r, \phi) = V_i(r, \phi) + V_e(r, \phi), \tag{C.1.11}$$

$$V_i(r, \phi) = -\frac{4\pi G}{3r} \int_0^u du' \, \rho(u')$$

$$\times \frac{\partial}{\partial u'} \left[u'^3 - \frac{3}{5} \left(\frac{u'^5}{r^2} \right) \varepsilon(u') P_2(\sin \phi) \right], \tag{C.1.12}$$

$$V_e(r, \phi) = -\frac{4\pi G}{3} \int_u^{u_s} du' \, \rho(u')$$

$$\times \frac{\partial}{\partial u'} \left[\frac{3}{2} u'^2 - \frac{3}{5} r^2 \varepsilon(u') P_2(\sin \phi) \right]. \tag{C.1.13}$$

Here V_i denotes the potential arising from the mass interior to the oblate spheroid passing through (r, ϕ), and V_e is the potential due to the mass exterior to (r, ϕ). Expanding these equations gives

$$V_i(r, \phi) = -\frac{4\pi G}{r} \int_0^u du' \, u'^2 \rho(u')$$

$$\times \left[1 - \left(\frac{u'}{r} \right)^2 \varepsilon(u') P_2(\sin \phi) \left(1 + \frac{1}{5} \eta(u') \right) \right], \tag{C.1.14}$$

$$V_e(r, \phi) = -4\pi G \int_u^{u_s} du' \, u' \rho(u')$$

$$\times \left[1 - \frac{1}{5} \left(\frac{r}{u'} \right)^2 \varepsilon(u') \eta(u') P_2(\sin \phi) \right], \tag{C.1.15}$$

with

$$\eta(u) \equiv \frac{u}{\varepsilon(u)} \frac{d\varepsilon(u)}{du}. \tag{C.1.16}$$

There is an additional contribution to the effective potential arising from the rotation of the oblate spheroid given by

$$V_\omega(r, \phi) = -\frac{1}{2} \omega^2 r^2 \cos^2 \phi = -\frac{1}{3} \omega^2 r^2 \left[1 - P_2(\sin \phi) \right]. \tag{C.1.17}$$

The effective gravitational potential is then given by

$$V_{\text{eff}}(r, \phi) = V_i(r, \phi) + V_e(r, \phi) + V_\omega(r, \phi). \tag{C.1.18}$$

The content of assumption (2) above is that V_{eff} must be a function of u only, for $u \leq u_s$. That is,

$$V_{\text{eff}}(r, \phi) = V_{\text{eff}}(u) = V_{\text{eff}}\big(r[1 + \varepsilon(r)P_2(\sin\phi)]\big). \qquad \text{(C.1.19)}$$

(We have used the fact that $\varepsilon(r) = \varepsilon(u) + \mathcal{O}(\varepsilon^2)$ to obtain the above relation.) This implies that the coefficient of $P_2(\sin\phi)$ in $V_{\text{eff}}(u)$ must vanish for points interior to the surface of the Earth. This requirement leads to Clairaut's equation (see for instance [TASSOUL, 1978]), which we write in the form

$$u\frac{d\eta}{du} + 6\frac{\rho(u)}{\rho_m(u)}(\eta + 1) + \eta(\eta - 1) = 6, \qquad \text{(C.1.20)}$$

where

$$\rho_m(u) = \frac{3}{u^3}\int_0^u \rho(u')u'^2 du', \qquad \text{(C.1.21)}$$

$$\eta(u = 0) = 0. \qquad \text{(C.1.22)}$$

From Eq. (C.1.16) we also have

$$\varepsilon(u) = \varepsilon(u_s)\exp\left\{-\int_u^{u_s} du' \frac{\eta(u')}{u'}\right\}, \qquad \text{(C.1.23)}$$

where

$$\varepsilon(u_s) = \frac{5f_0}{3[\eta(u_s) + 2]}, \qquad \text{(C.1.24)}$$

and

$$f_0 = \frac{\omega^2 u_s^3}{GM_s} \cong \frac{\omega^2 a^3}{GM_s}, \qquad \text{(C.1.25)}$$

and where u_s is the value of u on the surface of the Earth. (An alternative notation used by some authors is $m = \omega^2 a^3/GM_s$. We introduce the symbol f_0 to avoid confusion of m with the mass.)

As discussed above, the coefficient of $P_2(\sin\phi)$ in $V_{\text{eff}}(u)$ is required by assumption 2) to vanish, and when this requirement is enforced, we are left with

$$V_{\text{eff}}(u) = -\frac{4\pi G}{u}\int_0^u du'\, u'^2\rho(u') - 4\pi G\int_u^{u_s} du'\, u'\rho(u') - \frac{1}{3}\omega^2 u^2. \quad \text{(C.1.26)}$$

The gravitational acceleration $\vec{g}(r, \phi)$ is thus given by

$$\vec{g}(r, \phi) = -\vec{\nabla}V(r, \phi) = -\vec{\nabla}V_{\text{eff}}\big(r[1 + \varepsilon(r)P_2(\sin\phi)]\big), \quad \text{(C.1.27)}$$

$$= -\frac{dV_{\text{eff}}}{du}(u)\left(\hat{r}\frac{\partial u}{\partial r} + \hat{\phi}\frac{1}{r}\frac{\partial u}{\partial \phi}\right). \quad \text{(C.1.28)}$$

Using

$$\frac{dV_{\text{eff}}}{du}(u) = \frac{GM(u)}{u^2} - \frac{2}{3}\omega^2 u, \tag{C.1.29}$$

and

$$\frac{\partial u}{\partial r} = 1 + \left[\varepsilon(r) + r\frac{d\varepsilon(r)}{dr}\right] P_2(\sin\phi)$$
$$= 1 + \varepsilon(r)\left[1 + \eta(r)\right] P_2(\sin\phi), \tag{C.1.30}$$

$$\frac{\partial u}{\partial \phi} = -3\varepsilon(r)\sin\phi\cos\phi. \tag{C.1.31}$$

We find for $u \leq u_s$, upon dropping terms of higher order,

$$\vec{g}(r,\phi) = -\hat{r}\left[\frac{GM(u(r,\phi))}{r^2}\left[1 - \varepsilon(r)(1 - \eta(r))P_2(\sin\phi)\right] - \frac{2}{3}\omega^2 r\right]$$
$$+ \hat{\phi}\left[3\frac{GM(u(r,\phi))}{r^2}\varepsilon(r)\sin\phi\cos\phi\right], \tag{C.1.32}$$

$$u(r,\phi) \cong r\left[1 + \varepsilon(r)P_2(\sin\phi)\right]. \tag{C.1.33}$$

In the region $u \geq u_s$, Eq. (C.1.18) becomes

$$V_{\text{eff}}(r,\phi) = -\frac{4\pi G}{r}\int_0^{u_s} du' \left\{u'^2\rho(u')\right.$$
$$\times \left[1 - \left(\frac{u'}{r}\right)^2 \varepsilon(u')P_2(\sin\phi)\left(1 + \frac{1}{5}\eta(u')\right)\right]\right\}$$
$$- \frac{1}{2}\omega^2 r^2 \cos^2\phi. \tag{C.1.34}$$

This may be rewritten as

$$V_{\text{eff}}(r,\phi) = -\frac{GM_s}{r} + \frac{GM_s J_2 a^2}{r^3}P_2(\sin\phi) - \frac{1}{2}\omega^2 r^2 \cos^2\phi, \tag{C.1.35}$$

where the subscript "s" refers to a quantity evaluated at $u = u_s$, and where

$$M_s = 4\pi \int_0^{u_s} du'\, u'^2\rho(u'), \tag{C.1.36}$$

$$J_2 = \frac{1}{M_s a^2}\int_0^{u_s} du'\, u'^4\rho(u')\varepsilon(u')[1 + \eta(u')/5]. \tag{C.1.37}$$

From Eq. (C.1.36) we find for $u \geq u_s$

$$\vec{g}(r,\phi) = -\hat{r}\left[\frac{GM_s}{r^2}\left(1 - \frac{3J_2 a^2}{r^2}P_2(\sin\phi)\right) - \omega^2 r\cos^2\phi\right]$$
$$+ \hat{\phi}\left[\left(\frac{3GM_s J_2 a^2}{r^2} + \omega^2 r\right)\sin\phi\cos\phi\right]. \tag{C.1.38}$$

It is in principle possible to directly evaluate Eq. (C.1.37) to obtain an analytic result for J_2. In practice, however, it is much easier to obtain J_2 by imposing the requirement that $\vec{g}(r,\phi)$ be continuous across the boundary $r_s(\phi) = u_s[1 - \varepsilon_s P_2(\sin\phi)]$. For simplicity we look at only $g_\phi(r,\phi)$, from which we find at the point $(r=r_s(\phi),\ \phi)$:

$$\frac{3GM_s J_2 a^2}{u_s^4} + \omega^2 u_s = \frac{3GM_s \varepsilon(u_s)}{u_s^2}. \qquad (C.1.39)$$

Solving Eq. (C.1.39) for J_2 and using Eq. (C.1.25) gives

$$J_2 \cong \varepsilon(u_s) - f_0/3. \qquad (C.1.40)$$

The effective gravitational acceleration field in the frame of reference co-rotating with the Earth is given by Eq. (C.1.32) $[u \leq u_s]$ and Eq. (C.1.38) $[u \geq u_s]$ for all values of r and ϕ. Using Eq. (C.1.32) and the density distribution given by the Preliminary Reference Earth Model, [DZIEWONSKI, 1981], we can evaluate $g = |\vec{g}|$ as a function of depth z, and the result is shown in Fig. C.2. We note that for $z \lesssim 2500\,\mathrm{km}$, g is approximately constant as a function of depth. This well-known result [STACEY, 1983; FISCHBACH, 1987] can be understood as arising from the near cancellation of the free-air gradient and the double-Bouguer terms in the upper layers of the Earth.

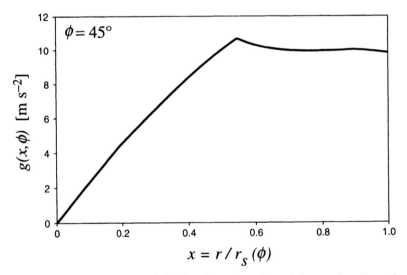

Figure C.2: Variation of the local acceleration $g(x)$ as a function of $x = r/r_s(\phi)$. As noted in the text, $g(x)$ is approximately constant for $x \gtrsim 0.6$, corresponding to depths $z \lesssim 2500\,\mathrm{km}$.

We also obtain from this first-order theory a calculated surface oblateness $f_s \cong 1/299.9$, which is in reasonable agreement with the results of earlier higher order analyses, such as that of Jeffreys [1963], who obtained $f_s \cong 1/299.67$. However, the values for f_s obtained from hydrostatic theory are not in good agreement with the value inferred from satellite observations [RAPP, 1987], which give $f_s = 1/298.257$. The 0.5% discrepancy between the results obtained from these two methods is well known in the geophysics literature [STACEY, 1977], and is commonly interpreted as a breakdown of the assumption of hydrostatic equilibrium. As is noted by Stacey [1977], the nonequilibrium component of the Earth's mass distribution appears to be constrained to reside in the upper mantle, and is probably dynamically maintained. If the only effect of the nonequilibrium distribution were to change f_s or ε_s by 0.5%, it is clear that these effects would be negligible on the scale of a first-order theory. However, if the nonequilibrium mass resides in the upper mantle—perhaps within a few hundred kilometers of the surface—then it may be necessary to consider the direct effects of this mass on the free-air gradient. Such a treatment is, however, beyond the scope of the present discussion.

C.2 Applications of the Earth Model

We first wish to demonstrate that Eq. (C.1.32) above, which is the interior solution to the effective gravitational acceleration in the Clairaut formalism, gives the "standard gravity equation" for the magnitude of the net gravitational acceleration at the surface of the Earth. Taking the magnitude of Eq. (C.1.32) and evaluating at the surface gives

$$
g_s(\phi) = |\vec{g}(r, \theta)||_{u=u_s} \cong g_r(r, \phi)
$$
$$
\cong \frac{GM_s}{u_s^2}\left[1 + \varepsilon_s(1 + \eta_s)P_2(\sin\phi) - \frac{2}{3}f_0\right], \qquad (\text{C.2.1})
$$

where as usual the subscript s denotes a quantity evaluated at $a - a_s$. We note that

$$
u_s(1 - \varepsilon_s P_2(\sin\phi)) \cong u_s(1 + \frac{1}{2}\varepsilon_s)(1 - \frac{3}{2}\varepsilon_s\sin^2\phi) \equiv a(1 - f_s\sin^2\phi), \quad (\text{C.2.2})
$$

and hence

$$
a = u_s(1 + \frac{1}{2}\varepsilon_s), \qquad (\text{C.2.3})
$$

and

$$
f_s \equiv \frac{(a - c)}{a} = \frac{3}{2}\varepsilon_s, \qquad (\text{C.2.4})
$$

where a is the equatorial radius and f_s is the oblateness. From Eq. (C.1.24), we also find

$$\varepsilon_s(1 + \eta_s) = \frac{5}{3}f_0 - \frac{2}{3}f_s. \tag{C.2.5}$$

Combining Eqs. (C.2.1)-(C.2.5) gives

$$g_s(\phi) \cong g_e \left[1 + \left(\frac{5}{2}f_0 - f_s\right)\sin^2\phi\right], \tag{C.2.6}$$

$$g_e \cong \frac{GM_s}{a^2}\left(1 + f_s - \frac{3}{2}f_0\right) = \frac{GM_s}{a^2}\left(1 + \frac{3}{2}J_2 - f_0\right). \tag{C.2.7}$$

This result is identical in first order to the standard surface gravity equation for the Earth [JEFFREYS, 1970; STACEY, 1977].

We next wish to rederive the results of Stacey et al. in Eqs. (C.1.8) and (C.1.9) starting from Eq. (C.1.32). Writing $z = r_s - r$, we have

$$g(z) = \frac{GM_s - G\Delta M(z)}{(r_s - z)^2}$$
$$\times \left[1 - \varepsilon(z)(1 - \eta(z))P_2(\sin\phi(z))\right] - \frac{2}{3}\omega^2(r_s - z), \tag{C.2.8}$$

where $\Delta M(z) \equiv M_s - M(z)$. We wish to expand this equation about the point $z = 0$ in small quantities. For this purpose, we treat z^2/r_s^2, ε_s, and $\omega^2 r_s/g_s$ as $\mathcal{O}(1)$ quantities. We write $\varepsilon(z)$ as

$$\varepsilon(z) \cong \varepsilon_s + z\left.\frac{d\varepsilon}{dz}\right|_{z=0} = \varepsilon_s\left(1 - \eta_s\frac{z}{r_s}\right). \tag{C.2.9}$$

Employing Eq. (C.1.20) and dropping higher order terms, we find for $\eta(z)$,

$$\eta(z) = \eta_s\left(1 - \eta_1\frac{z}{r_s}\right) + \frac{8\pi r_s^2(1 + \eta_s)}{M_s}\int_0^z dz'\,\rho(z'), \tag{C.2.10}$$

$$\eta_1 = 1 - \eta_s + 6/\eta_s. \tag{C.2.11}$$

We next note that while in principle $\phi = \phi(z)$, we have for the difference

$$\sin^2\phi_s - \sin^2\phi(z) = \frac{3z}{2r_s}\varepsilon_s\sin^2 2\phi_s, \tag{C.2.12}$$

which is of $\mathcal{O}(1)$. However since $\sin^2\phi(z)$ always multiplies quantities of $\mathcal{O}(1)$ or higher, then to first order we can write $\phi(z) \cong \phi_s$. The mass difference $\Delta M(z)$ may be obtained by first writing the mass as a function of u,

$$M(u) = 4\pi\int_0^u du'\,u'^2\rho(u'). \tag{C.2.13}$$

Upon substituting $u = r[1 + \varepsilon(r)P_2(\sin \phi_s)]$, this becomes

$$M(r) = 4\pi \int_0^r dr' r'^2 \rho(r') \left[1 + \varepsilon(r')(3 + \eta(r'))P_2(\sin \phi_s)\right]. \qquad (C.2.14)$$

Finally making the substitution $z = r_s - r$, we find for $\Delta M(z) = M_s - M(z)$,

$$\Delta M(z) \cong 4\pi r_s^2 \left[1 + \varepsilon_s(3 + \eta_s)P_2(\sin \phi_s)\right] \int_0^z dz' \rho(z')$$

$$- 8\pi r_s \int_0^z dz' z' \rho(z'), \qquad (C.2.15)$$

where we have again dropped higher order terms. The denominator of $(GM_s - G\Delta M(z))$ in Eq. (C.2.8) may be written to the necessary accuracy as

$$\frac{1}{(r_s - z)^2} \cong \frac{1}{r_s^2} \left(1 - \frac{2z}{r_s} + \frac{3z^2}{r_s^2}\right). \qquad (C.2.16)$$

Finally, we can substitute for GM_s in Eq. (C.2.8) above by evaluating that equation at $z = 0$, which yields

$$g_s = \frac{GM_s}{r_s^2}\left[1 - \varepsilon_s(1 - \eta_s)P_2(\sin \phi_s)\right] - \frac{2}{3}\omega^2 r_s. \qquad (C.2.17)$$

Solving Eq. (C.2.17) for GM_s, and expanding in small quantities, gives

$$GM_s = g_s r_s^2 \left[1 + \varepsilon_s(1 + \eta_s)P_2(\sin \phi_s)\right] + \frac{2}{3}\omega^2 r_s^3. \qquad (C.2.18)$$

Inserting Eqs. (C.2.9)–(C.2.11), (C.2.15), (C.2.16) and (C.2.18) into Eq. (C.2.8), we find

$$U(z) = \frac{2g_s z}{r_s}\left[1 + \frac{3z}{2r_s} - 3\varepsilon_s P_2(\sin \phi_s)\right] + 2\omega^2 z, \qquad (C.2.19)$$

$$X(z) = \left(1 + \frac{2z}{r_s}\right)\int_0^z dz' \rho(z') - \frac{2}{r_s}\int_0^z dz' z' \rho(z'). \qquad (C.2.20)$$

If we make the substitution $\varepsilon_s = J_2 + f_0/3$ in Eq. (C.2.19), we recover Stacey's expression for $U(z)$ given by Eq. (C.1.8). Similarly, we note that the only difference between Eq. (C.2.20) and Stacey's expression for $X(z)$ given by Eq. (C.1.9) is the coefficient of the first integral. This coefficient from Eq. (C.1.9) is

$$\frac{c}{a}\left[1 + \frac{2z}{r_s} + \frac{1}{2}\left(\frac{a^2 - c^2}{a^2}\right)\right]. \qquad (C.2.21)$$

Making the substitution $c/a = 1 - f_s$, Eq. (C.2.21) becomes

$$(1 - f_s) \left[1 + \frac{2z}{r_s} + \frac{1}{2}[(1 - (1 - f_s)^2)] \right] \cong (1 - f_s) \left[1 + \frac{2z}{r_s} + f_s \right]$$

$$= \left[1 + \frac{2z}{r_s} \right] + \mathcal{O}(f_s^2). \quad \text{(C.2.22)}$$

Thus to $\mathcal{O}(1)$ in f_s, Eq. (C.2.20) is identical to the result of Stacey et al. in Eq. (C.1.9).

C.3 Discussion

We have developed in Section C.1 a detailed model of the Earth's acceleration field $\vec{g}(r, \phi)$, from which $\vec{g}$ can be calculated at any point inside or outside the Earth. Our starting point is somewhat different from that of Stacey et al., in that we allow at the outset for a variation of ellipticity with depth, and employ a formulation valid for all values of r and ϕ, not just for those values for which $z^2/r_s^2 \ll 1$. However, our results as given in Eqs. (C.1.32) and (C.1.38) were shown in Section C.2 to be identical to those of Stacey et al., to lowest order in various small quantities (such as the oblateness f, $\omega^2 r/g(r, \phi)$, and z^2/r_s^2).

Although we have demonstrated the equivalence of the two models in first order, it should be kept in mind that this "equivalence" was obtained by making a number of simplifying assumptions. While the standard arguments for the validity of these assumptions seem quite compelling, they must be carefully scrutinized, since they might eventually lead to the suggestion of non-Newtonian gravity.

Bibliography

[ACHILLI, 1997] V. Achilli, et al., "A geophysical experiment on Newton's inverse-square law," *Nuovo Cimento* **112B**, 775–804 (1997).

[ADELBERGER, 1987] E. G. Adelberger et al., "New constraints on composition-dependent interactions weaker than gravity," *Phys. Rev. Lett.* **59**, 849–852 (1987).

[ADELBERGER, 1990] E. G. Adelberger et al., "Testing the equivalence principle in the field of the Earth: Particle physics at masses below 1 μeV?" *Phys. Rev. D* **42**, 3267–3292 (1990).

[ADELBERGER, 1991A] E. G. Adelberger, B. R. Heckel, C. W. Stubbs, and Y. Su, "Does antimatter fall with the same acceleration as ordinary matter?" *Phys. Rev. Lett.* **66**, 850–853 (1991).

[ADELBERGER, 1991B] E. G. Adelberger and B. R. Heckel, "Adelberger and Heckel Reply," *Phys. Rev. Lett.* **67**, 1049 (1991).

[ADELBERGER, 1991C] E. G. Adelberger, B. R. Heckel, C. W. Stubbs, and W. F. Rogers, "Searches for new macroscopic interactions," *Ann. Rev. Nucl. Part.* **41**, 269–320 (1991).

[ADLER, 1996] S. Adler et al., "Search for the decay $K^+ \to \pi^+ \nu \bar{\nu}$," *Phys. Rev. Lett.* **76**, 1421–1424 (1996).

[AIRY, 1856] G. B. Airy, "Account of pendulum experiments undertaken in the Harton Colliery, for the purpose of determining the mean density of the Earth," *Philos. Trans. R. Soc. London* **146**, 297–355 (1856).

[AKASAKA, 1989] N. Akasaka, H. Hirakawa, N. Mio, M. Ohashi, and K. Tsubono, "Dynamic null tests of the fifth force," In *Proceedings of the Fifth Marcel Grossmann Meeting on General Relativity* University of Western Australia, Perth, Australia, 8–13 August, 1988, edited by D. G. Blair and M. J. Buckingham (Singapore: World Scientific, 1989), pp. 1591–1594.

[ALIEV, 1989] T. M. Aliev, M. I. Dobroliubov, and A. Yu. Ignatiev, "Do kaon decays constrain the fifth force?" *Phys. Lett. B* **221**, 77–79 (1989).

[ANDER, 1989A]   M. E. Ander et al., "Test of Newton's inverse-square law in the Greenland ice cap," *Phys. Rev. Lett.* **62**, 985–988 (1989).

[ANDER, 1989B]   M. E. Ander et al., "A new field experiment in the Greenland ice cap to test Newton's inverse square law," In *Ann. NY Acad. Sci.* **571**, Fourteenth Texas Symposium on Relativistic Astrophysics, 11–16 December, 1988, Dallas, Texas, 672–680 (1989).

[ANSEL'M, 1982]   A. A. Ansel'm, "Possible new long-range interaction and methods for detecting it," *JETP Lett.* **36**, 55 (1982).

[ARONSON, 1982]   S. H. Aronson, G. J. Bock, H.-Y. Cheng, and E. Fischbach, "Determination of the fundamental parameters of the K^0–$\bar{K}^0$ system in the energy range 30–110 GeV," *Phys. Rev. Lett.* **48**, 1306–1309 (1982).

[ARONSON, 1983A]   S. H. Aronson, G. J. Bock, H.-Y. Cheng, and E. Fischbach, "Energy dependence of the fundamental parameters of the K^0–$\bar{K}^0$ system. I. Experimental analysis," *Phys. Rev. D* **28**, 476–494 (1983).

[ARONSON, 1983B]   S. H. Aronson, G. J. Bock, H.-Y. Cheng, and E. Fischbach, "Energy dependence of the fundamental parameters of the K^0–$\bar{K}^0$ system. II. Theoretical formalism," *Phys. Rev. D* **28**, 495–523 (1983).

[ARONSON, 1986]   S. H. Aronson, H.-Y. Cheng, E. Fischbach, and W. Haxton, "Experimental signals for hyperphotons," *Phys. Rev. Lett.* **56**, 1342–1345 (1986); **56**, 2334(E) (1986).

[ARONSON, 1988]   S. H. Aronson, E. Fischbach, D. Sudarsky, and C. Talmadge, "The compatibility of gravity and kaon results in the search for new forces," In *5th Force-Neutrino Physics* Proceedings of the XXIIIrd Rencontre de Moriond (VIIIth Moriond Workshop), Les Arcs, France, 23–30 January, 1989, edited by O. Fackler and J. Trân Thanh Vân (Gif-sur-Yvette: Editions Frontières, 1988), pp. 593–602.

[ASTONE, 1991]   P. Astone et al., "Evaluation and preliminary measurement of the interaction of a dynamical gravitational near field with a cryogenic gravitational wave antenna," *Z. Phys. C - Particles and Fields* **50**, 21–29 (1991).

[BAGLEY, 1997]   C. H. Bagley and G. G. Luther, "Preliminary results of a determination of the Newtonian constant of gravitation: A test of the Kuroda hypothesis," *Phys. Rev. Lett.* **78**, 3047–3050 (1997).

[BARKER, 1966]   B. M. Barker, S. N. Gupta, and R. D. Haracz, "One graviton exchange interaction of elementary particles," *Phys. Rev.* **149**, 1027–1032 (1966).

[BARTLETT, 1986]   D. F. Bartlett and D. Van Buren, "Equivalence of active and passive gravitational mass using the Moon," *Phys. Rev. Lett.* **57**, 21–24 (1986).

[BARTLETT, 1988]   D. F. Bartlett and S. Lögl, "Limits on an electromagnetic fifth force," *Phys. Rev. Lett.* **61**, 2285–2287 (1988).

[BARTLETT, 1989A]   D. F. Bartlett and W. L. Tew, "The fifth force: Terrain and pseudoterrain," In *Tests of Fundamental Laws of Physics* Proceedings of the XXIVth Rencontre de Moriond (IXth Moriond Workshop), Les Arcs, France, 21–28 January, 1989, edited by O. Fackler and J. Trân Thanh Vân (Gif-sur-Yvette: Editions Frontières, 1989), pp. 543–548.

[BARTLETT, 1989B]   D. F. Bartlett and W. L. Tew, "Possible effect of the local terrain on the Australian fifth-force measurement," *Phys. Rev. D* **40**, 673–675 (1989).

[BARTLETT, 1989C]   D. F. Bartlett and W. L. Tew, "Possible effect of the local terrain on the North Carolina tower gravity experiment," *Phys. Rev. Lett.* **63**, 1531 (1989).

[BARR, 1986]   S. M. Barr and R. N. Mohapatra, "Range of feeble forces from higher dimensions," *Phys. Rev. Lett.* **57**, 3129–3132 (1986).

[BARR, 1993]   G. D. Barr et al., "A new measurement of direct CP violation in the neutral kaon system," *Phys. Lett. B* **317**, 233–242 (1993).

[BARS, 1986]   I. Bars and M. Visser, "Feeble intermediate-range forces from higher dimensions," *Phys. Rev. Lett.* **57**, 25–28 (1986).

[BEKENSTEIN, 1984]   J. Bekenstein and M. Milgrom, "Does the missing mass problem signal the breakdown of Newtonian gravity?" *Astrophys. J.* **286**, 7–14 (1984).

[BELL, 1964]   J. S. Bell and J. K. Perring, "2π decay of the K_2^0 meson," *Phys. Rev. Lett.* **13**, 348–349 (1964).

[BENNETT, 1989]   W. R. Bennett, Jr., "Modulated-source Eötvös experiment at

Little Goose Lock," *Phys. Rev. Lett.* **62**, 365–368 (1989).

[BERNSTEIN, 1964]   J. Bernstein, N. Cabibbo, and T. D. Lee, "CP invariance and the 2π decay mode of the K_2^0," *Phys. Lett.* **12**, 146–148 (1964).

[BERTOTTI, 1991]   B. Bertotti and C. Sivaram, "Radiation of the 'fifth force' field," *Nuovo Cimento B* **106**, 1299–1304 (1991).

[BEVERINI, 1988]   N. Beverini, V. Lagomarsino, G. Manuzio, F. Scuri, and G. Torelli, "Possible measurements of the gravitational acceleration with neutral antimatter," *Hyperfine Interactions* **44**, 357–364 (1988).

[BIZZETI, 1986]   P. G. Bizzeti, "Significance of the Eötvös method for the investigation of intermediate-range forces," *Nuovo Cimento B* **94**, 80–86 (1986).

[BIZZETI, 1989]   P. G. Bizzeti, A. M. Bizzeti-Sona, T. Fazzini, A. Perego, and N. Taccetti, "Search for a composition-dependent fifth force," *Phys. Rev. Lett.* **62**, 2901–2904 (1989).

[BIZZETI, 1990]   P. G. Bizzeti, A. M. Bizzeti-Sona, T. Fazzini, A. Perego, and N. Taccetti, "Recent tests of the Vallombrosa experiment," In *New and Exotic Phenomena '90*, Proceedings of the Xth Moriond Workshop, Les Arcs, France, 20–27 January, 1990, edited by O. Fackler and J. Trân Thanh Vân (Gif-sur-Yvette: Editions Frontières, 1990), pp. 263–268.

[BLINNIKOV, 1978]   S. I. Blinnikov, "Constraints on the gravitational constant from the observations of white dwarfs," *Astrophys. and Space Sci.* **59**, 13–17 (1978).

[BOBRAKOV, 1991]   V. F. Bobrakov et al., "An experimental limit on the existence of the electron quasimagnetic (arion) interaction," *JETP Lett* **53**, 294–298 (1991).

[BOD, 1991]   L. Bod, E. Fischbach, G. Marx, and M. Náray-Ziegler, "One hundred years of the Eötvös experiment," *Acta Physica Hungarica* **69**, 335–355 (1991).

[BOHR, 1969]   A. Bohr and B. R. Mottelson, *Nuclear Structure, Vol. 1.* (New York: Benjamin, 1969).

[BONDI, 1957]   H. Bondi, "Negative mass in General Relativity," *Rev. Mod. Phys.* **29**, 423–428 (1957).

[BORDAG, 1994] M. Bordag, V. M. Mostepanenko, and I. Yu. Sokolov, "On strengthening the restrictions on hypothetical Yukawa-type forces with extremely small range range of action," *Phys. Lett. A* **187**, 35–39 (1994).

[BOSLOUGH, 1989] J. Boslough, "Searching for the secrets of gravity," *National Geographic* **175**, 563–583 (1989).

[BOUCHIAT, 1986] C. Bouchiat and J. Iliopoulos, "On the possible existence of a light vector meson coupled to the hypercharge current," *Phys. Lett. B* **169**, 447–449 (1986).

[BOULWARE, 1972] D. G. Boulware and S. Deser, "Can gravitation have a finite range?" *Phys. Rev. D* **6**, 3368–3382 (1972).

[BOWLER, 1976] M. G. Bowler, *Gravitation and Relativity* (Oxford: Pergamon, 1976).

[BOYNTON, 1987] P. Boynton, D. Crosby, P. Ekstrom, and A. Szumilo, "Search for an intermediate-range composition-dependent force," *Phys. Rev. Lett.* **59**, 1385–1389 (1987).

[BOYNTON, 1989] P. E. Boynton and P. Peters, "Torsion pendulums, fluid flows, and the Coriolis farce." In *Tests of Fundamental Laws of Physics* Proceedings of the XXIVth Rencontre de Moriond (IXth Moriond Workshop), Les Arcs, France, 21–28 January, 1989, edited by O. Fackler and J. Trân Thanh Vân (Gif-sur-Yvette: Editions Frontières, 1989), pp. 501–510.

[BOYNTON, 1990] P. E. Boynton and S. H. Aronson, "New limits on the detection of a composition-dependent macroscopic force." In *New and Exotic Phenomena '90*, Proceedings of the Xth Moriond Workshop, Les Arcs, France, 20–27 January, 1990, edited by O. Fackler and J. Trân Thanh Vân (Gif-sur-Yvette: Editions Frontières, 1990), pp. 207–224.

[BRAGINSKIĬ, 1971] V. B. Braginskiĭ and V. I. Panov, "Verification of the equivalence of inertial and gravitational mass," *Sov. Phys. JETP* **34**, 463–466 (1972). [Translation of *Zh. Eksp. Teor. Fiz.* **61**, 873–879 (1971).]

[BRAMANTI, 1992] D. Bramanti, A. M. Nobili, and G. Catastini, "Test of the equivalence principle in a non-drag-free spacecraft," *Phys. Lett. A* **164**, 243–254 (1992).

[BURGESS, 1988] C. P. Burgess and J. Cloutier, "Astrophysical evidence for a weak new force?" *Phys. Rev. D* **38**, 2944–2950 (1988).

[BUTLER, 1993] M. N. Butler, S. Nozawa, R. A. Malaney, and A. J. Boothroyd, "Gravitationally induced neutrino oscillations," *Phys. Rev. D* **47**, 2615–2618 (1993).

[CARLSON, 1987] E. D. Carlson, "Limits on a new U(1) coupling," *Nucl. Phys.* **286B**, 378–398 (1987).

[CAROSI, 1990] R. Carosi et al., "A measurement of the phases of the CP-violating amplitudes in $K^0 \to 2\pi$ decays and a test of CPT invariance," *Phys. Lett B* **237**, 303–312 (1990).

[CARUSOTTO, 1992] S. Carusotto et al., "Test of g universality with a Galileo type experiment," *Phys. Rev. Lett.* **69**, 1722–1725 (1992).

[CASIMIR, 1948] H. B. G. Casimir, "On the attraction between two perfectly conducting plates," *Kon. Akad. Wetenshappen* **B51**, 793 (1948).

[CAVASINNI, 1986] V. Cavasinni, E. Iacopini, E. Polacco, and G. Stefanini, "Galileo's experiment on free-falling bodies using modern optical techniques," *Phys. Lett. A* **116**, 157–161 (1986).

[CHAN, 1984] H. A. Chan and H. J. Paik, "Experimental test of a spatial variation of the Newtonian gravitational constant at large distances," In *Precision Measurement and Fundamental Constants II*, edited by B. N. Taylor and W. D. Phillips, Natl. Bureau of Standards Spec. Publ. **617**, pp. 601–606 (1984).

[CHAN, 1982] H. A. Chan, M. V. Moody, and H. J. Paik, "Null test of the gravitational inverse square law," *Phys. Rev. Lett.* **49**, 1745–1748 (1982).

[CHANDRASEKHAR, 1957] S. Chandrasekhar, *An Introduction to Stellar Structure* (New York: Dover, 1957).

[CHANG, 1990] D. Chang, W.-Y. Keung, and P. B. Pal, "Gauge hierarchy and attractive feeble long-range force," *Phys. Rev. D* **42**, 630–635 (1990).

[CHANMUGAM, 1970] G. Chanmugam and S. S. Schweber, "Electromagnetic many-body forces," *Phys. Rev.* **A1**, 1369–1375 (1970).

[CHARDIN, 1990] G. Chardin, "CP violation: A matter of gravity?" In *CP Violation in Particle and Astrophysics*, edited by J. Trân Thanh Vân (Gif-sur-Yvette: Editions Frontières, 1990), pp. 377–385.

[CHARDIN, 1992]   G. Chardin and J.-M. Rax, "CP violation: A matter of (anti) gravity?" *Phys. Rev. Lett.* **282**, 256–262 (1992).

[CHEN, 1984]   Y. T. Chen, A. H. Cook, and A. J. Metherell, "An experimental test of the inverse square law of gravitation at range of 0.1 m," *Proc. Soc. Lond. A* **394**, 47–68 (1984).

[CHEN, 1989]   S.-G. Chen, "Does vacuum polarization influence gravitation?" *Nuovo Cimento* **104B**, 611–619 (1989).

[CHEN, 1993]   Y. T. Chen and A. Cook, *Gravitational Experiments in the Laboratory*, (Cambridge: Cambridge University Press, 1993).

[CHENG, 1988]   H.-Y. Cheng, "The strong CP problem revisited," *Phys. Rep.* **158**, 1–89 (1988).

[CHO, 1990]   Y. M. Cho and D. H. Park, "Higher-dimensional unification and fifth force," *Nuovo Cimento* **105B**, 817–829 (1990).

[CHO, 1991]   Y. M. Cho and D. H. Park, "Fifth force from Kaluza-Klein unification," *Gen. Rev. Grav.* **23**, 741–757 (1991).

[CHRISTENSON, 1964]   J. H. Christenson, J. W. Cronin, V. L. Fitch, and R. Turlay, "Evidence for the 2π decay of the K_2^0 meson," *Phys. Rev. Lett.* **13**, 138–140 (1964).

[CHU, 1986]   S. Y. Chu and R. H. Dicke, "New force or thermal gradient in the Eötvös experiment?" *Phys. Rev. Lett.* **57**, 1823–1824 (1986).

[CHUI, 1993]   T. C. P. Chui and W.-T. Ni, "Experimental search for an anomalous spin-spin interaction between electrons," *Phys. Rev. Lett.* **71**, 3247–3250 (1993).

[CHUPP, 1989]   T. E. Chupp et al., "Results of a new test of local Lorentz invariance: A search for mass anisotropy in ^{21}Ne," *Phys. Rev. Lett.* **63**, 1541–1545 (1989).

[CHOU, 1990]   Y. Chou, W.-T. Ni, and S.-L. Wang, "Torsion balance equivalence principle experiment for the spin-polarized Dy_6Fe_{23}," *Mod. Phys. Lett. A* **5**, 2297–2303 (1990).

[CIUFOLINI, 1995] I. Ciufolini and J. A. Wheeler, *Gravitation and Inertia* (Princeton: Princeton University Press, 1995).

[COHEN, 1990] J. M. Cohen, "Intermediate-range forces?" *Int. J. Theor. Phys.* **29**, 157–160 (1990).

[COLELLA, 1975] R. Colella, A. W. Overhauser, and S. A. Werner, "Observation of gravitationally induced quantum interference," *Phys. Rev. Lett.* **34**, 1472–1474 (1975).

[CONDON, 1967] *Handbook of Physics*, edited by E. U. Condon and H. Odishaw (New York: McGraw-Hill, 1967), pp. **9**-66 – **9**-86.

[COOK, 1987] A. H. Cook, "Experiments on gravitation," In *Three Hundred Years of Gravitation*, edited by S. W. Hawking and W. Israel (Cambridge: Cambridge University Press, 1987), 50–79.

[COOK, 1988] A. H. Cook, "Experiments on gravitation," *Rep. Prog. Phys.* **51**, 707–757 (1988).

[CORNAZ, 1991] A. Cornaz, W. Kündig, and H. Stüssi, "Determination of the gravitational constant G at an effective distance of 125 m," In *Massive Neutrinos–Tests of Fundamental Symmetries*, Proceedings of the XXVIth Rencontre de Moriond (XIth Moriond Workshop), Las Arcs, France, 26 January – 2 February, 1991, edited by O. Fackler, G. Fontaine, and J. Trân Thanh Vân (Gif-sur-Yvette: Editions Frontières, 1991), pp. 275–278.

[CORNAZ, 1994] A. Cornaz, B. Hubler, and W. Kündig, "Determination of the gravitational constant G at an effective interaction distance of 112 m," *Phys. Rev. Lett.* **72**, 1152–1155 (1994).

[CORNWALL, 1990] J. M. Cornwall, "On the high-energy behavior of weakly-coupled gauge theories," *Phys. Lett. B* **243**, 271–278 (1990).

[COUPAL, 1985] D. P. Coupal et al., "Measurement of the ratio $\Gamma(K_L \rightarrow \pi^+\pi^-)/\Gamma(K_L \rightarrow \pi l\nu)$ for K_L with 65 GeV/c laboratory momentum," *Phys. Rev. Lett.* **55**, 566–569 (1985).

[COWSIK, 1988] R. Cowsik, N. Krishnan, S. N. Tandon, and C. S. Unnikrishnan, "Limit on the strength of intermediate-range forces coupling to isospin," *Phys. Rev. Lett.* **61**, 2179–2181 (1988).

[COWSIK, 1989A] R. Cowsik et al., "Torsion balance experiments for the measurement of weak forces in nature," *Indian J. Pure & Applied Phys.* **27**, 691–709 (1989).

[COWSIK, 1989B] R. Cowsik, N. Krishnan, P. Saraswat, S. N. Tandon, and C. S. Unnikrishnan, "Limits on the strength of the fifth force," *Adv. Space Res.* **9**, 123–132 (1989).

[COWSIK, 1990] R. Cowsik, N. Krishnan, S. N. Tandon, and C. S. Unnikrishnan, "Strength of intermediate-range forces coupling to isospin," *Phys. Rev. Lett.* **64**, 336–339 (1990).

[CRANSHAW, 1988] T. E. Cranshaw, "A new approach to the question of the fifth force," *Phys. Lett. A* **127**, 304 (1988).

[CVETIČ, 1989] M. Cvetič, "Low energy signals from moduli," *Phys. Lett. B* **229**, 41–44 (1989).

[DAHLEN, 1982] F. A. Dahlen, "Variation of gravity with depth in the Earth," *Phys. Rev. D* **25**, 1735–1736 (1982).

[DARLING, 1992] T. W. Darling, F. Rossi, G. I. Opat, and G. F. Moorhead, "The fall of charged particles under gravity: A study of experimental problems," *Rev. Mod. Phys.* **64**, 237–257 (1992).

[DERUJULA, 1986] A. de Rújula, "On weaker forces than gravity," *Phys. Lett. B.* **180**, 213–220 (1986).

[DE SABBATA, 1990] V. de Sabbata and C. Sivaram, "Fifth force as a manifestation of torsion," *Int. J. Theor. Phys.* **29**, 1–6 (1990).

[DESSLER, 1968] A. J. Dessler, F. C. Michel, H. E. Rorschach, and G. T. Trammell, "Gravitationally induced electric fields in conductors," *Phys. Rev.* **168**, 737–743 (1968).

[DICKE, 1961] R. H. Dicke, "The Eötvös experiment," *Sci. Am.* **205**, 81–94 (1961).

[DICKEY, 1994] J. O. Dickey et al., "Lunar laser ranging: A continuing legacy of the Apollo program," *Science* **265**, 482–490 (1994).

[DITTUS, 1991] H. Dittus, "Drop tower 'Bremem': A weightlessness laboratory on Earth," *Endeavour* **15**, 72–78 (1991).

[DONOGHUE, 1994]   J. F. Donoghue, "Leading quantum correction to the Newtonian potential," *Phys. Rev. Lett.* **72**, 2996–2999 (1974).

[DRAKE, 1978]   S. Drake, *Galileo at Work* (Chicago: Univ. of Chicago Press, 1978), pp. 19–20 and 413–416.

[DREVER, 1961]   R. W. P. Drever, "A Search for anisotropy of inertial mass using a free precession technique," *Phil. Mag.* **6**, 683 (1961).

[DYER, 1989]   P. Dyer, J. Camp, M. H. Holzscheiter, and G. Graessle, "Falling antimatter: An experiment to measure the gravitational acceleration of the antiproton," *Nucl. Instr. and Meth. in Phys. Res.* **B40/41**, Part I, 485–488 (1989).

[DYSON, 1920]   F. W. Dyson, A. S. Eddington, and C. Davidson, "A determination of the deflection of light by the Sun's gravitational field from observations made at the total eclipse of May 29, 1919," *Phil. Trans. Roy. Soc.* **220A**, 291 (1920); *Mem. Roy. Astron. Soc.* **62**, 291 (1920).

[DZIEWONSKI, 1981]   A. M. Dziewonski and D. L. Anderson, "Preliminary reference Earth model," *Phys. Earth and Planetary Interiors*, **25**, 297–356 (1981).

[ECKHARDT, 1988]   D. H. Eckhardt, C. Jekeli, A. R. Lazarewicz, A. J. Romaides, and R. W. Sands, "Tower gravity experiment: evidence for non-Newtonian gravity," *Phys. Rev. Lett.* **60**, 2567–2570 (1988).

[ECKHARDT, 1992]   D. Eckhardt, "The exponential potential and galactic dynamics," In *Progress in Atomic Physics, Neutrinos and Gravitation*, Proceedings of the XXVIIth Rencontre de Moriond (XIIth Moriond Workshop), edited by G. Chardin, O. Fackler, and J. Trân Thanh Vân (Gif-sur-Yvette: Editions Frontières, 1992), pp. 393–407.

[ECKHARDT, 1993]   D. Eckhardt, "The exponential potential versus dark matter," *Phys. Rev. D* **48**, 3762–3767 (1993).

[ELIZALDE, 1991]   E. Elizalde and A. Romeo, "Essentials of the Casimir effect and its computation," *Am. J. Phys.* **59**, 711–179 (1991).

[ELLIS, 1987]   J. Ellis, N. C. Tsamis, and M. Voloshin, "Could a dilaton solve the cosmological constant problem?" *Phys. Lett. B* **194**, 291–296 (1987).

[ELLIS, 1989]   J. Ellis, S. Kalara, K. A. Olive, and C. Wetterich, "Density-dependent couplings and astrophysical bounds on light scalar particles," *Phys. Lett. B* **228**, 264–272 (1989).

[EÖTVÖS, 1889]   R. v. Eötvös, "Über die Anziehung der Erde auf verschiedene Substanzen," In *Roland Eötvös Gesammelte Arbeiten*, edited by P. Selényi (Budapest: Akadémiai Kiado, 1953), pp. 15–20.

[EÖTVÖS, 1909]   R. v. Eötvös, "Bericht über geodätische Arbeiten in Ungarn besonders über Beobachtungen mit der Drehwaage," In *Roland Eötvös Gesammelte Arbeiten*, edited by P. Selényi (Budapest: Akadémiai Kiado, 1953), pp. 231–275.

[EÖTVÖS, 1922]   R. v. Eötvös, D. Pekár, and E. Fekete, "Beiträge zum gesetze der proportionalität von trägheit und gravität," *Ann. Phys. (Leipzig)* **68**, 11–66 (1922).

[EÖTVÖS, 1953]   R. v. Eötvös, D. Pekár, and E. Fekete, "Beiträge zum gesetze der proportionalität von trägheit und gravität," In *Roland Eötvös Gesammelte Arbeiten*, edited by P. Selényi (Budapest: Akadémiai Kiado, 1953), pp. 307–372. [This paper has been translated into English by J. Achzehnter, M. Bickeböller, K. Bräuer, P. Buck, E. Fischbach, G. Lübeck, and C. Talmadge, University of Washington preprint 40048-13-N6; for an earlier translation see *Annales Universitatis Scientiarum Budapestinensis de Rolando Eötvös Nominate, Sectio Geologica* **7**, 111 (1963).]

[ERICSON, 1990]   T. E. O. Ericson and A. Richter, "Empirical limits to antigravity," *Europhysics Letters* **11**, 295–300 (1990).

[EVERITT, 1994]   C. W. F. Everitt and S. Buchman, "Prospects for measuring γ to a part in 10^5 in the Gravity Probe B experiment," In *Particle Astrophysics, Atomic Physics, and Gravitation*, Proceedings of the XXIXth Rencontre de Moriond (XIVth Moriond Workshop), edited by J. Trân Thanh Vân, G. Fontaine, and E. Hinds (Gif-sur-Yvette: Editions Frontières, 1994), pp. 467–471.

[FAIRBANK, 1974]   W. M. Fairbank, F. C. Witteborn, J. M. J. Madey, and J. M. Lockhart, "Experiments to determine the force of gravity on single electrons and positrons," In *Experimental Gravitation*, Proceedings of the International School of Physics, Enrico Fermi, Course LVI, Lake Como, 17–29 July, 1972 edited by B. Bertotti (New York: Academic Press, 1974), pp. 310–330.

[FALLER, 1988] J. E. Faller, T. M. Niebauer, M. P. McHugh, and D. A. Van Baak, "Current research efforts at JILA to test the equivalence principle at short ranges," In *5th Force-Neutrino Physics*, Proceedings of the XXIIIrd Rencontre de Moriond (VIIIth Moriond Workshop), Les Arcs, France, 23–30 January, 1988 edited by O. Fackler and J. Trân Thanh Vân (Gif-sur-Yvette: Editions Frontières, 1988), pp. 457–470.

[FAYET, 1986A] P. Fayet, "A new long-range force?" *Phys. Lett.* B **171**, 261–266 (1986).

[FAYET, 1986B] "The Fifth Interaction in Grand-Unified Theories: A New Force Acting Mostly on Neutrons and Particle Spins," *Phys. Lett.* B **172**, 363–368 (1986).

[FAYET, 1989] P. Fayet, "The fifth force charge as a linear combination of baryonic, leptonic (or $B - L$) and electric charges," *Phys. Lett.* B **227**, 127–132 (1989).

[FAYET, 1990] P. Fayet, "Extra U(1)'s and new forces," *Nucl. Phys.* **B347**, 743–768 (1990).

[FEINBERG, 1968] G. Feinberg and J. Sucher, "Long-range forces from neutrino-pair exchanges," *Phys. Rev.* **166**, 1638–1644 (1968).

[FEINBERG, 1989] G. Feinberg, J. Sucher, and C.-K. Au, "The dispersion theory of dispersion forces," *Phys. Reports* **180**, 83–157 (1989).

[FEYNMAN, 1995] R. P. Feynman, F. B. Morinigo, and W. G. Wagner, *Feynman Lectures on Gravitation* (Reading: Addison-Wesley, 1995).

[FIORENTINI, 1989] G. Fiorentini and G. Mezzorani, "Neutrinos from SN1987A and long-range forces," *Phys. Lett.* B **221**, 353–356 (1989).

[FINZI, 1963] A. Finzi, "On the validity of Newton's law at a long distance," *Monthly Not. Royal Astron. Soc.* **127**, 21–30 (1963).

[FISCHBACH, 1981] E. Fischbach, B. S. Freeman, and W. K. Cheng, "General Relativistic Effects in Hydrogenic Systems," *Phys. Rev.* D **23**, 2157–2180 (1981).

[FISCHBACH, 1982] E. Fischbach, H.-Y. Cheng, S. H. Aronson, and G. J. Bock, "Interaction of the K^0–$\bar{K}^0$ system with external fields," *Phys. Lett.* B **116**,

73–76 (1982).

[FISCHBACH, 1985]   E. Fischbach, M. P. Haugan, D. Tadić, and H.-Y. Cheng, "Lorentz noninvariance and the Eötvös experiments," *Phys. Rev. D* **32**, 154–162 (1985).

[FISCHBACH, 1986A]   E. Fischbach, D. Sudarsky, A. Szafer, C. Talmadge, and S. H. Aronson, "Reanalysis of the Eötvös experiment," *Phys. Rev. Lett.* **56**, 3–6 (1986); **56**, 1427 (E) (1986).

[FISCHBACH, 1986B]   E. Fischbach, D. Sudarsky, A. Szafer, C. Talmadge, and S. H. Aronson, "Fischbach et al. respond," *Phys. Rev. Lett.* **56**, 2424 (1986).

[FISCHBACH, 1986C]   E. Fischbach, D. Sudarsky, A. Szafer, C. Talmadge, and S. H. Aronson, "A new force in nature?" In *Proceedings, 2nd Conference on Intersections between Particle and Nuclear Physics*, Lake Louise, Canada May 26–31, 1986, edited by D. Geesaman, AIP Conference Proceedings #150 (New York: American Institute of Physics, 1986), pp. 1102–1118.

[FISCHBACH, 1986D]   E. Fischbach, D. Sudarsky, A. Szafer, C. Talmadge, and S. H. Aronson, "Fischbach et al. reply," *Phys. Rev. Lett.* **56**, 2424 (1986).

[FISCHBACH, 1986E]   E. Fischbach, D. Sudarsky, A. Szafer, C. Talmadge, and S. H. Aronson, "Alternative explanations of the Eötvös results," *Phys. Rev. Lett.* **57**, 1959 (1986).

[FISCHBACH, 1987]   E. Fischbach, D. Sudarsky, A. Szafer, C. Talmadge, and S. H. Aronson, "The fifth force," In *Proceedings of the XXIII International Conference on High Energy Physics*, Berkeley, CA, 16–23 July, 1986, edited by S. C. Loken (Singapore: World Scientific, 1987), pp. 1021–1301.

[FISCHBACH, 1988]   E. Fischbach, H. T. Kloor, C. Talmadge, S. H. Aronson, and G. T. Gillies, "Possibility of shielding the fifth force," *Phys. Rev. Lett.* **60**, 74 (1988).

[FISCHBACH, 1988B]   E. Fischbach, D. Sudarsky, A. Szafer, C. Talmadge, and S. H. Aronson, "Long-range forces and the Eötvös experiment," *Ann. Phys. (NY)* **182**, 1–89 (1988).

[FISCHBACH, 1990]   E. Fischbach and C. Talmadge, "Finite-size effects in Eötvös-type experiments," In *New and Exotic Phenomena*, Proceedings of the 1990 Moriond Workshop, Les Arcs, France, 20–27 January, 1990, edited by J. Trân

Thânh Vân (Gif-Sur-Yvette: Editions Frontières, 1990), pp. 187–196.

[FISCHBACH, 1991]   E. Fischbach, C. Talmadge, and D. Krause, "Exponential models of non-Newtonian gravity," *Phys. Rev. D* **43**, 460–467 (1991).

[FISCHBACH, 1991B]   E. Fischbach, B. S. Freeman, and W. K. Cheng, "General-relativistic effects in hydrogenic systems," *Phys. Rev. D* **23**, 2157–2180 (1991).

[FISCHBACH, 1992A]   E. Fischbach and C. Talmadge, "Six years of the fifth force," *Nature* **356**, 207–215 (1992)

[FISCHBACH, 1992B]   E. Fischbach, G. T. Gillies, D. E. Krause, J. G. Schwan, and C. Talmadge, "Non-Newtonian gravity and new weak forces: An index of measurements and theory," *Metrologia* **29**, 213–260 (1992).

[FISCHBACH, 1994]   E. Fischbach, H. Kloor, R. Langel, A. T. Y. Lui, and M. Peredo, "New geomagnetic limits on the photon mass and on long-range fields coexisting with electromagnetism," *Phys. Rev. Lett.* **73**, 514–517 (1994).

[FISCHBACH, 1995]   E. Fischbach, D. E. Krause, C. Talmadge, and D. Tadić, "Higher-order weak interactions and the equivalence principle," *Phys. Rev. D* **52**, 5417–5427 (1995).

[FISCHBACH, 1996A]   E. Fischbach, "Long-range forces and neutrino mass," *Ann. of Phys. (NY)* **247**, 213–291 (1996).

[FISCHBACH, 1996B]   E. Fischbach, M. P. Haugan, and D. Tadić, "The equivalence principle and weak interactions," In *Proceedings of the STEP Symposium*, Pisa, Italy, 6–8 April, 1993, edited by R. Reinhard (European Space Agency publication ESA WPP-115, 1996), pp. 161–168.

[FITCH, 1988]   V. L. Fitch, M. V. Isaila, and M. A. Palmer, "Limits on the existence of a material-dependent intermediate-range force," *Phys. Rev. Lett.* **60**, 1801–1804 (1988).

[FRANKLIN, 1993]   A. Franklin, *The Rise and Fall of the Fifth Force* (New York: American Institute of Physics, 1993).

[FRIEMAN, 1991]   J. A. Frieman and B.-A. Gradwohl, "Dark matter and the equivalence principle," *Phys. Rev. Lett.* **67**, 2926–2929 (1991).

[FUJII, 1971]   Y. Fujii, "Dilaton and possible non-Newtonian gravity," *Nature*

(Phys. Sci.) **234**, 5–7 (1971).

[FUJII, 1972]   Y. Fujii, "Scale invariance and gravity of hadrons," *Ann. Phys. (NY)* **69**, 494–521 (1972).

[FUJII, 1974]   Y. Fujii, "Scalar-tensor theory of gravitation and spontaneous breakdown of scale invariance," *Phys. Rev. D* **9**, 874–876 (1974).

[FUJII, 1975]   Y. Fujii, "Spontaneously broken scale invariance and gravitation," *Gen. Rel. Grav.* **6**, 29–34 (1975).

[FUJII, 1986]   Y. Fujii, "Theoretical models for possible nonzero effect in the Eötvös experiment," *Progress of Theoretical Physics* **76**, 325–328 (1986).

[FUJII, 1988]   Y. Fujii, "On five-dimensional theories of the fifth force," *Mod. Phys. Lett. A* **3**, 19–22 (1988).

[FUJII, 1991A]   Y. Fujii, "Locally varying particle masses due to a scalar fifth-force field," *Phys. Lett. B* **255**, 439–444 (1991).

[FUJII, 1991B]   Y. Fujii, "The theoretical background of the fifth force," *Int. J. Mod. Phys. A* **6**, 3505–3557 (1991)

[FULIGNI, 1996]   F. Fuligni and V. Iafolla, "Galileo and the principle of equivalence," In *Proceedings of the STEP Symposium*, Pisa, Italy, 6–8 April, 1993, edited by R. Reinhard (European Space Agency publication ESA WPP-115, 1996), pp. 104–109.

[GABRIEL, 1990]   M. D. Gabriel and M. P. Haugan, "Testing the Einstein equivalence principle: Atomic clocks and local Lorentz invariance," *Phys. Rev. D* **41**, 2943–2955 (1990).

[GALIĆ, 1989]   H. Galić, "Weak decays of K and π mesons," *Phys. Rev. D* **40**, 2279–2289 (1989).

[GASPERINI, 1988]   M. Gasperini, "Testing the principle of equivalence with neutrino oscillations," *Phys. Rev. D* **38**, 2635–2637 (1988).

[GASPERINI, 1989A]   M. Gasperini, "Experimental constraints on a minimal and nonminimal violation of the equivalence principle in the oscillations of massive neutrinos," *Phys. Rev. D* **39**, 3606–3611 (1989).

[GASPERINI, 1989B]   M. Gasperini, "Phenomenological consequences of a direct fifth force coupling to photons," *Phys. Rev. D* **40**, 3525–3528 (1989).

[GELL-MANN, 1954]   M. Gell-Mann and F. E. Low, "Quantum electrodynamics at small distances," *Phys. Rev.* **95**, 1300–1312 (1954).

[GIBBONS, 1981]   G. W. Gibbons and B. F. Whiting, "Newtonian gravity measurements impose constraints on unification theories," *Nature* **291**, 636–638 (1981).

[GIBBONS, 1993A]   L. K. Gibbons et al., "New measurement of the neutral kaon parameters Δm, τ_s, $\phi_{00} - \phi_{+-}$, and ϕ_{+-}," *Phys. Rev. Lett.* **70**, 1199–1202 (1993).

[GIBBONS, 1993B]   L. K. Gibbons et al., "New measurement of the CP-violation parameter $\mathrm{Re}(\epsilon'/\epsilon)$," *Phys. Rev. Lett.* **70**, 1203–1206 (1993).

[GILLILAND, 1987]   R. L. Gilliland and W. Däppen, "Hypercharge, solar structure, and stellar evolution," *Astrophys. J.* **313**, 429–431 (1987).

[GILLIES, 1987]   G. T. Gillies, "The Newtonian gravitational constant," *Metrologia* **24** (Suppl.), 1–56 (1987).

[GILLIES, 1990]   G. T. Gillies, "Resource letter MNG-1: Measurements of Newtonian gravitation," *Am. J. Phys.* **58**, 525–534 (1990).

[GILLIES, 1992]   G. T. Gillies, *Measurements of Newtonian Gravitation: Selected Reprints*, College Park, MD, American Association of Physics Teachers (1992).

[GLASS, 1987]   E. N. Glass and G. Szamosi, "Intermediate-range forces and stellar structure," *Phys. Rev. D* **35**, 1205–1208 (1987).

[GLASS, 1989]   E. N. Glass and G. Szamosi, "Astrophysical treatment of intermediate-range forces," *Phys. Rev. D* **39**, 1054–1057 (1989).

[GOLDBERG, 1990]   H. Goldberg, "Breakdown of perturbation theory at tree level of theories with scalars," *Phys. Lett. B* **246**, 445–450 (1990).

[GOLDHABER, 1974]   A. S. Goldhaber and M. M. Nieto, "Mass of the graviton," *Phys. Rev. D* **9**, 1119–1121 (1974).

[GOLDMAN, 1982]   T. Goldman and M. M. Nieto, "Experiments to measure the gravitational acceleration of antimatter," *Phys. Lett.* **112B**, 437–440 (1982).

[GOLDMAN, 1986] T. Goldman, R. J. Hughes, and M. M. Nieto, "Experimental evidence for quantum gravity?" *Phys. Lett. B* **171**, 217–222 (1986).

[GOLDMAN, 1987] T. Goldman, R. J. Hughes, and M. M. Nieto, "Gravitational acceleration of antiprotons and of positrons," *Phys. Rev. D* **36**, 1254–1256 (1987).

[GOLDMAN, 1988] T. Goldman, R. J. Hughes, and M. M. Nieto, "Gravity and antimatter," *Sci. Am.* **258**, 48–56 (1988).

[GOLDMAN, 1991] T. Goldman et al., "Comment on: 'Does anti-matter fall with the same acceleration as ordinary matter?' " *Phys. Rev. Lett.* **67**, 1048 (1991).

[GOLDSTEIN, 1980] H. Goldstein, *Classical Mechanics* (Reading: Addison-Wesley, 1980).

[GOOD, 1961] M. L. Good, "K_2^0 and the equivalence principle," *Phys. Rev.* **121**, 311–313 (1961).

[GRAHAM, 1987] D. M. Graham, *Search for anomalous long-range spin-spin interaction*, Ph.D. Thesis, University of California, Irvine, unpublished (1987).

[GRAHAM, 1989] D. M. Graham, P. G. Nelson, and R. D. Newman, "A search for an anomalous intermediate range composition dependence in gravity," In *Abstracts of Contributed Papers, 12th International Conference on General Relativity and Gravitation*, Boulder, Colorado, 2–8 July, 1989, edited by N. Ashby et al. (International Society on General Relativity and Gravitation, 1989), p. 513.

[GRIFOLS, 1986] J. A. Grifols and E. Massó, "Constraints on finite-range baryonic and leptonic forces from stellar evolution," *Phys. Lett. B* **173**, 237 240 (1986).

[GROSSMAN, 1987] N. Grossman et al., "Measurement of the lifetime of K_S^0 mesons in the momentum range 100 to 350 GeV/c," *Phys. Rev. Lett.* **59**, 18–21 (1987).

[GUNDLACH, 1997] J. H. Gundlach, G. L. Smith, E. G. Adelberger, B. R. Heckel, and H. E. Swanson, "Short-range test of the equivalence principle," *Phys. Rev. Lett.* **78**, 2523–2526 (1997).

[HAGELIN, 1989]   J. S. Hagelin and L. S. Littenberg, "Rare kaon decays," *Prog. Part. Nucl. Phys.* **23**, 1–40 (1989).

[HALL, 1991]   A. M. Hall, H. Armbruster, E. Fischbach, and C. Talmadge, "Is the Eötvös experiment sensitive to spin?" In *Progress in High Energy Physics, Proceedings of the Second International Conference and Spring School on Medium and High Energy Nuclear Physics*, Taiwan, 8–18 May, 1990, edited by W.-Y. P. Hwang, S.-C. Lee, C.-E. Lee, and D. J. Ernst (New York: North-Holland, 1991), pp. 325–329.

[HALPRIN, 1991]   A. Halprin and C. N. Leung, "Can the Sun shed light on neutrino gravitational interactions?" *Phys. Rev. Lett.* **67**, 1833–1835 (1991).

[HALPRIN, 1996]   A. Halprin, C. N. Leung, and J. Pantaleone, "Possible violation of the equivalence principle by neutrinos," *Phys. Rev. D* **53**, 5365–5376 (1996).

[HARI DASS, 1976]   N. D. Hari Dass, "Test for C, P, and T nonconservation in gravitation," *Phys. Rev. Lett.* **36**, 393–395 (1976).

[HARI DASS, 1977]   N. D. Hari Dass, "A new spin test for the equivalence principle," *Gen. Rel. and Grav.* **8**, 89–93 (1977).

[HARTLE, 1970]   J. B. Hartle, "Long-range weak forces and cosmology," *Phys. Rev. D* **1**, 394–397 (1970).

[HARTLE, 1971]   J. B. Hartle, "Long-range neutrino forces exerted by Kerr black holes," *Phys. Rev.* **D3**, 2938–2940 (1971).

[HARTLE, 1972]   J. B. Hartle. In *Magic Without Magic: John Archibald Wheeler*, edited by J. R. Klauder (San Francisco: W. H. Freeman, 1972), pp. 259–275.

[HAUGAN, 1979]   M. P. Haugan, "Energy conservation and the principle of equivalence," *Ann. Phys.* **118**, 156–186 (1979).

[HAUGAN, 1976]   M. P. Haugan and C. M. Will, "Weak interactions and the Eötvös experiment," *Phys. Rev. Lett.* **37**, 1–4 (1976)

[HAUGAN, 1987]   M. P. Haugan and C. M. Will, "Modern tests of special relativity," *Phys. Today* **40**, 69–76 (May, 1987).

[HAYASHI, 1986]   K. Hayashi and T. Shirafuji, "Interpretations of geophysical and

Eötvös anomalies," *Prog. Theor. Phys.* **76**, 563–566 (1986).

[HAYASHI, 1987A]   K. Hayashi and T. Shirafuji, "Constraints for free fall experiments undertaken on a substance-dependent force," *Prog. Theor. Phys.* **78**, 22–26 (1987).

[HAYASHI, 1987B]   K. Hayashi, "A comment on space experiments of the 5th force," *Europhysics Letters* **4**, 959–962 (1987).

[HECKEL, 1989]   B. R. Heckel et al., "Experimental bounds on interactions mediated by ultralow-mass bosons," *Phys. Rev. Lett.* **63**, 2705–2708 (1989).

[HILL, 1988]   C. T. Hill and G. G. Ross, "Pseudo-Goldstone bosons and new macroscopic forces," *Phys. Lett. B* **203**, 125–131 (1988).

[HIPKIN, 1990]   R. G. Hipkin and B. Steinberger, "Testing Newton's law in the Megget water reservoir," In *Gravity, Gradiometry, and Gravimetry, Symposium No. 103*, Edinburgh, Scotland, 8–10 August, 1989, edited by R. Rummel and R. G. Hipkin (New York: Springer-Verlag, 1990), pp. 31–39.

[HIRAKAWA, 1980]   H. Hirakawa, K. Tsubono, and K. Oide, "Dynamical test of the law of gravitation," *Nature* **283**, 184–185 (1980).

[HOLDING, 1984]   S. C. Holding and G. J. Tuck, "A new mine determination of the Newtonian gravitational constant," *Nature* **307**, 714–716 (1984).

[HOLDING, 1986]   S. C. Holding, F. D. Stacey, and G. J. Tuck, "Gravity in mines–An investigations of Newton's law," *Phys. Rev. D* **33**, 3487–3494 (1986).

[HOLZSCHEITER, 1990]   M. H. Holzscheiter, "A measurement of the gravitational acceleration of the antiproton," In *New and Exotic Phenomena '90*, Proceedings of the XXVth Rencontre de Moriond (Xth Moriond Workshop), Les Arcs, France, 20–27 January, 1990, edited by O. Fackler and J. Trân Thanh Vân (Gif-sur-Yvette: Editions Frontières, 1990), pp. 227–282.

[HOLZSCHEITER, 1991]   M. H. Holzscheiter et al., "Are antiprotons forever?" *Phys. Lett. A* **214**, 279–284 (1996).

[HOROWITZ, 1993]   C. J. Horowitz and J. Pantaleone, "Long range forces from the cosmological neutrino background," *Phys. Lett. B* **319**, 186–190 (1993).

[HOSKINS, 1985]   J. K. Hoskins, R. D. Newman, R. Spero, and J. Schultz, "Experimental tests of the gravitational inverse-square law for mass separations from 2 to 105 cm," *Phys. Rev. D* **32**, 3084–3095 (1985).

[HSIEH, 1989]   C.-H. Hsieh et al., "The equivalence principle experiment for spin-polarized bodies," *Mod. Phys. Lett. A* **4**, 1597–1603 (1989).

[HSUI, 1987A]   A. Hsui, "Borehole measurement of the Newtonian gravitational constant," *Science* **237**, 881–883 (1987).

[HSUI, 1987B]   A. T. Hsui, "Response: Newtonian gravitational constant," *Science* **238**, 1027 (1987).

[HSU, 1994]   S. D. H. Hsu and P. Sikivie, "Long-range forces from two-neutrino exchange reexamined," *Phys. Rev. D* **49**, 4951–4953 (1994).

[HUBLER, 1995]   B. Hubler, A. Cornaz, and W. Kündig, "Determination of the gravitational constant with a lake experiment: New constraints for non-Newtonian gravity," *Phys. Rev. D* **51**, 4005–4016 (1995).

[HUGHES, 1960]   V. W. Hughes, H. G. Robinson, and V. Beltran-Lopez, "Upper limit for the anisotropy of inertial mass from nuclear resonance experiments," *Phys. Rev. Lett.* **4**, 342–344 (1960).

[HUGHES, 1991]   R. J. Hughes and M. H. Holzscheiter, "Constraints on the gravitational properties of antiprotons and positrons from cyclotron-frequency measurements," *Phys. Rev. Lett.* **66**, 854–857 (1991).

[HUGHES, 1992]   R. J. Hughes and M. H. Holzscheiter, "Tests of the weak equivalence principle with trapped antimatter," *J. Mod. Optics* **39**, 263–278 (1992).

[HUT, 1981]   P. Hut, "A constraint on the distance dependence of the gravitational constant," *Phys. Lett. B* **99**, 174–178 (1981).

[ILLY, 1989]   J. Illy, "Einstein and der Eötvös-Versuch: Ein Brief Albert Einsteins and Williy Wieu," *Ann. of Sci.* **46**, 417–422 (1989).

[ITZYKSON, 1980]   C. Itzykson and J. B. Zuber, *Quantum Field Theory* (New York: McGraw-Hill, 1980), p. 138*ff.*

[IVANOV, 1989]   B. Ivanov, "Composition dependent forces as superstring effects?" *Mod. Phys. Lett. A* **4**, 613–619 (1989).

[JACKSON, 1975]   J. D. Jackson, *Classical Electrodynamics*, 2nd edition (New York: J. Wiley & Sons, 1975).

[JAGANNATHAN, 1986]   K. Jagannathan and L. P. S. Singh, "Attraction/repulsion between like charges and the spin of the classical mediating field," *Phys. Rev. D* **33**, 2475–2477 (1986).

[JAFRY, 1996]   Y. Jafry, "STEP drag-free control," In *Proceedings of the STEP Symposium*, Pisa, Italy, 6–8 April, 1993, edited by R. Reinhard (European Space Agency publication ESA WPP-115, 1996), pp. 290–299.

[JEKELI, 1990]   C. Jekeli, D. H. Eckhardt, and A. J. Romaides, "Tower gravity experiment: No evidence for non-Newtonian gravity," *Phys. Rev. Lett.* **64**, 1204–1206 (1990).

[JEFFREYS, 1970]   H. Jeffreys, *The Earth, Its Origin, History, and Physical Constitution*, 5th Edition (Cambridge: Cambridge University Press, 1970).

[JEFFREYS, 1963]   H. Jeffreys, "On the hydrostatic theory of the figure of the Earth," *Geophys. J. Roy. Astron. Soc.* **8**, 196–202 (1963).

[JEN, 1992]   T.-H. Jen, W.-T. Ni, S.-S. Pan, and S.-L. Wang, "Torsion balance experiments searching for finite-range mass-spin interactions," In *Proceedings of the Sixth Marcel Grossmann Meeting on General Relativity*, Kyoto, Japan, 23–29 June, 1991, edited by H. Sato and T. Nakamura (Singapore: World Scientific, 1992), pp. 489–494.

[KAMMERAAD, 1990]   J. Kammeraad et al., "New results from Nevada: A test of Newton's law using the BREN tower and a high density ground gravity survey," In *New and Exotic Phenomena '90*, Proceedings of the Xth Moriond Workshop, Les Arcs, France, 20–27 January, 1990, edited by O. Fackler and J. Trân Thanh Vân (Gif-sur-Yvette: Editions Frontières, 1990), pp. 245–254.

[KASTENING, 1989]   B. Kastening, R. D. Peccei, and C. Wetterich, "Scalar interactions with intermediate range," *Phys. Rev. D* **39**, 1772–1775 (1989).

[KEYSER, 1989]   P. T. Keyser, "Forces on the Thieberger accelerometer," *Phys. Rev. Lett.* **62**, 2332 (1989).

[KEISER, 1982]   G. M. Keiser and J. E. Faller, "Eötvös experiment with a fluid fiber," In *Proceedings of the Second Marcel Grossmann Meeting on General Relativity*, edited by R. Ruffini (Amsterdam: North-Holland, 1982), pp. 969–976.

[KIM, 1986]   Y. E. Kim, "The local baryon gauge invariance and the Eötvös experiment," *Phys. Lett. B* **177**, 255–259 (1986).

[KIM, 1987]   Y. E. Kim, "New force or thermal convection in the differential-accelerometer experiment?" *Phys. Lett. B* **192**, 236–238 (1987).

[KLOOR, 1994A]   H. Kloor, E. Fischbach, C. Talmadge, and G. L. Greene, "Limits on new forces coexisting with electromagnetism," *Phys. Rev. D* **49**, 2098–2113 (1994).

[KLOOR, 1994B]   H. Kloor, *Limits on new forces coexisting with electromagnetism*, Ph.D. Thesis, Purdue University, unpublished (1994).

[KRAUSE, 1994]   D. Krause, H. Kloor, and E. Fischbach, "Multiple radiation from massive fields: Application to binary pulsar systems," *Phys. Rev. D* **49**, 6892–6906 (1994).

[KRAUSS, 1988]   L. Krauss and S. Tremaine, "Test of the weak equivalence principle for neutrinos and photons," *Phys. Rev. Lett* **60**, 176–177 (1988).

[KREUZER, 1968]   L. B. Kreuzer, "Experimental measurement of the equivalence of active and passive gravitational mass," *Phys. Rev.* **169**, 1007–1012 (1968).

[KUHN, 1987]   J. R. Kuhn and L. Kruglyak, "Non-Newtonian forces and the invisible mass problem," *Astrophys. J.* **313**, 1–12 (1987).

[KURODA, 1985]   K. Kuroda and H. Hirakawa, "Experimental test of the law of gravitation," *Phys. Rev. D* **32**, 342–346 (1985).

[KURODA, 1989]   K. Kuroda and N. Mio, "Test of a composition-dependent force by a free-fall interferometer," *Phys. Rev. Lett.* **62**, 1941–1944 (1989).

[KURODA, 1990]   K. Kuroda and N. Mio, "Limits on a possible composition-dependent force by a Galilean experiment," *Phys. Rev. D* **42**, 3903–3907 (1990).

[LAMOREAUX, 1986]   S. K. Lamoreaux, J. P. Jacobs, B. R. Heckel, F. J. Raab, and E. N. Fortson, "New limits on spatial anisotropy from optically pumped ^{201}Hg and ^{199}Hg," *Phys. Rev. Lett.* **57**, 3125–3128 (1986).

[LAMOREAUX, 1989]   S. K. Lamoreaux, J. P. Jacobs, B. R. Heckel, F. J. Raab, and E. N. Fortson, "Optical pumping technique for measuring small nuclear quadrupole shifts in $^{1}S_0$ atoms and testing spatial isotropy," *Phys. Rev. A* **39**, 1082–1111 (1989).

[LAMOREAUX, 1997] S. K. Lamoreaux, "Demonstration of the Casimir force in the 0.6 to 6 μm range," *Phys. Rev. Lett.* **78**, 5–8 (1997).

[LANGLOIS, 1964] W. E. Langlois, *Slow Viscous Flow* (New York: Macmillan, 1964), p. 152.

[LEE, 1955] T. D. Lee and C. N. Yang, "Conservation of heavy particles and generalized gauge transformations," *Phys. Rev.* **98**, 1501 (1955).

[LEITNER, 1964] J. Leitner and S. Okubo, "Parity, charge conjugation, and time reversal in the gravitational interaction," *Phys. Rev.* **136**, B1542–B1546 (1964).

[LI, 1986] M. Li and R. Ruffini, "Radiation of new particles of the fifth interaction," *Phys. Lett. A* **116**, 20–24 (1986).

[LIU, 1983] H. Liu, P. Zhang, and R. Qin, "A null experiment of gravitational inverse square law," In *Proceedings of the Third Marcel Grossmann Meeting On General Relativity*, Shanghai, China, 30 August – 3 September 1982, edited by N. Hu (Amsterdam: Science Press and North-Holland Publishing Company, 1983), 1501–1504.

[LOBOV, 1990] G. A. Lobov, "On the violation of the equivalence principle of General Relativity by the electroweak interaction," *Sov. J. Nucl. Phys.* **52**, 918–919 (1990).

[LONG, 1974] D. R. Long, "Why do we believe Newtonian gravitation at laboratory dimensions?" *Phys. Rev. D* **9**, 850–852 (1974).

[LONG, 1976] D. R. Long, "Experimental examination of the gravitational inverse square law," *Nature* **260**, 417–418 (1976).

[LONG, 1980] D. R. Long, "Vacuum polarization and non-Newtonian gravitation," *Nuovo Cimento* **55B**, 252–256 (1980).

[LONG, 1981] D. R. Long, "Current measurements of the gravitational 'constant' as a function of the mass separation," *Nuovo Cimento* **62B**, 130–138 (1981).

[LONG, 1988] D. R. Long, seminar given at conference on *5th Force-Neutrino Physics* (VIIIth Moriond Workshop), Les Arcs, France, January 23–30, 1988.

[LONGO, 1988] M. J. Longo, "New precision tests of the Einstein equivalence principle from SN1987A," *Phys. Rev. Lett.* **60**, 173–175 (1988).

[LUSIGNOLI, 1986]   M. Lusignoli and A. Pugliese, "Hyperphotons and K-meson decays" *Phys. Lett B* **171**, 468–470 (1986)

[LUTHER, 1982]   G. G. Luther and W. R. Towler, "Redetermination of the Newtonian gravitational constant G," *Phys. Rev. Lett.* **48**, 121–123 (1982).

[MACRAE, 1984]   K. I. Macrae and R. J. Riegert, "Long-range antigravity," *Nucl. Phys.* **B244**, 513–522 (1984).

[MALONEY, 1989]   F. P. Maloney, E. F. Guinan, and P. T. Boyd, "Eclipsing binary stars as tests of gravity theories: The apsidal motion of AS Camelopardalis," *Astron. J.* **98**, 1800–1813 (1989).

[MALANEY, 1995]   R. A. Malaney, G. D. Starkman, and S. Tremaine, "Time delays of supernova neutrinos from new long-range interactions," *Phys. Rev. D* **51**, 324–327 (1995).

[MANNHEIM, 1997]   P. D. Mannheim, "Are galactic rotation curves really flat?" *Ap. J.* **479**, 659–664 (1997).

[MARIS, 1988]   H. J. Maris, "Comment on 'Search for a substance-dependent force with a new differential accelerometer,' " *Phys. Rev. Lett.* **60**, 964 (1988).

[MAZILU, 1996]   P. Mazilu and H. Dittus, "The equivalence principle within the Lorentz-invariant scalar field theory of gravity—report on theoretical studies for experiments on drop tower 'Bremen'," In *Proceedings of the STEP Symposium*, Pisa, Italy, 6–8 April, 1993, edited by R. Reinhard (European Space Agency publication ESA WPP-115, 1996), pp. 85–95.

[MEMBRADO, 1988A]   M. C. Membrado and A. F. Pacheco, "Implication of Yukawa-like effects in a white dwarf structure," *Astrophys. J.* **327**, 726–731 (1988).

[MEMBRADO, 1988B]   M. C. Membrado and A. F. Pacheco, "Short-range effects in large white dwarfs," *Astrophys. J.* **331**, 394–396 (1988).

[MEMBRADO, 1990]   M. C. Membrado, A. F. Pacheco, and H. Vucetich, "Introduction of short-range effects in the Oppenheimer-Volkoff equation," *Astrophys. J.* **348**, 212–220 (1990).

[MIKHEYEV, 1985]   S. P. Mikheyev and A. Yu. Smirnov, "Resonance enhancement of oscillations in matter and solar neutrino spectroscopy," *Sov. J. Nucl. Phys.*

42, 913–917 (1985).

[MIKKELSEN, 1977]   D. R. Mikkelsen and M. J. Newman, "Constraints on the gravitational constant at large distances," *Phys. Rev. D* **16**, 919–926 (1977).

[MILGROM, 1983A]   M. Milgrom, "A modification of the Newtonian dynamics as a possible alternative to the hidden mass hypothesis," *Astrophys. J.* **270**, 365–370 (1983).

[MILGROM, 1983B]   M. Milgrom, "A modification of the Newtonian dynamics: Implications for galaxies," *Astrophys. J.* **270**, 371–383 (1983).

[MILGROM, 1983C]   M. Milgrom, "A modification of the Newtonian dynamics: Implications for galaxy systems," *Astrophys. J.* **270**, 384–389 (1983).

[MILGROM, 1986]   M. Milgrom, "On the use of Eötvös-type experiments to detect medium-range forces," *Nucl. Phys. B* **277**, 509–512 (1986).

[MINAKATA, 1995]   H. Minakata and H. Nunokawa, "Testing the principle of equivalence by solar neutrinos," *Phys. Rev. D* **51**, 6625–6634 (1995).

[MILYUKOV, 1985]   V. K. Milyukov, "Experimental verification of the law of gravity for laboratory distances," *Soviet Physics JETP* **61**, 187–191. [Translation of *Zh. Eksp. Teor. Fiz.* **88**, 321–328 (1985).]

[MIO, 1986]   N. Mio and H. Hirakawa, "Dynamic null experiment to test the law of gravitation," *J. Phys. Soc. Japan* **55**, 4143–4146 (1986).

[MIO, 1987]   N. Mio, K. Tsubono, and H. Hirakawa, "Experimental test of the law of gravitation at small distances," *Phys. Rev. D* **36**, 2321–2326 (1987).

[MISNER, 1973]   C. W. Misner, K. S. Thorne, and J. A. Wheeler, *Gravitation* (San Francisco: W. H. Freeman, 1973).

[MITROFANOV, 1988]   V. P. Mitrofanov and O. I. Ponomareva, "Experimental test of gravitation at small distances," *Sov. Phys. JETP* **67**, 1963–1966 (1988). [Translation of *Zh. Eksp. Teor. Fiz.* **94**, 16–22 (1988).]

[MOFFAT, 1987]   J. W. Moffat, "Nonsymmetric gravitation theory: A possible new force in nature," In *New and Exotic Phenomena*, Proceedings of the VIIth Moriond Workshop, Les Arcs, France, 24–31 January, 1987, edited by O. Fackler and J. Trân Thanh Vân (Gif-sur-Yvette: Editions Frontières, 1987), pp. 623–635.

[MOFFAT, 1988]   J. W. Moffat and E. Woolgar, "Motion of massive bodies: Testing the nonsymmetric gravitation theory," *Phys. Rev. D* **37**, 918–930 (1988).

[MOFFAT, 1989]   J. W. Moffat, "Detection of dark matter and tests of the weak equivalence principle," *Phys. Rev. D* **40**, 2499–2501 (1989).

[MOODY, 1984]   J. E. Moody and F. Wilczek, "New macroscopic forces?" *Phys. Rev. D* **30**, 130–138 (1984).

[MOODY, 1993]   M. V. Moody and H. J. Paik, "Gauss's law test of gravity at short range" *Phys. Rev. Lett.* **70**, 1195–1198 (1993).

[MOORE, 1988A]   G. I. Moore et al., "Determination of the gravitational constant at an effective mass separation of 22 m," *Phys. Rev. D* **38**, 1023–1029 (1988).

[MOORE, 1988B]   G. I. Moore et al., "A balance for precise weighing in a disturbed environment," *J. Phys. E: Sci. Inst.* **21**, 534–539 (1988).

[MORPURGO, 1991]   G. Morpurgo, "Comment on 'Does antimatter fall with the same acceleration as ordinary matter?' " *Phys. Rev. Lett.* **67**, 1047 (1991).

[MORRISON, 1957]   P. Morrison and T. Gold, In *Essays on Gravity* (New Boston: Gravity Research Foundation, 1957), pp. 45–50.

[MORRISON, 1958]   P. Morrison, "Approximate nature of physical symmetries," *Am. J. Phys.* **26**, 358–368 (1958).

[MOSTEPANENKO, 1987A]   V. M. Mostepanenko and I. Yu. Sokolov, "Restrictions on long-range forces following from the Casimir effect," *Sov. J. of Nucl. Phys.* **46**, 685–688 (1987). [Translation of Yad. Fiz **46**, 1174–1180 (1987).]

[MOSTEPANENKO, 1987B]   V. M. Mostepanenko and I. Yu. Sokolov, "The Casimir effect leads to new restrictions on long-range force constants," *Phys. Lett. A* **125**, 405–408 (1987).

[MOSTEPANENKO, 1988]   V. M. Mostepanenko and I. Yu. Sokolov, "New restrictions on the parameters of the spin-1 antigraviton following from the Casimir effect, Eötvös and Cavendish experiments," *Phys. Lett. A* **132**, 313–315 (1988).

[MOSTEPANENKO, 1989]   V. M. Mostepanenko and I. Yu. Sokolov, "Restrictions on the parameters of the spin-1 antigraviton and the dilaton resulting from the Casimir effect and from the Eötvös and Cavendish experiments," *Sov. J.*

of Nucl. Phys. **49**, 1118–1120 (1989). [Translation of *Yad. Fiz.* **49**, No. 6, 1807–1811 (1989).]

[MOSTEPANENKO, 1993] V. M. Mostepanenko and I. Yu. Sokolov, "Hypothetical long-range interactions and restrictions on their parameters from force measurements," *Phys. Rev. D* **47**, 2882–2891 (1993).

[MULLER, 1989] G. Müller, W. Zürn, K. Lindner, and N. Rösch," "Determination of the gravitational constant by an experiment at a pumped-storage reservoir," *Phys. Rev. Lett.* **63**, 2621–2624 (1989).

[MULLER, 1990] G. Müller, W. Zürn, K. Lindner, and N. Rösch," "Search for non-Newtonian gravitation—a gravimetric experiment in a hydroelectric lake," *Geophys. J. International* **101**, 329–344 (1990).

[NACHTMANN, 1969] O. Nachtmann, "CP violation and cosmological fields," In *Particle Physics*, edited by P. Urban (Berlin: Springer, 1969), pp. 485–500.

[NELSON, 1988] P. Nelson, D. Graham, and R. Newman, "A 'fifth force' search using a controlled local mass," In *5th Force-Neutrino Physics*, Proceedings of the XXIIIrd Rencontre de Moriond (VIIIth Moriond Workshop), Les Arcs, France, 23–30 January, 1988 edited by O. Fackler and J. Trân Thanh Vân (Gif-sur-Yvette: Editions Frontières, 1988), pp. 427–430.

[NELSON, 1990] P. G. Nelson, D. M. Graham, and R. D. Newman, "Search for an intermediate-range composition-dependent force coupling to $N - Z$," *Phys. Rev. D* **42**, 963–976 (1990).

[NEUFELD, 1986] D. A. Neufeld, "Upper limit on any intermediate-range force associated with baryon number," *Phys. Rev. Lett.* **56**, 2344–2346 (1986).

[NEWMAN, 1955] J. R. Newman, *The World of Mathematics, Volume Two* (New York: Simon and Schuster, 1956), pp. 828–839.

[NEWMAN, 1987] R. D. Newman, D. M. Graham, and P. G. Nelson, "Searches for anomalous long-range forces." In *New and Exotic Phenomena*, Proceedings of the VIIth Moriond Workshop, Les Arcs, France, 24–31 January, 1987, edited by O. Fackler and J. Trân Thanh Vân (Gif-sur-Yvette: Editions Frontières, 1987), pp. 599–606.

[NEWTON, 1960] I. Newton, *Principia*, Book 3, Proposition 6, Theorem 6, (University of California Press, Cajori Edition, 1960), p. 411.

[NI, 1977]   W.-T. Ni, "Equivalence principles and gauge fields," *Phys. Rev. Lett.* **38**, 301–304 (1977).

[NI, 1987]   W.-T. Ni, "Equivalence principles and gauge fields," *Phys. Lett. A* **120**, 174–178 (1987).

[NI, 1990]   W.-T. Ni, "Test of the equivalence principle for nuclear-polarized bodies at low temperature," *Physica B* **165, 166**, Part I, 157–158 (1990).

[NIEBAUER, 1987]   T. M. Niebauer, M. P. McHugh, and J. E. Faller, "Galilean test for the fifth force," *Phys. Rev. Lett.* **59**, 609–612 (1987).

[NIETO, 1988]   M. M. Nieto, T. Goldman, and R. J. Hughes, "The Principle of equivalence, quantum gravity, and new gravitational forces," *Australian Physicist* **25**, 259–262 (1988).

[NIETO, 1991]   M. M. Nieto and T. Goldman, "The arguments against 'antigravity' and the gravitational acceleration of antimatter," *Phys. Rep.* **205**, 221–281 (1991).

[NOBILI, 1987]   A. M. Nobili, A. Milani, and P. Farinella, "Testing Newtonian gravity in space," *Phys. Lett. A* **120**, 437–441 (1987).

[NOBILI, 1988]   A. M. Nobili, A. Milani, and P. Farinella, "The orbit of a space laboratory for the measurement of G," *Astron. J.* **95**, 576–578 (1988).

[NOBILI, 1990]   A. M. Nobili et al., "The Newton mission—A proposed man-made planetary system in space to measure the gravitational constant," *ESA Journal* **14**, 389–408 (1990).

[NOBILI, 1996]   A. M. Nobili, D. Bramanti, E. Polacco, and G. Catastini, "Galileo Galilei (GG): Test of the equivalence principle at room temperature," In *Proceedings of the STEP Symposium*, Pisa, Italy, 6–8 April, 1993, edited by R. Reinhard (European Space Agency publication ESA WPP-115, 1996), p. 374.

[NORDTVEDT, 1968A]   K. Nordtvedt, "Equivalence principle for massive bodies, I: Phenomenology," *Phys. Rev.* **169**, 1014–1016 (1968).

[NORDTVEDT, 1968B]   K. Nordtvedt, "Equivalence principle for massive bodies, II: Theory," *Phys. Rev.* **169**, 1017–1025 (1968).

[NORDTVEDT, 1972]   K. Nordtvedt, Jr., "Gravitation theory: Empirical status from solar system experiments," *Science* **178**, 1157–1164 (1972).

[NORDTVEDT, 1988]   K. Nordtvedt, "Lunar laser ranging and laboratory Eötvös-type experiments," *Phys. Rev. D* **37**, 1070–1071 (1988).

[NUSSINOV, 1986]   S. Nussinov, "Further tests and possible interpretations of a suggested new vectorial interaction," *Phys. Rev. Lett.* **56**, 2350–2351 (1986).

[O'CONNELL, 1974]   R. F. O'Connell, "Spin, rotation, and C, P and T effects in the gravitational interaction and related experiments," In *Experimental Gravitation*, Proceedings of the International School of Physics, Enrico Fermi, Course LVI, edited by B. Bertotti (New York: Academic Press, 1974), pp. 496–514.

[OGAWA, 1982]   Y. Ogawa, K. Tsubono, and H. Hirakawa, "Experimental test of the law of gravitation," *Phys. Rev. D* **26**, 729–733 (1982).

[O'HANLON, 1972]   J. O'Hanlon, "Intermediate-range gravity: A generally covariant model," *Phys. Rev. Lett.* **29**, 137–138 (1972).

[OLDHAM, 1991]   M. Oldham, *Testing for non-Newtonian gravity using pumped storage reservoirs*, Ph.D. Thesis, University of Newcastle-Upon-Tyne, unpublished (1991).

[OLDHAM, 1993]   M. Oldham, F. J. Lowes, and R. J. Edge, "A decametric scale investigation of the gravitational constant," *Geophys. J. Int.* **113**, 83–94 (1993).

[OLIVE, 1996]   K. Olive, "Why do we need non-baryonic dark matter?" In *Dark Matter in Cosmology, Quantum Measurements, Experimental Gravitation*, Proceedings of the XXXIst Rencontre de Moriond, Les Arcs, France, 20–27 January, 1996 edited by R. Ansari, Y. Giraud-Héraud, and J. Trân Thanh Vân (Gif-sur-Yvette: Editions Frontières, 1996), pp. 3–24.

[OVERHAUSER, 1952]   A. W. Overhauser, unpublished (1952).

[PAIK, 1979]   H. J. Paik, "New null experiment to test the inverse square law of gravitation," *Phys. Rev.* **19**, 2320–2324 (1979).

[PAKVASA, 1989]   S. Pakvasa, W. A. Simmons, and T. J. Weiler, "Test of equivalence principle for neutrinos and antineutrinos," *Phys. Rev. D* **39**, 1761–1763 (1989).

[PAN, 1992A]   S.-S. Pan, W.-T. Ni, and S.-C. Chen, "Polarized-body vs. polarized-body torsion balance experiment for measuring possible anomalous spin-spin interactions," In *Proceedings of the Sixth Marcel Grossmann Meeting on General Relativity*, Kyoto, Japan, 23–29 June, 1991, edited by H. Sato and T. Nakamura (Singapore: World Scientific, 1992), 364–370.

[PAN, 1992B]   S.-S. Pan, W.-T. Ni, and S.-C. Chen, "Experimental search for anomalous spin-spin interactions," *Mod. Phys. Lett. A* **7**, 1287–1299 (1992).

[PANOV, 1979]   V. I. Panov and V. N. Frontov, "The Cavendish experiment at large distances," *Sov. Phys. JETP* **50**, 852–856 (1979). [Translation of *Zh. Eksp. Teor. Fiz.* **77**, 1701–1707 (1979).]

[PANTALEONE, 1993]   J. Pantaleone, A. Halprin, and C. Leung, "Neutrino mixing due to a violation of the equivalence principle," *Phys. Rev. D* **47**, R4199–4202 (1993).

[PARKER, 1989]   R. L. Parker and M. A. Zumberge, "An analysis of geophysical experiments to test Newton's law of gravity," *Nature* **342**, 29–32 (1989).

[PDG, 1982]   Particle Data Group, "Review of particle properties," *Phys. Lett.* **111B**, 1–294 (1982).

[PDG, 1996]   Particle Data Group, "Review of Particle Properties," *Phys. Rev. D* **54**, 1–720 (1996).

[PAVER, 1989]   N. Paver, "Rare kaon decays: Theoretical overview," *Il Nuovo Cimento* **102A**, 97–111 (1989).

[PECCEI, 1987]   R. D. Peccei, J. Solà, and C. Wetterich, "Adjusting the cosmological constant dynamically: Cosmons and a new force weaker than gravity," *Phys. Lett. B* **195**, 183–190 (1987).

[PECHLANER, 1966]   E. Pechlaner and R. Sexl, "On quadratic lagrangians in General Relativity," *Communications in Mathematical Physics* **2**, 165–175 (1966).

[PHILLIPS, 1987]   P. R. Phillips, "Test of spatial isotropy using a cryogenic torsion pendulum," *Phys. Rev. Lett.* **59**, 1784–1787 (1987).

[PRESTAGE, 1985]   J. D. Prestage, J. J. Bollinger, W. M. Itano, and D. J. Wineland, "Limits for spatial anisotropy by use of nuclear-spin-polarized ^{9}Be ions," *Phys. Rev. Lett.* **54**, 2387–2390 (1985).

[PRICE, 1972A] R. H. Price, "Nonspherical perturbations of relativistic gravitational collapse. I. Scalar and gravitational perturbations," *Phys. Rev. D* **5**, 2419–2438 (1972).

[PRICE, 1972B] R. H. Price, "Nonspherical perturbations of relativistic gravitational collapse. II. Integer spin, zero-rest-mass fields," *Phys. Rev. D* **5**, 2439–2454 (1972).

[PRICE, 1988] J. C. Price, "Gravitational strength forces below 1 cm," In *International Symposium on Experimental Gravitational Physics*, edited by P. F. Michelson, H. En-ke and G. Pizzella (Singapore: World Press, 1988), 436–439 (1988).

[PRIMAKOFF, 1939] H. Primakoff and T. Holstein, "Many-body interactions in atomic and nuclear systems," *Phys. Rev.* **55**, 1218–1234 (1939).

[RAPP, 1974] R. H. Rapp, "Current estimates of mean earth ellipsoid parameters," *Geophys. Res. Lett.* **1**, 35–38 (1974).

[RAPP, 1977] R. H. Rapp, "Determination of potential coefficients to degree 52 from 5° mean gravity anomalies," *Bull. Geod.* **51**, 301–323 (1977).

[RAPP, 1987] R. H. Rapp, "An estimate of equatorial gravity from terrestrial and satellite data," *Geophys. Res. Lett.* **14**, 730–732 (1987).

[REINHARD, 1996] *Proceedings of the STEP Symposium*, Pisa, Italy, 6–8 April, 1993, edited by R. Reinhard (European Space Agency publication ESA WPP-115, 1996).

[RENNER, 1935] J. Renner, "Kísérleti vizsgálatok a tömegvonzás és a tehetetlenség arányosságáról," *Matematikai és Természettudományi Értesitő* **53**, 542–568 (1935)

[ROMAIDES, 1994] A. J. Romaides et al., "Second tower experiment: Further evidence for Newtonian gravity," *Phys. Rev. D* **50**, 3613–3617 (1994).

[ROMAIDES, 1997] A. J. Romaides, R. W. Sands, E. Fischbach, and C. Talmadge, "Final results from the WABG tower gravity experiment," *Phys. Rev. D* **55**, 4532–4536 (1997).

[ROZSA, 1931] M. Rózsa and P. Selenyi, "Über eine experimentalle methode zur prüfung der proportionalität der trägen und gravitierenden masse," *Z. für*

Physik **71**, 814–816 (1931).

[RITTER, 1990]   R. C. Ritter, C. E. Goldblum, W.-T. Ni, G. T. Gillies, and C. C. Speake, "Experimental test of equivalence principle with polarized masses," *Phys. Rev. D* **42**, 977–991 (1990).

[RIVEROS, 1986]   C. Riveros and H. Vucetich, "Bounds on the validity of Newton's gravitational law from electromagnetic solar deflection," *Phys. Rev. D* **34**, 321–326 (1986).

[RIZZO, 1986]   T. G. Rizzo, "Hyperphoton production in W-boson decay," *Phys. Rev. D* **34**, 3519–3520 (1986).

[ROLL, 1964]   P. G. Roll, R. Krotkov, and R. H. Dicke, "The equivalence of inertia and passive gravitational mass," *Ann. Phys. (NY)* **26**, 442–517 (1964).

[SAKURAI, 1967]   J. J. Sakurai, *Advanced Quantum Mechanics* (Reading: Addison-Wesley, 1967).

[SANDERS, 1984]   R. H. Sanders, "Anti-gravity and galaxy rotation curves," *Astron. Astrophys.* **136**, L21–L23 (1984).

[SANDERS, 1986A]   R. H. Sanders, "Alternatives to dark matter," *Monthly Not. Royal Astron. Soc.* **223**, 539–555 (1986).

[SANDERS, 1986B]   R. H. Sanders, "Finite length-scale anti-gravity and observations of mass discrepancies in galaxies," *Astron. Astrophys.* **154**, 135–144 (1986).

[SANDERS, 1992]   A. J. Sanders and W. E. Deeds, "Proposed new determination of the gravitational constant G and tests of Newtonian gravitation," *Phys. Rev. D* **46**, 489–504 (1992).

[SANTALÓ, 1976]   L. A. Santaló, *Integral Geometry and Geometric Probability* (Reading: Addison-Wesley, 1976), p. 212.

[SCHECTER, 1987]   B. Schecter, "May the force be with you," *Omni* **9**, 36–43 and 68–71 (1987).

[SCHERK, 1979A]   J. Scherk, "Antigravity: A crazy idea?" *Phys. Lett. B* **88**, 265–267 (1979)

[SCHERK, 1979B]   J. Scherk, "From supergravity to antigravity," In *Supergravity*,

Stony Brook, NY, September 27–29, 1979, edited by D. Freedman and P. van Nieuwenhuizen (Amsterdam: North Holland, 1979), pp. 43–51.

[SCHMIEDMAYER, 1989]   J. Schmiedmayer, "The equivalence of the gravitational and inertial mass of the neutron," *Nucl. Instr. Meth. Phys. Res. A* **284**, 59–62 (1989).

[SCHIFF, 1958]   L. I. Schiff, "Sign of the gravitational mass of a positron," *Phys. Rev. Lett.* **1**, 254–255 (1958).

[SCHIFF, 1959]   L. I. Schiff, "Gravitational properties of antimatter," *Proceedings of the National Academy of Sciences (USA)* **45**, 69–80 (1959).

[SCHIFF, 1960]   L. I. Schiff, "On experimental tests of the general theory of relativity," *Am. J. Phys.* **28**, 340–343 (1960).

[SCHIFF, 1966]   L. I. Schiff and M. V. Barnhill, "Gravitation-induced electric field near a metal," *Phys. Rev.* **151**, 1067–1071 (1966).

[SCHINDEL, 1986]   Ulrich Schindel (private communication) has brought the following reference to our attention: "Geschäftliche Mitteilungen der Königlichen Gessellschaft der Wissenschaft zu Göttingen," pp. 37–41 (1909).

[SCHWARZSCHILD, 1986]   B. Schwarzschild, "Reanalysis of old Eötvös data suggests fifth force... to some," *Physics Today* **39**, p. 17–20 (1986).

[SCHWARZSCHILD, 1988]   B. Schwarzschild, "From mine shafts to cliffs—the 'fifth force' remains elusive," *Physics Today* **41**, p. 21–24 (1988).

[SCHURR, 1991]   J. Schurr, H. Meyer, H. Piel, and H. Walesch, "A new laboratory experiment for testing Newton's gravitational law," In *Relativistic Gravity Research*, edited by J. Elhers and G. Schäfer (Berlin: Springer Verlag, 1991), pp. 341–347.

[SCHWINGER, 1954]   J. Schwinger, "Theory of quantized fields. VI," *Phys. Rev.* **94**, 1362–1384 (1954).

[SILVERMAN, 1987]   M. P. Silverman, "Satellite test of intermediate-range deviation from Newton's law of gravity," *Gen. Rel. Grav.* **19**, 511–514 (1987).

[SMITH, 1985]   D. E. Smith et al., "A global geodetic reference frame from LAGEOS ranging in (SL5.1AP)," *J. Geophys. Res.* **90**, 9221–9235 (1985).

[SPALLICCI, 1990]   A. D. A. M. Spallicci, "Orbiting test masses for an equivalence principle space experiment," *Gen. Rel. Grav.* **22**, 863–871 (1990).

[SPEAKE, 1986]   C. C. Speake and T. J. Quinn, "Beam balance test of weak equivalence principle," *Nature* **321**, 567–568 (1986).

[SPEAKE, 1988]   C. C. Speake and T. J. Quinn, "Search for a short-range, isospin-coupling component of the fifth force with use of a beam balance," *Phys. Rev. Lett.* **61**, 1340–1343 (1988).

[SPEAKE, 1990]   C. C. Speake et al., "Test of the inverse-square law of gravitation using the 300 m tower at Erie, Colorado," *Phys. Rev. Lett.* **65**, 1967–1971 (1990).

[SPERO, 1980]   R. Spero, J. K. Hoskins, R. Newman, J. Pellam, and J. Schultz, "Test of the gravitation inverse-square law of laboratory distances," *Phys. Rev. Lett.* **44**, 1645–1648 (1980).

[SPRUCH, 1986]   L. Spruch, "Retarded, or Casimir, long-range potentials," *Phys. Today* **39**, 37–49 (1986).

[STACEY, 1977]   F. D. Stacey, *Physics of the Earth*, 2nd edition (New York: J. Wiley & Sons, 1977).

[STACEY, 1981]   F. D. Stacey and G. J. Tuck, "Geophysical evidence for non-Newtonian gravity," *Nature* **292**, 230–232 (1981).

[STACEY, 1983]   F. D. Stacey, "Subterranean gravity and other deep hole geo-physics," In *Science Underground*, Los Alamos, 1982, edited by M. M. Nieto et al., AIP Conference Proceedings #96 (New York: American Institute of Physics, 1983), pp. 285–297.

[STACEY, 1984]   F. D. Stacey, "Gravity," *Sci. Prog. Oxf.* **69**, 1–17 (1984).

[STACEY, 1987A]   F. D. Stacey et al., "Geophysics and the law of gravity," *Rev. Mod. Phys.* **59**, 157–174 (1987).

[STACEY, 1987B]   F. D. Stacey, G. J. Tuck, and G. I. Moore, "Geophysical tests of the inverse square law of gravity," In *New and Exotic Phenomena*, Proceedings of the XXIIrd Rencontre de Moriond (VIIth Moriond Workshop), Les Arcs, France, 24–31 January, 1987 edited by O. Fackler and J. Trân Thanh Vân, (Gif-sur-Yvette: Editions Frontières, 1987), pp. 557–565.

[STUBBS, 1987]   C. W. Stubbs et al., "Search for an intermediate-range interaction," *Phys. Rev. Lett.* **58**, 1070–1073 (1987).

[STUBBS, 1988A]   C. W. Stubbs, *A search for a new composition-dependent interaction: An experimental test of the "fifth force" hypothesis*, Ph.D. Thesis, University of Washington, unpublished (1988).

[STUBBS, 1988B]   C. W. Stubbs, E. G. Adelberger, and E. C. Gregory, "Constraints of proposed spin-0 and spin-1 partners of the graviton," *Phys. Rev. Lett.* **61**, 2409–2411 (1988).

[STUBBS, 1989A]   C. W. Stubbs et al., "Limits on composition-dependent interactions using a laboratory source: Is there a 'fifth force' coupled to isospin?" *Phys. Rev. Lett.* **62**, 609–612 (1989).

[STUBBS, 1989B]   C. W. Stubbs, "Eöt-Wash constraints on multiple Yukawa interactions and on a coupling to 'isospin'," In *Tests of Fundamental Laws of Physics*, Proceedings of the IXth Moriond Workshop, Les Arcs, France, 21–28 January, 1989, edited by O. Fackler and J. Trân Thanh Vân (Gif-sur-Yvette: Editions Frontières, 1989), pp. 473–484.

[SU, 1994]   Y. Su et al., "New tests of the universality of free fall," *Phys. Rev.* *D* **50**, 3614–3636 (1994); *D* **51**, 3135(E) (1995).

[SUDARSKY, 1991]   D. Sudarsky, E. Fischbach, and C. Talmadge, "Effects of external fields on the neutral kaon system," *Ann. Phys. (NY)* **207**, 103–139 (1991).

[SUGIMOTO, 1972]   D. Sugimoto, "Astrophysical test for dilaton theory in non-Newtonian gravity," *Prog. Theor. Phys.* **48**, 699–700 (1972).

[SUTTON, 1938]   R. M. Sutton, *Demonstration Experiments in Physics* (New York: McGraw Hill, 1938), p. 123.

[SUZUKI, 1986]   M. Suzuki, "Bound on the mass and coupling of the hyperphoton by particle physics," *Phys. Rev. Lett.* **56**, 1339–1341 (1986).

[SYMON, 1971]   K. R. Symon, *Mechanics*, 3rd edition (Reading: Addison-Wesley, 1971), Chapter 3.

[TALMADGE, 1986]   C. Talmadge, E. Fischbach, and S. H. Aronson, "Effects of local mass anomalies in Eötvös-type experiments," In *Progress in Elec-*

troweak Interactions, Proceedings of the XXI Rencontre de Moriond, Les Arcs, France, 9–16 March, 1986, edited by J. Trân Thanh Vân, (Gif-sur-Yvette: Editions Frontières, 1986), pp. 228–240.

[TALMADGE, 1987A]   C. L. Talmadge, *Reanalysis of the Eötvös Experiment*, Ph.D. Thesis, Purdue University, unpublished (1987).

[TALMADGE, 1987B]   C. Talmadge, E. Fischbach, and S. H. Aronson, "Multicomponent models of the fifth force," In *New and Exotic Phenomena*, Proceedings of the XXIInd Rencontre de Moriond (VIIth Moriond Workshop), Les Arcs, France, 24–31 January, 1987, edited by O. Fackler and J. Trân Thanh Vân (Gif-sur-Yvette: Editions Frontières, 1987), pp. 541–555.

[TALMADGE, 1988]   C. Talmadge, J.-B. Berthias, R. W. Hellings, and E. M. Standish, "Model-independent constraints on possible modifications of Newtonian gravity," *Phys. Rev. Lett.* **61**, 1159–1162 (1988).

[TALMADGE, 1989A]   C. Talmadge, E. Fischbach, and D. Sudarsky, "Alternative models of the fifth force," In *Tests of Fundamental Laws of Physics*, Proceedings of the IXth Moriond Workshop, Les Arcs, France, 21–28 January, 1989, edited by O. Fackler and J. Trân Thanh Vân (Gif-sur-Yvette: Editions Frontières, 1989), pp. 445–458.

[TALMADGE, 1989B]   C. Talmadge and E. Fischbach, "The Earth's Gravity and the Fifth Force," In *Proceedings of the Fifth Marcel Grossmann Meeting on General Relativity*, University of Western Australia, Perth, Australia, 8–13 August, 1988, edited by D. G. Blair and M. J. Buckingham (Singapore: World Scientific, 1989), pp. 1553–1568.

[TASSOUL, 1978]   J. L. Tassoul, *Theory of Rotating Stars* (Princeton: Princeton University Press, 1978).

[TAYLOR, 1989]   J. H. Taylor and J. M. Weisberg, "Further experimental tests of relativistic gravity using the binary pulsar PSR 1913+16," *Ap. J.* **345**, 434–450 (1989).

[TAYLOR, 1991]   J. H. Taylor, A. Wolszcan, T. Damour, and J. M. Weisberg, "Experimental constraints on strong-field relativistic gravity," *Nature (London)* **355**, 132–136 (1991).

[TAYLOR, 1993]   J. H. Taylor, "Pulsar timing and relativistic gravity," *Class. Quantum Gravity* **10**, S167–S174 (1993).

[TEW, 1989] W. L. Tew, *Development of a He II supported torsion balance* Ph.D. Thesis, University of Colorado at Boulder, 1989, unpublished (1989).

[THODBERG, 1986] H. H. Thodberg, "Comment on the sign in the reanalysis of the Eötvös experiment," *Phys. Rev. Lett.* **56**, 2423 (1986); **57**, 1192 (1986).

[THOMAS, 1989] J. Thomas et al., "Testing the inverse-square law of gravity on a 465-m tower," *Phys. Rev. Lett.* **63**, 1902–1905 (1989).

[THOMAS, 1990] J. Thomas and P. Vogel, "Testing the inverse-square law of gravity in boreholes at the Nevada test site," *Phys. Rev. Lett.* **65**, 1173–1176 (1990); **65**, 2478 (E) (1990).

[THIEBERGER, 1986] P. Thieberger, "Hypercharge fields and Eötvös-type experiments," *Phys. Rev. Lett.* **56**, 2347–2349 (1986).

[THIEBERGER, 1987A] P. Thieberger, "Search for a substance-dependent force with a new differential accelerometer," *Phys. Rev. Lett.* **58**, 1066–1069 (1987).

[THIEBERGER, 1987B] P. Thieberger, "Search for a new force," In *New and Exotic Phenomena*, Proceedings of the VIIth Moriond Workshop, Les Arcs, France, 24–31 January, 1987, edited by O. Fackler and J. Trân Thanh Vân (Gif-sur-Yvette: Editions Frontières, 1987), pp. 579–589.

[THIEBERGER, 1988] P. Thieberger, "Thieberger replies," *Phys. Rev. Lett.* **60**, 965 (1988).

[THIEBERGER, 1989] P. Thieberger, "Thieberger replies," *Phys. Rev. Lett.* **62**, 2333 (1989).

[THIRRING, 1972] W. Thirring, "Gravitation," In *Essays in Physics*, Vol. 4, edited by G. K. T. Conn and G. N. Fowler (New York: Academic, 1972), pp. 125–163.

[TOHLINE, 1983] J. E. Tohline, "Stabilizing a cold disk with a $1/r$ force law," In *Internal Kinematics and Dynamics of Galaxies*, IAU Symposium 100, edited by E. Athanassoula (Dordrecht: Reidel, 1983), pp. 205–206.

[TRAMPETIĆ, 1989] J. Trampetić, S. H. Aronson, H.-Y. Cheng, E. Fischbach, and C. Talmadge, "Detecting hyperphotons in kaon decays," *Phys. Rev. D* **40**, 1716–1719 (1989).

[TUCK, 1988]   G. J. Tuck, M. A. Barton, G. D. Agnew, G. I. Moore, and F. D. Stacey, "A lake experiment for measurement of the gravitational constant on a scale of tens of metres," In *Proceedings of the Fifth Marcel Grossmann Meeting on General Relativity*, edited by D. G. Blair and M. J. Buckingham, University of Western Australia, Perth, Australia, 8–13 August, 1988, (Singapore: World Scientific, 1989), pp. 1605–1612.

[UEHLING, 1935]   A. E. Uehling, "Polarization effects in the positron theory," *Phys. Rev.* **48**, 55–62 (1935).

[VAN DAM, 1970]   H. van Dam and M. Veltman, "Massive and massless Yang-Mills and gravitational fields," *Nucl. Phys.* **B22**, 397–411 (1970).

[VANIČEK, 1986]   P. Vaniček and E. Krakiwsky, *Geodosy*, 2nd edition (Amsterdam: North-Holland, 1986).

[VENEMA, 1992]   B. J. Venema et al., "Search for a coupling of the Earth's gravitational field to nuclear spins in atomic mercury," *Phys. Rev. Lett.* **68**, 135–138 (1992).

[VECSERNYES, 1987]   P. Vecsernyés, "Constraints on a vector coupling to baryon number from the Eötvös experiment," *Phys. Rev. D* **35**, 4018–4019 (1987).

[VOROBYOV, 1988]   P. V. Vorobyov and Ya. I. Gitarts, "A new limit on the arion interaction constant," *Phys. Lett.* **208B**, 146–148 (1988).

[WAGONER, 1970]   R. V. Wagoner, "Scalar-tensor theory and gravitational waves," *Phys. Rev. D* **1**, 3209–3216 (1970).

[WAPSTRA, 1955]   A. H. Wapstra and G. J. Nijgh, "The ratio of gravitational to kinetic mass for the constituents of matter," *Physica* **21**, 796–798 (1955).

[WATANABE, 1988]   R. Watanabe, C. W. Stubbs, and E. G. Adelberger, "Shielding the 'fifth force'?" *Phys. Rev. Lett.* **61**, 2152 (1988).

[WEINBERG, 1964]   S. Weinberg, "Do hyperphotons exist?" *Phys. Rev. Lett.* **13**, 495–497 (1964).

[WEINBERG, 1972]   S. Weinberg, *Gravitation and Cosmology: Principles and Applications of the General Theory of Relativity* (New York: J. Wiley & Sons, 1972).

[WILL, 1987]   C. M. Will, "Experimental gravitation from Newton's Principia to Einstein's General Relativity," In *Three Hundred Years of Gravitation*, edited by S. W. Hawking and W. Israel (Cambridge: Cambridge University Press, 1987), pp. 80–127

[WILL, 1989]   C. M. Will, "Experimental gravitation in space: is there a future?" *Advances in Space Research* **9**, 147–155 (1989).

[WILL, 1990]   C. M. Will, "Twilight time for the fifth force?" *Sky & Telescope* **80**, 472–479 (1990).

[WILL, 1993]   C. M. Will, *Theory and Experiment in Gravitational Physics* (Cambridge: Cambridge University Press, 1993).

[WINELAND, 1991]   D. J. Wineland, J. J. Bollinger, D. J. Heinzen, W. M. Itano, and M. G. Raizen, "Search for anomalous spin-dependent forces using stored-ion spectroscopy," *Phys. Rev. Lett.* **67**, 1735–1738 (1991).

[WITTEBORN, 1967]   F. C. Witteborn and W. M. Fairbank, "Experimental comparison of the gravitational force on freely falling electrons and metallic electrons," *Phys. Rev. Lett.* **19**, 1049–1052 (1967).

[WITTEBORN, 1968]   F. C. Witteborn and W. M. Fairbank, "Experiments to determine the force of gravity on single electrons and positrons," *Nature* **220**, 436–440 (1968).

[WOLFENSTEIN, 1978]   L. Wolfenstein, "Neutrino oscillations in matter," *Phys. Rev. D* **17**, 2369–2374 (1978).

[WORDEN, 1996]   P. W. Worden, Jr. and M. Bye, "The Stanford equivalence principle experiment," In *Proceedings of the STEP Symposium*, Pisa, Italy, 6–8 April, 1993, edited by R. Reinhard (European Space Agency publication ESA WPP-115, 1996).

[YU, 1979]   H.-T. Yu et al., "Experimental determination of the gravitational forces at separations around 10 meters," *Phys. Rev. D* **20**, 1813–1815 (1979).

[ZACHOS, 1978]   K. Zachos, "$N = 2$ supergravity theory with a gauged central charge," *Phys. Lett. B* **76**, 329–332 (1978).

[ZAKHAROV, 1970]   V. I. Zakharov, "Linearized gravitation theory and the graviton mass," *JETP Lett* **12**, 312–314 (1970).

[ZAKHAROV, 1991]   V. I. Zakharov, "Unitarity constraints on multiparticle weak production," *Nucl. Phys. B* **353**, 683–688 (1991).

[ZUMBERGE, 1991]   M. A. Zumberge et al., "Submarine measurement of the Newtonian gravitational constant," *Phys. Rev. Lett.* **67**, 3051–3054 (1991).

Author Index

C

D

E

Subject Index

A

Accelerometer, 90, 169, 174, 185, 267, 268, 270, 283

Adelberger sensitivity function, 26–29

Air resistance, 185

Airy method, 4, 91, 214, 215, 216

Antigravity, 5, 94, 189, 195, 257, 270, 272, 274, 278

Antimatter
free-fall experiments, *viii*, 45, 189, 193, 247, 250, 256, 262, 263, 266, 272, 274
indirect tests of weak equivalence principle, 189, 192, 193–195
matter-antimatter asymmetry, 6
Schiff's argument, 189–192, 279

Antiprotons, 14, 192, 193, 256, 263, 265, 266

Archimedes' principle, 170

Arion, 208, 250, 284

Astronomical unit, 114

Astrophysical constraints
Earth-LAGEOS, 5, 116–117
LAGEOS-lunar, 118
lunar motion, 16, 118, 140–141, 249
planetary motion, 4, 67, 112–115, 217, 218
pulsars, 18, 180–184
solar, 137–141, 146–147, 185, 217, 262
sources (*see* Sources)
stellar structure, 4, 217–218

Atomic number (*see* Proton number)

Atomic tests, 12, 212, 261, 277, 284

Axion, 12, 205, 208

B

Baryon coupling (*see* Non-Newtonian interactions)

Baryon number (B), 6, 12, 14, 17, 19–26, 130, 197, 218

Beam balance experiments, 167–169, 280

Benecke Foundation, 130, 131

Binary pulsar, 18, 59, 119, 180–184, 203, 268, 282

Binomial coefficient, 57

Borehole experiments (*see* Mine-borehole experiments)

Bouguer correction (*see* Double-Bouguer term)

C

CP symmetry (*see also* Kaons), 6, 17, 198, 199, 211, 253, 262

CPT symmetry, 6, 17, 198, 199, 252

Cartesian diver, 178

Casimir effect, 74, 256, 269, 272, 273

Center of mass, 42, 91, 95, 132, 140, 150, 165, 172, 176, 219, 226

M

QC 178 .F53 1999
Fischbach, Ephraim.
The search for non-Newtonian
gravity

9 780387 984902

DATE DUE